Disability Discrimination Law and Practice

Sixth Edition

Disability Discrimination Law and Practice

Sixth Edition

Brian J. Doyle LLB, LLM, PhD, *Barrister*
Regional Employment Judge

2008

JORDANS

Published by
Jordan Publishing Limited
21 St Thomas Street
Bristol BS1 6JS

British Library Cataloguing-in-Publication Data
A catalogue record for this book is available from the British Library.

ISBN 978 1 84661 083 7

Typeset by Letterpart Ltd, Reigate, Surrey
Printed in Great Britain by Antony Rowe Limited, Chippenham, Wiltshire

DEDICATION

For Helen

PREFACE

In the three years since the last edition, the development of disability discrimination law has continued apace. The Disability Rights Commission has been replaced by the Equality and Human Rights Commission, while the Disability Discrimination Act 2005 and the Equality Act 2006 have made extensive and important changes to the Disability Discrimination Act 1995, already extensively amended. Further alterations have been made in passing by other legislation and by a raft of new statutory instruments. New or revised codes of practice, supporting separate parts of the Act, have also been published.

Unfortunately, the result is that the parent Act is now a difficult statute to navigate, with far too many exotically numbered new sections, important materials buried in schedules and confusing modifications made in relation to devolved government. The Act is sorely in need of re-codification and simplification. Whether that will be achieved by the Discrimination Law Review and the proposed Single Equality Act (see Chapter 1) remains to be seen.

Major changes to the structure of this edition are necessitated by the 2005 and 2006 legislation. With the dissolution of the Disability Rights Commission, the disability-specific institutional structure has been significantly altered and no longer requires the same level of treatment. Accordingly, that discussion is now to be found (in radically reduced form) in Chapter 1, which also examines those aspects of the Equality Act 2006 and the Equality and Human Rights Commission that are relevant to the topic of disability discrimination.

The definition of 'disability' in respect of people with mental illnesses has been amended and persons with HIV infection, multiple sclerosis or cancer are now deemed to be disabled (see Chapter 2). In the employment field, there are new provisions on discriminatory advertisements and group insurance arrangements (see Chapters 3 to 4). Important changes are made to Part 3 on provision of services so as to bring within its scope private clubs (see Chapter 5). A new duty is also imposed on landlords to provide reasonable adjustments to let premises, while particular provision is made for commonhold properties and in respect of improvements to dwelling houses (see Chapter 6).

It has also become unlawful for general qualifications bodies to discriminate against disabled persons in relation to the award of prescribed qualifications (see Chapter 7). The current exemption for transport in relation to services provision has been clarified and narrowed, while the executive is enabled to make rail vehicle accessibility regulations (see Chapter 8). A wholly new chapter (now Chapter 9) is offered to deal with disability discrimination law as it affects public authorities. Here is to be found the analysis of the new law affecting members of locally-elected authorities; the carrying out of functions by public authorities; and the disability equality duty.

Throughout, the discussion and analysis is up-dated to take account of new developments in secondary legislation, case law and the extra-statutory materials, including new or revised codes of practice.

Of particular note among the former are: Disability Discrimination (Private Clubs etc) Regulations 2005; Disability Discrimination (Transport Vehicles) Regulations 2005; Disability Discrimination (Public Authorities) (Statutory Duties) Regulations 2005; Disability Discrimination (Service Providers and Public Authorities Carrying Out Functions) Regulations 2005; Disability Discrimination (Questions and Replies) Order 2005; Disability Discrimination (Educational Institutions) (Alteration of Leasehold Premises) Regulations 2005; Disability Discrimination Act 1995 (Amendment) (Further and Higher Education) Regulations 2006; Disability Discrimination (Premises) Regulations 2006; Disability Discrimination Act 1995 (Amendment etc) (General Qualifications Bodies) (Alteration of Premises and Enforcement) Regulations 2007; Disability Discrimination Act 1995 (Amendment) (Further Education) Regulations 2007; and various regulations that amend earlier statutory instruments. These are all dealt with at appropriate points in the text (including their devolved equivalents).

The most active areas of evolving case law are on the meaning of disability and in respect of discrimination in the employment field. There are too many such cases to note here but, where relevant, they are accounted for in Chapters 2 to 4. Of particular note is *Coleman v Attridge Law* (on discrimination by association). There is less case law activity in other areas, but new cases affecting the discussion of let premises, education in schools and the functions and duties of public authorities are recorded in the appropriate chapters. Of particular importance are *Chavda v Harrow LBC* (on the disability equality duty) and *Eisai v NICE* (on the functions of public authorities).

I have endeavoured to state the law as I understand it to be as at 5 February 2008.

I am grateful for the support and assistance of Tony Hawitt and Gillian Wright of Jordan Publishing Ltd in bringing this edition to press.

Brian Doyle
February 2008

CONTENTS

TABLE OF ABBREVIATIONS

1994 Green Paper	*A Consultation on Government Measures to Tackle Discrimination Against Disabled People* (July 1994)
1995 White Paper	*Ending Discrimination Against Disabled People,* Cm 2729 (January 1995)
ACAS	Advisory, Conciliation and Arbitration Service
CEHR	Commission for Equality and Human Rights
CRE	Commission for Racial Equality
DARAS	Disability Access Rights Advisory Service
DDA 1995	Disability Discrimination Act 1995
DDA 2005	Disability Discrimination Act 2005
DLR	Disability Law Review
DPTAC	Disabled Persons' Transport Advisory Committee
DRC	Disability Rights Commission
DRCA 1999	Disability Rights Commission Act 1999
DRTF	Disability Rights Task Force
DRTF Report	*From Exclusion to Inclusion: A Report of the Disability Rights Task Force for Disabled People* (1999, London: DfEE)
EA 2002	Employment Act 2002
EAT	Employment Appeal Tribunal
EC Framework Employment Directive	Council Directive 2000/78/EC of 27 November 2000, establishing a general framework for equal treatment in employment and occupation
ECHR	European Convention for the Protection of Human Rights and Fundamental Freedoms 1950
Employment Code of Practice	*Code of practice for the elimination of discrimination in the field of employment against disabled persons or persons who have a disability* (1996, London: HMSO)
EOC	Equal Opportunities Commission
ERA 1996	Employment Rights Act 1996
ERA 1999	Employment Relations Act 1999
ETA 1996	Employment Tribunals Act 1996
EU	European Union
FEFCE	Further Education Funding Council for England
FEFCs	further education funding councils
GMC	General Medical Council

Government Response to DRTF Report	*Towards Inclusion – Civil Rights for Disabled People: Government Response to the Disability Rights Task Force* (2001, London: DfEE)
Guidance	*Guidance on matters to be taken into account in determining questions relating to the definition of disability* (1996, London: HMSO)
HEFCE	Higher Education Funding Council for England
HEFCW	Higher Education Funding Council for Wales
ILO	International Labour Organization
LEA	local education authority
NACEDP	National Advisory Council on the Employment of Disabled People
NDC	National Disability Council
NIDC	Northern Ireland Disability Council
Post-16 Code of Practice	*Disability Discrimination Act 1995 Part 4 Code of Practice for Providers of Post-16 Education and Related Services* (2002: Disability Rights Commission)
PSV	public service vehicle
Rights of Access Code of Practice 2002	*Code of Practice: Rights of Access: Goods, Facilities, Services and Premises* (2002, London: HMSO)
RRA 1976	Race Relations Act 1976
Schools Code of Practice	*Disability Discrimination Act 1995 Part 4 Code of Practice for Schools* (2002: Disability Rights Commission)
SDA 1975	Sex Discrimination Act 1975
SEN	special educational needs
SENDA 2001	Special Educational Needs and Disability Act 2001
SENDIST	Special Educational Needs and Disability Tribunal
SHEFC	Scottish Higher Education Funding Council
TULR(C)A 1992	Trade Union and Labour Relations (Consolidation) Act 1992
UN	United Nations
WHO	World Health Organization

TABLE OF CASES

References are to paragraph numbers.

TABLE OF STATUTES

References are to paragraph numbers.

TABLE OF STATUTORY INSTRUMENTS

References are to paragraph numbers.

TABLE OF CODES OF PRACTICE, GUIDANCE ETC

References are to paragraph numbers.

TABLE OF EUROPEAN, UN AND INTERNATIONAL LEGISLATION

References are to paragraph numbers.

CHAPTER 1

INTRODUCTION

1.1 INTRODUCTION

In more than a decade since the Disability Discrimination Act 1995 (DDA 1995) began to be brought into force, it has begun, slowly but surely, to provide disabled people in the UK with legal processes and remedies to challenge disability discrimination. There is no general agreement on the size of the population of disabled persons in the UK, although the former Disability Rights Commission (DRC) estimated it at approximately 10 million persons – more than one in five of the general population. Research had long-established evidence that disabled people face discrimination and barriers to equal participation and opportunity in education, employment, health and social services, housing, transport, the built environment, leisure and social activities, and civic rights.[1]

1.2 DISABILITY DISCRIMINATION ACT 1995

1.2.1 Moving the Third Reading of the Disability Discrimination Bill in the House of Commons on 28 March 1995, the then Minister for Social Security and Disabled People, Mr William Hague, claimed:

> 'It is a landmark Bill. It is the only comprehensive Bill for disabled people ever introduced by a British Government. It will mark the United Kingdom out as one of the world leaders and the leader in Europe in the move towards comprehensive anti-discrimination legislation for disabled people. It is a profound measure with significant implications for every part of the economy .... It sets this country on a clear, workable and unambiguous course to ending discrimination against disabled people. It will make a genuine difference to the opportunities and lives of millions of our fellow citizens ...'[2]

---

[1] See the references in previous editions of this book. I have continued to reduce or eliminate the contextual, comparative and international materials in this book in order to make space for the enlarged commentary of the DDA 1995 that follows in subsequent chapters.

[2] HC Deb, vol 257, cols 904 and 928; HL Deb, vol 566, col 1070. The Bill had been preceded by a Green Paper and a White Paper: *A Consultation on Government Measures*

More than a decade, and a change of government, later, the DDA 1995 – as amended on more than one occasion – remains the foundation stone of disability discrimination law.

1.2.2 The present Labour Government promised comprehensive civil rights legislation for disabled people and established the Disability Rights Task Force to examine the question. It reported in December 1999 and received a mainly positive response from the Government.[3] As a result, the DDA 1995 has been extensively amended by the Disability Rights Commission Act 1999 (DRCA 1999), the Special Educational Needs and Disability Act 2001 (SENDA 2001), the Disability Discrimination Act 1995 (Amendment) Regulations 2003[4] and the Disability Discrimination Act 2005, as well as a host of amending regulations made under other primary legislation.

Scope and extent

1.2.3 With the exception of some of the provisions on public transport and education, the DDA 1995 (as amended) is largely in force. Part 1 of the DDA 1995 defines the meanings of 'disability' and 'disabled person' and is dealt with in Chapter 2. Part 2 deals with discrimination and harassment in the employment field. This is addressed in Chapters 3 and 4. Part 3 deals with disability discrimination in relation to the provision of services, the functions of public authorities, private clubs and premises. Services and private clubs are dealt with in Chapter 5; premises in Chapter 6; and public authorities in a new Chapter 9. Education is dealt with in Part 4 of the Act (see Chapter 7). The Part 5 measures on public transport are examined in Chapter 8. New provisions affecting public authorities (including the disability equality duty) are examined in Chapter 9. The institutional framework that supports the Act is surveyed in the present Chapter below. General questions of liability and remedies are approached in Chapter 10.

---

to *Tackle Discrimination Against Disabled People* (1994, London: Department of Social Security); *Ending Discrimination Against Disabled People*, Cm 2729 (1995, London: HMSO).

[3]   Disability Rights Task Force, *From Exclusion to Inclusion: A Report of the Disability Rights Task Force on Civil Rights for Disabled People* (1999, London: DfEE); Better Regulation Task Force, *Anti-Discrimination Legislation* (May 1999); *Interim Government Response to the Report of the Disability Rights Task Force* (March 2000, DfEE); *Towards Inclusion – Civil Rights for Disabled People: Government Response to the Disability Rights Task Force* (March 2001, DfEE).

[4]   This enactment is a result of the requirement to amend the provisions of the DDA 1995 in the employment field in order to comply with the EC Framework Employment Directive 2000/78/EC made under the EC Treaty, art 13 (as amended). See *Towards Equality and Diversity: Implementing the Employment and Race Directives: Consultation Document* (Cabinet Office, 2001); *Equality and Diversity – The Way Ahead* (2002, Department of Trade and Industry).

Northern Ireland

1.2.4   The DDA 1995 is expressed to apply only to England, Wales and Scotland. However, its provisions also extend to Northern Ireland, with certain modifications and exceptions.[5] The application of the DDA 1995 in Northern Ireland has effect to the extent of and subject to the textual modifications set out in Sch 8 to the Act.[6] Where appropriate, these are indicated in the text.[7]

Application to the Crown

1.2.5   The Crown is bound by ss 21B–21E (discrimination by public authorities) and Part 5A (duties of public authorities) of the DDA 1995, and the other provisions of the Act so far as applying for those purposes.[8] Otherwise, the DDA 1995 applies to any act (or deliberate omission) done by (or for the purposes of) a Minister of the Crown or Government department in exactly the same way as it would apply to an act (or deliberate omission) done by a private person.[9] It also similarly applies to an act (or deliberate omission) done on behalf of the Crown by a statutory body or a person holding a statutory office.[10] The Crown Proceedings Act 1947 applies to proceedings against the Crown brought under the 1995 Act.[11]

1.2.6   Part 2 of the DDA 1995 (the employment field) now applies to service for the purposes of a Minister of the Crown or Government department (other than service of a person holding a statutory office) as it applies to employment by a private person.[12] Service for the purposes of a Minister of the Crown or Government department does not include service in certain ministerial offices or service as the head of a Northern Ireland department.[13] Part 2 also applies to service on behalf of the Crown for the purposes of a person holding a statutory office or for the purposes of a statutory body as it applies to employment by a private person.[14] A 'statutory body' is one set up by or under an enactment and a

---

[5]   DDA 1995, s 70(6).

[6]   Ibid, Sch 8, as amended by Northern Ireland Act 1998, Sch 13, para 16.

[7]   Note the effect of the Departments (Northern Ireland) Order 1999, SI 1999/283, and the Departments (Transfer and Assignment of Functions) Order (Northern Ireland) 1999, SR 1999/481. This is reflected in the text.

[8]   DDA 1995, s 64(A1), as inserted by DDA 2005 from 4 December 2006. Sections 57 and 58 shall apply for purposes of these provisions as if service as a Crown servant were employment by the Crown.

[9]   DDA 1995, ss 64(1)(a) and 68(1) and Sch 8, para 44.

[10]   Ibid.

[11]   Ibid, s 64(3)–(4), (8) and Sch 8, para 44(1) and (4)(b); Crown Proceedings Act 1947, s 23 and Parts II to V, but not ss 20 and 44 (removal of proceedings from the county court to the High Court or from the sheriff court to the Court of Session).

[12]   DDA 1995, s 64(2)(a), as amended.

[13]   Ibid, s 64(8) and Sch 8, para 44; House of Commons Disqualification Act 1975, Sch 2.

[14]   Ibid, s 64(2)(b).

'statutory office' is construed accordingly.[15] The effect is to provide that civil servants are to be regarded as employees, but not a person holding a statutory office (although a person employed by an office-holder is covered).[16] However, office-holders are now explicitly included within Part 2 of the Act from 1 October 2004.[17]

1.2.7   The explicit exclusion of service as a prison officer and as a fire-fighting member of a fire brigade has been revoked from 1 October 2004. However, the exclusion of service in the naval, military or air forces remains.[18] Originally, police officers were implicitly outside the scope of the Act, as they were neither employees nor Crown servants.[19] In addition, Part 2 of the Act did not apply to service in certain statutory police forces.[20] These exclusions have also been revoked from 1 October 2004 (and have been discussed in Chapter 4).

Application to Parliament

1.2.8   The DDA 1995 applies to an act (or deliberate omission) done by (or for the purposes of) the House of Lords or the House of Commons.[21] In other words, the Act is equally applicable to Parliament as it would be to a private person. Nothing in any rule of law or the law or practice of Parliament prevents proceedings being instituted under the DDA 1995 against either of the Houses of Parliament in an employment tribunal or a court. Otherwise parliamentary privilege would dictate that the Act would not apply to the legislature itself.

1.2.9   As far as the employment discrimination provisions of Part 2 of the DDA 1995 are concerned, the Corporate Officer of the House of Commons is to be treated as the employer of any person who is (or would be) a relevant member of the House of Commons staff.[22] In respect of discrimination in relation to the provision of goods, facilities or services to members of the public under Part 3 of the Act, the relevant provider of any services in question would be the Corporate Officer of the House of Commons and the Corporate Officer of the House of Lords respectively.[23] The two Houses provide a number of obvious services to visitors, such as refreshment facilities and information services. However,

---

[15]   DDA 1995, s 64(8).

[16]   HC Deb Standing Committee E, cols 441–442. See *Photis and Bruce v (1) KMC International Search & Selection and (2) Department of Trade & Industry; Heyes v Lord Chancellor's Department* (EAT/732/00, 766/00 and 960/00).

[17]   DDA 1995, ss 4C–4F, as amended (discussed in Chapter 4). The previous provisions on statutory office-holders in s 66 are now repealed.

[18]   Ibid, s 64(7).

[19]   See now DDA 1995, s 64A (subject to which s 64(1) and (2) have effect).

[20]   Ibid, s 64(5) (now repealed); Ministry of Defence Police Act 1987, s 1; British Transport Commission Act 1949, s 53; Parks Regulation Act 1872; Special Constables Act 1923, s 3.

[21]   DDA 1995, s 65(1).

[22]   Ibid, s 65(2) for the purposes of Employment Rights Act 1996, s 195.

[23]   Ibid, s 65(3).

where the service at issue is the access to and use of any place in the Palace of Westminster which members of the public are permitted to enter (such as the public galleries in the debating chambers), the Corporate Officers of both Houses are treated as joint providers of such a service.[24] This makes it plain that physical access to the political process of the legislature itself is a matter that can be addressed and redressed under the relevant provisions of the DDA 1995.

Application to police

1.2.10 For the purposes of Part 2 of the DDA 1995 (the employment field), the holding of the office of constable shall be treated as employment by the chief officer of police[25] as respects any act done by him or her in relation to a constable or that office and by the police authority as respects any act done by it in relation to a constable or that office.[26] For the purposes of s 58 (liability of employers and principals), the holding of the office of constable shall be treated as employment by the chief officer of police (and as not being employment by any other person); and anything done by a person holding such an office in the performance (or purported performance) of his or her functions shall be treated as done in the course of that employment.[27] These provisions apply to a police cadet and appointment as a police cadet as they apply to a constable and the office of constable.[28]

1.2.11 There shall be paid out of the police fund any compensation, costs or expenses awarded against a chief officer of police in any proceedings brought against him or her under Part 2 (employment) or Part 3 (services, public authority functions, private clubs and premises), and any costs or expenses incurred by him or her in any such proceedings so far as not recovered by him or her in the proceedings.[29] This also applies to any sum required by a chief officer of police for the settlement of any claim made against him or her under Part 2 or 3 if the settlement is approved by the police authority.[30]

1.2.12 Any proceedings under Part 2 or 3 which would lie against a chief officer of police shall be brought against the chief officer of police for the time being, or in the case of a vacancy in that office, against the person for the time being performing the functions of that office.[31] A police authority may, in such cases and to such extent as appear to it to be appropriate, pay out of the police fund any compensation, costs or expenses awarded in proceedings under Part 2 or 3 against a person under

---

24   DDA 1995, s 65(4).
25   As defined in the Police Act 1996 or Police (Scotland) Act 1967: DDA 1995, s 64A(7).
26   DDA 1995, s 64A(1).
27   Ibid, s 64A(2).
28   Ibid, s 64A(6).
29   Ibid, s 64A(3)(a).
30   Ibid, s 64A(3)(b).
31   Ibid, s 64A(4).

the direction and control of the chief officer of police.[32] This also applies to any costs or expenses incurred and not recovered by such a person in such proceedings; and any sum required in connection with the settlement of a claim that has or might have given rise to such proceedings.[33]

Regulations and orders

1.2.13   The DDA 1995 makes provision in several places for the enactment of regulations and orders which amplify the substantive provisions of the legislation. Any power under the Act to make regulations or orders is to be exercised by statutory instrument.[34] The term 'regulations' means regulations made by the Secretary of State.[35] Any such power may be exercised to make different provision for different cases, including different provision for different areas.[36] The power to make regulations and orders under the Act includes the power to make incidental, supplemental, consequential or transitional provisions.[37] That power is exercised by the person by whom the power is exercisable (which will include the Secretary of State, the Scottish Ministers and the Welsh Ministers) as appears to him or her as expedient. The power to make regulations and orders may also provide for a person to exercise a discretion in dealing with any matter.[38] A statutory instrument made under the DDA 1995 is subject to annulment by a resolution of either House of Parliament.[39] Particular provision is made in respect of regulations made under specific sections of the Act.[40]

1.3   COMMISSION FOR EQUALITY AND HUMAN RIGHTS

1.3.1   In December 2001, as part of its consultation on implementing the EC Employment and Race Directives, the Government mooted the

---

[32]   DDA 1995, s 64A(5)(a).

[33]   Ibid, s 64A(5)(b) and (c).

[34]   Ibid, s 67(1). An exception is provided for under s 67(6) in respect of an order under s 43 by which the Secretary of State may authorise the use on roads of a regulated public service vehicle (PSV) which does not comply with the PSV accessibility regulations or which does not possess an accessibility or approval certificate under ss 40–42 of the Act. See Chapter 8.

[35]   Ibid, s 68(1).

[36]   Ibid, s 67(2).

[37]   Ibid, s 67(3)(a).

[38]   Ibid, s 67(3)(b). Nothing in s 34(4) (licensing of taxis in compliance with taxi accessibility regulations) or s 40(6) (public service vehicle accessibility regulations) or s 46(5) (rail vehicle accessibility regulations) affects the powers conferred by s 67(2) or (3) above.

[39]   Ibid, s 67(5). However, that annulment procedure does not apply to a statutory instrument made under s 3(9) (an order appointing the date on which any s 3 guidance as to the meaning of disability is to come into force), s 53A(6)(a) (an order appointing the day on which a code of practice shall come into force) or s 70(3) (an order appointing the date when the provisions of the Act come into force).

[40]   DDA 1995, ss 67(3A)–(5A), 67A and 67B. This is not considered further.

possibility of a single equality commission (effectively combining the Disability Rights Commission (DRC), Commission for Racial Equality (CRE) and Equal Opportunities Commission (EOC) and embracing the new areas of discrimination law introduced in recent years).[41] That led to further consultation in October 2002 on refined plans to that end.[42] As a result, in May 2004, the Government published a White Paper proposing the establishment of a Commission for Equality and Human Rights (CEHR).[43] The proposed establishment of the CEHR was broadly welcomed by the DRC, although it would also have liked to see all discrimination legislation codified in a single equalities statute, so as best to protect the interests of disabled people in the new umbrella commission.[44]

1.3.2 The Equality Act 2006 now establishes the CEHR.[45] As a consequence, the DRC is dissolved and transitional arrangements have been made.[46] The Disability Rights Commission Act 1999 (DRCA 1999) ceases to have effect.

Commissioners

1.3.3 In appointing Commissioners to the CEHR, the Secretary of State shall appoint an individual only if the Secretary of State thinks that the individual has experience or knowledge relating to a relevant matter, or is suitable for appointment for some other special reason, and having regard to the desirability of the Commissioners together having experience and knowledge relating to the relevant matters.[47] For these purposes, the relevant matters are those matters in respect of which the CEHR has

---

[41] *Towards Equality and Diversity: Implementing the Employment and Race Directives: Consultation Document* (Cabinet Office, 2001), paras 7.1–7.5. See also the announcement on 15 May 2002 of a review of the equality framework (including a proposal of a single equality body) by Barbara Roche, Cabinet Office minister: Cabinet Office press release (CAB 053/02).

[42] *Equality and Diversity: The Way Ahead* (Department of Trade and Industry, 2002); *Equality and Diversity: Making It Happen* (Cabinet Office, 2002). See also: Parliamentary Joint Committee on Human Rights, *The Case for a Human Rights Commission: Interim Report* (22nd Report, 2001–02, HL 160 and HC 1142); Parliamentary Joint Committee on Human Rights, *The Case for a Human Rights Commission* (6th Report, 2002–03, HL 67 and HC 489).

[43] *Fairness for All: A New Commission for Equality and Human Rights* (Cm 6185). See also: Parliamentary Joint Committee on Human Rights, *Commission for Equality and Human Rights: Structure, Functions and Powers* (11th Report, 2003–04, HL 78 and HC 536); *Government Response to Joint Committee on Human Rights: 11th Report of Session 2003–04*, Cm 6295 (2004); Parliamentary Joint Committee on Human Rights, *Commission for Equality and Human Rights: The Government's White Paper* (16th Report, 2003–04, HL 156 and HC 998).

[44] DRC, *Government White Paper: Fairness for All – A New Commission for Equality and Human Rights: Response from the Disability Rights Commission* (DRC, August 2004); DRC, *Provisional Position on the CEHR White Paper* (DRC, May 2004).

[45] Equality Act 2006, s 1.

[46] Ibid, s 40 and Sch 3, para 59; s 91 and Sch 4.

[47] Ibid, Sch 1, para 2(1).

functions including, in particular, disability discrimination.[48] The Secretary of State shall ensure that the CEHR includes a Commissioner who is (or has been) a disabled person.[49] During the transitional period, Transition Commissioners are appointed as additional members of the CEHR. One of the Transition Commissioners is a commissioner of the DRC appointed by the former chairman of the DRC.[50]

Disability Committee

1.3.4 The CEHR is required to establish from the outset a decision-making committee to be known as the Disability Committee.[51] It shall ensure that there are not less than 7 or more than 9 members of the Disability Committee, that at least one half of the members are (or have been) disabled persons, and that the Chairman is (or has been) a disabled person.[52] The Transition Commissioner nominated by the chairman of the DRC may not be a member of the Disability Committee.[53] The appointment of each member of the Disability Committee shall be for a period of not less than two years or more than five years, subject to the possibilities of reappointment, dismissal in accordance with the terms of appointment, and the lapsing of the appointment upon the dissolution of the Disability Committee.[54]

1.3.5 The CEHR is deemed to have delegated to the Disability Committee the CEHR's specific duties in relation to diversity and equality, and to groups, insofar as they relate to disability matters.[55] This deemed delegation does not prevent the exercise by the CEHR of a power (or the fulfilment by it of a duty) by action which relates partly to disability matters and partly to other matters.[56] Before exercising a power or fulfilling a duty in relation to a matter affecting disabled persons, the CEHR shall consult the Disability Committee.[57] The Disability Committee shall advise the CEHR about the exercise of its functions insofar as they affect disabled persons.[58]

---

[48] Equality Act 2006, Sch 1, para 2(2).
[49] Ibid, Sch 1, para 2(3).
[50] Ibid, s 41(3).
[51] Ibid, Sch 1, para 49(1) and (2).
[52] Ibid, Sch 1, para 50(1).
[53] Ibid, Sch 1, para 50(2).
[54] Ibid, Sch 1, para 51.
[55] Ibid, Sch 1, para 52(1). See ss 8, 10–11, 13–15, 19, 27–28 and 30.
[56] Ibid, Sch 1, para 52(2). In both these contexts, 'disability matters' means matters provided for in Parts 1, 3, 4, 5 and 5B of the DDA 1995; the Equality Act 2006, ss 8 and 10, in so far as they relate to disability and the matters addressed, the Equality Act 2006, ss 14(3) and (4), 27(2) and (3) and 28(2) and (3).
[57] Equality Act 2006, Sch 1, para 53. This includes, in particular, any matter provided for in Part 2 of the DDA 1995.
[58] Equality Act 2006, Sch 1, para 54. This includes, in particular, any matter provided for in Part 2 of the DDA 1995.

1.3.6 In allocating its resources, the CEHR shall ensure that the Disability Committee receives a share sufficient to enable it to exercise its functions.[59] The Disability Committee shall submit to the CEHR a report of its activities for each financial year and this is to be incorporated into the CEHR's annual report.[60] The CEHR shall arrange for a review of the activities of the Disability Committee to be conducted as soon as is reasonably practicable after five years.[61] As soon as is reasonably practicable after receiving that report, the CEHR shall recommend to the Secretary of State for how long the Disability Committee should continue in existence and provision is made for the dissolution of the Committee.[62]

General duty

1.3.7 The CEHR's general duty is to exercise its functions with a view to encouraging and supporting the development of a society in which people's ability to achieve their potential is not limited by prejudice or discrimination; there is respect for and protection of each individual's human rights; there is respect for the dignity and worth of each individual; each individual has an equal opportunity to participate in society; and there is mutual respect between groups based on understanding and valuing of diversity and on shared respect for equality and human rights.[63]

Equality and diversity

1.3.8 The CEHR has specific duties in relation to equality and diversity. The term 'diversity' means the fact that individuals are different, while 'equality' means equality between individuals.[64] When exercising its powers it shall promote understanding of the importance of equality and diversity; encourage good practice in relation to equality and diversity; promote equality of opportunity; promote awareness and understanding of rights under the equality enactments; enforce the equality enactments; work towards the elimination of 'unlawful' discrimination; and work towards the elimination of 'unlawful' harassment.[65] In promoting equality of opportunity between disabled persons and others, the CEHR may, in particular, promote the favourable treatment of disabled persons.[66]

---

[59] Equality Act 2006, Sch 1, para 55.
[60] Ibid, Sch 1, para 56.
[61] Ibid, Sch 1, paras 57–59.
[62] Ibid, Sch 1, paras 60–64.
[63] Ibid, s 3.
[64] Ibid, s 8(2).
[65] Ibid, s 8(1). The 'equality enactments' include the DDA 1995: Equality Act 2006, s 33(1). The term 'unlawful' means contrary to a provision of the equality enactments: Equality Act 2006, ss 8(2) and 34(1). However, action is not unlawful for these purposes by reason only of the fact that it contravenes a duty under or by virtue of the DDA 1995, Part 5 (public transport), ss 49A and 49D (public authorities), and s 49G (consent to tenant's improvements): Equality Act 2006, s 34(2).
[66] Equality Act 2006, s 8(3). A 'disabled person' means a person who is a disabled person

Groups

1.3.9 In exercising its powers, the CEHR shall promote understanding of the importance of good relations between members of different groups and between members of groups and others.[67] It shall encourage good practice in relation to relations between members of different groups, and between members of groups and others.[68] It shall also work towards the elimination of prejudice against, hatred of and hostility towards members of groups, and work towards enabling members of groups to participate in society.[69] For these purposes, 'group' means a group or class of persons who share a common attribute in respect of specified matters, including disability.[70] A reference to a group includes a reference to a smaller group or smaller class, within a group, of persons who share a common attribute (in addition to the attribute by reference to which the group is defined) in respect of specified matters, including disability.[71] In taking action in respect of groups defined by reference to disability and others, the CEHR may promote or encourage the favourable treatment of disabled persons.[72]

Codes of practice

1.3.10 The CEHR may issue a code of practice in connection with a matter addressed by Parts 2 to 4 and 5A of the Disability Discrimination Act 1995, except for ss 28D and 28E (accessibility in schools).[73] Such a code of practice shall contain provision designed to ensure or facilitate compliance with those provisions of the DDA 1995 or to promote equality of opportunity.[74] In particular, the CEHR may issue a code of practice giving practical guidance to landlords and tenants in England or Wales and in Scotland about various matters relating to their duties under the DDA 1995.[75] A failure to comply with a provision of a code shall not of itself make a person liable to criminal or civil proceedings; but a code shall be admissible in evidence in criminal or civil proceedings, and shall be taken into account by a court or tribunal in any case in which it appears to the court or tribunal to be relevant.[76]

---

within the meaning of the DDA 1995 or has been a disabled person within that meaning (whether or not at a time when that Act had effect): Equality Act 2006, s 8(4).

[67] Equality Act 2006, s 10(1)(a). This is without prejudice to its duties under s 8 (equality and diversity): s 10(7).

[68] Ibid, s 10(1)(b).

[69] Ibid, s 10(1)(c) and (d).

[70] Ibid, s 10(2).

[71] Ibid, s 10(3).

[72] Ibid, s 10(5).

[73] Ibid, s 14(1)(d).

[74] Ibid, s 14(2).

[75] Ibid, s 14(3) and (4).

[76] Ibid, s 15(4).

Functions and powers

1.3.11 Previous editions of this book paid particular attention to the description and analysis of the functions and powers of the former Disability Rights Commission (DRC), particularly in relation to enforcement powers.[77] The CEHR has an extensive range of enforcement powers similar to those previously enjoyed by the DRC. However, they are now cross-jurisdictional rather than disability-specific. A discussion of the CEHR's enforcement powers is now beyond the scope of this book. It is sufficient to note that the CEHR has duties to monitor the law and progress towards achieving its goals.[78] It may engage in providing education, training, advice and information, as well as commissioning research.[79] Its enforcement powers extend to investigations, unlawful act notices, action plans and related agreements, applications to the court, and application to restrain unlawful advertising, pressure, etc.[80] It may make arrangements for conciliation services and for legal assistance.[81] It has powers in relation to judicial review and other legal proceedings.[82] As will be seen in Chapter 9, it also has powers of assessment and compliance concerning the new public sector duties.[83]

1.4　GUIDANCE ON MEANING OF DISABILITY

1.4.1 The Secretary of State is empowered to issue statutory guidance about the matters to be taken into account in determining whether an impairment has a substantial adverse effect on a person's ability to carry out normal day-to-day activities or whether such an impairment has a long-term adverse effect.[84] An 'adjudicating body' addressing these questions, for any purpose of the legislation, is obliged to take account of any statutory guidance issued by the Secretary of State which appears to it to be relevant.[85] If any such statutory guidance has been issued, the Secretary of State may from time to time revise the whole or any part of such guidance and reissue it.[86] The Secretary of State also has authority to revoke any guidance by order.[87]

---

[77]　See for example chapter 9 in the 5th edition.

[78]　Equality Act 2006, ss 11–12.

[79]　Ibid, s 13.

[80]　Ibid, ss 20–26 and Sch 2.

[81]　Ibid, ss 27–29.

[82]　Ibid, s 30.

[83]　Ibid, s 31–32.

[84]　DDA 1995, s 3(1). In Northern Ireland, see ibid, Sch 8, para 2.

[85]　Ibid, s 3(3) and (12), as amended. An 'adjudicating body' is a court or a tribunal, but also includes any other person who (or body which) may decide a claim under the new education provisions of DDA 1995, Part 4: DDA 1995, s 3(3A). This would obviously include the SENDIST.

[86]　DDA 1995, s 3(11)(a).

[87]　Ibid, s 3(11)(b).

1.4.2   The Secretary of State has issued statutory guidance on the meaning of disability which came into force on 31 July 1996.[88] This guidance was revised and up-dated in 2006.[89] The substance of this guidance is considered in Chapter 2.

1.5   FUTURE DEVELOPMENTS

1.5.1   The EC Commission has proposed a new Directive that would, among other things, extend disability discrimination law at the EU level beyond the workplace and into goods, services and housing. This proposal (which relies upon Article 13 of the EC Treaty) is still in a very early stage of development.[90]

1.5.2   More significant is the UK Government's Discrimination Law Review (DLR).[91] Its purpose is to harmonise and to simplify the law across the many anti-discrimination strands (including disability), to make the law more effective and to modernise it. Its proposals would effectively codify or consolidate existing anti-discrimination law into a Single Equality Act. It proposes a simplified definition of disability by removing the references to particular normal day-to-day activities (or 'capacities'). However, it rejects the idea that a concept of indirect disability discrimination should be adopted (preferring the approach taken by the duty to make reasonable adjustments and proposing a single threshold point at which this duty would be triggered). The DLR proposes a single objective justification test in disability discrimination cases based upon the standard of a proportionate means of achieving a legitimate aim. It also proposes a single public sector equality duty rather than separate duties for disability, race, gender, etc. The DLR further seeks to improve access to the common parts of let residential premises for disabled persons.

---

[88]   *Guidance on matters to be taken into account in determining questions relating to the definition of disability* (1996, London: HMSO). The Guidance came into force on 31 July 1996. A separate edition of the Guidance has been issued in Northern Ireland.

[89]   See the revised *Guidance on Matters to be Taken into Account in Determining Questions Relating to the Definition of Disability* (2006) replacing the 1996 version with effect from 1 May 2006.

[90]   Commission of the European Communities, *Commission legislative and work programme 2008* COM (2007) 640 final (13 October 2007).

[91]   Communities and Local Government, *Discrimination Law Review: A Framework for Fairness: Proposals for a Single Equality Bill for Great Britain: A Consultation Paper* (12 June 2007). Consultation closed on 4 September 2007 and the next stage of the process is awaited.

CHAPTER 2

DISABILITY AND DISABLED PERSON

2.1 INTRODUCTION

2.1.1 The twin concepts of 'disability' and 'disabled person' are central to the operation of disability discrimination law. These are the terms that determine who has rights and expectations under the DDA 1995. Only someone who can satisfy the definition of a disabled person within the meaning of the legislation can enjoy the protection of its framework. This will often be treated as an issue to be determined at a preliminary hearing.[1]

2.1.2 Part 1 of the DDA 1995 (ss 1–3) and Schs 1 and 2 to the Act furnish definitions of 'disability' and 'disabled person' for the purposes of the statute. A 'disabled person' is defined as 'a person who has a disability'.[2] A person has a disability if he or she has a physical or mental impairment which has a substantial and long-term adverse effect on his or her ability to carry out normal day-to-day activities.[3] These provisions are supplemented by regulations[4] and by the revised statutory guidance issued by the Secretary of State under s 3 (referred to hereafter as the 'Guidance').[5] The revised Guidance does not impose any legal obligations in itself and is not designed to be an authoritative statement of law. Nevertheless, an employment tribunal or court is required to take account of the revised Guidance, where relevant, when determining certain questions arising from the statutory definition of disability.[6] The revised

---

[1] *Greenwood v British Airways plc* [1999] IRLR 600, EAT. In employment cases, application may be made to the Tribunals Service for funding a medical report addressing the preliminary issue.

[2] DDA 1995, s 1(2).

[3] Ibid, s 1(1). Note that the definition is also extended to include persons who had such a disability in the past (s 2 and Sch 2, as amended by the Disability Discrimination Act 1995 (Amendment) Regulations 2003, SI 2003/1673).

[4] Disability Discrimination (Meaning of Disability) Regulations 1996, SI 1996/1455, which came into force on 30 July 1996 and were made under the authority of Sch 1, paras 1(2), 2(4), 3(2)–(3), 4(2)(a) and 5(a). See also the Disability Discrimination (Meaning of Disability) Regulations (Northern Ireland) 1996, SR 1996/421.

[5] See the revised *Guidance on Matters to be Taken into Account in Determining Questions Relating to the Definition of Disability* (2006) replacing the 1996 version with effect from 1 May 2006. A separate edition of the Guidance has been issued in Northern Ireland.

[6] See s 3(3), and *Goodwin v The Patent Office* [1999] IRLR 4, EAT.

Guidance is likely to be of assistance in marginal cases. It is not to be used in a literal fashion to reach conclusions that overturn the obvious impression of someone as being disabled within the meaning of the Act.[7]

2.1.3 Considerable care must be exercised in any attempt to use existing definitions of disability employed in other legal contexts (such as social welfare or social security law) as a means of identifying disabled persons protected under the DDA 1995. In order to enjoy protection from disability discrimination, claimants must bring themselves fairly and squarely within the definitional provisions of the 1995 legislation and the revised statutory guidance. However, with that necessary caveat, it is likely that many (but not all) individuals who satisfy the definition of disability or disabled person in other statutory contexts will be able to do so under disability discrimination law. Indeed, in one particular case – that of a person registered as disabled under the Disabled Persons (Employment) Act 1944 at specified times – there was a deeming provision by which the existing status of an individual as a legally recognised disabled person was preserved for that purpose.[8] In any event, the fact that a person has been assessed as disabled for some other statutory purpose may be relevant evidence to be taken into account as part of the evidence that the person is disabled for the purposes of the DDA 1995. It is then a question of the weight to be attached to that evidence.[9]

2.1.4 The burden of proof that a claimant was a disabled person at the time of the alleged act of discrimination lies with the claimant on the conventional balance of probabilities.[10] A claimant in tribunal or court proceedings under the DDA 1995 will be expected to lead evidence which relates to his or her status at the time of the events which have given rise to the complaint. This is a question of fact. Provided the tribunal or court directs itself carefully as to the statutory definition, considers the revised Guidance, and weighs the evidence appropriately, it is unlikely that its decision on this question will be interfered with on appeal, unless on grounds of perversity.[11] However, a tribunal (or court) cannot simply ignore uncontested medical evidence, unless it rejects the evidence on the

---

[7] *Vicary v British Telecommunications plc* [1999] IRLR 680, EAT; *Leonard v Southern Derbyshire Chamber of Commerce* [2001] IRLR 19, EAT.

[8] DDA 1995, Sch 1, para 7.

[9] *Abadeh v British Telecommunications plc* [2001] IRLR 23, EAT (the fact that a medical appeal tribunal had assessed the person as having an 18 per cent disablement for the purposes of statutory benefits could not be disregarded as wholly irrelevant in determining whether that person was disabled under the DDA 1995).

[10] *Morgan v Staffordshire University* [2002] IRLR 190, EAT. While a tribunal or court cannot order a claimant to disclose his or her medical records, it can order that the claimant consent to such disclosure. If the claimant fails to do so, the tribunal or court might stay the proceedings or strike them out. To do so would not offend the right to privacy under Art 8 of the European Convention on Human Rights when balanced against the respondent's right to a fair trial under Art 6: *Hanlon v Kirkless Metropolitan Council* EAT 0119/04 (IDS Brief 767).

[11] See *Quinlan v B & Q plc* [1999] Disc LR 76, EAT, and *Foster v Hampshire Fire and Rescue Service* (1998) 43 BMLR 186, EAT.

basis of which the medical opinion has been formed or where it is clear that the medical witness has misunderstood that evidence.[12] On the other hand, it is not the task of the medical expert to tell the tribunal (or court) whether the claimant satisfies the statutory definition. That is a matter for the tribunal (or court) to decide in the light of the medical evidence.[13] Equally, it is inadvisable for a tribunal to conduct its own tests of the status or extent of an applicant's disability.[14] Knowledge of the disability by the respondent or defendant is not an ingredient of the test of whether there is a disability or not.[15]

2.2 MEANING OF 'DISABILITY' AND 'DISABLED PERSON'

2.2.1 As already noted, a 'disabled person' is a person who has a 'disability'. A person has a 'disability' if he or she has a physical or mental impairment which has a substantial and long-term adverse effect on his or her ability to carry out normal day-to-day activities.[16] It might be useful to take account of what the legislature hoped to achieve in defining the protected class in this way. The apparent intention was to create a common-sense definition which fitted the generally accepted perception of what is a disability and who is a disabled person, and which provided certainty and avoided vagueness.[17] It was thought that the definition, and the legislation which it underpins, would not be credible if it embraced individuals who were not fairly or generally recognised as disabled. The government of the day believed that the definition would cover the vast majority of the 6.5 million disabled persons in Britain identified by the 1988 Office of Population Census and Surveys report.[18]

---

[12] *Kapadia v London Borough of Lambeth* [2000] IRLR 14, EAT, and [2000] IRLR 699, CA. Once a claimant consents to a medical examination in the course of litigation no further consent is required for the resultant medical report to be disclosed as part of the proceedings.

[13] *Abadeh v British Telecommunications plc* [2001] IRLR 23, EAT. The medical report should address the medical diagnosis of the impairment, the expert's observations of the person carrying out normal day-to-day activities (and the ease with which the person is able to perform those functions), together with any relevant opinion as to prognosis and the effect of medication.

[14] *London Underground Ltd v Bragg* (1999) EAT/847/98.

[15] *Barker v Westbridge International Ltd* (2000) EAT/1180/98.

[16] DDA 1995, s 1 (subject to the provisions of Sch 1, the revised statutory guidance and the Disability Discrimination (Meaning of Disability) Regulations 1996, SI 1996/1455).

[17] HC Deb Standing Committee E, col 73. However, tribunals and courts must be aware that a relatively small proportion of disabled people are visibly disabled. They should avoid approaching this issue with a stereotypical image of a disabled person as someone who uses a wheelchair or has severely impaired mobility: *Vicary v British Telecommunications* [1999] IRLR 680, EAT.

[18] Martin, Meltzer and Elliott, *The Prevalence of Disability Among Adults: OPCS Surveys of Disability in Great Britain Report 1* (1988, London: HMSO). More recently, it has been estimated that approximately 11.7 million adults (20 per cent of the population) are covered by the Act: Whitfield, *The Disability Discrimination Act: Analysis of Data from an Omnibus Survey* (1997, London: Department of Social Security).

2.2.2   The Employment Appeal Tribunal (EAT) in *Goodwin v The Patent Office*[19] has set out the correct approach to the question of whether a claimant is a disabled person within the meaning of the DDA 1995. This is a decision equally relevant in non-employment cases. The tribunal (or court) should look carefully at what the parties say in the documents setting out the claim and the defence. Whether the issue of disability is in contention should be identified before the hearing. Standard directions or a case management hearing will often be appropriate. Where expert evidence is to be called, advance notice should be given to the other party and a copy of any expert report provided.[20] Above all, the tribunal (or court) should adopt an inquisitorial or interventionist approach to the question of disability,[21] while a purposive approach to the construction of the statute should be taken so as to construe the language of the Act in a way which gives effect to Parliament's intention. Explicit reference should always be made to any relevant provision of the revised Guidance or the relevant Code of Practice, but without creating an extra hurdle over which the claimant must jump. The tribunal (or court) should look at the evidence by reference to four different conditions:

(1)   Does the claimant have an impairment?

(2)   Does it have an adverse effect on the ability to carry out normal day-to-day activities?

(3)   Is the adverse effect substantial?

(4)   Is the adverse effect long-term?

---

[19]   [1999] IRLR 4, EAT.

[20]   In employment cases, see the judicial guidance on the use of expert evidence provided in *De Keyser v Wilson* [2001] IRLR 324, EAT and *Morgan v Staffordshire University* [2002] IRLR 190, EAT. A party may be entitled to call rebutting expert evidence where it does not accept the findings of a jointly commissioned expert medical report as to the existence (as opposed to the cause) of an alleged impairment: *Hospice of St Mary of Furness v Howard* [2007] IRLR 944, EAT. In non-employment proceedings, account will be taken of Civil Procedure Rules 1998 (CPR 1998), Part 35 and the associated Practice Direction on expert evidence.

[21]   This has been interpreted as meaning that the tribunal is obliged to conduct the hearing in a fair and balanced manner, intervening and making its own inquiries of the parties and witnesses in the course of the hearing as it considers appropriate: *Rugamer v Sony Music Entertainment UK Ltd; McNicol v Balfour Beatty Rail Maintenance Ltd* [2001] IRLR 644, EAT; upheld on appeal, *McNicol v Balfour Beatty Rail Maintenance Ltd* [2002] EWCA Civ 1074, [2002] IRLR 711, CA (the Court of Appeal rejecting a contention that the tribunal should take a more inquisitorial and proactive role other than to adjudicate on the issues of fact and law). It is not its duty to conduct a free-standing inquiry of its own or to attempt to obtain further evidence beyond that adduced by the parties. Its inquisitorial role is limited to the consideration of the issues raised by the parties. See also *Morgan v Staffordshire University* [2002] IRLR 190, EAT; *Woodrup v London Borough of Southwark* [2002] EWCA Civ 1716, [2003] IRLR 111, CA.

Each of these elements of the definition of disability is considered in turn below.

2.3 IMPAIRMENT

2.3.1 The term 'impairment' is vital to an understanding of the concept of disability. Yet it is not defined in the legislation. A literal interpretation of the word would suggest a condition of weakness, injury or damage, but the term has a more precise meaning in medical circles. The World Health Organization (WHO) 1980 classification of impairment, disability and handicap defined impairment as 'any loss or abnormality of psychological, physiological, or anatomical structure or function'.[22] The tenor of the parliamentary debates on the DDA 1995 suggests that the intention was to base the framework of disability discrimination law upon a medical model of disability. In that regard, the WHO definition may be a helpful one (although not necessarily one that would be embraced by disabled people themselves).

2.3.2 The revised Guidance anticipates that in many cases there will be no dispute over whether or not a person has an impairment. It makes clear that the question of how an impairment was caused is not a relevant consideration.[23] However, the revised Guidance does not go any further in explaining the term 'impairment'.[24]

Physical impairment

2.3.3 The term 'physical impairment' is also not defined or further explained in the DDA 1995.[25] However, an addiction to (including dependency upon) alcohol, nicotine or any other substance does not

---

[22] World Health Organization, *International Classification of Impairments, Disabilities and Handicaps: A Manual of Classification Relating to the Consequences of Disease* (1980, Geneva: WHO). This has now been revised and superseded by WHO, *International Classification of Functioning, Disability and Health* (2001, Geneva: WHO), which gives greater recognition to the social and environmental model of disability. It complements the ICD-10: WHO, *International Statistical Classification of Diseases and Related Health Problems* (10th Revision) (1990, Geneva: WHO).

[23] See also *Millar v Inland Revenue Commissioners* [2006] IRLR 112, Ct of Sess. Following an accident at work, the claimant developed a vision impairment. The medical evidence could not establish a physical cause. On appeal, the court ruled that a physical impairment can be established without proof of causation or reference to an illness.

[24] Guidance (2006), Part 2, paras A3–A8. Note that an impairment includes one which is controlled or corrected by medical treatment, medication, prosthesis, auxiliary devices or other aids: DDA 1995, Sch 1, para 6. The Court of Appeal has held that the term 'impairment' should be given its ordinary and natural meaning: *McNicol v Balfour Beatty Rail Maintenance Ltd* [2002] EWCA Civ 1074, [2002] IRLR 711 (noting that an impairment may result from or consist of an illness and that it is not necessary to consider how the impairment has been caused).

[25] Although note that the Act treats a severe disfigurement as a relevant impairment in defined circumstances (see Sch 1, para 3 and the more detailed discussion of this provision below). Many commonly accepted conditions (such as orthopaedic

amount to an impairment for the purposes of the Act.[26] That does not prevent, for example, liver disease resulting from alcohol dependency or abuse from counting as an impairment, even though alcoholism itself would not be so treated.[27] This exclusion also does not prevent an addiction which was originally the result of administration of medically prescribed drugs or other medical treatment from amounting to an impairment, all other things being equal.[28] So, for example, an addiction to pain-killers, to sedatives or to a mood-altering drug may amount to an impairment provided that the drug in question was *medically prescribed* and not simply bought over-the-counter without prescription or otherwise acquired. Seasonal allergic rhinitis (a form of severe hay fever) is also treated as not amounting to an impairment.[29] In this case, however, account might be taken of the condition so far as it aggravates the effect of another condition which does amount to an impairment (for example, a breathing impairment, such as asthma).[30]

Mental impairment

2.3.4　　The term 'mental impairment' is also not defined in the DDA 1995.[31] The revised Guidance is of little further assistance, indicating that the term will include developmental disabilities, learning difficulties, mental health conditions and mental illness.[32] Clearly, it is intended that learning, psychiatric and psychological impairments are to be included,[33] but regulation-making powers have been used to exclude certain anti-social disorders and addictions.[34] To that end, the conditions of a tendency to set fires, to steal or to physical or sexual abuse of other persons, together with the conditions of exhibitionism and voyeurism, are treated as not amounting to impairments.[35]

---

impairments, cerebral palsy, epilepsy, muscular dystrophy, multiple sclerosis, cancer, heart disease, diabetes and tuberculosis) will almost invariably qualify as impairments.

[26] Disability Discrimination (Meaning of Disability) Regulations 1996, SI 1996/1455, regs 2 and 3(1), made under DDA 1995, Sch 1, para 1(2)(a) and (3). This regulation-making power provides flexibility to deal with future medical developments and to resolve problems of interpretation that arise through case-law or medically disputed or controversial conditions: HC Deb Standing Committee E, cols 105 and 109.

[27] Guidance (2006), Part 2, para A14. See *Power v Panasonic UK Ltd* [2003] IRLR 151, EAT (depression caused by alcoholism capable of amounting to a disability).

[28] Disability Discrimination (Meaning of Disability) Regulations 1996, SI 1996/1455, reg 3(2).

[29] Ibid, reg 4(2).

[30] Ibid, reg 4(3).

[31] But see the previous provision in DDA 1995, Sch 1, para 1(1) discussed below.

[32] Guidance (2006), Part 2, para A6. In *Dunham v Ashford Windows* [2006] IRLR 608 the EAT recognised that a claimant with learning difficulties could establish a mental impairment. However, what is frequently required is expert evidence (such as that of a psychologist) of an identified condition (such as dyslexia) rather than a mere assertion of difficulties at school.

[33] Although, as already noted, addiction to alcohol, nicotine or any other substance has been excluded (whether this amounts to a mental or a physical impairment).

[34] HC Deb Standing Committee E, cols 72 and 105.

[35] Disability Discrimination (Meaning of Disability) Regulations 1996, SI 1996/1455,

2.3.5 Prior to 5 December 2005, a mental impairment *included* an impairment resulting from or consisting of a mental illness – but only if the illness was a *clinically well-recognised* illness.[36] This provision is now repealed and does not merit further consideration here. Anyone now relying upon a mental illness to establish disability must do so in the usual way and without an additional hurdle to surmount.

2.3.6 The definition of 'mental impairment' used in the DDA 1995 is not the same as that used in other mental health legislation.[37] The fact that an impairment would be a mental impairment for other purposes does not prevent it from being a mental impairment under the Act, but it is not to be treated as automatically so.

Physical impairment or mental impairment?

2.3.7 Just as the term 'impairment' is not defined, the distinction between a physical and a mental impairment might not always be clear. In two cases,[38] the applicants relied upon a condition described in medical terms as 'functional or psychological overlay'. The applicants claimed to have a physical injury. The medical evidence suggested that their symptoms were not the manifestation of any organic physical pathology, but were a manifestation of each individual's psychological state. In both cases, the applicants relied upon a physical impairment (rather than mental impairment) as the basis of their claim to be disabled persons. The EAT held that functional or psychological overlay was not a physical impairment for the purposes of the DDA 1995. In the EAT's view, the dividing line between physical and mental impairment depended upon whether the nature of the impairment was physical or mental. The

---

reg 4(1), made under DDA 1995, Sch 1, para 1(2)–(3). See HC Deb Standing Committee E, col 109. However, in *Murray v Newham Citizens Advice Bureau Ltd* [2003] IRLR 340, the EAT held that a person with a past history of violence resulting from paranoid schizophrenia was a disabled person within the DDA 1995, even though a tendency to violence was an excluded condition. It held that the tendency to violence was a consequence of a recognised illness and thus a manifestation of a disability, rather than a free-standing condition as contemplated by the exclusion in the regulations. In contrast, the EAT in *Edmund Nuttall Ltd v Butterfield* [2005] IRLR 751 found this distinction unhelpful. It recognised that the claimant might have both a legitimate impairment (here, depression) and an excluded condition (here, exhibitionism). The question is then what was the reason for the discriminatory treatment – the excluded condition or the legitimate impairment?

[36] DDA 1995, Sch 1, para 1(1) (emphasis added), now repealed. See *Goodwin v The Patent Office* [1999] IRLR 4, EAT; *Morgan v Staffordshire University* [2002] IRLR 190, EAT.

[37] DDA 1995, s 68(1). See e g Mental Health Act 1983, s 1(2).

[38] *Rugamer v Sony Music Entertainment UK Ltd; McNicol v Balfour Beatty Rail Maintenance Ltd* [2001] IRLR 644, EAT. The decision is a controversial one as it appears to require an applicant to prove the cause of the impairment, thus adding an additional hurdle to the test of disability. The decision has been upheld on appeal: *McNicol v Balfour Beatty Rail Maintenance Ltd* [2002] EWCA Civ 1074, [2002] IRLR 711, CA. The Court of Appeal stressed the importance of the applicant making clear the nature of his or her claim to be a disabled person, and for both parties to obtain relevant medical evidence on the issue of impairment.

distinction did not depend upon whether a physical or mental function or activity was affected. As there was no evidence in the cases that the applicants had (what was then required to be) a clinically well-recognised illness, and as they had not relied upon a mental impairment in any event, their cases could not succeed. In contrast, in a later case,[39] the claimant claimed to have experienced slow, progressive muscle weakness and wasting. The medical evidence suggested that there was no organic disease process causing the symptoms described. The claimant did not rely upon a mental impairment. The EAT held that an employment tribunal was entitled to conclude that the claimant had a physical impairment. There was no requirement to draw a distinction between an underlying fault, shortcoming or defect of or in the body and evidence of the manifestations or effects thereof. The Act contemplated that an impairment can be something that results from an illness as opposed to itself being an illness, ie an impairment may be cause or effect. The three cases are difficult to reconcile. It is suggested that the reasoning in the later case is to be preferred.

2.3.8 This debate aside, there remains some ground for doubt and argument about what impairments are of a physical or mental nature. Undoubtedly there will be difficult cases where the point will be taken in litigation. For example, the condition of chronic fatigue syndrome (so-called 'ME') is one which is not universally recognised in medicine. Where it is, there is doubt about whether its origins are physical, viral or psychological.[40] It is important to note that the DDA 1995 does not recognise the concept of a generic disability. In each case, the individual will have to show how his or her condition and its effects fit into the definitional framework erected by the statute.[41]

Sensory and other impairments

2.3.9 Individuals with sensory impairments are embraced by the definition of impairment used in the DDA 1995. Sensory impairments include deafness, other hearing impairments or loss, blindness, partial sightedness and dual sensory impairments (such as combined loss of speech and hearing). The legislature intended that persons with sensory impairments should be covered by the legislation:

---

[39] *College of Ripon & York St John v Hobbs* [2002] IRLR 185, EAT. On appeal in *McNicol v Balfour Beatty Rail Maintenance Ltd* (above), the Court of Appeal agreed with the EAT in *Hobbs* that an impairment can result from an illness rather than being an illness itself. That *McNicol* is likely to be restricted to its particular facts and easily distinguishable is recognised in *Millar v Inland Revenue Commissioners* [2006] IRLR 112, Ct of Sess.

[40] The condition was recognised as amounting to a disability for the individual applicant in *O'Neill v Symm & Co Ltd* [1998] IRLR 233, EAT, where the tribunal at first instance placed reliance upon expert evidence and the (then relevant) WHO *International Classification of Diseases*.

[41] See eg *Gittins v Oxford Radcliffe NHS Trust* (2000) EAT/193/99 (bulimia is not a generic disability; it is the effects of bulimia on the individual applicant which are in issue).

'The terms physical and mental are intended to be seen in their widest sense and should comprehensively cover all forms of impairment . . . [A] third category, in addition to physical and mental impairment, might imply that those categories are not all-embracing . . . Sensory conditions would generally be covered as physical conditions or, exceptionally, in cases such as hysterical deafness, as mental conditions.'[42]

In any event, the revised Guidance makes it plain that the concept of a physical or mental impairment includes sensory impairments, such as those affecting sight or hearing.[43]

2.3.10 The Disability Discrimination (Blind and Partially Sighted Persons) Regulations 2003 came into force on 14 April 2003.[44] They state that a person who is certified as blind or partially sighted by a consultant ophthalmologist is deemed to be a disabled person for the purposes of the DDA 1995. A person registered as blind or partially sighted in a register maintained by or on behalf of a local authority is also covered by this deeming provision. The regulations provide for conclusive evidence of certified status by the production of a certificate signed by the consultant ophthalmologist. Alternatively, a person's registered status is presumed by a certificate issued by (or on behalf of) the local authority stating that the person is registered as blind or partially sighted with that authority.

2.4 ABILITY TO CARRY OUT NORMAL DAY-TO-DAY ACTIVITIES

2.4.1 A person is a disabled person only if possessing an impairment that has an adverse effect, of the degree required, upon that person's 'ability to carry out normal day-to-day activities'.[45] An impairment is treated as affecting the ability of the person concerned to carry out normal day-to-day activities *only* if it affects one of the following:[46]

- mobility;[47]

- manual dexterity;

- physical co-ordination;

- continence;[48]

---

[42] HC Deb Standing Committee E, col 71.
[43] Guidance (2006), Part 2, para A6.
[44] SI 2003/712.
[45] DDA 1995, s 1(1).
[46] Ibid, Sch 1, para 4(1). Note the power to make regulations under Sch 1, para 4(2). No regulations have been made at the time of writing.
[47] In *Ashton v Chief Constable of West Mercia Constabulary* [2001] ICR 67, EAT, the personal choice of a person with gender identity dysphoria not to socialise outside work did not result in her condition having a substantial adverse effect on her mobility.
[48] A rare example is *Thornhill v London Central Bus Co Ltd* (2000) EAT/463/99 (an unduly

- ability to lift, carry or otherwise move everyday objects;

- speech,[49] hearing or eyesight;

- memory or ability to concentrate, learn or understand;[50]

- perception of the risk of physical danger.

The revised Guidance explains what is meant by the scope of the eight listed activities or 'capacities'.[51] It is not intended to reproduce this here. The focus is upon whether an impairment affects *any* of the abilities or capacities listed above. If it does, then it will be almost inevitable that there will be some adverse effect upon normal day-to-day activities.[52]

2.4.2   It is clear that it is the effect upon the claimant (and not persons generally) that matters. The EAT in *Goodwin v The Patent Office* has given important guidance on this question:

> 'What the Act is concerned with is an impairment on the person's *ability* to carry out activities. The fact that a person can carry out such activities does not mean that his ability to carry them out has not been impaired . . . In order to constitute an adverse effect, it is not the doing of the acts which is the focus of attention but rather the ability to do (or not do) the acts . . . The focus of attention required by the Act is on the things that the applicant either cannot do or can only do with difficulty, rather than on the things the person can do.'[53]

The tribunal (or court) should consider matters in the round and make an overall assessment of whether the adverse effect is substantial. However, it is not a question of weighing in the balance things which a person can do against things that person cannot do.[54] This should mean that, contrary to trends in some of the early first instance decisions, a claimant should

---

frequent desire to urinate, which did not lead to incontinence, was not a disability). See also *Kirton v Tetrosyl Ltd* [2003] EWCA Civ 619, [2003] IRLR 353, CA (an impairment of urinary incontinence as a result of surgery for cancer was a disability).

[49]   In *Ashton* (above) there was no evidence that the applicant's ability to speak was affected by her decision to alter the way in which she spoke (as part of preparation for gender reassignment).

[50]   An 'ability to understand' is not limited to an ability to understand information, knowledge or instructions. A broad approach to 'understanding' is required. See *Hewett v Motorola Ltd* [2004] IRLR 545, EAT (a person who has difficulty in understanding normal social interaction among people or the subtleties of human non-factual communication – for example, as may be the case of a person with Asperger's Syndrome – can be regarded as having his or her understanding affected).

[51]   Guidance (2006), Part 2, parasD20–D27. The revised Guidance uses the term 'capacities' rather than 'activities'.

[52]   *Ekpe v Commissioner of Police of the Metropolis* [2001] IRLR 605, EAT.

[53]   [1999] IRLR 4, EAT. See also *Leonard v Southern Derbyshire Chamber of Commerce* [2001] IRLR 19, EAT; *Ekpe v Commissioner of Police of the Metropolis* [2001] IRLR 605, EAT.

[54]   *Leonard v Southern Derbyshire Chamber of Commerce* [2001] IRLR 19, EAT.

find it relatively easier to establish his or her status as a disabled person, despite having adopted means of neutralising the effects of a disabling condition or environment (for example, by modifying their behaviour or adopting coping strategies).[55]

2.4.3 Expert evidence of what the claimant can and cannot do (and the circumstances of that capability) will be important. Often this will be in the form of a report or evidence from a medical specialist (such as a consultant or occupational health professional). However, the tribunal (or a court) must not delegate the decision as to what are normal day-to-day activities to the expert witness. That is a judicial decision, to be arrived at using basic common sense, and in the light of the evidence, the statute and the revised Guidance.[56] But there is a 'Catch-22' for many claimants in arguing that they are sufficiently disabled to be covered by the DDA 1995, but not so disabled as to be prevented from carrying out, for example, the duties of employment.[57] Yet, as a matter of principle, evidence of the nature of a claimant's duties at work and the way in which they are performed can be relevant to the assessment of whether the claimant is a disabled person.[58] Duties while at work will often encompass normal day-to-day activities. At the very least, evidence of ability or inability to carry out normal day-to-day activities while at work goes to the credibility of any evidence that those activities cannot be carried on outside work (or can only be done so with difficulty).

2.4.4 The reference to the effect which an impairment has upon the ability to carry out normal day-to-day activities is designed to exclude mild or trivial conditions from the scope of the DDA 1995. For example, individuals with temporary and non-chronic conditions, such as sprains or influenza, most obviously fall outside the boundaries of the statute.[59] Moreover, a person who, because of some physical or mental limitation, is effectively excluded from participating in a specialised activity or pursuit – which the majority of people would be incapable of enjoying in any event – enjoys no protection under the Act. Thus, a person with colour blindness, who is disqualified from being a commercial airline pilot, cannot usually be said to experience adverse effects on his or her ability to carry out normal day-to-day activities. A person who is left-handed will be disabled in using industrial machinery designed for right-handed use, but left-handedness is not usually recognised as a disability. An individual

---

[55] Guidance (2006), Part 2, paras B7–B9.

[56] *Vicary v British Telecommunications plc* [1999] IRLR 680, EAT; *Adabeh v British Telecommunications plc* [2001] IRLR 23, EAT.

[57] See *London Underground Ltd v Bragg* (1999) EAT/847/98.

[58] *Law Hospital NHS Trust v Rush* [2001] IRLR 611, Ct of Sess; *Cruickshank v VAW Motorcast Ltd* [2002] IRLR 24, EAT (a case where the adverse effects of the claimant's medical condition or impairment – occupational asthma – on his normal day-to-day activities were exacerbated by his working conditions or environment). See also *Paterson v Commissioner of Police of the Metropolis* [2007] IRLR 763, EAT.

[59] This is also be underlined by the 'substantial and long-term adverse effect' formula discussed below.

with a poor educational record because of comparatively low or average intelligence will be effectively disqualified from aspiring to the position of heart surgeon, but the majority of the population can be said to be 'disabled' to that extent also. It is not thought that colour blindness, left-handedness or indifferent educational attainment are within the scope of the Act.[60]

2.4.5   It is also not intended that activities which are normal only for a particular person or group of people should be included.[61] Account must be taken of how far the activity is normal for most people and carried out by most people on a daily or frequent and fairly regular basis.[62] However, it is equally the case that what is normal does not depend on whether the majority of people do it.[63] Thus travelling on the London Underground or by plane is a normal day-to-day activity, but if the individual does not use these modes of transport in practice, it will be difficult to show that an inability to use them can be regarded as a substantial adverse effect.[64]

2.4.6   Where a child under six years of age has an impairment which does not have an effect on the child's ability to carry out one of the listed normal day-to-day activities, the impairment is nevertheless to be taken to have a substantial and long-term adverse effect on the child's ability to carry out normal day-to-day activities if it would normally have such an effect on the ability of a person aged six years or over.[65]

2.4.7   Although the DDA 1995 clearly covers mental illnesses and impairments, it might be difficult for persons with such conditions to be able to show that they have an adverse effect on normal day-to-day activities, as those activities are defined in the Act. In the employment sphere, many mental illnesses or impairments might have an adverse effect upon a person's full working capacity, but work is not one of the listed normal day-to-day activities.[66] Nevertheless, in one case, the EAT has held that a police officer with dyslexia, who was disadvantaged in taking employment-related assessments and examinations, was a disabled person. It said, somewhat controversially, that carrying out an assessment

---

[60]   See, for example, Guidance (2006), Part 2, para D25.

[61]   *Abadeh v British Telecommunications plc* [2001] IRLR 23, EAT (what is a normal day-to-day activity must be addressed without regard to whether it is normal to the particular applicant).

[62]   See Guidance (2006), Part 2, paras D4 *et seq.*

[63]   *Ekpe v Commissioner of Police of the Metropolis* [2001] IRLR 605, EAT (what is normal is anything which is not abnormal or unusual, judged by an objective population standard).

[64]   *Abadeh v British Telecommunications plc* [2001] IRLR 23, EAT.

[65]   Disability Discrimination (Meaning of Disability) Regulations 1996, SI 1996/1455, reg 6.

[66]   See Guidance (2006), Part 2, paras D7–D10 and *Law Hospital NHS Trust v Rush* [2001] IRLR 611, Ct of Sess.

or examination can be described as a normal day-to-day activity, which encompasses activities which are relevant to participation in professional life.[67]

2.5 SUBSTANTIAL ADVERSE EFFECT

2.5.1 To satisfy the definition of a disability, the putative disabled person must demonstrate that he or she has a physical or mental impairment 'which has a substantial and long-term adverse effect' on the ability to carry out normal day-to-day activities.[68] The revised statutory guidance specifically refers to the matters which a court or tribunal ought to take into account when determining whether an impairment has a substantial adverse effect on a person's ability to carry out normal day-to-day activities[69] or whether such an impairment has a long-term adverse effect.[70]

Meaning of 'substantial'

2.5.2 Whether an impairment has a substantial adverse effect upon a person is not explained in the DDA 1995.[71] It was intended that minor impairments should not provide a cause of action. The use of the word 'substantial' is designed to ensure that trivial conditions are beyond the scope of the legislation.[72] Someone whose hearing impairment merely requires them to view television with the volume up and results in occasional difficulty in hearing speech may have difficulty in showing substantial adverse effect.[73] The revised Guidance confirms that a substantial effect is one that is more than minor or trivial. It indicates that the requirement that an adverse effect be substantial is designed to reflect the general understanding of disability as being a limitation going beyond the normal differences in ability between people.[74] The word 'substantial' is not to be given its ordinary dictionary definition. The Guidance is to be followed so that, for example, the ability to prepare vegetables, cut up meat and carry a tray are all examples of normal day-to-day activities, as would be various DIY and household tasks. An inability to carry out these functions was regarded as 'obviously' amounting to a substantial

---

[67] *Paterson v Commissioner of Police of the* Metropolis [2007] IRLR 763, EAT, purporting to apply *ChacóNavas v Eurest Colectividades SA* C-13/05 [2006] IRLR 706, ECJ.

[68] DDA 1995, s 1(1).

[69] Guidance (2006) Section B.

[70] Guidance (2006) Section C.

[71] The word 'substantial' is also used, for example, in the employment provisions of Part 2, and there is no suggestion that this should be interpreted in different ways in different contexts. See the discussion of this question in Chapter 3.

[72] HC Deb Standing Committee E, col 114; HC Deb, vol 566, col 174.

[73] See the *obiter dicta* in *London Underground Ltd v Bragg* (1999) EAT/847/98.

[74] Guidance (2006), Part 2, para B1. An example of a tribunal applying the wrong test on substantial effect (under the Part 4 provisions on education) can be seen in *M and M v SW School and the Special Educational Needs and Disability Tribunal* [2004] EWHC Admin 2587.

adverse effect on the ability to carry out normal day-to-day activities.[75] However, it is for the tribunal (or the court) to assess what adverse effects are substantial or not. In the final analysis, what is and what is not a 'substantial' adverse effect will be a matter for judicial interpretation of the statutory language, albeit assisted by the provisions of the revised Guidance and any appropriate regulations.[76]

2.5.3   The revised Guidance states that, in judging whether the adverse effects of an impairment upon a normal day-to-day activity are substantial, account should be taken of the time taken to carry out the activity and the way in which the activity is carried out.[77] If the impairment adversely affects the speed or manner in which that person can perform a particular activity in comparison with other persons, that is a relevant consideration. Environmental considerations will also be important (for example, the effect which temperature or stress has upon the impairment).[78] The EAT has said that, in judging whether an impairment has a *substantial* adverse effect, a tribunal may take into account how the claimant appears to the tribunal to manage, 'although tribunals will be slow to regard a person's capabilities in the relatively strange adversarial environment as an entirely reliable guide to the level of ability to perform normal day-to-day activities'.[79] It will also be appropriate to take account of the cumulative effects of an impairment.[80] For example, someone with depression may experience only minor effects upon any of a number of the listed normal day-to-day activities, but the aggregate effect may be quite disabling and should be treated as so under the DDA 1995.[81] The cumulative effect of two or more impairments might also produce the adverse substantial adverse effect on normal day-to-day activities called for by the statute – even if, in isolation, each impairment could not be said to have such an effect.[82]

2.5.4   Account should also be taken of how far a person might reasonably be expected to modify his or her behaviour so as to prevent or reduce the adverse effects of an impairment on normal day-to-day

---

[75]   *Vicary v British Telecommunications plc* [1999] IRLR 680, EAT.

[76]   DDA 1995, Sch 1, para 5 provides that regulations may be made to provide for an effect of a prescribed kind on the ability of a person to carry out normal day-to-day activities to be treated as being (or, alternatively, as not being) a substantial adverse effect. No general regulations have been made under this power; but see Disability Discrimination (Meaning of Disability) Regulations 1996, SI 1996/1455, reg 5 (on tattoos and body piercing, discussed below) and reg 6 (on babies and young children under six years of age, discussed above).

[77]   Guidance (2006), Part 2, paras B2–B3.

[78]   Guidance (2006), Part 2, para B10.

[79]   *Goodwin v The Patent Office* [1999] IRLR 4, EAT. See also *Ekpe v Commissioner of Police of the Metropolis* [2001] IRLR 605, EAT (a tribunal considering whether to draw any conclusions from a party's behaviour during the hearing would be expected to raise it at the hearing).

[80]   Guidance (2006), Part 2, paras B4–B6.

[81]   Guidance (2006), Part 2, para B5 and example.

[82]   Guidance (2006), Part 2, para B6.

activities.[83] For example, a person with a condition which manifests itself as an allergic reaction to certain substances might reasonably be expected to take steps to avoid those substances. To that extent, that person could not be said to experience a substantial adverse effect upon his or her normal day-to-day activities and would no longer satisfy the definition of disability. However, such avoidance or coping strategies must be subject to a test of reasonableness and might produce second order disabling effects in themselves. In any event, it must be recognised that such strategies might break down at times of stress and that must be weighed in the balance.[84] The fact that a person is able to mitigate the effects of a disability does not mean that they are not disabled within the meaning of the legislation.[85]

Recurring conditions

2.5.5 The DDA 1995 provides that if an impairment is one which has had a substantial adverse effect on a person's ability to carry out normal day-to-day activities, but subsequently ceased to have that effect, it will be treated as continuing to have such a substantial adverse effect (that is, during any intervening period of remission or good health) 'if that effect is likely to recur'.[86] This is an essential provision which recognises that there are many impairments whose effects upon day-to-day activities fluctuate. In the case of epilepsy, for example, the underlying condition is constant, but the adverse effects of the condition are variable, with periods of impairment or disability alternating with periods of good health and normal activity. Such conditions are within the Act.[87] Nevertheless, seasonal allergic rhinitis, a condition whose effects are recurring and can be substantial for a brief time, has been excluded by regulation.[88]

2.5.6 In respect of an impairment or condition with recurring effects, the revised Guidance states that an effect is likely to recur if 'it is more likely than not that the effect will recur'.[89] If the effects are likely to recur

---

[83]   Guidance (2006), Part 2, paras B7–B9 and example..

[84]   Guidance (2006), Part 2, para B9.

[85]   *Vicary v British Telecommunications plc* [1999] IRLR 680, EAT.

[86]   DDA 1995, Sch 1, para 2(2). The likelihood of an effect recurring shall be disregarded in circumstances which may be prescribed in regulations (ibid, Sch 1, para 2(3)). No such regulations have been made to date.

[87]   HC Deb Standing Committee E, col 113.

[88]   See above.

[89]   Guidance (2006), Part 2, para C4. It is likely an event will happen if it is more probable than not that it will happen: Guidance (2006), Part 2, para C2. That is to be assessed at the time at which the discriminatory behaviour occurred: *Latchman v Reed Business Information Ltd* [2002] ICR 1453, EAT (it is not what had actually later occurred but what could earlier have been expected to occur that was to be judged and the relevant time to examine the likelihood of a recurrence was at the point at which the impairment had ceased to have a substantial adverse effect). See also *Spence v Intype Libra Ltd* EAT 0617/06 (EAT) IDS Employment Law Brief 844; *McDougall v Richmond Adult Community College* [2008] EWCA Civ 4 (Court of Appeal).

beyond 12 months after the first occurrence, then they are to be treated as long term.[90] However, in judging the likelihood of recurrence, account should be taken of all the circumstances, including any reasonable expectation that the person concerned should take steps to prevent the recurrence.[91] The EAT in *Swift v Chief Constable of Wiltshire Constabulary* suggests that, when considering the recurring conditions provisions, a tribunal should ask itself the following questions.[92] First, at some stage was there an impairment which had a substantial adverse effect on the claimant's ability to carry out normal day-to-day activities? Secondly, did the impairment cease to have that effect and, if so, when? Thirdly, what was the substantial adverse effect? Fourthly, is that substantial adverse effect likely to recur (ie is it more probable than not that the effect will recur)? The tribunal must be satisfied that the same effect is likely to recur and will again amount to a substantial adverse effect on the claimant's ability to carry out normal day-to-day activities. The question for the tribunal is whether the substantial adverse effect is likely to recur (and not simply whether the impairment or illness is likely to recur). The effect is that the impairment is treated as continuing for as long as its substantial adverse effect is likely to recur.

Progressive conditions

2.5.7   Special provision is made for persons with progressive conditions. Progressive conditions include cancer, multiple sclerosis, muscular dystrophy or HIV infection,[93] but this list is not exhaustive. Where a person has a 'progressive condition' and, as a result of that condition,[94] he or she has an impairment which has (or had) an effect on his or her ability to carry out normal day-to-day activities, but that effect is not (or was not) a *substantial* adverse effect, such a person is treated as having an impairment which has such a substantial adverse effect if the condition is

---

[90]   Guidance (2006), Part 2, para C5.
[91]   Guidance (2006), Part 2, para C8.
[92]   [2004] IRLR 540.
[93]   DDA 1995, Sch 1, para 8(1)(a), as amended. HIV infection means infection by a virus capable of causing AIDS: DDA 1995, Sch 1, para 9, as amended. Regulations may provide (for the purposes of this provision only) that conditions of a prescribed description are to be treated as being or not being progressive conditions (Sch 1, para 8(2)). No such regulations have been made to date. Note that a person who has cancer, HIV infection or multiple sclerosis (but not muscular dystrophy) is also deemed to have a disability, in any event: DDA 1995, Sch 1, para 6A, as amended.
[94]   Because of this phrase, this provision does not embrace a progressive condition (such as cancer) which has been treated – and is thus asymptomatic – but does cover the situation where the treatment itself has resulted in an impairment having an adverse effect upon a person's ability to carry out normal day-to-day activities: *Kirton v Tetrosyl Ltd* [2003] EWCA Civ 619, [2003] IRLR 353, CA (an impairment of urinary incontinence as a result of surgery for cancer was a disability and fell within the progressive conditions provisions – the words 'as a result of that condition' are not to be interpreted narrowly). The adverse effects (if any) arising from the impairment resulting from the treatment have to be judged on their own merits.

likely to result in that person having such an impairment in the future.[95] However, the double-edged nature of this sword is that a degenerative condition might be seen as undermining a claimant's claim in a Part 2 case to be employable (with or without adjustments) for the future.[96] The answer must be that this is a question that goes to remedy rather than to establishing disability or liability for discrimination. In any event, in order to rely upon the progressive condition provision, the claimant must establish that the condition in his or her case is likely to have a substantial adverse effect, usually by medical evidence as to the likely prognosis or by the use of statistical evidence.[97]

2.5.8 It is apparent from the parliamentary debates that the legislature did not intend that this provision should protect individuals from discrimination where they possess asymptomatic conditions:[98]

> 'We recognise that there is a need to protect people where the effect of the condition is not yet substantial but is expected to be so in the future. That is why the [Act] specifically includes people with progressive conditions as soon as there are any effects on their ability to carry out normal day-to-day activities. However, we do not believe that it would be right to include people with conditions which may remain latent, possibly for a considerable number of years . . . The Disability Discrimination [Act] is designed to protect people who have, or . . . have had, an actual disability. It is not a general anti-discrimination [Act] nor a general health discrimination [Act]. If we extend it to cover people who may develop a disability at some unspecified time in the future we will undermine the effectiveness of the [Act] by creating uncertainty about who is covered.'[99]

A symptomless illness or condition is not an impairment which has yet affected one of the designated normal day-to-day activities.[100]

2.5.9 Despite the inclusive tone of the statute's treatment of progressive conditions, the wording of the DDA 1995 makes it plain that it is to be the *future* effects of a *presently existing* progressive condition only which the law intends to embrace. A person whose medical status or condition merely indicates that it is likely that he or she might suffer from a progressive condition *in the future* is not treated as having an impairment with substantial adverse effects on ability to carry out normal day-to-day

---

[95] DDA 1995, Sch 1, para 8(1).

[96] See *London Underground Ltd v Bragg* (1999) EAT/847/98.

[97] *Mowat-Brown v University of Surrey* [2002] IRLR 235, EAT (the fact that the applicant had multiple sclerosis was not in itself sufficient to bring him within the progressive condition provision without evidence of the future likely effects of his condition upon him).

[98] HL Deb, vol 566, col 1061.

[99] HL Deb, vol 564, col 1682.

[100] DDA 1995, Sch 1, para 4. Persons with asymptomatic conditions or conditions where it is unclear whether substantial adverse effects are likely to recur or initial effects are likely to worsen may have difficulty in satisfying the definition of disability used in the DDA 1995.

activities. Thus the 'progressive conditions' provision does not include within the protection of the Act individuals who merely have a genetic or other predisposition to (or risk of) a progressive condition in the future. Individuals who have undergone a medical test which indicated that they have a predictive propensity to develop an impairment at a later date are not protected from disability discrimination at this point. The Act also does not protect individuals who have a mistaken or erroneous reputation as a person who has (or had) a disability or might do so in the future.

Severe disfigurement

2.5.10   An impairment which consists of a severe disfigurement is treated as having a substantial adverse effect on the ability of the person concerned to carry out normal day-to-day activities.[101] The assessment of the severity of a disfigurement is a matter of degree and account may be taken of where on the body the feature in question is to be found.[102] The implication is that a facial disfigurement is more likely to pass the test of severity than one hidden by a person's clothing. The inclusion of severe disfigurements within the definition of disability for the purposes of the DDA 1995 is important. Persons with facial port wine stains, other birth marks, severe burns or scalds, and other disfiguring signs face discrimination based upon aesthetic appearance. The revised Guidance also refers to scars, limb or postural deformation and diseases of the skin.[103] Such impairments are rarely disabling in themselves. Rather, the disability experienced by disfigured individuals is as a result of society's reaction to perceived imperfection. This is a rare example of the legislation acknowledging a social model of disability rather than a purely medical one.

2.5.11   While the DDA 1995 does not automatically exclude deliberately acquired severe disfigurements, it does provide for their potential exclusion by regulations.[104] Regulations stipulate that a severe disfigurement is not to be treated as having a substantial adverse effect on the ability of the person concerned to carry out normal day-to-day activities if it consists of a tattoo (which has not been removed) or body piercing for decorative or other *non-medical purposes* (including any object attached through the piercing for such purposes).[105] The present writer suggests that a severe disfigurement resulting from an attempt to

---

[101] DDA 1995, Sch 1, para 3(1).

[102] Guidance (2006), Part 2, para B21.

[103] Guidance (2006), Part 2, para C21. In *Cosgrove v Northern Ireland Ambulance Service* [2007] IRLR 397, NI CA, a claimant with the skin condition psoriasis was rejected for employment because his skin condition created an increased risk of infection and cross-infection. Although his psoriasis was a severe disfigurement, his disability was not merely cosmetic. He had not been rejected because of the disfigurement but because of the skin condition itself. His claim failed.

[104] DDA 1995, Sch 1, para 3(3).

[105] Disability Discrimination (Meaning of Disability) Regulations 1996, SI 1996/1455, reg 5.

remove a tattoo would not be so excluded. For the moment, the regulations do not make any further exclusions. It should be noted that there is no general exclusion of deliberately acquired disfigurements (such as facial or bodily scarring caused by self-mutilation or self-administered injury).[106]

Effect of medical treatment

2.5.12 Does a person whose disability is controlled, corrected or adjusted by medical treatment, or by the use of medication, auxiliary devices or other aids, remain a person with an impairment for the purpose of protection against disability-related discrimination? In a strict sense, such a person might no longer be said to have an impairment which has an adverse effect on normal day-to-day activities. Yet, at the same time, the underlying condition or impairment remains and the person is disabled to the extent that the method of control or correction will involve residual or second order effects and inconveniences. Equally, such a person might experience continuing adverse treatment at the hands of others who might continue to regard the individual as disabled. That might be the case illustratively where an individual walks with the aid of a prosthesis or is mobile with the assistance of a motorised wheelchair.

2.5.13 The DDA 1995 provides that an impairment which would be likely to have a substantial adverse effect on the ability of the person concerned to carry out normal day-to-day activities – but for the fact that measures are being taken to treat or correct it – is nevertheless to be treated as continuing to be an impairment amounting to a disability.[107] The legislation gives examples of measures treating or correcting an impairment as including 'medical treatment and the use of a prosthesis or other aid'.[108]

2.5.14 The DDA 1995 does not define what is meant by an 'aid', but the EAT has offered the *obiter* view that this refers 'to aids such as zimmer frames or sticks or wheelchairs and not to household objects' (such as automatic can-openers).[109] Similarly, the term 'medical treatment' is not defined. The EAT has held that counselling sessions with a consultant clinical psychologist constitute such treatment.[110] Provided that the impairment would have had a substantial adverse effect on a person's ability to carry out normal day-to-day activities *but for* the fact that it has been treated or controlled or corrected in the manner described, then it is also to be treated as continuing to have such a substantial adverse effect

---

[106] HC Deb Standing Committee E, cols 110–111.
[107] DDA 1995, Sch 1, para 6(1).
[108] Ibid, Sch 1, para 6(2).
[109] *Vicary v British Telecommunications* [1999] IRLR 680, EAT. See also *Carden v Pickerings Europe Ltd* [2005] IRLR 720, EAT (a plate and pins surgically inserted in the claimant's ankle).
[110] *Kapadia v London Borough of Lambeth* [2000] IRLR 14, EAT, and [2000] IRLR 699, CA.

even though no such effect is actually experienced because of such treatment or control or correction. An example of such an impairment might include insulin-controlled diabetes or medication-regulated epilepsy. A further illustration would be hearing loss improved by a hearing aid.

2.5.15 The EAT has said that only continuing medical treatment (and not concluded treatment) is relevant.[111] Where the treatment has ceased the effects of that treatment should be taken into account in assessing the disability. If the medical evidence is that the treatment has created a permanent improvement then the effects of that treatment should be taken into account when assessing the disability. In contrast, where the treatment is continuing, it must be disregarded if the final outcome of the treatment cannot be determined or it is known that ceasing the treatment would result in a relapse of worsened condition.

2.5.16 The revised Guidance states that this provision applies even if the measures in question result in the effects being completely under control or not at all apparent.[112] The question of whether or not a person has an impairment which has a substantial adverse effect upon the ability to carry out normal day-to-day activities is to be answered by reference to what would be the effect of the impairment or condition but for the treatment, aid or medication.[113] A tribunal (or court) should examine how a claimant's abilities have been affected whilst on medication (or, by analogy, whilst receiving any other medical treatment). It should then consider the 'deduced effects': that is, what effects there would have been *without* the medication (or other medical intervention) and whether those effects are clearly more than minor or trivial.[114] Medical evidence as to what the deduced effects would be is essential.[115]

2.5.17 However, this provision does not extend to the impairment of a person's sight, to the extent that the impairment is, in the particular person's case, 'correctable by spectacles or contact lenses'.[116] Individuals with spectacles or contact lenses which compensate for an impairment to their sight do not usually regard themselves as disabled and are not treated as such for the purposes of the DDA 1995. The use of the word 'correctable' seems to suggest also that an individual who has a sight impairment, but does not use spectacles or contact lenses that might otherwise correct the sight loss, would not qualify as a 'disabled person'.

---

[111] *Abadeh v British Telecommunications plc* [2001] IRLR 23, EAT.

[112] Guidance (2006), Part 2, para B12.

[113] Guidance (2006), Part 2, para B13.

[114] See *Goodwin v The Patent Office* [1999] IRLR 4, EAT, *Kapadia v London Borough of Lambeth* [2000] IRLR 14, EAT, and [2000] IRLR 699, CA.

[115] *Woodrup v London Borough of Southwark* [2002] EWCA Civ 1716, [2003] IRLR 111, CA (the burden of proof is with the claimant).

[116] DDA 1995, Sch 1, para 6(3)(a). Regulations may also provide that this exception be extended to other impairments: ibid, Sch 1, para 6(3)(b). No such regulations have been made to date.

In other words, this provision of the Act only embraces involuntary disabilities. This might mean that a person who chooses not to take basic, non-surgical remedial action to correct a vision impairment cannot claim protection of the Act. The statute does not suggest that a sight impairment correctable by surgical techniques is presently excluded from the coverage of the legislation. However, the Guidance states that the only effects on ability to carry out normal day-to-day activities to be considered are *those which remain* when spectacles or contact lenses are used (or would remain if they were used).[117] There would seem to be some room for confusion here which will call for judicial resolution.

2.6   LONG-TERM ADVERSE EFFECT

2.6.1   The DDA 1995 is more expansive in its explication of what amounts to long-term effects of an impairment. It provides that the effect of an impairment is 'long-term' if:

- it has lasted for at least 12 months; or

- the period for which it lasts is likely to be at least 12 months; or

- it is likely to last for the rest of the life of the person affected.[118]

The intention is to exclude from the protection of the anti-discrimination principle those persons whose impairment or disability is merely short-term or temporary.[119]

2.6.2   Suppose that an employee suffered a sudden onset of deafness and was dismissed within six months of medical diagnosis. Would the employee have redress under the law, all other things being equal? Even though at the time of dismissal the impairment had not lasted at least 12 months, nevertheless the employee should be able to show that the period for which the hearing impairment is likely to last is at least 12 months, and so the employee would be enabled to seek a remedy. However, a person refused access to a restaurant because he has a broken leg in plaster, or because she exhibits obvious signs of German measles, would not have redress because the impairments or conditions in question do not have, or are not likely to have, long-term effects.[120] How does the DDA 1995 treat a person diagnosed as having a terminal illness with a prognosis that he or she will not live for more than a few months and less than 12 months?[121]

---

[117] Guidance (2006), Part 2, para B14.
[118] DDA 1995, Sch 1, para 2(1). Regulations may prescribe circumstances in which an effect which would not otherwise be long term is to be treated as a long-term effect or an effect which would otherwise be long term is not to be treated as a long-term effect (ibid, Sch 1, para 2(4)). No such regulations have been made to date.
[119] HC Deb Standing Committee E, col 70.
[120] See further HC Deb Standing Committee E, cols 77–78.
[121] Ibid, col 78.

Could such a person be lawfully refused, for example, provision of goods or services in a shop or restaurant? Terminal illnesses are within the definition and, in this case, the impairment can reasonably be expected to last for the rest of the life of the person affected.

2.6.3   The revised Guidance states that, in judging whether the adverse effects of an impairment are long-term, it is not necessary for the effect to be the same throughout the period in question. The effect may be variable or progressive. Provided the impairment continues to have (or is likely to have) an adverse effect on ability to carry out normal day-to-day activities throughout the period, there is a long-term effect.[122] The Guidance also states:

> 'In assessing the likelihood of an effect lasting for 12 months, account should be taken of the total period for which the effect exists. This includes any time before the point at which the alleged incident of discriminatory behaviour which is being considered by the adjudicating body occurred. Account should also be taken of both the typical length of such an effect on an individual, and any relevant factors specific to this individual (for example, general state of health or age).'[123]

Note, however, that provision is also made for recurring effects.[124] If the adverse effects are likely to recur beyond 12 months after the first occurrence, they are to be treated as long-term.[125] It is likely that an event will happen if it is more probable than not that it will happen.[126]

2.6.4   In an early case, it was held that an employment tribunal in a Part 2 case should consider the adverse effects of the applicant's condition up to and including the date of the hearing.[127] That was a curious case where it would seem that the act of disability discrimination complained of triggered a recurrence of the applicant's disability which had appeared to have been successfully treated or at least under control. It is suggested that the proper approach is to judge whether the applicant or claimant satisfied the definition of a disabled person as at the date of the alleged act of unlawful discrimination, effectively ignoring such evidence as may have become available by the time of the date of the hearing.[128]

---

[122]   Guidance (2006), Part 2, para C6.

[123]   Guidance (2006), Part 2, para C3.

[124]   See DDA 1995, Sch 1, para 2(2), discussed above.

[125]   Guidance (2006), Part 2, paras C4–C6.

[126]   Guidance (2006), Part 2, para C4.

[127]   *Greenwood v British Airways plc* [1999] IRLR 600, EAT, purporting to rely upon the original Guidance (1996), Part II, para B8.

[128]   *Cruickshank v VAW Motorcast Ltd* [2002] IRLR 24, EAT; *Spence v Intype Libra Ltd* EAT 0617/06 (EAT) IDS Employment Law Brief 844; *McDougall v Richmond Adult Community College* [2008] EWCA Civ 4, Court of Appeal, allowing an appeal from [2007] IRLR 771, EAT.

Past disability and long-term adverse effect

2.6.5   Some modification of the meaning of 'long-term effect' is necessary in order to accommodate the inclusion of past disabilities.[129] When dealing with the question of whether a person with a past disability has experienced a long-term adverse effect on ability to carry out normal day-to-day activities, the effect of an impairment is a long-term effect if it has lasted for at least 12 months.[130] Where an impairment ceases to have a substantial adverse effect on a person's ability to carry out normal day-to-day activities, it is to be treated as continuing to have that effect if that effect recurs.[131]

2.7   PERSONS DEEMED TO BE DISABLED

2.7.1   There is no implicit assumption that a court or tribunal will regard a certification of a person as disabled under other disability legislation as conclusive or persuasive of their status under the DDA 1995. However, the Act contains one exceptional case in respect of a person who was a 'registered disabled person' under the Disabled Persons (Employment) Act 1944 (or its Northern Ireland equivalent).[132] A person who was on the register maintained under the 1944 Act on 12 January 1995, and who remained registered on 2 December 1996, was 'deemed to have a disability'. That person was treated as a disabled person for the purpose of the application of any provision of the DDA 1995 for 'the initial period'.[133] The certificate of registration was treated as conclusive evidence, in relation to the person with respect to whom it was issued, in respect of the matters certified and, unless the contrary was shown, its validity was entitled to be taken at face value.[134]

2.7.2   However, this deemed status only lasted for the so-called 'initial period'.[135] This was a period of three years beginning on 2 December 1996 (and thus ending on 1 December 1999).[136] Such a person will now need to meet the statutory definition of 'disabled person' contained in all its detail in the DDA 1995 and any accompanying guidance and regulations. In practice, that might not be an insurmountable task for a person who qualified under the Disabled Persons (Employment) Act 1944 and whose conditions and circumstances remain unchanged or

---

[129] By virtue of DDA 1995, s 2(2) and Sch 2, para 2. Note the amendments made by the Disability Discrimination Act 1995 (Amendment) Regulations 2003, SI 2003/1673.

[130] DDA 1995, Sch 2, para 5, modifying Sch 1, para 2(1)–(3).

[131] See Guidance (2006), Part 2, paras A15–A17 and C10.

[132] DDA 1995, Sch 1, para 7. For the modification of these provisions in the Northern Ireland context, see Sch 1, para 49. Prescribed descriptions of persons might also be deemed to have disabilities and to be disabled persons for the purposes of the Act: Sch 1, para 7(5)–(6). No such prescription has been made to date.

[133] DDA 1995, Sch 1, para 7(2)(a).

[134] Ibid, Sch 1, paras 7(3)–(4) and 7(7).

[135] Ibid, Sch 1, para 7(2)(a).

[136] Ibid, Sch 1, para 7(7).

comparable. In any event, such a person will be regarded as being a person who *had* a disability, and thus to have been a disabled person, during the initial period.[137] This means that he or she will be able to rely upon the extension of the DDA 1995 to include persons who have had a disability in the past.[138]

2.7.3 The Disability Discrimination (Blind and Partially Sighted Persons) Regulations 2003 provide that a person who is certified as blind or partially sighted by a consultant ophthalmologist, or registered as blind or partially sighted in a register maintained by or on behalf of a local authority, is deemed to be a disabled person for the purposes of the DDA 1995.[139]

2.7.4 With effect from 5 December 2005, a person who has cancer, HIV infection or multiple sclerosis is now also deemed to have a disability, without more inquiry.[140]

2.8   PAST DISABILITIES

2.8.1 Parts 2, 3 and 4 of the DDA 1995 (discrimination in relation to the employment field, goods, facilities and services, premises and education) apply *pari passu* in relation to a person 'who has had a disability' as if that person is a person who has that disability at the present or relevant time.[141] The thinking behind this provision is as follows:

> 'It has become clear that people who have had a disability, although they may be no longer disabled as such, share with people who are currently disabled, a need for protection against discrimination in relation to their disability . . . It is clearly a very important part of the whole process of recovery that someone who has been disabled is able not only to participate fully in employment and social activities but to feel confident in doing so . . . In addition, we have been persuaded that it is not always possible to tell when a person has fully recovered from a disability and when the condition is no longer likely to recur.'[142]

It ensures consistency of treatment between persons who are presently disabled and those individuals who have recovered from the same condition.[143]

---

[137] DDA 1995, Sch 1, para 7(2)(b).
[138] Ibid, s 2 and Sch 2 as discussed below.
[139] Discussed above.
[140] DDA 1995, Sch 1, para 6A, as amended. See Guidance (2006), Part 2, paras A10–A11.
[141] DDA 1995, s 2(1). The substantive provisions of the Act are appropriately modified (s 2(2) and Sch 2, as amended by the Disability Discrimination Act 1995 (Amendment) Regulations 2003, SI 2003/1673). In particular, references in Parts 2 to 4 of the Act to a disabled person are also to be read as references to a person who has had a disability (Sch 2, para 2).
[142] HL Deb, vol 564, col 1655.
[143] Ibid, vol 564, col 1656.

2.8.2 In a case of alleged discrimination against a person who complains of an act based upon that person's past disability, it does not matter that the relevant provisions of the DDA 1995 were not in force when that person was actually experiencing the disability in question. The question as to whether a person had a disability at a particular time is determined as if the relevant provisions of the DDA 1995 which were in force at the time of the discriminatory act had been in force at the relevant time (ie when the person had the disability in issue).[144] Furthermore, the past disability in question might have been experienced at a time before the passing of the new legislation.[145]

2.8.3 The inclusion of past disabilities within the protection of the DDA 1995 is an important concession. It provides a potential remedy for those persons who are discriminated against because of their history or record of disability. For example, a person with a history of depression or mental or emotional illness might be unreasonably excluded from employment opportunity. That person would otherwise have no cause of action unless the depression or mental or emotional illness was a clinically recognised condition which the individual had at the time the employment opportunity was denied. However, it is important to note that, where a person seeks to rely upon the status of being 'a person who has had a disability', it will still be necessary for that person to show that, at the relevant time in the past, he or she had a physical or mental impairment which had a substantial and long-term adverse effect on his or her ability to carry out normal day-to-day activities.

---

[144] DDA 1995, s 2(4).
[145] Ibid, s 2(5).

CHAPTER 3

THE EMPLOYMENT FIELD: COMMON CONCEPTS

3.1 INTRODUCTION

3.1.1 Part 2 of the Disability Discrimination Act 1995, as originally enacted, was concerned with disability discrimination in employment. That embraced discrimination by employers, against contract workers and by trade organisations.[1] Provision was also made in respect of charities and supported employment, discriminatory advertisements, occupational pension schemes and insurance services.[2] Part 2 contained its own measures for enforcement, remedies and procedure, the validity of certain agreements and the alteration to premises occupied under leases.[3]

Disability Discrimination Act 1995 (Amendment) Regulations 2003

3.1.2 These provisions have been amended by the Disability Discrimination Act 1995 (Amendment) Regulations 2003, with effect from 1 October 2004.[4] The amendments give effect to the EC Framework Employment Directive.[5] The purpose of the Directive is to lay down a general framework for combating discrimination on the ground (among others) of disability as regards employment and occupation, with a view to putting into effect in the Member States the principle of equal treatment.[6] As amended, Part 2 now addresses the problem of discrimination against disabled persons in the employment field at large. In particular, it covers applicants for employment, employees, contract workers, office-holders, police officers, partners in firms, barristers and advocates, practical work experience, occupational pensions and group insurance services. It also deals with discrimination in the provision of employment services, in relation to locally-electable authorities and their members, and by public

---

[1] DDA 1995, ss 4–7, 12 and 13–15, respectively.
[2] Ibid, ss 10, 11, 17 and 18, respectively.
[3] Ibid, ss 8 (and Sch 3, Part 1), 9 and 16 (and Sch 4, Part 1), respectively.
[4] SI 2003/1673. In Northern Ireland, see the Disability Discrimination Act 1995 (Amendment) (Northern Ireland) Regulations 2004, SR 2004/55. Amendments have also been effected by the Disability Discrimination Act 2005 and the Equality Act 2006. They are addressed here and in later chapters, as the need arises.
[5] Council Directive 2000/78/EC of 27 November 2000, establishing a general framework for equal treatment in employment and occupation: OJ (2 December 2000) L 303/16.
[6] Ibid, Art 1.

authorities.[7] The discussions in this chapter and the next are concerned with the relevant law, as in force from 1 October 2004.

3.1.3 To a large extent, the amended provisions in Part 2 are modelled after similar provisions in other employment discrimination legislation,[8] especially following the changes effected in discrimination law generally by the EC Framework Employment Directive. Where the statutory language is common or identical, case-law under related discrimination legislation will be instructive. However, there are important differences between the 1995 Act and the other legal provisions, although those differences are less marked now than they once were. In particular, the 1995 Act deals with direct and indirect forms of discrimination in a unique fashion, it uses a different comparative basis for detecting discrimination, it contains a limited but distinctive justification defence in particular circumstances and it imposes a positive duty upon employers to accommodate disabled persons. The Court of Appeal has expressly warned against approaching the 1995 Act with assumptions and concepts familiar from experience of the earlier equal opportunities statutes.[9]

Secondary sources

3.1.4 Part 2 of the Act, so far as it originally affected employment and contract work, first came into force on 2 December 1996. It has been the subject of regulations amplifying (and sometimes narrowing) the provisions on employment discrimination.[10] Two updated Codes of Practice have been issued by the former DRC to support the amended law, with effect from 1 October 2004.[11] They provide guidance and assistance in respect of the rights and obligations under Part 2. They do not impose

---

7   These are dealt with in later chapters.

8   See, in particular: Sex Discrimination Act 1975 (as amended); Race Relations Act 1976 (as amended); Part-time Workers (Prevention of Less Favourable Treatment) Regulations 2000 (as amended); Fixed-term Employees (Prevention of Less Favourable Treatment) Regulations 2002; Employment Equality (Religion or Belief) Regulations 2003 (as amended); Employment Equality (Sexual Orientation) Regulations 2003 (as amended); and Employment Equality (Age) Regulations 2006.

9   *Clark v TDG Ltd t/a Novacold* [1999] IRLR 318, CA.

10 Disability Discrimination (Employment) Regulations 1996, SI 1996/1456, and Disability Discrimination (Employment) Regulations (Northern Ireland) 1996, SR 1996/419. From 1 October 2004, these regulations are revoked and replaced in part by the Disability Discrimination (Employment Field) (Leasehold Premises) Regulations 2004, SI 2004/153, and the Disability Discrimination (Employment Field) (Leasehold Premises) Regulations (Northern Ireland) 2004, SR 2004/374. They in turn revoke and replace in full the Disability Discrimination (Sub-leases and Sub-tenancies) Regulations 1996, SI 1996/1333, and the Disability Discrimination (Sub-leases and Sub-tenancies) Regulations (Northern Ireland) 1996, SR 1996/420. See **6.3**.

11 DDA 1995, s 53A; *Code of Practice: Employment and Occupation* (2004); *Code of Practice: Trade Organisations and Qualifications Bodies* (2004). They replace the *Code of Practice for the Elimination of Discrimination in the Field of Employment Against Disabled Persons or Persons Who Have Had a Disability* (1996). Separate (but essentially identical) Codes of Practice apply in Northern Ireland, reflecting the different institutional context of the province.

legal obligations and are not intended to be an authoritative statement of the law. However, they are admissible in proceedings before an employment tribunal or court, which must take into account any provision of a Code of Practice which appears to be relevant to the determination of a question in those proceedings.[12]

The scheme of Part 2, as amended

3.1.5 The amendments made to the scheme of Part 2 call for a different treatment of the analysis of discrimination in the enlarged employment field than was adopted in early editions of this book. Part 2 now contains a number of sections that deal with legal concepts that are common across the employment field, regardless of the identity of the respondent. These common concepts are: (1) the meaning of discrimination; (2) the meaning of harassment; (3) general provisions on reasonable adjustments; (4) relationships which have come to an end; (5) discriminatory advertisements; and (6) instructions and pressure to discriminate.[13] In the litigation process, the natural starting-point is to identify the particular cause of action that arises on the alleged facts. However, to do so presupposes an understanding of the common concepts that underpin those causes of action, such as the meaning of discrimination or the scope of the duty to make reasonable adjustments.

3.1.6 Accordingly, in this chapter, the common concepts are described and explained. In Chapter 4, the individual causes of action are then examined. Enforcement, remedies and procedure will be dealt with in Chapter 10, as will the revised provisions on validity of contracts, collective agreements and rules of undertaking. Alterations to premises occupied by employers and others under leases are dealt with in Chapter 6.

3.2 DISCRIMINATION

3.2.1 For the purposes of establishing the unlawfulness of an act under Part 2 of the DDA 1995, as amended, a person might 'discriminate' against a disabled person in one of four ways.[14] In shorthand terms, these might be termed as: (1) disability-related discrimination; (2) direct discrimination; (3) failure to make reasonable adjustments; and (4) victimisation. Victimisation is a concept which is common to other parts of the Act and is dealt with in more detail in Chapter 10. Account will also be taken shortly of the provisions dealing with harassment. Consideration will also be given to discrimination by association and perceived discrimination.

---

[12] DDA 1995, s 53A(8).
[13] Ibid, ss 3A, 3B, 18B, 16A, 16B and 16C, respectively.
[14] Ibid, ss 3A and 55.

3.2.2 In the account which follows, the 'person' who discriminates will be – as the case may be: an employer; the relevant person in relation to an appointment to an office or post; the trustees or managers of an occupational pension scheme; a firm (or partnership); a barrister or barrister's clerk or an advocate; a person instructing a barrister or an advocate; a trade organisation; a qualifications body; or a person providing practical work experience. Discrimination by locally-electable authorities and public authorities, or by providers of employment services, is dealt with in later chapters. The statutory language refers to the person as 'he', but that person can equally be 'she' or 'it'. In many cases, the person will be a legal person, such as a limited company, a statutory body or an unincorporated association. Wherever appropriate, the term 'respondent' will be used in the analysis below to avoid confusion, unless a particular kind of respondent (such as an employer) needs to be identified in context.

Disability-related discrimination

3.2.3 For the purposes of Part 2, a person discriminates against a disabled person if, for a reason which relates to the disabled person's disability, the person treats the disabled person less favourably than the person treats (or would treat) others to whom that reason does not (or would not) apply and the person cannot show that the treatment in question is justified.[15] Treatment is justified for this purpose if, but only if, the reason for it is both material to the circumstances of the particular case and substantial.[16] However, treatment of a disabled person cannot be justified in this way if it amounts to direct discrimination.[17] Moreover, if a person is under a duty to make reasonable adjustments in relation to the disabled person, but fails to comply with that duty, the treatment of the disabled person cannot be justified unless it would have been justified even if that duty had been complied with.[18] This definition of 'disability discrimination' has been part of the statute since it was first enacted.

Less favourable treatment

3.2.4 The key concept is that of less favourable treatment. It is for the claimant to identify the less favourable treatment complained of.[19] A person only discriminates against a disabled person if he or she treats the disabled person 'less favourably than' the person 'treats or would treat others' to whom the reason which relates to the disabled person's

---

[15] DDA 1995, s 3A(1); *Code of Practice: Employment and Occupation* (2004), paras 4.27–4.32 (and examples); *Code of Practice: Trade Organisations and Qualifications Bodies* (2004), paras 4.26–4.31 (and examples).

[16] DDA 1995, s 3A(3).

[17] Ibid, s 3A(4). Direct discrimination is discrimination that falls within s 3A(5) and will be discussed below.

[18] Ibid, s 3A(6).

[19] *British Gas Services Ltd v McCaull* [2001] IRLR 60, EAT.

disability does not or would not apply.[20] This concept of less favourable treatment calls for a comparative approach. The question is: how has the disabled person been treated in comparison with other persons to whom the reason relating to the disabled person's disability does not apply? If the treatment of the comparator is more favourable than the treatment of the claimant, one of the necessary (but not sufficient) criteria for establishing unlawful discrimination is in place. A number of points should be noted about this definition of 'discrimination'.

3.2.5 First, a disabled person could seek to show that he or she has been treated less favourably than a hypothetical (rather than an actual) comparator. The double use of the word 'would' supports that reasoning.[21] This is especially important where a disabled person has been refused or denied opportunities in the employment field in a context which is not an immediately competitive one. For example, a disabled employee denied promotion would not need to show that a colleague was actually promoted instead. It might be sufficient to show that a similarly situated employee without a disability would have been promoted in those circumstances. A hypothetical comparator can be constructed by having regard to actual comparators whose circumstances were similar but not identical to those of the claimant.[22] Where a claimant can show that he or she was disadvantaged by reason of his or her disability, it may not be necessary at all to identify other comparators with whom to compare the treatment of the disabled person.[23]

3.2.6 Secondly, there will often be no 'smoking gun' or direct evidence of discrimination. Prior to 1 October 2004, an employment tribunal may have been able to draw inferences of discrimination from the primary facts.[24] The outcome in disability discrimination cases was often dependent upon the propriety of drawing inferences from primary facts in relation to the question of whether there has been less favourable treatment for a reason related to disability. If an employer gave an unsatisfactory explanation for the detrimental treatment of a disabled person (eg a dismissal), it was open to the tribunal to infer disability

---

[20] DDA 1995, s 3A(1)(a); *Code of Practice: Employment and Occupation* (2004), paras 4.30–4.31 (and examples); *Code of Practice: Trade Organisations and Qualifications Bodies* (2004), paras 4.29–4.30 (and examples).

[21] DDA 1995, s 3A(1)(a).

[22] The case-law in race and sex discrimination is instructive: *Chief Constable of West Yorkshire v Vento* [2001] IRLR 124, EAT; *Balamoody v United Kingdom Central Council for Nursing, Midwifery and Health Visiting* [2001] EWCA Civ 2097, [2002] IRLR 288, CA.

[23] *British Sugar plc v Kirker* [1998] IRLR 624, EAT (but for his or her disability, would the disabled person have been treated in that way?).

[24] *West Midlands Passenger Transport Executive v Singh* [1988] IRLR 186, CA; *King v Great Britain-China Centre* [1991] IRLR 513, CA; *Qureshi v London Borough of Newham* [1991] IRLR 264, CA; *Zafar v Glasgow City Council* [1998] ICR 125, HL; *Anya v University of Oxford* [2001] IRLR 364, CA; *Rihal v London Borough of Ealing* [2004] IRLR 642, CA; *Bahl v The Law Society* [2004] IRLR 799, CA.

discrimination.[25] From 1 October 2004, where the claimant proves facts from which the tribunal could conclude, in the absence of an adequate explanation, that the respondent has acted in a way which is unlawful under Part 2, the tribunal shall uphold the complaint, unless the respondent proves that it did not so act.[26]

3.2.7   Thirdly, a disabled person can seek to show that he or she has been treated less favourably than another disabled person has been or would be. The provision does not necessarily call for an analysis of discriminatory behaviour which distinguished between disabled and non-disabled individuals. For example, two equally well-qualified applicants might be in competition for an employment vacancy. One has a physical disability and the other a mental disability. If, without interviewing both candidates and considering their respective merits, the employer automatically rejects the applicant with a mental disability, that action could form the basis of a complaint of disability-related discrimination brought by the rejected applicant. Again, the employer might be able to justify the differential treatment, but the individual with a mental disability was entitled to be given due consideration.[27]

3.2.8   Fourthly, the actual or hypothetical comparison is between the disabled person and a comparator to whom the reason relating to the disabled person's disability does not or would not apply. The definition of disability-related discrimination does not call for a simplistic comparison between a disabled person and a person who is not disabled or who does not have the disability in question. During the parliamentary debates, the Minister gave the example of two employees who cannot type: one because he or she is disabled with arthritis and the other (who is not disabled) because he or she has never been taught to type. If the disabled person with arthritis is refused employment as a typist, that is not discriminatory treatment, provided the non-disabled person (who has never been taught to type) is also refused employment in such a position.[28] The disabled person has been refused employment because of a reason related to disability (the inability to type being due to arthritis). However, he or she has not been treated less favourably in comparison with the other person if the employer has rejected all candidates who cannot type. If the employer offers the position to someone who is able to

---

25 British Sugar plc v Kirker [1998] IRLR 624, EAT; Rowden v Dutton Gregory (a firm)

[25]   *British Sugar plc v Kirker* [1998] IRLR 624, EAT; *Rowden v Dutton Gregory (a firm)* [2002] ICR 971, EAT.

[26]   DDA 1995, s 17A(1C), implementing Council Directive 2000/78/EC, Art 10; *Barton v Investec Henderson Crosthwaite Securities Ltd* [2003] IRLR 332, EAT; *University of Huddersfield v Wolff* [2004] IRLR 534, EAT; *Chamberlin Solicitors v Emokpae* [2004] IRLR 592, EAT; *Sinclair Roche & Temperley v Heard* [2004] IRLR 763, EAT; *Code of Practice: Employment and Occupation* (2004), paras 4.41–4.43 (and examples); *Code of Practice: Trade Organisations and Qualifications Bodies* (2004), paras 4.40–4.42 (and examples).

[27]   It is also likely to be direct discrimination but, if so, that cannot be justified.

[28]   HL Deb, vol 566, col 1200; *Code of Practice: Employment and Occupation* (2004), para 4.30 (example); *Code of Practice: Trade Organisations and Qualifications Bodies* (2004), para 4.29 (example).

type, that may be less favourable treatment of the person with arthritis for a reason related to his or her disability. Nevertheless, subject to the duty to make adjustments, the employer will probably be able to explain the treatment if typing skills are a requirement of the position applied for.

3.2.9 Fifthly, is the basis of the comparison to be drawn widely or narrowly? This depends upon the interpretation to be placed upon the phrase 'that reason'.[29] Take, for example, a disabled employee who is dismissed for absenteeism, including disability-related absences. With whom should the employee be compared for the purpose of establishing less favourable treatment? One possibility is to compare how the disabled employee has been treated relative to an employee also absent from work for the same length of time, but for a reason which is not related to disability. This would reflect the usual expectation in discrimination cases that like should be compared with like.[30]

3.2.10 However, disability-related discrimination (unlike direct discrimination) does not require the comparison to be based upon a consideration of the comparators in relevant circumstances which are the same or not materially different. Thus, a second possibility is to compare how the disabled employee (who is unable to perform the functions of his or her job) has been treated in comparison with other employees who were not absent from work at all (ie who are performing the main functions of their jobs). This focuses upon the reason for the treatment (ie the reason for the dismissal) and not the reason for the absence which led to the dismissal. The disabled employee has been dismissed for absenteeism. Some of those absences are related to his or her disability, so the dismissal is for a reason (ie absenteeism) which relates to the disabled person's disability. For the purposes of establishing less favourable treatment, the comparison must be with others to whom that reason (ie absenteeism) does not (or would not) apply. Attention would then switch to the employer's justification defence.[31]

3.2.11 That is the approach favoured by the Court of Appeal in *Clark v TDG Ltd t/a Novacold* and is now the authoritative one.[32] It has been explained as requiring the tribunal to determine the material reason for the treatment complained of; then to ask whether that material reason related to the disability in question; and finally to consider whether the respondent would have treated in the same way some other person to whom that material reason would not apply.[33]

---

[29] DDA 1995, s 3A(1)(a).

[30] *Clark v Novacold Ltd* [1998] IRLR 420, EAT.

[31] DDA 1995, s 3A(1)(b), subject to the duty to make reasonable adjustments.

[32] [1999] IRLR 318, CA. The Court of Appeal did not comment upon the EAT's approach in *Kirker v British Sugar plc* [1998] IRLR 624. The 'but for' test in *Kirker* is not without the attraction of simplicity, but *Novacold* navigates the statutory language more assuredly.

[33] *Cosgrove v Caesar & Howie* [2001] IRLR 653, EAT. Despite *Novacold*, in *Abbey National plc v Fairbrother* [2007] IRLR 320, EAT an employee with obsessive

Reason related to disability

3.2.12   The less favourable treatment of a disabled person must be 'for a reason which relates to the disabled person's disability'.[34] The intention, purpose or motive for so acting is not relevant. However, there must be a nexus or causal connection between the less favourable treatment and the claimant's disability.[35] The Act does not prohibit an employer from appointing the best person for the job. Equally, it does not prevent employers or others in the employment field from treating disabled people more favourably than those without a disability. A disabled person who is refused or denied an opportunity in the employment field because he or she does not have the necessary vocational qualifications, or is not the best person on merit, has not been discriminated against. That person has been treated less favourably than the person who was awarded the opportunity, at least in the sense that his or her employment aspirations have been disappointed. Nevertheless, the reason for the apparently less favourable treatment is not that person's disability, but rather a reason which is unrelated to disability, namely merit or qualification.

3.2.13   The test of causation under the DDA 1995 appears to be the same as that under the other discrimination statutes – was the person's disability the effective and predominant cause or the real and efficient cause of the less favourable treatment?[36] If an employment tribunal is to conclude that there is no connection between the disability and the discriminatory treatment, this must be explained by reference to the evidence (including medical evidence) and its findings of fact.[37] It is equally important for the tribunal to identify correctly what is the treatment that is the subject of the complaint.

3.2.14   For example, in one case, the payment of contractual sick pay was discretionary.[38] The claimant previously had been paid contractual sick pay during disability-related absences. However, due to high sickness levels among its workforce, the employer then exercised its discretion not to pay sick pay generally. It refused to pay sick pay to the claimant when he experienced further disability-related absences. He would be treated no

---

compulsive disorder (OCD) was bullied and taunted by colleagues at work. Some, but not all, of that treatment was related to her disability. However, another, non-disabled colleague was also subjected to this treatment. The EAT ruled that the disabled employee had not been treated less favourably than the non-disabled employee. The present author suggests that the correct approach, required by *Novacold*, would be a comparison with the treatment of a non-disabled employee who was not bullied.

[34]   DDA 1995, s 3A(1)(a).

[35]   *British Gas Services Ltd v McCaull* [2001] IRLR 60, EAT. Whether intention, purpose or motive is wholly irrelevant has been thrown into controversial doubt by *Taylor v OCS Group Ltd* [2006] IRLR 613, CA (discussed below).

[36]   *Nagarajan v London Regional Transport* [1999] IRLR 572, HL; *Murphy v Sheffield Hallam University* (2000) EAT/6/99; *Rowden v Dutton Gregory (a firm)* [2002] ICR 971, EAT.

[37]   *Edwards v Mid Suffolk District Council* [2001] IRLR 190, EAT.

[38]   *London Clubs Management Ltd v Hood* [2001] IRLR 719, EAT.

differently from other employees in this respect. The EAT said that the treatment complained of was not the non-payment of wages ordinarily due, but rather the non-payment of discretionary sick pay. The claimant had not been refused sick pay for a reason related to his disability. The reason was the employer's application of its revised policy on discretionary sick pay and that was not a reason related to the claimant's disability (nor, it might be added, was he being treated less favourably than comparable other employees). However, in another case, an employer who reduced a disabled person's sick pay to half pay in accordance with its sickness absence policy was held to have failed to comply with its duty to make reasonable adjustments and committed unjustified disability-related discrimination.[39]

3.2.15 The concept of 'a reason which relates to the disabled person's disability' is a deliberately wide one and should be interpreted broadly. It is noticeably wider and more inclusive than the phrases 'on the ground of' or 'by reason of' which are found elsewhere in discrimination law. It is permissible to adopt a width to the expression 'which relates to' which is inclusive of causative links beyond those which would fall within phrases such as 'on the ground of disability' or 'by reason of disability'.[40] For example, a disabled employee whose disability worsens, creating difficulty in carrying out his or her work, might have been dismissed by an employer for incompetence or poor performance. However, although the reason for dismissal is a performance-related reason, it is also a reason related to the employee's disability. But for the employee's disability, his or her work performance would not have deteriorated and dismissal would not have resulted. The question will then arise as to whether the disabled employee has been treated less favourably than others to whom that reason does not apply and, if so, whether the employer can justify the treatment. In one case,[41] a teacher had a congenital heart disorder which meant that pregnancy would endanger her life. She had a child by a surrogate mother, but the school refused her paid post-natal leave because of a budget deficit. The EAT held that the refusal amounted to disability-related less favourable treatment. Her comparators were others who gave birth to their own children. The reason for the treatment was her inability to have children. That was a reason that related to her disability. However, the school succeeded in justifying the treatment on the ground of its financial position.

---

[39] *Nottinghamshire County Council v Meikle* [2004] IRLR 703, CA.

[40] *Rowden v Dutton Gregory (a firm)* [2002] ICR 971, EAT.

[41] *Murphy v Slough Borough Council* [2004] ICR 1163, EAT. The case also decided that a governing body of a school, rather than the local education authority, was the correct respondent by virtue of Education (Modification of Enactments Relating to Employment) Order 1999, SI 1999/2256, arts 2(2) and 6. See now: Education (Modification of Enactments Relating to Employment) Order 2003, SI 2003/1964.

Knowledge of disability

3.2.16 Although the concept of 'a reason which relates to the disabled person's disability' may be at large, is it essential to be able to show that the respondent was aware of the disability? The issue of knowledge is a separate one from the issues of motive and intention (which are irrelevant). There are two possible views.

3.2.17 The first view is that the respondent's knowledge of the disability is irrelevant. The test is whether, with the benefit of hindsight, it can be seen that the disabled person has been treated less favourably for a reason which is related to disability, as a matter of fact. The relevant statutory provision is silent on the question of knowledge. In contrast, in the context of the duty to make reasonable adjustments, there is an express requirement that the respondent must know (or, at least, have reasonable means of knowing) that the claimant is a disabled person. If the statute in one context has made knowledge of disability relevant by express provision, then the statute must have intended, by its silence, in another context that knowledge of disability should be irrelevant. The question of the respondent's knowledge or ignorance of the claimant's disability then goes to justification rather than to the issue of *prima facie* discrimination.

3.2.18 The second view is that the respondent's knowledge (actual or constructive) is relevant. Can a respondent be said to have treated a person less favourably 'for a reason which relates to' that person's disability if the respondent did not know that the person was disabled? How can someone be said to have acted for a particular reason unless they are aware of the ingredients which inform that reason? A respondent cannot deliberately ignore the available evidence or facts and thereby argue that it did not know that the person was disabled. Equally, the fact that the respondent did not believe the person to be disabled, or did not understand the significance of the statutory definition, may not be an excuse. However, this second view does require the respondent to have some knowledge that the person is disabled before there is disability-related discrimination.[42]

3.2.19 How are these conflicting views to be reconciled? One division of the EAT has ruled in *O'Neill v Symm & Co Ltd* that the respondent's actual or constructive knowledge of the disability is relevant.[43] It reasoned that a respondent cannot be said to have treated a person less favourably *for a reason which relates to* that person's disability if the respondent did not know that the person was disabled. Knowledge of the material features of the disability will be enough, but not simply knowledge of one or other equivocal symptom. This approach might discourage employers from seeking information from employment

---

[42] See, in an analogous context: *Del Monte Foods Ltd v Mundon* [1980] ICR 694, EAT; *Simon v Brimham Associates* [1987] IRLR 307, CA.

[43] [1998] IRLR 233, EAT.

applicants and employees that might lead to a disclosure of disability. It is doubtful whether this view – that the word 'reason', as a matter of causation, involves knowledge of the matter which is material – was compatible with *Clark v TDG Ltd t/a Novacold*.[44]

3.2.20 Subsequently, another division of the EAT has reconsidered the position in *H J Heinz & Co Ltd v Kenrick*.[45] The EAT rejected the view that the respondent is required to have knowledge of the disability or its material features. It casts doubt upon whether the earlier decision is correct. The EAT ruled that the test of the relationship between the alleged less favourable treatment and a disability is objective (does the relationship exist?) rather than subjective (did the respondent know that the relationship existed?). Furthermore, a reason related to disability is a broad concept, which can include a reason which derives from how the disability manifests itself.

3.2.21 The reasoning in *Kenrick* is preferable to that in *O'Neill*. That view is supported by *London Borough of Hammersmith and Fulham v Farnsworth*,[46] where the EAT stated that the approach in *O'Neill* was no longer good law in the light of the decision of the Court of Appeal in *Clark*. The effect is that, for example, employers should pause to consider whether a proposed dismissal might be connected with a reason related to a disability (of which the employer might otherwise be unaware). As soon as factors exist which put the employer on guard (such as the employer's awareness that the employee had been receiving medical treatment), the employer must pause to determine whether a disability exists which requires to be addressed by the duty to make reasonable adjustments (eg by not dismissing or by taking other steps). The employer cannot rely upon its ignorance of the circumstances unless that is rationally based. If, at the relevant time, it would have been reasonable to have undertaken further investigation to discover the actual situation and to assess it in the light of the relevant law, the employer would be expected to do so.[47]

3.2.22 Furthermore, a respondent might be treated as being possessed of knowledge by virtue of what was known to an employee or agent of the respondent (such as a line manager, a personnel officer or an occupational health practitioner) at the relevant time. For example, an occupational health physician was treated as the relevant decision-maker as to whether an employment applicant should be employed where, following a provisional offer of employment, the employer acted upon the physician's medical report as to that person's employability and withdrew

---

[44] [1999] IRLR 318, CA.
[45] [2000] IRLR 144, EAT.
[46] [2000] IRLR 691, EAT.
[47] *Heggison v A & W Bernard* (2000) EAT/1276/99.

the offer.[48] The question of what the respondent knew of the disability may still be relevant to the issue of justification and the duty to make reasonable adjustments.

3.2.23   The present author felt confident in the above account and reconciliation of the authorities until the decision in *Taylor v OCS Group Ltd*.[49] The case concerned an employer's decision to dismiss a deaf employee for misconduct. The decision to dismiss was partly based on the employee's failure, on account of his deafness, to give an adequate explanation of his conduct. The Court of Appeal ruled that the EAT had erred in holding that the dismissal for misconduct was for a reason which related to disability. It held that the employment tribunal had been entitled to focus on the reason for dismissal which was present in the employers' mind, namely misconduct, and to find that this was not related to the claimant's disability. The court described as 'fallacious' the argument that it was not necessary to show that the disability-related reason was present in the employer's mind in order to demonstrate that the reason related to disability. The court also stated that discrimination requires that the employer should have a certain state of mind. This meant that the disability-related reason must be present in the employer's mind and must have a significant influence on the employer's decision. It is open to a tribunal to find that the employer's decision had been affected by the disability-related reason even though the employer had not consciously allowed that reason to affect its thinking. What is important is that the disability-related reason must affect the employer's mind, whether consciously or subconsciously. Unless that reason has affected its mind, the employer cannot discriminate.

Justification

3.2.24   A person discriminates against a disabled person if there is less favourable treatment of a disabled person for a reason related to the disabled person's disability *and* the alleged discriminator cannot show that the less favourable treatment is justified.[50] The burden of proof will be upon the person who relies upon the justification defence. Less favourable treatment is justified if, *but only if*, the reason for it is *both* material to the circumstances of the *particular* case *and* substantial.[51] However, the treatment of a disabled person cannot be justified if the respondent is under a duty to make reasonable adjustments in relation to the disabled person, but fails to comply with that duty, unless the treatment would have been justified even if the respondent had complied with the duty.[52]

---

[48]   *London Borough of Hammersmith and Fulham v Farnsworth* [2000] IRLR 691, EAT.
[49]   [2006] IRLR 613, CA.
[50]   DDA 1995, s 3A(1)(b).
[51]   Ibid, s 3A(3); *Code of Practice: Employment and Occupation* (2004), chapter 6; *Code of Practice: Trade Organisations and Qualifications Bodies* (2004), chapter 6.
[52]   DDA 1995, s 3A(6).

This is a novel defence in the context of discrimination law. The EAT has described the statutory test of justification in the 1995 Act as 'unique'.[53]

3.2.25 The justification defence goes beyond merely showing that a disabled person was treated less favourably than others for a reason unconnected with or unrelated to his or her disability. A respondent will always be able to defend a discrimination complaint of this kind by proving that the alleged discriminatory act was not for a reason which related to the disabled person's disability.[54] The justification defence clearly only applies where a respondent *has* treated a disabled person less favourably for a disability-related reason. In other words, the Act envisages that there will be cases where, despite the merit principle, a respondent could take lawful account of a person's disability. Two especially difficult areas are health and safety concerns and medical information.[55] The EC Framework Employment Directive explicitly anticipates that, with regard to disabled persons, the principle of equal treatment shall be without prejudice to the right of Member States to maintain or adopt provisions on the protection of health and safety at work or to measures aimed at creating or maintaining provisions or facilities for safeguarding or promoting their integration into the working environment.[56]

3.2.26 For example, the disabled person might be otherwise well qualified for an employment position. However, the evidence might support a real fear (as opposed to a stereotypical assumption) of a clear and unacceptable health and safety risk to the disabled person or others, or that the disability will prevent the disabled person from attending work regularly and predictably.[57] In one case, a school was held to be justified in dismissing an employee with schizophrenia because he was not taking medication prescribed to control his condition, and other staff or pupils could have been at risk if he had an acute relapse.[58] In another case, the dismissal of an employee was held to be justified in circumstances where the employee had a poor sickness and attendance record, failed to comply with sickness reporting procedures, failed to respond to the employer's attempts to accommodate him and was not fit to return to work within a predictable timescale.[59] Such conclusions must be based upon hard evidence and not merely assumptions or stereotypes.

---

[53] *Baynton v Saurus General Engineers Ltd* [1999] IRLR 604, EAT.

[54] That is implicit in the wording of s 3A(1)(a).

[55] See *Code of Practice: Employment and Occupation* (2004), paras 6.7–6.16; *Code of Practice: Trade Organisations and Qualifications Bodies* (2004), paras 6.8–6.18.

[56] Council Directive 2000/78/EC, Art 7(1).

[57] *Code of Practice: Employment and Occupation* (2004), paras 6.7–6.13 (and examples); *Code of Practice: Trade Organisations and Qualifications Bodies* (2004), paras 6.8–6.15 (and examples).

[58] *A v London Borough of Hounslow* (2001) EAT/1155/98, IDS Brief 694.

[59] *Callagan v Glasgow City Council* [2001] IRLR 724, EAT.

3.2.27 The justification defence is a particular, rather than general, defence. The use of the phrase 'if, but only if' clearly limits the scope for justifying less favourable treatment of a disabled person for a reason related to disability. A respondent might have no difficulty in subjectively justifying to itself or to others the discriminatory treatment of disabled persons, but that is not enough to satisfy the test of justification. Furthermore, where the respondent is under a statutory duty to make reasonable adjustments, the justification defence must take account of that duty. This is considered further below.

3.2.28 The statutory defence requires the respondent to show that the reason for the less favourable treatment of a disabled person, for a reason related to that person's disability, is both 'material' to the circumstances of the particular case and 'substantial'.[60] The defence of justification must take account of the circumstances of the particular case.[61] The proper interpretation of the terms 'material' and 'substantial' is crucial to an understanding of the justification defence. The word 'material' conveys a sense that the reason for the discriminatory treatment must be important, essential or relevant in the circumstances of the case. The word 'substantial' is also used in the 1995 Act to measure the adverse effect that a person's disability has upon normal day-to-day activities. In that context, 'substantial' denotes something which is more than minor or trivial. The term is also used to qualify the disadvantage that must be faced by a disabled person before a respondent's duty to make reasonable adjustments is triggered.

3.2.29 The Employment Code of Practice (1996) stated that the justification defence 'means that the reason has to relate to the individual circumstances in question and *not just be trivial or minor*'.[62] That suggests that the term 'substantial' should be interpreted consistently wherever it appears in the Act and simply denotes something that is more than minor or trivial. The 2004 versions of the Codes of Practice make it clear that the test is an objective one. It is stated that 'material' means that there must be a reasonably strong connection between the reason given for the treatment and the circumstances of the particular case, while 'substantial' means that the reason must carry real weight and be of substance.[63]

3.2.30 In *Baynton v Saurus General Engineers Ltd*,[64] the EAT noted the statutory sequence for establishing justification as follows:

- the disabled person shows less favourable treatment for a reason related to disability;

---

[60] DDA 1995, s 3A(3).
[61] HL Deb, vol 566, cols 118–119.
[62] *Employment Code of Practice* (1996), para 4.6 (emphasis added).
[63] *Code of Practice: Employment and Occupation* (2004), para 6.3 (and example); *Code of Practice: Trade Organisations and Qualifications Bodies* (2004), para 6.3.
[64] [1999] IRLR 604, EAT.

- that less favourable treatment is shown to amount to a potentially unlawful act;

- the respondent shows that the treatment is justified if the reason for the treatment is both material to the circumstances of the particular case and substantial:
    - *unless* the respondent is also under a statutory duty to make a reasonable adjustment in relation to the disabled person;
    - *and* the respondent fails to comply with that duty;[65]

- *subject to* the treatment being justified, *even if* the respondent had complied with that duty.[66]

The EAT held that, in applying the test of justification, the interests of the disabled person and the interests of the respondent must be weighed in the balance. All the circumstances of the case must be considered (including both those of the disabled person and those of the respondent) and not simply the justificatory reason offered by the respondent. This appears to emphasise not merely the objective nature of the justification defence, but also its even-handedness.

3.2.31 Subsequently, however, another division of the EAT re-examined the justification defence in *H J Heinz & Co Ltd v Kenrick*.[67] The EAT agreed that the relevant circumstances include the circumstances of both the claimant and the respondent. Whilst not ruling out the balancing exercise between the interests of the two parties, the EAT pointed to the comparatively limited requirements of the statutory provision that provides both a necessary and sufficient condition for the operation of the defence. The EAT said that the justification defence is not a general test of reasonableness. In fact, the threshold for justification of disability-related less favourable treatment is a very low one, although apparently compatible with the Human Rights Act 1998.[68] The treatment *is* justified (not merely *can* or *may be* justified) if the reason for it is both material to the circumstances of the case and substantial (in the sense of being more than minor or trivial). On the facts of *Kenrick*, the employer's treatment of the disabled employee was held not to be justified because there had not been an adequate consideration of alternative employment or shorter hours before he was dismissed for a disability-related period of absence. The EAT in *Kenrick* recognised that where there was also a duty to make reasonable adjustments, there may be a necessary but *not* sufficient

---

[65] A failure to comply with a duty to make reasonable adjustments can no longer be justified under the post-1 October 2004 law.

[66] DDA 1995, s 3A(6). See *Code of Practice: Employment and Occupation* (2004), paras 6.4–6.6 (and example); *Code of Practice: Trade Organisations and Qualifications Bodies* (2004), paras 6.5–6.7.

[67] [2000] IRLR 144, EAT.

[68] *A v London Borough of Hounslow* (2001) EAT/1155/98, IDS Brief 694 (in particular, Arts 8 and 14 of the European Convention on Human Rights and Art 1 of the First Protocol to the Convention).

condition for justification, because the test of whether a reasonable adjustment would have made any difference also has to be satisfied. The EAT suggested that whenever a tribunal is moving towards a view that less favourable treatment is justified, it should reflect upon whether the respondent was also under a duty to make reasonable adjustments. If so, and if the respondent has failed to comply with that duty, then the tribunal should consider whether the less favourable treatment would still have been justified *even if* the employer had complied with the duty to make reasonable adjustments.

3.2.32 The substance of the test of justification is now explained more fully and authoritatively by the Court of Appeal in *Jones v Post Office*.[69] The claimant had developed insulin-dependent diabetes. He was removed from driving duties in accordance with the employer's medical fitness standards for its drivers, which required insulin-dependent employees to cease driving duties. The employer conceded that this amounted to disability-related less favourable treatment, but sought to argue that it was justified. The employment tribunal approached the case on the basis that the decision as to what was justified was for it to make. It re-examined the medical evidence and concluded that he was not a safety risk when driving. It held that the employer had not established a material and substantial reason for removing the claimant from driving duties. The EAT allowed the employer's appeal, reasoning that the tribunal had misdirected itself when preferring the claimant's medical evidence at the hearing to that of the employer's own doctor considered at the time.[70]

3.2.33 The Court of Appeal in *Jones* dismissed a further appeal.[71] Its view was that the tribunal had been wrong to find that the employer's reason was not material or substantial simply because it preferred the claimant's medical evidence to that relied upon by the employer at the time of the risk assessment. The task of the tribunal is a limited one. The question is whether the reason given for less favourable treatment can properly be described as both material to the circumstances of the particular case and substantial. The employer has to satisfy the statutory criteria. That involves the tribunal investigating the facts and assessing whether there was evidence on the basis of which the employer's decision could properly be taken. For example, if the employer had not carried out a risk assessment,[72] or if the decision was taken without appropriate medical evidence, the tribunal could decide that the employer's reason was insufficient and the treatment unjustified. The tribunal could also so decide if the employer's decision was an irrational one, going beyond the range of reasonable responses open to a reasonable decision-maker. It was

---

[69]   [2001] EWCA Civ 558, [2001] IRLR 384, CA.

[70]   *Post Office v Jones* [2000] ICR 388, EAT.

[71]   [2001] EWCA Civ 558, [2001] IRLR 384, CA.

[72]   A risk assessment might be a reasonable adjustment made as part of a pro-active approach to the DDA 1995: *Mid-Staffordshire General Hospitals NHS Trust v Cambridge* [2003] IRLR 566, EAT.

not the function of the tribunal to decide whether the employer's assessment of the risk was correct, provided it had been conducted properly, was based upon appropriate evidence and was not irrational.[73] It did not matter that the tribunal might have come to a different conclusion itself. It was not its function to make up its own mind based upon its own appraisal of the evidence. Its role is said to be not very different from that which it has under s 98 of the Employment Rights Act 1996 in unfair dismissal cases (the so-called 'band of reasonable responses' test).

3.2.34 The test propounded by the Court of Appeal in *Jones* is thus very different from the objective justification test which applies in sex and race discrimination cases. EC law adopts an objective justification standard in relation to indirect discrimination. For that reason, the decision in *Jones* is a controversial one. From 1 October 2004, following the amendments made to the DDA 1995 to implement the disability discrimination provisions of the EC Framework Employment Directive, it may be necessary to revisit the justification test in *Jones*. An appropriate opportunity to do so has not yet arisen.

3.2.35 Prior to 1 October 2004, it was possible to justify a failure to comply with a duty to make reasonable adjustments.[74] The applicability of *Jones* in justifying a failure to make reasonable adjustments was questioned judicially in *Collins v Royal National Theatre Board Ltd.*[75] Subsequently, the EAT has held that there is nothing in *Jones* that prevents a tribunal from making findings of fact on medical evidence obtained after an employer had rejected an employment applicant.[76] That evidence was relevant as to whether there was material to hand at the time at which the decision was made upon which such a decision could properly be made and was one open to a reasonable decision-maker. In another case, the EAT emphasised that the respondent must have sufficient material and must have carried out adequate inquiries to justify a decision to reject an employment applicant on grounds of disability.[77] In a further case, the EAT said that the nature and quality of medical evidence would be in issue for the tribunal where the medical practitioner had never treated the disabled person for his condition, did not know him

---

[73]　*A v London Borough of Hounslow* (2001) EAT/1155/98, IDS Brief 694 (a school was justified in dismissing an employee with schizophrenia because he was not taking the medication prescribed to control his condition, and other staff or pupils could have been at risk if he had an acute relapse. The employer had sufficient information on which to assess the risk and its medical adviser had been properly qualified to carry out the risk assessment).

[74]　DDA 1995, s 5(2) and (4), now repealed.

[75]　[2004] EWCA Civ 144, [2004] IRLR 395, CA (a factor that has already been considered in relation to the reasonableness of an adjustment cannot also be relied upon as part of a justification of a failure to make a reasonable adjustment). See also: *Law v Pace Micro Technology plc* [2004] EWCA Civ 923, CA (noting that *Collins* was implicitly approved in *Archibald v Fife Council* [2004] UKHL 32, [2004] IRLR 651, HL).

[76]　*Surrey Police v Marshall* [2002] IRLR 843, EAT.

[77]　*Murray v Newham Citizens Advice Bureau Ltd* [2003] IRLR 340, EAT.

well and did not comment in his report on the disabled person's fitness for the post or his ability to cope with stress.[78]

3.2.36 Is knowledge of a claimant's disability an ingredient of the test of justification of disability-related less favourable treatment? One division of the EAT took the view that a respondent cannot discharge the onus of justifying disability discrimination where it maintained that it did not know that the claimant was disabled (and thus did not apply its mind to what reasonable adjustments should be made).[79] In other words, a respondent could not deploy an *ex post facto* justification defence. However, that view has now been resiled from.[80] The fact that the respondent did not know that the disabled person was disabled might affect the justification issue but does not preclude it. Whether a person knew or did not know that the claimant was a disabled person is not an issue.[81] A person can rely upon a justification defence regardless of what he or she knew of the claimant's disability. The fact that the person did not know that the claimant was a disabled person may itself be capable of forming the substance of the justification.[82]

Direct discrimination

3.2.37 From 1 October 2004, a new form of discrimination is introduced into the 1995 Act in order to implement the EC Framework Employment Directive. This is direct discrimination. For the purposes of the Directive, the principle of equal treatment means that there shall be no direct discrimination whatsoever on the ground of disability.[83] Direct discrimination is taken to occur where one person is treated less favourably than another is (or has been or would be) treated in a comparable situation on the ground of disability.[84] The amended Act provides that a person directly discriminates against a disabled person if, on the ground of the disabled person's disability, the person treats the disabled person less favourably than the person treats (or would treat) a person not having that particular disability (and who has not had that particular disability) whose relevant circumstances (including his or her abilities) are the same as (or not materially different from) those of the

---

[78] *Paul v National Probation Service Ltd* [2004] IRLR 190, EAT. See also *Williams v J Walter Thompson Group Ltd* [2005] EWCA Civ 133, [2005] IRLR 376, CA.

[79] *Quinn v Schwarzkopf Ltd* [2001] IRLR 67, EAT.

[80] *Callagan v Glasgow City Council* [2001] IRLR 724, EAT; *Quinn v Schwarzkopf Ltd* [2002] IRLR 602, Ct of Sess.

[81] *London Borough of Hammersmith & Fulham v Farnsworth* [2000] IRLR 691, EAT.

[82] *H J Heinz & Co Ltd v Kenrick* [2000] IRLR 144, EAT. See also *Johnson & Johnson Medical Ltd v Filmer* [2002] ICR 292, EAT; *Wright v Governors of Bilton High School and Warwickshire County Council* [2002] ICR 1463, EAT.

[83] 2000/78/EC, Art 2(1).

[84] Ibid, Art 2(2)(a).

disabled person.[85] Less favourable treatment of a disabled person for a reason related to disability cannot be justified if it amounts to direct discrimination.[86]

3.2.38   Direct discrimination is concerned with discrimination that is *on the ground of* a disabled person's disability, as opposed to a *reason related to* that disability. It reflects the definition of direct discrimination to be found in existing discrimination law. It remains to be seen what significance this new form of discrimination will assume in the context of the DDA 1995.[87] The former DRC placed direct discrimination at the top of its analysis of the meaning of discrimination.[88] Direct disability discrimination is likely to be a narrower concept than disability-related discrimination. However, direct disability discrimination cannot be justified (unlike disability-related discrimination). The comparator required to establish direct disability discrimination is also obviously different. The comparison is with the way in which a person not having the particular disability of the disabled person is or would be treated. That does not call for the same approach as is taken in disability-related discrimination following *Clark v TDG Ltd t/a Novacold*.[89]

On the ground of disability

3.2.39   The first point to note is that the less favourable treatment must be 'on the ground of' the disabled person's disability. This is a question of causation.[90] Was the treatment caused by the fact that the disabled person is disabled or has a particular disability? But for the disability, would the disabled person have been treated in the way that he or she was treated? Was the disability the effective (even if not the sole) cause of the treatment, judged objectively? Direct discrimination is likely to tackle discrimination based upon assumptions about and stereotypes of disabled people (such as unfounded health and safety concerns).[91] It will also deal with less favourable treatment that is disability-specific or based upon prejudice, especially where there is an apparently neutral reason for the

---

[85]   DDA 1995, s 3A(5) and Sch 2, para 2C (as amended).

[86]   Ibid, s 3A(4).

[87]   See the former DRC's illustration of how direct discrimination is to be distinguished from disability-related discrimination and discrimination by way of a failure to make reasonable adjustments: *Code of Practice: Employment and Occupation* (2004), para 4.37 (and examples); *Code of Practice: Trade Organisations and Qualifications Bodies* (2004), para 4.36 (and examples).

[88]   *Code of Practice: Employment and Occupation* (2004), paras 4.5–4.23 (and examples); *Code of Practice: Trade Organisations and Qualifications Bodies* (2004), paras 4.5–4.22 (and examples).

[89]   [1999] IRLR 318, CA; *Code of Practice: Employment and Occupation* (2004), para 4.19; *Code of Practice: Trade Organisations and Qualifications Bodies* (2004), para 4.19.

[90]   *Code of Practice: Employment and Occupation* (2004), para 4.7; *Code of Practice: Trade Organisations and Qualifications Bodies* (2004), para 4.7.

[91]   *Code of Practice: Employment and Occupation* (2004), paras 4.8 and 6.7 (and examples); *Code of Practice: Trade Organisations and Qualifications Bodies* (2004), paras 4.8 and 6.8 (and examples).

treatment, but which is a pretext for discrimination.[92] Knowledge that the person has a disability or is a disabled person does not appear to be required and the treatment in question might not be conscious.[93]

The comparator

3.2.40 The second point to make is that direct discrimination is concerned with the less favourable treatment of a disabled person compared with the treatment of a person not having that particular disability. The comparator may be actual or hypothetical.[94] The comparator must be a person who does not have a disability at all or a person who has another kind of disability.[95] Where a hypothetical comparator is selected, it may be necessary to construct such a comparator from evidence of other persons who have been treated differently in broadly similar circumstances.[96]

The relevant circumstances

3.2.41 The third issue to address is the relevant circumstances of the comparison. The comparator's relevant circumstances must be the same as, or not materially different from, those of the disabled person. Those relevant circumstances will include the respective abilities of the comparator and the disabled person. It is clear that the relevant circumstances do not have to be identical, provided that they are not materially different.[97] The identification of a comparator in direct discrimination is an exercise that is a familiar one in discrimination law generally.[98] Nevertheless, difficulty may arise in identifying the circumstances that are relevant to the comparison. The fact that the disabled person has a disability is not a relevant circumstance, although the effects of the disability might be.[99] However, the disabled person's

---

[92] *Code of Practice: Employment and Occupation* (2004), paras 4.9–4.10 (and examples); *Code of Practice: Trade Organisations and Qualifications Bodies* (2004), paras 4.9–4.10 (and examples).

[93] *Code of Practice: Employment and Occupation* (2004), para 4.11 (and example); *Code of Practice: Trade Organisations and Qualifications Bodies* (2004), paras 4.11–4.12.

[94] *Code of Practice: Employment and Occupation* (2004), para 4.12: *Code of Practice: Trade Organisations and Qualifications Bodies* (2004), para 4.12.

[95] *Code of Practice: Employment and Occupation* (2004), para 4.13 (and example); *Code of Practice: Trade Organisations and Qualifications Bodies* (2004), para 4.13.

[96] *Code of Practice: Employment and Occupation* (2004), para 4.18 (and example); *Code of Practice: Trade Organisations and Qualifications Bodies* (2004), para 4.18 (and example).

[97] *Code of Practice: Employment and Occupation* (2004), paras 4.14–4.16 (and examples); *Code of Practice: Trade Organisations and Qualifications Bodies* (2004), paras 4.14–4.16 (and examples).

[98] *Code of Practice: Employment and Occupation* (2004), para 4.17; *Code of Practice: Trade Organisations and Qualifications Bodies* (2004), para 4.17. See *Shamoon v Chief Constable of the Royal Ulster Constabulary* [2003] IRLR 285, HL.

[99] *Code of Practice: Employment and Occupation* (2004), paras 4.20–4.21 (and examples); *Code of Practice: Trade Organisations and Qualifications Bodies* (2004), para 4.20 (and example).

circumstances and abilities are to be considered as they actually are. That means that if any reasonable adjustments are already in place, it is the disabled person's circumstances or abilities as measured with the assistance of reasonable adjustments that are relevant. However, if no reasonable adjustments have yet been made, the comparison is to be made without consideration of what effect any reasonable adjustments might have on the disabled person's circumstances or abilities.[100]

3.2.42 In an early case testing this new provision a HIV positive employee was suspended and dismissed. The employer's reason was not the fact of the employee being HIV positive. The employer feared a risk of transmission to others. The EAT held that it was not enough for a claimant to show that the treatment was on the grounds of disability. The treatment must be less favourable than the treatment which would be afforded to a hypothetical comparator in circumstances which are 'not materially different'. The comparator may be (but need not be) the same comparator as is envisaged for the purpose of disability-related discrimination (because the comparison in direct discrimination is with a person who does not have 'that particular disability'). The circumstances of the claimant and of the comparator must be the same 'or not materially different'. If the comparator would have been dismissed in comparable circumstances (that is, other than being HIV positive), then the claimant was not less favourably treated.[101]

Justification

3.2.43 Finally, direct discrimination cannot be justified.[102] There is no justification defence contained within the definition of 'direct discrimination'. Furthermore, less favourable treatment of a disabled person for a reason related to disability cannot be justified if it amounts to direct discrimination.[103]

Failure to make reasonable adjustments

3.2.44 The EC Framework Employment Directive requires that the principle of equal treatment shall mean that there shall be no indirect discrimination whatsoever on the ground of disability.[104] Indirect discrimination shall be taken to occur where an apparently neutral provision, criterion or practice would put persons having a particular

---

[100] *Code of Practice: Employment and Occupation* (2004), para 4.22 (and examples); *Code of Practice: Trade Organisations and Qualifications Bodies* (2004), para 4.21 (and example).

[101] *High Quality Lifestyles Ltd v Watts* [2006] IRLR 850, EAT.

[102] *Code of Practice: Employment and Occupation* (2004), para 4.23; *Code of Practice: Trade Organisations and Qualifications Bodies* (2004), para 4.22.

[103] DDA 1995, s 3A(4); *Code of Practice: Employment and Occupation* (2004), para 6.3; *Code of Practice: Trade Organisations and Qualifications Bodies* (2004), para 6.3.

[104] Council Directive 2000/78/EC, Art 2(1).

disability at a particular disadvantage compared with other persons.[105] However, there is no indirect discrimination where that provision, criterion or practice is objectively justified by a legitimate aim and the means of achieving that aim are appropriate and necessary.[106] In addition, there is no indirect discrimination where, as regards persons with a particular disability, a person to whom the Directive applies is obliged under national legislation to take appropriate measures to eliminate disadvantages entailed by such provision, criterion or practice.[107] That anticipates reasonable accommodation for disabled persons. In order to guarantee compliance with the principle of equal treatment in relation to disabled persons with disabilities, reasonable accommodation shall be provided. This means that employers shall take appropriate measures, where needed in a particular case, to enable a person with a disability to have access to, participate in or advance in employment, or to undergo training, unless such measures would impose a disproportionate burden on the employer.[108]

3.2.45 What distinguishes disability discrimination legislation from other discrimination law is the explicit duty that the 1995 Act places upon employers and others in the employment field to make reasonable adjustments to their arrangements and physical environment so as to accommodate disabled persons. The DDA 1995 does not contain a definition of 'indirect discrimination'. However, the statutory provisions:

> 'already firmly cover – and are intended to cover – the use of standards, criteria, administrative methods, work practices or procedures that adversely affect a disabled person. That applies whether determining who should be employed or dismissed or establishing terms on the basis of which people are employed and their access to opportunities is structured.'[109]

This addresses work practices and procedures which have an indirectly adverse effect upon the employment opportunities of disabled persons. It was clearly intended that indirect discrimination would be prohibited and that this should be underlined by the duty to make reasonable adjustments.[110] Whether that complies with the EC Framework Employment Directive remains to be seen.

3.2.46 There is nothing in Part 2 of the Act to prevent employers and others voluntarily affording disabled persons preferential treatment. The duty to make reasonable adjustments is an essential part of the prohibition on disability-related discrimination. Without employers and

---

[105] Council Directive 2000/78/EC, Art 2(2)(b).

[106] Ibid, Art 2(2)(b)(i).

[107] Ibid, Art 2(2)(b)(ii).

[108] Ibid, Art 5. This burden shall not be disproportionate when it is sufficiently remedied by measures existing within the framework of the disability policy of the Member State concerned.

[109] HC Deb Standing Committee E, col 142.

[110] Ibid, col 143.

others in the employment field being required to adjust practices or policies and to modify physical features of premises, disabled persons would face potentially indirect discrimination in the employment field. For example, employers' requirements and conditions will frequently represent barriers to equal opportunity and might have a disproportionate adverse impact upon disabled persons. Unless respondents are required to re-examine norms and standards established by reference to the predominant society, culture or environment, historic discrimination and inequality of opportunity are merely perpetuated.

Discrimination and the duty to make reasonable adjustments

3.2.47 For the purposes of Part 2 of the DDA 1995, a person also discriminates against a disabled person if that person fails to comply with a duty to make reasonable adjustments imposed on that person in relation to the disabled person.[111] In a case of disability-related discrimination,[112] if the respondent is under a duty to make reasonable adjustments in relation to a disabled person, but fails to comply with that duty, the respondent's treatment of that disabled person cannot be justified unless it would have been justified even if the respondent had complied with that duty.[113] A breach of the statutory duty is not otherwise an actionable breach of duty in itself but is merely an ingredient of the meaning of discrimination.[114]

3.2.48 An action for disability discrimination by way of a complaint that the respondent has failed to discharge a duty to make reasonable adjustments does not depend upon the claimant also bringing or succeeding in a claim of direct discrimination or disability-related discrimination.[115] It is possible that a breach of the duty to make reasonable adjustments could also amount to less favourable treatment for a reason related to disability.[116] Nevertheless, they are separate claims and should be dealt with explicitly as such by an employment tribunal.[117]

---

[111] DDA 1995, s 3A(2). *Code of Practice: Employment and Occupation* (2004), paras 4.24–4.26; *Code of Practice: Trade Organisations and Qualifications Bodies* (2004), paras 4.23–4.25.

[112] Ibid, s 3A(1).

[113] Ibid, s 3A(6). In *Nottinghamshire County Council v Meikle* [2004] IRLR 704, CA, the claimant's sick pay was reduced to half pay after 100 days' sickness in accordance with the respondent's policy. The question was whether the respondent had shown that if reasonable adjustments had been made, the claimant would not have been absent for over 100 days and thereby liable to half pay.

[114] Ibid, s 18B(6).

[115] *Clark v TDG Ltd t/a Novacold* [1999] IRLR 318, CA.

[116] *Rowden v Dutton Gregory (a firm)* [2002] ICR 971, EAT (a disciplinary process conducted in breach of the duty to make reasonable adjustments, in that the employee's absence through illness made the process inadequate, could amount to less favourable treatment for a disability-related reason).

[117] *Butterfield v Rapidmark Ltd t/a 3 MV* (1998) EAT 131/98.

Justification

3.2.49   Prior to 1 October 2004, a failure *without justification* to comply with the statutory duty imposed on a person to make reasonable adjustments in relation to a disabled person amounted to an act of discrimination.[118] Prior to that date, a failure to comply with the duty could be justified if, but only if, the reason for the failure was both material to the circumstances of the particular case and substantial.[119] From 1 October 2004, however, a failure to comply with that duty can no longer be justified.[120] The sole test is one of reasonableness.[121]

3.2.50   Where a respondent has treated a disabled person less favourably for a reason which relates to disability,[122] but has failed to comply with a statutory duty to make reasonable adjustments, then the less favourable treatment cannot be justified[123] unless the respondent can show that it would have been justified even if the respondent had complied with the duty to make a reasonable adjustment.[124] The matter should not be tackled *de novo* by the tribunal and without reference to the steps actually taken by the respondent.[125] Before a respondent can seek to justify the less favourable treatment of a disabled person for a reason related to disability, it must first address its duty to make reasonable adjustments. The respondent cannot rely upon a material and substantial reason for less favourable treatment if that reason could have been rendered immaterial or insubstantial by carrying out a reasonable adjustment.

Victimisation

3.2.51   A person (A) discriminates against another person (B) if A treats B less favourably than A treats or would treat other persons whose

---

[118]   DDA 1995, ss 5(2)(b), (4) and 6 (now repealed).

[119]   The case-law is now of historic interest only. See: *HM Prison Service v Beart* [2003] IRLR 238, CA; *Collins v Royal National Theatre Board Ltd* [2004] EWCA Civ 144, [2004] IRLR 395 CA.

[120]   See the previous case-law, now no longer relevant: *Greater Manchester Fire & Civil Defence Authority v Bradley* (EAT, 27 April 2001, unreported); *British Gas Services v McCaull* [2001] IRLR 60, EAT; *Cosgrove v Caesar & Howie* [2001] IRLR 653, EAT; *Fu v London Borough of Camden* [2001] IRLR 186, EAT; *Callagan v Glasgow City Council* [2001] IRLR 724, EAT; *Quinn v Schwarzkopf Ltd* [2002] IRLR 602, Ct of Sess; *Johnson & Johnson Medical Ltd v Filmer* [2002] ICR 292, EAT; *Wright v Governors of Bilton High School and Warwickshire County Council* (2002) EAT/113/01, IDS Brief 711.

[121]   *Code of Practice: Employment and Occupation* (2004), paras 5.43–5.44; *Code of Practice: Trade Organisations and Qualifications Bodies* (2004), paras 5.26–5.27 (and examples).

[122]   DDA 1995, s 3A(1).

[123]   Ibid, s 3A(3).

[124]   Ibid, s 3A(6). See *Baynton v Saurus General Engineers Ltd* [1999] IRLR 604, EAT; *HJ Heinz Co Ltd v Kenrick* [2000] IRLR 144, EAT.

[125]   *Post Office v Jones* [2000] ICR 388, EAT (tribunal should not carry out the exercise based solely on the evidence tendered at the hearing). See now *Jones v Post Office* [2001] IRLR 384, CA; *Williams v J Walter Thompson Group Ltd* [2005] EWCA Civ 133, [2005] IRLR 376, CA; *Rothwell v Pelikan Hardcopy Scotland Ltd* [2006] IRLR 24, EAT.

circumstances are the same as B's, and A does so for one of a number of specified reasons.[126] The specified reasons are as follows.

3.2.52 First, that B has brought proceedings against A or any other person under the Act.[127] Secondly, that B has given evidence or information in connection with such proceedings brought by any person.[128] Thirdly, that B has otherwise done anything under (or by reference to) the Act in relation to A or any other person.[129] Fourthly, that B has alleged that A or any other person has (whether or not the allegation so states) contravened the Act.[130] Where B is a disabled person (or a person who has had a disability), the disability in question shall be disregarded in comparing his or her circumstances with those of any other person for any of the above purposes.[131] Fifthly, that A believes or suspects that B has done or intends to do any of the above things.[132] The provisions on victimisation do not apply to the treatment of a person because of an allegation made by him or her if the allegation was false and not made in good faith.[133] In the case of an act which constitutes discrimination by virtue of victimisation, the relevant causes of action also apply to discrimination against a person who is not disabled.[134]

Discrimination by association or perception

3.2.53 The Act, as originally drafted and as subsequently amended, does not address the problem of discrimination against non-disabled persons because of their association with (or relationship to) a disabled person.[135] That is because it is only unlawful where a person discriminates against a disabled person on the ground of the disabled person's disability, or for a reason which relates to the disabled person's disability, or fails to comply with a duty to make reasonable adjustments imposed in relation to the disabled person, or subjects a disabled person to harassment for a reason which relates to the disabled person's disability. By the same reasoning, perceived discrimination – where a person is discriminated

---

[126] DDA 1995, s 55(1); *Code of Practice: Employment and Occupation* (2004), paras 4.33–4.36 (and example); *Code of Practice: Trade Organisations and Qualifications Bodies* (2004), paras 4.32–4.35 (and example). Victimisation is not a free-standing legal wrong and can only succeed if the claimant can show that the victimisation has resulted in an act made unlawful by DDA 1995, s 4: *Bruce v Addleshaw Booth & Co* EAT 0404/03.

[127] DDA 1995, s 55(2)(a)(i).

[128] Ibid, s 55(2)(a)(ii).

[129] Ibid, s 55(2)(a)(iii) and (6).

[130] Ibid, s 55(2)(a)(iv).

[131] Ibid, s 55(3).

[132] Ibid, s 55(2)(b).

[133] Ibid, s 55(4).

[134] Ibid, s 55(5), modifying ss 4, 4B, 4D, 4G, 6A, 7A, 7C, 13, 14A, 14C and 16A for this purpose. The most recent review of the discrimination law authorities on victimisation is to be found in *St Helens Metropolitan Borough Council v Derbyshire* [2007] IRLR 540, HL.

[135] HC Deb Standing Committee E, cols 168 and 172.

against because he or she is wrongly perceived to be a disabled person –
falls outside the drafting of the Act. This is an obvious gap in the
disability discrimination legislation, not found in other discrimination
legislation, and may amount to a failure properly to implement the
provisions of the EC Framework Employment Directive.[136] The Advocate
General has opined that the Directive protects people who, although not
themselves disabled, suffer direct discrimination and/or harassment in the
field of employment and occupation because they are associated with a
disabled person.[137] The judgment of the ECJ is now awaited.

3.3 HARASSMENT

3.3.1 The EC Framework Employment Directive treats harassment as a
deemed form of discrimination. It arises when unwanted conduct related
to disability takes place, with the purpose or effect of violating the dignity
of a person and of creating an intimidating, hostile, degrading,
humiliating or offensive environment.[138] In this context, the concept of
harassment may be defined in accordance with the national laws and
practice of the Member States.

3.3.2 From 1 October 2004, for the purposes of Part 2 of the DDA
1995, a person subjects a disabled person to harassment where, for a
reason which relates to the disabled person's disability, the person engages
in unwanted conduct which has the purpose or effect of (a) violating the
disabled person's dignity or (b) creating an intimidating, hostile,
degrading, humiliating or offensive environment for him or her.[139]
Conduct shall be regarded as having either of those effects only if, having
regard to all the circumstances, including in particular the perception of
the disabled person, it should reasonably be considered as having that
effect.[140] However, if the conduct is engaged in with the purpose of having
either of those effects, then harassment is established, regardless of its
actual effect on the disabled person.[141]

---

[136] A question that is the subject of a current reference to the ECJ: *Attridge Law v Coleman* [2007] IRLR 88, EAT. See also *HM Prison Service v Johnson* [2007] IRLR 951, EAT (the disability to which the reasons for the treatment complained of relates must be a disability which the claimant actually has (not merely is believed to have)). Treating a disabled person badly is not enough. The question is whether his or her disability was part of the reason for it.

[137] Opinion of Advocate General Poiares Maduro delivered on 31 January 2008 in case C-303/06 *S. Coleman v Attridge Law and Steve Law*.

[138] 2000/78/EC, Art 2(3).

[139] DDA 1995, s 3B(1).

[140] Ibid, s 3B(2).

[141] *Code of Practice: Employment and Occupation* (2004), paras 4.38–4.39 (and examples); *Code of Practice: Trade Organisations and Qualifications Bodies* (2004), paras 4.37–4.38 (and examples).

3.4 DUTY TO MAKE REASONABLE ADJUSTMENTS

3.4.1 The duty to make reasonable adjustments pervades Part 2 of the DDA 1995. The House of Lords has stressed the positive nature of the duty to make reasonable adjustments and indicated that a respondent may be obliged to discriminate positively in favour of disabled persons.[142] As has been seen above, a person discriminates against a disabled person if that person fails to comply with a duty to make reasonable adjustments imposed on that person in relation to the disabled person.[143] In a case of disability-related discrimination,[144] if the respondent is under a duty to make reasonable adjustments in relation to a disabled person, but fails to comply with that duty, the respondent's treatment of that disabled person cannot be justified unless it would have been justified even if the respondent had complied with that duty.[145] The circumstances in which the duty to make reasonable adjustments is triggered will be examined in specific detail in the next chapter. Those circumstances differ according to whether the duty arises in the context of employment or in relation to the other occupational settings. However, there are some concepts of reasonable adjustment which are common to the employment field generally and these are examined here.

The duty illustrated

3.4.2 Unusually, the statute itself (rather than a Code of Practice) exemplifies the kinds of steps which a respondent might have to take in relation to a disabled person in order to comply with the duty to make reasonable adjustments.[146] The illustrations are as follows:

- making adjustments to premises;

- allocating some of the disabled person's duties to another person;

- transferring the disabled person to fill an existing vacancy;

- altering the disabled person's hours of working or training;

---

[142] *Archibald v Fife Council* [2004] UKHL 32, [2004] IRLR 651, HL. Where an employer recruits a disabled employee to do a specific job, knowing of that employee's disability and that adjustments would have to be made, that is a material feature in relation to direct discrimination, to the duty to make reasonable adjustments and to the justification defence (if available): *Williams v J Walter Thompson Group Ltd* [2005] EWCA Civ 133, CA.

[143] DDA 1995, s 3A(2). *Code of Practice: Employment and Occupation (2004)*, paras 4.24–4.26; *Code of Practice: Trade Organisations and Qualifications Bodies (2004)*, paras 4.23–4.25.

[144] Ibid, s 3A(1).

[145] Ibid, s 3A(6).

[146] Ibid, s 18B(2); *Code of Practice: Employment and Occupation* (2004), para 5.18 (and examples); *Code of Practice: Trade Organisations and Qualifications Bodies* (2004), para 5.12 (and examples).

- assigning the disabled person to a different place of work or training;

- allowing the disabled person to be absent during working or training hours for rehabilitation, assessment or treatment;

- giving or arranging for training or mentoring (whether for the disabled person or any other person);

- acquiring or modifying equipment;

- modifying instructions or reference manuals;

- modifying procedures for testing or assessment;

- providing a reader or interpreter;

- providing supervision or other support.

In addition, the making of alterations to occupational pension scheme rules is an example of a step which trustees or managers of such a scheme may have to take in order to comply with their duty to make reasonable adjustments.[147]

3.4.3   This list is illustrative only of the types of adjustments that might be made and the Codes of Practice suggest further examples.[148] The list is not intended to be exhaustive or to be treated as a checklist.[149] More than one adjustment or a combination of adjustments might be required.[150] However, once the respondent has made reasonable adjustments, the duty to make reasonable adjustments does not require the respondent to accept reduced performance from the disabled person.[151]

3.4.4   So far as transferring a disabled person to fill an existing vacancy is concerned, it is not suggested that a respondent must create a vacancy.[152] However, if there is an existing vacancy, it might be reasonable to make adjustments to that vacancy so as to allow the disabled person to fill it. The duty to make reasonable adjustments might include transferring a disabled person to another position for which he or she was

---

[147]   DDA 1995, s 4H(2) (ie in addition to the examples set out in s 18B(2)). See **4.5**.

[148]   *Code of Practice: Employment and Occupation* (2004), para 5.20 (and examples); *Code of Practice: Trade Organisations and Qualifications Bodies* (2004), para 5.13.

[149]   *Humphreys v Environment Agency* (1999) EAT/24/95.

[150]   *Code of Practice: Employment and Occupation* (2004), para 5.19 (and example); *Code of Practice: Trade Organisations and Qualifications Bodies* (2004), para 5.12.

[151]   *Mulligan v Commissioner for Inland Revenue* (1999) EAT/691/99 (eg by lowering the quantity or volume of work being demanded).

[152]   *Electronic Data Systems Ltd v Travis* [2004] EWCA Civ 1256, CA (it is for the employer to bring evidence to show that there was no available alternative employment).

suited, without the need for competitive interview and selection.[153] It is not for the employment tribunal to identify a particular vacancy that the disabled person could have been offered. Provided it addresses itself to the statutory provision, the extent to which the tribunal needs to spell out what steps it would have been reasonable for a respondent to take will depend upon how controversial those matters are.[154] It is for the respondent to show that it addressed its mind to this question.[155] If suitable alternative work is offered, even at a reduced wage, the respondent may have satisfied the duty to make reasonable adjustments.[156]

3.4.5 A reasonable adjustment might involve altering the disabled person's hours of working or training. An offer of part-time work might be a reasonable adjustment, but not in circumstances where the disabled person has not sought it, has a serious absence and sickness record, and was not fit for any form of work at the relevant time.[157] Assigning the disabled person to a different place of work or training might include allowing a disabled person to work from home during a period of rehabilitation or as part of a phased return to work.[158] In one case, disability discrimination occurred where an employer failed to transfer an employee to a different workplace in circumstances where the employee was off work with depression as a result of a difficult working relationship with a line manager.[159] The payment of sick pay during disability-related absences can be a reasonable adjustment, all other things being equal, although it is likely to be exceptional.[160] The Court of Appeal has ruled that the duty to make reasonable adjustments did not

---

[153] *Archibald v Fife Council* [2004] UKHL 32, [2004] IRLR 651, HL. A reasonable adjustment might require the creation of a new post in substitution for an existing post: *Southampton City College v Randall* [2006] IRLR 24, EAT.

[154] *Electronic Data Systems Ltd v Travis* [2004] EWCA Civ 1256, CA (it was enough for a tribunal to have found that a reasonable step would have been the provision of training to bring the skills of a disabled employee up to date following periods of disability-related absence and where that employee was at risk of redundancy).

[155] *London Borough of Hillingdon v Morgan* (1999) EAT/1493/98, IDS Brief 649 (if the matter had been approached correctly by the employer, would adjustments have enabled the employee to return to work?). While consulting a disabled employee before dismissal on ill health grounds might be a reasonable adjustment (*Rothwell v Pelikan Hardcopy Scotland Ltd*) [2006] IRLR 24, EAT), consultation about what reasonable adjustments to make is not a separate and distinct part of the duty (*Tarbuck v Sainsbury's Supermarkets Ltd* [2006] IRLR 664, EAT). The key issue is whether a reasonable adjustment has been made: *Spence v Intype Libra Ltd* EAT 0617/06 IDS Employment Law Brief 832 (EAT) (an employer's failure to obtain an up-to-date medical report before dismissal of a disabled employee was not a breach of the duty to make reasonable adjustments).

[156] *Arboshe v East London Bus & Coach Co Ltd* (1999) EAT/877/98 (unless an employee's wages would be protected in analogous circumstances?).

[157] *Callagan v Glasgow City Council* [2001] IRLR 724, EAT.

[158] *London Borough of Hillingdon v Morgan* (1999) EAT/1493/98, IDS Brief 649.

[159] *HM Prison Service v Beart* (2002) EAT 650/01, IDS Brief 713 and [2003] IRLR 238, CA.

[160] *London Clubs Management Ltd v Hood* [2001] IRLR 719, EAT; *Nottinghamshire County Council v Meikle* [2004] IRLR 703, CA.

require an employer to pay full pay to an employee absent from work for a disability-related illness and who had exhausted entitlement under the employer's sick pay scheme.[161]

3.4.6 During the parliamentary debates, the Minister confirmed that the examples of reasonable adjustments that might be undertaken could include the provision of a sign-language interpreter, Minicom facilities or alterations to working hours. Furthermore, a reasonable adjustment 'could be a modification to a working environment, to a term or condition of employment or to any similar matter relating to the employment'.[162] Where a respondent has existing car-parking facilities for employees and others, it might be a reasonable adjustment to allocate a dedicated car-parking space to a person with a mobility disability.[163] Support for such initiatives might be sought from funds available under the Government's Access to Work scheme. However, the Minister also indicated that the taxpayer could not be expected to meet all the costs of reasonable adjustments. Respondents are expected to take some financial responsibility, especially in respect of adjustments and costs relating to working hours and retraining.[164]

What are reasonable steps to take?

3.4.7 The duty upon the respondent is only to take such steps as it is reasonable, in all the circumstances of the case, to take in order to prevent the provision, criterion or practice or physical feature having an adverse effect on the disabled person. The test is an objective one.[165] The fact that a tribunal does not mention every type of adjustment which might theoretically have been made will not necessarily vitiate a conclusion that a reasonable adjustment could not have been made.[166]

3.4.8 The respondent is entitled to take account of all the circumstances when deciding what steps it would be reasonable to take. For example, it might be reasonable to weigh 'whether the benefit to the disabled person would be proportionate to the cost and the difficulty of the measures in question'.[167] On the other hand, in deciding whether to make a reasonable adjustment, there is no compulsion upon a respondent to take advice. However, a failure to take advice or to seek assistance (eg from an

---

[161] *O'Hanlon v HM Revenue & Customs* [2006] IRLR 840, EAT and [2007] IRLR 404, CA.

[162] HC Deb Standing Committee E, col 208.

[163] HL Deb, vol 566, col 209.

[164] HC Deb Standing Committee E, col 209.

[165] *Morse v Wiltshire CC* [1998] IRLR 352, EAT; *Jones v Post Office* [2001] EWCA Civ 558, [2001] IRLR 384, CA; *Williams v J Walter Thompson Group Ltd* [2005] EWCA Civ 133, [2005] IRLR 376, CA.

[166] *Quinn v Schwarzkopf Ltd* [2002] IRLR 602, Ct of Sess. The tribunal must identify with some particularity what steps it is said the employer has failed to take: *HM Prison Service v Johnson* [2007] IRLR 951, EAT. See also *Project Management Institute v Latif* [2007] IRLR 579, EAT.

[167] HC Deb Standing Committee E, col 196.

occupational medical adviser or disability employment adviser) before determining whether or not to make a reasonable adjustment could be taken into account by an employment tribunal in considering whether the respondent had acted reasonably in the circumstances.[168] Equally, the test of reasonableness might need to take account of the extent to which the disabled person has co-operated with the respondent who attempts to make a reasonable adjustment.

3.4.9 In determining whether it is reasonable for a person to have to take a particular step in order to comply with the duty to make adjustments, regard is to be had, in particular, to the following matters:[169]

- the extent to which taking the step would prevent the effect in relation to which the duty is imposed;

- the extent to which it is practicable for the person to take the step;

- the financial and other costs that would be incurred by the person in taking the step;[170]

- the extent to which taking it would disrupt any of the person's activities;[171]

- the extent of the person's financial and other resources;

- the availability to the person of financial or other assistance with respect to taking the step;

- the nature of the person's activities and the size of the person's undertaking;

- where the step would be taken in relation to a private household, the extent to which taking it would disrupt that household or disturb any person residing there.

3.4.10 The Codes of Practice suggest that these factors make a useful checklist. The effectiveness and practicability of the adjustment might be considered first, before looking at the cost of the adjustment and the

---

[168] Ibid, col 222.

[169] DDA 1995, s 18B(1); *Code of Practice: Employment and Occupation* (2004), paras 5.28–5.41 (and examples); *Code of Practice: Trade Organisations and Qualifications Bodies* (2004), paras 5.14–5.25 (and examples).

[170] *Code of Practice: Employment and Occupation* (2004), paras 5.25 and 5.32–5.35; *Code of Practice: Trade Organisations and Qualifications Bodies* (2004), para 5.21.

[171] The need to consider whether the adjustment would increase risks to health and safety arises and a risk assessment may be necessary: *Code of Practice: Employment and Occupation* (2004), para 5.26; *Code of Practice: Trade Organisations and Qualifications Bodies* (2004), para 5.17.

resources available to fund it.[172] The Codes of Practice also suggest that other factors might be relevant, such as the effect on other employees, adjustments made for other disabled employees and the extent to which the disabled person is willing to co-operate.[173]

3.4.11   In one case,[174] an employment tribunal erred by failing to consider the extent to which, if at all, adjustments proposed by the claimant could have overcome her medical symptoms which otherwise prevented her return to work. In another case,[175] the EAT held that these provisions do not require that the particular step should prevent the effect in question, but merely that the respondent is entitled to have regard to the extent to which taking that step would prevent the effect when considering whether it was under a duty to take that step. In that case, there was a substantial possibility that the step in question would have worked and the fact that it might not have succeeded totally did not assist the respondent. The significance of the cost of a step may depend in part on the value of the disabled person's experience and expertise to the respondent, including factors such as resources (such as training) already invested in the person and his or her length of service, level of skill and knowledge, quality of relationships with clients and level of pay. It is more likely to be reasonable for a respondent with substantial resources to have to make a significantly costly adjustment than it would be for a respondent with fewer resources.

3.4.12   Other factors might be relevant, depending upon the circumstances, including (in an employment context) the effect that an adjustment has upon other employees, any adjustments already made for other disabled employees, and the extent to which the disabled person is willing to co-operate with the employer's attempts to make an adjustment. It may also be reasonable for a respondent to have to make more than one adjustment. The above listed matters are the 'key criteria ... in no particular order of priority' by which the reasonableness of an adjustment

---

[172]   *Code of Practice: Employment and Occupation* (2004), para 5.27; *Code of Practice: Trade Organisations and Qualifications Bodies* (2004), para 5.18.

[173]   *Code of Practice: Employment and Occupation* (2004), para 5.42 (and examples); *Code of Practice: Trade Organisations and Qualifications Bodies* (2004), para 5.18.

[174]   *Fu v London Borough of Camden* [2001] IRLR 186, EAT. See also, on the same point: *Johnson & Johnson Medical Ltd v Filmer* [2002] ICR 292, EAT. It was not a breach of the duty to make reasonable adjustments where an employer failed to extend a disabled employee's return to work programme unless the tribunal could find that the extension would have removed the substantial disadvantage caused by the disability and enabled the employee to return to full-time work: *Romec Ltd v Rudham* EAT 0069/07 IDS Employment Law Brief 836 (EAT).

[175]   *HM Prison Service v Beart* EAT 650/01, (2002) IDS Brief 713 and [2003] IRLR 238, CA. In *Arthur v Northern Ireland Housing Executive* (2007) NICA 25 IDS Employment Law Brief 841 (NI CA), allowing a dyslexic job applicant extra time to complete a pre-employment aptitude test placed the applicant on the same footing as other applicants, but his test score was still too low to be interviewed. The employer's duty had thus been exhausted as the substantial disadvantage had been overcome.

will be judged.[176] For example, if the only possible adjustments that could be made to aid the output of a disabled person could result in no more than a small improvement in productivity, but at a price of cost or disruption, the adjustments might not be reasonable.[177] Similarly, if – after reasonable adjustments have been made – a disabled person's productivity is below normal, and where the person is paid according to performance, a respondent would not be expected to make further adjustments by compensating the disabled person for the loss of performance-related pay.

3.4.13 During the parliamentary debates, the Minister gave further illustrations.[178] It might not be reasonable for an employer (especially a small employer) needing an employee urgently to have to wait for an adjustment to be made to allow a disabled person to be employed. An adjustment that would involve a breach of safety laws or fire regulations could not be reasonable. However, health and safety law does not require the avoidance of all risks, but simply ensuring that risk is properly assessed, understood and managed.[179] The cost of the adjustment might also render it an unreasonable one to make. Cost will include use of staff and other resources, as well as direct monetary costs. The respondent's resources must be taken into account. It might be more reasonable for a respondent with considerable resources to make a significantly costly adjustment than for a respondent with fewer resources. Moreover, a step is not unreasonable if there is available compensatory help from an outside organisation or from the disabled person. For example, the respondent might not be expected to purchase specialist computer equipment adapted for use by a person with a sight disability. Such equipment might be available under the Access to Work scheme or from a disability charity. It would also be a reasonable adjustment to allow a disabled worker to use his or her own auxiliary aids or equipment at work.

3.5 RELATIONSHIPS WHICH HAVE COME TO AN END

3.5.1 Prior to 1 October 2004, post-employment acts of disability discrimination might also have been unlawful if there was a sufficient connection with the erstwhile employment relationship.[180] From 1 October 2004, explicit provision is made in Part 2 of the amended Act in respect of relationships which have come to an end.[181]

---

[176] HL Deb, vol 566, col 184.
[177] Ibid, vol 566, cols 184–185.
[178] Ibid, vol 566, col 185.
[179] *Code of Practice: Employment and Occupation* (2004), paras 6.8–6.13 (and examples); *Code of Practice: Trade Organisations and Qualifications Bodies* (2004), paras 6.8–6.17 (and examples).
[180] *Rhys-Harper v Relaxion Group plc; D'Souza v Lambeth London Borough Council; Jones v 3M Healthcare Ltd* [2003] UKHL 33, [2003] ICR 867, HL.
[181] DDA 1995, s 16A; *Code of Practice: Employment and Occupation (2004)*, paras 8.28–8.32 (and examples); *Code of Practice: Trade Organisations and Qualifications Bodies* (2004), paras 7.23, 7.28–7.29, 8.13 and 8.18–8.19.

3.5.2   This arises where there has been a relevant relationship between a disabled person and another person (the relevant person) and the relationship has come to an end.[182] A relevant relationship is a relationship during the course of which an act of discrimination against (or harassment of) one party to the relationship by the other party to it is unlawful under the provisions of Part 2.[183] It also includes a relationship between a person providing employment services (within the meaning of Part 3 of the Act) and a person receiving such services.[184] Reference to an act of discrimination or harassment which is unlawful includes, in the case of a relationship which has come to an end before 1 October 2004, reference to such an act which would, after 1 October 2004, be unlawful.[185] It is unlawful for the relevant person to discriminate against the disabled person by subjecting him or her to a detriment, or to subject the disabled person to harassment, where the discrimination or harassment arises out of and is closely connected to the relevant relationship.[186]

3.5.3   A duty to make reasonable adjustments also arises in this context. It arises where a provision, criterion or practice applied by the relevant person to the disabled person in relation to any matter arising out of the relevant relationship places the disabled person at a substantial disadvantage in comparison with persons who are not disabled, but are in the same position as the disabled person in relation to the relevant person.[187] It also arises where a physical feature of premises which are occupied by the relevant person places the disabled person at a substantial disadvantage in comparison with persons who are not disabled, but are in the same position as the disabled person in relation to the relevant person.[188] In either case, it is the duty of the relevant person to take such steps as it is reasonable, in all the circumstances of the case, for that person to have to take in order to prevent the provision, practice or criterion, or feature, having that effect.[189] However, no duty is imposed on the relevant person if that person does not know (and could not reasonably be expected to know) that the disabled person has a disability and is likely to be affected in the way required.[190]

---

[182]   DDA 1995, s 16A(1).
[183]   Ibid, s 16A(2)(a).
[184]   Ibid, s 16A(2)(b).
[185]   Ibid, s 16A(7).
[186]   Ibid, s 16A(3).
[187]   Ibid, s 16A(4)(a).
[188]   Ibid, s 16A(4)(b).
[189]   Ibid, s 16A(5).
[190]   Ibid, s 16A(6).

3.6 DISCRIMINATORY ADVERTISEMENTS

3.6.1 From 5 December 2005, new provisions apply to persons who publish certain advertisements.[191] These are advertisements that invite applications for a relevant appointment or benefit[192] and which give certain indications.[193] It is unlawful for such an advertisement to indicate (or be reasonably understood to indicate) that an application will or may be determined to any extent by reference to the applicant not having (or not having had) any disability or any particular disability. It is also unlawful for such an advertisement to indicate (or be reasonably understood to indicate) any reluctance of the person determining the application to comply with a duty to make reasonable adjustments.

3.6.2 However, the unlawfulness does not apply where it would not in fact be unlawful under the 1995 Act for an application to be determined in the manner indicated (or understood to be indicated) in the advertisement.[194] It is also a defence for the publisher to prove that the advertisement was published in reliance on a statement made by the person who caused it to be published to the effect that the publication would not be unlawful and that it was reasonable to rely on that statement.[195]

3.7 INSTRUCTIONS AND PRESSURE TO DISCRIMINATE

3.7.1 From 1 October 2004, it is unlawful for a person who has authority over another person (or in accordance with whose wishes that other person is accustomed to act) to instruct him or her to do any act which is unlawful under Part 2[196] or to procure (or attempt to procure) the doing by him of any such act.[197] It is also unlawful to induce (or attempt to induce) a person to do any act which contravenes Part 2[198] by providing

---

[191] The term 'advertisement' includes every form of advertisement or notice, whether to the public or not: DDA 1995, s 16B(4).

[192] A 'relevant appointment or benefit' means any employment, promotion or transfer of employment; membership of, or a benefit under, an occupational pension scheme; or an appointment to any office or post to which DDA 1995, s 4D applies: DDA 1995, s 16B(3).

[193] DDA 1995, s 16B(1) (as amended).

[194] Ibid, s 16B(2).

[195] Ibid, s 16B(2A).

[196] Or, to the extent that it relates to the provision of employment services, Part 3.

[197] DDA 1995, s 16C(1), implementing 2000/78/EC, Art 2(4). See *Code of Practice: Employment and Occupation* (2004), para 3.22; *Code of Practice: Trade Organisations and Qualifications Bodies* (2004), para 3.21 (and example).

[198] Or, to the extent that it relates to the provision of employment services, Part 3.

(or offering to provide) him or her with any benefit[199] or subjecting (or threatening to subject) him or her to any detriment.[200]

---

[199] DDA 1995, s 16C(2)(a). An attempted inducement is not prevented from falling within s 16C(2) because it is not made directly to the person in question, if it is made in such a way that he or she is likely to hear of it: s 16C(3).

[200] Ibid, s 16C(2)(b). The term 'detriment' (except in s 16C(2)(b)) does not include conduct of the nature referred to in s 3B (harassment): s 18D(2).

CHAPTER 4

THE EMPLOYMENT FIELD: UNLAWFUL ACTS

4.1 INTRODUCTION

4.1.1 The EC Framework Employment Directive applies to all persons in both the public and private sectors (including public bodies) in relation to:

- conditions for access to employment, to self-employment or to occupation (including selection criteria and recruitment conditions), whatever the branch of activity and at all levels of the professional hierarchy (including promotion);

- access to all types and to all levels of vocational guidance, vocational training, advanced vocational training and retraining (including practical work experience);

- employment and working conditions (including dismissals and pay); and

- membership of (and involvement in) an organisation of workers or employers, or any organisation whose members carry on a particular profession, including the benefits provided for by such organisations.[1]

Member States may provide that legislation addressing discrimination on the ground of disability shall not apply to the armed forces.[2]

4.1.2 As a result, from 1 October 2004, Part 2 of the DDA 1995 (as amended by the Disability Discrimination Act 1995 (Amendment) Regulations 2003) is concerned with prohibiting disability discrimination in the employment field at large.[3] This chapter deals with the causes of action created by Part 2 in complying with the Directive. This analysis will begin with discrimination and harassment by employers. Separate consideration will be given later in this chapter to discrimination and

---

[1]   2000/78/EC, Art 3(1).
[2]   Ibid, Art 3(4).
[3]   In Northern Ireland, see the Disability Discrimination Act 1995 (Amendment) (Northern Ireland) Regulations 2004, SR 2004/55.

harassment in relation to contract workers, office-holders, occupational pension schemes, insurance benefits, partnerships, barristers and advocates, trade organisations, qualifications bodies and practical work experience.

4.2   EMPLOYERS

Unlawful acts

4.2.1   What does the Act make unlawful in relation to employers? Disability discrimination does not take place in a vacuum. A claimant must show that the alleged act of disability discrimination falls within one of the unlawful acts of employment discrimination set out in s 4 of the Act.[4] Section 4 makes it unlawful for an employer to discriminate against a disabled person in specified circumstances. The meaning of 'discriminate' has been considered in Chapter 3. An employment tribunal may only deal with a complaint of unlawful discrimination as defined by the claimant.[5] It is thus important to state the scope of the complaint with sufficient particularity and detail in the claim. The Act begins by dealing with discrimination in recruitment and selection and in respect of employment applicants.

Recruitment and selection

4.2.2   First, it is unlawful for an employer to discriminate against a disabled person in the arrangements which the employer makes for the purpose of determining to whom the employer should offer employment.[6] The concept of 'arrangements' has a wide meaning.[7] It covers the recruitment and selection process, including job advertisements, application forms and information.[8] It includes job specifications, qualifications, the location and timing of interviews, the use of assessment techniques, the interview itself, selection criteria and pre-employment training.[9] For example, the inclusion of unnecessary or marginal requirements in a job specification (or blanket exclusions which do not take account of individual circumstances) can be discriminatory.[10] This

---

[4]   As amended by the Disability Discrimination Act 1995 (Amendment) Regulations 2003. See also *Code of Practice: Employment and Occupation* (2004), paras 3.15–3.21 and Chapters 7 and 8.

[5]   *British Gas Services Ltd v McCaull* [2001] IRLR 60, EAT.

[6]   DDA 1995, s 4(1)(a). The term 'employer' includes a person who has no employees but is seeking to employ another person: s 18D(2).

[7]   *Code of Practice: Employment and Occupation* (2004), para 7.6.

[8]   So far as job advertisements are concerned, see DDA 1995, s 16B and *Code of Practice: Employment and Occupation* (2004), paras 7.11–7.14 (and examples). In respect of application forms and information, see *Code of Practice: Employment and Occupation* (2004), paras 7.16–7.18 (and examples).

[9]   In respect of selection, assessment and interview arrangements, see *Code of Practice: Employment and Occupation* (2004), paras 7.19–7.31 (and examples).

[10]   *Code of Practice: Employment and Occupation* (2004), paras 7.7–7.8 (and examples).

does not prevent the employer from choosing the best person for the job.[11] However, if a disabled person is rejected for a job because he or she lacks a qualification specified by the employer, the rejection might be discriminatory if the lack of the particular qualification is related to that person's disability (eg because of the effect of dyslexia). The employer would need to justify the stipulation of that qualification (eg by reference to relevance and significance) or demonstrate that no reasonable adjustment in favour of the disabled applicant (eg re-allocating some duties to another employee or devising an alternative test of competence) could have been made.[12]

4.2.3 Secondly, it is unlawful for an employer to discriminate against a disabled person in the terms on which the employer offers that person employment.[13] Thirdly, it is unlawful for an employer to discriminate against a disabled person by refusing to offer (or deliberately not offering) him or her employment.[14] Discrimination by these means includes a deliberate failure or omission to offer employment to a disabled person. There does not have to be an express refusal to offer employment in order for potentially unlawful discrimination to have occurred. Next, the Act addresses discrimination in employment and against disabled employees.

Terms of employment

4.2.4 Fourthly, it is unlawful for an employer to discriminate against a disabled person whom the employer employs in the terms of employment which the employer affords the disabled employee.[15] Terms and conditions of service should not discriminate against disabled persons. That does not mean that an employer can never offer a disabled person a less favourable contract. However, subject to any duty to make reasonable adjustments, the employer must be prepared to justify the differential. Equally, employers must not discriminate in their induction procedures.[16] If necessary, a newly recruited disabled employee may need an individually tailored induction programme.

Employment opportunities and benefits

4.2.5 Fifthly, it is unlawful for an employer to discriminate against a disabled person whom the employer employs in the opportunities which the employer affords the disabled employee for promotion, a transfer,

---

[11] *Code of Practice: Employment and Occupation* (2004), para 7.4.
[12] Ibid, para 7.10 (and examples).
[13] DDA 1995, s 4(1)(b); *Code of Practice: Employment and Occupation* (2004), para 7.32 (and example).
[14] Ibid, s 4(1)(c).
[15] Ibid, s 4(2)(a); *Code of Practice: Employment and Occupation* (2004), paras 8.4–8.6 (and examples).
[16] *Code of Practice: Employment and Occupation* (2004), para 8.7 (and examples).

training or receiving any other benefit.[17] Sixthly, it is unlawful for an employer to discriminate against a disabled person whom the employer employs by refusing to afford the disabled employee (or deliberately not affording him or her) any such opportunity.[18] Benefits might include canteens, meal vouchers, social clubs and other recreational activities, dedicated car-parking spaces, discounts on products, bonuses, share options, hairdressing, clothes allowances, financial services, healthcare, private health insurance, medical assistance or insurance, transport to work, company cars, education assistance, workplace nurseries, rights to special leave and occupational pensions.[19] They will include facilities and services.[20]

4.2.6   The prohibitions on unlawful discrimination in relation to benefits do not apply to benefits of any description if the employer is concerned with the provision of benefits of that description to the public or to a section of the public which includes the employee in question.[21] It does not matter whether the benefits are being provided for payment or not. For example, the employer might be a bank providing loans to the public and loans to its employees (perhaps at favourable rates of interest) or a local authority providing welfare-related benefits to disabled persons in the community, including its own disabled employees. However, the prohibitions will apply where the provision differs in a material respect from the provision of the benefits by the employer to its employees.[22] They will also apply where the provision of the benefits to the employee in question is regulated by his or her contract of employment.[23] They will also apply where the benefits relate to training.[24]

4.2.7   These exceptions are designed to prevent unnecessary overlap with the provisions in Part 3 of the Act outlawing discrimination in the provision of goods, facilities and services. The intention is that if an employer offers goods, facilities or services to its employees in the same way as it offers them to members of the public, but disabled employees receive discriminatory treatment in that provision, then their right of action falls under Part 3 of the Act, if at all. Nevertheless, Part 2 of the Act will continue to apply to such discriminatory treatment if the provision of goods, facilities and services to the employer's employees is not identical to such provision to the public, or is an incident of the employment contract, or relates to training.

---

[17]   DDA 1995, s 4(2)(b); *Code of Practice: Employment and Occupation* (2004), paras 8.8 and 8.13–8.14 (and examples).

[18]   Ibid, s 4(2)(c).

[19]   HL Deb, vol 566, col 169; *Code of Practice: Employment and Occupation* (2004), paras 8.9–8.11 (and examples).

[20]   DDA 1995, s 18D(2).

[21]   Ibid, s 4(4); *Code of Practice: Employment and Occupation* (2004), para 8.12 (and example).

[22]   Ibid, s 4(4)(a).

[23]   Ibid, s 4(4)(b).

[24]   Ibid, s 4(4)(c).

Dismissal

4.2.8   Seventhly, it is unlawful for an employer to discriminate against a disabled person whom the employer employs by dismissing him or her.[25] A potentially unlawful dismissal of a disabled employee might arise in the context of capability or absence,[26] but might equally arise from an unfair redundancy selection exercise.[27] A dismissal for this purpose includes the non-renewal of a fixed-term contract.[28] That arises where there is a termination of a person's employment by the expiration of any period. That includes a period expiring by reference to an event or circumstance. However, it does not include a termination immediately after which the employment is renewed on the same terms.

4.2.9   A dismissal also includes a constructive dismissal.[29] That is where a person's employment is terminated by any act of that person, including the giving of notice. The termination must have occurred in circumstances such that he or she is entitled to terminate it without notice by reason of the conduct of the employer. This overcomes the earlier difficulties in the case-law as to whether a constructive dismissal was within the scope of Part 2.[30] A constructive dismissal is where the employee resigns in response to the employer's conduct amounting to a serious or fundamental or repudiatory breach of contract. In one case, the respondent was in fundamental breach of the contract of employment by its continuing failure to deal with disability discrimination against the claimant. The claimant had resigned in response to that breach. The breach comprised the respondent's persistent failure to agree to adjustments requested by the claimant in order to enable her to return to work after sickness absence.[31]

Any other detriment

4.2.10   Finally, it is unlawful for an employer to discriminate against a disabled person whom the employer employs by subjecting him or her to any other detriment.[32] The concept of 'any other detriment' is a potentially broad one.[33] It provides a catch-all for any other forms of

[25] DDA 1995, s 4(2)(d); *Code of Practice: Employment and Occupation* (2004), paras 8.15–8.27 (and examples).

[26] *Clark v TDG Ltd t/a Novacold* [1999] IRLR 318, CA.

[27] *British Sugar plc v Kirker* [1998] IRLR 624, EAT.

[28] DDA 1995, s 4(5)(a), as amended from 1 October 2004.

[29] Ibid, s 4(5)(b), as amended from 1 October 2004.

[30] *Commissioner of Police of the Metropolis v Harley* [2001] IRLR 263, EAT; *Catherall v Michelin Tyre plc* [2003] IRLR 61, EAT.

[31] *Nottinghamshire County Council v Meikle* [2004] EWCA Civ 859, [2004] IRLR 703, CA (the limitation period runs from the date of termination rather than from the date of the breach). See also: *Williams v J Walter Thompson Group Ltd* [2005] EWCA Civ 133, [2005] IRLR 376, CA.

[32] DDA 1995, s 4(2)(d).

[33] *Garry v London Borough of Ealing* [2001] IRLR 681, CA (a case decided under the comparable provision of the RRA 1976).

employment discrimination against disabled persons, if not already caught by the specific categories above. Prior to 1 October 2004, harassment of a disabled person fell within this provision. Harassment is now dealt with separately,[34] although acts that fail to satisfy the statutory definition of harassment might still fall to be treated as a detriment.

Post-employment discrimination

4.2.11 Prior to 1 October 2004, there was some doubt, although largely assuaged by late developments in the case-law,[35] as to whether these provisions were wholly apt to address post-employment discrimination (eg a refusal to provide a reference or discrimination occurring during post-termination appeal proceedings). Now, particular provision is made where there has been a relevant relationship between a disabled person and another person (the 'relevant person') and that relationship has come to an end.[36] This is considered in greater detail in Chapter 3.[37]

Harassment

4.2.12 It is also unlawful for an employer, in relation to employment by that employer, to subject to harassment a disabled person whom the employer employs or a disabled person who has applied to the employer for employment.[38] The meaning of 'harassment' has been considered in Chapter 3.[39]

Pre-employment health screening

4.2.13 The Act does not expressly address the question of pre-employment medical examinations and screening. Many employers utilise health-related questions in application forms or medical examinations as a pre-condition of employment. By screening employment applicants for disability or medical conditions, many employers effectively exclude a proportion of applicants from further competition in the selection process. An applicant with a disability might be prematurely excluded from further consideration and may lose the opportunity to demonstrate ability and merit.

4.2.14 An attempt was made during the original legislative process to prohibit pre-employment medical examinations or screening, but the

---

[34] DDA 1995, s 3B and 4(3). The term 'detriment' (except in s 16C(2)(b)) does not include conduct of the nature referred to in s 3B (harassment): s 18D(2).

[35] *Rhys-Harper v Relaxion Group plc; D'Souza v Lambeth London Borough Council; Jones v 3M Healthcare Ltd* [2003] UKHL 33, [2003] ICR 867, HL.

[36] DDA 1995, s 16A(1); *Code of Practice: Employment and Occupation* (2004), paras 8.28–8.32 (and examples).

[37] At **3.5**.

[38] DDA 1995, s 4(3).

[39] At **3.3**.

amendments were rejected. The Government's view was that 'in general, employers should be free to use whatever recruitment procedures best meet their needs and to conduct medical examinations of employees where that seems appropriate'.[40] It was unwilling to forbid medical examinations or to limit enquiries about disability. Indeed, employers might find it necessary to question disabled applicants about a disability where such questions are designed to assist the disabled person in competing for employment opportunities.[41]

4.2.15 Nevertheless, that does not mean that health screens and examinations might not fall foul of the Act. Occupational health practitioners are likely to be treated as acting as the agent of the employer for this purpose.[42] Medical examinations, enquiries, questions or screening would undoubtedly constitute 'arrangements' made for the purpose of determining who should be offered employment.[43] If the effect of such arrangements was to amount to less favourable treatment of a disabled person for a reason related to disability, the employer would have to show that that treatment was justifiable. Even if all applicants and employees were medically examined, the effect might be to discriminate indirectly against disabled persons if the employer uses the evidence gleaned from the examination without further individualised enquiry as to the ability to do the job (including reasonable adjustments). The relevant Code of Practice provides some useful guidance in this area.[44]

Scope of the employment provisions

4.2.16 Section 4 of the Act applies only in relation to employment at an establishment in Great Britain (or in Northern Ireland).[45] It is concerned with acts of discrimination by an employer against a disabled person. The task of identifying the employer is not usually problematic.[46] The liability

---

[40] HC Deb Standing Committee E, col 151.

[41] HL Deb, vol 564, cols 1935–1936.

[42] *London Borough of Hammersmith and Fulham v Farnsworth* [2000] IRLR 691, EAT (an occupational health report is unlikely to be treated as a confidential medical record where the examinee has consented to medical information being provided to the employer so as to enable it to reach an employment decision).

[43] DDA 1995, s 4(1)(a).

[44] *Code of Practice: Employment and Occupation* (2004), paras 6.14–6.16 (and examples), 7.9 (and example) and 7.27–7.31 (and examples).

[45] DDA 1995, s 4(6), as modified by s 70(6) and Sch 8, para 3.

[46] But see *Lancashire County Council v Mason* [1998] ICR 907, EAT, in which neither the school governors nor the local education authority were held to be liable for an alleged act of disability discrimination in employment selection arrangements in the context of a state maintained county school with a delegated budget. See now *Murphy v Slough Borough Council* [2004] ICR 1163, EAT, and [2005] EWCA Civ 122, CA (school governing body rather than local education authority liable for employment-related decision in breach of DDA 1995), and Education (Modification of Enactments Relating to Employment) Order 2003, SI 2003/1964, and Education (Modification of Enactments Relating to Employment) (England) (Amendment) Order 2004, SI 2004/2325. See also Education (Modification of Enactments Relating to Employment) (Wales) Order 2006, SI 2006/1073.

of an employer may be vicarious liability for the actions of employees in the course of employment.[47] The employer's liability may be shared with another person who knowingly aids in the commission of an unlawful act of discrimination.[48] These concepts are discussed in more detail in Chapter 10.

Employment

4.2.17   The term 'employment' has the same extended definition as used in other discrimination statutes. The DDA 1995 embraces discrimination in employment under a contract of service or a contract of apprenticeship, but it also includes employment under a contract personally to do any work.[49] The dominant purpose of the contract must be the execution of personal work or labour.[50] Because disability discrimination is a statutory tort, the fact that the contract of employment (or its performance) may be tainted with illegality (such as receiving wages without deduction of tax) assumes less significance than it would do in employment law generally.[51]

Employment at an establishment in Great Britain

4.2.18   The phrase 'employment at an establishment in Great Britain' (and, by extension, Northern Ireland) has a particular meaning.[52] Great Britain includes such territorial waters of the United Kingdom as are adjacent to Great Britain.[53] Employment (including employment on board a ship or on an aircraft or hovercraft) is regarded as being employment at an establishment in Great Britain if the employee does his or her work wholly or partly in Great Britain.[54] However, if the employee does his or her work wholly outside Great Britain, the employment is still regarded as being employment at an establishment in Great Britain in

---

[47]   DDA 1995, s 58.

[48]   Ibid, s 57.

[49]   Ibid, s 68(1) and Sch 8, para 47; *Code of Practice: Employment and Occupation* (2004), para 3.8.

[50]   *Sheehan v Post Office Counters Ltd* [1999] ICR 734, EAT; *Burton v Higham (t/a Ace Appointments)* [2003] IRLR 257, EAT; *South East Sheffield Citizens Advice Bureau v Grayson* [2004] IRLR 354, EAT; *Hawkins v Nigel Darken t/a Sawbridgeworth Motorcycles* [2004] EWCA Civ 1755, CA. See generally: *Quinnen v Hovells* [1984] IRLR 227, EAT; *Mirror Group Newspapers Ltd v Gunning* [1986] ICR 145, CA; *BP Chemicals Ltd v Gillick* [1995] IRLR 128, EAT; *Mingeley v Pennock and Ivory t/a Amber Cars* [2004] IRLR 373, CA.

[51]   *Hall v Woolston Hall Leisure Ltd* [2000] IRLR 578, CA (the question is whether the claim is so inextricably bound up with the illegal conduct that a tribunal could not award compensation without appearing to condone the illegality).

[52]   DDA 1995, s 68(1), applying s 68(2)–(4A), as substituted or inserted by the Disability Discrimination Act 1995 (Amendment) Regulations 2003, with effect from 1 October 2004. In Northern Ireland, see DDA 1998, s 68(2) and Sch 8, para 47(2).

[53]   Ibid, s 68(1).

[54]   Ibid, s 68(2)(a).

certain circumstances.[55] Those circumstances are that: (a) the employer has a place of business at an establishment in Great Britain; (b) the work is for the purposes of the business carried on at the establishment; and (c) the employee is ordinarily resident in Great Britain at the time at which he or she applies for or is offered the employment or at any time during the course of the employment.[56]

4.2.19 Employment on board a ship is also included if the ship is registered at a port of registry in Great Britain or it belongs to or is possessed by Her Majesty in right of the Government of the United Kingdom.[57] Employment on board an aircraft or hovercraft is also covered if it is registered in the United Kingdom and operated by a person who has his or her principal place of business (or is ordinarily resident) in Great Britain.[58] Alternatively, it is covered if it belongs to or is possessed by Her Majesty in right of the Government of the United Kingdom.[59] Otherwise, employment on board a ship or an aircraft or a hovercraft is not to be regarded as being employment at an establishment in Great Britain.[60] Special provision is made for employment of a prescribed kind or in prescribed circumstances to be regarded as not being employment at an establishment in Great Britain,[61] but no prescription has been made. A particular provision is also made for determining if employment concerned with the exploration of the seabed or sub-soil or the exploitation of their natural resources is outside Great Britain.[62]

Exclusion of small businesses

4.2.20 As originally enacted, the employment provisions of the DDA 1995 did not apply to small businesses. The threshold was first set in relation to employers with fewer than 20 employees.[63] From 1 December 1998, the threshold applied to employers with fewer than 15 employees.[64] From 1 October 2004, this exclusion is repealed by the Disability Discrimination Act 1995 (Amendment) Regulations 2003. Part 2 of the 1995 Act now applies to all employers (except the armed forces), regardless of size or the number of employees.

---

55 DDA 1995, s 68(2)(b).
56 Ibid, s 68(2A).
57 Ibid, s 68(2), (2B).
58 Ibid, s 68(2), (2C)(a).
59 Ibid, s 68(2), (2C)(b).
60 Ibid, s 68(2D).
61 Ibid, s 68(4).
62 Ibid, s 68(4A), applying Sex Discrimination Act 1975, s 10(1) and (5) and Sex Discrimination and Equal Pay (Offshore Employment) Order 1987, SI 1987/930.
63 Ibid, s 7(1). The case-law on this provision is now of academic interest only: *Taylor v Lifesign Ltd* (2000) EAT/1437/98; *Hardie v CD Northern Ltd* [2000] IRLR 87, EAT; *Colt Group Ltd v Couchman* [2000] ICR 327, EAT; *Burton v Higham (t/a Ace Appointments)* [2003] IRLR 257, EAT; *South East Sheffield Citizens Advice Bureau v Grayson* [2004] IRLR 354, EAT; *Hawkins v Nigel Darken t/a Sawbridgeworth Motorcycles* [2004] EWCA Civ 1755, CA.
64 Disability Discrimination (Exemption for Small Employers) Order 1998, SI 1998/2618.

Other exemptions

4.2.21 As originally enacted, although the Act applied to employment by the Crown, government departments, statutory bodies and statutory office-holders,[65] its employment provisions did not apply to employment as a statutory office-holder (such as a police officer);[66] a member of certain statutory police forces; a prison officer (except custody officers); a fire-fighting member of a fire brigade; and a member of the naval, military or air forces of the Crown.[67] From 1 October 2004, these exemptions have been largely repealed by the Disability Discrimination Act 1995 (Amendment) Regulations 2003. The only exemption remaining relates to service in any of the naval, military or air forces of the Crown.[68] The wider question of the application of the Act to the Crown and to Parliament is considered in more detail in Chapter 10.

Police

4.2.22 From 1 October 2004, for the purposes of Part 2, the holding of the office of constable is to be treated as employment by the chief officer of police[69] as respects any act done by him or her in relation to a constable or that office.[70] For the same purposes, the holding of the office of constable is to be treated as employment by the police authority[71] as respects any act done by them in relation to a constable or that office.[72] This means that police officers now have the same rights as other employees under Part 2 of the DDA 1995.[73] So far as establishing vicarious liability for the acts of a police officer,[74] the holding of the office of constable shall be treated as employment by the chief officer of police (and as not being employment by any other person).[75] Anything done by a person holding such an office in the performance (or purported performance) of his or her functions shall be treated as done in the course of that employment.[76] The whole of this analysis immediately above applies equally to a police cadet[77] and appointment as a police cadet as it applies to a constable and the office of constable.[78]

---

[65] DDA 1995, s 64(1)–(2A) and (8).
[66] *Photis and Bruce v KMC International Search and Selection, Heyes v Lord Chancellor's Department* (EAT/732/00, EAT/766/00 and EAT/960/00).
[67] DDA 1995, s 64(5)–(8).
[68] Ibid, s 64(7); *Code of Practice: Employment and Occupation* (2004), para 3.9.
[69] Ibid, s 68A(4) and (7)–(8).
[70] Ibid, s 68A(1)(a).
[71] Ibid, s 68A(7)–(8).
[72] Ibid, s 68A(1)(b).
[73] *Code of Practice: Employment and Occupation* (2004), paras 3.11 and 9.23–9.24. See also Police (Appointments) Regulations (Northern Ireland) 2004, SR 2004/379.
[74] DDA 1995, s 58.
[75] Ibid, s 68A(2)(a).
[76] Ibid, s 68A(2)(b).
[77] Ibid, s 68A(7).
[78] Ibid, s 68A(6).

4.2.23 Any compensation, costs or expenses awarded against a chief officer of police in any proceedings brought against him or her under Part 2 shall be paid out of the police fund.[79] That includes any costs or expenses incurred by a chief officer of police in any such proceedings so far as not recovered in the proceedings. Any sum required by a chief officer of police for the settlement of any claim made against him or her under Part 2 if the settlement is approved by the police authority shall also be paid out of the police fund if the settlement is approved by the police authority.[80] In such cases and to such extent as appears to a police authority to be appropriate, a police authority may pay out of the police fund any compensation, costs or expenses awarded in proceedings under Part 2 against a person under the direction and control of the chief officer of police; any costs or expenses incurred and not recovered by such a person in such proceedings; and any sum required in connection with the settlement of a claim that has or might have given rise to such proceedings.[81]

Charities

4.2.24 Exceptional treatment under Part 2 of the Act is given to charities.[82] Nothing in Part 2 of the Act affects any charitable instrument which provides for conferring benefits on one or more categories of person determined by reference to any physical or mental capacity.[83] Moreover, nothing in the employment provisions of the 1995 Act makes unlawful any act done by a registered or non-registered charity[84] in pursuance of any of its charitable purposes, so far as those purposes are connected with persons determined by reference to any physical or mental capacity.[85] The term 'charity' has the same meaning as in the Charities Act 1993.[86] A 'charitable instrument' is an enactment or other instrument (whenever taking effect) so far as it relates to charitable purposes.[87]

Supported employment

4.2.25 Special provision is also made for persons providing supported employment under the Disabled Persons (Employment) Act 1944 or the

---

[79] DDA 1995, s 68A(3)(a) and (7).
[80] Ibid, s 68A(3)(b).
[81] Ibid, s 68A(5).
[82] Ibid, s 18C(1), originally enacted as s 10(1).
[83] Ibid, s 18C(1)(a).
[84] Ibid, s 18C(3) provides that a recognised body is one for the purposes of Part I of the Law Reform (Miscellaneous Provisions) (Scotland) Act 1990.
[85] Ibid, s 18C(1)(b).
[86] Ibid, s 18C(3). In Northern Ireland, see the Charities Act (Northern Ireland) 1964 (by virtue of DDA 1995, Sch 8, para 7(3)).
[87] Ibid, s 18C(3). In England and Wales (and Northern Ireland), charitable purposes are purposes which are exclusively charitable according to the law of England and Wales (and Northern Ireland) (s 18C(4) and Sch 8, para 7(4)). In Scotland only, charitable purposes are to be construed as if contained in the Income Tax Acts: s 18C(5).

Disabled Persons (Employment) Act (Northern Ireland) 1945. Nothing in Part 2 of the Act prevents a person who provides supported employment from treating members of a particular group of disabled persons (or persons who have had a disability in the past) more favourably than other persons in providing supported employment.[88] In this context, 'supported employment' means facilities provided or paid for under s 15 of the 1944 or 1945 Act.[89] Furthermore, nothing in Part 2 of the Act prevents the Secretary of State (or, in Northern Ireland, the Department of Higher and Further Education, Training and Employment) from agreeing to arrangements for the provision of supported employment which will (or may) have the effect of treating members of a particular group of disabled persons (or persons who have had a disability in the past) more favourably than other persons.[90]

4.2.26   The effect of these provisions is not to exclude persons employed under supported employment arrangements from the prohibition on disability discrimination *per se*. Rather, the intention is to allow employers providing supported employment to distinguish between different groups of disabled persons when extending supported employment opportunities. Providing supported employment opportunities for some disabled persons while excluding other persons with a disability would otherwise amount to disability-related discrimination or direct discrimination, contrary to the Act. For example, an employer is allowed to create a supported employment environment for workers with sight impairments and to do so without needing to provide similar facilities for other disabled workers. However, the supported employment in question must be within the framework provided by the 1944–1945 legislation. Moreover, this does not excuse acts of disability discrimination elsewhere in the employer's workplace.

Employer's duty to make reasonable adjustments

4.2.27   Section 4 of the DDA 1995 defines the circumstances in which an employer acts unlawfully by discriminating against a disabled person in relation to employment.[91] The definition of 'discrimination' for this purpose includes a failure to comply with a duty to make reasonable adjustments imposed on the employer in relation to the disabled person.[92] In the case of disability-related discrimination,[93] if an employer is under a duty to make reasonable adjustments in relation to a disabled person but fails to comply with that duty, the employer's treatment of that person

---

[88]   DDA 1995, s 18C(2)(a).
[89]   Ibid, s 18C(3) and Sch 8, para 7.
[90]   Ibid, s 18C(2)(b) and Sch 8, para 7(2).
[91]   Ibid, s 4(1) and (2).
[92]   Ibid, s 3A(2).
[93]   Ibid, s 3A(1).

cannot be justified,[94] unless it would have been justified even if the employer had complied with that duty.[95]

When does the duty to make reasonable adjustments arise?

4.2.28 The employer's duty to make reasonable adjustments arises in one of two circumstances.[96] The first arises where a provision, criterion or practice is applied by (or on behalf of) the employer. The effect might be to place the disabled person concerned at a substantial disadvantage in comparison with persons who are not disabled. If so, it is the duty of the employer to take such steps as it is reasonable (in all the circumstances of the case) for it to have to take in order to prevent the provision, criterion or practice having that effect.[97] The second arises where any physical feature of premises occupied by the employer places the disabled person concerned at a substantial disadvantage in comparison with persons who are not disabled. It is then the duty of the employer to take such steps as it is reasonable (in all the circumstances of the case) for it to have to take in order to prevent the feature having that effect.[98]

To whom is the duty owed?

4.2.29 Who is the 'disabled person concerned' in these contexts?[99] In the case of a provision, criterion or practice for determining to whom employment should be offered, it means any disabled person who is (or who has notified the employer that he or she may be) an applicant for that employment.[100] The length of notice given by the disabled applicant to the employer might play a part in determining whether the employer has satisfied the duty to make reasonable adjustments. In any other case, it means a disabled person who is an applicant for the employment concerned or an employee of the employer concerned.[101]

4.2.30 In the case of an applicant or potential applicant for employment, the duty to make reasonable adjustments is not imposed on an employer in relation to a disabled person if the employer does not know (and could not reasonably be expected to know) that the disabled person concerned is (or may be) an applicant for the employment.[102] Moreover, in any case, the duty to make reasonable adjustments is not imposed on an employer in relation to a disabled person if the employer does not know (and could not reasonably be expected to know) that that person has a disability and is likely to be placed at a substantial

---

[94] DDA 1995, s 3A(3).
[95] Ibid, s 3A(6). See generally the discussion at **3.2**.
[96] *Code of Practice: Employment and Occupation* (2004), para 5.3 (and example).
[97] DDA 1995, s 4A(1)(a).
[98] Ibid, s 4A(1)(b).
[99] *Code of Practice: Employment and Occupation* (2004), paras 5.5–5.7.
[100] DDA 1995, s 4A(2)(a).
[101] Ibid, s 4A(2)(b).
[102] Ibid, s 4A(3)(a).

disadvantage in comparison with persons who are not disabled.[103] The question of what the employer knew or could reasonably be expected to know is a question of fact for the tribunal.[104] What will be reasonable for an employer to know or expect will vary from case to case.

4.2.31 An employer may need to do all that it could reasonably be expected to do to find out whether a person has a disability which is likely to place him or her at a substantial disadvantage.[105] Of course, if a disabled person chooses to conceal a disability, that will lessen the possibility that the employer should be expected to carry out a reasonable adjustment, unless the circumstances are such that it would be reasonable for the employer to be expected to know of the disability without the necessity for revelation. Thus, employers need to be pro-active. They will not necessarily escape liability by simply not asking whether a person has a disability and whether the effects of any disability call for an adjustment to be made. The fact that the employer might not know of a person's disability will make no difference if, for example, a personnel officer, line manager or occupational health officer employed by the employer has that information.[106] The knowledge of an employee or agent of the employer is the vicarious knowledge of the employer itself.

4.2.32 It is recommended that employers should only ask disability-related questions if disability is (or may be) relevant to the ability to do the job. Equally, employers should be positive in welcoming applications from disabled persons. Asking about the effects of a disability is seen as a necessary part of the process of considering what reasonable adjustments might be made for a disabled person. In any event, if a person asks for an adjustment to be made, the employer will be entitled to ask for evidence that the person has a disability such as to trigger the statutory duty. Moreover, because a reasonable adjustment might not work in practice without the co-operation of other employees,[107] it may be necessary to reveal the fact of a person's disability (where otherwise not obvious) to some of that person's work colleagues (particularly a supervisor or manager) *in confidence* (eg where special assistance may be needed). This should be done on a selective and 'need-to-know' basis. Employers should be careful not to commit a separate act of discrimination by revealing such information without consulting the disabled person first or without a legitimate management purpose in doing so.

4.2.33 There does appear to be some onus on the applicant or employee to make known to the employer their need for a reasonable adjustment. Disabled people should not have a duty imposed upon them to give to an

---

[103] DDA 1995, s 4A(3)(b).
[104] *Hanlon v University of Huddersfield* (1998) EAT/166/98.
[105] *Code of Practice: Employment and Occupation* (2004), paras 5.12–5.14 (and examples).
[106] *London Borough of Hammersmith and Fulham v Farnsworth* [2000] IRLR 691, EAT; *Code of Practice: Employment and Occupation* (2004), paras 5.15–5.16 (and examples).
[107] *Code of Practice: Employment and Occupation* (2004), para 5.22 (and example).

employer a detailed account of their disability and its effects upon them, especially where this would only lead to an employer making adjustments that it would have been reasonable to make in any event.[108] However, it is equally undesirable to expect employers to ask intrusive questions of disabled people that would not have been asked of a non-disabled person. A tribunal has to measure the extent of the duty to make a reasonable adjustment, if any, against the actual or assumed knowledge of the employer, both as to the disability and its likelihood of causing the individual a substantial disadvantage in comparison with persons who are not disabled.

Provision, criterion or practice

4.2.34 The terms 'provision, criterion or practice' are not defined in the Act, except that they include any arrangements.[109] The Part 2 Code of Practice explains that they include arrangements for determining to whom employment should be offered, and terms, conditions or arrangements on which employment, promotion, transfer, training or any other benefit is offered or afforded.[110] Examples of such arrangements would include procedures for recruitment and selection or promotion (such as application forms, interviews or employment tests), and terms upon which employment opportunities are granted (such as insistence upon mobility or flexibility clauses or satisfaction of medical standards). It will be important for the claimant to identify the provision, criterion, practice or arrangement that is said to have the required comparative substantial disadvantage.[111]

4.2.35 In one case,[112] a need for occupational health clearance was held to be not in itself an arrangement that created a substantial disadvantage. However, the occupational health adviser's assessment as to the challenging and stressful nature of the post (and the claimant's unfitness for it) was part of the arrangements for determining to whom employment should be offered. That placed the claimant at a comparative substantial disadvantage and triggered the employer's duty to make reasonable adjustments. That duty would include obtaining specialist advice from the claimant's consultant, consulting the claimant, referring the matter back the occupational health adviser and adjusting the job.

4.2.36 The use of the terms 'provision, criterion or practice' is deliberately wider that the sole term 'arrangements' that was used before 1 October 2004. Prior to that date, the duty to make adjustments was held

---

[108] *Ridout v TC Group* [1998] IRLR 628, EAT.
[109] DDA 1995, s 18D(2). The pre-1 October 2004 term was 'arrangement': DDA 1995, s 6(1)(a) and (2) (prior to the 2004 amendments).
[110] *Code of Practice: Employment and Occupation (2004)*, para 5.8 (and examples) effectively adopting the previous statutory definition.
[111] *Paul v National Probation Service* [2004] IRLR 190, EAT.
[112] Ibid.

not to apply to a dismissal itself, although it did apply to the process leading to dismissal.[113] That distinction is doubtful. A decision to dismiss is capable of amounting to an arrangement on which employment is afforded. The list of examples of reasonable adjustments contains many illustrations of adjustments that are relevant to the retention of a disabled employee in lieu of dismissal.[114] However, not all arrangements that might be necessary to enable a disabled person to work fall within the duty to make adjustments.[115] The duty is not intended to cover everything an employer *could* do (eg arranging transport to and from work or providing a personal carer to assist with the disabled person's personal needs while at work). Only job-related arrangements (such as the way a job is structured or organised) are covered.

Physical features of premises

4.2.37　The Act defines the phrase 'physical feature of premises'.[116] The following are treated as physical features (whether permanent or temporary) of premises:

- any feature arising from the design or construction of a building on the premises;

- any feature on the premises of any approach to, exit from or access to such a building;

- any fixtures, fittings, furnishings, furniture, equipment or materials in or on the premises;

- any other physical element or quality of any land comprised in the premises.

The physical features of a building do not only include the physical fabric and structure of a building. Features such as lighting, air conditioning, building materials, fixtures and fittings, furniture and equipment are also included.[117] However, it is only the physical features of premises occupied by the employer which are in scope. The duty to make reasonable adjustments in respect of the physical features of premises does not extend to a disabled person's private house (eg in the case of a home-worker) or to the premises of another employer which a disabled

---

[113]　*Clark v TDG Ltd t/a Novacold* [1999] IRLR 318, CA.

[114]　DDA 1995, s 18B(2).

[115]　*Kenny v Hampshire Constabulary* [1999] IRLR 76, EAT.

[116]　DDA 1995, s 18D(2); *Code of Practice: Employment and Occupation* (2004), para 5.9 (and examples). The definition was previously in the Disability Discrimination (Employment) Regulations 1996, reg 9, now revoked (and the Disability Discrimination (Employment) Regulations (Northern Ireland) 1996).

[117]　A non-exhaustive list is provided in *Code of Practice: Employment and Occupation* (2004), para 5.10.

employee might have to visit in the course of employment (eg a travelling sales executive visiting a customer's premises).[118]

Substantial disadvantage

4.2.38 The duty to make reasonable adjustments arises only if the provision, criterion or practice or the physical feature in question places the disabled person concerned at a *substantial* disadvantage in comparison with persons who are not disabled.[119] The duty to make reasonable adjustments is an individualised duty.[120] It arises only where the disabled person in question suffers an actual or hypothetical comparative disadvantage. It does not necessarily arise generally or in respect of a class or group of disabled persons. The duty is only imposed following a comparative assessment of the adverse effect upon the disabled person. The comparators are persons who are not disabled (and, in the case of a person with a past disability, persons who have not had a disability).[121] The tribunal must address the comparison and make findings of fact to enable it to determine whether the disabled person has been placed at a substantial disadvantage.[122]

4.2.39 The use of the word 'substantial' appears to create quite a high threshold for the operation of the duty to make reasonable adjustments. Substantial disadvantages are those which are not minor or trivial.[123] The intention is that minor and trivial disadvantages do not cause the duty to be imposed on respondents. Only disadvantages of substance will call for accommodations.[124] Prior to 1 October 2004, a term or practice under which the amount of a person's pay was wholly or partly dependent on that person's performance was not to be taken to place disabled persons at a substantial disadvantage.[125] That will now be a question of fact and subject to the duty to make reasonable adjustments.[126]

Judicial guidance

4.2.40 The appellate courts have provided important guidance to employment tribunals on the practical approach to the issues raised by the

---

[118] HL Deb, vol 566, col 184.

[119] DDA 1995, s 4A(1), with emphasis added.

[120] *Code of Practice: Employment and Occupation* (2004), para 5.4.

[121] DDA 1995, s 2(2) and Sch 2, para 3, as amended.

[122] *London Clubs Management Ltd v Hood* [2001] IRLR 719, EAT; *Cave v Goodwin* [2001] All ER (D) 163 (Mar), IDS Brief 687, CA.

[123] *Code of Practice: Employment and Occupation* (2004), para 5.11.

[124] HC Deb Standing Committee E, col 196.

[125] Disability Discrimination (Employment) Regulations 1996, reg 3(2), now revoked (and Disability Discrimination (Employment) Regulations (Northern Ireland) 1996).

[126] *Code of Practice: Employment and Occupation* (2004), paras 8.5–8.6.

duty to make reasonable adjustments.[127] It is not an error of law for a tribunal to fail to follow these steps sequentially.[128] The judicial guidance has been modified in this discussion to reflect the October 2004 amendments to the statutory provisions.

4.2.41   The first question is whether, in the particular circumstances of the case, there is a duty to make reasonable adjustments imposed upon the employer.[129] If so, the next step is to enquire whether the employer has taken reasonable steps to prevent the 'provision, criterion or practice' or 'physical features of premises' having the effect of placing the disabled person at a comparative substantial disadvantage. That necessitates asking whether the employer reasonably could have taken any of the steps set out in the statutory provisions as illustrating the kinds of adjustments that might be made.[130] However, this does not mean that the employer is in breach of the duty to make reasonable adjustments if it was not aware of the statutory duty. The employer does not have to show that it consciously considered what steps it ought to take in the context of its statutory duty. The question is what steps the employer took and did not take. An employer may have taken all reasonable steps, despite being ignorant of its statutory duty or the statutory provisions. It may have taken no steps, but it will have a defence if it could not reasonably have taken any.[131] The duty is one placed upon the employer. If an employer has not turned its mind to what adjustments might be made, the fact that the claimant cannot suggest any reasonable adjustments does not mean that the duty has been discharged.[132]

4.2.42   In judging the reasonableness question, consideration will need to be given as to whether any of the factors set out in the Act apply.[133] A respondent is not prevented from arguing after the event or with the

---

[127]   *Morse v Wiltshire CC* [1998] IRLR 352, EAT; *British Gas Services Ltd v McCaull* [2001] IRLR 60, EAT; *Cosgrove v Caesar & Howie* [2001] IRLR 653, EAT; *Johnson & Johnson Medical Ltd v Filmer* [2002] ICR 292, EAT.

[128]   *Beart v HM Prison Service* [2003] IRLR 238, CA.

[129]   DDA 1995, s 4A(1). See *Environment Agency v Rowan* [2008] IRLR 20, EAT, discussed below. The duty might not arise at all: *NTL Group Ltd v Difolco* [2006] EWCA Civ 1508 (CA) (a disabled employee was to be made redundant, but as there was no link between her disability and her redundancy, no duty to make reasonable adjustments was engaged).

[130]   DDA 1995, s 18B(2). The tribunal must identify with some particularity the step the employer has failed to take. Unless it does so, it cannot assess the reasonableness of that step. The degree of specificity required will vary with the circumstances of the case: *HM Prison Service v Johnson* [2007] IRLR 951, EAT. See also *Project Management Institute v Latif* [2007] IRLR 579, EAT.

[131]   Under the pre-1 October 2004 law, it would have been very difficult for an employer to justify a failure to take reasonable steps if it had not considered what steps should be taken: *British Gas Services Ltd v McCaull* [2001] IRLR 60, EAT. However, the justification defence has now been repealed and the emphasis is upon the reasonableness of the steps taken or not taken.

[132]   *Cosgrove v Caesar & Howie* [2001] IRLR 653, EAT; *Code of Practice: Employment and Occupation* (2004), para 5.24.

[133]   DDA 1995, s 18B(1).

benefit of hindsight that a particular step was not a reasonable one to have to take simply because the respondent did not consider taking it at the time.[134] The test is an objective one of whether the respondent took such steps as it was reasonable in all the circumstances of the case for that respondent to have to take in order to prevent the application of a provision, criterion or practice or the physical features of premises placing the disabled person at a comparative substantial disadvantage.[135] The employment tribunal is not simply concerned with the reasonableness of the respondent's explanation. The tribunal can substitute its own judgment for that of the employer (or other person). It may not be sufficient for a respondent simply to assert that adjustments were considered and thought to be unreasonable. The tribunal might find that there were other reasonable adjustments which could have been made by that person.

4.2.43   Somewhat controversially, the Court of Session in *Archibald v Fife Council* held that the duty of reasonable adjustment only arises in respect of an existing employee where he or she is placed at a substantial disadvantage in the performance of his or her particular employment in comparison with persons who are not disabled.[136] The duty would then be triggered only if it was open to the employer to make adjustments to the arrangements of that particular post. On further appeal, however, the House of Lords has stressed the positive nature of the duty to make reasonable adjustments.[137] It indicated that an employer may be obliged to discriminate positively in favour of disabled persons. On the facts, the liability of a disabled employee to be dismissed because her disability meant that she was no longer able to carry out the duties that she was employed to do amounted to an 'arrangement' which placed her at a substantial disadvantage compared to other employees. That triggered the duty to make reasonable adjustments, which might include transferring her to another position for which she was suited, without the need for competitive interview and selection.

4.2.44   More recently still, the EAT has provided up-to-date and apparently prescriptive guidance on the sequence of steps that an employment tribunal should follow in judging whether the duty to make reasonable adjustments arises in the first place.[138] Without following this process, a tribunal cannot properly make findings of a failure to make

---

[134]   *British Gas Services Ltd v McCaull* [2001] IRLR 60, EAT.
[135]   *Morse v Wiltshire County Council* [1998] IRLR 352, EAT; *British Gas Services Ltd v McCaull* [2001] IRLR 60, EAT; *Johnson & Johnson Medical Ltd v Filmer* [2002] ICR 292, EAT.
[136]   [2004] IRLR 197, Ct of Sess.
[137]   [2004] UKHL 32, [2004] IRLR 651, HL.
[138]   *Environment Agency v Rowan* [2008] IRLR 20, EAT. Here the tribunal had failed to make appropriate findings of fact such as to identify clearly the nature and extent of the substantial disadvantage suffered by the claimant and so could not determine properly what reasonable adjustments should have been made to overcome that substantial disadvantage.

reasonable adjustments and cannot go on to judge whether any proposed adjustment is a reasonable one to make. First, the tribunal must identify the provision, criterion or practice applied by or on behalf of the employer. Alternatively, or in addition, it must identify the physical feature of the premises occupied by the employer that is in issue. Secondly, the tribunal must identify the non-disabled comparators, where appropriate. Thirdly, the tribunal should identify the nature and the extent of the substantial disadvantage suffered by the claimant. This may involve a consideration of the cumulative effect of *both* the provision, criterion or practice applied by or on behalf of the employer *and* any relevant physical feature of the employer's premises. The tribunal must look at the overall picture. What it cannot do is jump from a finding of substantial disadvantage to a finding of what adjustment it would have been reasonable to make without first considering how that proposed adjustment would overcome the substantial disadvantage in question.

4.2.45   As to the burden of proof in reasonable adjustment cases, one view is that it is enough for the claimant to prove facts from which it could be inferred that any provision, criterion or practice, or physical feature of premises, has placed the claimant at a comparative substantial disadvantage. On that view, the burden of proof then switches to the employer to prove that there is no relevant provision, criterion or practice, or physical feature of premises; or that there is but that the claimant has not been placed at a comparative substantial disadvantage. Alternatively, it is for the employer to prove that there are no (or no further) reasonable steps that it could have taken to reduce or eliminate any such disadvantage. The EAT appears to disagree.[139] It has ruled that it is not enough for the claimant to prove that the duty to make reasonable adjustments has been engaged. The claimant must also prove facts from which it can be inferred, in the absence of an explanation, that the duty has been breached. The claimant must bring some evidence of what reasonable adjustment should or could have been made. The detail required of the proposed adjustment will vary with the case, but the employer must be able to understand the broad nature of the proposal so as to allow it to engage with the issue of whether it was a reasonable one to make.

Unfair dismissal and disability discrimination

4.2.46   Nothing in the Act creates an obligation to provide disability leave, although one of the Codes of Practice suggests otherwise.[140] Nor does it place a requirement upon employers to retain newly disabled employees.[141] However, an employee absent from work on account of

---

[139]   *Project Management Institute v Latif* [2007] IRLR 579, EAT. See also DDA 1995, s 17A(1)(c); *Igen Ltd v Wong* [2005] IRLR 258, CA; *Code of Practice: Employment and Occupation* (2004), para 4.43.
[140]   *Code of Practice: Employment and Occupation* (2004), para 5.20 (and example).
[141]   HC Deb Standing Committee E, col 220.

disability or long-term chronic ill health will be entitled to the benefit of the duty upon employers to make reasonable adjustments, as well as the specific protection of unfair dismissal law. The combined effect of disability discrimination law and unfair dismissal standards produces an obligation upon employers to hesitate before dismissing an employee on the grounds of disability or incapacity. At the very least, such an employer will need to consider what reasonable adjustments might be made for the employee. This might have the effect of prolonging his or her employment tenure or of leading to redeployment. Nevertheless, many employers' existing redeployment policies (which tend to give preference to redundant workers) will be unable to deal sufficiently with the specific duty to make reasonable adjustments which arises in the context of disability. Treating a disabled worker as just another candidate for redeployment is likely to be insufficient.[142]

4.2.47 To enjoy statutory protection from unfair dismissal, a disabled employee must have one year's continuous employment with the dismissing employer.[143] There is no minimum service qualification required to bring a complaint in relation to dismissal under the DDA 1995. Disabled employees dismissed with less than one year's service must rely upon the DDA 1995 alone, but, for a longer-serving employee with a disability, a dual claim under the disability discrimination and unfair dismissal legislation will prove attractive. A tribunal must approach both claims separately and distinctly.[144] It does not inevitably follow that a discriminatory dismissal is an unfair dismissal.[145] An unfair dismissal is not necessarily a discriminatory dismissal. The tribunal should carefully address the statutory test of an unfair dismissal.[146] The rather subjective 'band of reasonable responses' test in unfair dismissal is not the same as the more objective questions that have to be asked in disability discrimination cases.

Performance-related pay

4.2.48 Prior to 1 October 2004, special provision was made by regulations for a justification defence in relation to performance-related pay.[147] These regulations have now been revoked and not replaced.[148]

---

[142] *London Borough of Hillingdon v Morgan* (1999) EAT/1493/98, IDS Brief 649; *Kent County Council v Mingo* [2000] IRLR 90, EAT; *Archibald v Fife Council* [2004] UKHL 32, [2004] IRLR 651, HL.

[143] Employment Rights Act 1996, ss 94 and 108 (with some exceptions).

[144] *British Sugar plc v Kirker* [1998] IRLR 624, EAT.

[145] *H J Heinz Co Ltd v Kenrick* [2000] IRLR 144, EAT.

[146] Employment Rights Act 1996, s 98; *Kent County Council v Mingo* [2000] IRLR 90, EAT.

[147] Disability Discrimination (Employment) Regulations 1996, SI 1996/1456, and Disability Discrimination (Employment) Regulations (Northern Ireland) 1996, SR 1996/419.

[148] Disability Discrimination (Employment Field) (Leasehold Premises) Regulations 2004, SI 2004/153; Disability Discrimination (Employment Field) (Leasehold Premises) Regulations (Northern Ireland) 2004, SR 2004/374.

Instead, provision is now made in the Code of Practice.[149] Employers must ensure that the way in which performance-related pay arrangements operate does not discriminate against disabled employees. If an employee is denied the opportunity to receive performance-related pay on the ground of disability or for a disability-related reason, that is likely to be discrimination (and, in the case of direct discrimination, will not be capable of being justified). An employee whose disability adversely affects his or her performance might receive less performance-related pay as a result. In that case, the employer must consider whether there are reasonable adjustments which would overcome this substantial disadvantage, such as modifying performance-related pay arrangements.

Agricultural wages

4.2.49   Prior to 1 October 2004, so far as agricultural wages were concerned, the Agricultural Wages Board was allowed to issue a permit to a disabled person incapable of earning the minimum wage set by the Board.[150] The permit allowed for the setting of a lower minimum wage for that person and/or the variation of other minimum terms and conditions (other than holidays) applicable to that worker. Because the payment of a lower rate of pay to a disabled worker might not be capable of justification under the 1995 Act simply by reason of the permit, special provision was made by regulations. Less favourable treatment of a disabled person was to be taken to be justified to the extent that it related to (and accorded with) a matter within the terms and conditions of a permit granted to incapacitated persons under the agricultural wages legislation.[151] A failure to take a step otherwise required to comply with a duty to make reasonable adjustments was also to be taken to be justified if that step would relate to a matter within the terms and conditions of the permit but would exceed the requirements of those terms and conditions.[152] These provisions did not allow employers in the agricultural sector to discriminate against disabled persons in employment matters other than pay and terms and conditions covered by a permit. However, the provisions in the Agricultural Wages Act 1948 relating to permits for incapacitated workers have been repealed with effect from 1 October 2004 and so these special provisions are no longer in place.[153]

---

[149] *Code of Practice: Employment and Occupation* (2004), paras 5.20 and 8.5–8.6 (and examples).

[150] Agricultural Wages Act 1948, s 5 and Agricultural Wages (Scotland) Act 1949, s 5. A new order came into effect on 1 October 2004: Agricultural Wages Order 2004 (No 1).

[151] Disability Discrimination (Employment) Regulations 1996, SI 1996/1456, reg 6(a) (and Disability Discrimination (Employment) Regulations (Northern Ireland) 1996).

[152] Ibid, reg 6(b).

[153] Department for Environment, Food and Rural Affairs, *Agricultural Wages: Repeal of the Permits for Incapacitated Persons Provisions* (March 2004); Agricultural Wages (Abolition of Permits to Incapacitated Persons) Regulations 2004, SI 2004/2178; Agricultural Wages (Permits to Infirm and Incapacitated Persons) (Repeals) (Scotland) Regulations 2004, SSI 2004/384. The provisions of the Disability Discrimination (Employment) Regulations 1996 were revoked by the Disability Discrimination

4.3   CONTRACT WORKERS

4.3.1   In what is now s 4B, the Act deals with discrimination by principals against contract workers in respect of the provision of contract work.[154] As originally enacted, the intention is to protect disabled persons 'working under employment business arrangements if a hirer either refuses to hire the disabled person or discriminates against the disabled person once he has begun working for the hirer'.[155] Such persons will be generally protected by Part 2 of the Act in respect of their relationship with their employer (perhaps an employment agency or labour supplier). That protection is extended as against a third party during the period when their services have been hired or contracted to the third party.[156] These provisions also apply to severely disabled workers supplied by a local authority or voluntary organisation to a host employer under the Workstep scheme (formerly known as the Supported Placement Scheme).[157]

Definitions

4.3.2   A 'principal' is a person who makes work available ('contract work') to be done by individuals who are employed by another person who supplies them under a contract made with the principal.[158] The existence of a contract between the principal and the contractor–employer for the supply of the employee's labour is crucial.[159] A 'contract worker' is any individual who is supplied to the principal under a contract made between the principal and the contractor–employer for contract work to be done.[160] Because of the expanded definition of 'employment' in the 1995 Act,[161] these provisions should be capable of applying to contract workers, whether or not they are employees of the contractor–employer or are self-employed but providing personal services under a contract with the contractor–employer.[162] The section applies

---

(Employment Field) (Leasehold Premises) Regulations 2004, SI 2004/153, and Disability Discrimination (Employment Field) (Leasehold Premises) Regulations (Northern Ireland) 2004, SR 2004/374.

[154] DDA 1995, s 4B replaces s 12 with amendments. See generally: *Code of Practice: Employment and Occupation* (2004), paras 9.3–9.13.

[155] HL Deb, vol 566, col 221.

[156] *Code of Practice: Employment and Occupation* (2004), para 9.6.

[157] Ibid, para 9.13.

[158] DDA 1995, s 4B(9); *Code of Practice: Employment and Occupation* (2004), para 9.5 (and example).

[159] *Rice v Fon-A-Car* [1980] ICR 133, EAT (a taxi driver was not a contract worker simply because his services were supplied to customers through a central agency, because the agency had no contractual relationship with the customers); *Harrods Ltd v Remick* [1997] IRLR 583, CA (employees of concessionaires in a department store were treated as contract workers, as they worked for the concessionaires but for the benefit of the store). See also: *CJ O'Shea Construction Ltd v Bassi* [1998] ICR 1130, EAT.

[160] DDA 1995, s 4B(9).

[161] Ibid, s 68(1).

[162] See *Construction Industry Training Board v Labour Force Ltd* [1970] 3 All ER 220; *Tanna*

only in relation to contract work done at an establishment in Great Britain (or Northern Ireland, as the case may be).[163]

4.3.3 The breadth of the contractual relationships envisaged by these provisions is illustrated by *MHC Consulting Services Ltd v Tansell*.[164] Mr Tansell (T) was a disabled person. He had formed a company (I) as a vehicle for offering his computer skills and services to third parties. T had placed his name with MHC Consulting Services Ltd (MHC), an employment agency specialising in placing computer personnel with third parties. Abbey Life Assurance Co Ltd (AL) entered into a contract with MHC whereby MHC contracted to provide computer personnel to AL. In pursuance of that relationship, MHC placed T's services with AL. It did so by entering into a contract with I for the supply of T's services to AL. However, it was alleged by T that AL rejected his services because of his disability. In the legal proceedings that followed, T was found not to be an employee of AL or MHC. If he was an employee at all, then he was employed by I. The EAT gave a purposive construction to the statutory provisions. It ruled that T could proceed with his action against AL. T was employed by I, which supplied T's services through MHC to AL. This amounted to an unbroken chain of contracts between the individual (T) and the end-user (AL). In these circumstances, the end-user was a principal within the meaning of the section.

Unlawful discrimination

4.3.4 First, it is unlawful for a principal, in relation to contract work, to discriminate against a disabled person who is a contract worker (a 'disabled contract worker') in the terms on which the principal allows him or her to do that work.[165] Secondly, it is unlawful for a principal, in relation to contract work, to discriminate against a disabled contract worker by not allowing him or her to do or continue to do the contract work.[166] Thirdly, it is unlawful for a principal, in relation to contract work, to discriminate against a disabled contract worker in the way the principal affords him or her access to any benefits or by refusing or deliberately omitting to afford him or her access to any benefits.[167] Fourthly, it is unlawful for a principal, in relation to contract work, to discriminate against a disabled contract worker by subjecting him or her to any other detriment.[168] Fifthly, it is also unlawful for a principal, in

---

v *Post Office* [1981] ICR 374; *Daley v Allied Suppliers Ltd* [1983] ICR 90, EAT; *Mirror Group Newspapers v Gunning* [1986] ICR 145.

[163] DDA 1995, s 4B(8), applying s 68 with appropriate modifications.

[164] [1999] IRLR 677, EAT, subsequently upheld *sub nom Abbey Life Assurance Co Ltd v Tansell* [2000] IRLR 387, CA.

[165] DDA 1995, ss 3A and 4B(1)(a).

[166] Ibid, ss 3A and 4B(1)(b); *BP Chemicals Ltd v Gillick* [1995] IRLR 128, EAT (the principal may have unlawfully discriminated by refusing to take on the contract worker).

[167] Ibid, ss 3A and 4B(1)(c).

[168] Ibid, ss 3A and 4B(1)(d).

relation to contract work, to subject a disabled contract worker to harassment.[169] The meanings of 'discriminate' and 'harassment' have been considered in Chapter 3.

4.3.5 These categories of unlawful acts are very similar to those that apply in relation to discrimination against employment applicants and employees.[170] However, they do not include discrimination in recruitment, selection, engagement and dismissal. Any disability discrimination in those areas will have been perpetrated by the contractor–employer rather than the principal for whom the contract work is to be done. A claimant would have a potential cause of action against the contractor–employer.

4.3.6 As is the case in the parallel employment provisions,[171] the contract worker provisions do not apply to benefits of any description if the principal is concerned with the provision (whether for payment or not) of benefits of that description to the public (or a section of the public, including the contract worker) unless that provision differs in a material respect from the provision of the benefits by the principal to contract workers.[172] The term 'benefits' includes facilities and services.[173] However, in such a case, a contract worker might have a cause of action under Part 3 of the Act.

Contract work and reasonable adjustments

4.3.7 The principal is subject to a duty to make reasonable adjustments in relation to disabled contract workers.[174] The broader issues raised by this duty have been considered in Chapter 3. First, the duty is addressed where a provision, criterion or practice is applied by or on behalf of all or most of the principals to whom the disabled contract worker is or might be supplied. If, as a result, the disabled contract worker is likely (on each occasion on which he or she is supplied to a principal to do contract work) to be placed at a substantial disadvantage in comparison with persons who are not disabled which is the same or similar in each case, the duty arises.[175] Secondly, the duty is also addressed where there is a physical feature of premises occupied by all or most of the principals to whom the disabled contract worker is or might be supplied. If, as a result, the disabled contract worker is likely (on each occasion on which he or she is supplied to a principal to do contract work) to be placed at a

---

[169] DDA 1995, ss 3B and 4B(2).

[170] Ibid, s 4.

[171] Ibid, s 4(4).

[172] Ibid, s 4B(3).

[173] Ibid, s 18B(2).

[174] *Code of Practice: Employment and Discrimination* (2004), paras 9.7–9.13. The complex provisions on contract workers in the Disability Discrimination (Employment) Regulations 1996, SI 1996/1456, reg 7 (and Disability Discrimination (Employment) Regulations (Northern Ireland) 1996, SR 1996/419) are revoked from 1 October 2004.

[175] DDA 1995, s 4B(4)(a).

substantial disadvantage in comparison with persons who are not disabled which is the same or similar in each case, the duty also arises.[176]

4.3.8   Where the duty arises in either case, the disabled contract worker's employer must take such steps as that employer would have to take if the provision, criterion or practice were applied by the employer (or on its behalf) or if the premises were occupied by the employer.[177] Furthermore, the employer's duty to make reasonable adjustments is also applied to the principal in relation to contract work as if the principal were (or would be) the employer of the disabled contract worker and as if any contract worker supplied to do work for the principal was an employee of the principal.[178] However, a principal is not required to take a step in relation to a disabled contract worker if the disabled contract worker's employer is required to take the step in relation to him or her.[179]

4.3.9   Thus, both the principal and the contractor–employer might be under separate (and sometimes overlapping) duties to make reasonable adjustments in relation to the disabled contract worker.[180] That imports an obligation on the principal and the contractor–employer to co-operate as far as is reasonable with adjustments already made for the contract worker by the employment business.[181] However, what will be a reasonable adjustment for a hirer to make will depend upon its individual circumstances and the rather limited, short-term nature of the labour-hiring relationship. For example, it might be unreasonable for a principal to have to make adjustments if the disabled contract worker is to be seconded to the principal for only a short time.[182] Also, in practice, it might be reasonable for the principal to allow an adjustment to be made in respect of the disabled contract worker, but for the employer to provide or pay for the necessary adjustment.

4.3.10   This might be best explained by adopting and modifying an example provided in the original Employment Code of Practice.[183] A disabled word-processor operator employed as a contract worker by a clerical agency requires a special keyboard as an adjustment for his or her disability. It can be anticipated that the contract worker will require such a keyboard wherever he or she is sent to work by the agency. It would be a reasonable step for the agency to supply the word-processor operator with the special keyboard. It would not be reasonable to expect any firm to

---

[176]   DDA 1995, s 4B(4)(b).

[177]   Ibid, s 4B(5), cross-referring to s 4A (and, by implication, s 18B).

[178]   Ibid, s 4B(6), cross-referring to s 4A (and, by implication, s 18B).

[179]   Ibid, s 4B(7), cross-referring to s 4A (and, by implication, s 18B).

[180]   *Code of Practice: Employment and Occupation* (2004), paras 9.9–9.12 (and examples).

[181]   HL Deb, vol 566, col 222; *Code of Practice: Employment and Occupation* (2004), para 9.12.

[182]   *Code of Practice: Employment and Occupation* (2004), para 9.8. No indication is given of what would amount to a short period of time, although the example accompanying para 9.8 suggests that two weeks would certainly be such a period.

[183]   *Employment Code of Practice* (1996), para 7.6.

whom that contract worker's services are supplied to have to acquire a special keyboard for him or her. However, those firms would be under a separate duty to co-operate with the adjustment made by the agency, eg by allowing the worker to carry and use the special keyboard at their premises. They might also have a residual duty to make a reasonable adjustment, eg by ensuring that the keyboard can be made compatible with their computer systems, such as might be achieved by installing the appropriate driver software.

4.4 OFFICE-HOLDERS

4.4.1 As a result of the EC Framework Employment Directive, office-holders are now explicitly covered by the DDA 1995, as amended by the Disability Discrimination Act 1995 (Amendment) Regulations 2003.[184] Unfortunately, the relevant provisions are amongst the most complex of the new amendments.[185]

Offices or posts

4.4.2 The new provisions apply to an 'office' or a 'post'. These terms are not defined. They will include company directors, judges and chairmen or members of non-departmental public bodies.[186] However, not all offices or posts are included. The provisions on discrimination and harassment,[187] and the duty to make reasonable adjustments,[188] apply to an office or post only if no 'relevant provision' of Part 2 applies in relation to an appointment to the office or post *and* one or more specified conditions is satisfied.[189] The relevant provisions of Part 2 for this purpose are those dealing with discrimination and harassment by employers, in relation to contract workers, by partnerships, by barristers and advocates and in relation to practical work experience, and members of locally-elected authorities.[190] In other words, if a claimant's case falls within one of the other identified areas of the employment field, the case cannot be brought under the office-holder provisions.

4.4.3 What are the specified conditions one or more of which must also be satisfied? There are three possibilities. First, the office or post is one to which persons are appointed to discharge functions personally under the

---

[184] See **4.2.21–4.2.23**.

[185] DDA 1995, ss 4C–4F.

[186] *Code of Practice: Employment and Occupation (2004)*, para 9.14. Tribunal appointments such as those considered in *Photis and Bruce v KMC International Search and Selection, Heyes v Lord Chancellor's Department* (EAT/732/00, EAT/766/00 and EAT/960/00) prior to 1 October 2004 will now be covered.

[187] DDA 1995, s 4D.

[188] Ibid, s 4E.

[189] Ibid, s 4C(1), subject to s 4C(5).

[190] Ibid, s 4C(2), as amended, referring to ss 4, 4B, 6A, 7A, 7C, 14C and 15B(3)(b), respectively. In Northern Ireland, see Disability Discrimination (Northern Ireland) Order 2006, SI 2006/312.

direction of another person and in respect of which they are entitled to remuneration.[191] For this purpose only, the holder of an office or post is to be regarded as discharging his or her functions under the direction of another person if that other person is entitled to direct him or her as to when and where he or she discharges those functions.[192] The holder of an office or post is not to be regarded as entitled to remuneration merely because he or she is entitled to payments in respect of expenses incurred by him or her in carrying out the functions of the office or post.[193] The holder of an office or post is also not to be regarded as entitled to remuneration merely because he or she is entitled to payments by way of compensation for the loss of income or benefits he or she would (or might) have received from any person had he or she not been carrying out the functions of the office or post.[194] Secondly, the office or post is one to which appointments are made by a Minister of the Crown, a government department, the Welsh Ministers, the First Minister for Wales, the Counsel General to the Welsh Assembly Government or any part of the Scottish Administration.[195] Thirdly, the office or post is one to which appointments are made on the recommendation of (or subject to the approval of) a Minister of the Crown, a government department, the Welsh Ministers, the First Minister for Wales, the Counsel General to the Welsh Assembly Government or any part of the Scottish Administration.[196] In Northern Ireland, the appropriate references are to appointments made by a Minister of the Crown, a Northern Ireland Minister or a government department, or to an office or post to which appointments are made on the recommendation of (or subject to the approval of) those persons or the Assembly.

Exclusions

4.4.4   The prohibitions on discrimination against (and the duty to make reasonable adjustments in relation to) office-holders do not apply to a raft of offices or posts.[197] The exclusions are as follows:

- any office of the House of Commons held by a member of it;

- a life peerage;[198]

- any office of the House of Lords held by a member of it;

- certain ministerial offices;[199]

---

[191]   DDA 1995, s 4C(3)(a).
[192]   Ibid, s 4C(4)(a).
[193]   Ibid, s 4C(4)(b)(i).
[194]   Ibid, s 4C(4)(b)(ii).
[195]   Ibid, s 4C(3)(b), as amended.
[196]   Ibid, s 4C(3)(c).
[197]   Ibid, s 4C(5), as amended.
[198]   Life Peerages Act 1958.
[199]   House of Commons Disqualification Act 1975, Sch 2.

- the offices of Leader of the Opposition, Chief Opposition Whip or Assistant Opposition Whip;[200]

- any office of the Scottish Parliament held by a member of it;

- a member of the Scottish Executive;[201]

- a junior Scottish Minister;[202]

- any office of the National Assembly for Wales held by a member of it;

- a member of the Welsh Assembly government;

- any office of a county council, a London borough council, a district council or a parish council held by a member of it (in England);

- any office of a county council, a county borough council or a community council held by a member of it (in Wales);

- any office of a council or community council held by a member of it (in Scotland);[203]

- any office of the Greater London Authority held by a member of it;

- any office of the Common Council of the City of London held by a member of it;

- any office of the Council of the Isles of Scilly held by a member of it;

- any office of a political party;

- any office of the Assembly held by a member of it (in Northern Ireland);

- any office of a district council held by a member of it (in Northern Ireland).

---

[200] Ministerial and other Salaries Act 1975.
[201] Scotland Act 1998, s 44.
[202] Ibid, s 49.
[203] Local Government etc (Scotland) Act 1994, s 2; Local Government (Scotland) Act 1973, s 51.

Unlawful acts

4.4.5 A number of unlawful acts of discrimination and harassment are created in relation to office-holders from 1 October 2004.[204] The unlawful acts are capable of being committed by 'a relevant person'. Who that relevant person is in relation to any particular unlawful act will become apparent as the unlawful acts are described.[205] Appointment to an office or post does not include election to such office or post.[206] The meanings of 'discrimination' and 'harassment' have been considered in Chapter 3.

Offer of appointment

4.4.6 First, it is unlawful for a relevant person in relation to an appointment to an office or post to discriminate against a disabled person in the arrangements which the relevant person makes for the purpose of determining who should be offered the appointment.[207] Secondly, it is unlawful for a relevant person in relation to an appointment to an office or post to discriminate against a disabled person in the terms on which the relevant person offers him or her an appointment.[208] Thirdly, it is unlawful for a relevant person in relation to an appointment to an office or post to discriminateagainst a disabled person by refusing to offer him or her an appointment.[209] A refusal includes a deliberate omission.[210] In a case relating to an appointment to an office or post, the relevant person is the person with power to make that appointment.[211]

Recommendation or approval of appointment

4.4.7 Fourthly, it is unlawful for a relevant person in relation to an appointment to an office or post to discriminate against a disabled person in the arrangements which the relevant person makes for the purpose of determining who should be recommended or approved in relation to the appointment.[212] Fifthly, it is unlawful for a relevant person in relation to an appointment to an office or post to discriminate against a disabled person in making or refusing to make a recommendation in relation to the appointment.[213] In both these cases, a recommendation includes the making of a negative recommendation.[214] Sixthly, it is unlawful for a relevant person in relation to an appointment to an office or post to

---

[204] DDA 1995, s 4D; *Code of Practice: Employment and Occupation* (2004), paras 9.15–9.20.

[205] *Code of Practice: Employment and Occupation* (2004), para 9.22.

[206] DDA 1995, s 4F(1).

[207] Ibid, s 4D(1)(a).

[208] Ibid, s 4D(1)(b).

[209] Ibid, s 4D(1)(c).

[210] Ibid, s 4D(7)(b).

[211] Ibid, s 4F(2)(a).

[212] Ibid, s 4D(2)(a).

[213] Ibid, s 4D(2)(b).

[214] Ibid, s 4D(7)(a).

discriminate against a disabled person in giving or refusing to give an approval in relation to the appointment.[215] In each of these three cases, the office or post must satisfy the particular condition that it is one to which appointments are made on the recommendation of (or subject to the approval of) a Minister of the Crown, a government department, the National Assembly for Wales or any part of the Scottish Administration.[216] In these three cases, the relevant person is the person or body with power to make that recommendation or (as the case may be) to give that approval.[217] A refusal includes a deliberate omission.[218]

Appointment terms and opportunities

4.4.8 Seventhly, it is unlawful for a relevant person, in relation to a disabled person who has been appointed to an office or post, to discriminate against him or her in the terms of the appointment.[219] In this case, the relevant person is the person with the power to determine those terms.[220] Eighthly, it is unlawful for a relevant person, in relation to a disabled person who has been appointed to an office or post, to discriminate against him or her in the opportunities which the relevant person affords him or her for promotion, a transfer, training or receiving any other benefit (or by refusing to afford him or her any such opportunity) – the so-called 'working conditions'.[221] In this case, the relevant person is the person with the power to determine those matters or, where there is no such person, the person with the power to make the appointment.[222] However, this provision does not apply to benefits of any description if the relevant person is concerned with the provision (for payment or not) of benefits of that description to the public (or a section of the public to which the disabled person belongs), except in three circumstances.[223] Those circumstances are that: (a) that provision differs in a material respect from the provision of the benefits to persons appointed to offices or posts which are the same as (or not materially different from) that to which the disabled person has been appointed; (b) the provision of the benefits to the person appointed is regulated by the terms and conditions of his or her appointment; or (c) the benefits relate to training.

Termination of appointment and any other detriment

4.4.9 Ninthly, it is unlawful for a relevant person, in relation to a disabled person who has been appointed to an office or post, to

---

[215] DDA 1995, s 4D(2)(b).
[216] Ibid, s 4D(2), by reference to s 4C(3)(c).
[217] Ibid, s 4F(2)(b), by reference to s 4C(3)(c).
[218] Ibid, s 4D(7)(b).
[219] Ibid, s 4D(3)(a).
[220] Ibid, s 4F(2)(c).
[221] Ibid, ss 4D(3)(b) and 4F(3)(a).
[222] Ibid, s 4F(2)(d) and (3)(a).
[223] Ibid, s 4D(5).

discriminate against him or her by terminating the appointment.[224] The
reference to the termination of the appointment includes a reference to
the expiry of a fixed term without non-renewal and a constructive
termination.[225] The relevant person is the person with power to terminate
the appointment.[226] Tenthly, it is unlawful for a relevant person, in
relation to a disabled person who has been appointed to an office or post,
to discriminate against him or her by subjecting him or her to any other
detriment in relation to the appointment.[227] The relevant person is any
person or body with power to make the appointment, to recommend or
approve the appointment, to determine the terms of appointment or its
working conditions, or to terminate the employment, as the case may
be.[228]

Harassment

4.4.10   Eleventhly, it is also unlawful for a relevant person, in relation to
an office or post, to subject to harassment a disabled person: (a) who has
been appointed to the office or post; (b) who is seeking or being
considered for appointment to the office or post; or (c) who is seeking or
being considered for a recommendation or approval in relation to an
appointment to an office or post.[229] In respect of (c), the office or post
must satisfy the particular condition that it is one to which appointments
are made on the recommendation of (or subject to the approval of) a
Minister of the Crown, a government department, the National Assembly
for Wales or any part of the Scottish Administration.[230] The relevant
person is any person or body with power to make the appointment, to
recommend or approve the appointment, to determine the terms of
appointment or its working conditions, or to terminate the employment,
as the case may be.[231]

Duty to make adjustments

4.4.11   Where a provision, criterion or practice applied by or on behalf
of a relevant person places the disabled person concerned at a substantial
disadvantage in comparison with persons who are not disabled, it is the
duty of the relevant person to take such steps as it is reasonable, in all the
circumstances of the case, for the relevant person to have to take in order
to prevent the provision, criterion or practice having that effect.[232]
Furthermore, where any physical feature of premises under the control of
a relevant person, and at or from which the functions of an office or post

---

[224] DDA 1995, s 4D(3)(c).
[225] Ibid, s 4D(6).
[226] Ibid, s 4F(2)(e).
[227] Ibid, s 4D(3)(d).
[228] Ibid, s 4F(2)(f).
[229] Ibid, s 4D(4).
[230] Ibid, s 4D(4)(c), by reference to s 4C(3)(c).
[231] Ibid, s 4F(2)(f).
[232] Ibid, s 4E(1)(a).

are performed, places the disabled person concerned at a substantial disadvantage in comparison with persons who are not disabled, it is the duty of the relevant person to take such steps as it is reasonable, in all the circumstances of the case, for the relevant person to have to take in order to prevent the feature having that effect.[233] This provision is very similar to that which applies in relation to employers and which has been discussed above. The broader issues raised by the duty to make reasonable adjustments have been discussed in Chapter 3.[234]

Relevant person

4.4.12 The relevant person for these purposes has already been identified above.[235] In particular, in respect of adjustments to physical features of premises, the relevant person will be the person with the power to determine the feature in question or the person with the power to make the appointment.[236]

Disabled person concerned

4.4.13 Who is 'the disabled person concerned' in the case of a provision, criterion or practice for determining who should be appointed to (or recommended or approved in relation to) an office or post? It is any disabled person who is (or who has notified the relevant person that he or she may be) seeking appointment to (or seeking a recommendation or approval in relation to) that office or post.[237] It also includes any disabled person who is being considered for appointment to (or for a recommendation or approval in relation to) that office or post.[238] In any other case, 'the disabled person concerned' is a disabled person who is seeking or being considered for appointment to (or a recommendation or approval in relation to) the office or post concerned,[239] or who has been appointed to the office or post concerned.[240]

4.4.14 What does the relevant person need to know of the disabled person in the case of a person who is being considered for, or is or may be seeking, appointment to, or a recommendation or approval in relation to, an office or post? No duty is imposed on the relevant person in relation to the disabled person if the relevant person does not know (and could not reasonably be expected to know) that the disabled person concerned is, or may be, seeking appointment to, or seeking a recommendation or

---

[233] DDA 1995, s 4E(1)(b).
[234] See also *Code of Practice: Employment and Occupation* (2004), para 9.21.
[235] DDA 1995, s 4F(2) and (3)(b).
[236] Ibid, s 4F(2)(d) and (3)(b).
[237] Ibid, s 4E(2)(a)(i).
[238] Ibid, s 4E(2)(a)(ii).
[239] Ibid, s 4E(2)(b)(i).
[240] Ibid, s 4E(2)(b)(ii).

approval in relation to, that office or post.[241] No duty is imposed on the relevant person in relation to the disabled person if the relevant person does not know (and could not reasonably be expected to know) that the disabled person concerned is being considered for appointment to, or (as the case may be) for a recommendation or approval in relation to, that office or post.[242] In any case, no duty is imposed on the relevant person in relation to the disabled person if the relevant person does not know (and could not reasonably be expected to know) that the disabled person concerned has a disability and is likely to be placed at a substantial disadvantage in comparison with persons who are not disabled.[243]

4.5   OCCUPATIONAL PENSION SCHEMES

Employers' obligations

4.5.1   Part 2 of the 1995 Act is capable of covering the actions of an employer who provides opportunities to employees for occupational pensions. Discrimination against disabled persons in the terms of employment and in the opportunities afforded for receiving any other benefit is unlawful, all other things being equal.[244] If an employer discriminates against a disabled person in respect of access to or benefits from an occupational pension scheme (including the terms of membership), that might amount to an unlawful act of discrimination, unless otherwise capable of justification. The pre-1 October 2004 special provision made for benefits provided under an occupational pension scheme in respect of termination of service, retirement, old age, death, accident, injury, sickness or invalidity has now been revoked.[245]

Trustees and managers of occupational pension schemes

4.5.2   Occupational pension schemes are run and managed by trustees and managers, rather than by the employer. At the time of enacting the DDA 1995, the then Government was concerned that disabled persons might be unfairly denied access to an employer's pension scheme arrangements by the decisions of the scheme trustees or managers (and not simply by the actions of employers). As originally enacted, the Act stated that every occupational pension scheme shall be taken to include a provision to be referred to as 'a non-discrimination rule'.[246] The effect of this implied non-discrimination rule related to the terms on which persons

---

[241]   DDA 1995, s 4E(3)(a)(i).

[242]   Ibid, s 4E(3)(a)(ii).

[243]   Ibid, s 4E(3)(b).

[244]   Ibid, s 4(2); *Code of Practice: Employment and Occupation* (2004), paras 10.2–10.5 (and example).

[245]   Disability Discrimination (Employment) Regulations 1996, SI 1996/1456, reg 4(3). See also Disability Discrimination (Employment) Regulations (Northern Ireland) 1996, SR 1996/419.

[246]   DDA 1995, s 17(1), now repealed; HL Deb, vol 566, cols 994–995.

become members of the scheme and the terms on which members of the scheme were treated. The non-discrimination rule also required the trustees or managers of the occupational pension scheme to refrain from any act or omission which, if done in relation to a person by an employer, would amount to unlawful discrimination under Part 2 of the Act. Moreover, the 'other provisions of the scheme' were to have effect subject to the implied non-discrimination rule. The effect of this provision meant that any discriminatory decision taken by trustees or managers would be contrary to the rules of the scheme. Any disabled person affected by such a discriminatory decision had to seek redress through the appropriate dispute resolution machinery for pension schemes, rather than in the employment tribunal.

4.5.3   The position is now changed as a result of the amendments made to the Act from 1 October 2004 by the Disability Discrimination Act 1995 (Pensions) Regulations 2003.[247]

Non-discrimination rule

4.5.4   Every occupational pension scheme shall be taken to include a provision called 'the non-discrimination rule'.[248] The rule does not apply in relation to rights accrued (or benefits payable) in respect of periods of service prior to 1 October 2004. It does apply to communications[249] with members[250] or prospective members[251] of the scheme in relation to such rights or benefits.[252] The rule contains two requirements. The first is that the trustees or managers[253] of the scheme refrain from discriminating against a relevant disabled person in carrying out any of their functions in

---

[247] SI 2003/2770, inserting DDA 1995, ss 4G–4K and repealing s 17. See also: *Code of Practice: Employment and Occupation* (2004), paras 10.6–10.15 (and examples).

[248] DDA 1995, s 4G(1).

[249] *Code of Practice: Employment and Occupation* (2004), para 10.10 (and example). In their application to communications, ss 4G–4J apply in relation to a disabled person who is entitled to the present payment of dependants' or survivors' benefits under an occupational pension scheme, or who is a pension credit member of such a scheme, as they apply in relation to a disabled person who is a pensioner member of the scheme: s 4K(1). Communications includes the provision of information and the operation of a dispute-resolution procedure: s 4K(2). A pension credit member and a pensioner member are defined by Pensions Act 1995, s 124(1), as at 1 October 2004: s 4K(2) (in Northern Ireland, Pensions (Northern Ireland) Order 1995, art 121(1)).

[250] A member in relation to an occupational pension scheme means any active, deferred or pensioner member, as defined in Pensions Act 1995, s 124(1) as at 1 October 2004: DDA 1995, s 4K(2) (in Northern Ireland, Pensions (Northern Ireland) Order 1995, art 121(1)).

[251] A prospective member is any person who, under the terms of his or her contract of employment or the scheme rules or both, is able (at his or her own option) to become a member of the scheme, or will become so able if he or she continues in the same employment for a sufficiently long period, or will be admitted to it automatically unless he or she makes an election not to become a member, or may be admitted to it subject to the consent of his or her employer: DDA 1995, s 4K(2).

[252] DDA 1995, s 4G(4). 'Benefits' does not include facilities or services for this purpose: s 18D(2).

[253] The terms 'managers' and 'trustees or managers' have the meanings given by Pensions

relation to the scheme.[254] That includes, in particular, their functions relating to the admission of members to the scheme and the treatment of members of the scheme. The second requirement is that the trustees or managers of the scheme do not subject a relevant disabled person to harassment in relation to the scheme. The other provisions of the scheme are to have effect subject to the non-discrimination rule.[255] That means that if there is a conflict between the non-discrimination rule and a rule of the scheme, the former prevails.[256] A relevant disabled person is a disabled person who is a member or prospective member of the scheme.[257]

Unlawful acts

4.5.5   It is unlawful for the trustees or managers of an occupational pension scheme to discriminate against a relevant disabled person contrary to the first requirement of the non-discrimination rule or to subject a relevant disabled person to harassment contrary to the second requirement of the non-discrimination rule.[258] The meanings of 'discrimination' and 'harassment' have been discussed in Chapter 3.

Alterations to a scheme

4.5.6   The trustees or managers of an occupational pension scheme may, by resolution, make such alterations to the scheme as may be required to secure conformity with the non-discrimination rule,[259] if they do not otherwise have power to make such alterations.[260] They may also make such alterations if they have such power, but where the procedure for doing so is liable to be unduly complex or protracted, or involves the obtaining of consents which cannot be obtained (or can only be obtained with undue delay or difficulty).[261] The alterations may have effect in relation to a period before the alterations are made (but may not have effect in relation to a period before 1 October 2004).[262]

Duty to make reasonable adjustments

4.5.7   The trustees or managers of an occupational pension scheme have a duty to make reasonable adjustments in two situations. First, where a provision, criterion or practice (including a scheme rule) applied by or on behalf of the trustees or managers of an occupational pension scheme

---

Act 1995, s 124(1) as at 1 October 2004: DDA 1995, s 4K(2) (in Northern Ireland, Pensions (Northern Ireland) Order 1995, art 121(1)).

[254] DDA 1995, s 4G(1)(a).
[255] Ibid, s 4G(2).
[256] *Code of Practice: Employment and Occupation* (2004), para 10.8.
[257] DDA 1995, s 4K(2).
[258] Ibid, s 4G(3).
[259] *Code of Practice: Employment and Occupation* (2004), para 10.8 (and example).
[260] DDA 1995, s 4G(5)(a).
[261] Ibid, s 4G(5)(b).
[262] Ibid, s 4G(6).

places a relevant disabled person at a substantial disadvantage in comparison with persons who are not disabled, it is the duty of the trustees or managers to take such steps as it is reasonable, in all the circumstances of the case, for them to have to take in order to prevent the provision, criterion or practice having that effect.[263] Secondly, where any physical feature of premises occupied by the trustees or managers places a relevant disabled person at a substantial disadvantage in comparison with persons who are not disabled, it is the duty of the trustees or managers to take such steps as it is reasonable, in all the circumstances of the case, for them to have to take in order to prevent the feature having that effect.[264] The making of alterations to scheme rules is an example of a step which trustees or managers may have to take in order to comply with the duty.[265] The duty is not imposed on trustees or managers in relation to a disabled person if they do not know (and could not reasonably be expected to know) that the disabled person is a relevant disabled person or that that person has a disability and is likely to be placed at a substantial disadvantage in comparison with persons who are not disabled.[266] The broader issues raised by the duty to make reasonable adjustment are addressed in Chapter 3.

Procedure and remedies

4.5.8 Particular provision is made where a relevant disabled person presents a complaint to an employment tribunal that the trustees or managers of an occupational pension scheme have acted in relation to him or her in a way which is unlawful under Part 2.[267] In such a case, the employer in relation to that scheme shall be treated as a party and be entitled to appear and be heard in the proceedings.[268] This is because the employer may be required to fund any award made against the scheme.[269]

4.5.9 Particular provision is also made in respect of remedies where a relevant disabled person presents to an employment tribunal a complaint that the trustees or managers of an occupational pension scheme have acted in relation to him or her in a way which is unlawful under Part 2 or an employer has so acted in relation to him or her.[270] The complaint must

---

[263] DDA 1995, s 4H(1)(a).

[264] Ibid, s 4H(1)(b).

[265] Ibid, s 4H(2) (ie in addition to the examples set out in s 18B(2)).

[266] Ibid, s 4H(3).

[267] Complaint may also be made via the dispute resolution mechanism of the scheme itself or to the Pensions Ombudsman or through the advice and conciliation service of the Pensions Advisory Service. See *Code of Practice: Employment and Occupation* (2004), para 10.15 and Appendix C.

[268] DDA 1995, s 4I(1) (ie in proceedings brought under s 17A and for the purposes of the Employment Tribunals Rules of Procedure 2004). The employer in relation to an occupational pension scheme has the meaning given by Pensions Act 1995, s 124(1), as at 1 October 2004 (in Northern Ireland, Pensions (Northern Ireland) Order 1995, art 121(1)).

[269] *Code of Practice: Employment and Occupation* (2004), para 10.12.

[270] DDA 1995, s 4J(1)(a).

relate to the terms on which persons become members of an occupational pension scheme or the terms on which members of the scheme are treated.[271] It assumes that the disabled person is not a pensioner member of the scheme[272] and that the tribunal finds that the complaint is well founded.[273] If so, the tribunal may make a declaration that the claimant has a right to be admitted to the scheme in question or to membership of the scheme without discrimination (as the case may be).[274] The declaration may be made in respect of such period as the declaration may specify (but may not be made in respect of any period before 1 October 2004).[275] It may make such provision as the tribunal considers appropriate as to the terms upon which (or the capacity in which) the disabled person is to enjoy such admission or membership.[276] The tribunal may not award the disabled person any compensation (whether in relation to arrears of benefits or otherwise) other than compensation for injury to feelings or initial or increased compensation pursuant to a failure to comply with the tribunal's recommendation.[277]

4.6   INSURANCE BENEFITS

4.6.1   Insurance benefits (such as private health insurance) offered to employees by an employer are within the scope of the prohibition on employment discrimination.[278] Before 5 December 2005, special provision was made where an employer made arrangements with an insurer for insurance-related benefits to be received by the employer's employees.[279] This was designed to address discrimination by the insurance company rather than by the employer itself. It was relevant where the insurer treated disabled persons differently from others for non-actuarial reasons.

4.6.2   The Disability Discrimination Act 2005 repealed the provisions concerning group insurance schemes contained in s 18 of the DDA 1995. The Government considered that s 18 was unnecessary and confusing. Its intention is that, following the repeal of s 18, it should be clear that a person who provides group insurance services to employees of particular employers is to be regarded as a provider of services. That person is then be liable for an act of discrimination contrary to Part 3 which he or she may commit against disabled persons employed by those employers. An act of discrimination by an employer in relation to a group insurance scheme falls within Part 2 of the Act. However, claims of discrimination against an insurer concerning the provision of group insurance services

---

[271] DDA 1995, s 4J(1)(b).

[272] Ibid, s 4J(1)(c).

[273] Ibid, s 4J(1)(d).

[274] Ibid, s 4J(2) (by reference to s 4J(1)(b)(i) or (ii), as the case may be). This is without prejudice to the generality of the tribunal's power under s 17A(2)(a).

[275] Ibid, s 4J(3)(a).

[276] Ibid, s 4J(3)(b).

[277] Ibid, s 4J(4), by reference to ss 17A(5) and 17A(2)(b).

[278] Ibid, s 4(2)(a)–(c) are particularly apposite.

[279] Ibid, s 18, now repealed.

are not subject to the Part 3 procedures and remedies in the county court or sheriff court (DDA 1995, s 25(6A)(a)). Instead, employment tribunals have jurisdiction to consider such claims. The definition of 'group insurance arrangements' in DDA 1995, s 68(1) is amended so that it covers all types of group insurance schemes – not just those relating to termination of service; retirement, old age or death; or accident, injury, sickness or invalidity.

4.7 PARTNERSHIPS

4.7.1 From 1 October 2004, partnerships were brought within the scope of Part 2 of the DDA 1995 as a result of the amendments made by the Disability Discrimination Act 1995 (Amendment) Regulations 2003.[280] These provisions apply in relation to persons proposing to form themselves into a partnership as they apply in relation to a firm.[281] They also apply to a limited liability partnership as they apply to a firm. References to a partner in a firm are references to a member of the limited liability partnership.[282] In the case of a limited partnership, references to a partner shall be construed as references to a general partner.[283] The effect of the new provisions is to give partners and applicants for partnership similar rights against a firm as those enjoyed by an employee or employment applicant against an employer.[284]

Unlawful acts

4.7.2 It is unlawful for a firm, in relation to a position as a partner in the firm, to discriminate against a disabled person in the arrangements which the firm makes for determining who should be offered a partnership or in the terms on which the firm offers him or her partnership or by refusing (or deliberately omitting) to offer him or her partnership.[285] In a case where the disabled person already is a partner in the firm, it is also unlawful for the firm to discriminate against him or her in the way the firm affords him or her access to any benefits (or by refusing or deliberately omitting to afford him or her access to them).[286] This does not apply to benefits of any description if the firm is concerned with the provision (whether or not for payment) of benefits of that description to the public (or to a section of the public which includes the partner in

---

[280] DDA 1995, ss 6A–6C; *Code of Practice: Employment and Occupation* (2004), paras 9.25–9.31.

[281] Ibid, s 6C(1).

[282] Ibid, s 6C(2).

[283] Ibid, s 6C(3); Limited Partnerships Act 1907, s 3. A 'firm' has the meaning given by Partnership Act 1890, s 4.

[284] *Code of Practice: Employment and Occupation* (2004), para 9.27 (and example).

[285] DDA 1995, s 6A(1)(a)–(c).This applies in relation to persons proposing to form themselves into a partnership as it applies in relation to a firm: s 6C(1).

[286] Ibid, s 6A(1)(d)(i).

question), unless that provision differs in a material respect from the provision of the benefits to the other partners.[287]

4.7.3 It is further unlawful for the firm to discriminate against the disabled person by expelling him or her as a partner or subjecting him or her to any other detriment.[288] Expulsion includes termination of a fixed-period partnership without renewal and constructive termination (where the disabled person is entitled to terminate the partnership without notice by reason of the conduct of the other partners).[289] Moreover, it is unlawful for the firm to subject to harassment a disabled person who is a partner or who has applied to be a partner.[290] Discrimination and harassment have been discussed in Chapter 3.

Duty to make reasonable adjustments

4.7.4 A duty to make reasonable adjustments applies to partnerships in much the same way as it applies elsewhere in the employment field.[291] The broader aspects of the duty have been discussed in Chapter 3. Where a provision, criterion or practice applied by or on behalf of a firm, or any physical feature of premises occupied by the firm, places the disabled person concerned at a substantial disadvantage in comparison with persons who are not disabled, it is the duty of the firm to take such steps as it is reasonable, in all the circumstances of the case, for it to have to take in order to prevent the provision, criterion or practice, or feature, having that effect.[292]

4.7.5 In the case of a provision, criterion or practice for determining to whom the position of partner should be offered, the disabled person concerned is any disabled person who is (or who has notified the firm that he or she may be) a candidate for that position.[293] In any other case, it is a disabled person who is a partner or a candidate for the position of partner.[294] In the case of a candidate or potential candidate for partnership, no duty is imposed on a firm in relation to a disabled person if the firm does not know (and could not reasonably be expected to know) that the disabled person concerned is (or may be) a candidate for the position of partner.[295] In any case, no duty is imposed if the firm does not know (and could not reasonably be expected to know) that the disabled

---

[287] DDA 1995, s 6A(3).

[288] Ibid, s 6A(1)(d)(ii).

[289] Ibid, s 6A(4).

[290] Ibid, s 6A(2). This applies in relation to persons proposing to form themselves into a partnership as it applies in relation to a firm: s 6C(1).

[291] Ibid, s 6B; *Code of Practice: Employment and Occupation* (2004), paras 9.30–9.31 (and example). This applies in relation to persons proposing to form themselves into a partnership as it applies in relation to a firm: s 6C(1).

[292] Ibid, s 6B(1).

[293] Ibid, s 6B(2)(a).

[294] Ibid, s 6B(2)(b).

[295] Ibid, s 6B(3)(a).

person has a disability and is likely to be placed at a substantial disadvantage in comparison with persons who are not disabled.[296]

4.7.6 Where a firm is required to take any steps in relation to the disabled person concerned, the cost of taking those steps shall be treated as an expense of the firm.[297] The extent to which such cost should be borne by the disabled person, where he or she is (or becomes) a partner in the firm, shall not exceed such amount as is reasonable, having regard in particular to the proportion in which he or she is entitled to share in the firm's profits.[298]

4.8 BARRISTERS AND ADVOCATES

England and Wales

4.8.1 Barristers (and, in Scotland, advocates) are already subject to Part 3 of the Act in relation to the provision of services to the public. They are also subject to Part 2 to the extent that they employ staff. From 1 October 2004, barristers and their clerks in England and Wales are more fully within the scope of Part 2 of the DDA 1995 as a result of the amendments made by the Disability Discrimination Act 1995 (Amendment) Regulations 2003.[299]

4.8.2 Prior to that date, an unsuccessful attempt had been made in legal proceedings to bring barristers and their pupils within the trade organisation provisions of the Act.[300] A barrister's chambers accepted an application for pupillage from a disabled person, but refused to defer the pupillage due to the prospective pupil's ill health. A claim was brought under the DDA 1995, contending that the chambers were a trade organisation and that the application for a pupillage was an application for membership of that trade organisation. At the Court of Appeal, it was not in dispute that the chambers were a trade organisation, but the Court held that the application for pupillage could not be construed as an application for membership of the chambers.[301]

---

[296] DDA 1995, s 6B(3)(b).

[297] Ibid, s 6B(4).

[298] *Code of Practice: Employment and Occupation* (2004), para 9.31 (and example).

[299] DDA 1995, ss 7A–7D; *Code of Practice: Employment and Occupation* (2004), paras 9.32–9.41 (and examples). The General Council of the Bar in England and Wales established its Equality and Diversity (Disability) Committee in 1991. The Bar's *Code of Conduct* (see paras 305 and 403) requires all barristers to have regard to the Bar's *Equality and Diversity Code* (revised 2004). It sets out the law and professional rules which prohibit discrimination. It also recommends good practice to chambers in relation to access to pupillages and tenancies, the conduct of work in chambers, complaints and grievances. See also The Law Society's *Solicitors Anti-Discrimination Rules 2004*.

[300] DDA 1995, ss 13–15 (prior to their recent repeal and replacement).

[301] *Paul Higham of 1 Pump Court Chambers v Horton* [2004] EWCA Civ 941. The legal or contractual position of a pupil and his or her chambers had been explored in *Edmonds v Lawson* [2000] ICR 567, CA.

4.8.3   The new provisions overcome the difficulties created by the need to attempt a forced construction of the trade organisation provisions. Throughout the new provisions, a barrister's clerk includes any person carrying out any of the functions of a barrister's clerk. The terms 'pupil', 'pupillage' and 'set of chambers' have the meanings commonly associated with their use in the context of barristers practising in independent practice. The terms 'tenancy' and 'tenant' have the meanings commonly associated with their use in the context of barristers practising in independent practice. However, they also include reference to any barrister permitted to practise from a set of chambers (ie a 'squatter' or non-tenant).[302]

Unlawful acts

4.8.4   It is unlawful for a barrister or a barrister's clerk, in relation to any offer of a pupillage or tenancy, to discriminate against a disabled person in the arrangements which are made for the purpose of determining to whom it should be offered; in respect of any terms on which it is offered; or by refusing, or deliberately omitting, to offer it to him or her.[303] The meaning of 'discrimination' has been considered in Chapter 3.

4.8.5   It is also unlawful for a barrister or a barrister's clerk, in relation to a disabled pupil or tenant in the set of chambers in question, to discriminate against him or her in respect of any terms applicable to him or her as a pupil or tenant; in the opportunities for training or gaining experience which are afforded or denied to him or her; in the benefits which are afforded or denied to him or her; by terminating his or her pupillage or by subjecting him or her to any pressure to leave the chambers; or by subjecting him or her to any other detriment.[304]

4.8.6   It is further unlawful for a barrister or barrister's clerk, in relation to a pupillage or tenancy, to subject to harassment a disabled person who is (or who has applied to be) a pupil or tenant in the set of chambers in question.[305] The meaning of 'harassment' has been considered in Chapter 3. Moreover, it is also unlawful for any person, in relation to the giving, withholding or acceptance of instructions to a barrister, to discriminate against a disabled person or to subject him or her to harassment.[306] Thus, it is unlawful for a solicitor (or other professional with direct access to the Bar) to refuse to instruct a barrister on the ground of the barrister's disability or for a reason related to his or her

---

[302] DDA 1995, s 7A(5); *Code of Practice: Employment and Occupation* (2004), para 9.35.
[303] Ibid, s 7A(1).
[304] Ibid, s 7A(2); *Code of Practice: Employment and Occupation* (2004), para 9.33 (and example).
[305] Ibid, s 7A(3).
[306] Ibid, s 7A(4).

disability.[307] However, the solicitor is not under a duty to make reasonable adjustments in relation to a barrister being instructed.[308]

Duty to make reasonable adjustments

4.8.7 A barrister or a barrister's clerk is subject to a duty to make reasonable adjustments. The broader concepts raised by this general duty have been discussed in Chapter 3. In the present context, it arises where a provision, criterion or practice applied by or on behalf of a barrister or barrister's clerk, or any physical feature of premises occupied by a barrister or a barrister's clerk, places the disabled person concerned at a substantial disadvantage in comparison with persons who are not disabled, it is the duty of the barrister or barrister's clerk to take such steps as it is reasonable, in all the circumstances of the case, for him or her to have to take in order to prevent the provision, criterion or practice, or feature, having that effect.[309] Where the duty arises in relation to two or more barristers in a set of chambers, the duty is on each of them to take such steps as it is reasonable, in all of the circumstances of the case, for him or her to have to take.[310]

4.8.8 In the case of a provision, criterion or practice for determining to whom a pupillage or tenancy should be offered, the disabled person concerned is any disabled person who is (or who has notified the barrister or the barrister's clerk concerned that he or she may be) an applicant for a pupillage or tenancy.[311] In any other case, it is a disabled person who is a tenant, a pupil, or an applicant for a pupillage or tenancy.[312] In the case of an applicant or potential applicant for pupillage or tenancy, no duty is imposed on a barrister or a barrister's clerk in relation to a disabled person if he or she does not know (and could not reasonably be expected to know) that the disabled person concerned is (or may be) such an applicant.[313] In any case, no duty is imposed on a barrister or a barrister's clerk in relation to a disabled person if he or she does not know (and could not reasonably be expected to know) that that person has a disability and is likely to be placed at a substantial disadvantage in comparison with persons who are not disabled.[314]

---

[307] *Code of Practice: Employment and Occupation* (2004), para 9.37.
[308] Ibid, para 9.39.
[309] DDA 1995, s 7B(1).
[310] Ibid, s 7B(2); *Code of Practice: Employment and Occupation* (2004), para 9.40.
[311] Ibid, s 7B(3)(a).
[312] Ibid, s 7B(3)(b).
[313] Ibid, s 7B(4)(a).
[314] Ibid, s 7B(4)(b).

Scotland

4.8.9 The provisions on barristers and barristers' clerks apply only in England and Wales.[315] Comparable provisions apply in Scotland in relation to advocates in relation to taking any person as a pupil or in relation to a disabled person who is a pupil or in relation to the giving, withholding or acceptance of instructions to an advocate.[316] These provisions are modified from those applying to barristers in recognition that in Scotland, advocates do not practise in sets of chambers.[317] That may affect the reasonableness of any adjustment that an advocate might otherwise be under a duty to make in relation to a disabled pupil. An advocate is a member of the Faculty of Advocates, practising as such. The term 'pupil' has the meaning commonly associated with its use in the context of a person training to be an advocate.[318]

Northern Ireland

4.8.10 Similar modifications are made in respect of barristers in Northern Ireland as are made in Scotland in respect of advocates.

4.9 TRADE ORGANISATIONS

4.9.1 As originally enacted, Part 2 of the DDA 1995 ensured that discrimination against disabled persons by trade organisations would be unlawful.[319] From 1 October 2004, the original provisions on trade organisations have been substituted.[320] Nevertheless, the effect of these provisions remains that:

> '... trade unions, employers' associations and analogous bodies would be covered by this [Act] in their relationship with their members or prospective members who are disabled or who have had a disability. Such organisations are already covered in the [Act] to the extent that they are employers. However, they are not covered by the access to services right because they are not providing services to members of the general public – just to their members.'[321]

A trade organisation will be covered by the employment provisions in Part 2 of the Act in so far as it employs persons. For example, a full-time

---

[315] DDA 1995, s 70(5A).

[316] Ibid, ss 7C, 7D and 70(5B).

[317] *Code of Practice: Employment and Occupation* (2004), paras 9.36 and 9.41.

[318] DDA 1995, s 7C(5); *Code of Practice: Employment and Occupation* (2004), para 9.36.

[319] DDA 1995, ss 13–15; *Code of Practice: Duties of Trade Organisations to their Disabled Members and Applicants* (1999) (a separate, but essentially identical, Code covered Northern Ireland).

[320] DDA 1995, ss 13–14. The relevant Code of Practice is now *Code of Practice: Trade Organisations and Qualifications Bodies (2004)* (a separate, but essentially identical, Code covers Northern Ireland).

[321] HL Deb, vol 566, cols 224–225.

officer of a trade union or a clerical worker employed by a trade association will be an employee (or would-be employee) of a trade organisation and will be protected from disability discrimination under Part 2.

4.9.2 However, there is nothing, in principle, to prevent trade organisations also being caught by Part 3 of the Act (the provisions on goods and services) where they also provide services to the public (as well as to their members).[322] For example, a trade union which allows its premises to be used as a meeting place by external groups (such as a local political party or community action group) will be subject to the duties and non-discrimination requirements contained in Part 3. Similarly, if a trade organisation allows its facilities to be used for social purposes (such as wedding receptions), open to individuals unconnected with that organisation, it will need to consider its Part 3 obligations. Nevertheless, the separate provisions of Part 2 in respect of discrimination by trade organisations against disabled members or disabled applicants for membership are largely self-contained measures and so warrant separate treatment.

Trade organisation

4.9.3 A 'trade organisation' is defined as 'an organisation of workers, an organisation of employers or any other organisation whose members carry on a particular profession or trade for the purposes of which the organisation exists'.[323] These terms are not further defined. There is no threshold of size or number of members. Part 2 thus applies to organisations of workers, organisations of employers and other organisations, but not qualifications bodies. However, some trade organisations (such as The Law Society) also confer qualifications and will also be subject to the Part 2 provisions on qualifications bodies, depending upon in which capacity the trade organisation is acting at the relevant time.[324]

Organisation of workers

4.9.4 This will obviously include trade unions.[325] A trade union is a temporary or permanent organisation of workers whose principal purposes include the regulation of relations between workers and employers or employers' associations.[326] A worker is a person who works (or seeks to work) under a contract of employment or under any other contract for the personal performance of any work or services (other than

---

[322] See Chapter 5.
[323] DDA 1995, ss 13(4) and 68(1).
[324] Ibid, ss 14A–14B; *Code of Practice: Trade Organisations and Qualifications Bodies (2004)*, paras 3.11 and 7.3–7.4.
[325] HL Deb, vol 566, cols 224–229.
[326] Trade Union and Labour Relations (Consolidation) Act 1992 (TULR(C)A 1992), s 1.

a professional and client relationship) or in Crown employment.[327] However, police officers are not 'workers', but office-holders, so that the Police Federation would not be an organisation of workers.[328] The position of the Prison Officers' Association is ambiguous.[329] The term does not exclude an organisation the majority of whose members practise a profession (such as medical or dental practitioners).[330]

4.9.5 The term 'organisation' imports form, structure and stability, so that a mere loose association of workers would be insufficient.[331] The 1995 Act does not appear to make a distinction between permanent or temporary organisations of workers. As a result, any branch or other division of a trade union might constitute an organisation of workers, including unofficial workplace co-ordinating committees. It was feared that the DDA 1995:

> '. . . might render unions liable for any failure to make adjustments by an informal group of union members of whose existence the union's officers are unaware . . . [including] groups of union members not recognising union rule books and with whom the national union does not communicate and who are given no powers or resources.'[332]

This concern is a real one, given the wording of the Act and the lack of a definition of 'organisation of workers' in the statute.

Organisation of employers

4.9.6 An 'organisation of employers' will include an employers' association. That is an organisation (whether temporary or permanent) which consists wholly or mainly of employers or individual owners of undertakings and whose principal purposes include the regulation of relations between employers and workers or trade unions.[333] It also includes an organisation which consists wholly or mainly of constituent or affiliated organisations (of the first kind or which themselves consist wholly or mainly of constituent or affiliated organisations of the first kind), or representatives of such constituent or affiliated organisations, and whose principal purposes include the regulation of relations between

---

[327] TULR(C)A 1992, s 296; *Writers' Guild of Great Britain v BBC* [1974] ICR 234; *Broadbent v Crisp* [1974] ICR 248; *Wiltshire Police Authority v Wynn* [1980] ICR 649.

[328] *Home Office v Evans* (Divisional Court, 18 November 1993, unreported).

[329] *Boddington v Lawton* [1994] ICR 478; but *cf* Criminal Justice and Public Order Act 1994, s 126.

[330] *Medical Protection Society v Sadek* [2004] EWCA Civ 865, [2004] ICR 1263, [2005] IRLR 57, CA.

[331] *Conservative and Unionist Central Office v Burrell* [1982] 1 WLR 522; *cf Midland Cold Storage Ltd v Turner* [1972] ICR 230.

[332] HL Deb, vol 566, cols 226–227.

[333] TULR(C)A 1992, s 122(1)(a).

employers and workers or between employers and trade unions, or the regulation of relations between its constituent or affiliated organisations.[334]

Other organisations

4.9.7 Part 2 applies equally to 'any other organisation whose members carry on a particular profession or trade for the purposes of which the organisation exists'. The term 'profession' includes any vocation or occupation, while the term 'trade' encompasses any business.[335] This category of trade organisations will include chartered professional institutions, other professional bodies and trade associations.[336]

Unlawful acts

4.9.8 First, it is unlawful for a trade organisation to discriminate against a disabled person: (a) in the arrangements which it makes for the purpose of determining who should be offered membership of the organisation; (b) in the terms on which it is prepared to admit him or her to membership of the organisation; or (c) by refusing to accept, or deliberately not accepting, his or her application for membership.[337] For example, a trade union which made it a condition of membership that a disabled person should pay a higher membership fee or joining fee than other applicants for membership would transgress this provision. Similarly, a professional body that would only admit disabled persons to membership after a longer period of apprenticeship or practice in the profession than in the normal case would also be in breach. A trade association which selectively or consistently refused membership of the association to disabled persons engaged in the relevant trade would commit a *prima facie* unlawful act. Similarly, a trade union which has received an application for membership from a disabled person, and deliberately fails to process that application, has committed a potential act of unlawful discrimination, even though it has not positively taken a step to reject the application. Its deliberate default in respect of the application might be tantamount to a non-acceptance.

4.9.9 Secondly, it is unlawful for a trade organisation, in the case of a disabled person who is a member of the organisation,[338] to discriminate

---

[334] TULR(C)A 1992, s 122(1)(b).

[335] DDA 1995, s 68(1).

[336] *Code of Practice: Trade Organisations and Qualifications Bodies* (2004), para 3.8 (giving as examples: The Law Society, the Royal College of Nursing, the Swimming Teachers' Association, the Society of Floristry, the British Computer Society and the Institute of Carpenters).

[337] DDA 1995, s 13(1); *Code of Practice: Trade Organisations and Qualifications Bodies* (2004), paras 7.5–7.14 (and examples).

[338] The Act does not protect corporate members of trade organisations, even where a disabled person is representing a corporate member: *Code of Practice: Trade Organisations and Qualifications Bodies* (2004), para 3.18 (and example).

against him or her: (a) in the way it affords him or her access to any benefits (or by refusing or deliberately omitting to afford him or her access to them); (b) by depriving him or her of membership, or varying the terms on which he or she is a member; or (c) by subjecting him or her to any other detriment.[339] In general, a trade organisation may not treat its disabled members as second-class members in respect of the rights and benefits of membership. This would include expulsion from membership where a non-disabled member would not be deprived of membership. Benefits include facilities and services.[340] That will include training facilities, welfare or insurance services, information about the organisation's activities, and assistance to members in an employer's disciplinary or dismissal procedure. Whether something is a benefit will depend upon the circumstances, including an organisation's rules and practice.[341]

4.9.10 Thirdly, it is also unlawful for a trade organisation, in relation to membership of that organisation, to subject to harassment a disabled person who is a member of the organisation or who has applied for membership of the organisation.[342] The meanings of 'discrimination' and 'harassment' have been considered in Chapter 3.

Duty to make reasonable adjustments

4.9.11 A trade organisation's duty to make reasonable adjustments arises where a provision, criterion or practice applied by or on behalf of a trade organisation, or any physical feature of premises occupied by the organisation, places the disabled person concerned at a substantial disadvantage in comparison with persons who are not disabled. It is then the duty of the organisation to take such steps as it is reasonable, in all the circumstances of the case, for it to have to take in order to prevent the provision, criterion or practice, or feature, having that effect.[343] The wider aspects of the duty to make reasonable adjustments have been considered in Chapter 3.

4.9.12 In the case of a provision, criterion or practice for determining to whom membership should be offered, the disabled person concerned is any disabled person who is (or who has notified the organisation that he

---

[339] DDA 1995, s 13(2); *Code of Practice: Trade Organisations and Qualifications Bodies* (2004), paras 7.15–7.29 (and examples).

[340] DDA 1995, s 18D(2); *Code of Practice: Trade Organisations and Qualifications Bodies* (2004), para 7.16 (and examples).

[341] There is no equivalent of DDA 1995, s 4(4) (which applies to employers providing benefits to their employees and to the public) to prevent any overlap between Part 2 and Part 3. It does not seem necessary.

[342] DDA 1995, s 13(3); *Code of Practice: Trade Organisations and Qualifications Bodies* (2004), paras 4.37–4.38 (and examples).

[343] DDA 1995, s 14(1); *Code of Practice: Trade Organisations and Qualifications Bodies* (2004), paras 5.2–5.3, 5.6–5.10, 7.10–7.14, 7.19–7.21 and 7.27–7.29 (and examples).

or she may be) an applicant for membership.[344] In any other case, the disabled person concerned is a disabled person who is a member of the organisation or who is an applicant for membership of the organisation.[345] In the case of an applicant or potential applicant, no duty is imposed on a trade organisation in relation to a disabled person if the organisation does not know (and could not reasonably be expected to know) that the disabled person concerned is (or may be) an applicant for membership of the organisation.[346] In any case, no duty is imposed on a trade organisation in relation to a disabled person if the organisation does not know (and could not reasonably be expected to know) that that person has a disability and is likely to be placed at a substantial disadvantage in comparison with persons who are not disabled.[347]

4.9.13 An interesting question concerns the overlap between the duty to make adjustments and the democratisation provisions in trade union law.[348] In particular, trade unions need to consider how to meet the stringent requirements upon unions in respect of ballots and elections while also complying with the duty to make reasonable adjustments for their disabled members. For example, elections to certain positions in a union are required to be conducted by secret postal ballot.[349] Union members must not be unreasonably excluded from candidature.[350] Union members with a disability may be able to use the 1995 Act to reinforce that right. The union is obliged to circulate election addresses for every candidate.[351] The DDA 1995 might require a union to ensure that Braille or large-print versions of such addresses are made available. The same is true of the scrutineer's report and the publication of the results of the ballot at the conclusion of the election process.

4.9.14 Voting in the election is to be by means of a fully postal secret ballot and no other form of voting is acceptable.[352] The system of fully postal voting works to the benefit of disabled members, some of whom might otherwise have been at a substantial disadvantage under a non-postal or partly postal voting system. However, a trade union might consider that the 1995 Act requires it to redesign the ballot paper so as to accommodate the needs of disabled members (especially those with visual or learning disabilities), while remaining within the form and content required by trade union law. Similar considerations in respect of the rights

---

[344] DDA 1995, s 14(2)(a); *Code of Practice: Trade Organisations and Qualifications Bodies* (2004), paras 5.4–5.5.

[345] DDA 1995, s 14(2)(b).

[346] Ibid, s 14(3)(a); *Code of Practice: Trade Organisations and Qualifications Bodies* (2004), paras 5.11 and 7.30–7.36 (and examples).

[347] Ibid, s 14(3)(b).

[348] TULR(C)A 1992. Examples are given in *Code of Practice: Trade Organisations and Qualifications Bodies* (2004), paras 5.12–5.25 (and examples).

[349] TULR(C)A 1992, Part I, Chapter IV.

[350] Ibid, s 47.

[351] Ibid, s 48.

[352] Ibid, s 51.

of trade union members with disabilities might also arise in respect of other aspects of trade union law relating to administration, elections, ballots before industrial action, union discipline, political fund resolutions and ballots, and so on.

4.10   QUALIFICATIONS BODIES

4.10.1   Prior to 1 October 2004, one area of doubt concerned the position of bodies which issue qualifications or authorisations required for (or facilitating engagement in) a trade or profession.[353] Examples might include The Law Society (in its regulatory capacity), the Council of Legal Education, or the General Medical Council (GMC).[354] Prior to the amendments to the DDA 1995 wrought by the Special Educational Needs and Disability Act 2001 (SENDA 2001), such bodies might have been excluded from DDA 1995 Part 3 (the provisions relating to goods and services) if they fell within the originally enacted exclusions in respect of education.[355] However, if they were not so excluded, they might have been caught by Part 3 in so far as they provide services to the public. Further or alternatively, they might be caught by the trade organisations provisions of the legislation in so far as they might be a professional or trade organisation.

4.10.2   Nevertheless, it was doubtful that qualifications bodies were covered by the DDA 1995 prior to 1 October 2004. There were no equivalent provisions in the DDA 1995 to those in the other discrimination statutes which explicitly dealt with discrimination by qualifications (or qualifying) bodies.[356] The Disability Rights Task Force recognised that there were no specific provisions in the DDA 1995 for qualifying bodies and recommended that this should be remedied.[357] In response,[358] the Government indicated that it wished to give further consideration to this recommendation about qualifying bodies in the light of the EC Framework Employment Directive.[359] In that context, the Government made it clear that it would ensure that all qualifying bodies are covered by the employment provisions of the DDA 1995, except to the

---

[353]   See HL Deb, vol 566, col 226.

[354]   In *General Medical Council v Cox* (2002) EAT/76/01, the EAT ruled that the GMC is not a trade organisation for the purposes of DDA 1995, s 13 (as it then was) because its statutory purpose under Medical Act 1983, s 1(1) is the protection of members of the public consulting a medical practitioner. Otherwise, the GMC is undoubtedly a qualifications body: *General Medical Council v Goba* [1988] IRLR 425, EAT.

[355]   DDA 1995, s 19(5)–(6). See Chapters 5 and 7.

[356]   SDA 1975, s 13; RRA 1976, s 12.

[357]   Disability Rights Task Force, *From Exclusion to Inclusion: A Report of the Disability Rights Task Force for Disabled People* (1999, London: DfEE), recommendation 5.13.

[358]   *Towards Inclusion – Civil Rights for Disabled People: Government Response to the Disability Rights Task Force* (March 2001: DfEE), para 3.68. See also *Interim Government Response to the Report of the Disability Rights Task Force* (March 2000: DfEE).

[359]   2000/78/EC.

extent that they are already covered by the provisions of the Act applying to further and higher education institutions.[360] Those changes have now been effected from 1 October 2004 as a result of the Disability Discrimination Act 1995 (Amendment) Regulations 2003.[361]

Qualifications bodies

4.10.3   A qualifications body is any authority or body which can confer (or renew or extend) a professional or trade qualification.[362] Examples of such bodies include the General Medical Council, the Nursing and Midwifery Council, the Driving Standards Agency, City and Guilds, the Institute of the Motor Industry, the Hospitality Awarding Body, and the Guild of Cleaners and Launders.[363] A professional or trade qualification is an authorisation, qualification, recognition, registration, enrolment, approval or certification which is needed for (or facilitates engagement in) a particular profession or trade.[364] However, to avoid overlap with the education provisions of Part 4 of the Act, a qualifications body does not include a responsible body in relation to a school or college or a local education authority in England or Wales, or an education authority in Scotland.[365]

Unlawful acts

4.10.4   It is unlawful for a qualifications body to discriminate against a disabled person: (a) in the arrangements which it makes for the purpose of determining upon whom to confer (or renew or extend) a professional or trade qualification; (b) in the terms on which it is prepared to confer (or renew or extend) a professional or trade qualification on him or her; (c) by refusing or deliberately omitting to grant any application by him or her for such a qualification; or (d) by withdrawing such a qualification from him or her or varying the terms on which he or she holds it.[366] It is also unlawful for a qualifications body, in relation to a professional or trade qualification conferred (or renewed or extended) by it, to subject to

---

[360]   See *Towards Equality and Diversity: Implementing the Employment and Race Directives: Consultation Document* (December 2001: Cabinet Office), paras 14.23–14.25. See also *Legislative Review: First Review of the Disability Discrimination Act 1995: Consultation* (May 2002: Disability Rights Commission), p 7.

[361]   DDA 1995, ss 14A–14B; *Code of Practice: Trade Organisations and Qualifications Bodies* (2004), chapters 3 and 8.

[362]   Ibid, s 14A(5).

[363]   *Code of Practice: Trade Organisations and Qualifications Bodies* (2004), paras 3.9–3.11. Some qualifications bodies will also be trade associations and *vice versa*. They will be subject to ss 13–14 and 14A–14B, as the circumstances require.

[364]   DDA 1995, s 14A(5); *Code of Practice: Trade Organisations and Qualifications Bodies* (2004), paras 8.5–8.8.

[365]   Ibid, s 14A(5). See Chapter 7.

[366]   Ibid, s 14A(1).

harassment a disabled person who holds or applies for such a qualification.[367] The meanings of 'discrimination' and 'harassment' have been addressed in Chapter 3.

Competence standards and justification

4.10.5 A competence standard is an academic, medical or other standard applied by or on behalf of a qualifications body for the purpose of determining whether or not a person has a particular level of competence or ability.[368] In determining whether the application by a qualifications body of a competence standard to a disabled person constitutes disability-related discrimination, the application of the standard is justified if, but only if, the qualifications body can show that the standard is (or would be) applied equally to persons who do not have his or her particular disability, and its application is a proportionate means of achieving a legitimate aim.[369] In this context, disability-related less favourable treatment of a disabled person cannot be justified in this way if it amounts to direct discrimination.[370] The justification defence is considered generally in Chapter 3.

Duty to make reasonable adjustments

4.10.6 Where a provision, criterion or practice (other than a competence standard) applied by or on behalf of a qualifications body, or any physical feature of premises occupied by a qualifications body, places the disabled person concerned at a substantial disadvantage in comparison with persons who are not disabled, it is the duty of the qualifications body to take such steps as it is reasonable, in all the circumstances of the case, for it to have to take in order to prevent the provision, criterion or practice, or feature, having that effect.[371] The broader issues raised by the duty to make reasonable adjustments were considered in Chapter 3.

4.10.7 In the case of a provision, criterion or practice for determining on whom a professional or trade qualification is to be conferred (or renewed or extended), the disabled person concerned is any disabled person who is (or who has notified the qualifications body that he or she may be) an applicant for the conferment (or renewal or extension) of that qualification.[372] In any other case, the disabled person concerned is a disabled person who holds a professional or trade qualification conferred

---

[367] DDA 1995, s 14A(2).

[368] Ibid, s 14A(5). For example, eyesight standards for airline pilots, but not length of service or experience: *Code of Practice: Trade Organisations and Qualifications Bodies* (2004), paras 8.27–8.31 (and examples).

[369] Ibid, s 14A(3), by reference to ss 3A and 3A(1)(b); *Code of Practice: Trade Organisations and Qualifications Bodies* (2004), paras 8.32–8.41 (and examples).

[370] Ibid, s 14A(4)(b), modifying s 3A(3).

[371] Ibid, s 14B(1); *Code of Practice: Trade Organisations and Qualifications Bodies (2004)*, chapter 5 and paras 8.15–8.26 (and examples).

[372] DDA 1995, s 14B(2)(a).

(or renewed or extended) by the qualifications body or who applies for a professional or trade qualification which it confers (or renews or extends).[373]

4.10.8 In the case of an applicant or potential applicant for a professional or trade qualification, no duty is imposed on the qualifications body in relation to a disabled person if the body does not know (and could not reasonably be expected to know) that the disabled person concerned is (or may be) an applicant for the conferment (or renewal or extension) of a professional or trade qualification.[374] In any case, no duty is imposed on the qualifications body in relation to a disabled person if the body does not know (and could not reasonably be expected to know) that that person has a disability and is likely to be placed at a substantial disadvantage in comparison with persons who are not disabled.[375]

4.10.9 There is no duty to make reasonable adjustments in relation to competence standards and no discrimination by way of a failure to make reasonable adjustments in that limited respect.[376]

4.11 PRACTICAL WORK EXPERIENCE

4.11.1 From 1 October 2004, providers of practical work experience are also covered by Part 2 of the DDA 1995.[377] These provisions are concerned with work placements and placement providers. A work placement is practical work experience undertaken for a limited period for the purposes of a person's vocational training. A placement provider is any person who provides a work placement to a person whom the placement provider does not employ.[378] The new law does not apply to anything made unlawful in relation to employers, or in respect of the provision of goods, facilities or services, or employment services, or private clubs, or in the education field.[379] It also does not apply to a work placement undertaken in any of the naval, military and air forces of the Crown.[380]

---

[373] DDA 1995, s 14B(2)(b).

[374] Ibid, s 14B(3)(a).

[375] Ibid, s 14B(3)(b).

[376] Ibid, s 14A(4)(a), disapplying s 3A(2) and (6); *Code of Practice: Trade Organisations and Qualifications Bodies* (2004), paras 8.32–8.41 (and examples).

[377] Ibid, ss 14C–14D.

[378] Ibid, s 14C(4); *Code of Practice: Trade Organisations and Qualifications Bodies* (2004), para 9.44.

[379] Ibid, s 14C(3), as amended, cross-referring to s 4 and Parts 3 and 4. The exclusion extends to anything which would be unlawful under s 4 or Parts 3 or 4 but for the operation of any other provision of the Act. See also *Code of Practice: Trade Organisations and Qualifications Bodies* (2004), para 9.45 (and examples). In Northern Ireland, see Disability Discrimination (Northern Ireland) Order 2006, SI 2006/312.

[380] Ibid, s 14C(5).

Unlawful acts

4.11.2   In the case of a disabled person seeking or undertaking a work placement, it is unlawful for a placement provider to discriminate against him or her: (a) in the arrangements which it makes for the purpose of determining who should be offered a work placement; (b) in the terms on which it affords him or her access to any work placement or any facilities concerned with such a placement; (c) by refusing or deliberately omitting to afford him or her such access; (d) by terminating the placement; or (e) by subjecting him or her to any other detriment in relation to the placement.[381] In relation to a work placement, it is also unlawful for a placement provider to subject to harassment a disabled person to whom it is providing a placement or a disabled person who has applied to it for a placement.[382] The concepts of discrimination and harassment were explained in Chapter 3.

Duty to make reasonable adjustments

4.11.3   Where a provision, criterion or practice applied by or on behalf of a placement provider, or any physical feature of premises occupied by the placement provider, places the disabled person concerned at a substantial disadvantage in comparison with persons who are not disabled, it is the duty of the placement provider to take such steps as it is reasonable, in all the circumstances of the case, for it to have to take in order to prevent the provision, criterion or practice, or feature, having that effect.[383] The larger questions raised by the duty to make reasonable adjustments were posed in Chapter 3. The organisation sending the disabled person on the work placement may also have its own duty to make reasonable adjustments in relation to the disabled person. This is likely to mean that that organisation and the placement provider will need to co-operate with one another in respect of any adjustments required.[384]

4.11.4   In the case of a provision, criterion or practice for determining to whom a work placement should be offered, the disabled person concerned is any disabled person who is (or who has notified the placement provider that he or she may be) an applicant for that work placement.[385] In any other case, it is a disabled person who is an applicant for the work placement concerned or who is undertaking a work placement with the placement provider.[386]

---

[381] DDA 1995, s 14C(1); *Code of Practice: Trade Organisations and Qualifications Bodies* (2004), para 9.42 (and examples).

[382] Ibid, s 14C(2); *Code of Practice: Trade Organisations and Qualifications Bodies* (2004), para 9.43 (and example).

[383] Ibid, s 14D(1); *Code of Practice: Trade Organisations and Qualifications Bodies* (2004), paras 9.47–9.50.

[384] *Code of Practice: Trade Organisations and Qualifications Bodies* (2004), paras 9.49–9.50.

[385] DDA 1995, s 14D(2)(a).

[386] Ibid, s 14D(2)(b).

4.11.5   In the case of an applicant or potential applicant for a work placement, no duty is imposed on a placement provider in relation to the disabled person concerned if it does not know (and could not reasonably be expected to know) that the disabled person concerned is (or may be) an applicant for the work placement.[387] In any case, no duty is imposed on a placement provider in relation to the disabled person concerned if it does not know (and could not reasonably be expected to know) that that person has a disability and is likely to be placed at a substantial disadvantage in comparison with persons who are not disabled.[388]

4.12   ENFORCEMENT, REMEDIES AND PROCEDURES

The question of enforcement, remedies and procedures in the employment field at large is considered in Chapter 10.

4.13   LOCALLY-ELECTED AUTHORITIES AND THEIR MEMBERS

4.13.1   Section 1 of the DDA 2005 inserted into the DDA 1995 new ss 15A–15C that deal with relationships between locally-electable authorities and their members (that is, the elected councillors). Although these are strictly-speaking part of the amended Part 2 of the Act, they more naturally fall to be treated as part of the discussion on public authorities in Chapter 9 below.

---

[387]   DDA 1995, s 14D(3)(a).
[388]   Ibid, s 14D(3)(b).

CHAPTER 5

GOODS, FACILITIES AND SERVICES

5.1 INTRODUCTION

5.1.1 The 1994 Green Paper[1] promised that consultation would take place on extending building regulations to ensure that physical barriers to access by disabled persons to public and domestic buildings would be removed or reduced. However, as the 1994 Green Paper acknowledged:

> '. . . removing physical impediments does nothing to banish the mental barriers of ignorance and prejudice. Making buildings easier to get into is of no avail if disabled people are kept outside because their appearance or behaviour is deemed too upsetting for other patrons or through misguided concern for their safety.'[2]

Instead, the 1994 Green Paper mooted a new right of access that would make it unlawful for providers of goods or services to treat an individual unfavourably because of that person's disability, except where there were physical barriers or genuine safety issues. In turn, the 1995 White Paper[3] proposed the introduction of a right of access to goods and services for disabled persons,[4] prohibiting discriminatory behaviour, while requiring reasonable and readily achievable positive action to overcome physical and communication barriers impeding access by disabled persons. Exceptionally, the new right would not apply to transport vehicles or to educational establishments (in the event, as will be seen, the DDA 1995 (as amended) now applies in these areas). It would also not apply where the supply of the goods or services in question would pose a risk to the health and safety of the disabled person or others.[5]

---

[1] A Consultation on Government Measures to Tackle Discrimination Against Disabled People (July 1994).
[2] Ibid, para 4.2.
[3] *Ending Discrimination Against Disabled People*, Cm 2729 (January 1995).
[4] Ibid, para 4.4.
[5] Ibid, para 4.6.

Timetable

5.1.2   These novel rights of access are set out in Part 3 of the DDA 1995.[6] The Major administration intended that there would be a long lead-in time for businesses to adapt to these new provisions, with these measures being brought into force in stages over a period as long as ten years.[7] The Blair Government then agreed to accelerate the timetable for implementation. The simple duties on service providers not to refuse service to a disabled person, and not to discriminate in the manner, standard or terms of service, came into force on 2 December 1996.[8] The next rights of access – requiring service providers to make reasonable adjustments to service delivery, short of physical alterations to premises – came into force on 1 October 1999.[9] The remaining duties to remove physical barriers came into force on 1 October 2004.[10] The extension of Part 3 to transport vehicles took place from 30 June 2005.[11] This is dealt with in Chapter 8.

Code and regulations

5.1.3   The provisions of Part 3 of the DDA 1995 are supported by a statutory Code of Practice.[12] The Code gives practical advice on how to comply with the legal duties in Part 3 and is designed to help both disabled persons and service providers to understand the law. However, it does not impose legal obligations and is not an authoritative statement of the law. It may be used in evidence in legal proceedings and an adjudicating body (primarily, in this context, a court) must take account of it where relevant.[13] Regulations under Part 3 have also been issued and will be considered at appropriate points in the text below or, as appropriate, in later chapters.[14]

---

[6]   DDA 1995, ss 19–21. Enforcement of the DDA 1995 rights and related questions are dealt with in ss 25–28. Part 3 of the DDA 1995 is broadly modelled after comparable provisions in SDA 1975, ss 29–36 and RRA 1976, ss 20–27. However, there are important and subtle differences between Part 3 of the DDA 1995 and the provisions of the earlier Acts: *Clark v TDG Ltd t/a Novacold* [1999] IRLR 318, CA.

[7]   HL Deb, vol 566, col 1031.

[8]   DDA 1995, s 19(1) (except ss 19(1)(b) and 20(1)): SI 1996/1474.

[9]   Ibid, ss 19(1)(b), 20(2) and 21 (except s 21(2)(a)–(c)): SI 1999/1190.

[10]   Ibid, s 21(2)(a)–(c): SI 2001/2030 (England, Wales and Scotland) and SR 2001/439 (Northern Ireland).

[11]   Ibid, s 21ZA as inserted by DDA 2005, s 5 and brought into force by SI 2005/1676. See also Disability Discrimination (Northern Ireland) Order 2006, SI 2006/312.

[12]   *Code of Practice: Rights of Access: Services to the Public, Public Authority Functions, Private Clubs and Premises* (2006, London: HMSO) referred to hereafter as the 'Rights of Access Code of Practice 2006'. The Code is prepared and issued by the DRC under DDA 1995, s 53A and came into effect on 4 December 2006: SI 2006/1966 and SI 2006/1967. It revises and replaces earlier versions of the Code of Practice published in 1996, 1999 and 2002. A separate, but largely identical, Code of Practice has been issued in Northern Ireland (where the Equality Commission is the responsible body).

[13]   DDA 1995, s 53A(8) and (8A), as amended. See generally Rights of Access Code of Practice 2006, Chapter 1.

[14]   Disability Discrimination (Service Providers and Public Authorities Carrying Out

Part 3 of the DDA 1995 outlined

5.1.4   The DDA 1995 applies to providers of goods, facilities or services.[15] It is unlawful for a service provider to discriminate against a disabled person by refusing to provide (or deliberately not providing) any service which it provides (or is prepared to provide) to members of the public;[16] or in the standard of service which it provides to the disabled person or the manner in which it provides it;[17] or in the terms on which it provides a service to the disabled person.[18] It is also unlawful for a service provider to discriminate by failing to comply with any statutory duty imposed on it to make reasonable adjustments in circumstances in which the effect of that failure is to make it impossible or unreasonably difficult for the disabled person to make use of goods, facilities or services.[19]

5.2   PROVISION OF SERVICES

Services

5.2.1   For the purposes of the present analysis, the provision of services includes the provision of any goods or facilities.[20] The terms are not defined in the statute or the extra-statutory sources, but the DDA 1995 provides a non-exhaustive list of examples of services to which the legislation applies:[21]

- access to and use of any place which members of the public are permitted to enter;

- access to and use of means of communication;

- access to and use of information services;

Functions) Regulations 2005, SI 2005/2901. The 2005 Regulations revoke and replace in part or in full a set of previous regulations made under Part 3, namely: Disability Discrimination (Services and Premises) Regulations 1996, SI 1996/1836; Disability Discrimination (Services and Premises) Regulations 1999, SI 1999/1191, as amended by SI 2002/1980; Disability Discrimination (Providers of Services) (Adjustment of Premises) Regulations 2001, SI 2001/3253, as amended by SI 2004/1429 and SI 2005/1121. See also: Disability Discrimination (Private Clubs etc) Regulations 2005, SI 2005/3258; Disability Discrimination (Transport Vehicles) Regulations 2005, SI 2005/3190; and Disability Discrimination (Premises) Regulations 2006, SI 2006/887.

[15]   Referred to throughout this chapter as 'service providers'. References to providing a service include providing goods or facilities (s 19(2)(a)). See generally Rights of Access Code of Practice 2006, Chapter 3.

[16]   DDA 1995, s 19(1)(a).

[17]   Ibid, s 19(1)(c).

[18]   Ibid, s 19(1)(d).

[19]   Ibid, ss 19(1)(b) and 21.

[20]   Ibid, s 19(2)(a).

[21]   Ibid, s 19(3); Rights of Access Code of Practice 2006, para 3.3.

- accommodation in a hotel, boarding house or other similar establishment;

- facilities by way of banking or insurance or for grants, loans, credit or finance;

- facilities for entertainment, recreation or refreshment;

- facilities provided by employment agencies;

- certain training facilities;[22]

- the services of any profession or trade, or any local or other public authority.

The Rights of Access Code of Practice 2006 adds considerably to this list by way of illustration.[23] A wide range of establishments and businesses are covered by the rights of access. What is also clear is that it is irrelevant whether the goods, facilities or services are provided on payment or without payment.[24]

5.2.2   The illustrative list of services does not explicitly include access to civic rights and duties, health services, broadcasting, the judicial system and legal proceedings, careers services, trade unions and employers' associations, trade and professional associations, or qualifying bodies,[25] but many of these examples are implicitly covered.[26] The apparent legislative intention was 'to provide a universal, all-embracing right of non-discrimination against disabled people that is applicable to all providers of goods, facilities and services to the general public'.[27] The list of services is thus not exhaustive.[28] It seems to have been intended that,

---

[22]   Provided under Employment and Training Act 1973, s 2 or Employment and Training Act (Northern Ireland) 1950, ss 1–2 (see DDA 1995, Sch 8, para 9(1)).

[23]   Rights of Access Code of Practice 2006, paras 10.2–10.17.

[24]   DDA 1995, s 19(2)(c).

[25]   Trade unions, employers' associations, trade associations and professional associations are the subject of ss 13–15 of Part 2 of the DDA 1995. See Chapter 4.

[26]   Rights of Access Code of Practice 2006, para 3.3.

[27]   HC Deb Standing Committee E, cols 290–291.

[28]   There is doubt about whether services provided by a company to its shareholders (eg information and meetings) are caught by Part 3 of the DDA 1995. The Disability Rights Task Force (DRTF) recommended that the Department of Trade and Industry should examine this issue as part of its fundamental review of company law: see *From Exclusion to Inclusion: A Report of the Disability Rights Task Force for Disabled People* (1999, London: DfEE) (DRTF Report), recommendation 6.11. The Government's response was broadly supportive of this recommendation: *Towards Inclusion – Civil Rights for Disabled People: Government Response to the Disability Rights Task Force* (2001, London: DfEE) (Government Response to DRTF Report), para 6.11. See the Companies Act 1985 (Electronic Communications) Order 2000, SI 2000/3373 (modifying various provisions of the Companies Act 1985 for the purpose of authorising or facilitating the use of electronic communications between companies and their members).

for example, facilities for telecommunication, the judicial system and legal proceedings,[29] broadcasting services,[30] medical and health services, and the constituency services of parliamentarians are covered.[31] However, where central or local government is acting in discharge of a statutory power or duty, there is a very strong argument – supported by case-law under comparable provisions[32] – that this does not entail the provision of a service (unless otherwise closely analogous to the kinds of services provided by a private sector undertaking) and thus is not covered by Part 3 of the DDA 1995.[33]

Goods and facilities

5.2.3 An everyday meaning of 'goods' as chattels or moveable property is probably intended and there seems no reason to import a definition from other statutory sources.[34] A refusal to supply goods which are in the nature of personal or moveable property will be covered. The literal meaning of 'facilities' suggests that the law is concerned with the provision of equipment or the physical means for doing something. For example, the provision of a telephone involves the provision of 'goods'; the supply of a link to the telecommunications network is the provision of a 'service'; while the means by which the service provider then bills the customer for the provision of the goods and service (and the medium by which the customer may settle that bill) would amount to 'facilities'. It may be that the distinction is merely artificial. The term 'facilities' simply embraces any matter not obviously amounting to goods or services.[35]

---

[29] Part 3 of the DDA 1995 probably does not apply to service as a juror or witness: HL Deb, vol 566, cols 259–262 (although the new 'public authority' provisions of the Act will assist).

[30] As to the requirements of television companies (other than the BBC) in respect of teletext and subtitling services, note the provisions of the Broadcasting Acts 1990 and 1996 (and the guidelines published by the Independent Television Commission). See also HL Deb, vol 566, cols 269–271.

[31] HC Deb Standing Committee E, cols 292–293; HL Deb, vol 564, col 1952.

[32] See *R v Entry Clearance Officer Bombay, ex parte Amin* [1983] 2 AC 818 where, under the similar provisions of the RRA 1976, the House of Lords held that an immigration officer exercising powers under immigration rules was not providing a service to the subject of an immigration decision. See also DDA 1995, s 59 (discussed in Chapter 10).

[33] The DRTF recommended that all functions of public authorities should be covered, subject only to careful consideration of the practical effect on those functions of the duty to make reasonable adjustments. It also recommended that the public sector should be under a statutory duty to promote the equalisation of opportunities for disabled people in the provision of services: DRTF Report, recommendations 6.12–6.13. The Government accepted these recommendations. See now the discussion of public authorities in Chapter 9.

[34] Sale of Goods Act 1979, s 61 defines goods as including 'all personal chattels other than things in action and money' excluding non-physical property (such as shares or intellectual property).

[35] The illustrations in the DDA 1995 (s 19(3)) of what amounts to 'services' appear to encompass 'facilities'.

Service providers

5.2.4 Part 3 of the DDA 1995 applies to 'a provider of services'. A person is a provider of services only if that person is concerned with the provision of services 'to the public or to a section of the public'.[36] The use of the word 'person' will include legal entities (such as companies or local authorities) as well as individuals or associations of individuals (such as trade unions or partnerships).[37] It is clear, for example, that in many circumstances Part 3 embraces the provision of services to the public or community by local and other public authorities.[38] In some cases, there might be more than one service provider – for example, where services are provided from multiple-occupancy premises (such as a department store or shopping centre) or appear to be provided by more than one service provider (as in the case of a conference held in an hotel) – and it is important to determine which service provider has liability or whether such liability is shared.[39]

5.2.5 The service provider must also be 'concerned with the provision, in the United Kingdom, of services to the public'. The meaning of this phrase is unclear and potentially ambiguous. It is capable of meaning that the services themselves must be provided within the UK (and thus, for example, an overseas holiday would not be covered). Equally, it might mean that it is sufficient that the service provider is based in the UK (even if the services themselves will be used outside the UK). Given the territorial nature of statutory jurisdiction, it seems likely that a British court would interpret this clause narrowly and in favour of the former interpretation rather than the latter. That does not mean that, for example, a British tour operator offering holidays abroad is entirely untouched by the DDA 1995. The brochure and booking services which it offers to the public in the UK are services within the Act, even if the actual holidays themselves may not be. This is a matter which awaits testing in litigation.

Manufacturers and designers

5.2.6 Part 3 of the DDA 1995 does not apply to manufacturers and designers, unless they supply goods or services directly to members of the public.[40] While such persons might wish to consider how to comply with the spirit of the legislation, they are not directly subject to its letter. There

---

[36] DDA 1995, s 19(2)(b).

[37] All those involved in the provision of services are affected: Rights of Access Code of Practice 2006, para 4.15.

[38] HL Deb, vol 565, col 672. This must be subject to what is said in **5.2.2** and the discussion of the duties of public authorities in Chapter 9.

[39] Rights of Access Code of Practice 2006, paras 10.4 and 10.6–10.16 (and examples) addressing the difficult questions of liability under the DDA 1995 in multi-occupancy premises with common areas and landlord–tenant relationships.

[40] HL Deb, vol 566, cols 241–242. See Rights of Access Code of Practice 2006, paras 3.30–3.31 (and examples).

is no obligation upon manufacturers or producers of goods or services (who are not also direct suppliers to the public) to consider the accessibility of the design, labelling or packaging of those goods or services to disabled consumers. For example, there is no legal obligation upon manufacturers under the Act to include any user instructions bundled with goods or products in accessible formats (such as Braille, large print or audio-visual medium) and there would appear to be no such duty placed upon the retail supplier either.[41]

To whom the service is provided

5.2.7 It is clear that Part 3 of the DDA 1995 only addresses discrimination in the provision of services to disabled persons as consumers themselves. It does not directly address discrimination against a person because of that individual's relationship to or association with a disabled person (perhaps as a spouse, parent or friend). Members of a family who are refused service in a restaurant because they are accompanied by a disabled child have no remedy under the Act (although the child will also have been discriminated against and will have a cause of action which will have to be pursued on his or her behalf).[42] However, the disabled person may be receiving services in his or her own right while acting on behalf of someone else or as a representative of a third party, and is likely to be covered by the DDA 1995 in those circumstances, all other things being equal.[43]

Excluded services

5.2.8 Part 3 of the DDA 1995 does not apply to education,[44] but it does apply to non-education services provided by educational institutions.[45]

---

[41] HL Deb, vol 566, col 251.

[42] A question that is the subject of a current reference to the ECJ: *Attridge Law v Coleman* [2007] IRLR 88, EAT under the employment provisions of the Act. The answer to the reference is likely to be only of indirect relevance to the service provisions of the Act as they do not reflect any legal obligation to implement a provision of EC equal treatment law.

[43] Rights of Access Code of Practice 2006, para 10.3.

[44] The exclusion of education was originally effected by DDA 1995, s 19(5)(a)–(ab) and (6) (as amended). This provision is now repealed by SENDA 2001, ss 38(1), (5)(a)–(b), 42(6) and Sch 9. The present position is that, by virtue of DDA 1995, s 19(5A) (inserted by SENDA 2001, s 38(1) and (6)), nothing in Part 3 of the DDA 1995 (the goods and services provisions) applies to the provision of a service which is made unlawful by DDA 1995, s 28A (discrimination against disabled pupils and prospective pupils), s 28F (duty of education authorities not to discriminate) or s 28R (discrimination against disabled students and prospective students), as inserted by SENDA 2001, ss 11, 16 and 26. See Rights of Access Code of Practice 2006, paras 3.22–3.25.

[45] As is illustrated by *White v Clitheroe Royal Grammar School* (2002) Preston County Court (District Judge Ashton), reported in *Equal Opportunities Review No 106* (June 2002) 26–28 (student with diabetes discriminated against contrary to DDA 1995, Part 3 when excluded from a school holiday for a reason connected with his disability).

Educational services are subject to the different regime provided by Part 4 of the Act and are discussed in Chapter 7.

5.2.9   As originally enacted, Part 3 also did not apply to transport.[46] However, the new s 21ZA applies ss 19–21 to transport vehicles. This is best discussed in the wider context of the law on disability accessible transport. See Chapter 8. Section 19(1) also does not apply to anything that is governed by EC Regulation No 1107/2006 concerning the rights of disabled persons and persons with reduced mobility when travelling by air.[47]

5.2.10   The Act also provides that the relevant provisions on services will not apply (or will apply only to a prescribed extent) in relation to a service of a prescribed description.[48] No such regulations have been made to date. It would appear that this is a precautionary piece of drafting and there has been no indication that this power will be used at any particular time or for any particular purpose.

5.3   UNLAWFUL DISCRIMINATION

5.3.1   Part 3 of the DDA 1995 provides that it is unlawful for a service provider to discriminate against a disabled person in a number of specified ways.[49]

Refusal to provide goods, facilities or services

5.3.2   First, it is an unlawful act for a service provider to discriminate against a disabled person in refusing to provide, or deliberately not providing, to a disabled person any service which the service provider provides, or is prepared to provide, to members of the public.[50] For example, a theatre which refuses to admit a person with cerebral palsy because of that individual's disability might be committing an unlawful act of discrimination.[51]

Standard or manner of service

5.3.3   Secondly, it is an unlawful act for a service provider to discriminate against a disabled person in the 'standard of service' which the service provider provides to the disabled person or by virtue of the 'manner in which' the service provider provides that service to the disabled

---

[46]   DDA 1995, s 19(5)(b) as originally enacted.

[47]   Ibid, s 19(4A) inserted by SI 2007/1895, reg 8 and in force from 26 July 2007.

[48]   DDA 1995, s 19(5), as substituted by DDA 2005.

[49]   See generally Rights of Access Code of Practice 2002, Chapters 2–4.

[50]   DDA 1995, s 19(1)(a).

[51]   See the further examples in Rights of Access Code of Practice 2006, paras 10.19–10.21.

person.[52] A restaurant that forces disabled customers to dine in a separate room unseen by other patrons might breach this provision.[53] A theatre which limits disabled patrons to matinee performances only might also fall foul of the Act, although there would be nothing to prevent a theatre arranging special matinee performances for disabled persons, provided they are also free to book seats for other times.[54] Similarly, providing inferior goods or services to disabled persons would be unlawful, although what would amount to *inferior* goods or services might be difficult to measure. For example, requiring wheelchair users to sit in a particular part of a theatre or restaurant when other customers or patrons have a comparatively free choice as to where they sit could be regarded as the provision of an inferior service.[55] Much will hinge upon the application of the defence of justification for the differential treatment in such cases,[56] but a service provider who adopts a deliberate policy to discourage disabled customers (for example, by deliberately surly, dilatory or inferior service) would have difficulty in justifying such discrimination.[57]

Terms on which service is provided

5.3.4   Thirdly, it is an unlawful act for a service provider to discriminate against a disabled person in the terms on which the service provider provides a service (or goods or facilities) to the disabled person.[58] An example of an act made unlawful by this provision would be a shop or entertainment outlet which charged higher prices for purchases by or admission to disabled persons in comparison with other customers.[59]

Failure to make reasonable adjustment

5.3.5   Finally, it is also an unlawful act for a service provider to discriminate against a disabled person by failing to comply with a duty imposed on it by the DDA 1995[60] to make reasonable adjustments in circumstances in which the effect of the failure is to make it impossible or unreasonably difficult for the disabled person to make use of any goods, facilities or services provided to other members of the public.[61] This is a pivotal duty under the Act and calls for separate and detailed explication below.[62]

---

[52]   DDA 1995, s 19(1)(c).
[53]   1994 Green Paper, para 4.3.
[54]   See the further examples in Rights of Access Code of Practice 2006, paras 10.22–10.23.
[55]   1994 Green Paper, para 4.4; Rights of Access Code of Practice 2006, para 10.22.
[56]   See **5.6**.
[57]   HL Deb, vol 566, col 267.
[58]   DDA 1995, s 19(1)(d).
[59]   1994 Green Paper, para 4.3. See the further examples in Rights of Access Code of Practice 2006, para 10.24.
[60]   DDA 1995, s 21.
[61]   Ibid, s 19(1)(b).
[62]   See **5.5**.

5.4 MEANING OF DISCRIMINATION

5.4.1 As has just been described, it is unlawful for a provider of services to 'discriminate' against a disabled person in a number of respects in relation to goods, facilities and services.[63] However, it is not sufficient to show that a disabled person has been badly or unreasonably treated in the outcomes set out above. It is also necessary to show that this is the result of discrimination by the service provider. What does 'discrimination' mean for this purpose and in this context? The definition of 'discrimination' in the context of Part 3 of the DDA 1995 is broadly similar to that used in Part 2 (discrimination in the employment field).[64] It contains two alternative bases for establishing discrimination: broadly, less favourable treatment and a failure to make a reasonable adjustment.[65] The Act also treats 'victimisation' as unlawful discrimination for present purposes (this is dealt with further in Chapter 10).[66]

Less favourable treatment

5.4.2 A provider of services discriminates against a disabled person if, for a reason which relates to the disabled person's disability, the service provider treats the disabled person less favourably than the service provider treats (or would treat) others to whom the reason which relates to the disabled person's disability does not or would not apply, and the service provider cannot show that the less favourable treatment in question is justified.[67] Although this definition allows less favourable treatment to be 'justified', it is closely related to the concept of 'direct discrimination' used in other discrimination legislation. However, the use of the phrase 'for a reason which relates to the disabled person's disability' suggests a more flexible test of discrimination.[68] This phraseology makes 'it clear that if a disabled person is refused service – for example, in a café

---

[63] DDA 1995, s 19(1), and see **5.3**.

[64] Ibid, s 20. Decisions and judicial interpretation under Part 2 will be of assistance in applying the parallel definition in s 20, but care must be taken to ensure that in Part 3 cases direct reference is made to the wording of s 20 itself.

[65] The DRTF recommended that the existing categories of discrimination should continue: DRTF Report, recommendation 6.1. The DRC suggests that an EU Directive is required with respect to discrimination on the grounds of disability in relation to a broad range of goods and services: DRC Legislative Review, recommendation 13.

[66] DDA 1995, s 55. An act of victimisation will constitute an act of discrimination for the purposes of discrimination in relation to goods, facilities and services and will provide a cause of action, whether or not the person victimised is a disabled person. This is achieved on the face of ss 19–21 by virtue of s 19(4).

[67] Ibid, s 20(1). See Rights of Access Code of Practice 2006, paras 4.5–4.9 and 5.4–5.13 (and the examples provided there). Part 3 of the Act does not prohibit positive action in favour of disabled people. Service providers may provide services to disabled people on more favourable terms: Rights of Access Code of Practice 2002, para 5.14.

[68] DDA 1995, s 20(1)(a).

– for a reason connected with his disability, where non-disabled people are happily served', that will be a prima facie case of discrimination, subject to any 'defence' of justification.[69]

5.4.3 This concept of discrimination requires proof that the disabled person has been treated less favourably than other persons to whom the reason related to disability does not apply. This calls for a comparison of how the disabled person was treated relative to such other persons.[70] The question is not merely whether the disabled person has experienced poor, inadequate or sub-standard provision in respect of goods, facilities or services. Rather the issue is whether there has been differential and unfavourable treatment of the disabled person in circumstances where other persons (to whom the reason related to disability does not apply) have not been so treated. The comparator is another member of the public (or a hypothetical member of the public). This might include a person with a disability of a different kind from the complainant because the wording of the DDA 1995 does not rule out the unlawfulness of differential treatment by service providers among disabled persons themselves.

5.4.4 The less favourable treatment must be related to the disabled person's disability. While the intention, purpose or motive with which the service provider acted is irrelevant, there must be a causal connection between the discriminatory action and the complainant's disability. A disabled person who is refused admission to a cinema because he or she does not have the means to pay for entry, or who is refused service in a public house because he or she is drunk and disorderly, has not been discriminated against contrary to the DDA 1995.[71] The reason for the apparently less favourable treatment is not that person's disability, but rather a reason which is unrelated to disability. Indeed, in any event, in these illustrations it might be claimed that there has been no less favourable treatment at all, because the service provider might be able to show that any member of the public in like circumstances would have been treated in the same way.

5.4.5 However, following the logic of the Court of Appeal's decision in the DDA 1995, Part 2 case of *Clark v TDG Ltd t/a Novacold*,[72] it is essential when approaching less favourable treatment discrimination under Part 3 to identify the reason why the disabled person is being treated less favourably than others. For example, suppose that a disabled person has cerebral palsy which causes her difficulty with physical co-ordination when eating. She is refused further service in a restaurant because the service provider objects to the messy way in which she eats.

---

[69] HL Deb, vol 566, col 120. Strictly, justification is not a defence, but rather is one of the component parts of the definition of discrimination.

[70] Rights of Access Code of Practice 2002, paras 5.4–5.10.

[71] Ibid, paras 5.8–5.10.

[72] [1999] IRLR 318, CA.

That is a refusal of service; the refusal is because of the way in which the customer eats; that is a reason which is related to the customer's disability (because her eating habits are affected by her disability); no other customers have been refused service in the restaurant; and so this amounts to less favourable treatment for a reason related to disability. It would not be sufficient for the restaurant to claim that it would have refused service to anyone who was a messy eater. The DDA 1995 does not require the comparison to be based upon a consideration of comparators in relevant circumstances which are the same or not materially different. This would be unlawful discrimination unless the restaurant can justify the treatment of the disabled customer.[73]

5.4.6   Nevertheless, in *R v Powys County Council, ex parte Hambidge (No 2)*,[74] the Court of Appeal has taken a narrower approach to the concept of less favourable treatment for a reason related to disability under Part 3 of the DDA 1995 than was taken in *Clark* under Part 2. The applicant was in receipt of disability living allowance and received home care services from the local authority.[75] The local authority introduced charges for home care services.[76] It did so by reference to three categories of service user: (A) those in receipt of income support only; (B) those in receipt of income support and either attendance allowance or disability living allowance; and (C) those not in receipt of income support (regardless of whether they were receiving any other benefits). Those in category (A) were not charged for home care services at all, while those in categories (B) and (C) were charged at differential rates. The applicant fell into category (B). She challenged the home care services charge by arguing that it amounted to less favourable treatment for a reason related to her disability.[77] Her argument was that the charges levied on category (B) were because those in category (B) had more income than those in category (A) and that the only reason for this was that those in category (B) received disability benefits by virtue of having a disability. The High Court and the Court of Appeal rejected the applicant's contention that this amounted to disability discrimination unless justified. The appellate court thought that it could not have been intended that such a case was to be covered by s 20(1)(a). The charges were based upon means or income rather than disability status or disability benefits as such. The case is probably best explained as being one based upon its particular facts.

5.4.7   Is it an essential ingredient of this limb of discrimination to be able to show that the service provider knew that the service user was a disabled person or that it was aware of the disability to which the reason for the alleged unlawful treatment was related? The question of whether

---

[73]   The question of justification is addressed at **5.6**.
[74]   [2000] 2 FCR 69, CA.
[75]   Under National Health Service Community Care Act 1990, s 47 and Chronically Sick and Disabled Persons Act 1970, s 2(1).
[76]   Under Health and Social Services and Social Security Adjudications Act 1983, s 17(2).
[77]   Relying upon DDA 1995, ss 19(1)(d), (2)(c), (3)(h) and 20(1)(a).

the service provider knew that the service user (being treated in a way which is allegedly unlawful) was disabled is likely to be an especially keen one under Part 3 of the DDA 1995. For example, a disability might affect the appearance or behaviour of the disabled person, leading the service provider to believe honestly, but wrongly, that the service user was drunk or was engaging in threatening or unacceptable behaviour. Can a service provider be said to have treated a person less favourably for a reason which relates to that person's disability if the service provider did not know that the person was disabled?

5.4.8 The issue of knowledge has been raised in the context of the employment provisions of Part 2 of the DDA 1995.[78] The wording of s 20(1) is for all intents and purposes virtually identical to that of the parallel provisions in s 3A(1). Under the employment provisions, the correct approach to the question of the knowledge of disability has divided opinion in the first tier appellate courts. One view is that an employer's knowledge of the disability is relevant.[79] An employer cannot be said to have treated a person less favourably *for a reason which relates to* that person's disability if the employer did not know that the person was disabled. Knowledge of the material features of the disability will be enough, but not simply knowledge of one or other equivocal symptom.[80] However, other judicial opinion has doubted the correctness of that view.[81] According to the later opinion, as the wording of the relevant statutory provision is silent on the question of knowledge, the test is an objective one of whether the disabled person has been treated less favourably for a reason which is related to disability *as a matter of fact*. The subjective question of the employer's knowledge or ignorance of the complainant's disability might then go to the issue of justification.

5.4.9 In the employment context, the latter view that knowledge of disability is not a requirement of establishing less favourable treatment discrimination is defensible both on policy grounds and in the framework of an employer's recourse to a broadly defined concept of justification.[82] However, in relation to provision of goods and services, a service provider will not usually be possessed of the same degree of actual or potential knowledge of an individual's disability as an employer might be. Unless the service user immediately informs the service provider that he or she is disabled and explains the effects of the disability, a service provider might make a snap decision (for example, to refuse service) for a reason (for example, the appearance of being drunk) which later turns out to be a disability-related reason. Unlike the potential knowledge-based justification open to an employer, the service provider's justification 'defence' is

---

[78]   See Chapter 3.
[79]   See e g *O'Neill v Symm & Co Ltd* [1998] IRLR 233, EAT.
[80]   Whether this view is compatible with the Court of Appeal's construction of s 3A(1) in *Clark v TDG Ltd t/a Novacold* [1999] IRLR 318, CA, is arguably questionable.
[81]   See e g *HJ Heinz Co Ltd v Kenrick* [2000] IRLR 144, EAT.
[82]   However, this legal clarity has been blurred by the decision under Part 2 in *OCS Group Ltd v Taylor* [2006] IRLR 613, CA, discussed at **3.2.23** above.

narrowly defined and limited to the circumstances set out in Part 3 of the DDA 1995.[83] A literal interpretation of s 20(1) would suggest that knowledge of the disability is not relevant, but whether a court in a Part 3 case will interpret this provision in a services environment in the same way as it might be construed in an employment setting remains to be seen.[84] In *Council of the City of Manchester v Romano and Samari*[85] the Court of Appeal thought that if knowledge of the disability was not relevant, that could lead to absurd and unfair consequences. It suggested that Parliament should review the legislation at an early date.

Indirect discrimination

5.4.10   A service provider providing services subject to a requirement or condition which a smaller proportion of disabled persons than non-disabled persons can meet could be said to have indirectly discriminated against disabled persons if they suffer a detriment as a result and if the service provider cannot justify the imposition of the requirement or condition. The DDA 1995 does not contain an explicit prohibition on indirect discrimination in relation to services, unlike the comparable provisions of the SDA 1975 and the RRA 1976. This is because the 1994 Green Paper took the view that indirect discrimination would be 'more difficult to tackle effectively where disabled people are involved because disability occurs in many forms' and should not be the subject of legislation.[86] That view was reiterated in the 1995 White Paper which stated that 'a general prohibition of indirect discrimination . . . could have unforeseen consequences which were unfairly burdensome for businesses'.[87] However, it was accepted that certain practices – which had an indirect effect upon the right of disabled persons to access to services – should be prevented. The White Paper gave the specific example of a service provider banning animals from its premises and the disproportionate adverse effect this would have on persons with visual impairments who rely upon guide dogs. This would be a case that would clearly call for

---

[83]   DDA 1995, s 20(1)(b), (3) and (4). See **5.6**. It would then be for the service provider to argue that it is enough that it reasonably believed that, for example, the disabled person's appearance or behaviour created a danger to health or safety (s 20(4)(a)) or would prevent other service users from being served (s 20(4)(c) or (d)).

[84]   The Rights of Access Code of Practice 2006 (at paras 5.11–5.13) prefers the test of whether, as a matter of fact, the treatment of the disabled person is for a reason related to disability. It counsels service providers that some disabilities are not visible and that staff should not attempt to make fine judgments as to whether an individual is disabled or not, but rather should focus on meeting the needs of each customer. It sets out helpful (non-statutory) guidance to service providers as to the steps they should consider taking so as to comply with the DDA 1995 and to prevent their employees from discriminating against disabled customers: para 4.16. See also paras 6.17–6.18 (in the context of the duty to make reasonable adjustments).

[85]   [2004] EWCA Civ 834.

[86]   1994 Green Paper, para 4.11.

[87]   1995 White Paper, para 4.5.

reasonable practical adjustments or modifications to be made by the service provider. That leads us to a consideration of the duty to make reasonable adjustments.

5.5 DUTY TO MAKE REASONABLE ADJUSTMENTS

Introduction

5.5.1 While many incidents of indirect discrimination in relation to goods, facilities or services will be caught by the 'less favourable treatment' formula,[88] the duty to make reasonable adjustments assumes even greater importance as a means to prevent (or to require the adjustment of) unjustified practices, rules, policies, requirements or conditions which have a harsh or adverse impact upon access by disabled persons. The 1995 White Paper proposed that it would not be enough simply to prohibit discriminatory behaviour. Legislation would also require 'positive action which is reasonable and readily achievable to overcome the physical and communication barriers that impede disabled people's access'.[89] This would mean that policies, practices and procedures which discriminated against disabled persons would have to be prohibited, unless fundamental to the nature of the business. Auxiliary aids and services (such as information on tape for blind customers or induction loops in places of entertainment for individuals with hearing disabilities) would have to be provided, if this was reasonable and readily achievable. Physical barriers might also have to be removed or alternative means of access be provided.

5.5.2 Accordingly, the DDA 1995 places a duty on service providers to amend policies, procedures and practices which prevent disabled persons using a service; to remove or alter physical barriers; and to provide auxiliary aids or services.[90] The statutory duty placed upon service providers to make reasonable adjustments to allow disabled persons meaningful access to the provision of services provided to the public is the keystone to the rights of access contained in Part 3 of the Act. A breach of the duty to make reasonable adjustments is not actionable in itself and a failure to observe the duty on the part of a service provider does not give an aggrieved disabled person a common law right in tort to sue for breach of a statutory duty. Nevertheless, the duty to make reasonable adjustments is important for determining whether a service provider has discriminated against a disabled person.[91] An *unjustified* failure to comply with a s 21 duty imposed upon a service provider in relation to a disabled person is treated as amounting to discrimination against the disabled person.[92] Such a failure is potentially an *unlawful* act of discrimination if

---

[88]   DDA 1995, s 20(1). See **5.4.2**.
[89]   1995 White Paper, para 4.4.
[90]   DDA 1995, s 21.
[91]   Ibid, s 21(10).
[92]   Ibid, s 20(2); Rights of Access Code of Practice 2006, paras 6.1–6.9 and 6.37.

the failure has the effect of making it 'impossible or unreasonably difficult' for the disabled person to make use of a service which the service provider provides (or is prepared to provide) to the public.[93]

5.5.3 The Rights of Access Code of Practice 2006 attempts to cast light upon the meaning of this complex provision.[94] For example, the DDA 1995 does not define what is meant by 'impossible or unreasonably difficult' in the context of the effect upon the accessibility of a service to a disabled person as a result of a failure to make a reasonable adjustment.[95] Instead the Code offers some factors (such as time, inconvenience, effort, discomfort, anxiety or loss of dignity entailed in using a service) which go to the question of what would be unreasonably difficult for a disabled person to have to endure when attempting to use a service.[96] Again, the statute does not say what are 'reasonable steps' in relation to the duty of the service provider to make adjustments. Filling the gap, the Rights of Access Code 2006 borrows from the Employment Code of Practice.[97] What is a reasonable step for a service provider to have to take will vary according to the type of services being provided; the nature of the service provider and its size and resources; and the effect of the disability on the individual disabled person.[98] Other factors which may be relevant include the effectiveness of the steps; their practicability; financial and other costs;[99] disruption to the service provider's business; the extent of the

---

[93]   DDA 1995, s 19(1)(b). The Act assumes that an action for a breach of the duty to make reasonable adjustments will be brought under the bespoke provision in s 19(1)(b). However, there seems to be no reason of statutory construction (reading ss 19(1), 20(2), (9) and 21 together) why such an action could not be brought within the other causes of action set out in s 19(1) (and where the threshold for action may not be so high). Similarly, it might be possible to pursue the breach via ss 19(1)(b) and 20(1) ('less favourable treatment' discrimination).

[94]   Rights of Access Code of Practice 2002, Chapters 6–7.

[95]   The former DRC recommended that the DDA 1995 should be amended to require adjustments either where they would enable and/or facilitate the use of a service or where a disabled customer is at a substantial disadvantage in accessing a service: DRC Legislative Review, recommendation 25.

[96]   Rights of Access Code of Practice 2002, paras 6.33–6.36 and Chapters 10 and 12 of the code. The DRTF considered that the trigger point for making a reasonable adjustment should be monitored to see whether it had been set too high: DRTF Report, recommendation 6.5. That was a matter which the Government asked the former DRC to keep under review: Government Response to DRTF Report, para 3.73. The DRC recommended that, rather than requiring reasonable adjustments where it is impossible or unreasonably difficult to access a service, the DDA 1995 should be altered to require these either where they would enable and facilitate the use of a service or where a disabled customer is at a substantial disadvantage in accessing a service: DRC Legislative Review, recommendation 25.

[97]   Employment and Occupation Code of Practice (2004), paras 5.24–5.42. There is a noticeable and important difference here, however, in that the Employment Code builds upon the factors identified in s 18B(1) in Part 2 of the DDA 1995 as being within the scope of the reasonable steps inquiry for the purposes of the employment-related duty to make adjustments. Part 3 contains no such statutory factors and so the Rights of Access Code 2006 strictly speaking is filling a vacuum.

[98]   Rights of Access Code of Practice 2006, paras 6.24–6.25.

[99]   The DDA 1995 allows for a future possibility that a service provider would not be

service provider's financial and other resources (including any resources already expended on adjustments); and the availability of financial or other assistance.[100] A service provider with substantial financial resources may be expected to take greater steps than a service provider with fewer resources. On the other hand, steps need not be taken if they would fundamentally alter the nature of the service in question or which would alter the nature of the trade, profession or business that the service provider runs or owns.[101]

5.5.4 Moreover, the Rights of Access Code of Practice 2006 describes the duty to make reasonable adjustments as one arising in relation to disabled people at large.[102] It counsels service providers to anticipate the requirements of disabled users of its services for reasonable adjustments to be made to the way in which its services are provided.[103] Section 21 of the DDA 1995 thus contains an anticipatory duty which is owed to disabled people at large, but the breach of which gives rise to a potential individual cause of action.[104] The duty is also a continuing and evolving one.[105] What may be a reasonable adjustment today may cease to be so in the future, especially as technological development gathers pace.

Practices, policies or procedures

5.5.5 The first aspect of the duty to make reasonable adjustments arises where a service provider has a 'practice, policy or procedure' which makes it 'impossible or unreasonably difficult' for disabled persons to make use of goods, facilities or services which the service provider provides or is prepared to provide to other members of the public.[106] In such a case, it is the duty of the service provider 'to take such steps as it is reasonable, in all

---

required to take any steps incurring expenditure exceeding a prescribed maximum sum: s 21(7). Any prescribed maximum might be calculated by reference to criteria set out in s 21(8) and the regulations may provide for expenditure incurred by one service provider to be treated as incurred by another: s 21(9). There is no present intention to use this power.

[100] Rights of Access Code of Practice 2006, para 6.25 (and example) and paras 6.26–6.27. The DRTF approved of these factors but recommended that they should be set out in legislation: DRTF Report, recommendation 6.2. The Government referred this question to the then DRC: Government Response to DRTF Report, para 3.73. The former DRC agreed with the DRTF: DRC Legislative Review, recommendation 32.

[101] DDA 1995, s 21(6); Rights of Access Code of Practice 2006, paras 10.39–10.40.

[102] Rights of Access Code of Practice 2006, para 6.14–6.15. See *Ross v Ryanair Ltd and Stansted Airport Ltd* [2004] EWCA Civ 1751, discussed at **8.5.2**.

[103] Ibid, paras 6.16 and 6.19–6.21.

[104] The description of the duty in s 21 speaks of its effect upon 'disabled persons' (in the plural), whereas ss 19(1)(b) and 20(2) – in defining what is unlawful discrimination – addresses 'the disabled person' (in the singular).

[105] Rights of Access Code of Practice 2006, paras 6.22–6.23. The DRTF approved of these principles, but recommended that they should be expressed in legislation in clearer terms: DRTF Report, recommendation 6.4. The Government asked the then DRC to look at this question: Government Response to DRTF Report, para 3.73. The former DRC agreed with the DRTF approach: DRC Legislative Review, recommendation 32.

[106] DDA 1995, s 21(1).

the circumstances of the case',[107] for the service provider to have to take 'in order to change' the policy, practice or procedure in question so that 'it no longer has' the effect described (that is, making it impossible or unreasonably difficult for disabled persons to access the goods, facilities or services in point).[108] This may simply involve waiving a practice, or amending or abandoning a particular policy (such as a dress code in a restaurant or a requirement of a driving licence as proof of identification) which creates difficulty for people with certain kinds of disabilities.[109]

5.5.6   The DDA 1995 provides no further guidance or interpretation as to the meaning of the s 21(1) duty or its component parts. Neither the 1994 Green Paper nor the 1995 White Paper cast further light on this duty. The parliamentary debates on the draft legislation are also unhelpful. The Code of Practice is a little bit more expansive.[110] However, the wording of the subsection is relatively unambiguous and the duty to make reasonable adjustments set out there is not likely to give rise to many disputes of legal interpretation. One obvious example that is caught by this duty is the policy or practice of shops or places of entertainment which exclude access to dogs accompanied by their owners. Such a policy or practice will need to be revisited and exception made (as was often the voluntary position previously) for service animals accompanied by a disabled person.[111] Similarly, cinemas or restaurants which refuse or limit access to wheelchair users have to rethink this practice.[112]

Physical features

5.5.7   The 1994 Green Paper referred to the fact that disabled persons cannot take access to non-domestic buildings for granted and pointed out that high steps, narrow doorways, and absence of lift access and aids to communication constituted typical physical barriers.[113] Accordingly, the second aspect of the duty to make reasonable adjustments applies where a physical feature makes it impossible or unreasonably difficult for disabled persons to make use of goods, facilities or services which a service provider provides or is prepared to provide to other members of the public.[114] Where a physical feature of this kind has the effect described,

---

[107]   See Rights of Access Code of Practice 2006, paras 7.7–7.9.

[108]   Regulations may make provision as to the circumstances in which it is reasonable (or not reasonable) for a service provider to have to take steps of a prescribed description (s 21(5)(a)–(b)). Moreover, such regulations may prescribe what is to be included or not included within the meaning of a 'practice, policy or procedure' (s 21(5)(c)–(d)). No such regulations have been made at the time of writing.

[109]   Rights of Access Code of Practice 2006, para 7.9 (and examples).

[110]   Ibid, paras 7.7–7.11.

[111]   Rights of Access Code of Practice 2002, para 6.22 (example).

[112]   Thus, there is an obvious overlap with the duty to provide auxiliary aids and services which arises under DDA 1995, s 21(4).

[113]   1994 Green Paper, para 3.3.

[114]   DDA 1995, s 21(2); Rights of Access Code of Practice 2006, para 7.32.

then there is a duty upon the service provider 'to take such steps as it is reasonable,[115] in all the circumstances of the case', for the service provider to have to take in order:

- to remove the feature;[116]

- to alter it so that it no longer has that effect;[117]

- to provide a reasonable means of avoiding the feature;[118]

- to provide a reasonable alternative method of making the service in question available to disabled persons.[119]

While the last of these aspects of this particular duty was brought into force on 1 October 1999, the remaining aspects of the duties in respect of physical features came into force on 1 October 2004.[120]

5.5.8 The 2002 revision of the Code of Practice was designed to assist service providers to prepare for the 2004 duties during the transitional period.[121] Now what a service provider did during that transitional period may be a relevant consideration for a court to take into account when judging whether a service provider has taken reasonable steps in relation to its duty after 1 October 2004.[122] The 2002 Code of Practice made the business case for planning and implementing changes to physical features

---

[115] Regulations have been made under DDA 1995, s 21(5)(a)–(b) prescribing particular circumstances for the purposes of s 21 in which it is or is not reasonable for a service provider to have to take certain steps in relation to premises occupied under a lease or other binding obligation: Disability Discrimination (Providers of Services) (Adjustment of Premises) Regulations 2001, SI 2001/3253, as amended by SI 2004/1429 and SI 2005/1121. See also Rights of Access Code of Practice 2006, Appendix B, paras 30–51, and the extended discussion in Chapter 6.

[116] DDA 1995, s 21(2)(a) (in force from 1 October 2004).

[117] Ibid, s 21(2)(b) (in force from 1 October 2004).

[118] Ibid, s 21(2)(c) (in force from 1 October 2004). Regulations yet to be enacted may prescribe matters which are to be taken into account in determining whether the providing of means to avoid a physical feature is 'reasonable' (s 21(3)(a)).

[119] DDA 1995, s 21(2)(d), in force since 1 October 1999. Regulations may prescribe matters which are to be taken into account in determining whether the providing of an alternative method of making the service available to disabled persons is 'reasonable' (s 21(3)(a)). When this subsection was brought into force in 1999, no such prescriptive regulations were made in support.

[120] SI 2001/2030 (England, Wales and Scotland) and SR 2001/439 (Northern Ireland). See **5.1.2**.

[121] Rights of Access Code of Practice 2002, para 5.33. Note that DDA 1995, s 27 and Sch 4, Part II and the Disability Discrimination (Providers of Services) (Adjustment of Premises) Regulations 2001, SI 2001/3253, as amended make special provision where a service provider occupies its premises under lease. Where the lease or the lessor prevents or hinders the occupier in making adjustments to the premises so as to comply with a s 21 duty, these provisions will modify the effect of the lease and place duties upon the lessor. See also Rights of Access Code of Practice 2006, Appendix B, paras 30–51 and the extended discussion in Chapter 6.

[122] Rights of Access Code of Practice 2002, para 5.34 (and example).

prior to 1 October 2004.[123] It also encouraged service providers to carry out an access audit of their premises and to draw up an access plan or strategy.[124]

5.5.9   By way of example in the statute itself, a 'physical feature' refers to a feature 'arising from the design or construction of a building or the approach or access to premises'.[125] However, regulations go further and for this purpose physical features include:[126]

- any feature arising from the design or construction of a building on the premises occupied by the service provider;

- any feature on those premises or any approach to, exit from or access to such a building;

- any fixtures, fittings, furnishings, furniture, equipment or materials in or on such premises;

- any fixtures, fittings, furnishings, furniture, equipment or materials brought onto premises (other than those occupied by the service provider) by or on behalf of the service provider in the course of (and for the purpose of) providing services to the public or to a section of the public;

- any other physical element or quality of land comprised in the premises occupied by the service provider.

All these features which are within the boundaries of a service provider's premises are covered, whether temporary or permanent, inside or outside.[127] A building means an erection or structure of any kind.[128]

5.5.10   It is worth noting that s 21(2) of the DDA 1995 leaves to the service provider the choice of steps to be taken to overcome the adverse

---

[123]   Rights of Access Code of Practice 2002, paras 5.33–5.35.

[124]   Ibid, paras 5.42–5.43. See now Rights of Access Code of Practice 2006, paras 7.41–7.42.

[125]   DDA 1995, s 21(2).

[126]   Disability Discrimination (Service Providers and Public Authorities Carrying Out Functions) Regulations 2005, SI 2005/2901, reg 9.

[127]   Rights of Access Code of Practice 2006, para 7.44. The Code of Practice illustrates physical features as including steps, stairways, kerbs, exterior surfaces and paving, parking areas, building entrances and exits (including emergency escape routes), internal and external doors, gates, toilet and washing facilities, public facilities (such as telephones, counters or service desks), lighting and ventilation, lifts and escalators, floor coverings, signs, furniture, and temporary or movable items (such as equipment and display racks): ibid, para 7.45. This is not an exhaustive list. Physical features also include the sheer scale of a premises (such as the size of an airport).

[128]   Disability Discrimination (Service Providers and Public Authorities Carrying Out Functions) Regulations 2005, SI 2005/2901, reg 2(1); Rights of Access Code of Practice 2006, para 7.44.

effects of a physical feature.[129] The duty itself might not be triggered at all if another reasonable adjustment has ensured that the physical feature does not make it impossible or unreasonably difficult for disabled persons to use the service.[130] The subsection does not require the service provider to remove or alter the physical feature as a priority and does not require a hierarchical approach to adjustments to physical features. Thus, somewhat controversially, the effect of this provision is not wholly integrationist or inclusive. Although the Code of Practice encourages service providers to adopt an inclusive approach,[131] the Act appears to permit (but does not require) a 'separate but equal' or segregated approach to the provision of services to disabled persons. For example, if access to a museum is by a front entrance which could not be made accessible to wheelchair users without rebuilding or physical alteration, it might be reasonable for the museum trustees to provide a wheelchair-accessible entrance at the side or back of the building. However, such alternative means of access to the building might not be reasonable where the disabled visitor has to negotiate rubbish bins or other detritus in the process.[132] In such a case, physical alterations to the main entrance might be the only reasonable solution.

5.5.11 Regulations may exempt categories of service providers from the duty to make reasonable adjustments in respect of physical features only.[133] This power of exemption has not been used to date. If it was to be used in the future, then it is likely that it would be used to safeguard limited groups of service providers – such as occupiers of listed buildings[134] – who might otherwise be faced with a disproportionately heavy burden under s 21(2) of the DDA 1995 or for whom it would not be possible or sensible to make physical alterations.[135] Regulations make provision for the interplay between the building regulations, disability access standards for buildings and any duty to make an adjustment to the physical features of premises occupied by a service provider.[136]

---

[129] Rights of Access Code of Practice 2006, paras 7.34–7.35 (and example).

[130] Ibid, paras 7.34–7.35.

[131] Rights of Access Code of Practice 2006, paras 7.36–7.40. The former DRC recommended that the DDA 1995 should require that when service providers make reasonable adjustments to their premises they must first consider removing or altering physical barriers, and only if this is not possible consider providing the service by an alternative means: DRC Legislative Review, recommendation 24.

[132] HL Deb, vol 564, cols 2022–2023. Rights of Access Code of Practice 2006, paras 7.39 and 7.50–7.51 stress the dignity of disabled persons as a relevant consideration.

[133] DDA 1995, s 21(3)(b).

[134] Who might be generally protected, in any event, by DDA 1995, s 59 (acts done in compliance with existing enactments, such as listed buildings regulations). That said, there is no general exemption for listed buildings from the application of the s 21 duties: HL Deb, vol 564, cols 2021–2024.

[135] HC Deb Standing Committee E, cols 358–359.

[136] Disability Discrimination (Providers of Services) (Adjustment of Premises) Regulations 2001, SI 2001/3253, reg 9 as amended; Disability Discrimination (Service Providers and Public Authorities Carrying Out Functions) Regulations 2005, SI 2005/2901. See also Rights of Access Code of Practice 2006, Appendix B, and the extended discussion in Chapter 6.

5.5.12   This aspect of the duty to make reasonable adjustments calls for some imagination from service providers.[137] For example, a supermarket might reasonably consider whether the aisles between shelves or between the check-out tills are sufficiently wide to accommodate wheelchair users. A restaurant might consider how its seating arrangements are designed, while an art gallery might reconsider the height at which exhibits are hung, in both cases so as to accommodate diners or art lovers who are wheelchair users. Signage in public buildings is also counted as a physical feature and is often poorly designed or sited, without the needs of disabled persons in mind. The height and design of points of sale or service in stores, banks or post offices also frequently cause physical barriers between disabled customers and sales assistants. Lighting and ventilation in buildings is also regarded as a 'physical feature', so that the needs of persons with vision or respiratory impairments might call for reasonable adjustments to be made in these areas. Often very little effort or modification is required to remove or ameliorate the ill effects of physical barriers. Installing simple ramps or repositioning fixtures and fittings can often make a lot of difference for little or no expense. Other alterations might involve some cost, but with attendant benefits for all, as well as increased custom for the service provider. These might include widening entrance doors or installing two-way door hinges to assist wheelchair users, creating designated parking spaces for disabled customers or removing high pile, low density carpeting to aid the mobility of customers using a prosthesis or walking aid.

Auxiliary aids and services

5.5.13   Where an 'auxiliary aid or service' would enable disabled persons to make use of a service which a service provider provides (or is prepared to provide) to members of the public, it is the duty of the service provider to take such steps as it is reasonable, in all the circumstances of the case, for the service provider to have to take in order to provide the auxiliary aid or service in question.[138] Where an 'auxiliary aid or service' would facilitate the use by disabled persons of such a service, the duty also arises.[139] In either case, a failure to comply with the duty is an act of unlawful discrimination if its effect is to make it impossible or unreasonably difficult for the disabled person to make use of any goods, facilities or services.[140]

---

[137] See the guidance and examples given in Rights of Access Code of Practice 2006, paras 7.47–7.51.

[138] DDA 1995, s 21(4)(a). Note how the trigger for this duty differs from the duties in s 21(1) and (2).

[139] Ibid, s 21(4)(b). See *Ross v Ryanair Ltd and Stansted Airport Ltd* [2004] EWCA Civ 1751, discussed at **8.5.2**.

[140] Ibid, s 19(1)(b). In principle, the duty to provide auxiliary aids or services could be the subject of an expenditure cap formulated by regulations: s 21(7)–(9). No such cap has been introduced.

5.5.14   The term 'auxiliary aid or service' is exemplified by reference to the provision of information on audio tape or the provision of a sign language interpreter.[141] Further illustrations include the provision of induction loops in theatres or cinemas, large print point of sale literature in shops or audio-visual telephones in hotel rooms for individuals with sensory impairments. However, in many cases, an auxiliary aid or service might amount to no more than the allocating of a particular member of staff to provide requested assistance to a disabled customer. For example, a blind customer in a self-service store might reasonably request that a store assistant should locate a particular item for purchase or should read out loud the description of goods from any product packaging. A training company organising a seminar for the legal profession would have to take reasonable steps to accommodate the known needs of disabled delegates attending the seminar (such as by providing a sign interpreter or a temporary induction loop system). It would need to choose the seminar location in a hotel or conference centre that was reasonably physically accessible for delegates with mobility disabilities.[142]

5.5.15   Until the balance of the duties in relation to reasonable adjustments and physical features came into force on 1 October 2004,[143] regulations provided that devices, structures or equipment – the installation, operation or maintenance of which would necessitate making a permanent alteration to (or which would have a permanent effect on) the physical fabric of premises, fixtures, fittings, furnishings, furniture, equipment or materials – were not to be treated as auxiliary aids or services.[144] The effect was that until 1 October 2004 service providers were not required to do (but were not prevented from doing) anything that would involve a permanent alteration to the physical fabric of premises (as broadly defined in the regulations) when providing an auxiliary aid.[145]

5.6   JUSTIFICATION

5.6.1   A provider of services discriminates against a disabled person in a case of disability-related less favourable treatment discrimination if it cannot show that the 'treatment in question is justified'.[146] Similarly, a service provider also discriminates against a disabled person in a case where it fails to comply with a duty to make reasonable adjustments in relation to the disabled person if it cannot show that the 'failure to

---

[141]   DDA 1995, s 21(4). Future regulations may provide as to things which are to be treated, or which are not to be treated, as auxiliary aids or services: s 21(5)(g)–(h).

[142]   See the general advice and the further illustrations given in Rights of Access Code of Practice 2006, paras 7.12–7.31.

[143]   DDA 1995, s 21(2)(a)–(c).

[144]   Disability Discrimination (Services and Premises) Regulations 1999, SI 1999/1191, reg 4.

[145]   But see the positive advice on good practice given by Rights of Access Code of Practice 2002, para 5.15.

[146]   DDA 1995, s 20(1)(b); Rights of Access Code of Practice 2006, para 8.6.

comply with that duty is justified'.[147] The discriminatory treatment of a disabled person (or a failure to comply with a duty to make reasonable adjustments[148]) will be justified only if, in the service provider's opinion, one or more statutory conditions are satisfied[149] and it is reasonable in all the circumstances of the case for the service provider to hold that opinion.[150]

5.6.2 This justification defence is a novel one.[151] First, discrimination law in the fields of sex, race and equal pay (and fair employment in Northern Ireland) does not contain an explicit justification defence to direct discrimination (as opposed to indirect discrimination). Secondly, it might be argued that a justification defence is implicit in the principle of direct discrimination, in the sense that a defendant can always seek to show that the less favourable treatment complained of was not based upon the protected characteristic of the claimant. However, the justification defence is truly relevant only when the protected characteristic of the claimant has played a part in the resultant discrimination, but there are factors or criteria present which nevertheless excuse what would be otherwise discriminatory treatment, impacts or effects. Under the DDA 1995, justification is relevant where a disabled person has been treated less favourably 'for a reason which relates to the disabled person's disability'.[152] In other words, a service provider may be allowed to justify discrimination in circumstances where the less favourable treatment has been informed by the complainant's disability. Thirdly, in existing discrimination legislation, the justification defence in indirect discrimination is the subject of an objective test (albeit one of variable quality in the decided cases). Part 3 of the DDA 1995 bucks that trend.

5.6.3 The justification defence also differs significantly from the parallel defence in Part 2 of the DDA 1995 (the employment provisions). The Government's view was that 'service providers often have to take very quick and perhaps less informed decisions when serving someone [so that] an opinion-based approach remains appropriate'.[153] Unlike the employment provisions in Part 2 of the Act,[154] there is no suggestion that, in

---

[147] DDA 1995, s 20(2)(b); Rights of Access Code of Practice 2006, paras 8.7–8.12.

[148] Ibid, s 20(9) states that in s 20(3), (4) and (8) 'treatment' includes a failure to comply with a s 21 duty.

[149] Ibid, s 20(3)(a).

[150] Ibid, s 20(3)(b).

[151] The DRTF recommended that the justification defence should be removed in the case of discrimination based upon a failure to comply with a duty to make reasonable adjustments and that the service provider should be able to rely only upon a set of expanded factors in the assessment of what is a 'reasonable' adjustment: DRTF Report, recommendation 6.7. The Government referred this question to the then DRC: Government Response to DRTF Report, para 3.73. The former DRC agreed with the DRTF: DRC Legislative Review, recommendation 31.

[152] DDA 1995, s 20(1)(a).

[153] HL Deb, vol 566, col 119.

[154] DDA 1995, s 3A(6).

cases of less favourable treatment discrimination, a service provider cannot justify the treatment if a reasonable adjustment would have made a difference.[155] The Part 3 defence also exhaustively identifies the key reasons that might justify less favourable treatment of a disabled person by a service provider, whereas the defence is at large under Part 2.

Subjective opinion and objective reasonableness

5.6.4   The justification defence in Part 3 of the DDA 1995 is based upon a mixture of a subjective test and an objective test. While an opinion-based approach has been seen as appropriate, 'the proper degree of objectivity is imposed because the opinion must be shown to be reasonably held'.[156] The dual subjective–objective nature of the defence has also been recognised judicially.[157] The Rights of Access Code of Practice 2006 also emphasises this point, acknowledging that a service provider does not have to be an expert on disability, but is expected to take account of all the circumstances.[158]

5.6.5   The burden of proof is on the service provider. The service provider must be able to show that, *at the time of* the act of alleged discrimination, it actually held the opinion that one of the statutory conditions for the operation of the defence was satisfied (a subjective test). The language and tense used in the statutory provision[159] make it clear that it is the service provider's opinion at the time of the discriminatory treatment that matters. An ex post facto rationalisation of events will not be sufficient or permissible.[160] In practice, the subjective test of opinion will not be difficult to pass. However, it must also be shown that it is reasonable, in all the circumstances of the case, for the service provider to hold that opinion (an objective test).[161] Again, the test

---

[155]   In earlier editions of this book, the author attempted to suggest otherwise, but has since recanted that view. The Rights of Access Code of Practice 2006 is largely silent on this point (but see paras 8.18, 8.22, 10.40, 10.45 and 10.48 , on good practice).

[156]   HL Deb, vol 566, col 119.

[157]   *Rose v Bouchet* [1999] IRLR 463 (Sheriff Principal Nicholson QC), a case under the similar provisions in DDA 1995, s 24 (the justification defence for discrimination in the disposal or management of premises). The court did not think that assistance could be summoned from cases under Part 2 (the employment provisions).

[158]   Rights of Access Code of Practice 2006, para 8.13. The circumstances will include the available information, whether it was possible to seek advice, and whether the disabled person's input was sought and taken account of. However, the need to seek further information or make further inquiry will vary with the circumstances, and it might be reasonable to expect the disabled person to volunteer further information: *Rose v Bouchet* (above).

[159]   DDA 1995, s 20(3)(a).

[160]   This is confirmed in *Rose v Bouchet* (above). See also Rights of Access Code of Practice 2006, paras 8.13–8.15.

[161]   In *White v Clitheroe Royal Grammar School* (2002) Preston County Court (District Judge Ashton) reported in *Equal Opportunities Review No 106* (June 2002) 26–28, the court found that a student with diabetes was discriminated against contrary to DDA 1995, Part 3 when excluded from a school holiday for a reason connected with his disability and in circumstances where the school had failed to check the assumptions

of the reasonableness of the service provider's subjectively held opinion should be judged in the light of the circumstances known at the time of the discriminatory act.[162] The concept of reasonableness is one that tribunals and courts are very experienced in applying. However, it will not be the reasonableness of the opinion itself that matters. Rather the question is whether it was reasonable of the particular service provider to hold that opinion in the particular circumstances of the case and in respect of the particular disabled person who is the subject of the less favourable treatment (or failure to comply with a s 21 duty).[163]

Conditions for justification defence

5.6.6 The conditions, one or more of which (in the service provider's reasonably held opinion) must be satisfied for the operation of the statutory defence of justification, are set out exhaustively in the statute.[164] Some of these conditions apply generally, but some apply only in the context of particular forms of discrimination in relation to goods, facilities or services. The DDA 1995 contemplates five conditions or circumstances in which the justification defence might be operable.[165]

Health and safety

5.6.7 First, in any case, disability discrimination might be justified where the less favourable treatment (or failure to comply with a duty to make reasonable adjustments) is 'necessary' (not merely reasonably necessary) in order not to endanger the health or safety of any person.[166] This may include endangerment to the health or safety of the disabled person who is alleging discriminatory treatment. For example, a local authority recreation centre could be justified in refusing the use of its

---

upon which the exclusion had been made, did not consult with the pupil or his parents, and carried out no risk assessment involving the holiday provider and the pupil's medical advisers.

[162] DDA 1995, s 20(3)(b).

[163] The wording of DDA 1995, s 20(3)(b) does not appear to admit a test of reasonableness based upon what a reasonable service provider faced with similar circumstances might have opined, although undoubtedly that will be a useful starting point.

[164] DDA 1995, s 20(4).

[165] The DRTF was generally content with the limited categories of justification available in Part 3 of the DDA 1995. It recommended that there should be better guidance to service providers on the appropriate use of the 'health and safety' and 'greater cost' justifications, and that the operation of the justification defence should be monitored: DRTF Report, recommendation 6.6. In its response, the Government recognised that in producing the 2002 version of the Code of Practice the DRC had already provided fuller guidance on the justifications (including those relating to health and safety and greater expense), but asked the DRC to review other guidance in the light of its monitoring of the justifications and developing case-law: Government Response to DRTF Report, para 3.75. The former DRC invited comments upon this issue: DRC Legislative Review, recommendation 26. See now: Rights of Access Code of Practice 2006, Chapter 8.

[166] DDA 1995, s 20(4)(a). See *White v Clitheroe Royal Grammar School* (2002) Preston County Court (District Judge Ashton) reported in *Equal Opportunities Review No 106* (June 2002) 26–28 and referred to above.

indoor climbing wall to a person with orthopaedic impairment, or in excluding a wheelchair user from its basketball league, on the ground of a risk to the health and safety of the individual or other participants. A swimming instructor might be justified in excluding a disabled person from a beginners' swimming class if, by having to focus most attention on the disabled learner, the safety of other members of the class would be put at risk.[167] It remains to be seen how narrowly this defence of justification will be interpreted and applied in practice. Health or safety risk is often relied upon by service providers as a blanket reason for excluding disabled persons from places of refreshment or entertainment (such as cinemas, theatres and restaurants). Inappropriate or unsupported reference is also frequently made to the requirements of fire regulations.[168] The use of the word 'necessary' calls for individual justification on the facts where a service provider seeks to rely upon health and safety as the grounds for compromising the civil rights of disabled persons.

Incapacity to contract

5.6.8 Secondly, in any case, the less favourable treatment of a disabled person (or failure to comply with a duty to make reasonable adjustments) can be justified if the disabled person is incapable of entering into an enforceable agreement, or of giving an informed consent, and for that reason the treatment (or failure) is reasonable in that case.[169] This provision generated some concern on behalf of persons with mental disabilities who, it was feared, might suffer discrimination in the provision of services on the basis of a service provider's perception that they lacked full legal capacity to make a contract. The Government's view was that:

> 'If a service provider has a reasonably held belief that a contract with a disabled customer might be invalid, he must be allowed, under this measure, to refuse to enter into an agreement until it is reasonably clear that it would be enforceable, without the fear of being accused of discrimination.'[170]

That would allow a service provider to refuse to sell goods to, or to enter into a consumer credit agreement with, a disabled person if it holds a reasonably held opinion that the customer lacks or might lack legal capacity (whether by virtue of age or mental incapacity). The test here is whether it is reasonable to discriminate within the particular

---

[167] HL Deb, vol 566, col 1025. See the further examples in Rights of Access Code of Practice 2006, paras 8.16–8.18. The revised Code of Practice stresses that health or safety reasons which are based on stereotypes or generalisations will provide no defence. Any action taken in relation to health and safety must be proportionate to the risk. Disabled persons are entitled to take risks within the same limits as other people.

[168] Rights of Access Code of Practice 2006, para 8.17. Restrictions produced by genuine requirements of local fire regulations will excuse otherwise discriminatory treatment by virtue of s 59 (actions done in pursuance of a statutory authority).

[169] DDA 1995, s 20(4)(b); Rights of Access Code of Practice 2002, paras 8.19–8.22.

[170] HC Deb Standing Committee E, col 349.

circumstances of the case.[171] The Government believed that this justification would only apply when the purchase of a product or service would normally be the subject of a written agreement or contract formality. It would thus apply in only a few cases (such as motor car hire purchase or consumer credit agreements).[172]

5.6.9 Regulations have been made to disapply this provision where another person is acting for the disabled person under an enduring power of attorney[173] or where, in Scotland, a guardian, tutor or judicial factor has been appointed in relation to the disabled person's property or affairs.[174]

Providing the service

5.6.10 Thirdly, where disability discrimination takes the form of a refusal (or deliberate omission) to provide to a disabled person any goods, facilities or services provided to members of the public,[175] such less favourable treatment (or failure to comply with a duty to make reasonable adjustments) might be justified if it is 'necessary' (not merely reasonably necessary) because the service provider would otherwise be unable to provide the goods, facilities or services to members of the public.[176] The 1995 White Paper gave as an example that it would no longer be possible to bar disabled persons from places of entertainment, but a coach training champion athletes would still be able to exclude the majority of the population from coaching classes.[177] The Government believed that it had introduced a strict test for the application of this defence and that it would apply 'only in circumstances in which, if a service provider were to serve a particular disabled person, he would not be able to continue to provide his service at all'.[178] However, the preferences of other customers are not a justification for discrimination.[179]

---

[171] HC Deb, vol 257, col 893.

[172] Ibid, col 350. It remains to be seen whether such cases are few (but what of contracts for holidays, which are typically made on written standard form conditions, for example, or car rental agreements?). It was doubted whether it would be reasonable for a shopkeeper to rely upon this exception when someone is buying a newspaper or confectionery (as opposed to a luxury car).

[173] Or functions conferred by or under Mental Capacity Act 2005.

[174] DDA 1995, s 20(7), as amended by DDA 2005 and Mental Capacity Act 2005; Disability Discrimination (Service Providers and Public Authorities Carrying Out Functions) Regulations 2005, SI 2005/2901, reg 3; Rights of Access Code of Practice 2006, para 8.21.

[175] Under DDA 1995, s 19(1)(a).

[176] DDA 1995, s 20(4)(c); Rights of Access Code of Practice 2006, paras 10.43–10.45.

[177] 1995 White Paper, para 4.4, and see the examples in Rights of Access Code of Practice 2006, paras 10.43–10.45.

[178] HC Deb Standing Committee E, col 354. The Minister could not think of a meaningful example of when this provision would be applicable and his opinion was that it would only apply in extreme and rare circumstances.

[179] Rights of Access Code of Practice 2006, para 10.44.

Standard of service

5.6.11 Fourthly, in a case where the discriminatory treatment (or failure to comply with a duty to make reasonable adjustments) arises in the standard of service provided to disabled persons, or the manner in which or terms on which the service provider provides goods, facilities or services to disabled persons,[180] that treatment may be justified if it is 'necessary' (not merely reasonably necessary) in order for the service provider to be able to provide the service to the disabled person or to other members of the public.[181] This is clearly linked to the third condition above and is likely to apply in exactly the same way, if at all. By way of illustration, a cinema which reserves seats at the end of rows for persons with mobility disabilities might rely upon this provision to justify what might amount to a differential standard or manner or service. Without making such arrangements, the cinema might argue that it could not admit such a disabled person at all without infringing fire regulations or otherwise causing greater inconvenience to other customers. Similarly, a museum which provides a daily guided tour of its exhibits might be justified in rostering a guide with sign language skills to assist deaf visitors on specified days of the week only.[182]

Greater cost

5.6.12 Fifthly, if the service provider has discriminated in the terms on which goods, facilities or services are provided to a disabled person,[183] that discrimination is capable of being justified where the difference in such terms as between that disabled person and other members of the public 'reflects the greater cost' to the service provider in providing the goods, facilities or services to the disabled person.[184] The Government indicated that this measure is aimed at small businesses, in particular, and gave as an example a shoe maker asked to make a shoe for a disabled person to an unusual design or in an unusual fabric.[185] If that task would involve greater labour or special equipment and materials, it might be reasonable for the shoe maker to charge the disabled customer a premium to reflect that.

5.6.13 Taken literally, however, this last condition might be thought to justify a hotelier charging a disabled person a room supplement for providing him or her with a room adapted to take a wheelchair or with an audio-visual fire alarm. It might also be taken to justify a service provider charging blind customers for the additional cost of providing Braille or tape formats of sales literature and so on. Nevertheless, a service provider

---

[180] Under DDA 1995, s 19(1)(c)–(d).

[181] Ibid, s 20(4)(d); Rights of Access Code of Practice 2006, paras 10.46–10.48.

[182] See the further examples in Rights of Access Code of Practice 2006, paras 10.46–10.48.

[183] Under DDA 1995, s 19(1)(d).

[184] Ibid, s 20(4)(e); Rights of Access Code of Practice 2006, paras 10.49–10.50.

[185] HC Deb Standing Committee E, col 357; HL Deb, vol 564, col 2009.

who attempts to pass on the costs of compliance with the DDA 1995 to disabled persons (as opposed to spreading those costs across all customers or clients) would not be facilitated in doing so by this provision.[186] The DDA 1995 does not permit surcharges upon disabled persons for extra expenses or opportunity costs incurred by service providers in complying with the legislation. Moreover, the Act explicitly provides that any increase in the cost of providing services to a disabled person, resulting from the service provider's compliance with the statutory duty to make reasonable adjustments, is to be disregarded for the purposes of the 'greater cost' justification.[187] A service provider is not able to pass the costs of complying with its duties under the DDA 1995 directly to a disabled customer.[188]

Insurance services

5.6.14   The DDA 1995 contemplates that regulations might be made so as to provide for other circumstances in which less favourable treatment of a disabled person for a reason relating to disability could be deemed to be justified.[189] Regulations address the circumstances where, for a reason which relates to a disabled person's disability, a provider of insurance services (in connection with an insurance business carried on by it) has treated a disabled person less favourably than it treats or would treat others to whom that reason does not or would not apply.[190] Insurance business means business which consists of effecting or carrying out contracts of insurance.[191] The treatment is to be taken as justified if it is based upon information which is relevant to the assessment of the risk to be insured and if it is reasonable having regard to the information relied upon and any other relevant factors.[192] The information, which might include actuarial or statistical data or a medical report, must be from a source upon which it is reasonable to rely.[193] This recognises that insurers may need to distinguish between individuals on the basis of the risks against which they seek to insure. The burden of proof will be upon the insurer to show that there was an additional risk associated with the disabled person which arises from his or her disability.[194]

---

[186]   HC Deb Standing Committee E, col 357.

[187]   DDA 1995, s 20(5); Rights of Access Code of Practice 2006, paras 6.31–6.32 and 10.50.

[188]   HL Deb, vol 564, cols 2009–2010; ibid, vol 566, col 119.

[189]   DDA 1995, s 20(8).

[190]   Disability Discrimination (Service Providers and Public Authorities Carrying Out Functions) Regulations 2005, SI 2005/2901, regs 2 and 4–6. See generally Rights of Access Code of Practice 2006, paras 9.2–9.8. The DRTF recommended that the special treatment of insurance services should continue: DRTF Report, recommendation 6.19.

[191]   Disability Discrimination (Service Providers and Public Authorities Carrying Out Functions) Regulations 2005, SI 2005/2901, reg 2(1). The definition is to be read with Financial Services and Markets Act 2000, s 22, any relevant order under that section and Sch 2 to that Act: ibid, reg 2(2).

[192]   Ibid, reg 4(2).

[193]   Ibid, reg 4(2).

[194]   The Regulations make special provision for insurance policies that came into existence before 2 December 1996: ibid, reg 5. The less favourable treatment of a disabled person

Guarantees

5.6.15 Regulations also deal with guarantees where, for a reason which relates to a disabled person's disability, a service provider treats that person less favourably in respect of a guarantee than it treats or would treat others to whom that reason does not or would not apply.[195] The guarantee, whether legally enforceable or not, must have been provided by the service provider. It must guarantee that the purchase price of services provided will be refunded if not of satisfactory quality or that services in the form of goods provided will be replaced or repaired if not of satisfactory quality.[196] The service provider must have refused to provide a replacement, repair or refund under the guarantee because damage (above the level at which the guarantee would normally be honoured) has occurred for a reason which relates to the disabled person's disability.[197] It must be reasonable in all the circumstances of the case for the service provider to refuse to provide a replacement, repair or refund under the guarantee.[198] If all these conditions are satisfied, the less favourable treatment is deemed to be automatically justified.[199] Accordingly, this provision deals with situations where a disabled person's disability results in higher than average wear or tear to goods or services supplied and where it would not be reasonable to expect service providers to honour a guarantee.[200]

Deposits

5.6.16 Regulations also deal with the question of deposits in respect of goods and facilities.[201] The circumstances in which this special provision operates are as follows. Goods or facilities have been provided to a disabled person for which that person is required to provide a deposit which is refundable if the goods or facilities are returned undamaged.[202]

---

which results from such a policy is treated as automatically justified, unless the policy fell for renewal or review on or after 4 December 2006, and the less favourable treatment occurred on or after the date when the renewal or review was due. Once renewed or reviewed, or once the date for renewal or review has passed, less favourable treatment in relation to the insurance policy falls within the usual rules concerning justification explained immediately. There are also similar provisions for cover documents and master policies: ibid, reg 6; Rights of Access Code of Practice 2006, para 9.8.

[195] Disability Discrimination (Service Providers and Public Authorities Carrying Out Functions) Regulations 2005, SI 2005/2901, reg 7; Rights of Access Code of Practice 2006, paras 9.9–9.13.

[196] Ibid, reg 7(2)(a). A guarantee includes any document which has the effect referred to in reg 7(2)(a), whether or not so described: reg 7(3).

[197] Ibid, reg 7(2)(b).

[198] Ibid, reg 7(2)(c).

[199] Ibid, reg 7(1).

[200] See generally Rights of Access Code of Practice 2006, paras 9.9–9.13.

[201] Disability Discrimination (Service Providers and Public Authorities Carrying Out Functions) Regulations 2005, SI 2005/2901, reg 8; Rights of Access Code of Practice 2006, paras 9.14–9.19.

[202] Ibid, reg 8(2)(a).

The service provider has refused to refund some or all of the deposit because damage has occurred to the goods or facilities for a reason which relates to the disabled person's disability.[203] That damage is above the level at which the provider would normally refund the deposit in full.[204] If it is reasonable in all the circumstances of the case for the service provider to refuse to repay the deposit in full,[205] then that less favourable treatment (for a reason related to disability) is deemed to be justified.[206]

5.7   EMPLOYMENT SERVICES

5.7.1   The Disability Discrimination Act 1995 (Amendment) Regulations 2003 inserted a new s 21A as part of Part 3 of the DDA 1995 in order to address disability discrimination in relation to employment services.[207] In the 1995 Act as amended, 'employment services' means vocational guidance or training. It also refers to services to assist a person to obtain or retain employment or to establish that person as self-employed.[208] It will include services provided by employment agencies, employment businesses and Jobcentre Plus.[209]

5.7.2   In relation to employment services, it is unlawful for a provider of employment services to subject to harassment a disabled person to whom the provider is providing such services or who has requested the provider to provide such services.[210] Otherwise, the provisions on discrimination in relation to goods, facilities and services in ss 19–21, already discussed above, apply to employment services.[211] However, there are some adjustments to those provisions as they apply to employment services only.

5.7.3   A bespoke s 19(1)(aa) provides that it is unlawful for a provider of employment services to discriminate against a disabled person in failing to comply with a s 21(1) duty to make reasonable adjustments (ie to practices, policies or procedures) in circumstances in which the effect of that failure is to place the disabled person at a substantial disadvantage in comparison with persons who are not disabled in relation to the provision

---

[203] Disability Discrimination (Service Providers and Public Authorities Carrying Out Functions) Regulations 2005, SI 2005/2901, reg 8(2)(b).

[204] Ibid, reg 8(2)(b).

[205] Ibid, reg 8(2)(c).

[206] Ibid, reg 8(1). See generally Rights of Access Code of Practice 2002, paras 9.14–9.19.

[207] SI 2003/1673, regs 3(1), 19(1) and in force from 1 October 2004. See generally Code of Practice: Employment and Occupation (2004), chapter 11; Rights of Access Code of Practice 2006, paras 3.29 and 20.14.

[208] DDA 1995, s 21A(1), as amended.

[209] Code of Practice: Employment and Occupation (2004), para 11.4.

[210] DDA 1995, s 21A(2). Section 3B (which defines 'harassment' in the context of the employment provisions in Part 2 of the Act) applies for this purpose. See Chapter 3. See generally Code of Practice: Employment and Occupation (2004), para 11.8 (and example).

[211] DDA 1995, s 21A(3).

of the service.[212] An amended s 19(1)(b) also applies (only for this purpose and not generally), making it unlawful for a provider of employment services to discriminate against a disabled person in failing to comply with s 21(2) or (4) duty to make reasonable adjustments (ie in relation to physical features or an auxiliary aid or service) in circumstances in which the effect of that failure is to make it impossible or unreasonably difficult for the disabled person to make use of any such service.[213]

5.7.4   In defining discrimination in this contest,[214] a bespoke s 20(1A) then provides that, for the purposes of s 19, a provider of services also discriminates against a disabled person if the provider fails to comply with a s 21(1) duty to make reasonable adjustments (ie to practices, policies or procedures) in relation to the disabled person.[215] Section 20(2)(a) is to be read as referring to the s 21(2) and (4) duties (ie in relation to physical features or an auxiliary aid or service).[216] A new s 20(3A) is then read down to provide that the treatment of a disabled person cannot be justified under s 20(3) if it amounts to direct discrimination.[217]

5.7.5   The duty to make reasonable adjustments in s 21(1) is then modified in relation to employment services only.[218] Where a provider of employment services has a practice, policy or procedure which places disabled persons at a substantial disadvantage in comparison with persons who are not disabled in relation to the provision of the service which the provider provides (or is prepared to provide) to other members of the public, it is the provider's duty to take such steps as it is reasonable, in all the circumstances of the case, for the provider to have to take in order to change that practice, policy or procedure so that it no longer has that effect.[219] A bespoke s 21(1A) then provides that a 'practice, policy or procedure' includes a provision or criterion for this purpose.[220]

---

[212] DDA 1995, s 21A(4)(a). Section 19(2) is read as including a reference to s 21A: s 21A(4)(c). See generally Code of Practice: Employment and Occupation (2004), paras 11.5–11.7 (and examples).

[213] DDA 1995, s 21A(4)(b). Section 19(2) is read as including a reference to s 21A: s 21A(4)(c).

[214] See Code of Practice: Employment and Occupation (2004), paras 11.11–11.14. Note that the provisions of the DDA 1995 on relationships that have come to an end (s 16A), discriminatory advertisements (s 16B), unlawful instructions and pressure to discriminate (s 16C) and victimisation (s 55) will apply equally to employment services. See Code of Practice: Employment and Occupation (2004), para 11.10.

[215] DDA 1995, s 21A(5)(a).

[216] Ibid, s 21A(5)(b).

[217] Ibid, s 21A(5)(c). Direct discrimination is defined in the DDA 1995, falling within s 3A(5). See Chapter 3. See Code of Practice: Employment and Occupation (2004), paras 11.20–11.22.

[218] See Code of Practice: Employment and Occupation (2004), paras 11.15–11.19 (and examples).

[219] DDA 1995, s 21A(6)(a).

[220] Ibid, s 21A(6)(b).

5.7.6 Normally, any term in a contract for the provision of goods, facilities or services (or in any other agreement) is void in so far as it purports to require a person to do anything which would contravene Part 3 or which would exclude or limit the operation of Part 3 or prevent any person from making a claim under Part 3.[221] However, that is not the case in relation to any term in a contract (or other agreement) for the provision of employment services.[222]

5.8 PRIVATE MEMBERS' CLUBS

5.8.1 As originally enacted, private members' clubs were not covered by Part 3 of the DDA 1995 because they did not provide services *to the public* or a section of the public.[223] Such clubs were free to discriminate against disabled persons seeking membership or access.[224] The 2002 Code of Practice defined a private club as one where membership was a condition of participation and where there was a genuine selection process (usually under the club's rules).[225] Nevertheless, even a private membership club would have been subject to Part 3 obligations if it used its premises to provide some services of a public nature. For example, a private golf club that provided facilities to non-members for wedding receptions would not have been able lawfully to discriminate against a disabled wedding guest. This remains the case and several examples in the Rights of Access Code of Practice 2006 illustrate this remaining area of liability for private clubs providing services to the public or a section of it.[226]

5.8.2 However, from 5 December 2005, Part 3 now applies to private clubs and analogous organisations.[227] The Rights of Access Code of

---

[221] DDA 1995, s 26(1).

[222] Ibid, s 26(1A), inserted by the Disability Discrimination Act 1995 (Amendment) Regulations 2003, SI 2003/1673, regs 3(1) and 19(3) (in force from 1 October 2004).

[223] DDA 1995, s 19(2)(b). See Rights of Access Code of Practice 2002, paras 2.38–2.39; Rights of Access Code of Practice 2006, para 1.2.

[224] See the case-law to like effect under the now repealed provisions of the Race Relations Act 1968: *Dockers Labour Club and Institute Ltd v Race Relations Board* [1976] AC 285; *Charter v Race Relations Board* [1973] AC 885. Cf RRA 1976, s 25 and *Applin v Race Relations Board* [1975] AC 259.

[225] See Rights of Access Code of Practice 2002, para 2.39. The DRTF recommended that private clubs should be covered, but without extending coverage to private social arrangements: DRTF Report, recommendation 6.10. The Government asked the then DRC to address the issue of whether to develop a voluntary approach instead of legislating to reduce any problems disabled people may face in joining private clubs (including the making of reasonable adjustments) once the provisions in Part 3 of the DDA 1995 were fully in force as part of its ongoing duty to review the DDA 1995: Government Response to DRTF Report, para 3.73. The former DRC endorsed the DRTF view. See *Legislative Review: First Review of the Disability Discrimination Act 1995: Consultation* (May 2002, Disability Rights Commission) (DRC Legislative Review), recommendation 23.

[226] See Rights of Access Code of Practice 2006, para 3.1.

[227] DDA 1995, ss 21F–21J, as inserted by DDA 2005, s 12. See SI 2005/1676 and 2774. In Northern Ireland, see also SI 2006/312, art 13. For the background to these new provisions, see Department for Work and Pensions, *Delivering Equality for Disabled*

Practice 2006 deals separately with the specific provisions that affect private clubs and organisations,[228] although throughout the Code there is helpful discussion and illustration of concepts that are common to private clubs, public authorities and service providers. The discussion of terms such as 'discrimination', 'justification' and 'reasonable adjustments' (and the relevant case law) in the earlier part of this chapter in the context of service providers will assist the understanding of the private club provisions.

Associations of persons

5.8.3 The new provisions apply to any association of persons (however described) if the association meets certain conditions.[229] The association may be incorporated or unincorporated. It might be a company or an unincorporated association or a friendly society. Its legal form or personality is not important.[230] It does not matter whether or not its activities are carried on for profit. It must have 25 or more members, whether in active membership or not.[231]

5.8.4 Admission to its membership must be regulated by its constitution and must be so conducted that the members do not constitute a section of the public.[232] The constitution may be written or unwritten but, without a constitutional regulation of its membership, it is unlikely to be a private club (or analogous association) and is more likely to be a service provider.[233] In practice, the club or association will be operating a policy of membership selection genuinely based on personal criteria. For example, applicants for membership may be required to make a personal application; to be sponsored or nominated by other members as to their good character; and to undergo a selection process, such as voting by existing members.[234] It must not be a trade organisation.[235]

5.8.5 In the remainder of this analysis, for simplicity, references to a private club are to be taken as including analogous organisations.

People: A Consultation on the Extension of the Disability Discrimination Act to Functions of Public Authorities and the Introduction of a Duty to Promote Equality for Disabled People, Cm 6255 (July 2004).

[228] Rights of Access Code of Practice 2006, Chapter 12.

[229] DDA 1995, s 21F(1); Rights of Access Code of Practice 2006, paras 3.9–3.13 and 12.2–12.4.

[230] Rights of Access Code of Practice 2006, para 12.7.

[231] DDA 1995, s 21F(1)(a); Rights of Access Code of Practice 2006, para 12.5.

[232] Ibid, s 21F(1)(b). A section of the public has the meaning ascribed in s 19(2).

[233] Rights of Access Code of Practice 2006, paras 12.8–12.9.

[234] Ibid, para 12.6 and example.

[235] That is, one to which s 13 applies: s 21F(1)(c).

Members, associates and guests

5.8.6 The provisions on private clubs afford rights to members, associates and guests of the club. A person is a 'member' if he or she belongs to the club by virtue of admission to any sort of membership provided for by the club's constitution.[236] It is not enough that the person has certain rights under the club's constitution by virtue of membership of some other association. A person is an 'associate' of a club where, although not a member of the club, under the club's constitution he or she has some or all of the rights enjoyed by members (or would have apart from any constitutional provision that authorises the refusal of those rights in particular cases).[237] A 'guest' includes a person who is a guest of the club by virtue of an invitation issued by a member or associate in circumstances permitted by the club.[238] Regulations may provide as to the circumstances in which a person is to be treated as being or not being a guest of a club.[239]

Unlawful acts: access to membership

5.8.7 It is unlawful for a private club to discriminate against a disabled person who is not a member of the club (a) in the terms on which it is prepared to admit him or her to membership or (b) by refusing or deliberately omitting to accept his or her application for membership.[240]

Unlawful acts: membership rights

5.8.9 It is unlawful for a private club to discriminate against a disabled person who is a member or associate of the club (a) in the way it affords that member access to a benefit, facility or service or (b) by refusing or deliberately omitting to afford him or her access to a benefit, facility or service.[241] In the case of a disabled member, it is unlawful to discriminate by depriving him or her of membership, or by varying the terms on which he or she is a member.[242] In the case of a disabled associate, it is unlawful to discriminate by depriving him or her of his rights as an associate, or by varying those rights.[243] It is unlawful to discriminate against a disabled member or associate by subjecting him or her to any other detriment.[244]

---

[236] DDA 1995, s 21J(1)(a).

[237] Ibid, s 21J(1)(b).

[238] Ibid, s 21J(2).

[239] Ibid, s 21J(3).

[240] Ibid, s 21F(2); Rights of Access Code of Practice 2006, para 12.14 and examples.

[241] DDA 1995, s 21F(3)(a)–(b) ; Rights of Access Code of Practice 2006, paras 12.15–12.16 and example.

[242] DDA 1995, s 21F(3)(c).

[243] Ibid, s 21F(3)(d).

[244] Ibid, s 21F(3)(e).

Unlawful acts: guests

5.8.10 It is unlawful for a private club to discriminate against a disabled person in his or her capacity as a guest of the club. Unlawful discrimination here arises in the way it affords him or her access to a benefit, facility or service, or by refusing or deliberately omitting to afford him or her access to a benefit, facility or service.[245] It is also unlawful to subject such a guest to any other detriment.[246]

5.8.11 It is unlawful for a private club to discriminate against a disabled person in the terms on which it is prepared to invite that disabled person (or permit a member or associate to invite him or her) to be a guest of the club.[247] In like manner, it is unlawful to discriminate by refusing or deliberately omitting to invite him or her to be a guest, or by not permitting a member or associate to invite him or her to be a guest.[248]

Unlawful acts: reasonable adjustments

5.8.12 It is unlawful for a private club to discriminate against a disabled person in failing in prescribed circumstances to comply with a duty to make reasonable adjustments imposed on it under s 21H.[249] This is discussed in further detail below at **5.8.18**.

Unlawful acts: victimisation

5.8.13 In the case of an act which constitutes discrimination by virtue of the victimisation provisions of s 55, s 21F also applies to discrimination against a person who is not disabled.[250]

Discrimination[251]

5.8.14 A private club discriminates against a disabled person if, for a reason which relates to the disabled person's disability, the club treats the disabled person less favourably than it treats (or would treat) others to whom that reason does not (or would not) apply, and it cannot show that the treatment in question is justified.[252] Such treatment is justified only if

---

[245] DDA 1995, s 21F(4)(a)–(b); Rights of Access Code of Practice 2006, paras 12.17–12.18 and example.

[246] Ibid, s 21F(4)(c).

[247] Ibid, s 21F(5)(a).

[248] Ibid, s 21F(5)(b)–(c).

[249] Ibid, s 21F(6).

[250] Ibid, s 21F(7); Rights of Access Code of Practice 2006, paras 20.2–20.4 and example.

[251] See generally Rights of Access Code of Practice 2006, Chapter 4.

[252] DDA 1995, s 21G(1). See generally Rights of Access Code of Practice 2006, Chapters 5 and 8, and the specific examples at paras 5.9 and 5.14. Regulations may make provision as to circumstances (other than any for the time being mentioned in s 21G(3)) in which treatment is to be taken to be justified for the purposes of s 21G(1): DDA 1995, s 21G(5)(c). Particular provision, similar to that applying in service providion cases, is

(a) in the opinion of the club, one or more of the conditions mentioned in s 21G(3) are satisfied, and (b) it is reasonable, in all the circumstances, for it to hold that opinion.[253] The s 21G(3) conditions are as follows.[254]

Justification[255]

5.8.15   First, that the treatment is necessary in order not to endanger the health or safety of any person (which may include that of the disabled person).[256] Secondly, that the disabled person is incapable of entering into an enforceable agreement, or giving an informed consent, and for that reason the treatment is reasonable in that case.[257] Thirdly, in certain cases only,[258] the treatment is necessary in order for the club to be able to afford its members, associates or guests, or the disabled person, access to a benefit, facility or service.[259] Fourthly, again in certain cases only,[260] the treatment is necessary because the club would otherwise be unable to afford its members, associates or guests access to a benefit, facility or service.[261]

5.8.16   Fifthly, in a case falling within s 21F(2)(a), the difference between (i) the terms on which membership is offered to the disabled person, and (ii) those on which it is offered to other persons, reflects the greater cost to the club of affording the disabled person access to a benefit, facility or service.[262] Sixthly, in certain cases only,[263] the difference between (i) the club's treatment of the disabled person, and (ii) its treatment of other members, associates or guests, reflects the greater cost to the club of affording the disabled person access to a benefit, facility or service.[264] Seventhly, in a case falling within s 21F(5)(a), the difference between (i)

---

made in respect of guarantees and deposits: Disability Discrimination (Private Clubs etc) Regulations 2005, SI 2005/3258, regs 4 and 5.

[253]   DDA 1995, s 21G(2). Regulations may make provision, for purposes of s 21G(2), as to circumstances in which it is (or as to circumstances in which it is not) reasonable for a club to hold that opinion: s 21G(5)(a).

[254]   Regulations may amend or omit a condition specified in s 21G(3) or make provision for it not to apply in prescribed circumstances: DDA 1995, s 21G(5)(b).

[255]   See Rights of Access Code of Practice 2006, paras 12.37–12.49 and examples.

[256]   DDA 1995, s 21G(3)(a).

[257]   Ibid, s 21G(3)(b). The conditions specified in s 21G(3)(b) shall not apply where another person is acting for a disabled person by virtue of a power of attorney or being a deputy appointed by the Court of Protection or powers exercisable in relation to the disabled person's property or affairs in consequence of the appointment (under the law of Scotland) of a guardian, tutor or judicial factor: Disability Discrimination (Private Clubs etc) Regulations 2005, SI 2005/3258, reg 3 (as amended by SI 2007/1898).

[258]   That is, cases falling within DDA 1995, ss 21F(2)(a), 21F(3)(a), 21F(3)(c)(ii), 21F(3)(d)(ii), 21F(3)(e), 21F(4)(a), 21F(4)(c) or 21F(5)(a).

[259]   Ibid, s 21G(3)(c).

[260]   That is, cases falling within ibid, ss 21F(2)(b), 21F(3)(b), 21F(3)(c)(i), 21F(3)(d)(i), 21F(4)(b), 21F(5)(b) or 21F(5)(c).

[261]   Ibid, s 21G(3)(d).

[262]   Ibid, s 21G(3)(e).

[263]   That is, cases falling within ibid, ss 21F(3)(a), 21F(3)(c)(ii), 21F(3)(d)(ii) or 21F(4)(a).

[264]   Ibid, s 21G(3)(f).

the terms on which the disabled person is invited (or permitted to be invited) to be a guest of the club, and (ii) those on which other persons are invited (or permitted to be invited) to be guests of the club, reflects the greater cost to the club of affording the disabled person access to a benefit, facility or service.[265]

5.8.17 In the group of three conditions discussed in **5.8.16** only, any increase in the cost of affording a disabled person access to a benefit, facility or service which results from compliance with a club's duty to make reasonable adhustments under s 21H shall be disregarded.[266]

Reasonable adjustments

5.8.18 A private club also discriminates against a disabled person if it fails to comply with a duty to make reasonable adjustments under s 21H imposed on it in relation to the disabled person, and it cannot show that its failure to comply with that duty is justified.[267] Regulations may make provision as to circumstances in which failure to comply with a duty under s 21H is to be taken to be justified for these purposes.[268]

5.8.19 Section 21H provides that regulations may impose on a private club a duty to take steps for a purpose relating to a policy, practice or procedure of the club, or a physical feature, which adversely affects disabled persons who are (or might wish to become) members or associates, or who are (or are likely to become) guests of the club.[269] Regulations may also impose on a private club a duty to take steps for the purpose of making an auxiliary aid or service available to any such disabled persons.[270] Any such regulations may (in particular) make provision as to the cases in which a duty is imposed, the steps which a duty requires to be taken, and the purpose for which a duty requires steps to be taken.[271] However, any duty imposed under s 21H is imposed only for the purpose of determining whether a club has discriminated against a disabled person. A breach of any such duty is not actionable as such.[272]

Benefits, facilities or services

5.8.20 Regulations apply where a private club has a practice, policy or procedure which makes (or would make) it impossible or unreasonably difficult for the club's disabled members, associates or guests to make use

---

[265] DDA 1995, s 21G(3)(g).

[266] Ibid, s 21G(4).

[267] Ibid, ss 21F(6) and 21G(6). See generally Rights of Access Code of Practice 2006, Chapters 6–8 and the specific examples at paras 6.16, 6.31, 7.9, 7.24, 7.27 and 7.48. See specifically Rights of Access Code of Practice 2006, paras 12.21–12.36 and examples.

[268] DDA 1995, s 21G(7).

[269] Ibid, s 21H(1)(a).

[270] Ibid, s 21H(1)(b).

[271] Ibid, s 21H(2).

[272] Ibid, s 21H(3).

of a benefit, facility or service which the club provides (or is prepared to provide) to other members, associates or guests. It is the duty of the club to take such steps as it is reasonable in all the circumstances to take in order to change that practice, policy or procedure so that it no longer has that effect.[273]

5.8.21 Regulations also apply where a physical feature[274] makes (or would make) it impossible or unreasonably difficult for a club's disabled members, associates or guests to make use of a benefit, facility or service which the club provides (or is prepared to provide) to other members, associates or guests. It is the duty of the club providing that benefit, facility or service to take such steps as it is reasonable in all the circumstances to take in order to (a) remove the feature; or (b) alter it so that it no longer has that effect; or (c) provide a reasonable means of avoiding the feature; or (d) provide a reasonable alternative method of making the benefit, facility or service in question available to disabled members, associates or guests.[275]

5.8.22 Regulations further apply where an auxiliary aid or service would enable a club's disabled members, associates or guests to make use of a benefit, facility or service which the club provides (or is prepared to provide) to other members, associates or guests.[276] Those regulations also apply where an auxiliary aid or service would facilitate the use by a club's disabled members, associates or guests of such a benefit, facility or service.[277] In both cases, it is the duty of the club to take such steps as it is reasonable in all the circumstances to take in order to provide that auxiliary aid or service (for example, the provision of information on audio tape or of a sign language interpreter).[278]

5.8.23 It is unlawful for a private club to discriminate against a disabled member, associate or guest by failing to comply with a duty imposed on it by the regulations in circumstances in which the effect of that failure is to make it impossible or unreasonably difficult for the disabled member, associate or guest to make use of any benefit, facility or service which the club provides (or is prepared to provide) to other members, associates or guests.[279]

---

[273] Disability Discrimination (Private Clubs etc) Regulations 2005, SI 2005/3258, reg 6(1).

[274] Ibid, reg 10. See reg 11 as to reasonableness where consent of a third party is necessary for an adjustment to physical features of a club's premises and reg 12 in respect of reasonableness and design standards.

[275] Ibid, reg 6(2).

[276] Ibid, reg 6(3)(a).

[277] Ibid, reg 6(3)(b).

[278] Ibid, reg 6(3).

[279] Ibid, reg 6(4).

Membership

5.8.24 Regulations apply where a private club has a practice, policy or procedure which makes (or would make) it impossible or unreasonably difficult for the club's disabled members (or associates) – in comparison with members (or associates) who are not disabled – to retain their membership (or rights as an associate), or to avoid having their membership (or rights as an associate) varied. It is the duty of the club to take such steps as it is reasonable in all the circumstances to take in order to change that practice, policy or procedure so that it no longer has that effect.[280]

5.8.25 The regulations also apply where an auxiliary aid or service would enable disabled members (or associates) to retain their membership (or rights as an associate), or to avoid having their membership (or rights as an associate) varied.[281] Moreover, they apply where an auxiliary aid or service would facilitate the retention by disabled members (or associates) of their membership (or rights as an associate), or facilitate such disabled persons avoiding having their membership (or rights as an associate) varied.[282] In both instances it is the duty of the club to take such steps as it is reasonable in all the circumstances to take in order to provide that auxiliary aid or service.[283]

5.8.26 It is unlawful for a private club to discriminate against a disabled member or associate by failing to comply with a duty imposed on it by these provisions in circumstances in which the effect of that failure is to make it impossible or unreasonably difficult for the disabled member or associate – in comparison with members or associates who are not disabled – to retain their membership or rights as an associate, or to avoid having their membership or rights as an associate varied.[284]

Prospective members

5.8.27 Where a private club has a practice, policy or procedure which makes it impossible or unreasonably difficult for disabled persons – in comparison with persons who are not disabled – to be admitted as members, it is the duty of the club to take such steps as it is reasonable in all the circumstances to take in order to change that practice, policy or procedure so that it no longer has that effect.[285] Where an auxiliary aid or service would enable disabled persons to be admitted as members, or would facilitate disabled persons being admitted as members, it is the duty of the club to take such steps as it is reasonable in all the circumstances to

---

[280] Disability Discrimination (Private Clubs etc) Regulations 2005, SI 2005/3258, reg 7(1).
[281] Ibid, reg 7(2)(a).
[282] Ibid, reg 7(2)(b).
[283] Ibid, reg 7(2).
[284] Ibid, reg 7(3).
[285] Ibid, reg 8(1).

take in order to provide that auxiliary aid or service.[286] It is unlawful for a club to discriminate against a disabled person by failing to comply with these duties in circumstances in which the effect of that failure is to make it impossible or unreasonably difficult for the disabled person – in comparison with persons who are not disabled – to be admitted as a member of the club.[287]

Prospective guests

5.8.28   Where a private club has a practice, policy or procedure which makes it impossible or unreasonably difficult for disabled persons – in comparison with persons who are not disabled – to be invited as guests of the club, it is the duty of the club to take such steps as it is reasonable in all the circumstances to take in order to change that practice, policy or procedure so that it no longer has that effect.[288] Where an auxiliary aid or service would enable disabled persons to be invited as guests, or would facilitate disabled persons being invited as guests, it is the club's duty to take such steps as it is reasonable in all the circumstances to take in order to provide that auxiliary aid or service.[289] It is unlawful for a club to discriminate against a disabled person by failing to comply with these duties in circumstances in which the effect of that failure is to make it impossible or unreasonably difficult for the disabled person – in comparison with persons who are not disabled – to be invited as a guest of the club.[290]

Justification

5.8.29   For the purposes of s 21G(6), failure to comply with a duty set out in the regulations above in respect of benefits, facilities or services; membership; prospective members; and prospective guests is justified only if, in the opinion of the club, one or both of two conditions are satisfied, and it is reasonable, in all the circumstances, for it to hold that opinion.[291] The first condition is that the non-compliance with the duty is necessary in order not to endanger the health or safety of any person (which may include that of the disabled person).[292] The second condition is that the disabled person is incapable of entering into an enforceable agreement (or of giving an informed consent) and for that reason the non-compliance with the duty is reasonable in that case.[293] However, that second condition does not apply where another person is acting for a disabled person by virtue of a power of attorney; or being a deputy appointed by the Court

---

[286]   Disability Discrimination (Private Clubs etc) Regulations 2005, SI 2005/3258, reg 8(2).
[287]   Ibid, reg 8(3).
[288]   Ibid, reg 9(1).
[289]   Ibid, reg 9(2).
[290]   Ibid, reg 9(3).
[291]   Ibid, reg 13(1).
[292]   Ibid, reg 13(2)(a).
[293]   Ibid, reg 13(2)(b).

of Protection; or powers exercisable in relation to the disabled person's property or affairs in consequence of the appointment (under the law of Scotland) of a guardian, tutor or judicial factor.[294]

Limitations

5.8.30 The reasonable adjustment duties set out in the Disability Discrimination (Private Clubs etc) Regulations 2005 do not require a private club to take any steps which would fundamentally alter the nature of the benefits, facilities or services in question or the nature of the club.[295] They also do not require a member or associate of a club which meets in that member's or associate's private house to make any adjustments to a physical feature in relation to that member's or associate's private house.[296]

5.9 ENFORCEMENT, REMEDIES AND PROCEDURES

5.9.1 A claim of unlawful discrimination in relation to the provision of goods, facilities or services, or in relation to private clubs, under Part 3 of the DDA 1995 is the subject of civil proceedings for tort in the county court (in England and Wales or Northern Ireland) or in reparation for breach of a statutory duty in the sheriff court (in Scotland).[297] The usual remedy will be damages (including injury to feelings),[298] but a claimant (or pursuer) might also seek a declaration or an injunction.[299] The question of enforcement procedures and remedies is considered in more detail in Chapter 10.

5.9.2 However, the usual enforcement provisions applying to Part 3 cases do not apply to employment services claims falling under s 21A.[300] These claims may be presented as a complaint to an employment tribunal.[301]

---

[294] Disability Discrimination (Private Clubs etc) Regulations 2005, SI 2005/3258, reg 13(3), as amended.

[295] Ibid, reg 14(a).

[296] Ibid, reg 14(b).

[297] DDA 1995, s 25(1), (3) and (4). The modification of s 25 for Northern Ireland is achieved in Sch 8, para 12.

[298] Ibid, s 25(2). An upper limit to compensation may be prescribed under Sch 3, para 7. No such cap on compensation has been set to date.

[299] Ibid, s 25(5).

[300] Ibid, s 25(7) as amended by the Disability Discrimination Act 1995 (Amendment) Regulations 2003, SI 2003/1673, regs 3(1) and 19(2) (in force from 1 October 2004).

[301] Ibid, s 25(8). Section 17A(1A)–(7) and Sch 3, paras 3–4 apply in relation to such a complaint as if it were a complaint under s 17A(1) (and Sch 3, paras 6–8 do not apply in relation to such a complaint): s 25(9). See Code of Practice: Employment and Occupation (2004), para 11.23.

CHAPTER 6

PROPERTY, PREMISES AND LEASES

6.1 INTRODUCTION

6.1.1 Part 3 of the DDA 1995 also makes it unlawful for landlords and other persons who are disposing of or selling property to discriminate against a disabled person.[1] While it is not thought that discrimination against disabled persons is as widespread as racial discrimination once was in the property market, the Government felt sufficiently moved by at least one case of landlord discrimination against a disabled person to introduce an amendment to the DDA 1995 during its progress as a Bill.[2] As the provisions on discrimination in relation to premises are a free-standing part of Part 3 of the Act, they warrant separate treatment in this chapter. However, much of the terminology used in relation to property discrimination echoes many of the concepts used elsewhere in the DDA 1995. Accordingly, decisions reached and precedents made in respect of other sections will be influential and of assistance in the interpretation of the law on discrimination in respect of premises.

6.1.2 The DDA 1995 also makes provision for the position where employers and trade organisations (and others covered by Part 2 of the Act), service providers (and others covered by Part 3 of the Act) and educational establishments (and others covered by Part 4 of the Act) occupy premises under the terms of a lease. It was recognised that such parties might find it difficult to discharge a duty to make reasonable adjustments for disabled persons, especially in respect of the physical features of premises, where the lease or the landlord prevented or hindered such adjustments. Accordingly, Parts 2, 3 and 4 adjust the respective rights of the landlord and tenant to a lease so as to accommodate the duties to make adjustments to premises. Questions also arise in this context in relation to building regulations. As these provisions affect property interests, they are logically dealt with in this chapter.

---

[1] DDA 1995, ss 22–24 (in force since 2 December 1996). These provisions mirror similar measures in the sex and race discrimination statutes, although they are not in identical terms: SDA 1975, ss 30–32; RRA 1976, ss 21–24. See generally Rights of Access Code of Practice 2006, Chapters 13–19 and Appendix B.

[2] HC Deb Standing Committee E, col 453.

6.1.3   Important changes are made to the premises provisions by the DDA 2005[3] and the Disability Discrimination (Premises) Regulations 2006.[4] These are dealt with in the text below. The 2005 Act imposes a duty to provide reasonable adjustments on landlords and others who manage rented premises. It also confers a power to modify or end the current small dwellings exemption.[5] The Act also provides regulation-making powers to deal with the practical consequences of the extension of the duty to make reasonable adjustments in relation to the physical features of premises in relation to local councillors, public authorities, general qualifications bodies and private clubs.

6.2   DISCRIMINATION IN RELATION TO PREMISES

6.2.1   The DDA 1995 makes it unlawful for 'a person with power to dispose of any premises' to discriminate against a disabled person in one of a number of ways.[6] It is also unlawful for 'a person managing any premises' to discriminate against a disabled person 'occupying those premises' in a similar fashion.[7] Furthermore, the legislation deals with discrimination which arises by the withholding of a licence or consent required for the disposal of premises to a disabled person.[8]

Unlawful acts of discrimination

6.2.2   First, it is unlawful to discriminate 'in the terms' on which a person with power to dispose of premises offers to dispose of those premises to a disabled person.[9] For example, a landlord cannot seek to charge a higher rent for premises to a disabled tenant than the landlord would otherwise charge to a non-disabled lessee.

6.2.3   Secondly, it is unlawful to discriminate where a person with power to dispose of premises refuses to dispose of those premises to a disabled person.[10] This is a self-evident measure designed to prevent a disabled person from being denied the right to own a legal interest in property solely because of a disability. It is analogous with the illegitimacy of a property owner's action in refusing to sell or lease property to a member of an ethnic minority. It does not prevent the property owner from

---

3   In Northern Ireland, see the comparable changes made by Disability Discrimination (Northern Ireland) Order 2006, SI 2006/312.

4   SI 2006/887.

5   See Department of Work and Pensions, *Disability Discrimination Bill: Consultation on private clubs; premises; the definition of disability; and the questions procedure*, Cm 6402 (December 2004).

6   DDA 1995, s 22(1). See generally Rights of Access Code of Practice 2006, chapter 13. The meaning of discrimination in this context is set out in s 24. See Rights of Access Code of Practice 2006, chapters 14 and 15.

7   Ibid, s 22(3).

8   Ibid, s 22(4).

9   Ibid, s 22(1)(a); Rights of Access Code of Practice 2006, para 14.14.

10   Ibid, s 22(1)(b); Rights of Access Code of Practice 2006, para 14.15.

refusing to dispose of the property to a disabled person for reasons unconnected with that person's disability (for example, their inability to meet the purchase price or evidence that as a tenant they would be a bad credit risk).

6.2.4 Thirdly, it is unlawful for a person with power to dispose of any premises to discriminate against a disabled person in his or her 'treatment' of that disabled person 'in relation to any list of persons in need of premises of that description'.[11] This prohibition most obviously addresses discrimination against disabled persons in relation to housing association or local authority housing lists or those of private letting agencies. For example, a refusal to include a disabled person on a housing list, or the removal of that person from such a list, or a failure to accord that person proper priority in accordance with their ranking on the list might all be acts of unlawful discrimination. Similarly, allocating less desirable property to a disabled person on a housing list where a non-disabled person is more favourably treated would constitute a likely act of discrimination.[12]

6.2.5 Fourthly, it is unlawful for a person managing any premises to discriminate against a disabled person occupying those premises 'in the way' the person managing the premises 'permits the disabled person to make use of any benefits or facilities' or by 'refusing or deliberately omitting' to permit the disabled person to make use of any benefits or facilities.[13] Inclusion of a person managing any premises clearly broadens the scope of this provision which is not solely concerned with discrimination by property owners. A property management agency, accommodation agency, housekeeper, estate agent or rent collection service could all constitute parties who might be liable under this provision (and those that follow below).[14] The terms 'benefits or facilities' are not defined and there is no express intention to include 'services' within these terms. However, the Code of Practice indicates that benefits or facilities include, for example, laundry facilities, access to a garden and parking facilities.[15]

---

[11] DDA 1995, s 22(1)(c); Rights of Access Code of Practice 2006, para 14.16.

[12] The DDA 1995 does not prohibit more favourable treatment or positive action in respect of disabled persons and housing lists.

[13] DDA 1995, s 22(3)(a) and (b); Rights of Access Code of Practice 2006, paras 14.17–14.20.

[14] Rights of Access Code of Practice 2006, para 14.18. Regulations may provide for the purpose of s 22(3) who is to be treated (or not treated) as being a person who manages premises or a person occupying premises: s 22(3A) inserted by DDA 2005, s 19(1) and Sch 1. The Disability Discrimination (Premises) Regulations 2006, SI 2006/887, reg 8(1) provides that a commonhold association, which exercises functions in relation to any commonhold premises, is to be treated as a person who manages the premises for the purposes of s 22(3).

[15] Ibid, para 14.20. For example, a property management agency, managing a residential block of flats on behalf of a landlord, may not discriminate by refusing a disabled tenant access to benefits or facilities, such as common garden or recreational areas.

6.2.6   Fifthly, it is unlawful for a person managing any premises to discriminate against a disabled person occupying those premises by 'evicting' the disabled person or by 'subjecting him [or her] to any other detriment'.[16] This does not prohibit the eviction of a disabled tenant in accordance with a lawful process where, for example, the disabled person has failed to pay rent or has breached the terms of the tenancy. Instead, it provides a disabled tenant, who has been evicted by a manager of premises because of a reason related to disability, an additional cause of action apart from any available under the law of landlord and tenant. The provision also obviously addresses harassment of a disabled tenant by the person managing the premises.

6.2.7   Finally, it is unlawful for any person 'whose licence or consent is required' for the disposal of any premises 'comprised in . . . a tenancy' to discriminate against a disabled person by withholding that licence or consent for the disposal of the premises to the disabled person.[17] In Scotland, this prohibition applies in respect of the disposal of any premises 'the subject of' a tenancy. This subsection applies to tenancies created before or after the passing of the DDA 1995.[18]

Person with power to dispose of any premises

6.2.8   The phrase 'a person with power to dispose of any premises'[19] is not defined in the DDA 1995. However, the word 'dispose' is defined,[20] and by this circuitous route some light can be cast upon the class of person whose potentially unlawful actions constitute the mischief at which this part of the Act is aimed. A person with the power to dispose of premises includes a person who has the power to grant a right to occupy the premises.[21] Where the premises are comprised in or the subject of a tenancy, the relevant party will be the person with the power to assign the tenancy or to sub-let or part with possession of the premises or any part

---

[16]   DDA 1995, s 22(3)(c); Rights of Access Code of Practice 2006, paras 14.21–14.22. The Court of Appeal in *Council of the City of Manchester v Romano and Samari* [2004] EWCA Civ 834 considered the example at (what was then) para 9.26 of 2002 version of the Code of Practice as inept in the context of the law relating to residential tenancies, but agreed that, if a landlord wished to obtain possession for a breach of tenancy agreement that has been committed for reasons relating to a disabled tenant's disability, the landlord will have to show that the action is justified under s 24. The example has now been amended in the 2006 Code of Practice.

[17]   DDA 1995, s 22(4); Rights of Access Code of Practice 2006, para 14.23.

[18]   DDA 1995, s 22(5).

[19]   As used in ibid, s 22(1).

[20]   In ibid, s 22(6), and see Rights of Access Code of Practice 2006, paras 14.8–14.9.

[21]   This does not include the hire of premises or the booking of rooms in hotels or guest houses or the hire of premises to members of a private club (which would be covered by the provisions of DDA 1995, Part 3, as amended): Rights of Access Code of Practice 2006, para 14.9. The boundary between ss 22–24 and ss 19–21J will not always be clear.

of them. The Act thus covers both the sale and lease of premises and, by implication, any other form of legal disposal (for example, by licence).[22]

6.2.9   The DDA 1995 does not automatically apply to private occupiers disposing of premises by private agreement or transaction.[23] This is because the statutory provisions preventing discrimination against disabled persons by a person with a power to dispose of premises do not apply to 'a person who owns an estate or interest in premises *and wholly occupies them*', unless further conditions are satisfied.[24] So the statute does not make any discrimination against a disabled person unlawful where a person with the power to dispose of premises is the owner (or owns a legal interest in the premises), wholly occupies the premises, and disposes of the premises by private agreement. However, the statutory prohibitions will still apply if such a person uses the services of an estate agent[25] or publishes an advertisement (or causes an advertisement to be published)[26] for the purpose of disposing of the premises.[27] That would cease to be a disposal by a purely private agreement.

Premises and tenancy

6.2.10   The term 'premises' is not statutorily defined.[28] Nevertheless, the ordinary or literal meaning of the word 'premises' suggests that the DDA 1995 is concerned with legal and equitable interests in houses, lands, tenements and buildings, while the Act makes no apparent distinction between commercial and non-commercial (or domestic) property. Thus the DDA 1995 would appear to cover, for example, dwelling-houses, office blocks, flats, bed-sits, factory premises, industrial or commercial sites,

---

[22]   *Quaere* whether the statute is also concerned with the disposal of premises by the operation of the law of succession or insolvency law.

[23]   See generally, Rights of Access Code of Practice 2006, paras 14.12–14.13. The DRTF saw no reason to interfere with this exemption. See *From Exclusion to Inclusion: A Report of the Disability Rights Task Force for Disabled People* (1999, London: DfEE) (DRTF Report), recommendation 6.23. The Government asked the former DRC to keep this question under review: *Towards Inclusion – Civil Rights for Disabled People: Government Response to the Disability Rights Task Force* (2001, London: DfEE) (Government Response to DRTF Report), para 3.73.

[24]   DDA 1995, s 22(2) (emphasis added) for the purposes of s 22(1).

[25]   An 'estate agent' for this purpose is a person carrying on the trade or profession of providing services 'for the purpose of finding premises for persons seeking to acquire them or assisting in the disposal of premises': DDA 1995, s 22(6). That definition would appear to be wide enough to include not only an estate agent per se, but also an accommodation bureau or agency.

[26]   An 'advertisement' includes every form of advertisement or notice, whether to the public or not: DDA 1995, s 22(6). So the circulation to a small or select number of persons of the details of premises for disposal would constitute an advertisement of the premises and would trigger the provisions prohibiting discrimination against disabled persons in the subsequent disposal.

[27]   DDA 1995, s 22(2) (these are the further conditions referred to above).

[28]   Except to the extent that s 68(1) of the DDA 1995 indicates that premises include land of any description and s 22(8) makes it clear that the Act is only concerned with premises in the UK.

agricultural land and so on – in other words, real property of any description.[29] The Act also clearly impinges upon the law of landlord and tenant.[30] A 'tenancy' means a tenancy created by a lease or sub-lease, by an agreement for a lease or sub-lease, by a tenancy agreement, or in pursuance of any 'enactment' (for example, a statutory tenancy).[31]

Commonholds

6.2.11 A new s 22A has been inserted into the DDA 1995, with effect from 4 December 2006.[32] The section applies only in relation to premises in England and Wales.[33] It provides that it is unlawful for any person whose licence or consent is required for the disposal of an interest in a commonhold unit by the unit-holder to discriminate against a disabled person by withholding that licence or consent for the disposal of the interest in favour of (or to) the disabled person.[34] Where it is not possible for an interest in a commonhold unit to be disposed of by the unit-holder unless some other person is a party to the disposal of the interest, it is unlawful for that other person to discriminate against a disabled person by deliberately not being a party to the disposal of the interest in favour of (or to) the disabled person.[35]

6.2.12 In the present context, the terms 'commonhold unit', and 'unit-holder' in relation to such a unit, have the same meaning as in Part 1 of the Commonhold and Leasehold Reform Act 2002.[36] Regulations may provide for s 22A(1) or (2) not to apply (or to apply only) in cases of a prescribed description.[37] Regulations may make provision for the purposes of s 22A as to what is (or is not) to be included within the meaning of 'dispose' (and 'disposal') and 'interest in a commonhold unit'.[38] The term 'dispose', in relation to an interest in a commonhold unit, includes granting a right to occupy the unit (and 'disposal' is

---

[29] Rights of Access Code of Practice 2006, para 14.10.

[30] DDA 1995, s 22 obviously and expressly applies to the granting of tenancies, their assignment and the right to sub-let.

[31] Ibid, ss 22(6) and 68(1); Rights of Access Code of Practice 2006, para 14.11.

[32] DDA 2005, Sch 1, para 17. In the case of an act which constitutes discrimination by virtue of DDA 1995, s 55 (victimisation), s 22A also applies to discrimination against a person who is not disabled: s 22A(6).

[33] DDA 1995, s 22A(7).

[34] Ibid, s 22A(1); Right of Access Code of Practice 2006, paras 16.6–16.7.

[35] Ibid, s 22A(2); Right of Access Code of Practice 2006, para 16.8. A commonhold association which exercises functions in relation to any commonhold premises is also to be treated as a person who manages the premises for the purposes of any liability under s 22(3): Disability Discrimination (Premises) Regulations 2006, SI 2006/887, reg 8(1).

[36] DDA 1995, s 22A(5). Similarly, the terms 'commonhold', 'commonhold association' and commonhold community statement' are to be interpreted in the light of the 2002 Act: Disability Discrimination (Premises) Regulations 2006, SI 2006/887, reg 1(2).

[37] DDA 1995, s 22A(3).

[38] Ibid, s 22A(4).

construed accordingly).[39] An 'interest in a commonhold unit' includes an interest in part only of a commonhold unit.[40]

Exemption for small dwellings

6.2.13   Where certain cumulative conditions are satisfied, there is a statutory exemption[41] for small dwellings in respect of the provisions prohibiting discrimination against disabled persons in the disposal or management of premises[42] or by the withholding of a licence or consent for the disposal of premises.[43] The exemption is likely to apply to a multi-occupancy residential building with shared accommodation.[44] A necessary but not sufficient condition for the operation of this exemption is that the premises must be 'small premises'.[45] Premises are 'small premises' if there is not normally residential accommodation on the premises for more than six persons in addition to the relevant occupier and any members of the relevant occupier's household.[46] Alternatively, premises are 'small premises' if the premises satisfy four conditions:[47]

- only the relevant occupier and members of his or her household reside in the accommodation occupied by him or her;

- in addition to the accommodation occupied by the relevant occupier, the premises must comprise residential accommodation for at least one other household;

- the residential accommodation for each other household must be let (or available for letting) on a separate tenancy or similar agreement; and

- there must be not normally more than two such other households.

For example, a large house where the basement and an annex have been converted into self-contained residential dwellings or flats would satisfy

---

[39]   Disability Discrimination (Premises) Regulations 2006, SI 2006/887, reg 8(2)(a).

[40]   Ibid, reg 8(2)(b).

[41]   DDA 1995, s 23(1). See generally Rights of Access Code of Practice 2006, paras 17.2–17.10. The DRTF saw no reason to interfere with this exemption, except possibly to allow the threshold for its operation to be lowered: DRTF Report, recommendation 6.24. The Government replied that, when legislative time allowed, it would create a power to reduce to below six persons the exemption figure for small dwellings in the private disposal of premises provisions, and would use that power if it was shown to be necessary: Government Response to DRTF Report, para 3.72.

[42]   DDA 1995, s 22(1) and (3).

[43]   Ibid, s 22(4).

[44]   Rights of Access Code of Practice 2006, para 17.10.

[45]   DDA 1995, s 23(2)(d); Rights of Access Code of Practice 2006, paras 17.8–17.9.

[46]   Ibid, s 23(3) and (5). A householder who has converted part of his or her dwelling-house into bed-sit accommodation would fall outside this exemption if such accommodation embraced more than six tenants.

[47]   Ibid, s 23(4).

these conditions if the owner also resides on the premises and there is an element of shared accommodation (other than for storage or access purposes).

6.2.14 The fact that the premises are a small dwelling is not enough. Three further conditions must also be satisfied. First, the relevant occupier must reside, and must intend to continue to reside, on the premises.[48] The use of the word 'reside' indicates that this exemption is only enjoyed in respect of dwelling-houses or other residential property and does not apply to commercial or industrial premises. A 'relevant occupier' means a person with the power to dispose of the premises[49] or the person managing the premises[50] or the person whose licence or consent is required for the disposal of the premises.[51] In all three cases, the relevant occupier will include 'a near relative'.[52] Secondly, the relevant occupier must be sharing accommodation on the premises with persons who reside on the premises and who are not members of the occupier's household.[53] This condition contemplates a multi-occupancy residential building with shared accommodation. This might include a large house, sub-divided into individually let bed-sits, with a resident landlord and shared accommodation, such as communal kitchens or bathrooms. Thirdly, the shared accommodation must not be storage accommodation or a means of access.[54] This underlines the last observation illustrating the notion of shared accommodation. It indicates that it is not enough that there is a common entrance door or passageway. Equally, the premises would not include shared accommodation only by virtue of there being a garage or cellar in which the tenants or occupiers may store their personal effects.

Meaning of discrimination

6.2.15 The provisions of Part 3 of the DDA 1995 dealing with discrimination in relation to premises include a self-contained definition

---

[48] DDA 1995, s 23(2)(a) and (6) (as amended).

[49] In a case where DDA 1995, s 22(1) would otherwise apply (discrimination in relation to the disposal of premises).

[50] In any case where DDA 1995, s 22(3) would otherwise apply (discrimination in relation to benefits or facilities).

[51] In any case where DDA 1995, s 22(4) would otherwise apply (discrimination by withholding a licence or consent for the disposal of tenancy premises).

[52] This term is exhaustively defined by DDA 1995, s 23(7) (as amended) to mean a person's spouse or civil partner, partner, child, grandparent, grandchild, or brother or sister (whether of full or half blood or by marriage or civil partnership). The term 'partner' means the other member of a couple consisting of a man and a woman who are not married to each other but are living together as husband and wife, or two people of the same sex who are not civil partners of each other but are living together as if they were civil partners. It only becomes necessary to identify whether someone is a partner if the relevant occupier is not actually present on the premises when discrimination is alleged (eg while temporarily away on business): HL Deb, vol 564, col 2029.

[53] DDA 1995, s 23(2)(b).

[54] Ibid, s 23(2)(c).

of discrimination.[55] This does not create a free-standing right to complain of discrimination and it will be necessary to show that discrimination has occurred in a way which is made unlawful.[56] While case-law on the meaning of discrimination as used elsewhere in the statute will be instructive, care must be taken to ensure that an action for alleged discrimination in the disposal or management of premises satisfies the definition of discrimination for present purposes.[57] In particular, until the amendments made by the DDA 2005 in relation to premises to let and let premises (discussed below) there was no explicit duty to make reasonable adjustments for disabled persons in the context of the disposal or management of premises.

6.2.16 Certainly, judicial interpretation of the meaning of discrimination pre-DDA 2005 did not give rise to an implicit duty of this nature.[58] The DRTF felt that the lack of a duty to make reasonable adjustments within ss 22–24 should be remedied. In particular, it recommended that there should be a duty on those covered by the disposal and management of premises provisions to make reasonable adjustments to policies, practices and procedures, and to provide auxiliary aids and services in the selling and letting process. It also recommended that covered persons should not be allowed to withhold consent unreasonably for a disabled person to make changes to the physical features of premises.[59] The Government agreed in principle to extending to those who let or manage premises duties relating to reasonable adjustments to policies, practices and procedures, and the provision of auxiliary aids and services, and undertook to consult on the factors which might determine reasonableness when a landlord is asked by a disabled tenant to consent to changes to physical features.[60] The change in the law is now effected by DDA 1995, ss 24A–24M in relation to premises to let and let premises (discussed below).

---

[55] DDA 1995, s 24.

[56] That is, under ibid, ss 22 or 22A. That is the effect of the opening words of s 24(1), as amended: 'For the purposes of sections 22 and 22A . . .'.

[57] See the detailed discussion of the meaning of discrimination in Chapter 3 and Chapter 5.

[58] *Richmond Court (Swansea) Ltd v Williams* [2006] EWCA Civ 1719 (Court of Appeal) (a landlord's refusal of consent to the installation of a stair-lift at the disabled tenant's expense did not constitute unlawful discrimination within DDA 1995, s 22(3)). The 2002 version of the Code of Practice anticipated that view, although it stressed that there was nothing in the DDA 1995 to prevent positive action: Rights of Access Code of Practice 2002, para 9.6. It also noted that persons managing or disposing of premises (such as estate agents, accommodation bureaux or management companies) may have parallel duties as service providers and might be subject to a duty to make reasonable adjustments to the way in which they provide their services in relation to premises. The boundary between these duties will not always be easily drawn, especially where the question of reasonable adjustments is being raised.

[59] DRTF Report, recommendations 6.25–6.27.

[60] Government Response to DRTF Report, para 3.83.

Less favourable treatment

6.2.17 A person discriminates against a disabled person if, for a reason which relates to the disabled person's disability, that person treats the disabled person less favourably than that person treats (or would treat) others to whom that reason does not or would not apply.[61] Such less favourable treatment for a reason related to disability will amount to potentially *unlawful* discrimination[62] if the alleged discriminator cannot show that the treatment in question is justified.[63]

Justification

6.2.18 The justification 'defence'[64] can only be made out if certain statutory criteria are met.[65] First, the alleged discriminator must hold the opinion that one or more statutory conditions are satisfied.[66] This is to be tested subjectively.[67] It must be shown that, at the time the treatment took place, *in the opinion* of the defendant, the treatment was necessary. It must be shown that this was an opinion held at that time and not an ex post facto rationalisation in the face of litigation. Secondly, it must be reasonable, in all the circumstances of the case, for that person to hold that opinion.[68] This calls for an objective assessment of all the relevant circumstances.[69] The objective reasonableness of the opinion may depend

---

[61]   DDA 1995, s 24(1)(a). See the discussion of the concept of disability-related less favourable treatment in Chapters 3 and 5. See also the examples given in Rights of Access Code of Practice 2006, paras 14.3–14.7.

[62]   For the purposes of DDA 1995, s 22.

[63]   Ibid, s 24(1)(b).

[64]   Strictly, the justification requirement is part of the definition of discrimination rather than an explicit defence.

[65]   DDA 1995, s 24(2). See generally Rights of Access Code of Practice 2006, paras 17.11–17.28.

[66]   Ibid, s 24(2)(a).

[67]   *Rose v Bouchet* [1999] IRLR 463 (Sheriff Principal Nicholson QC). This case concerned the refusal to let a flat to a blind person accompanied by a guide dog. The refusal was said by the landlord to be motivated by a concern for the disabled person's safety because of a missing handrail on the steps leading to the flat's entrance. The Sheriff Principal did not think it helpful to engage the assistance of cases decided under the employment provisions of the Act when construing s 24. See now *Council of the City of Manchester v Romano and Samari* [2004] EWCA Civ 834 (discussed at **6.2.24**).

[68]   DDA 1995, s 24(2)(b). Future regulations may amplify the circumstances in which it is reasonable (or not reasonable) for a person to hold the opinion that one or more of the statutory conditions are satisfied: s 24(4). No such regulations have been made at the time of writing.

[69]   *Rose v Bouchet* (above). On the facts, the landlord's opinion as to the safety issues arising from letting the flat to a blind person in the particular circumstances of the case was held to be objectively reasonable. See now *Council of the City of Manchester v Romano and Samari* [2004] EWCA Civ 834 (discussed at **6.2.24**).

upon what information was available at the time, what further reasonable inquiries might have been made and what, if any, information has been proffered by the disabled person.[70]

6.2.19 There are six possible statutory (and exhaustive) conditions about the satisfaction of which the alleged discriminator must hold a reasonably held opinion.[71] These conditions are very similar to the parallel conditions for the operation of the justification defence in respect of discrimination arising in the context of goods, facilities or services.[72] First, in any case, the person alleged to have discriminated may be able to justify less favourable treatment by showing that that person reasonably believed that the treatment was necessary in order not to endanger the health or safety of any person, including the disabled person.[73] Secondly, in any case, less favourable treatment might be justified by reference to a reasonably held opinion that the disabled person was incapable of entering into an enforceable agreement or of giving an informed consent, and for that reason the treatment was reasonable in the particular case.[74] Thirdly, in a case where a person managing premises has treated a disabled occupier less favourably in the way in which that occupier is allowed to make use of any benefits or facilities,[75] the alleged discriminator might be able to show a reasonably held opinion that the discriminatory treatment was necessary in order for the disabled person (or occupiers of other premises forming part of the building) to make use of a benefit or facility.[76] Fourthly, in a case where a person managing premises has treated a disabled occupier less favourably by refusing (or deliberately omitting) to permit that occupier to make use of any benefits

---

[70] *Rose v Bouchet* (above). See Rights of Access Code of Practice 2006, paras 8.13–8.15. See now *Council of the City of Manchester v Romano and Samari* [2004] EWCA Civ 834 (discussed at **6.2.24**).

[71] DDA 1995, s 24(3), as amended. Future regulations may also provide for additional circumstances in which less favourable treatment of a disabled person is to be taken to be justified: s 24(5). No such regulations have been made at the time of writing.

[72] DDA 1995, s 20(4). The justification defence in relation to the disposal or management of premises raises similar issues to those in respect of discrimination in the provision of goods, facilities or services. See Chapter 5 for a more considered analysis of these issues.

[73] Ibid, s 24(3)(a); Rights of Access Code of Practice 2006, para 17.16 (and examples). It is sufficient to show that a person's health or safety is endangered or threatened. It is not necessary to prove actual damage. Health is a state of complete physical, mental and social well-being and not merely the absence of disease and infirmity, but trivial risks are to be disregarded: *Council of the City of Manchester v Romano and Samari* [2004] EWCA Civ 834 (construing DDA 1995, s 24(3)(a) in the light of Human Rights Act 1998, s 3).

[74] DDA 1995, s 24(3)(b); Rights of Access Code of Practice 2006, paras 17.17–17.18 (and examples). Regulations may make provision for the condition specified in s 24(3)(b) not to apply in prescribed circumstances: s 24(4A), as amended. The condition does not apply where another person is acting for the disabled person by virtue of a power of attorney; or functions conferred by or under Part 7 of the Mental Health Act 1983; or (in Scotland) powers exercisable in relation to the disabled peron's property or affairs in consequence of the appointment of a guardian, tutor or judicial factor: Disability Discrimination (Premises) Regulations 2006, SI 2006/887, reg 2.

[75] DDA 1995, s 22(3)(a).

[76] Ibid, s 24(3)(c); Rights of Access Code of Practice 2006, para 17.19 (and examples).

or facilities,[77] less favourable treatment might be justified by demonstrating a reasonably held opinion that the treatment was necessary in order for the occupiers of other premises forming part of the building to make use of the benefit or facility.[78]

6.2.20   The fifth and sixth conditions arise from amendments made by DDA 2005 from 4 December 2006. The fifth condition applies in a case where a person with power to dispose of the premises discriminates against a disabled person in the terms on which disposal of the premises to the disabled person is offered.[79] If the premises are to let, and the person with power to dispose of the premises is a controller of them, and the proposed disposal of the premises would involve the disabled person becoming a person to whom they are let, the condition is that the terms are less favourable in order to recover costs which (i) as a result of the disabled person having a disability, are incurred in connection with the disposal of the premises, and (ii) are not costs incurred in connection with taking steps to avoid liability under s 24G(1) (duty to make reasonable adjustments).[80] The sixth condition applies in a case where a person managing the premises discriminates against a disabled person occupying those premises by subjecting him or her to any detriment other than eviction.[81] If the premises are let premises, and the person manging the premises is a controller of them, and the disabled person is a person to whom the premises are let (or, although not a person to whom they are let, is lawfully under the letting an occupier of them), the condition is that the disabled person is subjected to the detriment in order to recover costs which (i) as a result of the disabled person having a disability, are incurred in connection with the management of the premises, and (ii) are not costs incurred in connection with taking steps to avoid liability under s 24A(1) or 24G(1) (duty to make reasonable adjustments).[82]

6.2.21   Regulations may provide for additional circumstances in which less favourable treatment of a disabled person is to be taken to be justified.[83] The only such provision to date affects deposits. It arises where a person with power to dispose of any premises ('the provider') grants a disabled person a right to occupy the premises, whether by a formal tenancy agreement or otherwise.[84] The provider may have required the disabled person to provide a deposit in respect of his or her occupation of the premises. The deposit is intended to be refundable at the end of the

---

[77]   DDA 1995, s 22(3)(b).

[78]   Ibid, s 24(3)(d); Rights of Access Code of Practice 2006, para 17.19 (and examples).

[79]   Ibid, s 22(1)(a).

[80]   Ibid, s 24(3)(e), (3A) and (3C), as amended; Rights of Access Code of Practice 2006, paras 17.20–17.21.

[81]   Ibid, s 22(3)(c).

[82]   Ibid, s 24(3)(f), (3B) and (3C), as amended; Rights of Access Code of Practice 2006, paras 17.20–17.21.

[83]   Ibid, s 24(5).

[84]   Disability Discrimination (Services) Regulations 2006, SI 2006/887, reg 3(2)(a). See generally Rights of Access Code of Practice 2006, paras 17.22–17.27.

occupation provided that the premises and contents are not damaged.[85] Suppose that the provider refuses to refund some or all of the deposit because the premises or contents have been damaged for a reason which relates to the disabled person's disability.[86] If the damage is above the level at which the provider would normally refund the deposit in full,[87] and if it is reasonable in all the circumstances of the case for the provider to refuse to refund the deposit in full,[88] then that apparently less favourable treatment of the disabled person for a reason relating to his or her disability is deemed to be justified.[89]

Victimisation

6.2.22 For present purposes,[90] a person (X) also discriminates against another person (Y) if X treats Y less favourably than X treats (or would treat) other persons whose circumstances are the same as Y's, and X does so for one of a number of statutory reasons.[91] Those statutory reasons relate to the fact that Y has exercised (or is believed or suspected by X as having exercised or as intending to exercise) rights under the DDA 1995.[92] For example, Y may have brought proceedings against X or given evidence in respect of such proceedings. This is victimisation.[93] An act of victimisation amounts to discrimination.[94] A person (whether disabled or not) who is victimised in this way has a cause of action for an unlawful act in relation to the disposal or management of premises.[95] By way of illustration, if Y was employed by local authority X and brought a complaint of disability-related employment discrimination against X, it would be an act of discrimination if X then victimised Y by removing Y from the local authority's housing waiting list. In these particular circumstances, it is not strictly necessary that Y should be a disabled person. It is sufficient that he or she has been victimised for doing something in relation to the DDA 1995 and has suffered a discriminatory act.

Enforcement and remedies

6.2.23 The provisions in respect of disability-informed discrimination in the disposal or management of premises are enforced (and remedies are

---

[85] Disability Discrimination (Services) Regulations 2006, SI 2006/887, reg 3(2)(b).
[86] Ibid, reg 3(2)(c).
[87] Ibid, reg 3(2)(c).
[88] Ibid, reg 3(2)(d).
[89] Ibid, reg 3(1), for the purposes of DDA 1995, s 24(1).
[90] DDA 1995, ss 22–24 (as for Part 3 as a whole).
[91] Ibid, s 55(1).
[92] Ibid, s 55(2).
[93] The concept of victimisation is explained in more detail in Chapter 10.
[94] DDA 1995, s 22(7), for the purposes of ss 22–24.
[95] As outlined in ibid, s 22. See Rights of Access Code of Practice 2006, paras 20.2–20.4.

sought) in exactly the same way as complaints of discrimination in respect of the provision of goods, facilities and services.[96] Further discussion is pursued in Chapter 10.

Judicial consideration of sections 22–24

6.2.24 In *Council of the City of Manchester v Romano and Samari*,[97] the Court of Appeal has considered for the first time the interface of housing legislation, possession orders and ss 22–24 of the 1995 Act. The appeals concerned two secured tenants of the local authority. In each case, the local authority had obtained possession orders against the tenants under the Housing Act 1985 on the grounds of their anti-social behaviour. However, there was some evidence that their anti-social behaviour might be a product of a mental illness. The question was whether it was reasonable to make a possession order against a tenant with a mental impairment. That in turn raised the relevance of disability discrimination law to that question.[98]

6.2.25 The court considered that, in applying the definition of discrimination in s 24, it was bound by the approach that had been taken to the identical definition in the employment field.[99] It agreed that the eviction of the tenants would only be justified if, in the local authority's opinion, possession proceedings were necessary in order not to endanger the health or safety of neighbouring tenants *and* it was reasonable in all the circumstances of the case for it to hold that opinion. The case confirms that the test in s 24(2) is both subjective and objective. Did the landlord hold the opinion *and* was it reasonable for it to hold that opinion in all the circumstances of the case? The reasonableness of that opinion has to be tested by reference to the facts known to the landlord at the time of the alleged discriminatory treatment (rather than after the event).[100] The court anticipated that there might be features that the landlord did not appreciate at the time, but that a court could be satisfied that the landlord had made sufficient inquiry. The landlord's opinion might be objectively justified, but the court might subsequently consider that it was

---

[96] The relevant provisions are contained in DDA 1995, ss 25–28 and Sch 3, Part II.

[97] [2004] EWCA Civ 834 (Court of Appeal). See generally: *Croydon London Borough Council v Moody* (1998) 31 HLR 738, CA; *Knowsley Housing Trust v McMullen* [2006] EWCA Civ 539, CA. In *North Devon Homes Ltd v Brazier* [2003] EWHC 574, [2003] HLR 59, QBD, the court held that it was inappropriate to make an order for possession where an eviction was unlawful in the terms of the DDA 1995. The judge considered that the 1995 Act furnished its own code for justified eviction which required a higher threshold than merely to say that the degree of misbehaviour was significant and there was not much prospect of it abating. In addition, the limitations on interference with the defendant's right to respect for her home were set out in the 1995 Act, and the court's powers accorded by the Housing Act 1988 had to be read in a manner that was compatible with her rights under the Human Rights Act 1998.

[98] DDA 1995, s 6(1)(b). The detail of this duty has been considered in Chapters 3–5.

[99] Ibid, s 5 (prior to the October 2004 amendments) and *Clark v TDG Ltd t/a Novacold* [1999] IRLR 318, CA.

[100] See Rights of Access Code of Practice 2006, paras 8.13–8.15.

not reasonable to make a possession order. That might be because circumstances had changed or because there were other relevant features of the situation that could not reasonably have been known by the landlord at the relevant time which fell to be weighed in the balance at the time of the hearing.[101]

6.2.26 The court rejected a submission that the passage of ss 22–24 of the 1995 Act had been intended to leave the law on possession proceedings unaffected. However, it remarked that there were evident difficulties in ss 22–24 which needed to be remedied at an early date. It noted that the sections were not limited to residential tenancies and would apply equally to a business tenant. The court thought that a further difficulty arose from the fact that a tenant could assert that the landlord could not recover possession for non-payment of rent because the reason why the tenant could not manage his or her financial affairs related to a mental disability. Another difficulty was said to lie in the fact that a private landlord who does not have to establish a 'reasonableness' ground for possession may nevertheless be confronted by an assertion that he or she has caused detriment to a disabled tenant by selecting that tenant for eviction. The court suggested that unless Parliament took rapid remedial action, the courts may be confronted with a deluge of cases in which disabled tenants resisted possession proceedings by use of ss 22–24 of the Act.

6.2.27 *Romano* was distinguished in *Richmond Court (Swansea) Ltd v Williams* discussed at **6.2.16**.[102] *Williams* concerned whether the less favourable treatment provisions could be used in effect to construct a duty to make reasonable adjustments to let premises. To an extent, this is now overtaken by the new provisions on let premises discussed immediately below. In *London Borough of Lewisham v Malcolm* the court had to consider the situation where, unlike in *Romano*, the local authority landlord had an immediate right to possession and the court had no discretion to withhold a possession order.[103] The court concluded that the disabled tenant could rely on DDA 1995, s 22(3)(c) (eviction or other detriment) in the possession proceedings even though he had no security of tenure and the court had no discretion not to make a possession order. The court held that it should dismiss the proceedings if it was satisfied that their pursuit was unlawful under s 22(3)(c).

6.3 LET PREMISES AND PREMISES TO LET

6.3.1 The DDA 2005 amends the DDA 1995 in order to impose for the first time a duty to provide reasonable adjustments on landlords and

---

[101] Approving *Rose v Bouchet* [1999] IRLR 463 (Sheriff Principal Nicholson QC).

[102] [2006] EWCA Civ 1719 (Court of Appeal) (a landlord's refusal of consent to the installation of a stair-lift at the disabled tenant's expense did not constitute unlawful discrimination within DDA 1995, s 22(3)).

[103] [2007] EWCA Civ 763 (CA).

others who manage rented premises (so-called 'let premises').[104] These provisions (in ss 24A–24M) came into effect on 4 December 2006 and apply throughout the United Kingdom. They apply to let premises and premises to let.

6.3.2   For the purposes of these new provisions, a person is a controller of let premises if he or she is (a) a person by whom the premises are let; or (b) a person who manages the premises.[105] The term 'let' includes a sub-let and premises shall be treated as let by a person to another where a person has granted another a contractual licence to occupy them.[106]

Let premises: what is unlawful?

6.3.3   It is unlawful for a controller of let premises to discriminate against a disabled person (a) who is a person to whom the premises are let or (b) who, although not a person to whom the premises are let, is lawfully under the letting an occupier of the premises.[107] For this purpose, a controller of let premises discriminates against a disabled person if (a) he or she fails to comply with a duty under s 24C or 24D imposed on him or her by reference to the disabled person; and (b) he or she cannot show that failure to comply with the duty is justified under s 24K.[108]

6.3.4   However, s 24A(1) does not apply if (a) the premises are (or have at any time been) the only or principal home of an individual who is a person by whom they are let; and (b) since entering into the letting the individual has not (and where he or she is not the sole person by whom the premises are let, no other person by whom they are let has) used for the purpose of managing the premises the services of a person who (by profession or trade) manages let premises.[109] Section 24A(1) also does not apply if the premises are of a prescribed description.[110] Moreover, where

---

[104]   DDA 1995, ss 24A–24M, as inserted. Rights of Access Code of Practice 2006, paras 1.4, 3.16, 13.17–13.19 and chapter 15. See Disability Discrimination (Premises) Regulations 2006, SI 2006/887 (in force 4 December 2006); Disability Discrimination (Premises) Regulations (Northern Ireland) 2007, SR 2007/474 (in force 31 December 2007). The Disability Discrimination (Services and Premises) Regulations 1996 and the Disability Discrimination (Services and Premises) (Amendment) Regulations 2002 are revoked.

[105]   DDA 1995, s 24A(3), as inserted. Rights of Access Code of Practice 2006, paras 15.5–15.7.

[106]   Ibid, s 24A(4), as inserted. Rights of Access Code of Practice 2006, para 15.8.

[107]   Ibid, s 24A(1), as inserted. Rights of Access Code of Practice 2006, paras 15.9–15.11. Section 24A applies only in relation to premises in the United Kingdom: s 24A(5). For the purposes of s 23, 'the relevant occupier' means, in a case falling within s 24A(1), a controller of the let premises, or a near relative of his or her; and 'near relative' has here the same meaning as in s 23: s 24B(4), as inserted. Rights of Access Code of Practice 2006, para 17.4.

[108]   DDA 1995, s 24A(2), as inserted. Rights of Access Code of Practice 2006, para 13.17.

[109]   Ibid, s 24B(1), as inserted. Rights of Access Code of Practice 2006, paras 15.21–15.23.

[110]   Ibid, s 24B(2), as inserted.

the conditions mentioned in s 23(2) are satisfied (the exemption for small dwellings), s 24A(1) does not apply.[111]

Duties of controller of let premises

Auxiliary aids or services

6.3.5 It is the duty of the controller of let premises to take such steps as it is reasonable,[112] in all the circumstances of the case, for him or her to have to take in order to provide an auxiliary aid or service under certain conditions.[113] This duty arises where (a) a controller of let premises receives a request made by or on behalf of a person to whom the premises are let; (b) it is reasonable to regard the request as a request that the controller take steps in order to provide an auxiliary aid or service; and (c) either of two further conditions is satisfied.

6.3.6 The first condition is that (a) the auxiliary aid or service would enable a relevant disabled person to enjoy (or facilitate such a person's enjoyment of) the premises, but would be of little or no practical use to the relevant disabled person concerned if he or she were neither a person to whom the premises are let nor an occupier of them; and (b) it would, were the auxiliary aid or service not to be provided, be impossible or unreasonably difficult[114] for the relevant disabled person concerned to enjoy the premises.[115]

6.3.7 The second condition is that (a) the auxiliary aid or service would enable a relevant disabled person to make use (or facilitate such a person's making use) of any benefit or facility, which by reason of the letting is one of which he or she is entitled to make use, but would be of little or no practical use to the relevant disabled person concerned if he or she were neither a person to whom the premises are let nor an occupier of them; and (b) it would, were the auxiliary aid or service not to be provided, be impossible or unreasonably difficult for the relevant disabled person concerned to make use of any benefit or facility, which by reason of the letting is one of which he or she is entitled to make use.[116]

6.3.8 The following are treated as auxiliary aids or services for present purposes: (a) the removal, replacement or provision of any furniture, furnishings, materials, equipment or other chattels;[117] (b) the replacement or provision of any signs or notices; (c) the replacement of any taps or

---

[111] DDA 1995, s 24B(3), as inserted.
[112] Rights of Access Code of Practice 2006, paras 15.45–15.46.
[113] DDA 1995, s 24C(2), as inserted, but subject to s 24E(1). Rights of Access Code of Practice 2006, paras 15.12–15.13 and 15.33–15.34.
[114] Rights of Access Code of Practice 2006, paras 15.47–15.48.
[115] DDA 1995, s 24C(3), as inserted.
[116] Ibid, s 24C(4), as inserted.
[117] But not including the provision of any item which would be a fixture when installed: Disability Discrimination (Premises) Regulations 2006, SI 2006/887, reg 5(2).

door handles; (d) the replacement, provision or adaptation of any door bell or door entry system; and (e) changes to the colour of any surface (such as, for example, a wall or door).[118] It is reasonable to regard a request for a matter falling within the above list as a request for the controller of premises to take steps in order to provide an auxiliary aid or service.[119]

Practices, policies, procedures or terms

6.3.9 It is also the duty of the controller of let premises to take such steps as it is reasonable, in all the circumstances of the case, for him or her to have to take in order to change a practice, policy, procedure or term so as to stop it having a disadvantageous effect.[120] The duty applies where (a) the controller of let premises has a practice, policy or procedure which has the effect of making it impossible, or unreasonably difficult, for a relevant disabled person to enjoy the premises, or to make use of any benefit or facility, which by reason of the letting is one of which he or she is entitled to make use, or (b) a term of the letting has that effect, and (in either case) the specified conditions are satisfied.[121]

6.3.10 The specified conditions are (a) that the practice, policy, procedure or term would not have that effect if the relevant disabled person concerned did not have a disability; and (b) that the controller receives a request made by or on behalf of a person to whom the premises are let; and (c) that it is reasonable to regard the request as a request that the controller take steps in order to change the practice, policy, procedure or term so as to stop it having that effect.[122]

Physical features

6.3.11 For the purposes of ss 24C and 24D, it is never reasonable for a controller of let premises to have to take steps consisting of, or including, the removal or alteration of a physical feature.[123] The term 'physical features' is defined in the way familiar in other parts of the DDA 1995: (a) any feature arising from the design or construction of the premises; (b) any feature of any approach to, exit from, or access to the premises; (c) any fixtures in or on the premises; (d) any other physical element or

---

[118] Disability Discrimination (Premises) Regulations 2006, SI 2006/887, reg 5(1); Rights of Access Code of Practice 2006, paras 15.29–15.30.

[119] Ibid, reg 5(3). The 'controller of premises' here means the controller of let premises: reg 5(4).

[120] DDA 1995, s 24D(3), as inserted, but subject to s 24E(1).

[121] Ibid, s 24D(1), as inserted; Rights of Access Code of Practice 2006, paras 15.12–15.13, 15.36–15.38 and 15.41. Note also Unfair Terms in Consumer Contracts Regulations 1999, SI 1999/2083.

[122] DDA 1995, s 24D(2), as inserted; Rights of Access Code of Practice 2006, paras 15.26–15.28.

[123] Ibid, s 24E(1), as inserted; Rights of Access Code of Practice 2006, para 15.13.

quality of any land comprised in the premises.[124] In the present context, physical features do not include any furniture, furnishings, materials, equipment or other chattels in or on the premises.[125] The following are not to be treated as alterations of physical features: (a) the replacement or provision of any signs or notices; (b) the replacement of any taps or door handles; (c) the replacement, provision or adaptation of any door bell or door entry system; and (d) changes to the colour of any surface (such as, for example, a wall or door).[126]

Let premises: scope of the duties

6.3.12 Sections 24C and 24D impose duties only for the purpose of determining whether a person has, for the purposes of s 24A, discriminated against another and a breach of any such duty is not actionable as such.[127] In these sections, a 'relevant disabled person' in relation to let premises means a particular disabled person who is a person to whom the premises are let; or who, although not a person to whom the premises are let, is lawfully under the letting an occupier of the premises.[128] For the purposes of ss 24C and 24D, the terms of a letting of premises include the terms of any agreement which relates to the letting of the premises.[129]

Let premises: victimisation

6.3.13 Where a duty under s 24C or 24D is imposed on a controller of let premises by reference to a person who, although not a person to whom the premises are let, is lawfully under the letting an occupier of the premises, it is unlawful for a controller of the let premises to discriminate against a person to whom the premises are let.[130] For this purpose, a controller of the let premises discriminates against a person to whom the premises are let if (a) the controller treats that person ('T') less favourably than he or she treats or would treat other persons whose circumstances are the same as T's; and (b) he or she does so because of costs incurred in connection with taking steps to avoid liability under s 24A(1) for failure to comply with the duty.[131]

6.3.14 In comparing T's circumstances with those of any other person for these purposes, the following (as well as the costs having been incurred) shall be disregarded: (a) the making of the request that gave rise

---

[124] Disability Discrimination (Premises) Regulations 2006, SI 2006/887, reg 4(1) and (2). Rights of Access Code of Practice 2006, paras 15.14–15.15.

[125] Ibid, reg 4(3).

[126] Ibid, reg 4(4); Rights of Access Code of Practice 2006, paras 15.16–15.20.

[127] DDA 1995, s 24E(2), as inserted.

[128] Ibid, s 24E(3), as inserted; Rights of Access Code of Practice 2006, paras 15.24–15.25.

[129] Ibid, s 24E(4), as inserted.

[130] Ibid, s 24F(1), as inserted.

[131] Ibid, s 24F(2), as inserted; Rights of Access Code of Practice 2006, para 13.17.

to the imposition of the duty; and (b) the disability of each person who (i) is a disabled person or a person who has had a disability, and (ii) is a person to whom the premises are let or, although not a person to whom the premises are let, is lawfully under the letting an occupier of the premises.[132]

Premises to let

6.3.15   A person is a controller of premises that are to let if he or she is a person who has the premises to let or a person who manages the premises.[133] The term 'let' includes a sub-let.[134] Premises shall be treated as to let by a person to another where a person proposes to grant another a contractual licence to occupy them.[135] References to a person considering taking a letting of premises shall be construed accordingly. Section 24G applies only in relation to premises in the United Kingdom.[136]

Premises to let: what is unlawful?

6.3.16   By virtue of s 24G(1), where a person has premises to let, and a disabled person is considering taking a letting of the premises, it is unlawful for a controller of the premises to discriminate against the disabled person.[137] In these circumstances, by virtue of s 24G(2), a controller of premises that are to let discriminates against a disabled person if (a) he or she fails to comply with a duty under s 24J imposed on him or her by reference to the disabled person; and (b) he or she cannot show that failure to comply with the duty is justified under s 24K.[138]

6.3.17   Section 24G(1) does not apply if the premises to let are (or have been) the only or principal home of a person who has them to let and that individual does not use (and where he or she is not the sole person who has the premises to let, no other person who has the premises to let uses) the services of an estate agent[139] for the purposes of letting the premises.[140] Section 24G(1) also does not apply if the premises are of a prescribed description.[141] Moreover, where the conditions mentioned in s 23(2) are satisfied, s 24G(1) does not apply.[142] For the purposes of s 23,

---

[132] DDA 1995, s 24F(3), as inserted; Rights of Access Code of Practice 2006, paras 15.49–15.52.

[133] Ibid, s 24G(3), as inserted; Rights of Access Code of Practice 2006, paras 15.5–15.7.

[134] Ibid, s 24G(4)(a), as inserted.

[135] Ibid, s 24G(4)(b), as inserted.

[136] Ibid, s 24G(5), as inserted.

[137] Ibid, s 24G(1), as inserted; Rights of Access Code of Practice 2006, paras 15.9–15.11.

[138] Ibid, s 24G(2), as inserted.

[139] Within the meaning given by s 22(6) above.

[140] DDA 1995, s 24H(1), as inserted; Rights of Access Code of Practice 2006, paras 15.21–15.23.

[141] Ibid, s 24H(2), as inserted.

[142] Ibid, s 24H(3), as inserted.

'the relevant occupier' means, in a case falling within s 24G(1), a controller of the premises that are to let, or a near relative of his or (and 'near relative' has here the same meaning as in s 23.[143]

Duties of controller of premises to let

6.3.18   What are the duties for the purpose of s 24G(2)? Section 24J explains.

Auxiliary aids or services

6.3.19   It is the duty of the controller of premises to take such steps as it is reasonable, in all the circumstances of the case, for the controller to have to take in order to provide an auxiliary aid or service in the following circumstances.[144] First, a controller of premises that are to let receives a request made by or on behalf of a relevant disabled person.[145] Secondly, it is reasonable to regard the request as a request that the controller take steps in order to provide an auxiliary aid or service.[146] Thirdly, the auxiliary aid or service would enable the relevant disabled person to become (or facilitate his or her becoming) a person to whom the premises are let, but would be of little or no practical use to him or her if he or she were not considering taking a letting of the premises.[147] Fourthly, were the auxiliary aid or service not to be provided, it would be impossible or unreasonably difficult for the relevant disabled person to become a person to whom the premises are let.[148]

6.3.20   The following are treated as auxiliary aids or services for present purposes: (a) the removal, replacement or provision of any furniture, furnishings, materials, equipment or other chattels;[149] (b) the replacement or provision of any signs or notices; (c) the replacement of any taps or door handles; (d) the replacement, provision or adaptation of any door bell or door entry system; and (e) changes to the colour of any surface (such as, for example, a wall or door).[150] It is reasonable to regard a request for a matter falling within the above list as a request for the controller of premises to take steps in order to provide an auxiliary aid or service.[151]

---

[143]   DDA 1995, s 24H(4), as inserted; Rights of Access Code of Practice 2006, para 17.4.

[144]   Ibid, s 24J(2), as inserted, but subject to s 24J(5).

[145]   Ibid, s 24J(1)(a), as inserted; Rights of Access Code of Practice 2006, paras 15.12–15.13 and 15.35.

[146]   Ibid, s 24J(1)(b), as inserted.

[147]   Ibid, s 24J(1)(c), as inserted.

[148]   Ibid, s 24J(1)(d), as inserted.

[149]   But not including the provision of any item which would be a fixture when installed: Disability Discrimination (Premises) Regulations 2006, SI 2006/887, reg 5(2); Rights of Access Code of Practice 2006, para 15.31-15.32.

[150]   Ibid, reg 5(1); Rights of Access Code of Practice 2006, paras 15.20–15.30.

[151]   Ibid, reg 5(3). The 'controller of premises' here means the controller of premises that are to let: reg 5(4).

Practices, policies or procedures

6.3.21 It is also the duty of the controller of premises to take such steps as it is reasonable, in all the circumstances of the case, for him or her to have to take in order to change a practice, policy or procedure so as to stop it having the following effect.[152] This duty arises where a controller of premises that are to let has a practice, policy or procedure which has the effect of making it impossible (or unreasonably difficult) for a relevant disabled person to become a person to whom the premises are let.[153] The practice, policy or procedure must be one that would not have that effect if the relevant disabled person did not have a disability.[154] The controller must have received a request made by or on behalf of the relevant disabled person.[155] It must be reasonable to regard the request as a request that the controller take steps in order to change the practice, policy or procedure so as to stop it having that effect.[156]

Physical features

6.3.22 For the purposes of s 24J, it is never reasonable for a controller of premises that are to let to have to take steps consisting of (or including) the removal or alteration of a physical feature.[157] The term 'physical features' is defined in the way familiar in other parts of the DDA 1995 (see **6.3.11**).[158] In the present context, physical features do not include any furniture, furnishings, materials, equipment or other chattels in or on the premises.[159] The following are not to be treated as alterations of physical features: (a) the replacement or provision of any signs or notices; (b) the replacement of any taps or door handles; (c) the replacement, provision or adaptation of any door bell or door entry system; and (d) changes to the colour of any surface (such as, for example, a wall or door).[160]

Premises to let: scope of the duties

6.3.23 In s 24J 'relevant disabled person', in relation to premises that are to let, means a particular disabled person who is considering taking a letting of the premises.[161] The section imposes duties only for the purpose

---

[152] DDA 1995, s 24J(4), as inserted, but subject to s 24J(5); Rights of Access Code of Practice 2006, paras 15.36–15.38.
[153] Ibid, s 24J(3)(a), as inserted.
[154] Ibid, s 24J(3)(b), as inserted.
[155] Ibid, s 24J(3)(c), as inserted.
[156] Ibid, s 24J(3)(d), as inserted.
[157] Ibid, s 24J(5), as inserted; Rights of Access Code of Practice 2006, para 15.13.
[158] Disability Discrimination (Premises) Regulations 2006, SI 2006/887, reg 4(1) and (2).
[159] Ibid, reg 4(3).
[160] Ibid, reg 4(4).
[161] DDA 1995, s 24J(6), as inserted; Rights of Access Code of Practice 2006, para 15.24–15.25.

of determining whether a person has, for the purposes of s 24G, discriminated against another. Accordingly, a breach of any such duty is not actionable as such.[162]

Let premises and premises to let: justification

6.3.24 For the purposes of ss 24A(2) and 24G(2), a person's failure to comply with a duty is justified only if (a) in his or her opinion,[163] one of the conditions mentioned in s 24K(2) is satisfied;[164] and (b) it is reasonable, in all the circumstances of the case, for him or her to hold that opinion.[165]

6.3.25 The first possible condition is that it is necessary to refrain from complying with the duty in order not to endanger the health or safety of any person (which may include that of the disabled person concerned).[166] The second possible condition is that the disabled person concerned is incapable of entering into an enforceable agreement, or of giving informed consent, and for that reason the failure is reasonable.[167] However, this second condition does not apply where another person is acting for a disabled person by virtue of a power of attorney; or functions conferred by or under Part 7 of the Mental Health Act 1983; or, in Scotland, powers exercisable in relation to the disabled person's property or affairs in consequence of the appointment of a guardian, tutor or judicial factor.[168]

Regulations and exclusions

6.3.26 Section 24L contains a general regulation-making power in relation to ss 24–24K.[169]

6.3.27 Section 24M anticipates that the premises provisions should not apply where other provisions operate. First, ss 22–24L do not apply in relation to the provision of premises by a provider of services where it

---

[162] DDA 1995, s 24J(7), as inserted.

[163] Regulations may make provision as to circumstances in which it is (or is not) reasonable for a person to hold the opinion: DDA 1995, s 24K(3)(a), as inserted.

[164] Regulations may amend or omit a specified condition or make provision for it not to apply in prescribed circumstances: DDA 1995, s 24K(3)(b), as inserted.

[165] DDA 1995, s 24K(1), as inserted; Rights of Acess Code of Practice 2006, chapter 17. Regulations may make provision as to circumstances (other than any for the time being mentioned in s 24K(2)) in which a failure is to be taken to be justified: s 24K(3)(c), as inserted.

[166] Ibid, s 24K(2)(a), as inserted.

[167] Ibid, s 24K(2)(b), as inserted.

[168] Disability Discrimination (Premises) Regulations 2006, SI 2006/887, reg 2.

[169] See Disability Discrimination (Premises) Regulations 2006, SI 2006/887 (in force 4 December 2006); Disability Discrimination (Premises) Regulations (Northern Ireland) 2007, SR 2007/474 (in force 31 December 2007).

provides the premises in providing services to members of the public.[170] Secondly, those provisions do not apply in relation to the provision, in the course of a Part 2 relationship (that is, a relationship in the employment field), of premises by the regulated party to the other party.[171]

6.3.28   Thirdly, the sections do not apply in relation to the provision of premises to a student or prospective student (a) by a responsible body within the meaning of Chapter 1 or 2 of Part 4 (the education provisions of the Act), or (b) by an authority in discharging any functions mentioned in s 28F(1).[172] Fourthly, ss 22–24L do not apply to anything which is unlawful under s 21F (discrimination by private clubs, etc) or which would be unlawful under that section but for the operation of any provision in or made under this Act.[173]

The problem of leases

6.3.29   Under the terms of a lease or other binding obligation,[174] a controller of let premises might be required to obtain the consent of another person to change a term of a letting. But for that requirement, it might be reasonable for the controller of let premises to change the term in order to comply with a duty under s 24D(3) (the duty of the controller of let premises to take such steps as it is reasonable, in all the circumstances of the case, for him or her to have to take in order to change a practice, policy, procedure or term so as to stop it having a disadvantageous effect). It is reasonable for the controller of let premises to have to request that consent, but it is not reasonable for him or her to have to change the term of the letting before that consent is obtained.[175]

6.3.30   Subject to the discussion in **6.3.29**,[176] the Disability Discrimination (Premises) Regulations 2006 prescribe circumstances in which it is reasonable for the purposes of s 24D(3) for a controller of let premises to have to take specified steps.[177]

---

[170]   DDA 1995, s 24M(1)(a), as inserted. This has effect subject to any prescribed exceptions: s 24M(2). The terms 'provider of services' and 'providing services' have the same meaning as in DDA 1995, s 19. See Chapter 5.

[171]   Ibid, s 24M(1)(b), as inserted. A 'Part 2 relationship' means a relationship during the course of which an act of discrimination against, or harassment of, one party to the relationship by the other party to it is unlawful under ss 4–15C; and in relation to a Part 2 relationship, 'regulated party' means the party whose acts of discrimination, or harassment, are made unlawful by ss 4–15C: DDA 1995, s 24M(4). See Chapters 3 and 4.

[172]   Ibid, s 24M(1)(c), as inserted. The term 'student' includes 'pupil': s 24M(5). See Chapter 7.

[173]   Ibid, s 24M(1)(d), as inserted. See Chapter 5.

[174]   In this context, 'binding obligation' means any legally binding obligation in relation to premises, whether arising from an agreement or otherwise: Disability Discrimination (Premises) Regulations 2006, SI 2006/887, reg 6(2).

[175]   Ibid, reg 6(1). Rights of Access Code of Practice 2006, para 15.44.

[176]   Ibid, reg 7(4).

[177]   Ibid, reg 7(1). See Rights of Access Code of Practice 2006, paras 15.42–15.43.

6.3.31 First, the controller of let premises must be subject to a duty under s 24D(3) in relation to a term of the letting of a dwelling house.[178] Secondly, the duty must have arisen because a term of the letting prohibits the person to whom the premises are let from making alterations or improvements to the premises.[179] Thirdly, the terms of the letting must contain no exception to that prohibition for alterations or improvements to be made with the consent of the controller of let premises.[180] Fourthly, the person to whom the premises are let must have requested permission to make an improvement to the premises.[181] Fifthly, if the improvement in question were excluded from the prohibition, the term must no longer have the effect of making it impossible or unreasonably difficult for a relevant disabled person to enjoy the premises or make use of any benefit or facility which by reason of the letting is one of which he or she is entitled to make use.[182] Finally, it must be reasonable in all the circumstances for the person to whom the premises are let to make the improvement in question.[183]

6.3.32 Where all the above prescribed circumstances are satisfied, it is reasonable for the controller of let premises to have to take steps to change the term of the letting that prohibits the person to whom the premises are let from making alterations or improvements to the premises. That means that, so far as the term relates to the improvement in question, it becomes a term which permits the making of that improvement, subject to the imposition of reasonable conditions by the controller of let premises.[184]

Commonholds and let premises

6.3.33 Premises which are a commonhold unit, of which a person is a unit-holder, are treated as premises which are let to that person for the purposes of ss 24A–24F.[185] In these circumstances, a commonhold association which exercises functions in relation to the premises is treated as a person who manages the premises.[186] For the purposes of ss 24D and 24E, any reference to a term of the letting is to be treated as including a reference to a term of the commonhold community statement and any other term applicable by virtue of the transfer of the unit to the

---

[178] Disability Discrimination (Premises) Regulations 2006, SI 2006/887, reg 7(2)(a).
[179] Ibid, reg 7(2)(b).
[180] Ibid, reg 7(2)(c).
[181] Ibid, reg 7(2)(d).
[182] Ibid, reg 7(2)(e).
[183] Ibid, reg 7(2)(f).
[184] Ibid, reg 7(3). Rights of Access Code of Practice 2006, paras 15.42–15.43.
[185] Ibid, regs 1(2) and 9(1); Commonhold and Leasehold Reform Act 2002, Part 1; Rights of Access Code of Practice 2006, paras 16.11–16.14 and 16.11–16.14.
[186] Disability Discrimination (Premises) Regulations 2006, SI 2006/887, regs 1(2) and 9(2)(a); Commonhold and Leasehold Reform Act 2002, Part 1.

unit-holder.[187] For the purposes of ss 24C(4) and 24D(1), any benefit or facility which, by reason of the letting, is one of which a relevant disabled person is entitled to make use, shall be treated as including any benefit or facility which by reason of any term of the commonhold community statement and any other term applicable by virtue of the transfer of the unit to the unit-holder is one of which a relevant disabled person is entitled to make use.[188] A person who is lawfully an occupier of the unit, although not a unit-holder nor a person lawfully occupying the unit under a letting of it, is to be treated as a person who, although not a person to whom the premises are let, is lawfully under a letting an occupier of them.[189]

6.4 ALTERATIONS TO PREMISES

The duty to make reasonable adjustments to premises

6.4.1 In respect of Part 2 of the DDA 1995, in relation to the employment field generally, where any physical features of premises occupied by a respondent place a disabled person at a substantial disadvantage in comparison with non-disabled persons, it is the duty of the respondent to take such steps as it is reasonable in all the circumstances of the case to take in order to prevent the physical feature in question having that effect.[190] That duty might require the respondent to make adjustments to the premises, subject to considerations such as practicability, cost and resources. A failure to consider or discharge that duty can amount to an act of unlawful discrimination.

6.4.2 In respect of Part 3 of the DDA 1995, a detailed duty to make reasonable adjustments is also placed upon service providers, public authorities and private clubs.[191] Where a physical feature of a building makes it impossible or unreasonably difficult for disabled persons to make use of a service provided to the public by a service provider (including public authorities and private clubs in this phrase), it is the duty of the service provider to make reasonable adjustments. A service provider's unjustified failure to discharge a duty to make reasonable adjustments to its premises in these ways is a potential act of discrimination.[192]

---

[187] Disability Discrimination (Premises) Regulations 2006, SI 2006/887, regs 1(2) and 9(2)(b); Commonhold and Leasehold Reform Act 2002, Part 1.

[188] Disability Discrimination (Premises) Regulations 2006, SI 2006/887, reg 9(2)(c).

[189] Ibid, reg 9(2)(d).

[190] Ibid, s 4A(1)(b). See Chapters 3 and 4.

[191] Ibid, ss 21, 21E and 21H; Disability Discrimination (Private Clubs, etc) Regulations 2005. See Chapters 5 and 9.

[192] Ibid, ss 20, 21D and 21G; Rights of Access Code of Practice 2006, chapters 6–7 and Appendix B. See also the Disability Discrimination (Providers of Services) (Adjustment of Premises) Regulations 2001, SI 2001/3253 (as amended by SI 2004/1429 and 2005/2901), in force from 1 October 2004, but not extending to Northern Ireland.

6.4.3 Until recently, there was no comparable duty to make reasonable adjustments to premises in respect of the disposal or management of premises.[193] Now, as discussed above, there is a limited duty to make reasonable adjustments in respect of premises to let and let premises.[194] In Part 4 cases, there is also a duty to make reasonable adjustments in respect of the physical features of premises in further and higher education, and in respect of general qualifications bodies (but not schools or education authorities).[195]

Building regulations: employment field

6.4.4 For the purposes of the statutory duty to make adjustments to premises occupied by a Part 2 respondent in the employment field, the fact that the design or construction of a building meets the requirements of Part M of the Building Regulations[196] does not diminish a respondent's duty to make reasonable adjustments in respect of its physical features.[197] It is unlikely to be reasonable for a respondent to have to make an adjustment to a physical feature of a building that it occupies if the design and construction of that physical feature are in accordance with the relevant British Standard.[198] It is also unlikely to be reasonable for a respondent to have to make an adjustment to a physical feature that accords with the relevant provisions of the most up-to-date version of Approved Document M (the guidance accompanying the Building Regulations).[199] It might also be necessary to obtain statutory consents to an alteration (planning permission, listed building consent, fire regulations approval, etc) and an adjustment would not be a reasonable one to make if the occupier has applied for such consent and it has been refused. In such a case, the duty to make adjustments should take account of alternative ways of achieving a viable adjustment.[200]

---

[193] DDA 1995, ss 22–24 (discussed at **6.2**).

[194] Ibid, ss 24G and 24J (discussed at **6.3**).

[195] Ibid, s 28T.

[196] Building Act 1984, s 122; Building Regulations 2000, SI 2000/2531, Sch 1; (in Scotland) Part T of the Technical Standards for compliance with the Building Standards (Scotland) Regulations 1990, SI 1990/2179 (amended by SI 1993/1457, SI 1994/1266, SI 1996/2251 and SI 1997/2157). In April 2000, in Scotland, Part T was discontinued and its general requirements were integrated into the general Technical Standards (SSI 1999/173 and SSI 2001/320).

[197] Code of Practice: Employment and Occupation (2004), paras 12.6–12.11; Code of Practice: Trade Organisations and Qualifications Bodies (2004), paras 9.6–9.10. See previously: Disability Discrimination (Employment) Regulations 1996, SI 1996/1456, regs 2 and 8 (now revoked).

[198] British Standard 8300:2001, *Design of Buildings and their Approaches to Meet the Needs of Disabled People – Code of Practice*.

[199] The most recent version is the 2004 edition.

[200] Code of Practice: Employment and Occupation (2004), paras 12.3–12.5 (and example); Code of Practice: Trade Organisations and Qualifications Bodies (2004), paras 9.3–9.5 (and example).

Building regulations: service providers

6.4.5   In relation to service providers and Part 3 of the DDA 1995 in general, the revised Rights of Access Code of Practice 2006 gives helpful guidance on the interaction of the building regulations with the service provider's prospective duty to make adjustments to premises.[201] In general terms, if the physical features of a building in England and Wales accord with Approved Document M,[202] then it will comply with Part M (access and facilities for disabled people) of the building regulations by making reasonable provision for disabled people to gain access to and use the building with reasonable safety and convenience.[203] Part M applies to new buildings and some extensions to buildings since 1985. Provided the relevant physical feature of a building meets the requirements of Part M by according with the guidance in Approved Document M, the service provider will enjoy an exemption from having to make adjustments to that feature if 10 years or less have passed since it was installed. Even if the feature in question does not accord with Approved Document M, it may have been accepted by the relevant authority (such as a building control officer) as meeting the requirements of Part M. If the feature in question enables disabled persons to access and use the building with comparable ease, it is unlikely to be reasonable for the service provider to have to make an adjustment to it within 10 years of its installation or construction.[204]

6.4.6   The position in Scotland is similar but not identical. In Scotland, between April 1991 and April 2000, the appropriate reference was to Part T of the Technical Standards for compliance with the Building Standards (Scotland) Regulations 1990.[205] In April 2000, Part T was discontinued and its general requirements were integrated into the general Technical Standards.[206] In 2003, the Building (Scotland) Act 2003 was passed and a new system of building standards, based upon the Building (Scotland) Regulations 2004, came into operation in May 2005. Guidance on compliance with the functional standards set out in the Regulations is given in the Scottish Building Standards Agency (SBSA) Technical Handbooks.

---

[201] Rights of Access Code of Practice 2006, Appendix B. This account draws from that source. The Code's explanation of what are complex provisions is difficult to improve upon.

[202] This is the guidance issued to accompany the Building Regulations 1991 or 2000. Approved Document M for these purposes means the 1992 or 1999 or 2004 edition of that document. The 2004 edition came into force on 1 May 2004. It is more detailed than the earlier editions and might achieve greater accessibility for disabled persons.

[203] The latest version of Part M of the Building Regulations is now found in Sch 1 to the Building Regulations 2000, SI 2000/2531.

[204] If the feature is not covered by Approved Document M, then the service provider may have to make an adjustment to it.

[205] SI 1990/2179, issued by the Scottish Office in 1990 and subsequently amended (see SI 1993/1457, SI 1994/1266, SI 1996/2251 and SI 1997/2157).

[206] See SSI 1999/173 and SSI 2001/320.

6.4.7 The Disability Discrimination (Service Providers and Public Authorities Carrying Out Functions) Regulations 2005[207] prescribe particular circumstances (for the purposes of DDA 1995, ss 21 and 21E) in which it is not reasonable for a provider of services or a public authority carrying out its functions to have to take the steps specified in this regulation.[208] It is not reasonable for a provider of services or a public authority carrying out its functions to have to remove or alter a physical feature where the feature concerned (a) was provided in or in connection with a building for the purpose of assisting people to have access to the building or to use facilities provided in the building; and (b) satisfies the relevant design standard.[209] Whether a physical feature satisfies the relevant design standard shall be determined in accordance with Schedule 1 to the Regulations.[210]

6.4.8 A physical feature does not satisfy the relevant design standard where more than 10 years have elapsed since (a) the day on which the construction or installation of the feature was completed; or (b) in the case of a physical feature provided as part of a larger building project, the day on which the works in relation to that project were completed.[211] Subject to that proviso, a physical feature (in relation to a building situated in England or Wales) satisfies the relevant design standard where it accords with the relevant objectives, design considerations and provisions in Approved Document M.[212] in relation to a building situated in Scotland a physical feature satisfies the relevant design standard where (a) it was provided in or in connection with the building on or after 30 June 1994 and before 1 May 2005 in accordance with the Technical Standards relevant in relation to that feature; or (b) it was provided in or in connection with the building on or after 1 May 2005 in accordance with the relevant functional standards and guidance in the Technical Handbook.[213]

---

[207] The Regulations revoke and replace (in part) the Disability Discrimination (Services and Premises) Regulations 1996, (in full) the Disability Discrimination (Services and Premises) Regulations 1999, (in full) the Disability Discrimination (Providers of Services) (Adjustment of Premises) (Amendment) Regulations 2004 and (in full) the Disability Discrimination (Providers of Services) (Adjustment of Premises) (Amendment) Regulations 2005. In addition, they amend the application of the Disability Discrimination (Providers of Services) (Adjustment of Premises) Regulations 2001 and revoke and replace reg 3 of and the Sch to those Regulations. These changes partially consolidate provisions in relation to providers of services. In addition, the Regulations make provision in relation to public authorities, which arises out of new duties on public authorities carrying out their functions, introduced by the DDA 2005.

[208] SI 2005/2901, reg 11(1).

[209] Ibid, reg 11(2).

[210] Ibid, reg 11(3).

[211] Ibid, Sch 1, para 1(3).

[212] Ibid, Sch 1, para 1(1).

[213] Ibid, Sch 1, para 1(2).

6.4.9   In England and Wales, 'Approved Document M' means the 1992 or 1999 or 2004 edition of that document.[214] The reference to 'the Building Regulations' means the Building Regulations 1991 or the Building Regulations 2000.[215] In the case of a physical feature provided as part of building works to which the Building Regulations applied, Approved Document M is whichever edition is the practical guidance which was relevant in relation to meeting the requirements of the Building Regulations which applied to those building works.[216] In any other case, Approved Document M is whichever edition was the last edition published at the time when the physical feature was provided in or in connection with the building.[217] A physical feature is deemed to be provided in or in connection with the building on (a) the day upon which the works to install or construct the feature were commenced; or (b) in the case of a physical feature provided as part of a larger building project, the day upon which the works in relation to that project were commenced.[218] Where in relation to the physical feature in question any provision of Approved Document M refers to a standard or specification (in whole or in part), that standard or specification shall be construed as referring to any equivalent standard or specification recognised for use in any member state of the European Community or European Economic Area.[219]

6.4.10   In Scotland, 'Technical Standards' means the Technical Standards as defined by reg 2(1) of the Building Standards (Scotland) Regulations 1990 in effect at the time when the physical feature was provided in or in connection with the building. The term 'Technical Handbook' means the Scottish Building Standards Agency Technical Handbook for non-domestic buildings approved by the Scottish Ministers as guidance meeting the requirements of the Building (Scotland) Regulations 2004.[220] A physical feature is deemed to be provided in or in connection with the building on (a) the day upon which the works to install or construct the feature were commenced; or (b) in the case of a physical feature provided as part of a larger building project, the day upon which the works in relation to that project were commenced.[221] In a case where the physical feature is provided as part of building works in relation to which an application for a warrant for the construction or change of use of the building has been made and granted, the works are deemed to have commenced on the day upon which the application for the warrant was made.[222] Where in relation to the physical feature in question any provision of the Technical Standards or Technical Handbook refers to a standard or specification (in whole or in part), that standard or

---

[214]   SI 2005/2901, Sch 1, para 2(1)(a).
[215]   Ibid, Sch 1, para 2(1)(b).
[216]   Ibid, Sch 1, para 2(2).
[217]   Ibid, Sch 1, para 2(3).
[218]   Ibid, Sch 1, para 2(4).
[219]   Ibid, Sch 1, para 2(5).
[220]   Ibid, Sch 1, para 3(1).
[221]   Ibid, Sch 1, para 3(2).
[222]   Ibid, Sch 1, para 3(3).

specification shall be construed as referring to any equivalent standard or specification recognised for use in any member state of the European Community or European Economic Area.[223]

6.4.11 Similar provisions apply in relation to private clubs[224] and in relation to educational institutions in further and higher education.[225]

The problem of leases

6.4.12 The duty to make reasonable adjustments to premises is primarily imposed upon the person who occupies those premises. Where that person owns the premises there can be no question that the person has a right to make alterations to the premises, subject only to planning, building and environmental regulation. In such a case, if there is a duty to make an adjustment, and if an alteration to the fabric or a physical feature of the premises would otherwise be a reasonable adjustment to make, then the occupier will be expected to take such steps, all other things being equal.

6.4.13 Nevertheless, many persons occupy premises as tenants under a commercial lease. A term or covenant in that lease might forbid or restrict alterations to the property or might only permit such alterations with the prior consent of the landlord. In that latter case, consent under the lease might not be forthcoming if the landlord reasonably or unreasonably withholds permission. In these circumstances, the occupier might be unable to discharge its duty to a disabled person to make reasonable adjustments.[226] This could amount to an unlawful act of disability discrimination, although the restriction in the lease or the landlord's refusal to countenance an alteration to the occupied premises might bring a justification defence into play, where available.

The effect of the DDA 1995 upon premises occupied under leases

6.4.14 The DDA 1995 clarifies the relation between the potentially conflicting legal obligations of disability discrimination law and the law of landlord and tenant. Separate provision is made for Part 2 (the employment field)[227] and Part 3 (service providers, public authorities and

---

[223] SI 2005/2901, Sch 1, para 3(4).

[224] Disability Discrimination (Private Clubs etc) Regulations 2005, SI 2005/3258, reg 12 and Sch.

[225] Disability Discrimination (Educational Institutions) (Alteration of Leasehold Premises) Regulations 2005, SI 2005/1070; Post-16 Code of Practice 2007, chapter 12.

[226] It is arguable (but uncertain) that a restrictive clause or covenant in a commercial lease, which prevents a tenant carrying out an alteration in pursuit of a duty to make a reasonable adjustment under the DDA 1995, is invalid as being a term of an agreement which limits the operation of the statute. See also HL Deb, vol 566, col 1016.

[227] DDA 1995, s 18A and Sch 4, Part 1 (occupation by employer etc). See also Code of Practice: Employment and Occupation (2004), paras 12.13–12.31 and Code of Practice: Trade Organisations and Qualifications Bodies (2004), paras 9.12–9.30.

private clubs) and Part 4 (in the educational field).[228] The effect may be to prevent landlords of commercial or industrial premises thwarting or undermining the objectives of the legislation. The relevant statutory provisions apply where the occupier occupies premises under a 'lease'.[229] A 'lease' for this purpose includes a tenancy, sub-lease or sub-tenancy, and an agreement for a lease, tenancy, sub-lease or sub-tenancy.[230] The term 'sub-lease' means any sub-term created out of or deriving from a (superior) leasehold interest and 'sub-tenancy' means any tenancy created out of or deriving from a superior tenancy.[231] Where there are references in the statute[232] to a 'lessor', that reference is to be taken as referring to the lessor who is the occupier's immediate landlord in the case of an occupier occupying premises under a sub-lease or sub-tenancy.[233]

6.4.15 The statutory provisions apply if the effect of the lease would otherwise be that the occupier would not be entitled to make a particular alteration to the premises,[234] and if the alteration is one which the occupier proposes to make in order to comply with a statutory duty to make reasonable adjustments.[235] If the terms and conditions of a lease impose conditions which are to apply if the occupier alters the premises, then the occupier is treated[236] as not being entitled to make the alteration.[237] Similarly, if the terms and conditions of the lease entitle the lessor to impose conditions when giving any consent to the occupier to alter the premises, the occupier is treated[238] as not being entitled to make the alteration.[239] If the above conditions are satisfied,[240] the DDA 1995 provides that the lease shall have effect as if it provided for the occupier to be entitled to make the alteration with the written consent of the lessor.[241] In other words, a statutory term is implied into the lease or agreement at

---

[228] DDA 1995, s 27 Sch 4, Part 2 (occupation by persons subject to a duty under ss 21 (service providers), 21E (public authorities) or 21H (private clubs)), Part 3 (occupation by educational institutions) and Part 4 (occupation by general qualifications bodies). See Rights of Access Code of Practice (2006), Appendix B and Post-16 Code of Practice, Chapter 12.

[229] DDA 1995, ss 18A(1)(a) and 27(1)(a).

[230] Ibid, ss 18A(3) and 27(3). The Act provides that regulations may further define the meaning of these terms.

[231] Disability Discrimination (Employment Field) (Leasehold Premises) Regulations 2004, SI 2004/153, reg 8 (for the purposes of DDA 1995, s 18A); Disability Discrimination (Providers of Services) (Adjustments of Premises) Regulations 2001, SI 2001/3253, reg 4 (for the purposes of DDA 1995, s 27).

[232] DDA 1995, s 18A and Sch 4, para 1; s 27 and Sch 4, paras 5, 10 and 15.

[233] Disability Discrimination (Employment Field) (Leasehold Premises) Regulations 2004, SI 2004/153, reg 9 (for the purposes of DDA 1995, s 18A); Disability Discrimination (Providers of Services) (Adjustment of Premises) Regulations 2001, SI 2001/3253, reg 9 (for the purposes of s 27 and Sch 4, paras 5-7).

[234] DDA 1995, ss 18A(1)(b) and 27(1)(b).

[235] Ibid, ss 18A(1)(c) and 27(1)(c).

[236] For the purposes of ibid, ss 18A(1)(b) and 27(1)(b).

[237] Ibid, ss 18A(4)(a) and 27(4)(a).

[238] For the purposes of ibid, ss 18A(1)(b) and 27(1)(b).

[239] Ibid, ss 18A(4)(b) and 27(4)(b).

[240] Ibid, s 18A(1) or s 27(1).

[241] Ibid, ss 18A(2)(a) and 27(2)(a). See Code of Practice: Employment and Occupation

issue. The statutory term requires that, if the occupier wishes to make an alteration to the premises, the occupier must first make a written application to the lessor for consent.[242] Furthermore, the Act implies into the terms of the lease a requirement that, if a written application for consent is made by the occupier, the lessor will not withhold consent unreasonably.[243] In turn, the lessor is deemed to be entitled to make any consent the subject of reasonable conditions.[244]

6.4.16 Where the occupier occupies premises under a sub-lease or sub-tenancy, any superior lease under which the premises are held has effect (except to the extent to which it expressly so provides) in relation to the lessor and lessee who are parties to the superior lease as if it provided for the lessee to have to make a written application to the lessor for consent to the alteration.[245] If such an application is made, the superior lease has effect as if it provided for the lessor not to withhold its consent unreasonably and for the lessor to be entitled to make its consent subject to reasonable conditions.

6.4.17 Rather puzzlingly, the statutory wording appears to restrict the vigour of this otherwise quite far-reaching adjustment of the rights of commercial landlord and tenant. It is apparent that a lease is to have effect as modified by the statutory implied terms 'except to the extent to which it expressly so provides'.[246] The reference to 'it' must be taken to be a reference to the lease.[247] This suggests that the landlord might impose express terms in the lease that have the intent and effect of thwarting the statutory implications made in the lease. If that is right – and the author does not believe that this is what was intended – then it may be that such express terms would have to surmount the test of an invalid agreement.

Employment field cases

6.4.18 Prior to 1 October 2004, in cases in the employment field, it was not reasonable for a person (in relation to premises occupied by it) to have

---

(2004), para 12.13; Code of Practice: Trade Organisations and Qualifications Bodies (2004), para 9.12; Rights of Access Code of Practice (2002), para 6.32.

[242] DDA 1995, ss 18A(2)(b) and 27(2)(b).

[243] Ibid, ss 18A(2)(c) and 27(2)(c).

[244] Ibid, ss 18A(2)(d) and 27(2)(d).

[245] Ibid, s 18A(2A), inserted by Disability Discrimination (Employment Field) (Leasehold Premises) Regulations 2004, SI 2004/153, reg 9(b) and modifying s 18A (from 1 October 2004); DDA 1995, s 27(2A) inserted by Disability Discrimination (Providers of Services) (Adjustments of Premises) Regulations 2001, SI 2001/3253 (as amended by SI 2004/1429), reg 9(1) and (3) and modifying s 27 (in force from 1 October 2004). The former provisions made by the Disability Discrimination (Employment) Regulations 1996 and the Disability Discrimination (Sub-leases and Sub-tenancies) Regulations 1996 have been revoked from 1 October 2004.

[246] DDA 1995, ss 18A(2) and 27(2).

[247] It is possible that it is a drafting error and that the reference was intended to be to the subsection rather than to the lease (the phrase 'except to the extent to which [the sub-section] expressly so provides' might make better sense).

to take a step to comply with a statutory duty to make reasonable adjustments, if this would be contrary to the terms of any lease under which the person occupied the premises, in the following circumstances. The occupier had applied to the lessor in writing to take the step; the occupier had indicated in writing that it proposed to take the step (subject to the lessor's consent) in order to comply with its statutory duty; the lessor had withheld that consent; and the occupier had informed the disabled person that it had applied for the consent of the lessor and that the lessor had withheld that consent.[248] This provision has now been revoked and not replaced. It is nevertheless clear that the occupier must write to the lessor to seek consent to the proposed step under the lease.

6.4.19 Where, under any binding obligation, a person is required to obtain the consent of any person to any alteration of the premises occupied by it, it is always reasonable for the occupier to have to take steps (not including an application to a court or tribunal) to obtain that consent. It is never reasonable for the occupier to have to make that alteration before that consent is obtained.[249] In this context, a binding obligation means a legally binding obligation (not contained in a lease) in relation to the premises (whether arising from an agreement or otherwise).[250] An example of such an obligation would include a mortgage or a charge or, in Scotland, a feu disposition.[251]

6.4.20 It is implied that the lessor will not withhold consent unreasonably.[252] The landlord is entitled to make any consent the subject of reasonable conditions.[253] If so, the occupier must carry out the alteration, subject to those conditions. A lessor is to be taken to have withheld consent to an alteration where the lessor has received a written application by or on behalf of the occupier for consent to make the alteration and the lessor has failed within a period of 21 days (or such longer period as is reasonable) either (a) to reply consenting to or refusing the application; or (b) to reply consenting to the application, subject to obtaining the consent of another person required under a superior lease or binding obligation (such as a mortgage or charge or, in Scotland, a feu disposition) *and* seek that consent.[254] If the lessor belatedly meets the

---

[248]   Disability Discrimination (Employment) Regulations 1996, SI 1996/1456, reg 15 (now revoked).

[249]   DDA 1995, s 18B(3) and (4), replacing Disability Discrimination (Employment) Regulations 1996, reg 10 (from 1 October 2004).

[250]   DDA 1995, s 18B(5), replacing Disability Discrimination (Employment) Regulations 1996, reg 2 (from 1 October 2004).

[251]   Code of Practice: Employment and Occupation (2004) para 12.12 (and example); Code of Practice: Trade Organisations and Qualifications Bodies (2004), para 9.11.

[252]   DDA 1995, s 18A(2)(c).

[253]   Ibid, s 18A(2)(d).

[254]   Disability Discrimination (Employment Field) (Leasehold Premises) Regulations 2004, SI 2004/153, reg 4(1) and (2) for the purposes of DDA 1995, s 18A and Sch 4, Part I. In this context, a binding obligation is a legally binding obligation (not contained in a lease) in relation to the premises, whether arising from an agreement or otherwise: reg 2. The period of 21 days begins with the day on which the application is received. See

above requirements, it shall be taken to have withheld its consent from the date of the failure to meet the requirements on time, but then shall be treated as having not withheld its consent from the time when it belatedly met the requirements.[255] A lessor is treated as not having sought the consent of another person (if so required) unless the lessor has applied in writing to that person indicating that the lessor's consent to the alteration has been applied for in order to comply with a statutory duty to make a reasonable adjustment and that the lessor has given its consent conditionally upon obtaining the other person's consent.[256]

6.4.21 A lessor withholds consent unreasonably where the lease provides that consent shall or will be given to an alteration of the kind in question.[257] Consent is also withheld unreasonably where the lease provides that consent shall or will be given to an alteration of the kind in question if the consent is sought in a particular way and that has been complied with.[258] Moreover, a lessor withholds consent unreasonably where the lessor is treated as withholding consent.[259] On the other hand, a lessor is regarded as acting reasonably in withholding consent where there is a binding obligation (for example, a mortgage or charge) requiring the consent of a third party to an alteration; the lessor has taken steps to seek that consent; and that consent has not been given or has been given subject to a condition making it reasonable for the lessor to withhold consent.[260] Alternatively, a lessor acts reasonably in withholding consent where the lessor is bound by an agreement allowing the lessor to consent to the alteration subject to a condition that the lessor makes a payment and that condition does not permit the lessor to make its consent subject to a condition that the occupier reimburse that payment.[261] If it would be reasonable for the lessor to withhold consent, but consent has nevertheless been given, it would be reasonable to impose a condition on that consent that upon expiry of the lease the occupier (or any assignee or successor) must reinstate any relevant part of the premises to its prior state.[262]

---

further Code of Practice: Employment and Occupation (2004), paras 12.16–12.21; Code of Practice: Trade Organisations and Qualifications Bodies (2004), paras 9.16–9.20.

[255] Disability Discrimination (Employment Field) (Leasehold Premises) Regulations 2004, SI 2004/153, reg 4(3).

[256] Ibid, reg 4(4).

[257] Ibid, reg 5(1) and (2).

[258] Ibid, reg 5(1) and (3).

[259] Ibid, reg 5(1) and (4) by reference to reg 4. See further Code of Practice: Employment and Occupation (2004), paras 12.22–12.24 (and examples); Code of Practice: Trade Organisations and Qualifications Bodies (2004), paras 9.21–9.23 (and examples).

[260] Disability Discrimination (Employment Field) (Leasehold Premises) Regulations 2004, SI 2004/153, reg 6(1). In this context, a binding obligation is a legally binding obligation (not contained in a lease) in relation to the premises whether arising from an agreement or otherwise: reg 2. See further Code of Practice: Employment and Occupation (2004), para 12.25; Code of Practice: Trade Organisations and Qualifications Bodies (2004), para 9.24.

[261] Disability Discrimination (Employment Field) (Leasehold Premises) Regulations 2004, SI 2004/153, reg 6(2).

[262] Ibid, reg 7(2).

6.4.22 Where the lessor gives consent to an alteration, but subject to a condition, such a condition is regarded as *reasonable* if it is any of the following conditions (or a condition to a similar effect):

- the occupier must obtain any necessary planning permission (and any other consent or permission) required by or under any enactment;[263]

- the occupier must submit any plans or specifications for the alteration to the lessor for approval (provided the condition binds the lessor not to withhold approval unreasonably) and that the work is carried out in accordance with such plans or specifications;[264]

- the lessor must be permitted a reasonable opportunity to inspect the work when complete;[265] or

- the occupier must repay to the lessor the costs reasonably incurred in connection with the giving of the consent.[266]

6.4.23 Special provisions deal with a failure by an occupier to obtain consent to the alteration.[267] These apply where any question arises as to whether an occupier occupying premises under a lease has failed to comply with its statutory duty to make a reasonable adjustment by failing to make a particular alteration to premises. In answering that question, the employment tribunal must ignore any constraint attributable to the fact that the occupier occupies the premises under a lease, unless the occupier has applied to the lessor in writing for consent to make the alteration. The occupier is denied recourse to a justification defence based upon the restrictive terms or covenants of a lease unless and until it has sought to obtain the landlord's consent to the making of the alteration despite that restriction.[268] In other words, the occupier of the premises cannot plead justification by pointing to the negative terms of a lease alone.[269] The occupier is expected to rely upon the statutory provisions and to seek the landlord's consent to the alteration by means of written application.

---

[263] Disability Discrimination (Employment Field) (Leasehold Premises) Regulations 2004, SI 2004/153, reg 7(1)(a).

[264] Ibid, reg 7(1)(b).

[265] Ibid, reg 7(1)(c).

[266] Ibid, reg 7(1)(d). See generally Code of Practice: Employment and Occupation (2004), paras 12.26–12.27; Code of Practice: Trade Organisations and Qualifications Bodies (2004), paras 9.25–9.26.

[267] DDA 1995, Sch 4, Part I, supplementing s 18A.

[268] Ibid, Sch 4, para 1.

[269] Code of Practice: Employment and Occupation (2004), para 12.14; Code of Practice: Trade Organisations and Qualifications Bodies (2004), para 9.13.

6.4.24 The sting in the tail of this provision is as follows.[270] In employment tribunal proceedings, where a question arises about a duty to make a reasonable adjustment by an alteration to premises occupied under a lease, either the claimant or the occupier may request the tribunal to join (in Scotland, sist) the lessor as a party to the proceedings.[271] The tribunal must grant such a request if it is made before the hearing commences,[272] otherwise the granting of such a request is at the tribunal's discretion.[273] Such a request to join the lessor to proceedings cannot be made once the tribunal has determined the complaint.[274] If the lessor has been thus joined (or sisted) as a party to the tribunal proceedings, the tribunal has certain powers in relation to the lessor if certain conditions are satisfied. It may determine whether the lessor has refused consent to the alteration or consented subject to one or more conditions.[275] If so, the tribunal may then determine whether the refusal or any of the conditions were unreasonable.[276] Where the tribunal has so determined, it may take one or more steps.[277] The tribunal may make such a declaration as it considers appropriate or make an order authorising the occupier to make an alteration specified in the order.[278] This latter power is quite novel and is likely to prove important in practice. An order made under this power may require the occupier to comply with any conditions specified in the order.[279] Alternatively or additionally, the tribunal may order the lessor to pay compensation to the claimant.[280] Any step taken by the tribunal above may be in substitution for or in addition to the usual statutory remedies available against the respondent.[281] However, if the tribunal decides to order the lessor to pay compensation to the claimant, it may not make a compensation order against the occupier (respondent).[282]

Goods and services cases

6.4.25 Where under any 'binding obligation' a provider of services or a public authority carrying out its functions is required to obtain the consent of any person to an alteration to premises which it occupies, and that alteration is one which, but for that requirement, it would be reasonable for the provider of services or a public authority carrying out its functions to have to make in order to comply with a duty under s 21 or

---

[270] See generally Code of Practice: Employment and Occupation (2004), paras 12.28–12.30; Code of Practice: Trade Organisations and Qualifications Bodies (2004), paras 9.27–9.29.

[271] DDA 1995, Sch 4, para 2(1).

[272] Ibid, Sch 4, para 2(2).

[273] Ibid, Sch 4, para 2(3).

[274] Ibid, Sch 4, para 2(4).

[275] Ibid, Sch 4, para 2(5)(a).

[276] Ibid, Sch 4, para 2(5)(b).

[277] Ibid, Sch 4, para 2(6).

[278] Ibid, Sch 4, para 2(6)(a) and (b).

[279] Ibid, Sch 4, para 2(7).

[280] Ibid, Sch 4, para 2(6)(c).

[281] Ibid, Sch 4, para 2(8).

[282] Ibid, Sch 4, para 2(9).

21E of the 1995 Act, it is reasonable for the provider of services or public authority carrying out its functions to have to request that consent.[283] It is not reasonable for it to have to make that alteration before that consent is obtained. In this context, a binding obligation means a legally binding obligation (not contained in a lease) in relation to the premises (whether arising from an agreement or otherwise).[284] An example of such an obligation would include a mortgage, a charge, a restrictive covenant or, in Scotland, a feu disposition.

6.4.26   As has been explained above, where a service provider occupies premises under a lease, a statutory term is implied that, if the service provider wishes to make an alteration to the premises, the occupier must first make a written application to the lessor for consent.[285] If a written application for consent is made by the service provider, the lessor will not withhold consent unreasonably.[286] In turn, the lessor is deemed to be entitled to make any consent the subject of reasonable conditions.[287] Regulations deal with the further consequences of these provisions as follows.[288]

6.4.27   The lessor is treated as having withheld its consent where it fails to reply in writing (consenting to or refusing the alteration) within 42 days of receipt of the application for consent.[289] The same result arises where within the same timescale the lessor replies in writing consenting to the alteration subject to the consent of another person required under a superior lease (or pursuant to a binding obligation), but the lessor fails to seek that consent.[290] However, in either case, the lessor is not treated as having withheld consent where the service provider fails to submit with the application such plans and specifications as it is reasonable for the lessor to require before consenting to the alteration, provided the lessor has requested such a submission within 21 days of receiving the application.[291] However, where such plans and specifications are submitted to the lessor in response to a timely request, the lessor is treated as withholding consent to the alteration where it fails to reply in writing (consenting to or refusing the alteration) within 42 days of receiving those plans and specifications.[292] The same result accrues where within that

---

[283]   Disability Discrimination (Service Providers and Public Authorities Carrying Out Functions) Regulations 2005, reg 10(2).

[284]   Ibid, reg 10(3).

[285]   DDA 1995, s 27(2)(b).

[286]   Ibid, s 27(2)(c).

[287]   Ibid, s 27(2)(d).

[288]   Disability Discrimination (Providers of Services) (Adjustment of Premises) Regulations 2001, reg 5.

[289]   Ibid, regs 5(2)(a) and (7)(b). A lessor who complies outside the statutory time period is treated as having withheld its consent until such time as it did comply: ibid, reg 5(6).

[290]   Ibid, reg 5(2)(b) and (7)(b). A lessor who complies outside the statutory time period is treated as having withheld its consent until such time as it did comply: ibid, reg 5(6).

[291]   Ibid, reg 5(3).

[292]   Ibid, reg 5(4)(a) and (7)(b). A lessor who complies outside the statutory time period is treated as having withheld its consent until such time as it did comply: ibid, reg 5(6).

timescale the lessor replies in writing consenting to the alteration subject to the consent of another person required under a superior lease (or pursuant to a binding obligation), but the lessor fails to seek that consent.[293]

6.4.28 As can be seen immediately above, the regulations envisage circumstances where the lessor might reply in writing to the service provider consenting to the alteration subject to the consent of another person required under a superior lease (or pursuant to a binding obligation). Assuming the lessor has sought that consent, and has received it, the lessor is nevertheless treated as having withheld consent to the alteration where it fails to inform the service provider in writing of that fact within 14 days of the receipt of that consent.[294] The lessor is treated as not having sought the other person's consent unless it has applied in writing to that person indicating that the occupier (service provider) has applied for consent to the alteration of the premises in order to comply with a DDA 1995, s 21 duty. In addition, the lessor must indicate to that other person that it has given its consent conditionally upon obtaining that other person's consent. The lessor must also submit to that other person any plans and specifications which have been submitted by the occupier (service provider) to the lessor.[295]

6.4.29 When can a lessor be said to have withheld its consent to an alteration reasonably or unreasonably?[296] A lessor is treated as acting unreasonably in withholding its consent for an alteration to premises where the lease provides that it shall give its consent to an alteration of the kind in question and it has withheld its consent to that alteration.[297] In contrast, the lessor will be taken to have acted reasonably in withholding consent where there is a binding obligation requiring the consent of any person to the alteration, it has taken steps to seek that consent, and that consent has not been given or has been given subject to a condition making it reasonable to withhold the consent.[298] The lessor will also be taken to have acted reasonably in withholding consent where the lessor does not know, and could not be reasonably expected to know, that the alteration is one which the occupier (service provider) proposes to make in order to comply with a DDA 1995, s 21 duty.[299] Circumstances

---

[293] Disability Discrimination (Providers of Services) (Adjustment of Premises) Regulations 2001, reg 5(4)(b) and (7)(b). A lessor who complies outside the statutory time period is treated as having withheld its consent until such time as it did comply: ibid, reg 5(6).

[294] Ibid, reg 5(5). A lessor who complies outside the statutory time period is treated as having withheld its consent until such time as it did comply: ibid, reg 5(6).

[295] Ibid, reg 5(7).

[296] Ibid, regs 6–7.

[297] Ibid, reg 6.

[298] Ibid, reg 7(2)(a).

[299] Ibid, reg 7(2)(b).

are also prescribed where the giving of the lessor's consent subject to a condition is to be treated as reasonable.[300] If a condition is to the effect that:

- the occupier (service provider) must obtain any necessary planning permission (and any other consent or permission) required by or under any enactment;[301]

- the work must be carried out in accordance with any plans or specifications approved by the lessor;[302]

- the lessor must be permitted a reasonable opportunity to inspect the work (whether before or after it is completed);[303]

- the consent of another person required under a superior lease or a binding agreement must be obtained;[304] or

- the occupier must repay to the lessor the costs reasonably incurred in connection with the giving of the consent,[305]

it is regarded as reasonable.

6.4.30   Enforcement provisions in respect of a duty to make alterations to premises by providers of services under DDA 1995, Part 3 are similar, but slightly different, to those applicable to employers under Part 2.[306] Where any question arises as to whether a service provider occupying premises under a lease has failed to comply with a duty to make reasonable adjustments by failing to make a particular alteration to premises, any constraint attributable to the fact that the service provider occupies the premises under a lease must be ignored, unless the occupier has applied to the lessor in writing for consent to make the alteration.[307] A novelty is the provision for a reference to be made to the court where the lessor has refused consent for such an alteration to be made by the occupier.[308] A reference may also be made where the lessor has given consent to the alteration but has made the consent subject to one or more conditions. In both cases, the occupier must have applied in writing to the lessor for the necessary consent. In these circumstances, the occupier or a

---

[300] Disability Discrimination (Providers of Services) (Adjustment of Premises) Regulations 2001, reg 8(1).

[301] Ibid, reg 8(2)(a).

[302] Ibid, reg 8(2)(b).

[303] Ibid, reg 8(2)(c).

[304] Ibid, reg 8(2)(d).

[305] Ibid, reg 8(2)(e).

[306] DDA 1995, s 27 and Sch 4, Part II. The differences are explained in Code of Practice: Employment and Occupation (2004), para 12.31, and Code of Practice: Trade Organisations and Qualifications Bodies (2004), para 9.30.

[307] Ibid, Sch 4, para 5.

[308] Ibid, Sch 4, para 6(1). There is no equivalent in employment cases.

disabled person (who has an interest in the proposed alteration to the premises being made) may refer the matter to the county court.[309] It does not seem to be contemplated that such a reference can be made only where legal proceedings have been commenced.[310] These provisions would appear to provide for a preliminary clarification of the rights of the parties concerned by the court, even where litigation based upon a complaint of unlawful disability discrimination has not been initiated or contemplated.

6.4.31 Regulations provide for the modification of these provisions where the occupier (service provider) occupies the premises under a sub-lease or sub-tenancy.[311] In those circumstances, references to a 'lessor' are treated as a reference to the 'immediate landlord'.[312] The regulations then provide that, except to the extent which it expressly so provides, any superior lease in respect of the premises shall have effect in relation to the lessor and the lessee who are parties to the superior lease as if it provided:

- for the lessee to be entitled to give its consent to the alteration with the written consent of the lessor;

- for the lessee to have to make a written application to the lessor for consent if it wishes to give its consent to the alteration;

- for the lessor not to withhold its consent unreasonably if such an application is made; and

- for the lessor to be entitled to make its consent subject to reasonable conditions.[313]

Where the lessee of any superior lease in relation to the premises has applied in writing to its lessor for consent to the alteration, and that consent has been refused or the lessor has made its consent subject to one or more conditions, then the occupier (service provider), lessee or a disabled person who has an interest in the proposed alteration to the premises being made may refer the matter to a county court (or, in Scotland, to the sheriff).[314]

6.4.32 Where the matter has been referred to the court by these various means, the court shall determine whether the refusal of the lessor (or the immediate landlord, as the case might be) was unreasonable or whether

---

[309] In Scotland, the sheriff court. See DDA 1995, Sch 4, para 6(2).

[310] Under DDA 1995, s 25.

[311] Disability Discrimination (Providers of Services) (Adjustment of Premises) Regulations 2001, SI 2001/3253, reg 9(1), modifying DDA 1995, s 27 and Sch 5, paras 5–7.

[312] Ibid, reg 9(2), modifying DDA 1995, s 27(2).

[313] Ibid, reg 9(3), inserting DDA 1995, s 27(2A).

[314] Ibid, reg 9(5), inserting DDA 1995, Sch 4, para 6(1A).

any conditions imposed upon consent are unreasonable.[315] If the court decides that the refusal of consent to the alteration (or any conditions imposed upon the consent) by the lessor (or the immediate landlord, as the case might be) was unreasonable, then the court may make an appropriate declaration at its discretion. It may also make an order authorising the occupier to make an alteration specified in the order.[316] Such an order may require the occupier to comply with specified conditions.[317]

6.4.33　If litigation has been commenced, then in any court proceedings where a question arises about a duty to make a reasonable adjustment by an alteration to premises occupied under a lease, either the claimant (in Scotland, the pursuer) or the occupier may ask the court to join (in Scotland, sist) any lessor (including a superior landlord, as the case might be) as a party to the proceedings.[318] The court must grant such a request if it is made before the hearing commences,[319] otherwise the granting of such a request is at the court's discretion.[320] Such a request to join the lessor to proceedings cannot be made once the court has determined the claim.[321] If the lessor has been joined (or sisted) as a party to the proceedings, then the court has certain powers in relation to the lessor if certain conditions are satisfied.

6.4.34　The court may determine whether the lessor has refused consent to the alteration at issue or whether the lessor has consented to the alteration but subject to one or more conditions.[322] If so, in either case, the tribunal may then determine whether the refusal (or any of the conditions) was unreasonable.[323] Where such a finding has been made, the court may make such a declaration as it considers appropriate or order the lessor to pay compensation to the claimant or pursuer.[324] Although this is not made explicit, it seems logical that any such remedy against the lessor may be made in addition to or instead of any remedy that the court would be able to make against the occupier who is the defendant (or

---

[315] DDA 1995, Sch 4, para 6(3); Disability Discrimination (Providers of Services) (Adjustment of Premises) Regulations 2001, reg 9(6).

[316] DDA 1995, Sch 4, para 6(4); Disability Discrimination (Providers of Services) (Adjustment of Premises) Regulations 2001, reg 9(6).

[317] DDA 1995, Sch 4, para 6(5).

[318] Ibid, Sch 4, para 7(1); Disability Discrimination (Providers of Services) (Adjustment of Premises) Regulations 2001, reg 9(7)(a).

[319] DDA 1995, Sch 4, para 7(2). Where the premises are occupied under a sub-lease or sub-tenancy, the request shall be granted if it is made before the hearing of the claim begins, unless it appears to the court that another lessor should be joined or sisted as a party to the proceedings: Disability Discrimination (Providers of Services) (Adjustment of Premises) Regulations 2001, SI 2001/3253, reg 9(7)(b), substituting DDA 1995, Sch 4, para 7(2).

[320] DDA 1995, Sch 4, para 7(3).

[321] Ibid, Sch 4, para 7(4).

[322] Ibid, Sch 4, para 7(4)(a).

[323] Ibid, Sch 4, para 7(4)(b).

[324] Ibid, Sch 4, para 7(6)(a) or (c).

defender) to the proceedings. However, if the court decides to order the lessor to pay compensation to the claimant or pursuer, it may not make a parallel compensation order against the occupier.[325] Moreover, the court is also given an additional or alternative power which might prove quite radical in practice. If the court has determined that the lessor's refusal of consent to (or conditions imposed upon) an alteration was unreasonable, it may make an order authorising the occupier to make an alteration specified in the order.[326] Such an order may require the occupier to comply with any conditions specified in the order.[327]

Other provisions

6.4.35 Similar provisions as those discussed above in relation to service providers and public authorities (and, by inference, private clubs[328]) apply in relation to educational institutions and general qualifications bodies.[329] Further discussion in those contexts would be repetitive and unnecessary. The problem of making alterations to premises to let or let premises has already been discussed at **6.3.29–6.3.32** above.

Improvements to dwelling houses

6.4.36 However, some account should be given of the new provisions on improvements to dwelling houses in the new s 49G inserted by the DDA 2005 and in force from 4 December 2006. These provisions apply in England and Wales only. They affect the way in which the DDA 1995 interacts with the Landlord and Tenant Act 1927 and the Housing Acts 1980 and 1985, which might provide a disabled tenant with a statutory right to make improvements to his or her home in way that is more effective than the new ss 24A–24M on let premises (discussed at **6.3** above).[330] In Scotland, the new s 49G does not apply. Tenants in Scotland must rely on ss 24A–24M or the Housing (Scotland) Acts 2001 and 2006.[331]

6.4.36 Section 49G applies in relation to a lease of a dwelling house if (a) the tenancy is not a protected tenancy, a statutory tenancy or a secure tenancy; (b) the tenant or any other person who lawfully occupies or is intended lawfully to occupy the premises is a disabled person; (c) the person mentioned in paragraph (b) occupies or is intended to occupy the premises as his or her only or principal home; (d) the tenant is entitled under the lease to make improvements to the premises with the consent of

---

[325] DDA 1995, Sch 4, para 7(8).
[326] Ibid, Sch 4, para 7(6)(b).
[327] Ibid, Sch 4, para 7(7).
[328] Disability Discrimination (Private Clubs, etc) Regulations 2005, SI 2005/ 3258, reg 11.
[329] DDA 1995, Sch 4, Parts 3 and 4; Disability Discrimination (Educational Institutions (Alteration of Leasehold Premises) Regulations 2005, SI 2005/1070.
[330] See the more detailed discussion in Rights of Access Code of Practice 2006, chapter 18.
[331] See the more detailed discussion in Rights of Access Code of Practice 2006, chapter 19.

the landlord, and (e) the tenant applies to the landlord for his or her consent to make a relevant improvement.[332] An improvement to premises is a relevant improvement if, having regard to the disability which the disabled person mentioned has, it is likely to facilitate his or her enjoyment of the premises.[333] An 'improvement' means any alteration in or addition to premises and includes (a) any addition to or alteration in landlord's fittings and fixtures; (b) any addition or alteration connected with the provision of services to the premises; (c) the erection of a wireless or television aerial; and (d) the carrying out of external decoration.[334]

6.4.36   The following apply to a lease only to the extent that provision of a like nature is not made by the lease itself.[335] If the consent of the landlord is unreasonably withheld it must be taken to have been given.[336] Where the tenant applies in writing for the consent, if the landlord refuses to give consent, he or she must give the tenant a written statement of the reason why the consent was withheld.[337] If the landlord neither gives nor refuses to give consent within a reasonable time, consent must be taken to have been withheld.[338] If the landlord gives consent to the making of an improvement subject to a condition which is unreasonable, the consent must be taken to have been unreasonably withheld.[339] In any question as to whether (a) the consent of the landlord was unreasonably withheld, or (b) a condition imposed by the landlord is unreasonable, it is for the landlord to show that it was not.[340] If the tenant fails to comply with a reasonable condition imposed by the landlord on the making of a relevant improvement, the failure is to be treated as a breach by the tenant of an obligation of his or her tenancy.[341]

---

[332] DDA 1995, s 49G(1). A 'lease' includes a sub-lease or other tenancy (and 'landlord' and 'tenant' must be construed accordingly); a 'protected tenancy' has the same meaning as in Rent Act 1977, s 1; 'statutory tenancy' must be construed in accordance with Rent Act 1977, s 2; and 'secure tenancy' has the same meaning as in Housing Act 1985, s 79: DDA 1995, s 49G(9).

[333] DDA 1995, s 49G(7).

[334] Ibid, s 49G(9).

[335] Ibid, s 49G(8).

[336] Ibid, s 49G(2).

[337] Ibid, s 49G(3)(a).

[338] Ibid, s 49G(3)(b).

[339] Ibid, s 49G(4).

[340] Ibid, s 49G(5).

[341] Ibid, s 49G(6).

CHAPTER 7

EDUCATION

7.1 INTRODUCTION

7.1.1 The 1994 Green Paper anticipated that the right of access to goods and services would not apply to educational facilities.[1] It was thought that provision for disabled pupils and students was already best served by being the subject of other legislation.[2] This disapplication of the right of access was confirmed by the 1995 White Paper, which went on to promise fresh initiatives in respect of educational opportunities for disabled persons.[3] The exclusion of access to education from the right not to be discriminated against as a disabled person in relation to the provision of goods, facilities and services was envisaged.

7.1.2 Thus, somewhat controversially, the DDA 1995 *as originally enacted* did not include access to education within the scope of its anti-discrimination provisions. Instead, in contrast to the position in discrimination law generally,[4] education was explicitly excluded from the scope of services for the purposes of Part 3 of the Act.[5] The controversial aspect of this exclusion was that education is recognised as being crucial to the aspirations of disabled persons to enjoy full and equal opportunities.[6] In many respects, the right to freedom from discrimination in employment[7] may be undermined if educational opportunities are not equally available to disabled persons to enable them to compete with a well-qualified labour force as they seek to enter the competitive labour market. Nevertheless, the Act did address the question of access to education by means other than via the anti-discrimination framework

---

[1]   *A Consultation on Government Measures to Tackle Discrimination Against Disabled People* (July 1994), para 4.9.

[2]   As this book is a text on disability discrimination law, it is not proposed to explore the relevant law of education in any detail.

[3]   *Ending Discrimination Against Disabled People*, Cm 2729 (1995), para 4.6, and Chapter 6.

[4]   See Part III of the SDA 1975 and Part III of the RRA 1976.

[5]   DDA 1995, s 19(5). As to the provisions on services generally, see ss 19–21, and Chapter 5.

[6]   See generally Disability Rights Task Force, *From Exclusion to Inclusion: A Report of the Disability Rights Task Force for Disabled People* (1999, London: DfEE) (DRTF Report), Chapter 4.

[7]   DDA 1995, Part 2. See Chapters 3 and 4.

contained in Part 3 of the Act. This was achieved in Part IV of the Act (now referred to as Part 4), provisions of which are now found in other statutes (but discussed below).

7.1.3 The DRTF regarded the lack of protection from unfair discrimination in education for disabled children as unacceptable, but rejected the simplistic solution of removing the education exclusion from the DDA 1995.[8] Instead, it recommended that providers of school education of all descriptions should be placed under a statutory duty not to discriminate unfairly against a disabled pupil, for a reason relating to his or her disability, in the provision of education. It also recommended that the pupil's parents should have a right of redress and that there should be a defence of *acceptable* less favourable treatment.[9] The DRTF went further by advocating a statutory duty on school education providers to review policies, practices and procedures and to make reasonable adjustments to any that discriminate against or have an adverse impact upon disabled pupils.[10] Moreover, a duty to make reasonable adjustments – by taking reasonable steps to provide education by an alternative method – was suggested to overcome physical barriers which place disabled pupils at a substantial disadvantage in comparison with non-disabled pupils.[11] Furthermore, a right to adjustments to achieve physical access and access to the curriculum was urged.[12] Similar proposals affecting further, higher and adult education (and the Youth Service provision of local authorities) were also made.[13]

7.1.4 The Government broadly (but not completely) accepted the DRTF recommendations on education and enacted the Special Educational Needs and Disability Act 2001 (SENDA 2001) in response. Accordingly, from 1 September 2002,[14] the position is somewhat changed. The exclusion of education was originally effected by DDA 1995, s 19(5).[15] This provision is now repealed.[16] The present position is that, by virtue of DDA 1995, s 19(5A) as amended,[17] nothing in Part 3 of the DDA 1995 applies to the provision of a service which is made unlawful by Part 4 of the DDA 1995 designed to prohibit discrimination in education generally.

---

[8]   DRTF Report, p 48, para 14.
[9]   Ibid, recommendation 4.4.
[10] Ibid, recommendations 4.5 and 4.6.
[11] Ibid, recommendation 4.7.
[12] Ibid, recommendation 4.10.
[13] Ibid, recommendations 4.13 and 4.17.
[14] See Special Educational Needs and Disability Act 2001 (Commencement No 5) Order 2002, SI 2002/2217 and Special Educational Needs and Disability Act 2001 (Commencement No 2) (Wales) Order 2003, SI 2003/2532 (W 247).
[15] DDA 1995, s 19(5)(a)–(ab) and (6) (as amended).
[16] SENDA 2001, ss 38(1), 38(5)(a)–(b), 42(6) and Sch 9.
[17] Inserted by ibid, s 38(1) and (6), and then substituted by DDA 2005, s 19(1) and Sch 1, Part 1, paras 1, 13(1) and 13(4) from 4 December 2006.

7.1.5 The previous edition of this book reviewed the pre-September 2002 law on disability discrimination in the educational field as background to the law post-September 2002. That account is no longer necessary.

7.2 THE LAW POST-SEPTEMBER 2002

Special Educational Needs and Disability Act 2001

7.2.1 The SENDA 2001 received the Royal Assent on 11 May 2001. Part 2 of the SENDA 2001 is the result of the Government's response to the Final Report of the DRTF.[18] It addresses the key recommendations in the DRTF Final Report on education. It amends Part IV of the DDA 1995 (now to be known as Part 4) to introduce rights for disabled persons in education. It applies in England, Wales and Scotland, but not Northern Ireland, which has separate legislation to similar effect.[19] The exemption of publicly funded providers of education services and private schools from Part 3 of the DDA 1995 is removed. As a result, any provider of education previously exempted from Part 3 and not covered by the Part 4 duties becomes subject to the duties in Part 3 of the DDA 1995.[20] SENDA 2001, Part 2 contains the provisions on disability discrimination in education which amend Part 4 of the DDA 1995.[21] Chapter 1 of DDA 1995, Part 4 deals with schools and education authorities and Chapter 2 of Part 4 deals with further and higher education.[22] Each Part is dealt

---

[18] Disability Rights Task Force, *From Exclusion to Inclusion: A Report of the Disability Rights Task Force for Disabled People* (1999, London: DfEE); *Interim Government Response to the Report of the Disability Rights Task Force* (2000, London: DfEE); *Towards Inclusion – Civil Rights for Disabled People: Government Response to the Disability Rights Task Force* (2001, London: DfEE).

[19] Special Educational Needs and Disability (Northern Ireland) Order 2005, SI 2005/1117 (NI 6), Parts III and IV making provision against discrimination, on grounds of disability, in schools and other educational institutions and by other educational and qualifications bodies in Northern Ireland with effect from 1 September 2005. See also Special Educational Needs and Disability Tribunal (Northern Ireland) Regulations 2005, SR 2005/339. Separate Codes of Practice for Schools and for Further and Higher Education have been issued in Northern Ireland in 2006 by the Equality Commission.

[20] *Explanatory Notes to Special Educational Needs and Disability Act 2001*. See the discussion of DDA 1995, Part 3 in Chapter 5. Notably, this will include local authority day nurseries and family centres, private and voluntary playgroups and pre-schools, and accredited childminders which would not otherwise be covered by the provisions of DDA 1995, Part 4. See *Disability Discrimination Act 1995 Part 4 Code of Practice for Schools*, paras 10.7–10.9.

[21] SENDA 2001, Part 1 amends the law relating to special educational needs and is beyond the scope of this book.

[22] Chapter 3 of SENDA 2001, Part 2 deals with miscellaneous matters, including extending the role of the DRC, providing for codes of practices and making provision for conciliation of disputes. Various schedules deal with the consequential effects of the changes to the DDA 1995. These provisions are addressed in appropriate chapters of this book.

with in turn below. New provisions introduced by the DDA 2005 deal with discrimination by general qualification bodies and is also dealt with below.

7.3 SCHOOLS AND EDUCATION AUTHORITIES

7.3.1 As a result of the changes brought about by the SENDA 2001 there are now three sources of support available to disabled pupils in school. These are:

(1) the disability discrimination duties;

(2) the planning duties; and

(3) the existing and amended SEN framework.

A discussion of the SEN framework is beyond the scope of this book, but it is important to note that the duties in DDA 1995, Part 4, Chapter 1 are designed to dovetail with it. The statutory provisions containing the duties are supported by the *Disability Discrimination Act 1995 Part 4 Code of Practice for Schools* (Schools Code of Practice) (2002) issued by the DRC under DDA 1995, s 53A at the request of the Secretary of State for Education and Skills.[23] The Schools Code of Practice applies to all schools and LEAs (known as education authorities in Scotland) in England, Wales and Scotland, and to young people over the age of 16 when in school.[24] Further guidance is also available from various other sources.[25]

---

[23] See the overview of the legislation provided in the Schools Code of Practice, Chapters 2 (Scotland) and 3 (England and Wales). As well as describing the interaction of the DDA 1995 with the SEN framework, the Schools Code of Practice (Chapter 10) usefully explains the relationship of the DDA 1995 with other legislation and responsibilities (such as data protection legislation, health and safety law and regulations, fire safety legislation, occupiers' liability, defective premises law, the Human Rights Act 1998, sex and race discrimination legislation, etc). See also *Accompanying Guidance for the DRC's Code of Practice for Schools (Scotland)* (2006).

[24] Schools Code of Practice, paras 1.2–1.3. Its purpose and status is set out in paras 1.4–1.7 (and see further the discussion in **9.3**). It does not apply in Northern Ireland, but takes account of devolved government and the differences between the education systems in the different parts of Great Britain: paras 1.8–1.10.

[25] See the guidance issued to local authorities, LEAs and schools in England by the Department for Education and Skills: *Accessible Schools: Planning to Increase Access to Schools for Disabled Pupils* (LEA/0168/2002: July 2002). See also DRC, *A Guide for Schools: Part 4 of the DDA 1995 as amended by SENDA 2001* (2003) (separate editions of which are available for England, Wales and Scotland); Disability Rights Commission, *Information for School Governors in England; A Guide for Parents: Part 4 if the DDA 1995 as amended by SENDA 2001* (2003) (separate editions of which are available for England, Wales and Scotland). The DRC has also published a number of good practice guides respectively for governors and senior managers, and in respect of admissions and marketing, examinations, central services, residential services, learning and teaching, staff development, libraries, estates and careers.

Disability discrimination duties

7.3.2 By virtue of s 28A(1) of the DDA 1995,[26] it is unlawful for 'the body responsible for a school' to discriminate against a 'disabled person':[27]

- in the arrangements it makes for determining admission to the school as a pupil;[28]

- in the terms on which it offers to admit him or her to the school as a pupil; or

- by refusing or deliberately omitting to accept an application for his or her admission to the school as a pupil.

It is also unlawful for 'the body responsible for a school' to discriminate against a disabled pupil[29] in the education or associated services provided for (or offered to) pupils at the school by that body.[30] It is further unlawful for 'the body responsible for a school' to discriminate against a disabled pupil by excluding him or her from the school, whether permanently or temporarily.[31] A school's failure to provide a pupil with autistic spectrum disorder with such personal guidance and support within the school's

---

[26] See Schools Code of Practice, para 4.22. For early examples of appellate courts considering these provisions, see: *McAuley Catholic High School v (1) CC; (2) PC; and (3) Special Educational Needs and Disability Tribunal* [2003] EWHC 3045 (Admin), [2004] ICR 1543, QBD, and *R (on the application of D) v Governing Body of Plymouth High School for Girls* [2004] EWHC 1923 (Admin), Collins J.

[27] A 'disabled person' is a person falling within DDA 1995, ss 1–2 and Schs 1–2 (discussed in Chapter 2). This section also applies to discrimination against a person who is not disabled in the case of an act which constitutes discrimination by virtue of DDA 1995, s 55 (victimisation): DDA 1995, s 28A(6). See Schools Code of Practice, Chapter 4 and paras 10.10–10.14 (and examples).

[28] This includes any criteria for deciding who will be admitted to the school when it is over-subscribed and includes the operation of those criteria: Schools Code of Practice, para 4.22. By virtue of DDA 1995, s 28Q(3), the term 'pupil' (as used throughout this analysis) has the meaning assigned to it by Education Act 1996, s 3(1) and Education (Scotland) Act 1980, s 135(1). See Schools Code of Practice, Chapter 4.

[29] By virtue of DDA 1995, s 28Q(2), the term 'disabled pupil' (as used throughout this analysis) means a pupil who is a disabled person. See Schools Code of Practice, Chapter 4.

[30] DDA 1995, s 28A(2). The Secretary of State may by regulations prescribe services which are or are not to be regarded for this purpose as being 'education' or 'an associated service': DDA 1995, s 28A(3). See Schools Code of Practice, paras 4.23–4.26 which define education and associated services (without intending to be exhaustive) as including: preparation for entry to the school; the curriculum; teaching and learning; classroom organisation; timetabling; grouping of pupils; homework; access to school facilities; activities to supplement the curriculum (eg a drama group visiting the school); school sports; school policies; breaks and lunchtimes; the serving of school meals; interaction with peers; assessment and exam arrangements; school discipline and sanctions; exclusion procedures; school clubs and activities; school trips; the school's arrangements for working with other agencies; preparation of pupils for the next phase of education.

[31] DDA 1995, s 28A(4). It does not matter whether the exclusion takes the form (in

pastoral care system as he required has been hold to amount to an unlawful act of disability discrimination.[32]

7.3.3 The meaning of the term 'the body responsible for a school' (referred to as the 'responsible body') depends upon the kind of school involved.[33] In England and Wales, in the case of a maintained school or maintained nursery school, it is the LEA[34] or governing body,[35] according to which has the function in question; in the case of a pupil referral unit, it is the LEA; and in the case of an independent school or a special school not maintained by the LEA, it is the proprietor of the school.[36] In Scotland,[37] in the case of a school managed by an education authority, it is the education authority; in the case of an independent school, it is the proprietor of the school; in the case of a self-governing school, it is the board of management of the school; and in the case of a school in respect of which the managers are for the time being receiving grants,[38] it is the managers of the school.

Discrimination

7.3.4 The meaning of discrimination for this purpose is set out in DDA 1995, s 28B. There are two kinds of discrimination contemplated by the section. They might be referred to in shorthand as (1) less favourable treatment, and (2) failure to make reasonable adjustments.

Scotland) of a temporary exclusion or an exclusion/removal from the register or (in England and Wales) a permanent or fixed-term exclusion: Schools Code of Practice, para 4.27.

[32] *McAuley Catholic High School v (1) CC; (2) PC; and (3) Special Educational Needs and Disability Tribunal* [2003] EWHC 3045 (Admin), [2004] ICR 1563, QBD.

[33] DDA 1995, ss 28A(5) and 28Q(6), and Sch 4A, as amended by Education Act 2002. In Scotland, the term 'school' (used throughout this analysis) has the meaning assigned by Education (Scotland) Act 1980, s 135(1). In England and Wales, the term 'school' (used throughout this analysis) means a maintained school (within the meaning of School Standards and Framework Act 1998, s 20(7)); a maintained nursery school (within the meaning of School Standards and Framework Act 1998, s 22(9)); an independent school (within the meaning of Education Act 1996, s 463); a special school which is not a maintained special school but which is approved by the Secretary of State (in England) or by the Welsh Ministers (in Wales) under Education Act 1996, s 342; or a pupil referral unit (within the meaning of Education Act 1996, s 19(2)). See DDA 1995, s 28Q(4)–(5). See Schools Code of Practice, Chapter 4.

[34] As defined in School Standards and Framework Act 1998, s 22(8).

[35] The 'governing body' in relation to a maintained school means the body corporate which the school has as a result of Education Act 2002, s 19; DDA 1995, s 28Q(7).

[36] As defined in Education Act 1996, s 579.

[37] In this account, the terms 'board of management', 'education authority', 'managers' and 'proprietor' are defined in Education (Scotland) Act, s 135(1).

[38] Under Education (Scotland) Act 1980, s 73(c) or (d).

Less favourable treatment

7.3.5 A responsible body discriminates against a disabled person if, for a reason which relates to his or her disability,[39] it treats him or her less favourably than it treats or would treat others to whom that reason does not (or would not apply)[40] and it cannot show that the treatment in question is justified.[41] Less favourable treatment of a person is justified if it is the result of a permitted form of selection.[42] Otherwise, less favourable treatment is justified only if the reason for it is both material to the circumstances of the particular case and substantial (that is, more than minor or trivial).[43] If the responsible body is under a duty to make reasonable adjustments (imposed by DDA 1995, s 28C) in relation to the disabled person, but it fails without justification to comply with that duty, its treatment of that person cannot be justified by reference to a material and substantial reason[44] unless that treatment would have been justified

---

[39] There has to be a link between the reason and the disability: Schools Code of Practice, paras 5.7–5.8 (and examples).

[40] This calls for a real or hypothetical comparison: Schools Code of Practice, paras 5.9–5.10 (and examples). The comparison is between a disabled pupil and a pupil who is not disabled: *R (on the application of D) v Governing Body of Plymouth High School for Girls* [2004] EWHC 1923 (Admin).

[41] DDA 1995, s 28B(1). See Schools Code of Practice, Chapter 5. See *R (on the application of D) v Governing Body of Plymouth High School for Girls* [2004] EWHC 1923 (Admin). A school discriminated against a disabled pupil without justification by failing to assist her properly in relation to a work placement. The pupil had filled in her work placement form incompletely by failing to answer a question about her disability, but the school failed to take steps to remedy the position. Her disability appeared to be a factor in her failure to obtain a placement. Her treatment was for a reason related to her disability.

[42] DDA 1995, s 28B(6) by virtue of s 28B(5) and see Schools Code of Practice, paras 5.18–5.23 (and examples). In England and Wales, the term 'permitted form of selection' in relation to a maintained school which is not designated as a grammar school (under School Standards and Framework Act 1998, s 104) means any form of selection mentioned in School Standards and Framework Act 1998, s 99(2) or (4); in relation to a maintained school which is so designated as a grammar school it means any of its selective admission arrangements; and in relation to an independent school it means any arrangements which make provision for any or all of its pupils to be selected by reference to general or special ability or aptitude with a view to admitting only pupils of high ability or aptitude: DDA 1995, s 28Q(9). In Scotland, the term 'permitted form of selection' in relation to a school managed by an education authority (within the meaning of Education (Scotland) Act 1980, s 135(1)) means such arrangements as have been approved by the Scottish Ministers for the selection of pupils for admission; and in relation to an independent school or a self-governing school (within the meaning of Education (Scotland) Act 1980, s 135(1)) it means any arrangements which make provision for any or all of its pupils to be selected by reference to general or special ability or aptitude with a view to admitting only pupils of high ability or aptitude: DDA 1995, s 28Q(10)–(11). See further Department for Education and Skills, *Code of Practice on School Admissions* (1999); Welsh Office, *School Admissions Code of Practice* (1999).

[43] DDA 1995, s 28B(7), by virtue of s 28B(5). See Schools Code of Practice, paras 5.11–5.15 (and examples). See also: *K v (1) The School and (2) SENDIST* [2007] EWCA Civ 165 (CA).

[44] DDA 1995, s 28B(7).

even if it had complied with that duty.[45] The concept of unjustified less favourable treatment discrimination arising here is broadly similar to the parallel provision in Part 2 of the DDA 1995 (discrimination in employment) and the case-law there is likely to be instructive.[46]

Failure to make reasonable adjustments

7.3.6 A responsible body also discriminates against a disabled person if it fails, to his or her detriment, to comply with the duty to make reasonable adjustments contained in DDA 1995, s 28C and it cannot show that its failure to comply is justified.[47] Before this kind of discrimination can be explored further it is necessary to examine the duty to make reasonable adjustments in this context.[48]

7.3.7 There are two aspects to the duty to make reasonable adjustments upon schools.[49] First, the responsible body for a school must take such steps as it is reasonable for it to have to take to ensure that, in relation to the arrangements it makes for determining the admission of pupils to the school, disabled persons are not placed at a substantial disadvantage in comparison with persons who are not disabled.[50] Secondly, it must also take such steps as it is reasonable for it to have to take to ensure that, in relation to education and associated services provided for (or offered to) pupils at the school by it, disabled pupils are not placed at a substantial disadvantage in comparison with pupils who are not disabled.[51] The duty is an anticipatory duty and a continuing one.[52] However, neither aspect of the duty requires the responsible body to remove or alter a physical feature (for example, one arising from the design or construction of the

---

[45] DDA 1995, s 28B(8). See Schools Code of Practice, para 5.16 (and example). See also *The Governing Body of Olchfa Comprehensive School v (1) IE & EE and (2) Rimington* [2006] EWHC 1468 (Admin), Crane J.

[46] This has been confirmed in *McAuley Catholic High School v (1) CC; (2) PC; and (3) Special Educational Needs and Disability Tribunal* [2003] EWHC 3045 (Admin), [2004] ICR 1563, QBD, applying *Clark v TDG Ltd t/a Novacold* [1999] ICR 951, CA, and *Rowden v Dutton Gregory (a firm)* [2002] ICR 971, EAT, to the terms of s 28B(1). See Chapter 3 and see the further examples in Schools Code of Practice, para 5.17. See also: *VK v Norfolk County Council and the Special Educational Needs and Disability Tribunal* [2004] EWHC 2921 (Admin), Stanley Burnton J.

[47] That is, the reason for failing to comply with the duty to make reasonable adjustments is both material to the circumstances of the particular case and substantial: DDA 1995, s 28B(7). See Schools Code of Practice, paras 6.35–6.36.

[48] See Schools Code of Practice, Chapter 6.

[49] DDA 1995, s 28C imposes duties only for the purpose of determining whether a responsible body has discriminated against a disabled person. A breach of any duty under s 28C is not actionable as such. See ibid, s 28C(8).

[50] Ibid, s 28C(1)(a).

[51] Ibid, s 28C(1)(b). See *R (on the application of D) v Governing Body of Plymouth High School for Girls* [2004] EWHC 1923 (Admin), discussed at **7.4.5**, footnote 6. See also *McAuley Catholic High School v (1) CC; (2) PC; and (3) Special Educational Needs and Disability Tribunal* [2003] EWHC 3045 (Admin), [2004] ICR 1563, QBD, discussed at **7.4.2**.

[52] Schools Code of Practice, paras 6.12–6.18 (and examples).

school premises or the location of resources) or to provide auxiliary aids or services.[53] What triggers the duty is the requirement for a comparative substantial (that is, more than minor or trivial) disadvantage. A number of factors may have to be taken into account in measuring that requirement, including the time and effort that might need to be expended by a disabled child; the inconvenience, indignity or discomfort a disabled child might suffer; the loss of opportunity or the diminished progress that a disabled child may make in comparison with his or her peers who are not disabled.[54]

7.3.8 Regulations may make provision for these purposes as to circumstances in which it is (or is not) reasonable for a responsible body to have to take steps of a prescribed description or as to steps which it is always or never reasonable for a responsible body to have to take.[55] A responsible body must have regard to any relevant provisions of a code of practice[56] in considering whether it is reasonable for it to have to take a particular step in order to comply with its duty to make reasonable adjustments.[57]

7.3.9 Particular provision is made where a 'confidentiality request' has been made in relation to a person and the responsible body is aware of it.[58] A 'confidentiality request' is a request which asks for the nature of (or the existence of) a disabled person's disability to be treated as confidential.[59] It must have been made by that person's parent[60] or by that person himself (in which case the responsible body must reasonably believe that he or she has sufficient understanding of the nature of the

---

[53] DDA 1995, s 28C(2). As the code of practice explains, the reasonable adjustments duty does not apply to auxiliary aids and services. It is anticipated that in schools in the maintained sector (in England and Wales) or the publicly funded sector (in Scotland) such provision will be made through the SEN framework. While physical alterations to schools are not required under the reasonable adjustments duty as it is anticipated that these will be achieved through a longer-term and more strategic approach to improving access for disabled pupils: Schools Code of Practice, paras 2.8, 3.8 and 6.19–6.27 (and examples).

[54] Schools Code of Practice, paras 6.9–6.11 (and examples).

[55] DDA 1995, s 28C(3). No regulations have been made at the time of writing, but Schools Code of Practice, paras 6.28–6.34 (and examples) suggest that the following factors may be relevant: the need to maintain academic, musical, sporting and other standards; the financial resources available to the responsible body; the cost of taking a particular step; the extent to which it is practicable to take a particular step; the extent to which aids and services will be provided to disabled pupils at the school (under Education Act 1996, Part IV or Education (Scotland) Act 1980, ss 60–65G); health and safety requirements; and the interests of other pupils and persons who may be admitted to the school as pupils.

[56] Issued under DDA 1995, s 53A or, now, Equality Act 2006, s 14.

[57] DDA 1995, s 28C(4), as amended.

[58] Ibid, s 28C(5). See Schools Code of Practice, paras 7.13–7.17 (and examples).

[59] Ibid, s 28C(7).

[60] Ibid, s 28C(7)(a). The term 'parent' has the meaning assigned to it by Education Act 1996, s 576 and Education (Scotland) Act 1980, s 135(1): DDA 1995, s 28Q(8).

request and of its effect).[61] In determining whether it is reasonable for the responsible body to have to take a particular step in relation to that person in order to comply with its duty to make reasonable adjustments, regard shall be had to the extent to which taking the step in question is consistent with compliance with that request.[62]

Knowledge of disability

7.3.10   The question of the relevance of what an alleged discriminator knew or did not know about the fact of a disabled person's disability has bedevilled the interpretation of the employment and services provisions of the DDA 1995.[63] The provisions in Part 4 of the Act attempt to address that question head on. In relation to a failure to take a particular step, a responsible body does not 'discriminate' against a person if it shows that, at the time in question, it did not know and could not reasonably have been expected to know, that he or she was disabled, and that its failure to take the step was attributable to that lack of knowledge.[64] Knowledge might be actual or constructive. Furthermore, the taking of a particular step by a responsible body in relation to a person does not amount to 'less favourable treatment' if it shows that at the time in question it did not know, and could not reasonably have been expected to know, that he or she was disabled.[65]

Justification

7.3.11   As has been noted, less favourable treatment of a person is justified if it is the result of a permitted form of selection.[66] Otherwise, less favourable treatment or a failure to comply with the duty to make reasonable adjustments is justified only if the reason for it is both material to the circumstances of the particular case and substantial.[67] However, in a case of less favourable treatment discrimination, if the responsible body is under a duty to make reasonable adjustments under DDA 1995, s 28C in relation to the disabled person, but it fails without justification to comply with that duty, its treatment of that person cannot be justified[68] unless that treatment would have been justified even if it had complied

---

[61]   DDA 1995, s 28C(7)(b).

[62]   Ibid, s 28C(6).

[63]   Parts 2 and 3. See Chapters 3–5.

[64]   DDA 1995, s 28B(3). See Schools Code of Practice, paras 7.4–7.12. The use of the word 'discriminate' here clearly suggests that knowledge of the disability is a necessary ingredient of both less favourable treatment discrimination and failure to make reasonable adjustments discrimination arising from an act of omission.

[65]   DDA 1995, s 28B(4). See Schools Code of Practice, paras 7.4–7.12. Clearly, this provision is only concerned with an act of commission which would otherwise amount to less favourable treatment discrimination.

[66]   DDA 1995, s 28B(6), by virtue of s 28B(5).

[67]   Ibid, s 28B(7), by virtue of s 28B(5).

[68]   Under ibid, s 28B(7).

with that duty.[69] Again, the parallels with the comparable provisions of DDA 1995, Part 2 (discrimination in employment) will be apparent and instructive.[70]

Accessibility strategies and plans

7.3.12 Complementing the anti-discrimination provisions of the amended DDA 1995 as they affect schools are provisions[71] placing a duty on LEAs[72] and schools in England and Wales to develop 'accessibility strategies' and 'accessibility plans'[73] for disabled pupils.[74] Broadly comparable (but not identical) duties have been introduced in Scotland by the Scottish Parliament as a result of the Education (Disability Strategies and Pupils' Records) (Scotland) Act 2002.[75] The discussion below is based upon the legislation in England and Wales, with cross-references to the Scottish legislation in the footnotes.

7.3.13 Each LEA must prepare an 'accessibility strategy' in relation to schools for which it is responsible.[76] An accessibility strategy is a strategy for:

---

[69] DDA 1995, s 28B(8).

[70] See Chapter 3. See: *VK v Norfolk County Council and the Special Educational Needs and Disability Tribunal* [2004] EWHC 2921 (Admin), Stanley Burnton J, applying *Post Office v Jones* [2001] EWCA Civ 558, [2001] IRLR 384, CA.

[71] See generally DDA 1995, ss 28D–28E. These provisions came into force in England on 1 September 2002 by virtue of Special Educational Needs and Disability Act 2001 (Commencement No 5) Order 2002, SI 2002/2217, art 4 and Sch 1, Part 2. These provisions did not come into force in Wales on 1 September 2002 because SENDA 2001, s 43(6)(d) provides that the relevant provisions will be brought into force as respects Wales on such day as the Welsh Ministers may appoint by order. The operative date in Wales was 8 October 2003: Special Educational Needs and Disability Act 2001 (Commencement No 2) (Wales) Order 2003, SI 2003/2532 (W 247).

[72] A 'local education authority' (LEA) is defined in Education Act 1996, s 12: DDA 1995, s 28D(16). See the comparable provisions in Education (Disability Strategies and Pupils' Records) (Scotland) Act 2002, s 6(1).

[73] By virtue of DDA 1995, s 28Q(13), these terms have the meaning assigned to them in DDA 1995, s 28D.

[74] A 'disabled pupil' includes a disabled person who may be admitted to a school as a pupil: DDA 1995, s 28D(18). See the comparable provisions in Education (Disability Strategies and Pupils' Records) (Scotland) Act 2002, s 6(1).

[75] The relevant provisions of this Act (ss 1–3) came into force on 15 August 2002 by virtue of the Education (Disability Strategies and Pupils' Records) (Scotland) Act 2002 (Commencement) Order 2002, SSI 2002/367, the remainder of the Act having come into force with the Royal Assent on 30 April 2002. The Act is supported by the Education (Disability Strategies) (Scotland) Regulations 2002, SSI 2002/391, in force on 1 October 2002 and the *Guidance on Planning to Improve Access to Education for Pupils with Disabilities* issued by the Scottish Executive.

[76] DDA 1995, s 28D(1)(a). Each LEA must also prepare 'further such strategies' at such times as may be prescribed: DDA 1995, s 28D(1)(b). In Scotland, the obligation of a school's responsible body to prepare an 'accessibility strategy' is found in Education (Disability Strategies and Pupils' Records) (Scotland) Act 2002, s 1. For this purpose, the responsible body will be the education authority, the proprietor of an independent school, the managers of a grant-receiving school, or the board of management of a self-governing school, as the case may be: Education (Disability Strategies and Pupils'

- increasing the extent to which disabled pupils can participate in the schools' curriculums;[77]

- improving the physical environment of the schools for the purpose of increasing the extent to which disabled pupils are able to take advantage of education and associated services provided or offered by the schools;[78] and

- improving the delivery to disabled pupils of information which is provided in writing for pupils who are not disabled, within a reasonable time and in ways which are determined after taking account of their disabilities and any preferences expressed by them or their parents.[79]

The accessibility strategy must be in writing[80] and relate to a prescribed period.[81] In England, the original prescribed period to which an accessibility strategy must relate is the period of three years from 1 April 2003 to 31 March 2006.[82] The subsequent prescribed period is three years

---

Records) (Scotland) Act 2002, s 6(1). In Scotland, an education authority also has additional responsibilities for developing accessibility strategies in relation to the education of children under school age (or who are of school age and are travelling people) outwith schools: Education (Disability Strategies and Pupils' Records) (Scotland) Act 2002, s 2.

[77] DDA 1995, s 28D(2)(a). See the comparable provisions in Education (Disability Strategies and Pupils' Records) (Scotland) Act 2002, s 1(2)(a).

[78] DDA 1995, s 28D(2)(b). Regulations may prescribe services which are (or which are not) to be regarded for these purposes as being education or an associated service: DDA 1995, s 28D(15). See the comparable provisions in Education (Disability Strategies and Pupils' Records) (Scotland) Act 2002, s 1(2)(b) and (6).

[79] DDA 1995, s 28D(2)(c). See the comparable provisions in the Education (Disability Strategies and Pupils' Records) (Scotland) Act 2002, s 1(2)(c).

[80] In Scotland, the law provides for the provision of accessibility strategies in alternative forms (ie orally, on audio tape, through sign language or lip speaking, on video tape (using signing and/or lip speaking), in Braille, in large print, on CD-ROM or other means of electronic communication, or in any other form which the responsible body regards as a reasonable form in which to provide information): Education (Disability Strategies and Pupils' Education Records) (Scotland) Act 2002, s 3(5)(b) and Education (Disability Strategies) (Scotland) Regulations 2002, SSI 2002/391, reg 3.

[81] DDA 1995, s 28D(2) and (3). In relation to Wales, this means prescribed in regulations made by the Welsh Ministers: DDA 1995, s 28D(17), as amended. See the comparable provisions in Education (Disability Strategies and Pupils' Records) (Scotland) Act 2002, s 1(2) and (3).

[82] Disability Discrimination (Prescribed Periods for Accessibility Strategies and Plans for Schools) (England) Regulations 2002, SI 2002/1981, reg 2. These regulations came into force on 1 September 2002 and apply only in relation to England: reg 1. In Scotland, the responsible body shall prepare its first accessibility strategy by 1 April 2003 for a period of up to three years starting by 1 April 2003, and further accessibility strategies shall be prepared by a date not more than three years after the date of preparation of the previous strategy and shall be for a further period of three years commencing immediately on the expiry of the period to which the previous strategy related: Education (Disability Strategies) (Scotland) Regulations 2002, SSI 2002/391, reg 2. In Wales, see Disability Discrimination (Prescribed Periods for Accessibility Strategies and

from 1 April 2006.[83] The LEA must keep the accessibility strategy under review during the period to which it relates and revise it if necessary.[84] In preparing the accessibility strategy, the LEA must have regard to:

- the need to allocate adequate resources for implementing it;[85]

- any guidance issued as to its content, the form in which it is to be produced and the persons to be consulted in its preparation;[86] and

- any guidance issued as to compliance with the requirement to keep the strategy under review.[87]

It is the statutory duty of the LEA to implement its accessibility strategy.[88] Previously, a statutory inspection of an LEA[89] may extend to the performance by it of its functions in relation to the preparation, review, revision and implementation of its accessibility strategy.[90] The LEA must provide a copy of its accessibility strategy if the Secretary of State (in England) or the Welsh Ministers (in Wales) ask for a copy.[91]

7.3.14 Maintained schools, maintained nursery schools (in Wales only), independent schools and approved non-maintained special schools[92] are

---

Plans for Schools) (Wales) Regulations 2003, SI 2003/2531 (W 246) (in force 8 October 2003) where the first accessibility strategies are to commence on 1 April 2004 for a three-year period.

[83]   Disability Discrimination (Prescribed Periods for Accessibility Strategies and Plans for Schools) (England) Regulations 2005, SI 2005/3221, reg 2.

[84]   DDA 1995, s 28D(4). See the comparable provisions in Education (Disability Strategies and Pupils' Records) (Scotland) Act 2002, s 1(4).

[85]   DDA 1995, s 28E(1)(a). See the comparable provisions in Education (Disability Strategies and Pupils' Records) (Scotland) Act 2002, s 3(1)(a).

[86]   DDA 1995, s 28E(1)(b). Such guidance may be issued by the Secretary of State (in relation to England) or by the Welsh Minister (in relation to Wales): DDA 1995, s 28E(3), as amended. See the comparable provisions in Education (Disability Strategies and Pupils' Records) (Scotland) Act 2002, s 3(1)(b)–(c) and (2).

[87]   DDA 1995, s 28E(2), cross-referencing to s 28D(4). Such guidance may be issued by the Secretary of State (in relation to England) or by the Welsh Ministers (in relation to Wales): DDA 1995, s 28E(3), as amended. See the comparable provisions in Education (Disability Strategies and Pupils' Records) (Scotland) Act 2002, s 3(3).

[88]   DDA 1995, s 28D(5). See the comparable provisions in Education (Disability Strategies and Pupils' Records) (Scotland) Act 2002, s 1(5).

[89]   Under Education Act 1997, s 38.

[90]   DDA 1995, s 28D(6). This provision was repealed in England from 1 April 2005 (and in Wales from a date yet to be appointed) by the Children Act 2004. Note that in relation to schools and accessibility plans (s 28D(13)) there is an additional function of 'publication' which is not found in the comparable provision relating to LEAs and accessibility strategies. However, if asked to do so, an LEA must make a copy of its accessibility strategy available for inspection at such reasonable times as it may determine: DDA 1995, s 28E(7). See the comparable provisions in Education (Disability Strategies and Pupils' Records) (Scotland) Act 2002, s 3(4)–(6).

[91]   DDA 1995, ss 28E(5)–(6) (as amended). See the comparable provisions in Education (Disability Strategies and Pupils' Records) (Scotland) Act 2002, s 3(4)–(6).

[92]   The terms 'maintained school' and 'independent school' are defined in School Standards and Framework Act 1998, s 20(7) and Education Act 1996, s 463 respectively: DDA

subject to parallel duties in relation to the development of an 'accessibility plan'.[93] The body responsible for such a school (the responsible body or, in the case of a maintained school or maintained nursery school, the governing body[94]) must prepare an 'accessibility plan' in relation to the school.[95] An accessibility plan is a plan for:

- increasing the extent to which disabled pupils can participate in the school's curriculum;[96]

- improving the physical environment of the school for the purpose of increasing the extent to which disabled pupils are able to take advantage of education and associated services provided or offered by the school;[97] and

- improving the delivery to disabled pupils of information which is provided in writing for pupils who are not disabled, within a reasonable time and in ways which are determined after taking account of their disabilities and any preferences expressed by them or their parents.[98]

It must be in writing and relates to a prescribed period.[99] In England only, the original prescribed period to which an accessibility plan must relate is

---

1995, ss 28D(19) and 28Q(5). The term 'approved non-maintained special school' is coined by the author to describe special schools which are not maintained schools but which are approved by the Secretary of State (or by the Welsh Ministers) under Education Act 1996, s 342: see DDA 1995, s 28D(7)(c) and SI 2007/1388.

[93] DDA 1995, s 28D(7)–(13), as amended by SI 2005/2913. In Scotland, the obligation of a school's responsible body to prepare an 'accessibility strategy' (as opposed to a 'plan') is found in Education (Disability Strategies and Pupils' Records) (Scotland) Act 2002, s 1. For this purpose, the responsible body will be the education authority, the proprietor of an independent school, the managers of a grant-receiving school, or the board of management of a self-governing school, as the case may be: Education (Disability Strategies and Pupils' Records) (Scotland) Act 2002, s 6(1).

[94] DDA 1995, s 28D(14), as amended by Education Act 2002, s 215(1) and Sch 21, para 26 (from 1 September 2003 in England only, at the time of writing). As has been seen, the meaning of the term 'the body responsible for a school' (referred to as the 'responsible body') depends upon the kind of school involved: DDA 1995, s 28A(5) and Sch 4A, as amended by Education Act 2002. See **7.4.3**.

[95] DDA 1995, s 28D(8)(a). The responsible body must also prepare 'further such plans' at such times as may be prescribed: DDA 1995, s 28D(8)(b). See the comparable provisions in Education (Disability Strategies and Pupils' Records) (Scotland) Act 2002, s 1(1).

[96] DDA 1995, s 28D(9)(a). See the comparable provisions in Education (Disability Strategies and Pupils' Records) (Scotland) Act 2002, s 1(2)(a).

[97] DDA 1995, s 28D(9)(b). Regulations may prescribe services which are (or which are not) to be regarded for these purposes as being education or an associated service: DDA 1995, s 28D(15). See the comparable provisions in Education (Disability Strategies and Pupils' Records) (Scotland) Act 2002, s 1(2)(b) and (6).

[98] DDA 1995, s 28D(9)(c). See the comparable provisions in Education (Disability Strategies and Pupils' Records) (Scotland) Act 2002, s 1(2)(c).

[99] DDA 1995, s 28D(9) and (10). In relation to Wales, this means prescribed in regulations made by the Welsh Ministers: DDA 1995, s 28D(17), as amended. See the comparable provisions in Education (Disability Strategies and Pupils' Records) (Scotland) Act 2002, s 1(2) and (3).

the period of three years from 1 April 2003 to 31 March 2006.[100] The subsequent period is from 1 April 2006 and at three yearly intervals.[101] The responsible body must keep the accessibility plan under review during the period to which it relates and revise it if necessary.[102] In preparing the accessibility strategy, the responsible body must have regard to the need to allocate adequate resources for implementing it.[103] It is the statutory duty of the responsible body to implement its accessibility plan.[104] A statutory inspection of a school[105] may extend to the performance by the responsible body of its functions in relation to the preparation, publication, review, revision and implementation of its accessibility plan.[106] The proprietor of an independent school (other than a city academy[107]) must provide a copy of its accessibility plan if the Secretary of State (in England) or the Welsh Ministers (in Wales) ask for a copy.[108] If asked to do so, such a proprietor must also make a copy of its accessibility plan available for inspection at such reasonable times as it may determine.[109]

7.3.15   As has been seen,[110] since 1 January 1997, the 'annual report' for a relevant school has been required to include a report containing certain information relating to disabled pupils.[111] From 1 September 2002, the governors' report[112] shall include information as to:

---

[100] Disability Discrimination (Prescribed Periods for Accessibility Strategies and Plans for Schools) (England) Regulations 2002, SI 2002/1981, reg 2. These regulations came into force on 1 September 2002 and apply only in relation to England: reg 1. In respect of a school established after 1 April 2003, the prescribed period begins with the date on which the school is established and ends on 31 March 2006: reg 3. In Wales, see the Disability Discrimination (Prescribed Periods for Accessibility Strategies and Plans for Schools) (Wales) Regulations 2003, SI 2003/2531 (W 246).

[101] Disability Discrimination (Prescribed Periods for Accessibility Strategies and Plans for Schools) (England) Regulations 2005, SI 2005/3221, reg 3.

[102] DDA 1995, s 28D(11). See the comparable provisions in Education (Disability Strategies and Pupils' Records) (Scotland) Act 2002, s 1(4).

[103] DDA 1995, s 28E(4).

[104] Ibid, s 28D(12). See the comparable provisions in Education (Disability Strategies and Pupils' Records) (Scotland) Act 2002, s 1(5).

[105] Under Part 1 of the Education Act 2005.

[106] DDA 1995, s 28D(13), as amended by Education Act 2005. Note the additional function of 'publication' which is not found in the comparable provision (s 28D(6), but repealed in England from 1 April 2005, and in Wales from a date yet to be appointed, by the Children Act 2004) relating to LEAs and accessibility strategies.

[107] The term 'city academy' means a school which is known as a city academy as a result of Education Act 1996, s 482(3) or (3A): DDA 1995, s 28Q(12).

[108] DDA 1995, s 28E(5)–(6), as amended.

[109] Ibid, s 28E(8).

[110] See **7.2.10**.

[111] Education Act 1993, s 161(6), as inserted by DDA 1995, s 29(2) (which was repealed by Education Act 1996, s 582(2) and Sch 38, Part I); see now Education Act 1996, s 317(6)–(7). See *School Prospectuses and Governors' Annual Reports* (DfEE Circulars 11/96 (primary schools) and 12/96 (secondary schools)).

[112] The report prepared under School Standards and Framework Act 1998, s 42(1): Education Act 1996, s 317(7), as amended by SENDA 2001, s 14(2).

- the arrangements for the admission of disabled persons[113] as pupils at the school;

- the steps taken to prevent disabled pupils from being treated less favourably than other pupils;

- the facilities provided to assist access to the school by disabled pupils; and

- the accessibility plan prepared by the governing body.[114]

This is as a result of the amendments made by the SENDA 2001.[115]

Residual duty of education authorities

7.3.16   Education authorities have residual duties under DDA 1995, ss 28F–28G.[116] These duties arise in relation to the functions – other than functions that may be prescribed[117] – of LEAs in England and Wales[118] and education authorities in Scotland.[119] In discharging the relevant functions, it is unlawful for the authority to discriminate against a disabled pupil or a disabled person who may be admitted to a school as a pupil,[120] but only if no other provision of DDA 1995, Part 4, Chapter 1 (that is, ss 28A–28Q) applies.[121] The meaning of discrimination for this purpose is set out in DDA 1995, s 28B. This is achieved by applying s 28B for the purposes of s 28F with modifications.[122]

---

[113] As defined in the DDA 1995: Education Act 1996, s 317(7A), as amended by SENDA 2001, s 14(2).

[114] That is, the accessibility plan prepared under DDA 1995, s 28D.

[115] Education Act 1996, s 317(6)–(7), as amended by SENDA 2001, s 14(2).

[116] See Schools Code of Practice, paras 10.1–10.6 (and examples).

[117] DDA 1995, s 28F(2). No such functions have been prescribed at the time of writing. Schools Code of Practice, para 10.3 suggests that the functions which are covered include policies such as the authority's policies on SEN, capital building programmes, sports, cultural activities, transport and early years provision; the education authority's policy and arrangements on school admissions and exclusions, and (in England and Wales) the school's admissions policy and arrangements; the deployment of the authority's non-delegated budget and any other arrangements which might directly affect disabled pupils; and services to pupils (such as weekend or after-school leisure and sporting activities, school trips, and cultural activities).

[118] Under the Education Acts as defined in Education Act 1996, s 578: DDA 1995, s 28F(1)(a) and (7). See Education Act 1996, s 12: DDA 1995, s 28F(6).

[119] Under the Education (Scotland) Act 1980; the Education (Scotland) Act 1996; the Standards in Scotland's Schools etc Act 2000; and the Education (Additional Support For Learning) (Scotland) Act 2004: DDA 1995, s 28F(1)(b), as amended. See Education (Scotland) Act 1980, s 135(1) and DDA 1995, s 28F(8).

[120] DDA 1995, s 28F(3). In the case of an act which constitutes discrimination by virtue of ibid, s 55 (ie victimisation), these provisions also apply to discrimination against a person who is not disabled: ibid, s 28F(5).

[121] Ibid, s 28F(4).

[122] Ibid, s 28G(1).

7.3.17 Thus, an authority[123] discriminates against a disabled person if, for a reason which relates to his or her disability, it treats him or her less favourably than it treats or would treat others to whom that reason does not (or would not) apply and it cannot show that the treatment in question is justified.[124] Less favourable treatment of a person is justified if it is the result of a permitted form of selection.[125] Otherwise, less favourable treatment is justified only if the reason for it is both material to the circumstances of the particular case and substantial.[126] If the authority is under a duty to make reasonable adjustments[127] in relation to the disabled person, but it fails without justification to comply with that duty, its treatment of that person cannot be justified by reference to a material and substantial reason[128] unless that treatment would have been justified even if it had complied with that duty.[129]

7.3.18 An authority also discriminates against a disabled person if it fails, to his or her detriment, to comply with the duty to make reasonable adjustments contained in DDA 1995, s 28G(2)–(4), and it cannot show that its failure to comply is justified. An authority must take such steps as it is reasonable for it to have to take to ensure that, in discharging any function to which s 28F above applies, disabled persons who may be admitted to a school as pupils are not placed at a substantial disadvantage in comparison with persons who are not disabled.[130] It must also take such steps as it is reasonable for it to have to take to ensure that, in discharging any function to which s 28F above applies, disabled pupils are not placed at a substantial disadvantage in comparison with pupils who are not disabled.[131] However, neither aspect of the duty requires the authority to remove or alter a physical feature or to provide auxiliary aids or services.[132] In relation to a failure to take a particular step, an authority does not discriminate against a person if it shows that, at the time in question, it did not know and could not reasonably have been expected to know that he or she was disabled, and that its failure to take the step was attributable to that lack of knowledge.[133] Furthermore, the taking of a particular step by an authority in relation to a person does not amount to less favourable treatment if it shows that at the time in question it did not know, and could not reasonably have been expected to know, that he or she was disabled.[134]

---

[123] An LEA in England and Wales or an education authority in Scotland: DDA 1995, s 28G(7).
[124] Ibid, s 28B(1).
[125] Ibid, s 28B(6), as modified by virtue of s 28B(5).
[126] Ibid, s 28B(7), as modified by virtue of s 28B(5).
[127] Imposed by ibid, s 28G(2)–(4), by virtue of the modifications in s 28G(1)(b).
[128] Ibid, s 28B(7), as modified.
[129] Ibid, s 28B(8), as modified.
[130] Ibid, s 28G(2)(a).
[131] Ibid, s 28G(2)(b).
[132] Ibid, s 28G(3).
[133] Ibid, s 28B(3), as modified.
[134] Ibid, s 28B(4), as modified.

7.4 FURTHER AND HIGHER EDUCATION

7.4.1 The DDA 1995, Part 4, Chapter 2 addressed the rights of disabled students in relation to further and higher education – broadly post-16 education and related services.[135] The Government implemented the duties in three stages.[136] The main provisions came into force on 1 September 2002 and make it unlawful to discriminate against disabled people or students by treating them less favourably than others. In addition, they require responsible bodies to provide certain types of reasonable adjustments to provision where disabled students or other disabled people might otherwise be substantially disadvantaged. The duty on responsible bodies to make adjustments involving the provision of auxiliary aids and services came into effect on 1 September 2003. The duty on responsible bodies to make adjustments to physical features of premises where these put disabled people or students at a substantial disadvantage has been in force from 1 September 2005.

7.4.2 The statutory provisions containing the duties placed upon the providers of post-16 education services are supported by the *Disability Discrimination Act 1995 Part 4 Code of Practice for Providers of Post-16 Education and Related Services* (Post-16 Code of Practice) (2002) issued by the DRC under DDA 1995, s 53A at the request of the Secretary of State for Education and Skills, and revised in 2007.[137] The law and the Code of Practice apply throughout Great Britain (but not Northern Ireland) to a variety of further and higher education institutions; LEAs (known as education authorities in Scotland) in relation to the provision by them of further education, adult and community education, and youth and community services; and schools providing further education for adults.[138] Further guidance is also available from various other sources.[139]

---

[135] SENDA 2001, Part 2, Chapter 2, inserting new ss 28R–28X and 31A into the DDA 1995. Important amendments are made by the Disability Discrimination Act 1995 (Amendment) (Further and Higher Education) Regulations 2006, SI 2006/1721.

[136] See Special Educational Needs and Disability Act 2001 (Commencement No 5) Order 2002, SI 2002/2217, arts 3 and 5–6, and Schs 1 (Part 1) and 2.

[137] Post-16 Code of Practice (Revised 2007), Chapter 1. It usefully explains how discrimination can be avoided: ibid, Chapter 2.

[138] Where a school makes provision for pupils post-16 that provision is covered by DDA 1995, Part 4, Chapter 1 and the Schools Code of Practice.

[139] Association of Colleges, *Rights to Access: A Toolkit to Help Colleges Meet or Exceed the Requirements of the Disability Discrimination Act*; Learning and Skills Council, *The Special Educational Needs and Disability Act 2001* (Equality and Diversity Guidance 02/2002); Education and Learning Wales, *Disability Access Planning* (NC/C/01/11LL); Department for Education and Skills, *Guidance for LEAs and Adult Education Providers on the Implementation of the Disability Discrimination Act Part 4*. See also the DRC publications (now available from the CEHR): *A guide for disabled students and learners: Part 4 of the DDA 1995: Post-16* (2005); *Understanding the DDA; a guide for colleges, universities and adult community learning providers in GB* (2007).

Wholly privately funded post-16 providers and providers of work-based training are not covered by these provisions but will be within the scope of Part 3 of the DDA 1995.[140]

Disability discrimination duties

7.4.3 By virtue of s 28R(1) of the DDA 1995, it is unlawful for 'the body responsible for an educational institution' to discriminate against a 'disabled person':[141]

- in the arrangements it makes for determining admissions to the institution;[142]

- in the terms on which it offers to admit him or her to the institution; or

- by refusing or deliberately omitting to accept an application for his or her admission to the institution.

It is further unlawful for 'the body responsible for an educational institution' to discriminate against a disabled student[143] by excluding him or her from the institution, whether permanently or temporarily.[144] New provisions from 1 September 2006 make it unlawful for the body responsible for an educational institution to discriminate against a disabled person (a) in the arrangements which it makes for the purpose of determining upon whom to confer a qualification; (b) in the terms on which it is prepared to confer a qualification on him or her; (c) by refusing or deliberately omitting to grant any application by him or her for a qualification; or (d) by withdrawing a qualification from him or her, or varying the terms on which he or she holds it.[145] It is also unlawful for the body responsible for an educational institution to subject to harassment a disabled person who (a) holds or applies for a qualification conferred by

---

[140] See Chapter 5. In particular, non-statutory youth services (e g clubs and activities run by voluntary organisations, the scouts or youth clubs) will be covered by DDA 1995, Part 3 rather than Part 4.

[141] See generally Post-16 Code of Practice (Revised 2007) Chapter 3. A 'disabled person' is a person falling within DDA 1995, ss 1–2 and Schs 1–2 (discussed in Chapter 2). This section also applies to discrimination against a person who is not disabled in the case of an act which constitutes discrimination by virtue of DDA 1995, s 55 (victimisation): DDA 1995, s 28R(4).

[142] See generally Post-16 Code of Practice (Revised 2007), Chapter 8.

[143] By virtue of DDA 1995, s 31A(2), the term 'disabled student' (as used throughout this analysis) means a student who is a disabled person. A 'student' means a person who is attending or undertaking a course of study at an educational institution: DDA 1995, s 31A(3). It does not matter whether that person is completing an entire course. Someone enquiring about, applying to, attending or undertaking a course of study (however short or long) at an educational institution is covered.

[144] DDA 1995, s 28R(3).

[145] Ibid, s 28R(3A) inserted by SI 2006/1721. See generally Post-16 Code of Practice (Revised 2007), Chapter 10.

the institution; (b) is a student at the institution; or (c) seeks admission as a student to the institution.[146] A responsible body subjects a disabled person to harassment where, for a reason which relates to the disabled person's disability, that body engages in unwanted conduct which has the purpose or effect of (a) violating the disabled person's dignity, or (b) creating an intimidating, hostile, degrading, humiliating or offensive environment for him or her. Conduct shall be regarded as having the effect referred to in the latter case only if, having regard to all the circumstances, including in particular the perception of the disabled person, it should reasonably be considered as having that effect.[147]

7.4.4 It is also unlawful for 'the body responsible for an educational institution' to discriminate against a disabled student in the student services[148] it provides (or offers to provide).[149] Such services might include: teaching (including classes, lectures, seminars, practical sessions); curriculum design; examinations and assessments; field trips and outdoor education; arranging study abroad or work placements; outings and trips; research degrees and research facilities; informal/optional study skills sessions; short courses; day or evening adult education courses; training courses; distance learning; independent learning opportunities (such as e-learning); learning facilities (such as classrooms, lecture theatres, laboratories, studios, darkrooms, etc); learning equipment and materials (such as laboratory equipment, computer facilities, class handouts, etc); libraries, learning centres, and information centres and their resources; information and communication technology and resources; placement finding services; careers advice and training; careers libraries; job references; job shops and employment-finding services; graduation and certificate ceremonies; leisure, recreation, entertainment and sports facilities; the physical environment; chaplaincies and prayer areas; health services; counselling services; catering facilities; childcare facilities; campus or college shops; car parking; residential accommodation; accommodation-finding services; financial advice; and welfare services.[150] Many (but not all) of these services would have been caught by DDA 1995, Part 3 prior to 1 September 2002,[151] but now will be within the exclusive scope of DDA 1995, Part 4.

7.4.5 In England and Wales, an 'educational institution' is an institution within the further education or higher education sector or designated as such by an Order (where the Secretary of State is satisfied that the

---

[146] DDA 1995, s 28R(3B) inserted by SI 2006/1721.

[147] Ibid, s 28SA inserted by SI 2006/1721.

[148] The term 'student services' means services of any description which are provided wholly or mainly for students: ibid, s 28R(11). Regulations may prescribe services which are (or are not) to be regarded for this purpose as being 'student services': ibid, s 28R(3).

[149] Ibid, s 28R(2). See generally Post-16 Code of Practice (Revised 2007), Chapter 9.

[150] See generally Post-16 Code of Practice (Revised 2007), Chapters 8–10.

[151] They will continue to be caught where they are being provided to persons other than students (such as the provision by an educational institution of commercial conference facilities or commercial research and consultancy services).

institution is wholly or partly funded from public funds).[152] In Scotland, it is an institution within the higher education sector;[153] a college of further education with a board of management;[154] a central institution;[155] a college of further education maintained by an education authority;[156] or an institution designated as such by an order (where the Secretary of State is satisfied that the institution is wholly or partly funded from public funds).[157] The 'body responsible for an educational institution' (referred to as the 'responsible body') is to be determined in accordance with DDA 1995, s 28R.[158] In England and Wales, the responsible body will be the governing body of the institution[159] or, in the case of an institution designated by order, the body specified in the order. In Scotland, as the case might be, the responsible body will usually be the governing body, the board of management, an education authority, the managers of a school or, in the case of an institution designated by order, the body specified in the order.

Discrimination

7.4.6 The meaning of discrimination for this purpose is set out in DDA 1995, s 28S. There are two kinds of discrimination contemplated by the section. They might be referred to in shorthand as (1) less favourable treatment, and (2) failure to make reasonable adjustments.[160]

Less favourable treatment

7.4.7 A responsible body discriminates against a disabled person if, for a reason which relates to his disability,[161] it treats him less favourably than it treats or would treat others to whom that reason does not (or would not) apply[162] and it cannot show that the treatment in question is justified.[163] Prior to 1 September 2006, less favourable treatment of a person was justified if it was necessary in order to maintain academic standards (or

---

[152] DDA 1995, s 28R(6) (to be read with Further and Higher Education Act 1992, s 91) and (9). See the Disability Discrimination (Designation of Educational Institutions) Order 2002, SI 2002/1459. See generally Post-16 Code of Practice (Revised 2007), Chapter 11.
[153] Within the meaning of Further and Higher Education (Scotland) Act 1992, s 56(2).
[154] Within the meaning of Further and Higher Education (Scotland) Act 1992, s 36.
[155] Within the meaning of Education (Scotland) Act 1980, s 135.
[156] In the exercise of its further education functions in providing courses of further education within the meaning of ibid, s 1(5)(b)(ii).
[157] DDA 1995, s 28R(7), (9)–(10). See the Disability Discrimination (Designation of Educational Institutions) Order 2002, SI 2002/1459.
[158] Ibid, ss 28R(5) and 31A(4).
[159] As defined in Further and Higher Education Act 1992, s 90.
[160] See generally Post-16 Code of Practice (Revised 2007), Chapter 3. DDA 1995, Part 4 does not prohibit more favourable treatment of disabled persons.
[161] There has to be a link between the reason and the disability.
[162] This calls for a real or hypothetical comparison.
[163] DDA 1995, s 28S(1). See generally Post-16 Code of Practice (Revised 2007) Chapter 6.

standards of any other prescribed kind).[164] It was also justified where it was of a prescribed kind, or it occured in prescribed circumstances, or where it was both of a prescribed kind *and* occurred in prescribed circumstances.[165] Otherwise, less favourable treatment was justified only if the reason for it was both material to the circumstances of the particular case and substantial (that is, more than minor or trivial).[166] If the responsible body was under a duty to make reasonable adjustments (imposed by DDA 1995, s 28T) in relation to the disabled person, but it failed without justification to comply with that duty, its treatment of that person could not be justified by reference to a material and substantial reason[167] unless that treatment would have been justified even if it had complied with that duty.[168] The concept of unjustified less favourable treatment discrimination arising here is broadly similar to the parallel provision in Part 2 of the DDA 1995 (discrimination in employment) and the case-law there is likely to be instructive.[169]

7.4.8   From 1 September 2006,[170] treatment (other than the application of a competence standard) is justified if, but only if, the reason for it is both material to the circumstances of the particular case and substantial. However, if a responsible body is under a duty under s 28T or s 28UA(5) in relation to the disabled person, but fails to comply with that duty, its treatment of that person cannot be justified unless that treatment would have been justified even if it had complied with that duty. The application by a responsible body of a competence standard to a disabled person is justified if, but only if, the body can show that (a) the standard is (or would be) applied equally to persons who do not have his particular disability, and (b) its application is a proportionate means of achieving a legitimate aim. A competence standard means an academic, medical or other standard applied by or on behalf of a responsible body for the purpose of determining whether or not a person has a particular level of competence or ability In any event, treatment of a disabled person by a responsible body cannot be justified if it amounts to direct discrimination. A responsible body directly discriminates against a disabled person if, on the ground of the disabled person's disability, it treats the disabled person less favourably than it treats or would treat a person not having that particular disability whose relevant circumstances, including his abilities, are the same as, or not materially different from, those of the disabled person.

---

[164] DDA 1995, s 28S(6), by virtue of s 28S(5).

[165] Ibid, s 28S(7), by virtue of s 28S(5).

[166] Ibid, s 28S(8), by virtue of s 28S(5).

[167] Ibid, s 28S(8).

[168] Ibid, s 28S(9).

[169] See Chapter 3.

[170] DDA 1995, s 28S(5)–(11) as substituted by SI 2006/1721.

Failure to make reasonable adjustments

7.4.9 By virtue of DDA 1995, s 28S(2) a responsible body also discriminates against a disabled person if it fails, to his or her detriment, to comply with the duty to make reasonable adjustments contained in DDA 1995, s 28T or s 28UA(5) and it cannot show that its failure to comply is justified.[171] Before this kind of discrimination can be explored further, it is necessary to examine the duty to make reasonable adjustments in this context.[172]

7.4.10 First, the duty to make reasonable adjustments arises where a provision, criterion or practice (other than a competence standard) is applied by or on behalf of a responsible body. The provision, criterion or practice must relate to the arrangements it makes for determining admissions to the institution, or student services provided for (or offered to) students by the responsible body. If that provision, criterion or practice places disabled persons at a substantial disadvantage in comparison with persons who are not disabled, it is the duty of the responsible body to take such steps as it is reasonable, in all the circumstances of the case, for it to have to take in order to prevent the provision, criterion or practice having that effect.[173]

7.4.11 Secondly, the duty to make reasonable adjustments arises where a provision, criterion or practice (other than a competence standard) is applied by or on behalf of a responsible body. It must be a provision, criterion or practice for determining on whom a qualification is to be conferred and a disabled person is (or has notified the body that he or she may be) an applicant for the conferment of that qualification. If the provision, criterion or practice places the disabled person at a substantial disadvantage in comparison with persons who are not disabled, it is the duty of the responsible body to take such steps as it is reasonable, in all the circumstances of the case, for it to have to take in order to prevent the provision, criterion or practice having that effect.[174]

7.4.12 Thirdly, the duty to make reasonable adjustments arises where a provision, criterion or practice (other than a competence standard) is applied by or on behalf of a responsible body. The provision, criterion or practice must be one other than one mentioned in the first and second cases above. It must have the effect of placing a disabled person who holds a qualification conferred by the responsible body, or applies for a qualification which the responsible body confers, at a substantial disadvantage in comparison with persons who are not disabled. If so, it is

---

[171] That is, the reason for failing to comply with the duty to make reasonable adjustments is both material to the circumstances of the particular case and substantial: DDA 1995, s 28S(8), by virtue of s 28S(5).

[172] Ibid, s 28S(2), as amended by SI 2006/1721. See generally Post-16 Code of Practice (Revised 2007) Chapter 5.

[173] Ibid, s 28T(1), as amended by SI 2006/1721.

[174] Ibid, s 28T(1A), as amended by SI 2006/1721.

the duty of the responsible body to take such steps as it is reasonable, in all the circumstances of the case, for it to have to take in order to prevent the provision, criterion or practice having that effect.[175]

7.4.13 Fourthly, the duty to make reasonable adjustments arises where any physical feature of premises occupied by a responsible body places disabled persons at a substantial disadvantage in comparison with persons who are not disabled in relation to (a) the arrangements which that body makes for determining admissions to the institution, or (b) student services provided for (or offered to) students by that body. It is then the duty of the body to take such steps as it is reasonable, in all the circumstances of the case, for it to have to take in order to prevent the feature having that effect.[176]

7.4.14 Fifthly, the duty to make reasonable adjustments arises where any physical feature of premises occupied by a responsible body places a disabled person who (a) applies for a qualification which that body confers, or (b) holds a qualification which was conferred by that body, at a substantial disadvantage in comparison with persons who are not disabled. It is then the duty of the body to take such steps as it is reasonable, in all the circumstances of the case, for it to have to take in order to prevent the feature having that effect.[177]

7.4.15 What reasonable steps might the responsible body of an educational institution have to take to discharge its DDA 1995, s 28T duty? The responsible body must have regard to any relevant provisions of a code of practice[178] in considering whether it is reasonable for it to have to take a particular step in order to comply with its duty to make reasonable adjustments.[179] Obviously, the Post-16 Code of Practice (Revised 2007) is relevant here, especially as the Act does not define what are reasonable steps. The Code anticipates that responsible bodies will have to consider a wide range of adjustments. However, the duty to make reasonable adjustments is being introduced in stages. While the main duty came into force on 1 September 2002, there was no obligation to provide auxiliary aids or services until 1 September 2003, and there will be no obligation to make adjustments to physical features of premises until 1 September 2005.[180]

7.4.16 Nevertheless, those temporal limits aside, the Code of Practice does suggest some criteria that might be taken into account when

---

[175] DDA 1995, s 28T(1B), as amended SI 2006/1721.
[176] Ibid, s 28T(1C)), as amended by SI 2006/1721. See generally Post-16 Code of Practice (Revised 2007), Chapter 12.
[177] Ibid, s 28T(1D), as amended SI 2006/1721.
[178] Issued under DDA 1995, s 53A, as amended by SENDA 2001, s 36; now Equality Act 2006, s 14.
[179] DDA 1995, s 28T(2), as amended.
[180] Post-16 Code of Practice (Revised 2007), paras 5.3–5.4.

determining what is reasonable.[181] In particular, the Code of Practice speculates that what is reasonable will depend on all the circumstances of the case and will vary according to the type of services being offered; the nature of the institution or service and its size and resources; and the effect of the disability on the individual disabled person or student. Some of the factors that might be taken into account are suggested as including: whether taking any particular steps would be effective in overcoming the difficulty that disabled people face in accessing the student services in question; the type of service being provided; the nature of the institution or service and its size and resources; the effect of the disability on the individual disabled person or student; the extent to which it is practicable for the education provider to take the steps; the financial and other costs of making the adjustment; the financial resources available to the education provider; the availability of grants, loans and other assistance to disabled students (and only disabled students) for the purpose of enabling them to receive student services (such as Disabled Students' Allowances); the extent to which aids and services will otherwise be provided to disabled people or students; health and safety requirements; and the relevant interests of other people including other students.

7.4.17   Particular provision is made where a 'confidentiality request' has been made in relation to a person and the responsible body is aware of it.[182] A 'confidentiality request' is a request made by a disabled person which asks for the nature of (or the existence of) his or her disability to be treated as confidential.[183] In determining whether it is reasonable for the responsible body to have to take a particular step in relation to that person in order to comply with its duty to make reasonable adjustments, regard shall be had to the extent to which taking the step in question is consistent with compliance with that request.[184]

Knowledge of disability

7.4.18   The question of the relevance of what an alleged discriminator knew or did not know about the fact of a disabled person's disability has bedevilled the interpretation of the employment and services provisions of the DDA 1995.[185] The provisions in Part 4 of the Act attempt to address that question head on. In relation to a failure to take a particular step, a responsible body does not 'discriminate' against a person if it shows that, at the time in question, it did not know and could not reasonably have been expected to know, that he or she was disabled, and that its failure to take the step was attributable to that lack of knowledge.[186] Knowledge

---

[181]   Post-16 Code of Practice (Revised 2007), pp 78–93.
[182]   DDA 1995, s 28T(3).
[183]   Ibid, s 28T(5).
[184]   Ibid, s 28T(4), as amended.
[185]   Parts 2 and 3. See Chapters 3–5.
[186]   DDA 1995, s 28S(3). The use of the word 'discriminate' here clearly suggests that

might be actual or constructive.[187] Previously, the taking of a particular step by a responsible body in relation to a person did not amount to 'less favourable treatment' if it showed that at the time in question it did not know, and could not reasonably have been expected to know, that he or she was disabled.[188]

Justification

7.4.19   As has been noted, less favourable treatment of a person or a failure to make reasonable adjustments may be justified in specified circumstances.[189] Prior to 1 September 2006, those circumstances included the maintenance of academic or other prescribed standards, or other prescribed kinds or circumstances of treatment. Otherwise, less favourable treatment or a failure to comply with the duty to make reasonable adjustments was justified only if the reason for it was both material to the circumstances of the particular case and substantial.[190] However, in a case of less favourable treatment discrimination, if the responsible body was under a duty to make reasonable adjustments under DDA 1995, s 28T in relation to the disabled person, but it failed without justification to comply with that duty, its treatment of that person could not be justified[191] unless that treatment would have been justified even if it had complied with that duty.[192] Again, the parallels with the comparable provisions of DDA 1995, Part 2 (discrimination in employment) will be apparent and instructive.[193]

7.4.20   From 1 September 2006,[194] treatment (other than the application of a competence standard) is justified if, but only if, the reason for it is both material to the circumstances of the particular case and substantial. However, if a responsible body is under a duty under s 28T or s 28UA(5) in relation to the disabled person, but fails to comply with that duty, its treatment of that person cannot be justified unless that treatment would have been justified even if it had complied with that duty. The application by a responsible body of a competence standard to a disabled person is justified if, but only if, the body can show that (a) the standard is (or would be) applied equally to persons who do not have his particular disability, and (b) its application is a proportionate means of achieving a

knowledge of the disability is a necessary ingredient of both less favourable treatment discrimination and failure to make reasonable adjustments discrimination arising from an act of omission.

[187] See also Department for Education and Skills, *Finding Out About People's Disability: A Good Practice Guide for Further and Higher Education Institutions* (DfES/0024/2002).

[188] DDA 1995, s 28S(4), now repealed by SI 2006/1721 from 1 September 2006. Clearly, this provision is only concerned with an act of commission which would otherwise amount to less favourable treatment discrimination.

[189] DDA 1995, s 28S(5)–(9), as originally enacted.

[190] Ibid, s 28S(8), by virtue of s 28S(5).

[191] Under ibid, s 28S(8).

[192] Ibid, s 28S(9).

[193] See Chapter 3.

[194] DDA 1995, s 28S(5)–(11) as substituted by SI 2006/1721.

legitimate aim. A competence standard means an academic, medical or other standard applied by or on behalf of a responsible body for the purpose of determining whether or not a person has a particular level of competence or ability.

Direct discrimination

7.4.21 In any event, treatment of a disabled person by a responsible body cannot be justified if it amounts to direct discrimination.[195] A responsible body directly discriminates against a disabled person if, on the ground of the disabled person's disability, it treats the disabled person less favourably than it treats or would treat a person not having that particular disability whose relevant circumstances, including his abilities, are the same as, or not materially different from, those of the disabled person.

Harassment

7.4.22 Also from 1 September 2006, it is unlawful for an education provider to subject a disabled person who is a student at that institution, or seeks admission as a student to that institution, to harassment for a reason which relates to his or her disability. It is also unlawful to subject a disabled person who holds or applies for a qualification conferred by the education provider to harassment.[196] Harassment occurs where, for a reason which relates to a person's disability, an education provider engages in unwanted conduct which has the purpose or effect of violating the disabled person's dignity or creating an intimidating, hostile, degrading, humiliating or offensive environment for him or her.[197] If the relevant conduct was engaged in with the purpose or intention that it should have either of these effects, then it amounts to harassment irrespective of its actual effect on the disabled person. In the absence of such intention, the conduct will only amount to harassment if it should reasonably be considered as having either of these effects, having regard to all the circumstances, including the perception of the disabled person.[198]

Other providers of further education or training facilities

7.4.23 The provisions of DDA 1995, ss 28R and 28T are modified for the purpose of their application in England and Wales in relation to higher and further education secured by an LEA; further education provided by the governing body of a maintained school; or recreational or training facilities secured by an LEA.[199] Similar modifications are made in respect of the comparable provision of further education or training

---

[195] DDA 1995, s 28S(10). See generally Post-16 Code of Practice (Revised 2007) Chapter 4.
[196] Ibid, s 28SA. See generally Post-16 Code of Practice (Revised 2007) Chapter 7.
[197] Ibid, s 28SA(1).
[198] Ibid, s 28SA(2).
[199] Ibid, s 28U(1) and (2), and Sch 4C, Parts 1 and 1A, as substituted by SI 2006/1721. See generally Post-16 Code of Practice (Revised 2007) Appendix A.

facilities in Scotland.[200] These modifications are rehearsed here only to show the differences which arise in the relevant statutory provisions. Otherwise, reference should be made to the discussion above.

7.4.24   The modified s 28R of the DDA 1995[201] applies to any course[202] of further education[203] or higher education[204] secured by an LEA[205] and any course of further education provided by the governing body of a maintained school in England and Wales.[206] It is unlawful for the LEA to discriminate against a disabled person:

- in the arrangements it makes for determining who should be enrolled on the course;

- in the terms on which it offers to enrol him or her on the course; or

- by refusing or deliberately omitting to accept an application for his or her enrolment on the course.[207]

It is also unlawful for the LEA to discriminate against a disabled person who has enrolled on the course in the services[208] which it provides (or offers to provide).[209] It is also unlawful for the LEA to subject to harassment a disabled person who seeks enrolment on the course; is enrolled on the course; or is a user of any services provided by the LEA in relation to the course.[210]

7.4.25   The meaning of discrimination for this purpose is set out in DDA 1995, s 28S without modification. As already discussed, the kinds of discrimination contemplated by the section include a failure to make reasonable adjustments. The duty to make reasonable adjustments is that which arises under s 28T, with the following modification to s 28T(1) only (s 28T(1A) to (1D) being omitted here). The responsible body[211] must

---

[200]   DDA 1995, s 28U(3) and (4), and Sch 4C, Parts 2 and 2A, as substituted.

[201]   Modified by ibid, s 28U and Sch 4C, as substituted.

[202]   The term 'course' in relation to further education secured by an LEA includes each of the component parts of a course of further education if there is no requirement imposed on persons registered for any component part of the course to register for any other component part of that course. The term 'enrolment' in relation to such a course includes registration for any one of those parts. See DDA 1995, s 28R(6), as modified.

[203]   As defined in Education Act 1996, s 2(3): DDA 1995, s 28R(7), as modified.

[204]   The term 'higher education' is defined in Education Act 1996, s 579(1): DDA 1995, s 28R(9), as modified.

[205]   'Local education authority' is defined in Education Act 1996, s 12: DDA 1995, s 28R(10), as modified.

[206]   DDA 1995, s 28R(1), as modified. Note the references in this modified section to Education Reform Act 1988, s 120.

[207]   DDA 1995, s 28R(2), as modified.

[208]   The term 'services' means services of any description which are provided wholly or mainly for persons enrolled on the course: DDA 1995, s 28R(5), as modified.

[209]   Ibid, s 28R(3).

[210]   Ibid, s 28R(4), as modified.

[211]   That is, the LEA: DDA 1995, s 28R(7), as modified.

take such steps as it is reasonable for it to have to take to ensure that, in relation to its arrangements for enrolling persons on a course of further or higher education provided by it, and in relation to services provided (or offered) by it, disabled persons are not placed at a substantial disadvantage in comparison with persons who are not disabled.[212]

7.4.26 Section 28R is substituted (and ss 28S and 28T are modified) as it applies in relation to further education provided by schools, and recreational or training facilities provided by local education authorities.[213] The provisions on further education and on recreational and training facilities in Scotland are also the subject of substitution and modification.[214] The details of these modified provisions are not considered further here.

Other unlawful acts

7.4.27 As in other areas of disability discrimination law, provision is made in the educational field for unlawful acts in relation to relationships which have come to an end, instructions and pressure to discriminate, and discriminatory advertisements. These are not considered further here.[215]

7.5 GENERAL QUALIFICATIONS BODIES

Introduction

7.5.1 The DDA 2005 inserts new provisions into Part 4 of the DDA 1995 so as to deal with discrimination and harassment by general qualifications bodies.[216] A general qualifications body means any authority or body which can confer a relevant qualification. However, it does not include, in the educational context, a responsible body, a local education authority in England or Wales, an education authority in Scotland, or an authority or body of a prescribed description or in prescribed circumstances.[217] References to the conferment of a qualification on a person include the renewal or extension of a qualification, and the authentication of a qualification awarded to him by another person.[218]

---

[212] DDA 1995, s 28T(1) as modified.
[213] Ibid, Sch 4C, Parts 2 and 2A, as substituted by SI 2006/1721..
[214] Ibid, Sch 4C, Part 1A, as substituted by SI 2006/1721.
[215] Ibid, ss 28UA, 28UB and 28UC, as inserted by SI 2006/1721. See, for example, the discussion of these concepts in the employment field in Chapters 3 and 4.
[216] See also the provisions inserted by Disability Discrimination (General Qualifications Bodies) (Alteration of Premises and Enforcement) Regulations 2007, SI 2007/2405. The new law is supported by the Revised Draft Code of Practice: Trade Organisations, Qualifications Bodies and General Qualifications Bodies (2007) prepared by the former DRC. At present it lacks statutory force and has been issued in form of non-statutory guidance.
[217] DDA 1995, s 31AA(6)(a).
[218] Ibid, s 31AA(6)(b).

7.5.2 These provisions apply to relevant qualifications. A relevant qualification means an authorisation, qualification, approval or certification of a prescribed description.[219] An authorisation, qualification, approval or certification may not be so prescribed if it is a professional or trade qualification (within DDA 1995, s 14A(5)).[220] The prescribed qualifications are at present as follows: Advanced Extension Awards; Entry level qualifications; Free Standing Maths Qualifications; General Certificate of Education Advanced level (A and AS levels); General Certificate of Secondary Education; General National Vocational Qualifications; the International Baccalaureate; Key Skills; Certificate in Adult Literacy—Entry levels 1, 2 and 3; Certificate in Adult Numeracy—Entry levels 1, 2 and 3; The National Qualifications framework in Scotland; Vocational Certificate of Education; and the Welsh Baccalaureate Qualification.[221]

Unlawful acts

7.5.3 It is unlawful for a general qualifications body to discriminate against a disabled person (a) in the arrangements which it makes for the purpose of determining upon whom to confer a relevant qualification; (b) in the terms on which it is prepared to confer a relevant qualification on him or her; (c) by refusing or deliberately omitting to grant any application by him or for such a qualification; or (d) by withdrawing such a qualification from him or her, or varying the terms on which he or she holds it.[222]

7.5.4 It is also unlawful for a general qualifications body, in relation to a relevant qualification conferred by it, to subject to harassment a disabled person who holds or applies for such a qualification.[223] A body subjects a disabled person to harassment where, for a reason which relates to the disabled person's disability, the body engages in unwanted conduct which has the purpose or effect of (a) violating the disabled person's dignity; or (b) creating an intimidating, hostile, degrading, humiliating or offensive environment for him or her.[224] Conduct shall be regarded as having that effect only if, having regard to all the circumstances, including in particular the perception of the disabled person, it should reasonably be considered as having that effect.[225]

---

[219] DDA 1995, s 31AA(4). See Disability Discrimination (General Qualifications Bodies) (Relevant Qualifications, Reasonable Steps and Physical Features) Regulations 2007, SI2007/1764, in force on 1 September 2007. The regulations do not extend to Northern Ireland.

[220] DDA 1995, s 31AA(5). See Chapters 3 and 4.

[221] Disability Discrimination (General Qualifications Bodies) (Relevant Qualifications, Reasonable Steps and Physical Features) Regulations 2007, SI 2007/1764, reg 2 and Sch.

[222] DDA 1995, s 31AA(1).

[223] Ibid, s 31AA(2).

[224] Ibid, s 31AC(1).

[225] Ibid, s 31AC(2).

7.5.5 In the case of an act which constitutes discrimination by virtue of DDA 1995, s 55 (that is victimisation), s 31AA also applies to discrimination against a person who is not disabled.[226]

Discrimination

7.5.6 A general qualifications body discriminates against a disabled person if (a) for a reason which relates to the disabled person's disability, it treats him or her less favourably than it treats (or would treat) others to whom that reason does not (or would not) apply; and (b) it cannot show that the treatment in question is justified.[227] A body also discriminates against a disabled person if it fails to comply with a duty to make reasonable adjustments imposed on it by s 31AD in relation to the disabled person.[228] Moreover, a body directly discriminates against a disabled person if, on the ground of the disabled person's disability, it treats the disabled person less favourably than it treats (or would treat) a person not having that particular disability whose relevant circumstances, including his or her abilities, are the same as (or not materially different from) those of the disabled person.[229]

Justification

7.5.7 Disability-related less favourable treatment (other than the application of a competence standard) is justified if, but only if, the reason for it is both material to the circumstances of the particular case and substantial.[230] However, in this case, if a body is under a duty to make reasonable adjustments under s 31AD in relation to the disabled person, but fails to comply with that duty, its treatment of that person cannot be justified unless it would have been justified even if the body had complied with that duty.[231] The application by a general qualifications body of a competence standard[232] to a disabled person is justified if, but only if, the body can show that (a) the standard is (or would be) applied equally to persons who do not have his or her particular disability; and (b) its application is a proportionate means of achieving a legitimate aim.[233] However, in any case, treatment of a disabled person cannot be justified if

---

226 DDA 1995, s31AA(3).

227 Ibid, s 31AB(1).

228 Ibid, s 31AB(2).

229 Ibid, s 31AB(8).

230 Ibid, s 31AB(3).

231 Ibid, s 31AB(5).

232 In s 31AB, 'competence standard' means an academic, medical or other standard applied by or on behalf of a general qualifications body for the purpose of determining whether or not a person has a particular level of competence or ability: DDA 1995, s 31AB(9).

233 Ibid, s 31AB(4).

it amounts to direct discrimination.[234] Subject to that, regulations may make provision as to circumstances in which treatment is or is not to be taken to be justified.[235]

Duty to make reasonable adjustments

7.5.8 A duty to make reasonable adjustments arises where a provision, criterion or practice[236] (other than a competence standard) is applied by or on behalf of a general qualifications body.[237] The provision, criterion or practice must be one for determining on whom a relevant qualification is to be conferred.[238] The disabled person in question must be (or has notified the body that he or she may be) an applicant for the conferment of that qualification.[239] If the provision, criterion or practice places the disabled person at a substantial disadvantage in comparison with persons who are not disabled,[240] it is the duty of the body to take such steps as it is reasonable, in all the circumstances of the case, for it to have to take in order to prevent the provision, criterion or practice having that effect.[241]

7.5.9 A duty may also arise where a provision, criterion or practice (other than a competence standard) is applied by or on behalf of a general qualifications body and is a provision, criterion or practice other than one for determining on whom a relevant qualification is to be conferred.[242] The question then is whether it places a disabled person who (i) holds a relevant qualification conferred by the body, or (ii) applies for a relevant qualification which the body confers, at a substantial disadvantage in comparison with persons who are not disabled.[243] If so, it is then the duty of the body to take such steps as it is reasonable, in all the circumstances of the case, for it to have to take in order to prevent the provision, criterion or practice having that effect.[244]

7.5.10 In the above cases, the granting of an exemption from one or more of the components of any examination or assessment shall be a step

---

[234] DDA 1995, s 31AB(7).

[235] Ibid, s 31AB(6). No regulations have been made to date.

[236] The terms 'provision, criterion or practice' includes (subject to any provision under s 31AD(6)(e)) any arrangements: DDA 1995, s 31AD(5)(a). Regulations may make provision as to what is or is not to be included within the meaning of 'provision, criterion or practice': s 31AD(6)(e).

[237] Ibid, s 31AD(1)(a).

[238] Ibid, s 31AD(1)(b).

[239] Ibid, s 31AD(1)(c).

[240] Ibid, s 31AD(1)(d). Regulations may make provision as to circumstances in which a provision, criterion or practice is to be taken to have or not to have this effect: s 31AD(6)(a).

[241] Ibid, s 31AD(1).

[242] Ibid, s 31AD(2)(a) and (b).

[243] Ibid, s 31AD(2)(c). Regulations may make provision as to circumstances in which a provision, criterion or practice is to be taken to have or not to have this effect: s 31AD(6)(a).

[244] Ibid, s 31AD(2).

which it is always reasonable for a general qualifications body to have to take.[245] This concession arises where the provision, criterion or practice is the requirement for candidates to undertake one or more components of an examination or assessment for the purposes of determining on whom a relevant qualification is to be conferred.[246] It will apply where the granting of an exemption from the component is the only reasonable step that could be taken to prevent the disabled person from being placed at a substantial disadvantage.[247]

7.5.11 The duty also comes into play where any physical feature[248] of premises occupied by a general qualifications body places a relevant disabled person at a substantial disadvantage in comparison with persons who are not disabled.[249] A relevant disabled person is one who holds a relevant qualification conferred by the body, or applies for a relevant qualification which the body confers. In these circumstances, it is the duty of the body to take such steps as it is reasonable, in all the circumstances of the case, for it to have to take in order to prevent the feature having that effect. The problem of alterations to premises occupied under leases arises here as it does elsewhere in the DDA 1995.[250]

7.5.12 However, none of the above duties are imposed on a general qualifications body in relation to a disabled person if the body does not know (and could not reasonably be expected to know) in the case of an applicant (or potential applicant) for the conferment of a relevant qualification, that the disabled person concerned is (or may be) such an applicant.[251] They are also not imposed, in any case, if the body does not know (and could not reasonably be expected to know) that that person has a disability and is likely to be affected in the way required by the duty.[252]

7.5.13 Regulations may make provision as to circumstances in which it is or is not reasonable for a body to have to take steps of a prescribed description.[253] They may also make provision as to steps which it is always or is never reasonable for a body to have to take.[254]

---

[245] Disability Discrimination (General Qualifications Bodies) (Relevant Qualifications, Reasonable Steps and Physical Features) Regulations 2007, SI 2007/1764, reg 3(1).

[246] Ibid, reg 3(2)(a).

[247] Ibid, reg 3(2)(b).

[248] Ibid, SI 2007/1764, reg 4.

[249] DDA 1995, s 31AD(3). Regulations may make provision as to circumstances in which a physical feature is to be taken to have or not to have this effect: s 31AD(6)(b). Regulations may also make provision as to things which are or which are not to be treated as physical features: s 31AD(6)(f).

[250] See ibid, ss 31ADB, 31AE and 31AF, and Sch 4, Part 4; Disability Discrimination (General Qualifications Bodies) (Relevant Qualifications, Reasonable Steps and Physical Features) Regulations 2007, SI 2007/1764, reg 5.

[251] DDA 1995, s 31AD(4)(a).

[252] Ibid, s 31AD(4)(b).

[253] Ibid, s 31AD(6)(c).

[254] Ibid, s 31AD(6)(d).

Enforcement, remedies and procedures

7.5.14   The enforcement of the provisions on general qualifications bodies, and the applicable remedies and procedures, is dealt with in ss 31ADA and 31AE, and Sch 3, Part 5.[255] This explained further in Chapter 10 below. Section 31AD imposes duties only for the purpose of determining whether a body has, for the purposes of s 31AA, discriminated against a disabled person. A breach of any such duty is not actionable as such.[256]

7.6   REASONABLE ADJUSTMENTS AND THE PROBLEM OF LEASES

7.6.1   As is already the case in the employment and services field,[257] the education provisions of the DDA 1995 deal with the potentially conflicting legal obligations of disability discrimination law and the law of landlord and tenant which will arise when the duty to make reasonable adjustments embraces potential alterations to physical features of premises from 1 September 2005.[258] As these provisions are broadly similar to those that apply in employment, and in goods and services cases, further analysis is not called for here.

---

[255] See also: Disability Discrimination (General Qualifications Bodies) (Relevant Qualifications, Reasonable Steps and Physical Features) Regulations 2007, SI 2007/1764; Disability Discrimination (General Qualifications Bodies) (Alteration of Premises and Enforcement) Regulations 2007, SI 2007/2405.

[256] DDA 1995, s 31AD(7).

[257] See **6.3**.

[258] DDA 1995, s 28W and Sch 4, Part 3; Disability Discrimination (Educational Institutions) (Alteration of Leasehold Premises) Regulations 2005, SI 2005/1070.

CHAPTER 8

PUBLIC TRANSPORT

8.1 INTRODUCTION

8.1.1 The 1994 Green Paper considered whether the proposed general right of access should be extended to facilities for transport or travel.[1] It anticipated that the new right would not require modifications to transport systems where existing physical barriers prevented access. The 1995 White Paper confirmed that the new right would not apply to transport vehicles but would apply to stations.[2] It suggested that further initiatives would take place outside the framework of the proposed disability discrimination legislation. In the event, the initiatives were taken in Part 5 of the DDA 1995.

Transport services and Part 3 of the DDA 1995

8.1.2 As originally enacted, the goods, facilities and services provisions in Part 3[3] did not apply to any service 'so far as it consists of the use of any means of transport'.[4] This meant that the original Part 3 rights of access to services merely required transport providers to make some (but not all) of their facilities or services accessible without discrimination to disabled people.[5] For example, facilities and services (so-called 'infrastructure') such as timetables, ticketing arrangements, booking facilities, waiting areas, toilet facilities, platforms and other public areas were subject to the anti-discrimination provisions of the DDA 1995. Transport providers had to consider what reasonable adjustments might be made in order to ensure that disabled passengers enjoy effective access to such facilities or services.[6]

---

1   *A Consultation on Government Measures to Tackle Discrimination Against Disabled People* (July 1994), para 4.5.
2   *Ending Discrimination Against Disabled People*, Cm 2729 (1995), para 4.6.
3   DDA 1995, ss 19–21.
4   Ibid, s 19(5)(b) (in its original form), subject to any provision to the contrary in future regulations (no such regulations have been proposed to date).
5   See (during the relevant period) Rights of Access Code of Practice 2002, paras 2.36–2.37.
6   See the rather artificial example in *Roads v Central Trains Ltd* [2004] EWCA Civ 1541, CA. A train operator was required to make an adjustment for a wheelchair-user passenger where a station's platforms were not otherwise easily accessible. That involved the provision of an accessible taxi from another town to ferry the passenger from one

8.1.3 However, in its original form, Part 3 did not require buses, coaches, taxis, trains, aeroplanes, ferries, ships or other forms of public transport (including heritage vehicles) to be accessible without discrimination or to be accommodating of the needs of disabled passengers.[7] There were other legal or extra-legal sources which assisted disabled persons to achieve a right of access in respect of transport vehicles. For example, some local authorities already made the accessibility of taxis the subject of licensing conditions. Nevertheless, from its inception the DDA 1995 did not create a general right of transport accessibility. For example, hire car and breakdown recovery services were not fully subject to the Part 3 duty to make reasonable adjustments (so far as they consisted of the use of a means of transport, such as the hire car itself or a breakdown relay vehicle). Furthermore, discriminatory behaviour on board a transport vehicle (such as refusal to serve a disabled person in a restaurant car of a train) was not unlawful.

8.1.4 The Disability Rights Task Force (DRTF) recommended that the exemption for transport operators from the pre-2004 rights of access[8] should be removed, and that car hire and breakdown recovery services should be brought within the fold.[9] The Government expressed its intention to act on these recommendations and consulted on the proposal to do so.[10] Measures to effect the change were included in the Disability Discrimination Act 2005 and were fully implemented from 4 December 2006.[11]

---

side of the station to the other. The artificiality of the agreed facts of the case (including a concession that cost was not a factor) reduces its value as a precedent.

[7]   HL Deb, vol 566, col 463. See (during the relevant period) Rights of Access Code of Practice 2002, paras 2.36–2.37.

[8]   That is, the original provisions of ss 19–21 with the exception of s 21(2)(a)–(c). See Chapter 5.

[9]   Disability Rights Task Force, *From Exclusion to Inclusion: A Report of the Disability Rights Task Force for Disabled People* (1999, London: DfEE) (DRTF Report). See, ibid, recommendations 7.2 and 7.5.See now also: DRC, *Avoiding disability discrimination in transport: a practical guide for breakdown recovery operators* (2007) and DRC, *Avoiding disability discrimination in transport: a practical guide for vehicle rental firms* (2007).

[10]   See Department for Transport, *Consultation on the Government's Proposals to Lift the Exemption for Transport Services from Some of the Civil Rights Duties in Part III of the Disability Discrimination Act 1995* (November 2002); Department for Transport, *Disability Discrimination Act 1995: Access to Goods, Services and Facilities: Consultation on the Government's proposals to lift the exemption for transport services from some of the civil rights duties in Part III of the Disability Discrimination Act* (2005). See generally: Department for Transport, *Inclusive Mobility* (undated).

[11]   For the background, see: Department for Work and Pensions, *Draft Disability Discrimination Bill*, Cm 6058 (December 2003); *Explanatory Notes*, Cm 6058-ii; *Draft Regulatory Impact Assessment*, Cm 6058-iii. See, in particular: Joint Committee on the Draft Disability Discrimination Bill, *First Report* (April 2004); Department for Work and Pensions, *The Government's Response to the Report of the Joint Committee on the Draft Disability Discrimination Bill*, Cm 6276 (July 2004).

8.1.5 The exclusionary reference to transport services in the old s 19(5)(b) has now been repealed.[12] Transport services are thus no longer explicitly excluded from Part 3. Instead, a new s 21ZA provides for the application of ss 19–21 to transport vehicles.[13] The presumption is that the provision of services in transport is covered, unless excluded to any extent by s 21ZA or re-included by regulations.[14] The section is concerned with the provision of a transport service. A transport service means a service which (to any extent) involves transport of people by vehicle. A vehicle is one for transporting people by land, air or water. It includes (in particular) a vehicle not having wheels, and a vehicle constructed or adapted to carry passengers on a system using a mode of guided transport.[15]

8.1.6 Sections 19(1)(a) (refusal of service), 19(1)(c) (standard or manner of service) and 19(1)(d) (terms on which service is provided) do not apply to a transport service where the provider of that service discriminates against a disabled person (a) in providing (or not providing) him or her with a vehicle; or (b) in providing (or not providing) him or her with services when he or she is travelling in a vehicle provided in the course of the transport service.[16]

8.1.7 For the purposes of ss 21(1),[17] 21(2),[18] and 21(4),[19] it is never reasonable for a provider of a transport service to have to take steps

---

12 By DDA 2005, s 19(1) and Sch 1. Section 19(5) now merely provides that regulations may provide for ss 19(1) and 21(1), (2) and (4) not to apply (or to apply only to a prescribed extent) in relation to a service of a prescribed description.

13 Inserted by DDA 2005, s 5 and in force 30 June 2005. Similar provision is made in Northern Ireland: SI 2006/312.

14 See Rights of Access Code of Practice 2006, paras 3.14–3.15 and example. The particular way in which s 21ZA interacts with ss 19–21 has called for separate supporting regulations and a supplementary code of practice: Disability Discrimination (Transport Vehicles) Regulations 2005, SI 2005/3190 (in force 4 December 2006); *Provision and Use of Transport Vehicles: Statutory Code of Practice: Supplement to Part 3 Code of Practice* (2006) (referred to below as the 'Transport Vehicles Code of Practice'.

15 DDA 1995, s 21ZA(4). The term 'guided transport' has the same meaning as in the Transport and Works Act 1992.

16 DDA 1995, s 21ZA(1). See Transport Vehicles Code of Practice Chapters 3 and 4.

17 The duty to make reasonable adjustments where a service provider has a practice, policy or procedure which makes it impossible or unreasonably difficult for disabled persons to make use of goods, facilities or services which the service provider provides or is prepared to provide to other members of the public.

18 The duty to make reasonable adjustments where a physical feature makes it impossible or unreasonably difficult for disabled persons to make use of goods, facilities or services which a service provider provides or is prepared to provide to other members of the public.

19 Where an 'auxiliary aid or service' would enable disabled persons to make use of a service (or would facilitate his or her use of such a service) which a service provider provides (or is prepared to provide) to members of the public, it is the duty of the service provider to take such steps as it is reasonable, in all the circumstances of the case, for the service provider to have to take in order to provide the auxiliary aid or service in question.

which would involve the alteration or removal of a physical feature of a vehicle used in providing the service.[20] For these purposes also, it is never reasonable for a provider of a transport service to have to take steps which would affect whether vehicles are provided in the course of the service or what vehicles are so provided.[21] Moreover, it is never reasonable for a provider of a transport service to have to take steps which would, where a vehicle is provided in the course of the service, affect what happens in the vehicle while someone is travelling in it.[22]

8.1.8 Regulations may provide for ss 21ZA(1) or (2) above not to apply (or to apply only to a prescribed extent) in relation to vehicles of a prescribed description – effectively to re-include certain vehicles within the disability discrimination provisions.[23] The Disability Discrimination (Transport Vehicles) Regulations 2005 have been made to that end.[24]

8.1.9 The regulations provide[25] that s 21ZA(1) does not apply to a provider of transport services who provides such services by way of the following descriptions of vehicles:[26] (a) M1, M2 or N1 hire vehicles;[27] (b) private hire vehicles;[28] (c) public service vehicles;[29] (d) rail vehicles;[30] (e)

---

[20] DDA 1995, s 21ZA(2)(a). See Transport Vehicles Code of Practice Chapter 5.
[21] Ibid, s 21ZA(2)(b)(i).
[22] Ibid, s 21ZA(2)(b)(ii).
[23] Ibid, s 21ZA(3).
[24] SI 2005/3190. See Transport Vehicles Code of Practice Chapters 1 and 2.
[25] Disability Discrimination (Transport Vehicles) Regulations 2005, reg 3(1).
[26] Ibid, reg 3(2).
[27] 'M1', in relation to a vehicle, means a vehicle designed and constructed for the carriage of passengers and comprising no more than eight seats in addition to the driver's seat; 'M2', in relation to a vehicle, means a vehicle designed and constructed for the carriage of passengers, comprising more than eight seats in addition to the driver's seat and having a maximum mass not exceeding 5 tonnes; and 'N1', in relation to a vehicle, means a vehicle designed and constructed for the carriage of goods and having a maximum mass not exceeding 3.5 tonnes. The term 'hire vehicle' means an M1, M2 or N1 vehicle which is hired out by a vehicle-hire firm under a hiring agreement. The term 'vehicle-hire firm' means any person engaged in hiring vehicles in the course of a business. The term 'hiring agreement' means an agreement for the hire of an M1, M2 or N1 vehicle being an agreement which contains such particulars as may be prescribed under the Road Traffic Offenders Act 1988, s 84 but does not include a hire-purchase agreement within the meaning of the Consumer Credit Act 1974, s 189. See Disability Discrimination (Transport Vehicles) Regulations 2005, reg 2. The definitions of M1, M2 and N1 hire vehicles derive from the definition of vehicle categories in Annex II(A) of Council Directive 70/156/EEC (OJ L42 23.2.1970 p 1), last amended by Council Directive 2004/3/EC (OJ L49 19.2.2004 p 36).
[28] The term 'private hire vehicle' means (in relation to England and Wales) a vehicle licensed under Private Hire Vehicles (London) Act 1998, s 7, Local Government (Miscellaneous Provisions) Act 1976, s 48 or an equivalent provision of a local enactment; and (in relation to Scotland) a hire car other than a taxi within the meaning of Civic Government (Scotland) Act 1982, s 23. See Disability Discrimination (Transport Vehicles) Regulations 2005, reg 2.
[29] The term 'public service vehicle' has the same meaning as in Public Passenger Vehicles Act 1981, s 1: Disability Discrimination (Transport Vehicles) Regulations 2005, reg 2.
[30] The term 'rail vehicle' means a vehicle constructed or adapted to carry passengers on

taxis;[31] (f) vehicles deployed by a breakdown or recovery operator,[32] whether or not through a third party, the sole or partial purpose of which is to transport the driver and occupants of a broken down vehicle from the scene of an accident or breakdown; and (g) vehicles deployed on a system using a mode of guided transport.

8.1.10   The regulations also provide that s 21ZA(2)(b), insofar as it relates to the application of ss 21(1) and (4), does not apply to a provider of transport services who provides such services by way of a particular description of vehicle.[33] Those vehicles are (a) M2 and N1 hire vehicles; (b) private hire vehicles; (c) public service vehicles; (d) rail vehicles; (e) taxis; and (f) vehicles deployed on a system using a mode of guided transport.[34]

8.1.11   The regulations further provide that s 21ZA(2)(b), insofar as it relates to the application of ss 21(1), 21(2)(d) and 21(4), does not apply to a vehicle deployed by a breakdown or recovery operator, whether or not through a third party, the sole or partial purpose of which is to transport the driver and occupants of a broken down vehicle from the scene of an accident or breakdown.[35] Furthermore, s 21ZA(2) does not apply to a provider of transport services who provides such services by way of an M1 hire vehicle.[36]

8.1.12   So far as auxiliary aids and services are concerned, the regulations state that, for the purposes of s 21(4), as applied to the vehicles described in regulations 4 and 5, the following are not to be treated as auxiliary aids or services, namely, devices, structures or equipment the installation, operation or maintenance of which would

---

any railway or tramway (and 'railway' and 'tramway' have the same meaning as in the Transport and Works Act 1992, s 67): Disability Discrimination (Transport Vehicles) Regulations 2005, reg 2.

[31]   The term 'taxi' means (in relation to England and Wales) a vehicle licensed under the Town Police Clauses Act 1847, s 37, licensed under the Metropolitan Public Carriage Act 1869, s 6 or which is drawn by one or more person, horse or other animal; and (in relation to Scotland) a hire car which is engaged, by arrangements made in a public place between the person to be conveyed in it (or a person acting on his behalf) and its driver for a journey beginning there and then, or a non-motorised vehicle which is drawn by one or more person, horse or other animal: Disability Discrimination (Transport Vehicles) Regulations 2005, reg 2.

[32]   The term 'breakdown or recovery operator' means a provider of roadside assistance services for the purpose of recovering or repairing a broken down vehicle: Disability Discrimination (Transport Vehicles) Regulations 2005, reg 2.

[33]   Ibid, reg 4(1).

[34]   Ibid, reg 4(2) and see the definition of these terms already provided above.

[35]   Ibid, reg 5 and see the definition of these terms already provided above. See Transport Vehicles Code of Practice Chapters 5 and 6.

[36]   Disability Discrimination (Transport Vehicles) Regulations 2005, reg 6 and see the definition of these terms already provided above. See Transport Vehicles Code of Practice Chapters 5 and 6.

necessitate making a permanent alteration to or which would have a permanent effect on either the internal or external physical fabric of a vehicle.[37]

8.1.13   So far as physical features of premises are concerned, the regulations provide, for the purposes of s 21(2), as applied to M1 hire vehicles by regulation 6, that any part of the vehicle which requires alteration in order to facilitate the provision of (a) hand controls to enable a disabled person to operate braking and accelerator systems in the vehicle and (b) facilities for the stowage of a wheelchair, is to be treated as a physical feature.[38] However, for this purpose, the following are not to be treated as physical features: (1) for the purposes of (a), fixed seating and in-built electrical systems; and (2) for the purposes of (b), fixed seating.[39]

8.1.14   These are undoubtedly difficult provisions. Drawing from the explanatory note to the regulations, they provide for certain provisions in DDA 1995, Part 3 to apply to the providers of certain transport services. The exemption from the application of certain parts of ss 19(1) and 21 is disapplied in respect of the provision of transport services by way of one of the described vehicles. The exemption from the application of that part of s 21(2) of the Act relating to the duty of providers of services to take reasonable steps, where a physical feature makes it impossible or unreasonably difficult for a disabled person to use that service, to provide a reasonable alternative method of making the service available, is disapplied in respect of breakdown and recovery vehicles. The exemption from the application of s 21(2) of the Act relating to the duty of providers of services to take various reasonable steps to overcome physical impediments to the use of a service by disabled persons is disapplied in respect of hire vehicles for the carriage of passengers which have no more than eight passenger seats (M1 hire vehicles). For the purposes of the application of s 21(4) to the vehicles described, the regulations provide for what should not be classified as an auxiliary aid or service. For the purposes of the application of s 21(2) to M1 hire vehicles, the regulations prescribe those parts of the vehicles which are to be treated as physical features, and those which are not.

8.1.15   The effect is thus. To a specified extent, the provision or use of a means of transport is exempted from Part 3 of the DDA 1995. Section 21ZA clarifies the scope of this exemption and enables it to be lifted in respect of the use or provision of certain vehicles. The regulations then lift the exemption for certain types of vehicle.[40]

---

[37]   Disability Discrimination (Transport Vehicles) Regulations 2005, reg 7. See Transport Vehicles Code of Practice Chapter 6.

[38]   Disability Discrimination (Transport Vehicles) Regulations 2005, reg 8(1). See Transport Vehicles Code of Practice Chapter 6.

[39]   Disability Discrimination (Transport Vehicles) Regulations 2005, reg 8(2).

[40]   Transport Vehicles Code of Practice, paras 1.2–1.7 and 2.2–2.21.

Transport employers and Part 2 of the DDA 1995

8.1.16 The original exclusion of transport services from Part 3 of the DDA 1995 did not prevent disabled persons from enjoying a right to equal employment opportunity under Part 2 of the Act in respect of transport employers. By way of illustration, a disabled bus driver would be entitled not to be discriminated against by the transport provider in its guise as employer. That might have called for modifications to be made to a vehicle if that would be a reasonable adjustment required under the provisions of Part 2 of the DDA 1995.[41] For example, a driver with impaired hearing might be entitled to the installation of a simple audio-visual signalling system that indicated when a passenger wished to alight.

Public transport and Part 5 of the DDA 1995

8.1.17 Although transport systems are not exhaustively covered by the anti-discrimination measures in the DDA 1995, the Act empowered the Government to enact accessibility standards for public transport. These accessibility standards apply to taxis, public service vehicles and rail vehicles. They apply only to land-based transport services and do not apply to aircraft or ferries. These are the measures set out in Part 5 of the Act which provides a statutory framework for accessibility regulations. Each of the methods of transport covered by Part 5 is now examined in turn.[42]

8.2 TAXIS

8.2.1 The Part 3 duties apply to operators and drivers of taxis as the provider of services.[43] However, as with other transport vehicles, the Part 3 duties are not sufficient to overcome the superstructural problems associated with the design, manufacture and accessibility of taxi vehicles. While many local authorities have attempted to improve the accessibility of taxis to disabled passengers through licensing conditions, the Government took the view during the passage of the DDA 1995 that such a piecemeal approach had been tried and failed. The sponsors of the Act

---

[41]   DDA 1995, s 6. See Chapter 3.

[42]   See generally: Department for Transport, *Inclusive Mobility* (undated). Note also that when the Government announced its 10-year Transport Plan in July 2000, it indicated that access for disabled persons would be a condition of all new investment in public transport. See further: House of Commons Transport Select Committee, *6th Report: Disabled People's Access to Transport* (March 2004, HC 439); Department for Transport, *The Government's Response to the Transport Select Committee 6th Report: Disabled People's Access to Transport*, Cm 6184 (June 2004).

[43]   By virtue of DDA 1995, ss 19–21 and 21ZA, read together with the Disability Discrimination (Transport Vehicles) Regulations 2005. The Transport Vehicles Code of Practice contains numerous examples of how the Part 3 duties apply to taxis. See also: DRC, *Avoiding disability discrimination in transport: a practical guide for taxi and private hire services* (2007).

expressed their 'clear intention' to introduce 'provisions to require that, from days to be determined, taxis newly licensed must, as a condition of licence, be accessible to all disabled people, including those who use wheelchairs'.[44] Whilst accepting that there had been criticism of the current models of wheelchair-accessible taxis, it was also made 'absolutely clear that we are not talking about a universal requirement for the current purpose-built taxi design'.[45]

Taxi accessibility regulations

8.2.2   The Secretary of State is given power by the DDA 1995 to make 'taxi accessibility regulations'.[46] This power has not yet been brought into force and no regulations have been made to date. The purpose of the regulations when made will be to secure that it is possible for disabled persons:

- to get into and out of taxis in safety;

- to be carried in taxis in safety and in reasonable comfort;

- to be conveyed in safety into and out of taxis while remaining in their wheelchairs (where a wheelchair user);

- to be carried in taxis in safety and in reasonable comfort while remaining in their wheelchairs (where a wheelchair user).

The regulations are intended to 'focus clearly on the needs of all disabled people and will be drawn up in close consultation with the Disabled Persons' Transport Advisory Committee' (DPTAC). Design parameters will be defined based on research and experience to provide 'optimum levels of accessibility' and manufacturers will be expected to meet the new market demand so created.[47]

8.2.3   Such taxi accessibility regulations may in particular require 'regulated taxis' to conform with regulations as to:

- the size of door openings for passenger use;

- the floor area of 'passenger compartments';[48]

- the amount of headroom in passenger compartments; and

---

[44]   HL Deb, vol 564, col 2034. A date for the implementation of the taxi accessibility standards was not indicated at the time: ibid, vol 566, cols 453–454.

[45]   HL Deb, vol 564, cols 2034–2035.

[46]   DDA 1995, s 32(1). A commencement date has not been appointed. In Scotland, the powers to introduce the regulations are contained in s 20 of the Civic Government (Scotland) Act 1982, as amended by the DDA 1995.

[47]   HL Deb, vol 564, col 2035.

[48]   The meaning of this term is to be prescribed in future regulations: DDA 1995, s 32(5).

- the fitting of restraining devices designed to ensure the stability of a wheelchair while the taxi is moving.[49]

Moreover, the regulations may require drivers of regulated taxis plying for hire (or under hire) to comply with regulations as to the carrying of ramps or other devices designed to facilitate the loading and unloading of wheelchairs.[50] The regulations might also require the driver of a regulated taxi, in which a disabled person in a wheelchair is being carried (while remaining in the wheelchair), to comply with regulations as to the position in which the wheelchair is to be secured.[51] The effect of these provisions is that taxi drivers must recognise their duty to carry disabled customers. It would not be lawful for drivers to refuse to pick up a disabled passenger in a wheelchair 'on the pretext . . . that they are not carrying the ramps'.[52] A failure to comply with such accessibility regulations by a driver plying for hire (or under hire) will be a criminal offence.[53]

Taxis to be covered by the regulations

8.2.4 To what taxis will these new regulations and duties apply? The regulations will define which taxis are to be regulated for these purposes. However, the regulations can only apply to a 'taxi' as narrowly defined.[54] A 'taxi' for this purpose means only a licensed vehicle.[55] It does not include a taxi which is drawn by a horse or other animal. The effect is that any new accessibility standards for taxis will apply only to hackney cabs or so-called 'black cabs' and will not apply to private hire cars or 'minicabs'.[56] At the same time, it is not intended that the taxi trade will in future be expected to make universal use of the London-style black cab or that the legislation (when in force) will produce a universal purpose-built taxi design.[57]

8.2.5 In order 'to ensure an orderly transition to the new requirements without damaging the viability of the taxi trade',[58] when these provisions

---

[49]   DDA 1995, s 32(2)(a).
[50]   Ibid, s 32(2)(b).
[51]   Ibid, s 32(2)(c).
[52]   HL Deb, vol 564, col 2035.
[53]   DDA 1995, s 32(3). On summary conviction, a person guilty of such an offence will be liable to a fine not exceeding level 3 on the standard scale: ibid, s 32(4).
[54]   Ibid, s 32(5).
[55]   That is, one licensed under Town Police Clauses Act 1847, s 37 or Metropolitan Public Carriage Act 1869, s 6. In Northern Ireland, a taxi is a vehicle licensed to stand or ply for hire under Road Traffic (Northern Ireland) Order 1981, art 61 and which seats not more than eight passengers in addition to the driver: DDA 1995, Sch 8, para 16(2).
[56]   HL Deb, vol 566, col 451. The DRTF recommended that the former DRC should consider mechanisms for increasing the availability of accessible private hire vehicles (including the carrying of registered assistance dogs): DRTF Report, recommendation 7.3.
[57]   Ibid, col 453.
[58]   Ibid, vol 564, col 2035.

are in force taxi licensing authorities[59] shall not grant a taxi licence unless the taxi conforms with the relevant taxi accessibility regulations.[60] However, the licensing requirements by reference to any taxi accessibility regulations apply only to newly licensed taxis, as opposed to taxis with existing licences and seeking renewal.[61] The intention is to regulate only new entrants to the taxi trade (or newly acquired taxis). It does not prevent the relicensing of non-accessible taxis provided that, subject to 28 days' grace, the new licence comes into force immediately on the expiry of the previous licence.[62] As the relevant Minister put it, this:

> '... provides that a licensing authority may, after a certain date, only license taxis which comply with the construction requirements that will be set out in the regulations ... We are also mindful of the need to protect the interests of the cab trade, much of which comprises small businesses. While it is reasonable to expect new taxis to be fully accessible, it would ... be unreasonable to require someone who had recently purchased and licensed a new non-accessible vehicle to dispose of it prematurely.'[63]

However, it is not intended that this exceptional treatment should continue indefinitely. The Secretary of State may provide by order that this exemption shall cease to have effect on a specified date.[64] The effect of such an order may be varied for different areas or localities.[65] Thus it is contemplated that there will be a future date beyond which no non-accessible vehicle can be relicensed as a taxi. That date is to be the subject of consultation with the trade.

Exemption regulations

8.2.6 When in force, it is hoped that these provisions will open up new markets for the taxi trade. However, it is acknowledged that compliance with the new standards could create difficulties. The Government recognised 'the enormously wide variations in types of area and of taxi use in this country'.[66] The 'strong presumption must be that, whatever the area, there will be now, or may be in the future, disabled people whose mobility would be enhanced by the availability of accessible vehicles'.[67] However, at the same time, the possibility that Part 5 of the DDA 1995 'could jeopardise the viability of the trade in a particular area to the point

---

[59] See DDA 1995, s 68(1) as to the meaning of this term.
[60] Ibid, s 34(1). Like s 32, s 34 is not yet in force and no date for its commencement has been appointed.
[61] Ibid, s 34(2). The provisions of s 34 are applied to Northern Ireland with appropriate substitutions: Sch 8, para 18.
[62] HL Deb, vol 566, cols 440–441.
[63] Ibid, vol 564, col 2035.
[64] DDA 1995, s 34(3).
[65] Ibid, s 34(4). By virtue of s 67(7), this is without prejudice to the generality of the powers to make regulations or orders by statutory instrument conferred by s 67(2)–(3).
[66] HL Deb, vol 564, col 2036.
[67] Ibid, col 2036.

at which there ceased to be taxi provision for anyone' was recognised.[68] The legislature wished to avoid that result.

8.2.7 Accordingly, when the substantive provisions are brought into effect, the Secretary of State may make 'exemption regulations' to enable taxi licensing authorities[69] to apply for an order to be exempt from the new licensing provisions.[70] This is so if the licensing authority believes that, having regard to 'circumstances prevailing in its area', the application of the licensing conditions would be 'inappropriate' and if their application would result in 'an unacceptable reduction in the number of taxis' in that area.[71] The exemption regulations may make particular provision and prescriptions requiring a licensing authority proposing to apply for an exemption order to carry out consultations,[72] to publish its proposal, to consider any representations made about the proposal (before it applies for an order), and to make its application in a prescribed form.[73] The Secretary of State must consider any application for an exemption order and consult DPTAC (and any other persons the Secretary of State considers appropriate). Then the Secretary of State may make an exemption order (in the terms applied for or in such other terms as the Secretary of State considers appropriate) or refuse to make such an order.[74]

Swivel seat regulations

8.2.8 Even if a taxi is exempted from any future taxi accessibility regulations, there will still be a power to require an 'exempt taxi' to comply with 'swivel seat regulations' as to the fitting and use of swivel seats in the taxi. The Secretary of State is given a power to make 'swivel seat regulations' requiring any 'exempt taxi' plying for hire in an area in respect of which an exemption order[75] is in force to conform with provisions as to the fitting and use of swivel seats.[76] The term 'swivel seats' will be defined in regulations.[77] No further light on these proposed

---

68 HL Deb, vol 564, col 2036.
69 That is, a licensing authority responsible for licensing taxis in any area of England and Wales other than the area to which the Metropolitan Public Carriage Act 1869 applies: DDA 1995, s 35(7).
70 DDA 1995, s 35(1). Section 35 does not apply in Northern Ireland: DDA 1995, Sch 8, para 19. Like ss 32 and 34, s 35 is not yet in force and no date for its commencement has been appointed.
71 Ibid, s 35(3).
72 Including 'as a matter of course, disabled people and the taxi trade': HL Deb, vol 564, col 2036.
73 DDA 1995, s 35(2).
74 Ibid, s 35(4).
75 That is, an order made under DDA 1995, s 35.
76 Ibid, s 35(5). An 'exempt taxi' is a taxi in relation to which s 34(1) would apply if there was not a s 35 exemption order in force: ibid, s 35(7). Note s 35(6) which cross-refers to s 34.
77 Ibid, s 35(7).

regulations is cast by the parliamentary debates on the legislation.[78] The power to make such regulations is not yet in force, and no such regulations have been proposed or made.

Duties of taxi drivers towards disabled passengers

8.2.9   At some future date, drivers of regulated taxis will be placed under new duties in respect of a taxi which has been hired by or for a disabled person in a wheelchair; or by a person who wishes to be accompanied by a disabled person in a wheelchair.[79] These duties (which are not yet in force) will be:

- to carry in the taxi the passenger while he or she remains in the wheelchair;

- to make no additional charge for doing so;

- to carry the wheelchair in the taxi if the passenger chooses to sit in a passenger seat; and

- to take such steps as are necessary to ensure that the passenger is carried in the taxi in safety and in reasonable comfort.[80]

In addition, it will be the driver's statutory duty to give such assistance as may be reasonably required:

- to enable the passenger to get into or out of the taxi;

- to enable the passenger to be conveyed into and out of the taxi while in the wheelchair if the passenger wishes to remain in the wheelchair;

- to load the passenger's luggage into or out of the taxi; and

- to load the wheelchair into or out of the taxi if the passenger does not wish to remain in the wheelchair.[81]

A failure to comply with any of these duties without lawful excuse will be a criminal offence punishable upon summary conviction by a fine not exceeding level 3 on the standard scale.[82] However, there are certain defences and exemptions as follows.

---

[78]   Although see HL Deb, vol 566, cols 1042–1043.
[79]   DDA 1995, s 36(1). Like ss 32 and 34–35, s 36 is not yet in force and no date for its commencement has been appointed.
[80]   Ibid, s 36(3)(a)–(d). The term 'the passenger' means the disabled person concerned and 'carry' means carry in the taxi concerned: s 36(2).
[81]   Ibid, s 36(3)(e).
[82]   Ibid, s 36(5).

8.2.10 Under these provisions when in force, the driver of a taxi is not required to carry more than one person in a wheelchair, or more than one wheelchair, on any one journey.[83] A taxi driver is not required to carry any person in circumstances in which it would otherwise be lawful for the driver to refuse to carry that person.[84] For example, a taxi driver could not be required to carry a disabled passenger where the taxi is already exceeding the number of passengers who may be carried in accordance with its licence. It will also be a defence to show that, even though the taxi conformed with any taxi accessibility regulations,[85] it would not have been possible for the wheelchair of the disabled passenger concerned to be carried in safety in the taxi.[86]

8.2.11 Provision will also be made for the exemption of taxi drivers from these new statutory duties on medical grounds. A taxi licensing authority shall issue a driver with a certificate of exemption from the duties above if it is satisfied that it is appropriate to exempt the driver on medical grounds.[87] An exemption certificate may also be issued on the ground that the driver's physical condition makes it impossible or unreasonably difficult for him or her to comply with a taxi driver's duties imposed under the DDA 1995.[88] The Government felt that this exception was important, especially for taxi drivers who themselves had a disability.[89] Provision is made for an appeal against a refusal to grant an exemption certificate.[90] The currency of the certificate of exemption shall be for such period as the licensing authority specifies in the certificate when issued.[91] Once an exemption certificate has been issued to a taxi driver, and so long as it remains in force, the driver is exempt from the statutory duties imposed,[92] provided an exemption notice (in a prescribed form and in a prescribed manner) is exhibited on the taxi.[93]

---

[83] DDA 1995, s 36(4)(a) which also contemplates an exception in the case of a taxi of a prescribed description. No such prescription has been made at the time of writing.

[84] DDA 1995, s 36(4)(b).

[85] That is, under ibid, s 32.

[86] Ibid, s 36(6).

[87] Ibid, s 36(7)(a). In Northern Ireland, this power lies with the Department of the Environment: ibid, Sch 8, para 20. Provision is made in s 49 for criminal offences committed in connection with exemption certificates (e g forgery or the making of false statements).

[88] Ibid, s 36(7)(b).

[89] HL Deb, vol 564, col 2036.

[90] DDA 1995, s 38(1), as amended by the Private Hire Vehicles (Carriage of Guide Dogs etc) Act 2002 and the Courts Act 2003. Any person who is aggrieved by a refusal of a licensing authority to issue an exemption certificate under s 36 (or ss 37 and 37A, discussed at **8.2.12** to **8.2.21**) may appeal to a magistrates' court. An appeal must be made within 28 days of the refusal: s 38(1). If the court allows such an appeal, it may direct the licensing authority to issue an exemption certificate and may specify the period of the currency of the exemption: s 38(2).

[91] Ibid, s 36(8).

[92] Under ibid, s 36(3).

[93] Ibid, s 36(9). The necessary prescriptions have yet to be made.

Carrying of guide dogs and hearing dogs in taxis

8.2.12 In order to address the problem of persons with sensory impairments (who use guide or hearing dogs) being refused access to taxis because they wish to be accompanied by their animal, the DDA 1995 imposes additional duties on taxi drivers.[94] This aspect of the provisions of Part 5 affecting taxis has been fully in force from 31 March 2001 in England and Wales, and from 1 August 2001 in Northern Ireland.[95] Comparable provisions came into force in Scotland on 2 December 2002 and have since been updated. The statutory provisions are amplified by regulations.[96]

8.2.13 These duties arise where the taxi has been hired by or for a disabled person ('the passenger') accompanied by a guide dog or hearing dog.[97] The duties also apply where the taxi has been hired by a person who wishes to be accompanied in the taxi by a disabled person ('the passenger') accompanied by a guide or hearing dog.[98] A guide dog is a dog trained to guide a blind person, while a hearing dog is a dog trained to assist a deaf person.[99] The statute provides for this section (DDA 1995, s 37) to be applied by regulations to any other category of dog trained to assist a disabled person with a prescribed disability.[100] The regulations provide that an 'assistance dog' is prescribed as a category of dog for this purpose.[101] An 'assistance dog' is a dog which is trained by a 'specified charity' to assist a disabled person with a physical impairment[102] which consists of epilepsy or otherwise affects his or her mobility, manual dexterity, physical coordination or ability to lift, carry or otherwise move everyday objects.[103] At the time that the disabled person whom the assistance dog is assisting hires a taxi, the dog must be wearing a jacket on

---

[94] DDA 1995, s 37.

[95] Disability Discrimination Act 1995 (Commencement No 8) Order 2000, SI 2000/2989; Disability Discrimination Act 1995 (Commencement No 7) Order (Northern Ireland) 2001, SR 2001/163.

[96] Disability Discrimination Act 1995 (Taxis) (Carrying of Guide Dogs etc) (England and Wales) Regulations 2000, SI 2000/2990, as amended by SI 2006/1616 from 17 July 2006; Disability Discrimination Act 1995 (Taxis) (Carrying of Guide Dogs etc) (Northern Ireland) Regulations 2001, SR 2001/169. See also Department for Transport, Carriage of Guide, Hearing and Other Assistance Dogs in Taxis (advice leaflet for taxi drivers) and Travelling with Assistance Dogs in Taxis (advice leaflet for disabled people).

[97] DDA 1995, s 37(1)(a) and (2).

[98] Ibid, s 37(1)(b) and (2).

[99] Ibid, s 37(11).

[100] Ibid, s 37(9)–(10) and Sch 8, para 21(3).

[101] Disability Discrimination Act 1995 (Taxis) (Carrying of Guide Dogs etc) (England and Wales) Regulations 2000, SI 2000/2990, reg 3(1); Disability Discrimination Act 1995 (Taxis) (Carrying of Guide Dogs etc) (Northern Ireland) Regulations 2001, SR 2001/169, reg 3(1).

[102] That is, for the purpose of DDA 1995, s 1.

[103] Disability Discrimination Act 1995 (Taxis) (Carrying of Guide Dogs etc) (England and Wales) Regulations 2000, SI 2000/2990, reg 3(2)(a); Disability Discrimination Act 1995 (Taxis) (Carrying of Guide Dogs etc) (Northern Ireland) Regulations 2001, SR 2001/169, reg 3(2)(a).

which is prominently inscribed the name of a 'specified charity'.[104] A 'specified charity' for this purpose means one of three charities registered with the Charity Commission, namely: Dogs for the Disabled; Support Dogs; or Canine Partners for Independence.[105]

8.2.14   The duties of a taxi driver in the above situations are to carry the disabled passenger's dog, allowing it to remain with the passenger in the taxi, and not to make any additional charge for so doing.[106] A breach of these duties is a criminal offence punishable on summary conviction by a fine not exceeding level 3 on the standard scale.[107] It is noteworthy that these duties apply to all taxis and not just to regulated taxis.

8.2.15   However, in like manner to the excusal from the duties relating to the carrying of passengers in wheelchairs,[108] a licensing authority may exempt a driver from the duties in respect of a disabled passenger accompanied by a guide dog, hearing dog or prescribed assistance dog.[109] This is achieved by means of an exemption certificate if the licensing authority is satisfied that such exemption is appropriate on medical grounds.[110] In deciding that question, the authority must have particular regard to the physical characteristics of the taxi in question.[111] For example, this exemption might cover a driver who has a medical condition

---

[104]   Disability Discrimination Act 1995 (Taxis) (Carrying of Guide Dogs etc) (England and Wales) Regulations 2000, SI 2000/2990, reg 3(2)(b); Disability Discrimination Act 1995 (Taxis) (Carrying of Guide Dogs etc) (Northern Ireland) Regulations 2001, SR 2001/169, reg 3(2)(b).

[105]   Disability Discrimination Act 1995 (Taxis) (Carrying of Guide Dogs etc) (England and Wales) Regulations 2000, SI 2000/2990, reg 3(3); Disability Discrimination Act 1995 (Taxis) (Carrying of Guide Dogs etc) (Northern Ireland) Regulations 2001, SR 2001/169, reg 3(3).

[106]   DDA 1995, s 37(3).

[107]   Ibid, s 37(4).

[108]   Ibid, s 36.

[109]   Ibid, s 37. Provisions are made as to the issue and currency of a s 37 exemption certificate and the display of such certificate in the taxi: s 37(7)–(8). See Disability Discrimination Act 1995 (Taxis) (Carrying of Guide Dogs etc) (England and Wales) Regulations 2000, SI 2000/2990, reg 2 and Schs 1–2 (as amended in respect of the manner in which the exemption notice should be displayed by the exempted taxi driver and the wording on the back of the exemption notice: the notice must be displayed on the windscreen, while display on the dashboard is no longer permitted); Disability Discrimination Act 1995 (Taxis) (Carrying of Guide Dogs etc) (Northern Ireland) Regulations 2001, SR 2001/169, reg 2 and Schedule. See also Department for Transport, 'Carriage of Guide, Hearing and Other Assistance Dogs in Taxis' (guidance leaflet for licensing authorities).

[110]   DDA 1995, s 37(5). In Northern Ireland, this power lies with the Department of the Environment: Sch 8, para 21. Provision is made in s 49 for criminal offences committed in connection with exemption certificates (e g forgery or the making of false statements). See further: Department for Transport, *Carriage of Assistance Dogs in Taxis: Medical Exemption for Drivers: Regulatory Impact Assessment* (November 2000; modified January 2004).

[111]   DDA 1995, s 37(6).

that is aggravated by dogs, such as an asthmatic condition or an allergy.[112] Provision is made for an appeal against a refusal to grant an exemption certificate.[113]

Carrying of assistance dogs in private hire vehicles

8.2.16   The DDA 1995 has been amended by the Private Hire Vehicles (Carriage of Guide Dogs etc) Act 2002. As a result,[114] s 37A deals with the carrying of an 'assistance dog' in private hire vehicles in England and Wales.[115] For this purpose, an 'assistance dog' is a dog which has been trained to guide a blind person or to assist a deaf person, or which has been trained by a prescribed charity to assist a disabled person who has a disability which consists of epilepsy or otherwise affects his or her mobility, manual dexterity, physical co-ordination or ability to lift, carry or otherwise move everyday objects.[116] A 'private hire vehicle' means a vehicle licensed under specified statutory provisions.[117] Section 37A creates a number of criminal offences. A person who is guilty of an offence under s 37A is liable on summary conviction to a fine not exceeding level 3 on the standard scale.[118]

8.2.17   First, it is an offence for the operator of a private hire vehicle to fail (or refuse) to accept a booking for a private hire vehicle if the booking is requested by (or on behalf of) a disabled person (or a person who wishes a disabled person to accompany him or her) and the reason for the failure (or refusal) is that the disabled person will be accompanied by his or her assistance dog.[119] Secondly, it is an offence for the operator of a private hire vehicle to make an additional charge for carrying an assistance dog which is accompanying a disabled person.[120] In both cases,

---

[112]   HL Deb, vol 564, col 2037.

[113]   See **8.2.11**.

[114]   From 31 March 2004 in England and Wales; from 1 June 2008 in Northern Ireland; and from a date to be appointed in Scotland. Section 37A is supported by the Disability Discrimination Act 1995 (Private Hire Vehicles) (Carriage of Guide Dogs etc) (England and Wales) Regulations 2003, SI 2003/3122, as amended from 17 July 2006 by SI 2006/1617.

[115]   Inserted by the Private Hire Vehicles (Carriage of Guide Dogs etc) Act 2002, s 1(1). See generally: Department for Transport, *Carriage of Assistance Dogs in Private Hire Vehicles: Consultation Paper* (November 2003); Department for Transport, *Carriage of Assistance Dogs in Private Hire Vehicles: Regulatory Impact Assessment* (December 2003); DPTAC, *Making Private Hire Services More Accessible to Disabled People: A Good Practice Guide for Private Hire Vehicle Operators and Drivers* (December 2003).

[116]   DDA 1995, s 37A(9). The prescribed charities for this purpose are Dogs for the Disabled, Support Dogs, and Canine Partners for Independence: Disability Discrimination Act 1995 (Private Hire Vehicles) (Carriage of Guide Dogs etc) (England and Wales) Regulations 2003, SI 2003/3122, reg 3.

[117]   DDA 1995, s 37A(9). The statutory provisions are Private Hire Vehicles (London) Act 1998, s 6; Local Government (Miscellaneous Provisions) Act 1976, s 48; or an equivalent provision of a local enactment.

[118]   DDA 1995, s 37A(4).

[119]   DDA 1995, s 37A(1).

[120]   Ibid, s 37A(2).

the term 'operator' means a person who holds a licence granted under specified statutory provisions.[121] Thirdly, it is an offence for the driver of a private hire vehicle to fail (or refuse) to carry out a booking accepted by the operator of the vehicle if the booking was made by (or on behalf of) a disabled person (or a person who wishes a disabled person to accompany him or her) and the reason for the failure (or refusal) is that the disabled person is accompanied by his or her assistance dog.[122] For this purpose, a 'driver' means a person who holds a licence granted under specific statutory provisions.[123]

8.2.18 However, in this third case only, if the licensing authority[124] is satisfied that it is appropriate on medical grounds to issue a certificate of exemption to a driver in respect of this provision, it must do so.[125] In determining whether to issue a certificate of exemption, the licensing authority shall have particular regard to the physical characteristics of the private hire vehicle which the applicant drives or those of any kind of private hire vehicle in relation to which he or she requires the certificate.[126] A certificate of exemption shall be issued with respect to a specified private hire vehicle (or a specified kind of private hire vehicle) and for such period as may be specified in the certificate.[127] No offence is committed by a driver[128] if a certificate of exemption issued to him or her is in force with respect to the private hire vehicle and the prescribed notice is exhibited on the private hire vehicle in the prescribed manner.[129] Provision is made for an appeal against a refusal to grant an exemption certificate.[130]

---

[121] DDA 1995, s 37A(9). The statutory provisions are Private Hire Vehicles (London) Act 1998, s 3; Local Government (Miscellaneous Provisions) Act 1976, s 55; or an equivalent provision of a local enactment.

[122] Ibid, s 37A(3).

[123] Ibid, s 37A(9). The statutory provisions are Private Hire Vehicles (London) Act 1998, s 13; Local Government (Miscellaneous Provisions) Act 1976, s 51; or an equivalent provision of a local enactment.

[124] Ibid, s 37A(9): licensing authority, in relation to any area of England and Wales, means the authority responsible for licensing private hire vehicles in that area.

[125] Ibid, s 37A(5).

[126] Ibid, s 37A(6).

[127] Ibid, s 37A(7).

[128] That is, under s 37A(3).

[129] Ibid, s 37A(8). See Disability Discrimination Act 1995 (Private Hire Vehicles) (Carriage of Guide Dogs etc) (England and Wales) Regulations 2003, SI 2003/3122, reg 2 (as amended in respect of the manner in which the exemption notice should be displayed by the exempted private hire vehicle driver and the wording on the back of the exemption notice: the notice must be displayed on the windscreen, while display on the dashboard is no longer permitted).

[130] See **8.2.11**. Provision is also made by s 49 (as amended) for criminal offences committed in connection with exemption certificates (e g forgery or the making of false statements).

Taxi accessibility at designated transport facilities

8.2.19 At a future date yet to be appointed, the 'appropriate national authority'[131] may by regulations provide for the application of any provision of the DDA 1995 relating to taxis or taxi drivers (that is, those described above) to be extended to vehicles (or their drivers) used for the provision of services under 'a franchise agreement'.[132] These regulations may apply any such taxi provisions with such modifications as the appropriate national authority considers appropriate.[133] A 'franchise agreement' is a contract entered into by the 'operator' of a 'designated transport facility' for the provision by the other party to the contract of 'hire car' services for members of the public using any part of the transport facility and which involves vehicles entering any part of that facility.[134] A 'designated transport facility' means any premises which form part of any port, airport, railway station or bus station which has been designated for the present purpose by an order made by the appropriate national authority.[135] The 'operator' of such a facility means any person who is concerned with the management or operation of the facility.[136] The definition of 'hire car' will be prescribed by regulations.[137]

8.2.20 The intention behind this provision, when brought into force, is to ensure that 'taxis' (using that term here in the popular, loose sense) that ply for hire at airports, railway stations and other transport termini could be brought within the accessibility regime for taxis.[138] It is not designed to capture those taxis that already fall within the definition of a taxi regulated for any of the purposes of the taxi provisions of Part 5 of the DDA 1995. They will be already subject to the new duties and standards. Instead, it is intended to embrace those taxis that are private hire cars or mini-cabs and which are entitled to provide car hire services to passengers under a monopoly contract or franchise with the operator of the transport terminus in question (such as, for example, the British Airports Authority at London Gatwick Airport).[139]

---

[131] In England and Wales, this is the Secretary of State; in Scotland, this is the Scottish Ministers: DDA 1995, s 33(4), as amended. However, so far as s 33 might require the implementation of EC obligations, the Secretary of State may exercise these powers on behalf of the Scottish Ministers: s 33(5), as amended.

[132] DDA 1995, s 33(2) (as amended by the DDA 2005), as read with s 33(4). This power also applies to the potential extension of regulations made in pursuance of the Civic Government (Scotland) Act 1982, s 20(2A). Under the Scotland Act 1998, functions under this section are transferred to the Scottish Ministers (insofar as they are exercisable in or as regards Scotland) by Transfer of Functions to the Scottish Ministers etc Order 1999, SI 1999/1750, art 2, Sch 1.

[133] Ibid, s 33(3), as amended.

[134] Ibid, s 33(1).

[135] Ibid, s 33(4), as amended.

[136] Ibid.

[137] Ibid.

[138] Created by ibid, ss 32–39.

[139] HC Deb, vol 265, cols 159–160.

Application to Scotland and Northern Ireland

8.2.21 On the face of the DDA 1995, the new duties and statutory framework affecting taxis apply only in England and Wales. However, these provisions also apply to Northern Ireland.[140] From 5 February 2003, the Civic Government (Scotland) Act 1982 has been amended so as to enable these provisions to be extended to Scotland by means of regulatory powers.[141]

Implementation

8.2.22 With the exception of the provisions relating to the carrying of guide dogs, hearing dogs and prescribed assistance dogs in taxis, the remaining provisions of DDA 1995, Part 5 (ss 32–39) affecting taxis are not yet in force. In July 1997, various government departments jointly issued an informal consultation document covering the features which could be included in regulations and suggesting dates for implementation of the proposed regulations.[142] The Government was expected to commence formal consultation on the implementation of these proposals during the course of 2000 or 2001, but that did not occur. Draft regulations have not been published. The informal consultation document proposed that taxi accessibility regulations would come into force for newly licensed vehicles in January 2002. At the same time, interim regulations would come into force for previously licensed wheelchair-accessible taxis. By January 2012, all taxis would be required to comply with the main taxi accessibility regulations. It is clear that this timetable has not been adhered to.

8.2.23 The latest position is recorded in a Government policy document issued in October 2003.[143] The Government intends to vary the application of the proposed regulations to target areas in which it is thought that accessible taxis will best meet the needs of disabled people without causing a disparate impact from additional costs. These areas are being referred to as 'first phase' authorities. It is proposed to introduce

---

[140] With the appropriate modifications contained in DDA 1995, Sch 8, paras 16–23.

[141] DDA 1995, s 39 and Disability Discrimination Act 1995 (Commencement No 10) (Scotland) Order 2003, SI 2003/215. See: Taxi Drivers' Licences (Carrying of Guide Dogs and Hearing Dogs) (Scotland) Regulations 2003, SSI 2003/73 (revoking earlier regulations and in force 3 March 2003); Private Hire Car Drivers' Licences (Carrying of Guide Dogs and Hearing Dogs) (Scotland) Regulations 2004, SSI 2004/88 (in force 31 March 2004). The duties in Scotland are imposed through a condition in the taxi or private hire car driver's licence.

[142] 'The Government's Proposals for Taxis' (1997, London: DETR).

[143] *Taxi Accessibility Regulations – Policy Proposals* (2003, London: Department for Transport). See also: House of Commons Transport Committee, *6th Report: Disabled People's Access to Transport* HC 439 (March 2004); Department for Transport, *The Government's Response to Transport Select Committee 6th Report: Disabled People's Access to Transport*, Cm 6184 (June 2004). See further: Department for Transport, *Determination of Accessible Taxi Requirements: Phase 1* (November 2003) and *Phase 2* (June 2004).

taxi accessibility regulations in these areas between 2010 and 2020. Those authorities meet one or more of the following criteria: a licensing authority population of at least 120,000 people; a major transport interchange; a major tourist attraction; or an existing mandatory policy resulting in 100 per cent accessible vehicles. Licensing authorities outside the first phase would not be subject to the regulations in the first instance, but would be subject to voluntary guidance on establishing an appropriate mix of vehicles and on the design parameters. The Government will monitor the introduction of accessible vehicles in these areas to determine whether the guidance is effective, so that a view would then be taken on the necessity of extending the regulations to these areas. The proposals will be the subject of a public consultation process in due course. Separate consultation exercises will be held in Scotland and Northern Ireland.

8.3 PUBLIC SERVICE VEHICLES

8.3.1 Introducing the provisions of the DDA 1995 dealing with access to buses, coaches and rail services,[144] the relevant Minister stated that they 'add up to a very significant change in the field of transport' and acknowledged that the transport industry had worked closely with the Department of Transport for many years 'to promote and encourage the introduction of better designs and operating practices to meet the needs of disabled people'.[145] Nevertheless, the then Government believed that legislation was necessary to continue progress towards an accessible transport system. At the same time, however, these new statutory measures are not retrospective and are designed to apply only to new vehicles.[146] It is intended to provide a legal framework compatible with existing transport requirements, but flexible enough to allow the introduction of new requirements that are workable and viable in a technical, operational and economic sense.

8.3.2 From 30 August 2000, these provisions apply to 'public service vehicles' (PSVs).[147] A PSV is a vehicle adapted to carry more than eight passengers (in addition to the driver) and which is in public service.[148] These provisions thus apply to buses and coaches of the required capacity offering a public transport service.[149]

---

[144] DDA 1995, ss 40–48.

[145] HL Deb, vol 565, cols 714–715.

[146] Ibid, vol 566, col 463. Heritage and replica vehicles are thus implicitly outside the new regime.

[147] DDA 1995, ss 40–45, which came into force on 30 August 2000: SI 2000/1969.

[148] Ibid, s 40(5) and Sch 8, para 24(2). See also the provisions of the Public Passenger Vehicles Act 1981 and the Road Traffic (Northern Ireland) Order 1981.

[149] To understand how the Part 3 access duties apply to bus and coach operators as service providers and interact with the Part 5 public service vehicles accessibility regulations, see: DRC, *Avoiding disability discrimination in transport: a practical guide for buses and scheduled coaches* (2007) and DRC, *Avoiding disability discrimination in transport: a practical guide for tour coach operators* (2007).

PSV accessibility regulations

8.3.3   The Secretary of State is empowered to make 'PSV accessibility regulations'.[150] In England and Wales, regulations have been enacted in the form of the Public Service Vehicles Accessibility Regulations 2000.[151] The regulations came into force on 30 August 2000. Much of the content of the Public Service Vehicles Accessibility Regulations 2000 is technical in nature and it is not proposed to reproduce it here. Appropriate cross-references to the regulations are made below.

8.3.4   The purpose of the regulations is to secure that it is possible for disabled persons to get on to and off 'regulated public service vehicles' in safety and without unreasonable difficulty. In the case of disabled persons in wheelchairs, the regulations seek to achieve this purpose while a disabled person remains in his or her wheelchair.[152] Furthermore, the regulations attempt to secure that it is possible for disabled persons to be carried in 'regulated public service vehicles' in safety and reasonable comfort.[153] As used in this context, a 'regulated public service vehicle' means a PSV to which the PSV accessibility regulations are expressed to apply.[154] This implies that the Secretary of State has discretion in defining which vehicles or kinds of public service are covered by the accessibility regulations. Moreover, the regulations may make different provision as respects different classes or descriptions of vehicle and as respects the same class or description of vehicle in different circumstances.[155] For example, in the case of full-size single-deck buses, an access solution might be low floors, whereas, in the case of coaches, a lift might be appropriate.[156] It was anticipated that local and regional variations might also be necessary, as might flexibility of timescales for implementation.

8.3.5   In fact, the Public Service Vehicles Accessibility Regulations 2000 apply to single-deck and double-deck buses and to single-deck and double-deck coaches with a capacity of more than 22 passengers which

---

[150]   DDA 1995, s 40(1), after due consultation with the DPTAC and other representative organisations: ibid, s 40(7) and Sch 8, para 24(3). The power to make such regulations in Northern Ireland is vested with the Department of the Environment: Sch 8, para 24(1).

[151]   SI 2000/1970, as amended SI 2000/3318, SI 2002/2981, SI 2004/1881, SI 2005/2988 and SI 2007/500. The 2000 Regulations have been modified so that compliance with Directive 2001/85/EC is offered as an alternative. The Directive requires that the UK may not refuse or prohibit sale or entry into service of a vehicle if the requirements of the Directive and its Annexes are met. Accordingly, the requirements of the 2000 Regulations may alternatively be met by a vehicle satisfying the requirements of the Directive. See further Department for Transport, 'The Public Service Vehicles Accessibility Regulations 2000 Guidance'. See further: Department for Transport, *Proposed PSV accessibility regulations: regulatory impact assessment* (February 2001, modified May 2003).

[152]   DDA 1995, s 40(1)(a).

[153]   Ibid, s 40(1)(b).

[154]   Ibid, s 40(5).

[155]   Ibid, s 40(6). By virtue of s 67(7), this is without prejudice to the generality of the powers to make regulations or orders by statutory instrument conferred by s 67(2)–(3).

[156]   HL Deb, vol 565, col 716.

are used to provide local and scheduled services (so-called 'regulated public service vehicles').[157] The Regulations recognise the impact their provisions will have on the bus manufacturing and operating industry by providing for a phased implementation of their requirements. The detailed technical requirements to be met by regulated public service vehicles are contained in three Schedules dealing with wheelchair accessibility requirements (Sch 1) and with the general accessibility requirements for buses (Sch 2) and coaches (Sch 3) respectively. These requirements are then applied to the various types of PSV according to the date when they are first used.[158] New buses weighing more than 7.5 tonnes and new double-deck buses must comply with both Sch 1 and Sch 2 from 31 December 2000 and all such buses which are in use must meet these requirements after 2016 and 2017. New buses weighing 7.5 tonnes or less and new coaches must comply with Sch 2 or Sch 3 respectively from 31 December 2000 until 1 January 2005, after which new vehicles of these kinds must also comply with Sch 1. All these regulated PSVs must meet the wheelchair accessibility requirements and those of the appropriate general accessibility requirements if in use after 1 January 2015 (for buses weighing 7.5 tonnes or less) or 2020 (for coaches). There is an exception in the case of regulated PSVs that are manufactured before 1 October 2000 and 1 October 2004. They are not required to comply with the requirements of the relevant Schedules unless and until they are in use on or after 1 January in either 2015 or 2016 or 2017 or 2020 as appropriate.

8.3.6 The PSV accessibility regulations may, in particular, make provision as to the construction, use and maintenance of regulated PSVs.[159] Such provision may include:

- provision as to the fitting of equipment to vehicles;

- equipment to be carried by vehicles;

- the design of such equipment;

- the fitting and use of restraining devices designed to ensure the stability of wheelchairs while vehicles are moving;

- the position in which wheelchairs are to be secured while vehicles are moving.

---

[157] It is clear that the regulations do not apply to small buses carrying less than 22 passengers, but see the non-statutory initiative of DPTAC, 'Accessibility Specification for Small Buses' (revised in November 2007).

[158] Public Service Vehicles Accessibility Regulations 2000, SI 2000/1970 (as amended), reg 3, subject to certain exemptions or delayed implementation set out in reg 4. Regulation 5 provides for the recognition of EEA (European Economic Area) equivalent requirements.

[159] DDA 1995, s 40(2).

It is not intended that this list should be exhaustive.[160]

8.3.7   In the event, the Public Service Vehicle Accessibility Regulations 2000 address the following matters in relation to relevant PSVs and disabled passengers in respect of wheelchair accessibility requirements:

- wheelchair spaces and provisions;[161]

- boarding lifts and ramps;[162]

- entrances and exits;[163]

- gangways;[164]

- signs and markings;[165]

- communication devices;[166]

- lighting.[167]

They also lay down general accessibility requirements for single-deck and double-deck buses and coaches covering the following areas:

- floors and gangways;[168]

- seats or priority seats;[169]

- steps;[170]

- handrails and handholds;[171]

- communication devices;[172]

---

[160] HL Deb, vol 565, col 716.
[161] Public Service Vehicles Accessibility Regulations 2000, SI 2000/1970 (as amended), reg 3 and Sch 1, paras 2–4. Schedule 1, para 1 supplies definitions for the purposes of Sch 1, paras 2–10.
[162] Ibid, Sch 1, para 5.
[163] Ibid, Sch 1, para 6.
[164] Ibid, Sch 1, para 7.
[165] Ibid, Sch 1, para 8.
[166] Ibid, Sch 1, para 9.
[167] Ibid, Sch 1, para 10 (as amended).
[168] Ibid, reg 3, Sch 2, para 2 and Sch 3, para 2. Schedule 2, para 1 (as amended) and Sch 3, para 1 (as amended) supply definitions for the purposes of Sch 2, paras 2–8 and Sch 3, paras 2–7.
[169] Ibid, reg 3, Sch 2, para 3 and Sch 3, para 3.
[170] Ibid, reg 3, Sch 2, para 4 (as amended) and Sch 3, para 4.
[171] Ibid, Sch 2, para 5 (as amended) and Sch 3, para 5.
[172] Ibid, Sch 2, para 6 (buses only).

- kneeling systems;[173]

- route and destination displays.[174]

8.3.8 Although frequent reference is made here to the needs of wheelchair users, the accessibility regulations are intended to make provision for the needs of other disabled travellers, including those with sensory impairments (for example, by the use of colour contrast on handrails and seating and improved lighting levels).[175] The general power to make codes of practice under the DDA 1995 might also be used to give guidance to transport staff on assistance to disabled persons (for example, in respect of audible announcements).[176] As a further consequence of the Public Service Vehicles Accessibility Regulations 2000, amendments have been made to the Public Service Vehicles (Conditions of Fitness, Equipment, Use and Certification) Regulations 1981 so as to ensure greater consistency between the two sets of regulations as they affect the use of PSVs by disabled persons.[177]

8.3.9 A regulated PSV shall not be used on the road unless it conforms with the provisions of any PSV accessibility regulations.[178] To do otherwise is a criminal offence punishable on summary conviction by a fine not exceeding level 4 on the standard scale.[179] It is also a criminal offence of like weight to contravene or fail to comply with any provision of the PSV accessibility regulations or to cause or permit a regulated PSV to be used on a road in non-conformity with such regulations.[180]

8.3.10 Provision is made for offences committed by a body corporate.[181] If such an offence is committed with the consent or connivance of a

---

[173] Public Service Vehicles Accessibility Regulations 2000, SI 2000/1970, Sch 2, para 7 and Sch 3, para 6. A kneeling system is one which enables a PSV to be raised and/or lowered relative to its normal height of travel.

[174] Ibid, Sch 2, para 8 and Sch 3, para 7.

[175] HL Deb, vol 566, cols 459–460.

[176] See Department for Transport, *Guidance on the Public Service Vehicles (Conduct of Drivers, Inspectors, Conductors and Passengers) (Amendment) Regulations 2002* (December 2002) and Department for Transport, *Conduct of Drivers, Inspectors and Conductors – A Guide for Bus and Coach Staff* (October 2003), published to support new duties introduced on 1 October 2002 as a result of the Public Service Vehicles (Conduct of Drivers, Inspectors, Conductors and Passengers) (Amendment) Regulations 2002, SI 2002/1724, that amend the Public Service Vehicles (Conduct of Drivers, Inspectors, Conductors and Passengers) Regulations 1990, SI 1990/1020.

[177] Public Service Vehicles (Conditions of Fitness, Equipment, Use and Certification) Regulations 1981, SI 1981/257, as amended by the Public Service Vehicles (Conditions of Fitness, Equipment, Use and Certification) (Amendment) Regulations 2002, SI 2002/335.

[178] DDA 1995, s 40(3)(b).

[179] Ibid, s 40(4).

[180] Ibid, s 40(3)(a),(c).

[181] Ibid, ss 40 and 48.

director,[182] manager, secretary or other similar officer, then there is joint liability for the offence.[183] Joint liability may also arise where the offence is attributable to any neglect on the part of any such officers. The position is also the same where the offence is committed with the consent or connivance (or is attributable to any neglect on the part) of a person purporting to act in such a capacity. In addition, in Scotland only, an offence committed by a partnership or other unincorporated association in the above circumstances can lead to a partner or a person concerned in the management or control of the association incurring joint criminal liability.[184]

Accessibility certificates

8.3.11 Without prejudice to the generality of the restraints and offences created above,[185] a regulated PSV shall not be used on a road unless a vehicle examiner[186] has issued an 'accessibility certificate'.[187] An 'accessibility certificate' is a certificate which certifies that the prescribed provisions of the PSV accessibility regulations have been satisfied in respect of the vehicle in question.[188] This will parallel the existing initial roadworthiness certification procedure for PSVs and it is envisaged that accessibility certificates will be issued at the same time as certificates of initial fitness.[189] A fee may be payable on application or issue.[190] If a regulated PSV is used on a road without an accessibility certificate, the operator of the vehicle is guilty of an offence and is liable on summary conviction to a fine not exceeding level 4 on the standard scale.[191]

8.3.12 After due consultation,[192] the Secretary of State has made regulations with respect to applications for accessibility certificates and their issue.[193] Their technical detail is not explored further here.

---

[182] Where the affairs of a body corporate are managed by its members, a director will include any such member: DDA 1995, s 48(2).

[183] Ibid, s 48(1).

[184] Ibid, s 48(3).

[185] By ibid, s 40.

[186] Appointed under Road Traffic Act 1988, s 66A.

[187] DDA 1995, s 41(1)(a). Provision is made for appeal to the Secretary of State against the refusal of a vehicle examiner to issue an accessibility certificate: s 44(3)–(6). A fee may be charged for such an appeal: s 45.

[188] Provision is made in DDA 1995, s 49 for criminal offences committed in connection with accessibility certificates (e g forgery or the making of false statements).

[189] HL Deb, vol 565, col 716 and vol 566, col 463.

[190] DDA 1995, s 45(1)(b).

[191] Ibid, s 41(3). This is subject to s 41(1)(b) and the provisions of s 42. See **8.2.13**. By virtue of s 41(4), the term 'operator' has the same meaning as in the Public Passenger Vehicles Act 1981. The appropriate modification of s 41(3)–(4) for Northern Ireland is made by Sch 8, para 25(2).

[192] DDA 1995, s 40(7).

[193] Ibid, s 41(2) (in Northern Ireland, the Department of the Environment: Sch 8, para 25(1)). See Public Service Vehicles Accessibility Regulations 2000, SI 2000/1970 (as amended), regs 6–8 and Sch 4.

8.3.13   Where the Secretary of State[194] is satisfied that prescribed provisions of the PSV accessibility regulations for the purposes of accessibility certificates have been satisfied in respect of a particular vehicle, that vehicle may be given approval on application and payment of a fee.[195] A vehicle approved in this manner is referred to as a 'type vehicle'.[196] This provision will clearly apply to vehicles produced in large numbers. The Secretary of State may at any time withdraw approval of a type vehicle.[197]

8.3.14   If the Secretary of State refuses an application for the approval of a vehicle,[198] provision is made for a review of that decision.[199] A request for review must be made within 28 days.[200] In reviewing the original decision, the Secretary of State must consider any written representations made by the applicant before the end of the prescribed period.[201]

Type approval certificates

8.3.15   If a person authorised by the Secretary of State has made a declaration in the prescribed form that a particular vehicle conforms in design, construction and equipment with a type vehicle (a 'declaration of conformity'), then a vehicle examiner may issue 'an approval certificate' to the effect that subsequent individual vehicles conform to the type vehicle.[202] The vehicle examiner may issue such an approval certificate after examining the vehicle to which the statutory declaration applies, if

---

[194]   In Northern Ireland, the Department of the Environment.

[195]   DDA 1995, ss 42(1) and 45(1)(a). The Northern Ireland modifications to s 42 are contained in Sch 8, para 26. In accordance with s 42(5)(a), the Secretary of State may make regulations with respect to applications for (and grants of) approval under s 42(1): see Public Service Vehicles Accessibility Regulations 2000, SI 2000/1970 (as amended), regs 9–12.

[196]   DDA 1995, s 42(2).

[197]   Ibid, s 42(6).

[198]   Ibid, s 42(1).

[199]   Ibid, s 44; Public Service Vehicles Accessibility Regulations 2000, SI 2000/1970 (as amended), reg 19.

[200]   Ibid, s 44(1); Public Service Vehicles Accessibility Regulations 2000, SI 2000/1970 (as amended), reg 19(3). The applicant for review must pay any fee fixed under s 45.

[201]   Ibid, s 44(2). The provisions appertaining to reviews, appeals and fees generally under ss 44–45 are modified for the purposes of Northern Ireland by Sch 8, paras 28–29.

[202]   DDA 1995, s 42(3), (4) and (8). Regulations may make general provision in respect of approval certificates: s 42(5) and see Public Service Vehicles Accessibility Regulations 2000, SI 2000/1970 (as amended), regs 13–17, 19(3) and Schs 5–6. Note the consultation requirements of s 40(7). Provision is made in s 49 for criminal offences committed in connection with approval certificates (eg forgery or the making of false statements).

he or she thinks fit.[203] However, these provisions are clearly designed to avoid the need for each vehicle of the same type to be individually inspected.[204]

8.3.16 If the Secretary of State withdraws approval of a type vehicle,[205] then a vehicle examiner may not issue any further approval certificates by reference to the type vehicle.[206] However, any approval certificate issued by reference to the type vehicle before such withdrawal of approval shall continue to have effect.[207]

Offences and exemptions

8.3.17 A regulated PSV shall not be used on a road unless it has an accessibility certificate[208] or unless, alternatively, an approval certificate[209] has been issued in respect of the vehicle.[210] Use of a regulated PSV in contravention of these alternative conditions is a criminal offence punishable on summary conviction by a fine not exceeding level 4 on the standard scale.[211]

8.3.18 These provisions[212] do not prevent the use of a regulated PSV on the road if the Secretary of State has by order authorised its use by reference to the class or description of the vehicle or by explicit specification.[213] This allows special operating authorisation for vehicles which do not comply with the PSV accessibility regulations and for which an accessibility or approval certificate is not in force. The Government recognised that there might be circumstances in which an individual vehicle or class of vehicles could not reasonably be expected to meet the full requirements of the new vehicle accessibility standards.[214] Such circumstances might be used to recognise the difficulty or undesirability of attempting to make vintage or heritage vehicles fully accessible.[215] Special authorisation may be given subject to specified restrictions or conditions[216] and even an order authorising the use of a vehicle in these

---

[203] DDA 1995, s 42(4). Provision is made for appeal to the Secretary of State against the refusal of a vehicle examiner to issue an approval certificate: s 44(3)–(6). A fee may be charged for such an appeal: s 45.

[204] HL Deb, vol 565, col 717.

[205] Under DDA 1995, s 42(6).

[206] Ibid, s 42(7)(a).

[207] For s 41 purposes: ibid, s 42(7)(b).

[208] Under ibid, s 41.

[209] Under ibid, s 42.

[210] Ibid, s 41(1).

[211] Ibid, s 41(3).

[212] Ibid, ss 40–42.

[213] Ibid, s 43(1). In Northern Ireland, the s 43 powers are vested in the Department of the Environment: Sch 8, para 27.

[214] HL Deb, vol 565, col 717.

[215] Ibid, vol 566, col 463.

[216] DDA 1995, s 43(2).

circumstances may require it to conform with certain aspects of the PSV accessibility regulations, with specified modifications or exceptions.[217]

8.3.19   Ordinarily, where the Secretary of State is given a power under the DDA 1995 to make an order, that power is exercisable by statutory instrument.[218] An exception is provided for[219] in respect of an order[220] by which the Secretary of State has authorised the use on roads of a regulated PSV which does not comply with the PSV accessibility regulations or which does not possess an accessibility or approval certificate.[221] Such an authorisation order need not be made by statutory instrument if it applies only to a specified vehicle or to vehicles of a specified person. Nevertheless, such an order is capable of being amended or revoked as if it was an order made by statutory instrument.[222]

8.4   RAIL VEHICLES

8.4.1   Although provision has already been made in railways legislation to ensure that rail transport operators have a duty to have regard to the needs of disabled passengers, the last Conservative Government regarded the provision of accessible rail services as 'a key link in the transport chain'.[223] Relevant provisions of the DDA 1995 are intended to strengthen the existing legislative framework by addressing access to rail services, including light rapid transit and tram systems.[224]

Rail vehicle accessibility regulations

8.4.2   The Secretary of State is empowered[225] to make 'rail vehicle accessibility regulations' after appropriate consultations.[226] The Rail Vehicle Accessibility Regulations 1998 came into force on 1 November

---

[217]   DDA 1995, s 43(3).
[218]   Ibid, s 67(1).
[219]   Under ibid, s 67(6).
[220]   Under ibid, s 43.
[221]   Under ibid, ss 40–42.
[222]   Ibid, s 67(6).
[223]   HL Deb, vol 565, col 717.
[224]   DDA 1995, ss 46–47. See also Strategic Rail Authority, *Train and Station Services for Disabled Passengers: A Code of Practice* (February 2002) and *Guidance on Disabled Persons' Protection Policies* (April 2002) (the latter made under the powers in the Railways Act 1993 (as amended), s 71B). See further National Rail, *Rail Travel for Disabled Passengers* (regularly updated) and Strategic Rail Authority, *Railways for All* (2005).
[225]   DDA 1995, s 46(1). To understand how the Part 3 access duties apply to rail services and interact with the Part 5 rail vehicle accessibility regulations, see: DRC, *Avoiding disability discrimination in transport: a practical guide for rail services* (2007).
[226]   Ibid, s 46(11) and Sch 8, para 30(4). In Northern Ireland, the s 46 powers are vested in the Department for Regional Development: Sch 8, para 30(1). Consultation upon the relevant regulations (discussed below) took place in May and June 1998. It took the form of the issue by the Mobility Unit of the DETR of draft regulations, together with a compliance cost assessment.

1998.[227] They are supported by non-statutory guidance for the railway industry indicating the scope of coverage of the regulations, detailed guidance on the regulatory requirements, best practice, how the exemption procedure works, and how the regulations will be enforced.[228] The purpose of the regulations is to secure that it is possible for disabled persons to get on to and off 'regulated rail vehicles' in safety and without unreasonable difficulty, and to be carried in such vehicles in safety and in reasonable comfort.[229] Moreover, the regulations make provision for securing that it is possible for disabled persons in wheelchairs to get on to and off 'regulated rail vehicles' in safety and without unreasonable difficulty while remaining in their wheelchairs, as well as to be carried in such vehicles in safety and reasonable comfort while remaining in their wheelchairs.[230]

8.4.3 The DDA 1995 anticipated that particular provision would be made in the rail vehicle accessibility regulations as to the construction, use and maintenance of 'regulated rail vehicles'.[231] Special provision might also be made in the regulations as to the fitting of equipment to rail vehicles; equipment to be carried by rail vehicles; the design of equipment to be fitted to or carried by rail vehicles; the use of equipment fitted to or carried by rail vehicles; the toilet facilities to be provided in rail vehicles; the location and floor area of the wheelchair accommodation to be provided in rail vehicles;[232] and assistance to be given to disabled persons.[233] While the statutory provisions make frequent reference to the needs of wheelchair users, the accessibility regulations are intended to make provision for the needs of other disabled travellers, including those with sensory impairments (for example, by the use of colour contrast on handrails and seating, and improved lighting levels).[234]

8.4.4 It is not proposed to reproduce the content of the 1998 Regulations (as amended) here. Much of their provision is technical and detailed. However, in summary, the rail vehicle accessibility regulations cover the following requirements:

---

[227] SI 1998/2456 (made under DDA 1995, s 46(1), (2) and (5)), as amended by the Rail Vehicle Accessibility (Amendment) Regulations 2000, SI 2000/3215 (applying the 1998 Regulations to an additional form of guided transport, namely systems which are track-based with side guidance, and making some other amendments to access requirements). In Northern Ireland, see the Rail Vehicle Accessibility Regulations (Northern Ireland) 2001, SR 2001/264 (in force 19 October 2001).

[228] Department for Transport, 'Rail Vehicle Accessibility Regulations 1998 (RVAR) Guidance'.

[229] DDA 1995, s 46(1)(a).

[230] Ibid, s 46(1)(b).

[231] Ibid, s 46(2).

[232] The meaning of the term 'wheelchair accommodation' is defined by regulations: ibid, s 46(6).

[233] DDA 1995, s 46(2)(a)–(g).

[234] HL Deb, vol 566, cols 459–460.

- for the marking of doors, their warning devices and their controls;[235]

- relating to steps on the exterior and in the interior of vehicles;[236]

- relating to floors;[237]

- for priority seating for the use of disabled persons;[238]

- for request-stop controls in a tramcar, if the tramcar is fitted with such controls;[239]

- relating to interior transparent surfaces;[240]

- for handrails and for handholds fitted to the backs of seats;[241]

- for the minimum force needed to operate a door handle;[242]

- for audible and visual announcements inside and outside the vehicle including their use and contents;[243]

- for any toilets which are fitted to a vehicle;[244]

- the provision of wheelchair spaces, their dimensions and other requirements;[245]

- the provision of wheelchair-compatible sleeping compartments;[246]

- the provision of tables in wheelchair spaces, if other passengers have them;[247]

- the provision of wheelchair-compatible doorways and passageways to wheelchair spaces and wheelchair-compatible sleeping compartments;[248]

- requirements relating to telephones for passengers' use;[249]

---

[235] Rail Vehicle Accessibility Regulations 1998, SI 1998/2456, regs 4 and 5 (as amended).
[236] Ibid, reg 6.
[237] Ibid, reg 7.
[238] Ibid, reg 8.
[239] Ibid, reg 9 (as amended).
[240] Ibid, reg 10.
[241] Ibid, reg 11.
[242] Ibid, reg 12.
[243] Ibid, reg 13.
[244] Ibid, regs 14 and 20 (as amended).
[245] Ibid, regs 15–16 (as amended).
[246] Ibid, reg 17.
[247] Ibid, reg 18.
[248] Ibid, reg 19.
[249] Ibid, reg 21.

- minimum internal door width;[250]

- the provision of boarding devices, which may be lifts or ramps, and requirements relating to them;[251]

- catering services, if such services are available for other passengers;[252] and

- wheelchair access to on-board facilities.[253]

in each case, for the benefit of disabled persons.

8.4.5 The statute anticipates that different provisions may be made in the regulations so as to differentiate between different classes or descriptions of rail vehicles and as respects different 'networks'.[254] Similarly, different provision may be made in the rail vehicle accessibility regulations as respects the same class or description of rail vehicle in different circumstances.[255] This apparently recognises that 'the design and use of rail vehicles will vary according to a range of factors' including locality, systems and uses. For example, the 1998 Regulations do make differing provisions for tramcars as opposed to trains.[256] It seems also to be intended that there should be future flexibility so that the 'accessibility regulations do not undermine the historic character of heritage railways'.[257] In addition, different provision might be made to reflect the different operating conditions and vehicle design on different parts of the London Underground railway (for example, those lines that use tubes rather than orthodox tunnels to carry rail vehicles).

Offences

8.4.6 If a 'regulated rail vehicle' is used for carriage while not conforming with any appropriate provisions of the rail vehicle

---

[250] Rail Vehicle Accessibility Regulations 1998, SI 1998/2456, reg 22.

[251] Ibid, reg 23.

[252] Ibid, reg 24.

[253] Ibid, reg 20A (as amended).

[254] DDA 1995, s 46(5)(a), (c). The term 'network' means any permanent way or other means of guiding or supporting rail vehicles or any section of such a network: s 46(6). From a date yet to be appointed, the Secretary of State shall exercise the power to make rail vehicle accessibility regulations so as to secure that on and after 1 January 2020 every rail vehicle is a regulated rail vehicle, but this does not affect the powers conferred by ss 46(5) or 47(1) or 67(2): DDA 1995, s 46(4A) inserted by DDA 2005, s 6(1) (but not yet in force).

[255] Ibid, s 46(5)(b). By virtue of s 67(7), these powers are without prejudice to the generality of the powers to make regulations or orders by statutory instrument conferred by s 67(2)–(3).

[256] See eg Rail Vehicle Accessibility Regulations 1998, SI 1998/2456, regs 9, 11 and 15 (as amended).

[257] HL Deb, vol 565, col 718.

accessibility regulations, the 'operator'[258] commits a criminal offence punishable on summary conviction by a fine not exceeding level 4 on the standard scale.[259] A person uses a rail vehicle for carriage if that person uses it for the carriage of members of the public for hire or reward at separate fares.[260] Provision is made for offences committed by a body corporate.[261] If such an offence is committed with the consent or connivance of a director,[262] manager, secretary or other similar officer, then there is joint liability for the offence.[263] Joint liability may also arise where the offence is attributable to any neglect on the part of any such officers. The position is also the same where the offence is committed with the consent or connivance (or is attributable to any neglect on the part) of a person purporting to act in such a capacity. In addition, in Scotland only, an offence committed by a partnership or other unincorporated association in the above circumstances can lead to a partner or a person concerned in the management or control of the association incurring joint criminal liability.[264]

Regulated rail vehicles

8.4.7   The key to an understanding of these access provisions is an appreciation of which rail vehicles are covered by the regulations. The rail vehicle accessibility regulations apply only to 'regulated rail vehicles'.[265] Thus, the scope of the regulations is determined in the accessibility regulations themselves as the term 'regulated rail vehicle' is said to be 'any rail vehicle to which the rail vehicle accessibility regulations are expressed to apply'.[266] It is clear that the Secretary of State has maximum flexibility to determine which rail vehicles are to be included or excluded from the access requirements. The 1998 Regulations apply to passenger-carrying vehicles used on railways, tramways, monorail systems, magnetic levitation systems or track-based with side guidance ('regulated rail vehicles'),[267] which are first brought into use, or belong to a class of vehicle first brought into use, on or after 1 January 1999.[268]

---

[258] The person having the management of that vehicle: DDA 1995, s 46(6). This definition is to be repealed from a date yet to be appointed: DDA 2005, s 19(2) and Sch 2.

[259] DDA 1995, s 46(3)–(4). These provisions are to be repealed from a date yet to be appointed: DDA 2005, s 19 and Schs 1 and 2.

[260] DDA 1995, s 46(10) (to be repealed in due course by DDA 2005, s 19(2) and Sch 2).

[261] Ibid, ss 46 and 48.

[262] Where the affairs of a body corporate are managed by its members, a director will include any such member: ibid, s 48(2).

[263] Ibid, s 48(1).

[264] Ibid, s 48(3).

[265] Ibid, s 46(6).

[266] Ibid.

[267] Rail Vehicle Accessibility Regulations 1998, SI 1998/2456, reg 3(1) (as amended). In accordance with reg 2(1), 'railway' and 'tramway' have the same meaning as in the Transport and Works Act 1992; 'magnetic levitation' and 'monorail' have the meaning provided for in the Transport and Works (Guided Transport Modes) Order 1992, SI 1992/3231.

[268] DDA 1995, s 46(1).

8.4.8 However, it is equally plain that the regulations can only apply to modes of passenger transport that satisfy the root definition of a 'rail vehicle': namely, a vehicle constructed or adapted to carry passengers on any railways, tramway or 'prescribed system'.[269] Except in Northern Ireland,[270] the terms 'railway' and 'tramway' have the same meaning as in the Transport and Works Act 1992. The use of the term 'prescribed system' means a transport system using a prescribed mode of guided transport within the meaning of the 1992 Act.[271]

8.4.9 Yet, however the term 'rail vehicle' is defined, it is also clear that the accessibility standards do not apply to any rail vehicle (or class of rail vehicle) first brought into use on or before 31 December 1998.[272] At the time of the passage of these provisions, the Government at that time made it clear in debate that it intended to use the regulation-making powers only in respect of new railway rolling stock and that there was no intention to require modifications to any existing rolling stock.[273] However, the DRTF recommends that an end date by which all passenger rail vehicles should comply with the 1998 Regulations should be introduced following consultation. It also recommends that the accessibility standards should be applied to the refurbishment of existing rolling stock.[274] This is likely to be the subject of future consultation.

Exemptions

8.4.10 General provision is made for exemptions from the rail vehicle accessibility regulations.[275] After due consideration and consultation,[276] the Secretary of State (in Northern Ireland, the Department for Regional Development) may make exemption orders[277] to authorise the use for carriage of a regulated rail vehicle even though that vehicle does not conform with the appropriate provisions of the rail vehicle accessibility regulations (or to authorise its use otherwise than in conformity with the

---

[269] DDA 1995, s 46(6). The DDA 2005 anticipates that the temporal limitation on the class of vehicle in question will be repealed at some future date: DDA 2005, s 6(2). In Northern Ireland, the term 'rail vehicle' means a vehicle constructed or adapted to carry passengers by rail: Sch 8, para 30(2).

[270] Ibid, Sch 8, para 30(3).

[271] Ibid, s 46(7).

[272] Ibid, s 46(6). The time at which a rail vehicle or class of rail vehicle is to be treated for s 46 purposes as first brought into use is determined by regulations made under s 46(8) (in due course, s 46(8)–(10) will be repealed by DDA 2005, s 19(2) and Sch 2). Such regulations may provide for the disregarding of periods of testing or other prescribed periods of use: s 46(9). The DDA 2005 anticipates that the temporal limitation on the class of vehicle in question will be repealed at some future date: DDA 2005, s 6(2).

[273] HL Deb, vol 565, col 717.

[274] DRTF Report, recommendation 7.1.

[275] DDA 1995, s 47.

[276] Ibid, s 47(3).

[277] Ibid, s 47(1), as substituted by DDA 2005, s 6(3) from 5 December 2005. Authority under s 47(1) may be for (a) any regulated rail vehicle that is specified or is of a specified description; or (b) use in specified circumstances of (i) any regulated rail vehicle, or (ii) any regulated rail vehicle that is specified or is of a specified description: s 47(1A).

regulations).[278] An exemption order may be made subject to specified restrictions or conditions.[279] The regulations may provide for procedural issues in respect of the application for, granting of, currency of or revocation of exemption orders.[280]

8.4.11   The Secretary of State has made the Rail Vehicle (Exemption Applications) Regulations 1998.[281] These regulations specify the manner in which applications for exemption from the Rail Vehicle Accessibility Regulations 1998 are to be made, including the information which is to be supplied with an application. An application must be in writing.[282] It must provide the following particulars with the application:[283]

• name and address of applicant;

• description of rail vehicle;

• applicable circumstances of the exemption;

• relevant requirements from which exemption is sought;

• the technical, economic and operational reasons why exemption is sought;

• the effect which the exemption would have on a disabled person's ability to use the rail vehicle so described;[284]

• any measures which could be taken to enable disabled persons to use such rail vehicles if exemption is granted;[285]

• any proposals for the later modification of such rail vehicles to secure compliance with the rail vehicle accessibility regulations within a stated period;

• the period of exemption (unless permanent exemption is sought).

---

[278]   At the time of writing, 49 exemptions orders have been made.

[279]   DDA 1995, s 47(4)–(5).

[280]   Ibid, s 47(2). It was not envisaged that the s 47 powers of exemption would be widely used: HL Deb, vol 565, col 718.

[281]   SI 1998/2457, made under DDA 1995, s 47 and in force from 1 November 1998. In Northern Ireland, see the Rail Vehicle (Exemption Applications) Regulations (Northern Ireland) 2001, SR 2001/265 (in force 19 October 2001).

[282]   Rail Vehicle (Exemption Applications) Regulations 1998, SI 1998/2457, reg 3.

[283]   Ibid, reg 3 and Schedule.

[284]   The meaning of 'use' is set out in Rail Vehicle (Exemption Applications) Regulations 1998, SI 1998/2457, Schedule, para 11.

[285]   The meaning of 'use' is set out in Rail Vehicle (Exemption Applications) Regulations 1998, SI 1998/2457, Schedule, para 11.

These regulations also make provision for the period and revocation of exemptions.[286] Numerous and various exemptions for particular descriptions of rail vehicles on particular rail systems have been sought and granted.[287]

Disability Discrimination Act 2005

8.4.12 The DDA 2005 prospectively makes amendments to ss 46–47 of the 1995 Act (on rail vehicle accessibility regulations and exemptions).[288] New ss 47A–47M will make provision for rail vehicle accessibility compliance certificates, inspection of rail vehicles, and associated fees and penalties. These changes to the law are not yet in force and are not discussed in further detail here. However, the background to these prospective changes is as follows.

8.4.13 In response to the DRTF Report, the Government consulted on a recommendation that called for the introduction of an end date by which all rail vehicles must comply with the Rail Vehicle Accessibility Regulations 1998 (and regulations covering the refurbishment of rail vehicles) and some associated questions (including changes to the enforcement regime and the removal of the requirement for exemptions to be granted by statutory instrument).[289] The consultation ended on 26 January 2004. The Disability Discrimination Act 2005 is the vehicle for change.[290]

8.4.14 The DDA 2005 enables the Secretary of State to achieve the policy objective of applying the rail vehicle accessibility regulations to rail vehicles first brought into use before 1 January 1999 and also to newer vehicles which are of the same type as ones first used before the regulations came into force on 1 January 1999. This change of definition enables the Secretary of State to set a date in the regulations by which time all rail vehicles must comply with their requirements. The 2005 Act continues to allow the Secretary of State to make exemption orders in respect of regulated rail vehicles, but clarifies the law by specifically allowing exemptions from the operational requirements of the rail vehicle accessibility regulations as well as construction requirements. It expressly

---

[286] Rail Vehicle (Exemption Applications) Regulations 1998, SI 1998/2457, reg 4.

[287] The details of these exemption orders are not reproduced here.

[288] DDA 2005, ss 7–8 and contextual amendments (signalled above) will be made to DDA 1995, ss 46–47 in the process.

[289] Department for Transport, *Consultation on Government's Proposals to Amend Rail Provisions in Part V of DDA* (November 2003).

[290] See: Department for Work and Pensions, *Draft Disability Discrimination Bill*, Cm 6058 (December 2003); *Explanatory Notes*, Cm 6058-ii, *Draft Regulatory Impact Assessment*, Cm 6058-iii. See, in particular: Joint Committee on the Draft Disability Discrimination Bill, *First Report* (April 2004); Department for Work and Pensions, *The Government's Response to the Report of the Joint Committee on the Draft Disability Discrimination Bill*, Cm 6276 (July 2004).

confers power to exempt the use of vehicles of a specified description in specified circumstances (eg a heritage railway).

8.4.15 The new provisions, when in force, will have the effect of requiring prescribed rail vehicles to have a rail vehicle accessibility compliance certificate. It is intended that the requirement to have a certificate will apply to all new rail vehicles and vehicles that are refurbished. The effect of this is to set up a rail vehicle accessibility regulations certification scheme. The provisions include power for the Secretary of State to make regulations providing for the appointment of independent assessors who will be responsible for checking regulated rail vehicles for compliance against each regulatory requirement to which that vehicle is required to conform. They also empower the Secretary of State to make regulations setting out the procedure for obtaining certificates, including provisions for assessors to charge fees, and a mechanism for disputes between assessors and applicants for certificates to be referred to the Secretary of State. A regulated rail vehicle would be prohibited from being used for carriage unless a valid compliance certificate has been issued for that vehicle. The provisions with which vehicles are required to conform will be prescribed in the regulations, including different requirements in the case of refurbished vehicles.

8.4.16 Much of this new law will be contained in regulations to be made under the new powers. The 2005 Act will also replace the existing criminal sanctions for non-compliance with the rail vehicle accessibility regulations with a civil enforcement regime which enables penalties to be levied. The Secretary of State will be enabled to issue an operator with an improvement notice, which sets a deadline for a non-compliance to be rectified. If the non-compliance continues after the improvement deadline, a final notice can be issued. If the final deadline is missed the Secretary of State can impose a penalty. An operator can lodge an objection with the Secretary of State against either the imposition or level of a penalty. The provisions also provide a right of appeal to the court.

8.4.17 The government intended that the supporting regulations and codes of practice would be in place by 31 December 2006.[291] Clearly this timetable has slipped and there is no present indication of when the DDA 2005 provisions will be brought into force.

8.5 AVIATION AND SHIPPING

8.5.1 The DDA 1995 does not directly address the rights of disabled people in respect of aviation or shipping services. Airports and passenger terminals are subject to Part 3 (on access to goods, facilities and services)

---

[291] See Department for Transport, *Consultation on draft Rail Vehicle Accessibility Exemption Order (Parliamentary Procedures) Regulations, Rail Vehicle Accessibility (Determination of Turnover) Regulations & Setting of Penalties: Code of Practice* (July 2006). See also Department for Transport, *Railways for All Strategy* (March 2006).

insofar as they are providing facilities or services. However, aeroplanes, helicopters, airships, ferries, hovercraft, boats and ships were previously excluded from Part 3, being 'the use of any means of transport'.[292] However, the new s 21ZA clarifies the exclusion of Part 3 in relation to the provision or use of a vehicle, including a vehicle for transporting people by air or water. The Disability Discrimination (Transport Vehicles) Regulations 2005 do not lift the exemption from Part 3 in relation to aircraft and ships.[293]

8.5.2   In addition, s 19(1) does not apply to anything that is governed by EC Regulation 1107/2006 concerning the rights of disabled persons and persons with reduced mobility when travelling by air.[294] This Regulation is designed to provide EC-level rules for the protection of disabled passengers and passengers with reduced mobility when travelling by air. The EC rules also apply to the provision of assistance to disabled passengers (and those with reduced mobility). It is intended to protect them from discrimination and to ensure they receive adequate assistance when travelling through an airport and on board an aircraft. The Regulation clarifies what assistance should be provided by the relevant airline and the relevant airport operator, and at whose cost. From 26 July 2007, subject to certain exceptions, it is illegal for an airline, travel agent or tour operator to refuse a booking on the grounds of disability, or to refuse to allow a disabled person to board an aircraft when they have a valid ticket and reservation. This applies to any flight leaving an airport in the European Union, and also to flights on European airlines arriving in the EU. Further rights for disabled passengers will be introduced in July 2008 to ensure a consistent and seamless level of service at airports and on board aircraft.[295]

8.5.3   Aircaft and shipping vessels are also not the subject of the framework for vehicle accessibility standards in Part 5 of the Act. The DRTF welcomed steps taken to develop a non-statutory code of practice on access for disabled people to air travel and suggests that the code might be given statutory backing.[296] It also recommends a formal review,

---

[292]   DDA 1995, s 19(5)(b) (as originally enacted).

[293]   Transport Vehicles Code of Practice, paras 2.22–2.23. To borrow the example given in the code, a wheelchair user has no protection under Part 3 of the Act if a ferry on which he or she wishes to travel is not accessible. However, if he or she is refused service in the buffet bar of the ferry terminal because of his or her disability, this is likely to be unlawful.

[294]   DDA 1995, s 19(4A) inserted by reg 8 of the Civil Aviation (Access to Air Travel for Disabled Persons and Persons with Reduced Mobility) Regulations 2007, SI 2007/1895 from 26 July 2007.

[295]   This account draws from the DfT factsheet on the regulation and a very helpful summary and analysis of it by the international law firm Bird & Bird (see www.twobirds.com). Those sources are acknowledged.

[296]   DRTF Report, recommendation 7.8. See Department for Transport, 'Code of Practice: Access to Air Travel for Disabled People'. The Government Response to the DRTF Report suggested that it might be prepared to give the code statutory backing. See also DPTAC, 'Design of Large Passenger Ships and Passenger Infrastructure: Guidance on

including the need for legislative provisions, for accelerating progress in compliance with the International Maritime Organization and the DPTAC guidance on access for disabled people in the shipping industry.[297] Both recommendations have been endorsed by the DRC.

8.5.4 In *Ross v Ryanair Ltd and Stansted Airport Ltd* the Court of Appeal held that an airline and an airport operator were jointly liable under Part 3 of the Act for a failure to provide wheelchair access through the airport to the airplane for a mobility-impaired passenger.[298] In addition, the airline was liable for seeking to charge the disabled passenger for providing the auxiliary aid of a wheelchair. Because the duty to make reasonable adjustments is owed to disabled persons as a class, and not to any particular individual, it was irrelevant that the claimant might have the financial means to meet the charge. Nor did it matter that the service provider might be said to have treated other disabled persons (such as disabled passengers with their own wheelchair) more favourably. The service in question was not excluded by the use of any means of transport exemption in (what was then) s 19(5)(b).

8.6   DISABLED PERSONS' PARKING BADGES

8.6.1   The Disability Discrimination Act 2005 amends the Chronically Sick and Disabled Persons Act 1970, which established the disabled persons' parking badge ('blue badge') scheme in England and Wales.[299] This scheme provides for certain parking concessions to operate in favour of disabled people whose vehicles display blue badges. The new provisions provide that the holders of foreign disabled persons' badges shall be afforded the same concessions as holders of domestic blue badges in respect of parking concessions. The Act makes provision to formalise existing (non-statutory) recognition of parking badges issued in the EU or in certain other European countries (for which there is reciprocal recognition) and to extend this recognition to badges issued in other countries. Further discussion of these provisions is outside the scope of this book.

Meeting the Needs of Disabled People' (reviewed in 2006). At the end of 2007, DPTAC was consulting on designing and operating passenger vessels and passenger shore infrastructure, with a view to producing up-dated guidance on meeting the needs of persons with reduced mobility.

[297] DRTF Report, recommendation 7.9.

[298] [2004] EWCA Civ 1751. DDA 1995, ss 19(1)(b), 19(2)(a), 21(2)(d) and 21(4)(b) applied. See also Department of Transport, *Code of Practice: Access to Air Travel for Disabled People* (2003), para 2.14; Rights of Access Code of Practice (2006), paras 6.29 and 10.17.

[299] DDA 2005, s 9 (which does not apply in Scotland and Northern Ireland) inserting new ss 21A21C into the 1970 Act with effect from 30 June 2205 in England and 30 March 2008 in Wales.

CHAPTER 9

PUBLIC AUTHORITIES

9.1 LOCALLY-ELECTABLE AUTHORITIES AND THEIR MEMBERS

Introduction

9.1.1 Section 1 of the DDA 2005 inserted into the DDA 1995 new ss 15A–15C that deal with relationships between locally-electable authorities and their members (that is, the elected councillors).[1] These provisions came largely into force on 5 December 2005 and are fully effective as at 4 December 2006.[2] They are not presently supported by a revised statutory Code of Practice, although the *Code of Practice: Employment and Occupation* (2004) will be relevant by analogy.

Locally-elected authorities

9.1.2 The new rights and duties apply only to the following authorities: (a) the Greater London Authority;[3] (b) a county council (in England or Wales); (c) a county borough council (in Wales); (d) a district council (in England); (e) a London borough council; (f) the Common Council of the City of London; (g) the Council of the Isles of Scilly; (h) a council constituted under s 2 of the Local Government etc (Scotland) Act 1994 (that is, a council for a defined local government area in Scotland); (i) a parish council (in England); and (j) a community council (in Wales or Scotland).[4] In Northern Ireland, they will apply to district councils.

Authorities and their members: discrimination and harassment

9.1.3 From 5 December 2005, the provisions of s 15B of the DDA 1995 relating to discrimination and harassment apply to disabled members of local authorities. A local councillor or local authority member will not be

---

[1] So far as Northern Ireland is concerned, see Disability Discrimination (Northern Ireland) Order 2006, SI 2006/312, art 3. This provision is not yet in force.

[2] Disability Discrimination Act 2005 (Commencement No 2) Order 2005 SI 2005/2774, arts 3(a) and 4(a).

[3] A 'member' in relation to the Greater London Authority means the Mayor of London or a member of the London Assembly: DDA 1995, s 15A(3).

[4] Ibid, s 15A(1).

able to take advantage of the provisions relating to office-holders[5] or relating to relationships that have come to an end.[6] The provisions on discriminatory advertisements also do not apply here.[7]

9.1.4   It is unlawful for a locally-electable authority (as defined above) to discriminate against a disabled person who is a member of the authority in the opportunities which it affords the disabled person to receive training (or any other facility) for the carrying-out of official business by that person.[8] It is also unlawful for a locally-electable authority to discriminate against a disabled person who is a member of the authority by refusing to afford (or deliberately not affording) the disabled person any such opportunities.[9]

9.1.5   It is further unlawful for a locally-electable authority to discriminate against a disabled person who is a member of the authority by subjecting the disabled person to any other detriment in connection with the carrying-out of official business by that person.[10] For these purposes, a member of an authority is not subjected to a detriment by reason of not being appointed or elected to an office of the authority.[11] Similarly, a detriment does not arise by not being appointed or elected to a committee or sub-committee of the authority (or to an office of such committee or sub-committee).[12] Equally, it is not a detriment by not being appointed or nominated in exercise of any power of the authority (or of a group of bodies that includes the authority) to appoint (or nominate for appointment) to any body.[13]

9.1.6   It is unlawful for a relevant authority to subject a disabled person who is a member of the authority to harassment in connection with his or her carrying-out of official business.[14]

Interpretation

9.1.7   In the above contexts, the carrying-out of official business is a reference to the disabled person doing anything as a member of the authority; or as a member of any body to which the person is appointed by (or is appointed following nomination by) the authority or a group of bodies that includes the authority; or as a member of any other body if it is a public body.[15]

---

5   DDA 1995, ss 4C–4F by virtue of s 4C(2) and (5) as amended.
6   Ibid, s 16A by virtue of s 16A(2) as amended.
7   Ibid, s 16B by virtue of s 16B(2C) as amended.
8   Ibid, s 15B(1)(a).
9   Ibid, s 15B(1)(b).
10   Ibid, s 15B(1)(c).
11   Ibid, s 15B(3)(a).
12   Ibid, s 15B(3)(b).
13   Ibid, s 15B(3)(c).
14   Ibid, s 15B(2).
15   Ibid, s 15A(2).

9.1.8 A 'disabled person' is a person who satisfies the conditions of Part 1 of the DDA.[16]

9.1.9 The terms 'discrimination' and 'harassment' have the same meanings as they command in the employment field provisions of Part 2 of the DDA 1995.[17] It is not intended to reproduce those provisions here. The case law on the meaning of disability and in the area of employment discrimination will be equally applicable in the present context.

9.1.10 Although none have yet been made, regulations may make provision as to the circumstances in which disability-related less favourable treatment of a disabled member is to be taken to be justified (or is to be taken not to be justified).[18] Such regulations may provide for the justification defence to apply with prescribed modifications (or not to apply) for those purposes. However, the disability-related treatment of a disabled member cannot be justified if it amounts to direct discrimination.[19] Moreover, in a case of disability-related discrimination, if an authority is under a duty to make reasonable adjustments in relation to a disabled member, but fails to comply with that duty, its treatment of that person cannot be justified unless it would have been justified even if it had complied with that duty.[20]

Authorities and their members: duty to make adjustments

9.1.11 From 4 December 2006, s 15C of the DDA 1995 places a duty to make reasonable adjustments upon an authority in relation to its disabled members. The duty arises where a provision, criterion or practice applied by or on behalf of an authority places a disabled member at a substantial disadvantage, in comparison with members of the authority who are not disabled persons, in connection with the disabled person's carrying-out of official business.[21] The duty also arises where any physical feature of premises occupied by, or under the control of, such an authority places a disabled member at a substantial disadvantage, in comparison with members of the authority who are not disabled persons, in connection with the disabled person's carrying-out of official business.[22]

9.1.12 Where the duty arises, the authority must take such steps as it is reasonable, in all the circumstances of the case, for it to have to take in order to prevent the provision, criterion or practice (or physical feature, as the case might be) having that effect.[23] This does not impose any duty on an authority in relation to a disabled member if the authority does not

---

16   DDA 1995, ss 1–3 and Schs 1–2. See the discussion in Chapter 2.
17   Ibid, ss 3A (discrimination) and 3B (harassment). See the discussion in Chapter 3.
18   Ibid, s 15B(4).
19   Ibid, s 15B(5).
20   Ibid, s 15B(c). See s 15C discussed below.
21   Ibid, s 15C(1)(a).
22   Ibid, s 15C(1)(b).
23   Ibid, s 15C(2).

know (and could not reasonably be expected to know) that the member has a disability and is likely to be affected in the way described above (the comparative substantial disadvantage).[24]

9.1.13   The provisions relating to the duty to make reasonable adjustments in the employment field will apply to the duty as it arises in the context of local authorities and their members.[25] The case law and Code of Practice under those provisions will be equally of assistance.

9.1.14   Regulations may make provision as to circumstances in which a provision, criterion or practice (or physical feature) is to be taken to have (or not to have) the required effect. Regulations may also provide as to circumstances in which it is (or is not) reasonable for an authority to have to take steps of a prescribed description. They may make provision as to steps which it is always (or never) reasonable for an authority to have to take and as to things which are (or are not) to be treated as physical features. No such regulations have been made to date.[26]

9.2   DISCRIMINATION BY PUBLIC AUTHORITIES

9.2.1   Section 2 of the DDA 2005 inserted into the DDA 1995 new ss 21B–21E that deal with discrimination by public authorities in relation to the carrying out of their functions.[27] These provisions came partly into force on 5 December 2005 and are fully effective as at 4 December 2006.[28]

Public authority

9.2.2   Every public authority is covered by these provisions unless specifically excluded.[29] A 'public authority' includes any person certain of whose functions are functions of a public nature.[30] The concept covers a wide range of public bodies, including central government departments and agencies and local authorities.

9.2.3   The Code of Practice illustrates public authorities as including government (and devolved government) ministers and departments; executive agencies (such as the Prison Service and the Immigration and Nationality Directorate); local authorities; governing bodies of higher education institutions, colleges and universities; NHS trusts and boards; chief officers of police, police authorities, the Police Complaints

---

[24]   DDA 1995, s 15C(3).
[25]   Ibid, ss 18A–18E by virtue of s 18D(2) as amended. See Chapter 3.
[26]   Ibid, s 15C(4).
[27]   So far as Northern Ireland is concerned, see Disability Discrimination (Northern Ireland) Order 2006, SI 2006/312, art 4. This provision is not yet in force.
[28]   Disability Discrimination Act 2005 (Commencement No 2) Order 2005, SI 2005/2774, art 4(a).
[29]   Rights of Access Code of Practice 2006, para 11.5.
[30]   DDA 1995, s 21B(2)(a).

Authority and the Criminal Injuries Compensation Authority; the Crown Prosecution Service and the Crown Office; courts and tribunals; inspection and audit agencies (such as the National Audit Office, Her Majesty's Inspectorate of Constabulary and the Healthcare Commission; the Housing Corporation; and certain publicly funded museums and other cultural bodies or institutions).[31] This list is merely illustrative and not exhaustive.

Exclusions

9.2.4   However, the term does not include the following persons: either House of Parliament; a person exercising functions in connection with proceedings in Parliament; the Security Service; the Secret Intelligence Service; the Government Communications Headquarters; and a unit (or part of a unit) of any of the naval, military or air forces of the Crown which is for the time being required by the Secretary of State to assist the Government Communications Headquarters in carrying out its functions.[32]

Public functions and private acts

9.2.5   The term 'function' is used to describe the activities of a public authority. As the Code of Practice explains it, 'in principle, all the activities of a public authority are functions – these include activities such as those relating to employment of staff, budgeting decisions, or decisions on entitlement to the payment of state benefits'.[33]

9.2.6   In relation to a particular act, a person is not a public authority – by virtue only of being a person certain of whose functions are functions of a public nature – if the nature of the act is private.[34] For example, 'a private security company which runs a prison will be covered in respect of functions relating to the running of that prison, but will not be covered in respect of anything it carries out in a private capacity, such as the provision of security for banks'.[35] Regulations yet to be made may provide for a person of a prescribed description to be treated as not being a public authority for these purposes.[36]

Exclusions

9.2.7   Section 21B(1) does not apply to a judicial act (whether done by a court, tribunal or other person) or to an act done on the instructions of

---

[31]   Rights of Access Code of Practice 2006, paras 11.5–11.6.

[32]   DDA 1995, s 21B(2)(b) and (3).

[33]   Rights of Access Code of Practice 2006, para 11.8.

[34]   DDA 1995, s 21B(4).

[35]   Rights of Access Code of Practice 2006, paras 11.5 and 11.8.

[36]   DDA 1995, s 21B(5).

(or on behalf of) a person acting in a judicial capacity.[37] This means that a disabled litigant cannot challenge a judicial decision as an alleged act of disability discrimination. It may only be challenged through the available routes of review, judicial review or appeal, as the case may be. Similarly, where the act complained of was done by an administrator of the court or tribunal, but for or on the instructions of a judicial office-holder, the DDA 1995 does not provide a cause of action, although there might be recourse to a complaints procedure.

9.2.8 Section 21B(1) does not apply to any act of (or relating to) making, confirming or approving primary or secondary legislation.[38] This includes an Act of Parliament, an Act of the Scottish Parliament, a Measure or Act of the National Assembly for Wales[39] and an Order in Council. It also encompasses an instrument made under an Act of Parliament or under an Act of the Scottish Parliament or under a Measure or Act of the National Assembly for Wales[40] by a Minister of the Crown, a member of the Scottish Executive or the Welsh Ministers, the First Minister for Wales or the Counsel General to the Welsh Assembly Government.[41]

9.2.9 Section 21B(1) also does not apply to any act of (or relating to) imposing conditions or requirements of a kind falling within s 59(1)(c) of the DDA 1995 (that is, any act done to comply with any condition or requirement imposed by a Minister of the Crown, whether before or after the passing of the Act, by virtue of any enactment).[42]

9.2.10 Section 21B(1) does not apply to a decision not to institute criminal proceedings and an act done for the purpose of enabling the decision to be made.[43] It does not apply to a decision not to continue criminal proceedings or an act done for the purpose of enabling the decision to be made or an act done for the purpose of securing that the proceedings are not continued.[44] While the DDA 1995 will not provide relief, there might be other avenues of redress, such as by way of judicial review.[45]

---

[37] DDA 1995, s 21C(1); Rights of Access Code of Practice 2006, para 11.9 and examples.
[38] Ibid, s 21C(2) as amended by SI 2007/1388, art 3, Sch 1, paras 47, 50(a).
[39] From 25 May 2007, by virtue of SI 2007/1388, arts 1(2) and 3, Sch 1, paras 47, 50(a) and the Government of Wales Act 2006, ss 46 and 161(5).
[40] From 25 May 2007, by virtue of SI 2007/1388, arts 1(2) and 3, Sch 1, paras 47, 50(b)(i) and the Government of Wales Act 2006, ss 46 and 161(5).
[41] From 25 May 2007, by virtue of SI 2007/1388, arts 1(2) and 3, Sch 1, paras 47, 50(b)(ii) and the Government of Wales Act 2006, ss 46 and 161(5).
[42] DDA 1995, s 21C(3).
[43] Ibid, s 21C(4)(a) and (b).
[44] Ibid, s 21C(4)(c) and (d).
[45] Rights of Access Code of Practice 2006, para 11.9 and examples.

9.2.11 Section 21B(1) does not apply to an act of a prescribed description.[46] No prescription has been made to date.

Residual provisions

9.2.12 As the Code of Practice puts it, 'these public authority function provisions only apply where the treatment is not covered by any other part of the Act – in this sense they are '"residual" provisions'.[47] They do not apply to anything which is unlawful under any other provision of the DDA 1995.[48] Otherwise, there would be considerable overlap between the provisions regulating a public authority as an employer or service provider or education authority and a public authority carrying out its other functions.[49] For example, if a public authority discriminates against one of its employees, the correct cause of action is under the employment provisions of Part 2 of the DDA 1995 and not the public functions provisions of Part 3.[50]

9.2.13 In practice, the most difficult distinction to make is likely to be between the functions of a public authority and the services which it provides to the public in the discharge of those functions. Drawing the distinction will depend on all the circumstances of the case.[51] The functions of a public authority might require it to provide services to the public (such as a local authority providing refuse collection services). If the activity can properly be characterised as the supply of a service, then the service provisions of Part 3 of the DDA 1995 will apply, rather than the public authority functions provisions. Similarly, the premises provisions of Part 3 will apply to a local authority landlord.

9.2.14 The Code of Practice suggests,[52] arguably correctly, that 'activities covered by the public authority provisions are those activities which can only be carried out by public authorities and which are not similar in kind to the services that can be performed by private persons' (for example, the law enforcement functions of the police, in contrast with its crime prevention services) and that 'often, an authority will be acting under a statutory power or duty when performing such a function'. That is a helpful test of the distinction between functions and services.

9.2.15 Furthermore, subject to what follows below, the public authority function provisions do not apply to anything which would be unlawful under any other provision of the DDA 1995 but for the operation of any

---

[46] DDA 1995, s 21C(5).
[47] Rights of Access Code of Practice 2006, para 3.6.
[48] DDA 1995, s 21B(7)(a).
[49] Rights of Access Code of Practice 2006, para 11.3.
[50] Ibid, para 11.15 and example.
[51] Ibid, paras 11.20–11.23 and examples.
[52] Ibid, para 11.21 and examples.

provision in (or made under) the 1995 Act.[53] The Code of Practice gives the following example to illustrate the point. Under Part 4 of the DDA 1995 a school is not required to make reasonable adjustments to the physical features of its premises. The public authority function provisions in s 21B(1) cannot be used to ensure that a school makes physical changes to its premises in relation to education and associated services. This is because of the limitation in Part 4 on making changes to the physical features of a school's premises.[54]

9.2.16 Nevertheless, s 21B(1) can apply in relation to a public authority's function of appointing a person to an office or post.[55] It can also apply in relation to a public authority's functions with respect to a person as holder of such an office or post. However, in either case, s 21B(1) only applies if none of the conditions specified in s 4C(3) is satisfied in relation to the office or post *and* ss 4D and 4E would apply in relation to an appointment to the office or post if any of those conditions was satisfied.

9.2.17 The Code of Practice provides a good explanation of this difficult interaction of different statutory provisions.[56] The employment provisions of Part 2 of the DDA 1995 cover appointment to certain offices or posts. These are offices or posts where the individual provides personal service under the direction of another person in return for remuneration or where appointment is made by or on the recommendation of the Government or subject to its approval. A good example would be the holding of a judicial office. However, certain post-holders are not included within Part 2 because of the voluntary nature of the post (for example, a school governor). These posts do not meet the conditions necessary for the employment provisions to apply. Instead, the public authority function provisions apply. They will cover both the appointment of a person to the post and the functions of the public authority in relation to the person when in post.

9.2.18 Section 21B(1) will also apply in relation to a public authority's functions with respect to a person as a candidate or prospective candidate for election to an office or post if certain criteria are met.[57] It will also apply in relation to a public authority's functions with respect to a person as elected holder of such an office or post. The office or post must not be membership of a House of Parliament, the Scottish Parliament, the National Assembly for Wales or a locally-electable authority.[58] None of

---

[53] DDA 1995, s 21B(7)(b).

[54] Rights of Access Code of Practice 2006, paras 11.12 and 11.24 and example.

[55] DDA 1995, s 21B(8), without prejudice to the generality of s 21B(1), but subject to s 21C(5) (exclusion of acts of a prescribed description), s 21B(10).

[56] Rights of Access Code of Practice 2006, paras 11.16–11.17.

[57] DDA 1995, s 21B(9), without prejudice to the generality of s 21B(1), but subject to s 21C(5) (exclusion of acts of a prescribed description), s 21B(10).

[58] Ibid, s 21B(9)(a). A locally-electable authority is one mentioned in s 15A(1), discussed above.

the conditions specified in s 4C(3) must be satisfied in relation to the office or post.[59] Sections 4D and 4E must apply in relation to an appointment to the office or post if any of those conditions was satisfied and s 4F(1) (but not s 4C(5)) was omitted.[60]

9.2.19 Again, the Code of Practice provides a helpful account of this complex provision.[61] The intention is to embrace persons who are elected to an office or post where the employment provisions do not apply to the office or post and it is not an excluded office or post. The public authority function provisions will apply to the relevant public authority in relation to a candidate or prospective candidate for such an office or post and in relation to the successful candidate once in office or post. Thus, an election of parent school governors is covered by the public authority provisions and they also apply to the parent governor once elected. However, this does not extend to local councillors because they are provided for separately in Part 2 of the DDA 1995.

Discrimination by a public authority in relation to its functions

9.2.20 By virtue of s 21B(1) of the DDA 1995,[62] it is unlawful for a public authority to discriminate against a disabled person in carrying out its functions.[63]

Disability-related less favourable treatment

9.2.21 A public authority discriminates against a disabled person if, for a reason which relates to the disabled person's disability, it treats him less favourably than it treats (or would treat others) to whom that reason does not (or would not) apply and it cannot show that the treatment in question is justified.[64] This is the classic definition of unjustified disability-related less favourable treatment discrimination discussed in the earlier chapters on employment, services and premises.

9.2.22 Disability-related less favourable treatment is justified if, in the opinion of the public authority, one or more of four specified conditions

---

59 DDA 1995, s 21B(9)(b).
60 Ibid, s 21B(9)(c).
61 Rights of Access Code of Practice 2006, paras 11.18–11.19 and example.
62 In respect of an unlawful act that amounts to discrimination by victimisation under DDA 1995, s 55(1), s 21B(1) also applies to discrimination against a person who is not disabled: DDA 1995, s 21B(6).
63 DDA 1995, ss 21B–21E have been used successfully to challenge as discriminatory guidance issued by the National Institute for Health and Clinical Excellence (NICE) in respect of the appraisal and cost effectiveness of drugs for treating Alzheimer's Disease: *Eisai Ltd v NICE and ors* [2007] EWHC 1941 (Admin) (no proper consideration was given to NICE's duties as a public authority to promote equal opportunities and to have due regard to the need to eliminate discrimination).
64 Ibid, s 21D(1) and Rights of Access Code of Practice 2006, paras 11.28–11.31 and examples.

are satisfied and it is reasonable, in all the circumstances of the case, for it to hold that opinion.[65] This justification defence has many similarities to that available in services and premises cases, discussed in earlier chapters. Regulations may provide as to the circumstances in which it is (or is not) reasonable for a public authority to hold the relevant opinion.[66] No regulations have been made to date.

9.2.23   The specified *alternative* conditions are as follows. First, that the treatment is necessary in order not to endanger the health or safety of any person (which may include that of the disabled person).[67] Secondly, that the disabled person is incapable of entering into an enforceable agreement, or of giving an informed consent, and for that reason the treatment is reasonable in the particular case.[68] However, this particular defence is not available where another person is acting for the disabled person by virtue of a power of attorney or its equivalent.[69] Thirdly, that treating the disabled person equally favourably would in the particular case involve substantial extra costs and, having regard to resources, the extra costs in that particular case would be too great.[70] Finally, that the treatment is necessary for the protection of rights and freedoms of other persons.[71]

9.2.24   Disability-related less favourable treatment is also justified if the acts of the public authority which give rise to the treatment are a proportionate means of achieving a legitimate aim.[72] Regulations may also make provision as to the circumstances in which disability-related less favourable treatment is to be taken to be justified.[73] No regulations have been made to date.

9.2.25   As the Code of Practice records, the principle of proportionality is an accepted principle of administrative law. Public authorities have to choose between a number of courses of action. The Code of Practice suggests that a public authority 'is only able to rely on this justification in relation to those matters of public interest (for example, the detection of

---

[65]   DDA 1995, s 21D(3).

[66]   Ibid, s 21D(6).

[67]   Ibid, s 21D(4)(a).

[68]   Ibid, s 21D(4)(b).

[69]   Disability Discrimination (Service Providers and Public Authorities Carrying Out Functions) Regulations 2005, SI 2005/2901, reg 3 (made under DDA 1995, s 21D(7)(a)). This exclusion also applies where a person is acting for the disabled person by virtue of functions conferred by or under Part 7 of the Mental Health Act 1983 or powers exercisable in relation to the disabled person's property or affairs in consequence of the appointment, under the law of Scotland, of a guardian, tutor or judicial factor.

[70]   DDA 1995, s 21D(4)(c) and Rights of Access Code of Practice 2006, paras 11.50–11.52 and example.

[71]   DDA 1995, s 21D(4)(d) and Rights of Access Code of Practice 2006, paras 11.53 and example.

[72]   DDA 1995, s 21D(5) and Rights of Access Code of Practice 2006, paras 11.54–11.56 and example.

[73]   DDA 1995, s 21D(7)(c).

crime) which, on an objective assessment of proportionality, can be said to be sufficiently important to override the right not to be discriminated against'.[74] It also asserts that 'to demonstrate that an act is a proportionate means of achieving a legitimate aim, the public authority must show that ... there is a pressing policy need that supports the aim which the treatment is designed to achieve, and it is therefore a "legitimate" aim; and the authority's action is causally related to achieving that aim; and there was no other way to achieve the aim that had a less detrimental impact on the rights of disabled people'.[75]

Failure to make reasonable adjustments

9.2.26 A public authority also discriminates against a disabled person if it unjustifiably fails to comply with its duty to make reasonable adjustments under s 21E of the DDA 1995.[76] Discrimination arises where the effect of that failure is to make it impossible or unreasonably difficult for the disabled person to receive any benefit that is or may be conferred by the carrying-out of a function by the authority. Discrimination also arises where the effect of that failure is to make it unreasonably adverse for the disabled person to experience being subjected to any detriment to which a person is (or may be) subjected by the carrying-out of a function by the authority.[77]

9.2.27 It is for the public authority to show that its failure to comply with the duty to make reasonable adjustments is justified. A failure to comply with the duty to make reasonable adjustments is justified if, in the opinion of the public authority, one or more of three specified conditions are satisfied and it is reasonable, in all the circumstances of the case, for it to hold that opinion.[78] This justification defence has many similarities to that available in services and premises cases, discussed in earlier chapters. Regulations may provide as to the circumstances in which it is (or is not) reasonable for a public authority to hold the relevant opinion.[79] No regulations have been made to date.

9.2.28 The specified *alternative* conditions are as follows. First, that the non-compliance is necessary in order not to endanger the health or safety of any person (which may include that of the disabled person).[80]

---

74   Rights of Access Code of Practice 2006, para 11.55.
75   Rights of Access Code of Practice 2006, para 11.56 and example.
76   DDA 1995, s 21D(2) and Rights of Access Code of Practice 2006, para 11.32. Nothing in s 21E requires a public authority to take any steps which, apart from s 21E, it has no power to take: s 21E(9) and Rights of Access Code of Practice 2006, para 11.57 and example. It imposes duties only for the purposes of determining whether a public authority has, for the purposes of s 21B(1), discriminated against a disabled person. A breach of any such duty is not actionable as such: s 21E(1).
77   Rights of Access Code of Practice 2006, paras 11.33–11.40.
78   DDA 1995, s 21D(3).
79   Ibid, s 21D(6).
80   Ibid, s 21D(4)(a).

Secondly, that the disabled person is incapable of entering into an enforceable agreement, or of giving an informed consent, and for that reason the non-compliance is reasonable in the particular case.[81] However, this particular defence is not available where another person is acting for the disabled person by virtue of a power of attorney or its equivalent.[82] Finally, that the non-compliance is necessary for the protection of rights and freedoms of other persons.[83]

9.2.29 A failure to comply with the duty to make reasonable adjustments is also justified if the acts of the public authority which give rise to the failure are a proportionate means of achieving a legitimate aim.[84] Regulations may also make provision as to the circumstances in which a failure to comply is to be taken to be justified.[85] No regulations have been made to date. See the discussion at **9.2.25** above.

Duty to make reasonable adjustments

Practices, policies or procedures

9.2.30 The duty of a public authority to make reasonable adjustments when carrying out its functions arises where it has a practice, policy or procedure which makes it impossible or unreasonably difficult for disabled persons to receive any benefit that is (or may be) conferred by the carrying-out of a function by the authority.[86] It also arises where it has a practice, policy or procedure which makes it unreasonably adverse for disabled persons to experience being subjected to any detriment to which a person is (or may be) subjected by the carrying-out of a function by the authority.[87] Where the duty thus arises, it is the duty of the authority to take such steps as it is reasonable, in all the circumstances of the case, for the authority to have to take in order to change that practice, policy or procedure so that it no longer has that effect.[88]

---

[81] DDA 1995, s 21D(4)(b).

[82] Disability Discrimination (Service Providers and Public Authorities Carrying Out Functions) Regulations 2005, SI 2005/2901, reg 3 (made under DDA 1995, s 21D(7)(a)). This exclusion also applies where a person is acting for the disabled person by virtue of functions conferred by or under Part 7 of the Mental Health Act 1983 or powers exercisable in relation to the disabled person's property or affairs in consequence of the appointment, under the law of Scotland, of a guardian, tutor or judicial factor.

[83] DDA 1995, s 21D(4)(d) and Rights of Access Code of Practice 2006, para 11.53 and example.

[84] DDA 1995, s 21D(5) and Rights of Access Code of Practice 2006, paras 11.54–11.56 and example.

[85] DDA 1995, s 21D(7)(c).

[86] Ibid, s 21E(1)(a).

[87] Ibid, s 21E(1)(b).

[88] Ibid, s 21E(2) and Rights of Access Code of Practice 2006, para 11.41 and example.

Physical features of premises

9.2.31 The duty of a public authority to make reasonable adjustments when carrying out its functions also arises where a physical feature makes it impossible or unreasonably difficult for disabled persons to receive any benefit that is (or may be) conferred by the carrying-out of a function by a public authority.[89] It also arises where a physical feature makes it unreasonably adverse for disabled persons to experience being subjected to any detriment to which a person is (or may be subjected) by the carrying-out of a function by a public authority.[90] In either case, it is the duty of the authority to take such steps as it is reasonable, in all the circumstances of the case, for the authority to have to take in order to (a) remove the feature; or (b) alter it so that it no longer has that effect; or (c) provide a reasonable means of avoiding the feature; or (d) adopt a reasonable alternative method of carrying out the function.[91]

9.2.32 The Disability Discrimination (Service Providers and Public Authorities Carrying Out Functions) Regulations 2005 make provision in respect of a public authority's duty to make reasonable adjustments to physical features of premises.[92] The regulations define what is meant by physical features, prescribe what is reasonable where the consent of a third party is necessary for an adjustment to physical features of premises and prescribe reasonableness in relation to design standards (including removal or alteration of physical features). They also amend the Disability Discrimination (Providers of Services) (Adjustments of Premises) Regulations 2001 so that they apply equally to a public authority carrying out its functions as they do to a provider of services. The result is a common code in respect of reasonable adjustments to physical features of premises applying to service providers, public authorities and private clubs. These provisions have been discussed in Chapter 6 and are not rehearsed here.

Auxiliary aids or services

9.2.33 The duty of a public authority to make reasonable adjustments when carrying out its functions further arises where an auxiliary aid or service would enable disabled persons to receive (or facilitate the receiving by disabled persons of) any benefit that is or may be conferred by the carrying-out of a function by a public authority.[93] It also arises where an

---

[89] DDA 1995, s 21E(3)(a).

[90] Ibid, s 21E(3)(b).

[91] Ibid, s 21E(4) and Rights of Access Code of Practice 2006, paras 11.44–11.45 and examples. Regulations may prescribe matters which are to be taken into account in determining whether any provision of a kind mentioned in s 21E(4)(c) or (d) is reasonable or categories of public authorities to whom s 21E(4) does not apply: s 21E(5). No regulations have been made to date.

[92] SI 2005/2901, regs 9–11 and 13, and Sch 1, made under DDA 1995, s 21E(8)(a) and (d). In Northern Ireland, see SR 2007/473.

[93] DDA 1995, s 21E(6)(a).

auxiliary aid or service would reduce the extent to which it is adverse for disabled persons to experience being subjected to any detriment to which a person is or may be subjected by the carrying-out of a function by a public authority.[94] In either case, it is the duty of the authority to take such steps as it is reasonable, in all the circumstances of the case, for the authority to have to take in order to provide that auxiliary aid or service.[95]

9.3 DUTIES OF PUBLIC AUTHORITIES

9.3.1 Section 3 of the DDA 2005 inserted a new Part 5A into the DDA 1995. This new part comprises ss 49A–49F. These sections deal with the duties of public authorities in relation to disabled persons and disability discrimination. These provisions have been brought into force in stages, but are fully effective from 4 December 2006.[96]

General duty

9.3.2 Section 49A(1) places a general duty upon every public authority when carrying out its functions to have due regard to certain matters. Those matters are the need to:

- eliminate discrimination that is unlawful under this Act;

- eliminate harassment of disabled persons that is related to their disabilities;

- promote equality of opportunity between disabled persons and other persons;

- take steps to take account of disabled persons' disabilities, even where that involves treating disabled persons more favourably than other persons;

- promote positive attitudes towards disabled persons; and

- encourage participation by disabled persons in public life.[97]

The general duty is without prejudice to any obligation of a public authority to comply with any other provision of the DDA 1995.[98]

---

[94] DDA 1995, s 21E(6)(b).

[95] Ibid, s 21E(7) and Rights of Access Code of Practice 2006, paras 11.42–11.43 and examples.

[96] See SI 2005/1676 and SI 2005/2774. Similar, but extensively modified, provision is made in Northern Ireland by the Disability Discrimination (Northern Ireland) Order 2006, SI 2006/312, art 5. The account below should be read with care in the Northern Ireland context, where in any event the relevant duties are not yet in force.

[97] DDA 1995, s 49A(1)(a)–(f).

[98] Ibid, s 49A(2).

Public authority

9.3.3 For this purpose, a 'public authority' includes any person certain of whose functions are functions of a public nature.[99] In relation to a particular act, a person is not a public authority by virtue only of this provision if the nature of the act is private.[100]

9.3.4 A 'public authority' does not include either House of Parliament; a person exercising functions in connection with proceedings in Parliament; the Security Service; the Secret Intelligence Service; the Government Communications Headquarters; a unit (or part of a unit) of any of the naval, military or air forces of the Crown which is for the time being required by the Secretary of State to assist the Government Communications Headquarters in carrying out its functions; the Scottish Parliament; a person, other than the Scottish Parliamentary Corporate Body, exercising functions in connection with proceedings in the Scottish Parliament; the National Assembly for Wales; or a person, other than the National Assembly for Wales Commission, exercising functions in connection with proceedings in the National Assembly for Wales.[101] Regulations may provide for a person of a prescribed description to be treated as not being a public authority for these purposes, but no regulations have been made to date.[102]

Exclusions

9.3.5 The general duty in s 49A(1) does not apply to a judicial act (whether done by a court, tribunal or other person) or an act done on the instructions (or on behalf) of a person acting in a judicial capacity.[103] It does not apply to any act of (or relating to) making or approving an Act of Parliament, an Act of the Scottish Parliament, a Measure or Act of the National Assembly for Wales or an Order in Council.[104] Regulations may provide for the general duty not to apply to a relevant act of a prescribed description, but no prescription has been made to date.[105]

9.3.6 So far as an act done in connection with recruitment to any of the naval, military or air forces of the Crown or an act done in relation to a person in connection with service by him or her as a member of any of those forces is concerned, the general duty is not as extensive as usual. In those cases only, the general duty does not extend to the need to promote equality of opportunity between disabled persons and other persons or to

---

[99] DDA 1995, s 49B(1)(a).
[100] Ibid, s 49B(2).
[101] Ibid, s 49B(1)(b) (as amended from 25 May 2007 by SI 2007/1388), including a cross-reference to s 21B(3).
[102] Ibid, s 49B(3).
[103] Ibid, s 49C(1).
[104] Ibid, s 49C(2) as amended by SI 2007/1388 from 25 May 2007.
[105] Ibid, s 49C(4) as amended by the Equality Act 2006, s 88 from 18 April 2006.

take steps to take account of disabled persons' disabilities (that is, even where that involves treating disabled persons more favourably than other persons).[106]

Specific duties

9.3.7   By the use of regulations, the Secretary of State may impose on a public authority (other than a relevant Scottish authority or a cross-border authority[107]) such duties as the Secretary of State considers appropriate for the purpose of ensuring the better performance by that authority of its general duty in relation to disabled persons.[108] Separate regulation-making powers are vested in the Secretary of State and the Scottish Ministers in relation to a relevant Scottish authority or a cross-border authority.[109] In any of these cases, the person making the regulations shall first consult the Commission for Equality and Human Rights (originally the Disability Rights Commission).[110] Provision is also made for consultation with or the consent of the Welsh or Scottish Ministers (and the Secretary of State) in the appropriate case.[111]

9.3.8   Regulations have been made. So far as Great Britain as a whole is concerned, the relevant regulations are the Disability Discrimination (Public Authorities) (Statutory Duties) Regulations 2005 as amended.[112] In Scotland, the Disability Discrimination (Public Authorities) (Statutory Duties) (Scotland) Regulations 2005 have been made and amended.[113] The account below focuses upon the position in the UK and not upon the particular provisions made in Scotland, although the position in Scotland is analogous. The prospective position in Northern Ireland is outlined further below. The regulations are supported by very extensive statutory codes of practice prepared by the Disability Rights Commission.[114]

Disability Equality Schemes

9.3.9   The Disability Discrimination (Public Authorities) (Statutory Duties) Regulations 2005 came into force on 5 December 2005. The regulations apply to those public authorities that are listed in Sch 1 to the

---

[106] DDA 1995, s 49C(3) by cross-reference to s 49A(1)(c) and (d).
[107] Ibid, s 49D(10).
[108] Ibid, s 49D(1).
[109] Ibid, s 49D(2)–(4).
[110] Ibid, s 49D(5) as amended by the Equality Act 2006, s 40 and Sch 3, paras 41 and 48.
[111] Ibid, s 49D(6)–(9).
[112] SI 2005/2966 as amended by the Disability Discrimination (Public Authorities) (Statutory Duties) (Amendment) Regulations 2007, SI 2007/618.
[113] SSI 2005/565 as amended by the Disability Discrimination (Public Authorities) (Statutory Duties) (Scotland) Amendment Regulations 2007, SSI 2007/195.
[114] The Duty to Promote Disability Equality: Statutory Code of Practice: England and Wales (2005) and The Duty to Promote Disability Equality: Statutory Code of Practice: Scotland (2006).

regulations.[115] This ensures that a very wide range of public bodies and authorities, including educational authorities and establishments, are embraced by the duty to publish a Disability Equality Scheme, explained below. The Disability Rights Commission estimated that some 45,000 public authorities in Great Britain would be covered.

Publication of a Disability Equality Scheme

9.3.10 A listed public authority shall publish a Disability Equality Scheme.[116] A Disability Equality Scheme is a scheme showing how the public authority intends to fulfil its duty under s 49A(1) of the DDA 1995 and its duties under the 2005 Regulations. The obligation to publish such a scheme is to be fulfilled on or before the relevant publication date. That date varies according to where the public authority is listed in Sch 1 and will be on a specified date between 4 December 2006 and 3 December 2007.[117] A public authority may comply with the duty to publish its scheme by setting it out as part of another published document or within a number of other published documents.[118]

Involvement of disabled people

9.3.11 A public authority obliged to publish a Disability Equality Scheme shall involve in the development of the scheme disabled people who appear to that authority to have an interest in the way it carries out its functions.[119] The scheme shall include a statement of the ways in which such interested disabled people have been involved in its development.[120] The scheme shall state the public authority's methods for assessing the impact of its policies and practices (or the likely impact of its proposed policies and practices) on equality for disabled persons.[121] It must also set out the steps which that authority proposes to take towards the fulfilment of its s 49A(1) duty (in other words, an action plan).[122]

Information

9.3.12 The scheme must contain a statement of the public authority's arrangements for gathering information on the effect of its policies and practices on disabled persons.[123] Particular attention must be given to its arrangements for gathering information on the effect of its policies and practices on the recruitment, development and retention of its disabled

---

[115] As amended by SI 2006/594 and SI 2007/618.
[116] SI 2005/2966, reg 2(1).
[117] Ibid, reg 2(6).
[118] Ibid, reg 2(5).
[119] Ibid, reg 2(2).
[120] Ibid, reg 2(3)(a).
[121] Ibid, reg 2(3)(b).
[122] Ibid, reg 2(3)(c).
[123] Ibid, reg 2(3)(d).

employees;[124] for specified authorities, on the educational opportunities available to (and on the achievements of) disabled pupils and students;[125] and for specified authorities, the extent to which the services it provides and those other functions it performs take account of the needs of disabled persons.[126] Finally, the statement must address that authority's arrangements for making use of such information to assist it in the performance of its s 49A(1) duty and, in particular, its arrangements for reviewing on a regular basis the effectiveness of the steps which it proposes to take towards the fulfilment of that duty, and preparing subsequent schemes.[127]

Review and revision of a Disability Equality Scheme

9.3.13 A relevant public authority must review its Disability Equality Scheme not later than the end of the period of three years beginning with the date of publication of its first scheme.[128] It must then publish a revised scheme within the same timescale. Thereafter it must review the scheme (and publish a revised scheme) subsequently at intervals of not more than three years beginning with the date of publication of the last revision of the scheme.[129] A public authority may comply with the duty to publish its revised scheme by setting it out as part of another published document or within a number of other published documents.[130]

Implementation of a Disability Equality Scheme

9.3.14 Within three years of the relevant publication date in relation to a Disability Equality Scheme, a listed public authority shall take the steps which it has been required to set out in the scheme – that is, the steps which that authority proposes to take towards the fulfilment of its s 49A(1) duty.[131] It shall also put into effect its arrangements (which it has been required to set out in the scheme) for gathering information and making use of such information.[132] However, these particular duties of implementation are not imposed on an authority where, in all the circumstances, it would be unreasonable or impracticable for it to perform the duty.[133]

---

[124] SI 2005/2966, reg 2(3)(d)(i).
[125] Ibid, reg 2(3)(d)(ii).
[126] Ibid, reg 2(3)(d)(iii).
[127] Ibid, reg 2(3)(e).
[128] Ibid, reg 2(4)(a).
[129] Ibid, reg 2(4)(b).
[130] Ibid, reg 2(5).
[131] Ibid, reg 3(1)(a).
[132] Ibid, reg 3(1)(b).
[133] Ibid, reg 3(2).

Annual reporting

9.3.15 A listed public authority shall publish a report not later than the end of the period of one year beginning with the date of publication of its first scheme and subsequently at intervals of not more than one year beginning with the date of publication of the last report.[134] Such a report may be set out in another published document.[135] The report shall contain a summary of the steps the authority has taken towards the fulfilment of its s 49A(1) duty.[136] It shall also summarise the results of the information-gathering it has carried out and the use it has made of such information it has gathered.[137]

Duty on reporting authorities

9.3.16 Certain public authorities – referred to as 'reporting authorities' – have additional reporting duties. These are the authorities set out in Sch 2 to the regulations.[138] They are the National Assembly for Wales and the Secretaries of State for Communities and Local Government; for Constitutional Affairs; for Culture, Media and Sport; for Education and Skills; for Environment, Food and Rural Affairs; for Health; for the Home Department; for Trade and Industry; for Transport; and for Work and Pensions.[139]

9.3.17 In respect of its 'policy sector', a reporting authority shall publish a report not later than 1 December 2008 and subsequently not later than the end of each successive period of three years beginning with 1 December 2008.[140] The term 'policy sector' means the sector of public activity in which the reporting authority carries out public functions.[141] The report shall give an overview of progress towards equality of opportunity between disabled persons and other persons made by public authorities operating in the policy sector.[142] It shall set out the reporting authority's proposals for the coordination of action by public authorities operating in that sector so as to bring about further progress towards equality of opportunity between disabled persons and other persons.[143]

Enforcement of general and specific duties of public authorities

9.3.18 The general and specific duties placed upon public authorities create no additional enforceable rights or remedies for individual disabled

---

[134] SI 2005/2966, reg 4(1).
[135] Ibid, reg 4(3).
[136] Ibid, reg 4(2)(a).
[137] Ibid, reg 4(2)(b) and (c).
[138] Ibid, reg 5(3).
[139] Ibid, Sch 2, as amended by SI 2006/1926.
[140] Ibid, reg 5(1).
[141] Ibid, reg 5(3).
[142] Ibid, reg 5(2)(a).
[143] Ibid, reg 5(2)(b).

persons. A failure by a public authority to comply with its general duty under s 49A(1) may be the subject of judicial review proceedings.[144] In addition, the Commission for Human Rights and Equality may assess the extent to which (or the manner in which) a public authority has complied with its general or specific duty in relation to disabled persons and report accordingly.[145]

9.3.19 Where the Commission thinks that a public authority has failed to comply with a general or specific duty in relation to disabled persons, it may give the public authority a notice requiring it to comply with the duty and to give the Commission, within the period of 28 days, written information of steps taken or proposed for the purpose of complying with the duty.[146] That notice may require the public authority to give the Commission information required by the Commission for the purposes of assessing compliance with the duty. If so, the notice shall specify the period within which the information is to be given (not exceeding three months), and the manner and form in which the information is to be given.[147] The Commission may not give such a notice unless it first carried out a s 31 assessment and the notice relates to the results of the assessment.[148]

9.3.20 The public authority is obliged to comply with the notice,[149] except to give information that it is prohibited from disclosing by virtue of an enactment or that it could not be compelled to give in proceedings before the High Court or the Court of Session.[150] If the Commission thinks that the public authority, to whom a notice has been given, has failed to comply with a requirement of the notice, it may apply to the High Court (or, in Scotland, the Court of Session) for an order requiring the person to comply.[151]

Public authorities in Northern Ireland

9.3.21 The general and specific duties of public authorities in Northern Ireland in relation to disabled people are not yet in force.[152] When they are

---

[144] In *R on the application of Chavda and ors v London Borough of Harrow* [2007] EWHC 3064 (Admin), a local authority's decision to restrict adult care services to people with critical needs only was challenged on a number of grounds, including that its decision-making process did not comply with its disability equality duty under DDA 1995, s 49A. The court concluded that the relevance of the duty had not been drawn to the attention of the decision-makers and that the consequent decision was unlawful.

[145] Equality Act 2006, s 31 and Sch 2.

[146] Ibid, s 32(1) and (2).

[147] Ibid, s 32(3).

[148] Ibid, s 32(4).

[149] Ibid, s 32(5).

[150] Ibid, s 32(6).

[151] Ibid, s 32(8) and (9).

[152] See the Disability Discrimination (Northern Ireland) Order 2006, SI 2006/312, art 5 inserting particularly worded ss 49A and 49B only into the DDA 1995 as it applies in Northern Ireland.

brought into force, they will operate in a slightly different way from the duties in Great Britain and in Scotland. That is because when carrying out its functions a Northern Ireland public authority is already obliged, among other duties to promote equality, to have due regard to the need to promote equality of opportunity between persons with a disability and persons without.[153]

9.3.22 In Northern Ireland, every public authority shall in carrying out its functions have due regard to the need to promote positive attitudes towards disabled persons and the need to encourage participation by disabled persons in public life.[154] This is without prejudice to any obligation of a public authority to comply with any other statutory provision.[155] The general duty will not apply to the functions of the Director of Public Prosecutions for Northern Ireland relating to the prosecution of offences or any act of a description prescribed by regulations.[156] It will apply to any public authority except one which is notified in writing by the Commission that the duty does not apply to it.[157]

9.3.23 The Equality Commission for Northern Ireland shall keep under review the effectiveness of the general duty and offer advice to public authorities and others in connection with that duty.[158] Not later than three years after the coming into force of these provisions in Northern Ireland (the appointed day), the Commission shall prepare and publish a report on the effectiveness of the duty imposed by this section.[159]

9.3.24 In Northern Ireland, from dates to be determined, a public authority shall prepare and submit to the Commission a plan showing how the public authority proposes to fulfil the duty imposed by s 49A in relation to its functions.[160] Any other public authority shall prepare and submit to the Commission such a plan if requested to do so by the Commission.[161] In that case, the request may specify particular functions that are to be the subject of the plan.[162]

9.3.25 A public authority in Northern Ireland may at any time revise its plan and submit the revised plan to the Commission.[163] In any event, the Commission may request it to revise its plan and submit the revised plan

---

[153] Northern Ireland Act 1998, s 75.
[154] DDA 1995, s 49A(1) (NI). A public authority is one defined in the Northern Ireland Act 1998, s 75.
[155] DDA 1995, s 49A(3) (NI).
[156] Ibid, s 49A(2) (NI).
[157] Ibid, s 49A(5) (NI).
[158] Ibid, s 49A(4) (NI).
[159] Ibid, s 49A(5) (NI).
[160] Ibid, s 49B(1) and (8) (NI).
[161] Ibid, s 49B(2) (NI).
[162] Ibid, s 49B(8) (NI).
[163] Ibid, s 49B(3)(a) (NI).

to the Commission.[164] A plan (or revised plan) shall conform to any guidelines as to form or content which are issued by the Commission with the approval of the Office of the First Minister and Deputy First Minister; specify a timetable for measures proposed in the plan; and include details of how it will be published.[165]

9.3.26 If a Northern Ireland public authority fails to submit a plan before the end of the period of six months beginning with the appointed day (or, if later, the establishment of the authority), the Commission shall lay before the Assembly a report of that failure containing such comments and other material as appear to the Commission to be appropriate to bring to the attention of the Assembly.[166] The same action will be taken where a public authority fails to submit a plan in response to a statutory request by the Commission before the end of the period of six months beginning with the date of the request; or fails to submit a revised plan in response to the Commission's request before the end of the period of three months beginning with the date of the request; or submits to the Commission a revised plan which in the opinion of the Commission fails to comply with the statutory requirements.[167]

9.3.27 In Northern Ireland, a public authority shall review its current plan under s 49B of the DDA 1995 at the same time as the authority reviews its current equality scheme in relation to the promotion of equal opportunities generally.[168] In the case of any other authority, it shall review its plan at such times as the Commission may request.[169] In either event, the public authority shall inform the Commission of the outcome of the review.[170]

---

[164] DDA 1995, s 49B(3)(b) (NI).
[165] Ibid, s 49B(4) (NI).
[166] Ibid, s 49B(6)(a) (NI).
[167] Ibid, s 49B(6)(b), (c) and (d) (NI).
[168] Ibid, s 49B(7)(a)(i) (NI). See Northern Ireland Act 1998, s 75 and Sch 9, para 8(3).
[169] DDA 1995, s 49B(7)(a)(ii) (NI).
[170] Ibid, s 49B(7)(b) (NI).

CHAPTER 10

LIABILITY AND REMEDIES

10.1 VICTIMISATION

10.1.1 For the purposes of Part 2 (the employment field) or Part 3 (provision of services, functions of public authorities, private clubs, and premises) and Part 4 (education) of the DDA 1995, a person is discriminated against if he or she is victimised by another person in connection with the exercise of any rights contained within the Act.[1] The concept of liability arising from the victimisation of a person because he or she sought to exercise statutory rights is one which is established in discrimination law and in employment law generally.[2] The victimisation provisions in the DDA 1995 are drafted in a slightly different way from the other discrimination statutes, but the case-law under the comparable provisions of other discrimination statutes will be informative.[3]

10.1.2 A complaint of victimisation is separate and different from any earlier complaint of discrimination which is said to have informed the later act of victimisation.[4] However, it does not create any cause of action in or of itself. It is not a free-standing provision. It merely defines an additional form of discrimination for the purposes of acts which are made unlawful (if at all) by Part 2, 3 or 4 of the Act. It does not (without more) provide that discrimination by way of victimisation is unlawful *per se*.[5]

10.1.3 A person (A) discriminates against another person (B) if A treats B less favourably than A treats or would treat other persons whose

---

[1] DDA 1995, s 55, as amended by SENDA 2001, Disability Discrimination Act 1995 (Amendment) Regulations 2003, Disability Discrimination Act (Pensions) Regulations 2003 and DDA 2005 (and in Northern Ireland by SI 2005/1117 and SI 2006/312). Separate provisions apply in relation to premises to let and let premises (ss 24A to 24M): DDA 1995, s 24F (discussed in Chapter 6).

[2] See, e g SDA 1975, s 4; RRA 1976, s 2; ERA 1996, s 104.

[3] HC Deb Standing Committee E, cols 425–426. See, e g *Bradford Hospitals NHS Trust v Al-Shabib* [2003] IRLR 4, EAT; *Jiad v Byford* [2003] IRLR 232, CA; *Visa International Service Association v Paul* [2004] IRLR 42, EAT; *St Helens MBC v Derbyshire* [2007] IRLR 540, HL.

[4] *Air Canada and Alpha Catering Services v Basra* [2000] IRLR 683, EAT.

[5] *Bruce v Addleshaw Booth & Co* (EAT/0404/03, 11 February 2004).

circumstances are the same as B's and A does so for one of a number of reasons.[6] Those alternative reasons are:[7]

- B has brought proceedings against A or any other person (C) under the Act;

- B has given evidence or information in connection with proceedings brought by a person (D) against A or C under the Act;

- B has otherwise done anything under or by reference to the Act in relation to A or any other person (C);

- B has alleged (expressly or impliedly) that A or C has contravened the Act;

- A believes or suspects that B has done or intends to do any of the above things.

The effect is to treat the listed forms of victimisation as amounting to acts of discrimination for the purpose of establishing an ingredient of acts made unlawful under the relevant provisions of Part 2, 3 or 4 of the DDA 1995.

10.1.4 However, victimisation of B by A in any of these circumstances is not made unlawful solely by virtue of the victimisation provisions if the less favourable treatment of B by A is because of an allegation made by B which was false and not made in good faith.[8] Furthermore, if the person being victimised (B) is a disabled person or a person who has had a disability, the disability in question is to be disregarded when comparing B's circumstances with those of any other person who is the comparator for judging A's less favourable treatment of B.[9] It is also clear that a tribunal or court could determine how B has been treated in comparison with a hypothetical comparator.[10]

10.1.5 Where B brings an action alleging unlawful discrimination by dint of victimisation, it does not matter whether B is or is not a disabled person within the meaning of the DDA 1995. The victimisation provisions provide the only basis for a cause of action under the Act for a person who either does not satisfy the definition of a disabled person in Part 1 or who is not a disabled person at all.[11]

---

[6]   DDA 1995, s 55(1), as amended.

[7]   Ibid, s 55(2), as amended. For the purposes of DDA 1995, Part 4, Chapter 1 only (ie the provisions affecting schools), references in s 55(2) to B include references to a person who is (for the purposes of that Chapter) B's parent, and a sibling of B: DDA 1995, s 55(3A), as inserted.

[8]   Ibid, s 55(4).

[9]   Ibid, s 55(3).

[10]   HC Deb Standing Committee E, col 426.

[11]   However, in the employment field, the Advocate General of the ECJ has opined that EU

10.1.6 The victimisation provisions of the DDA 1995 will or should catch the following illustrations:[12]

- B, a disabled person, is dismissed by A (his or her employer) because B took A to an employment tribunal under the Act for refusing him or her access to a training opportunity or a promotion;

- B, a non-disabled person, is demoted and receives a cut in pay because he or she gave evidence in court proceedings brought under the Act against A (B's employer) by C (a disabled person) who had been refused service in A's restaurant because C was a wheelchair-user;

- B, a disabled tenant of A (a local authority landlord), is evicted from his or her rented flat or removed from the housing list by A because B wrote to the local press complaining that A was failing to make provision under the Act to allow disabled persons physical access to the local community centre;

- B, a non-disabled activist on disability rights, is refused entry to A's cinema because B had picketed the cinema, alleging that it was physically inaccessible to disabled persons, contrary to the Act;

- B, a non-disabled pupil, is denied a part in a school play because he or she acted as a witness in support of a complaint against a school by a disabled pupil to the SENDIST.

10.1.7 However, judicial interpretation of the victimisation provisions in discrimination law at large demonstrates that not all forms of apparent victimisation will be caught. There must be a causal link between the victimisation and a protected act.[13] However, it is not necessary to show conscious or deliberate victimisation.[14] In *Chief Constable of West Yorkshire v Khan*, the House of Lords held that whether a claimant had been victimised by reason of having done a protected act was not to be

---

law protects people who, although not themselves disabled, suffer direct discrimination and/or harassment in the field of employment and occupation because they are associated with a disabled person: Opinion of Advocate General Poiares Maduro delivered on 31 January 2008 in case C-303/06 *S. Coleman v Attridge Law and Steve Law.* The judgment of the ECJ is now awaited.

[12] See also the various examples given in the relevant codes of practice. See also *National Probation Service v Kirby* [2006] IRLR 508, EAT.

[13] See, e g *British Airways Engine Overhaul Ltd v Francis* [1981] IRLR 9, EAT (there must be a connection between B's actions, A's actions and the provisions of the Act); *Aziz v Trinity Street Taxis Ltd* [1988] ICR 534, CA (there must be a causal link between the victimisation and a protected act).

[14] *Nagarajan v London Regional Transport* [1999] ICR 877, HL (motive is irrelevant and victimisation might be inferred from subconscious acts). See also: *Cornelius v University College of Swansea* [1987] IRLR 141, CA; *Kirby v Manpower Services Commission* [1980] ICR 420, EAT; *Waters v Metropolitan Police Commissioner* [1997] ICR 1073, CA; *Villalba v Merrill Lynch & Co Inc* [2006] IRLR, EAT.

determined simply by application of a 'but for' test.[15] In that case, a reference had been withheld by an employer. It was held that it had not been withheld by reason that the claimant had brought discrimination proceedings, but rather because the employer temporarily needed to preserve its position in the outstanding legal proceedings. Lord Nicholls suggested that the phrase 'by reason that' does not give rise to a test of causation in the usual way, but that the test is a subjective one (why did the alleged discriminator act as he or she did?). Lord Hoffmann considered that the test of causation was whether the fact that the proceedings had been brought was a reason why the person had been treated less favourably. Lord Scott suggested that it is necessary to look for the real reason or core reason or the motive for the treatment complained of.

10.2 LEGAL LIABILITY

10.2.1 The DDA 1995 established a number of ways upon which legal liability for acts of unlawful discrimination or harassment can be based. In particular, provision is made for the liability of employers and principals, and of those who aid unlawful acts. There are also cases where there is an exemption from liability which would otherwise arise (most notably in respect of the exceptions for statutory authority and national security).

Aiding unlawful acts

10.2.2 A person who knowingly aids another person to do an 'unlawful act' is treated for the purposes of the legislation as having done the same kind of unlawful act in his or her own right.[16] An 'unlawful act' means an act made unlawful by any provision of the DDA 1995 other than a provision contained in Part 4, Chapter 1 (the anti-discrimination provisions affecting education in schools).[17] The effect is that a person can become liable for a discriminatory act committed contrary to the DDA 1995 merely by aiding and abetting the person who is primarily responsible for the discriminatory conduct.[18] For example, if a company's personnel officer knowingly or deliberately discriminates against disabled applicants for employment, the company will be primarily responsible

---

[15] [2001] UKHL 48, [2001] IRLR 830, HL.

[16] DDA 1995, s 57(1), as amended. See generally the examples given in the relevant codes of practice and *Gilbank v Miles* [2006] IRLR 538, CA (the employee who aided the employer's unlawful acts was held jointly and severally liable for compensation).

[17] DDA 1995, s 57(6).

[18] By virtue of DDA 1995, s 57(2), the person aiding the unlawful act (such as an employee) might be solely and personally liable for the unlawful act if the person who would otherwise be primarily liable (such as an employer) escapes vicarious liability by showing that it took such steps as were reasonably practicable to prevent its employee from doing the act in question (ie under the statutory defence in DDA 1995, s 58(5)): *Yeboah v Crofton* [2002] EWCA Civ 794, [2002] IRLR 634, CA (a case decided under the comparable provisions of RRA 1976, ss 32(3) and 33(1)–(2)).

under the principle of statutory vicarious liability,[19] but the personnel officer may also be liable,[20] having aided the company to commit the discrimination in question. The word 'aids' bears no technical or special meaning in this context, and it does not matter who instigates or initiates the relationship.[21] However, difficulty may arise in proving that a person 'knowingly' aided an unlawful act. The mental element of knowledge or intention may be crucial.[22] Furthermore, there may be little to be gained in terms of remedies.

10.2.3 A person faced with an allegation of aiding another person to commit an act made unlawful by the legislation has an explicit defence.[23] For present purposes, a person does not knowingly aid another to do an unlawful act if he or she acts in reliance on a statement made to him or her by that other person. The statement must be to the effect that the act would not be unlawful because of any provision of the DDA 1995 and it must be reasonable to rely upon that statement. That other person is guilty of a criminal offence if he or she knowingly or recklessly makes such a statement which is false or misleading in a material respect.[24]

Liability of employers

10.2.4 Anything done by a person in the course of his or her employment is treated for the purposes of the DDA 1995 as also done by his or her employer, whether or not it was done with the employer's knowledge or approval.[25] This statutory principle of vicarious liability is

---

19   Under DDA 1995, s 58 (discussed below). In *London Borough of Hammersmith & Fulham v Farnsworth* [2000] IRLR 691, EAT, the vicarious liability of the local authority for the actions of an occupational health physician (as an agent of the authority) informing an employment decision by the authority (and the relevance of the provisions of DDA 1995, ss 57–58) would have been in issue but for a concession made during the appeal.

20   Under DDA 1995, s 57. See *AM v WC and SPV* [1999] IRLR 410, EAT.

21   *Anyanwu v South Bank Students' Union* [2001] UKHL 14, [2001] IRLR 305, HL (a person aids another person if he or she helps or assists, or co-operates or collaborates with that other person, and whether or not that help is substantial and productive, provided it is not so insignificant as to be negligible); *Hallam v Cheltenham Borough Council* [2001] UKHL 15, [2001] IRLR 312, HL (what is required is more than a general attitude of helpfulness and co-operation – what must be shown is aid to another to do the unlawful act); *Gilbank v Miles* [2006] IRLR 538, CA (merely creating an environment in which discrimination might occur does not amount to aiding an unlawful act).

22   However, if a fellow employee does an act in the course of employment which has the effect of discriminating against the claimant, and that is a result which can be concluded to have been within his or her knowledge at the time the act was carried out, the requirements of s 57 will be met: *Allaway v Reilly* [2007] IRLR 864, EAT (discrimination does not have to be what was intended nor is any particular motive required).

23   DDA 1995, s 57(3).

24   Ibid, s 57(4). A person guilty of that offence is liable upon summary conviction to a fine not exceeding level 5 on the standard scale (s 57(5)). An employer or principal cannot be made vicariously liable for such an offence committed by an employee or agent (s 58(4)).

25   Ibid, s 58(1). See generally the examples given in the various codes of practice. By virtue of s 58(4), vicarious liability cannot extend to an offence committed under s 57(4).

an important inclusion because the DDA 1995 speaks of unlawful acts committed by – by way of examples only – 'an employer', 'a trade organisation', 'a qualifications body', 'a provider of services', 'a person with power to dispose' (of any premises), 'the body responsible for a school', and so on. It reflects similar provisions in other discrimination statutes.[26] The effect is that while an employer will be liable in its own right for its own discriminatory acts,[27] the employer is also vicariously liable for the discriminatory acts of an employee during the course of employment. However, both the employer and the employee remain potentially liable, because the employee may have knowingly aided the employer in the commission of an unlawful act of discrimination.[28] The employee is not released from any individual liability that might arise.[29] So, even though the employee might not be capable of committing an act of discrimination made unlawful by the Act, he or she may be deemed to have aided the employer's unlawful act.[30]

10.2.5   At common law, the meaning of 'in the course of employment' has been the subject of a long line of case-law[31] which establishes that it is insufficient that the act was done while on duty or that the occasion to commit the act was provided in the context of employment, but it is enough that the act that gave rise to the discriminatory conduct was authorised by the employer, although carried out in an unauthorised or prohibited fashion.[32] Most recently, the House of Lords has ruled that the correct approach is to concentrate on the relative closeness of the connection between the nature of the employment and the employee's wrongdoing.[33] The question is whether the employee's tort is so closely connected with his or her employment that it would be fair and just to hold the employer vicariously liable. However, the common law principles on the meaning of 'in the course of employment' are not applicable to the

---

[26]   SDA 1975, s 41; RRA 1976, s 32. See also DDA 1995, s 64A (liability of a chief officer of police for the actions of a police officer).

[27]   The employer will be liable under the DDA 1995, but may also have liability in negligence at common law for any breach of a duty of care: *Waters v Commissioner of Police of the Metropolis* [2000] IRLR 720, HL (employer alleged to have behaved negligently in failing to deal with an employee's complaint that she had been sexually assaulted by a male colleague).

[28]   DDA 1995, s 57 (discussed at **10.2.2**). See under the SDA 1975: *Enterprise Glass Co Ltd v Miles* [1990] ICR 787, EAT; *AM v WC and SPV* [1999] IRLR 410, EAT.

[29]   *Yeboah v Crofton* [2002] EWCA Civ 794, [2002] IRLR 634, CA (a case decided under the comparable provisions of RRA 1976, ss 32(3) and 33(1)–(2)).

[30]   This is because DDA 1995, s 57(2) provides that an employee for whose act the employer is liable under s 58 shall be taken to have aided the employer to do the act. For an illustration of this under the SDA 1975, see *Read v Tiverton District Council* [1977] IRLR 202.

[31]   See most recently *Fennely v Connex South Eastern Ltd* [2001] IRLR 390, CA, and *Balfron Trustees Ltd v Peterson* [2001] IRLR 758, HC.

[32]   See eg *Irving and Irving v Post Office* [1987] IRLR 289, CA; *Aldred v Nacanco* [1987] IRLR 292, CA; *Heasmans v Clarity Cleaning Co Ltd* [1987] IRLR 286, CA.

[33]   *Lister v Hesley Hall Ltd* [2001] UKHL 22, [2001] IRLR 472, HL.

statutory concept of vicarious liability.[34] The test of what will amount to 'in the course of employment' for the purposes of establishing vicarious liability for acts of disability discrimination is more flexible and is ultimately a question of fact for the court or tribunal.[35]

10.2.6 In a case founded upon the vicarious liability provision, an employer has a possible defence. The employer might escape vicarious liability (but not any liability faced in its own right) by proving that it took such steps as were reasonably practicable to prevent the employee from doing the act complained of or doing acts of the same description in the course of employment.[36] It may be sufficient to avoid vicarious liability by showing, for example, that the employer was unaware of the discriminatory acts being perpetrated by the employee and that there was proper and adequate staff supervision, including appropriate training and the dissemination of an anti-discrimination or equal opportunities policy.[37] The burden of proof will be upon the employer. Case-law establishes that it is necessary to determine whether the employer took any steps at all to prevent the employee doing the act complained of in the course of employment and then to consider whether there were any further steps that could have been taken which were reasonably practicable. Whether taking any such steps would have prevented the discriminatory acts is not determinative of the question.[38]

Liability of principals

10.2.7 The statutory provision on vicarious liability also applies in part to the relationship of principal and agent. Anything done by a person as agent for a principal, and with the principal's express or implied authority,[39] is treated for the purposes of the DDA 1995 as also done by the principal, whether the authority was given before or after the act in question.[40] Once again, this means that the principal is vicariously liable

---

[34] *Jones v Tower Boot Co Ltd* [1997] IRLR 168, CA; *Sidhu v Aerospace Composite Technology Ltd* [2000] IRLR 602, CA.

[35] See e g *Chief Constable of Lincolnshire Police v Stubbs* [1999] IRLR 81, EAT (vicarious liability for sexual harassment during work-connected social activities).

[36] DDA 1995, s 58(5).

[37] *Balgobin and Francis v London Borough of Tower Hamlets* [1987] IRLR 401, EAT (a sex discrimination case under comparable provisions).

[38] *Canniffe v East Riding of Yorkshire Council* [2000] IRLR 555, EAT (a case decided under the comparable provisions of SDA 1975, s 41(3)). See also *Pearce v Governing Body of Mayfield Secondary School* [2000] IRLR 548, EAT.

[39] The authority referred to must be the authority to do an act which is capable of being done in a discriminatory manner just as it is capable of being done in a lawful manner: *Lana v Positive Action Training in Housing (London) Ltd* [2001] IRLR 501, EAT (ruling that SDA 1975, s 41(2), the equivalent of DDA 1995, s 58(2), is not restricted to situations in which the contract gives the agent authority to discriminate).

[40] DDA 1995, s 58(2)–(3). Whatever a person has power to do may be done by an agent. Without such a power vested in the principal, an agent has no power deriving from agency. See *Halsbury's Laws of England*, Vol 1(2) (4th edn, 1990), para 3. In a case brought under DDA 1995, s 4, the governing body of a state-maintained school with a

for the discriminatory actions of the agent and is jointly liable with the agent. The agent will be treated as having aided the principal to commit the unlawful act.[41] There is no defence available to the principal as there would be to an employer in a case of vicarious liability.[42]

Statutory authority

10.2.8 The DDA 1995 contains an exception to liability in respect of statutory authority. Nothing in the 1995 legislation causes an act or deliberate omission to be made unlawful where that act or omission is done in any of the following circumstances:[43]

- in pursuance of any 'enactment';

- in pursuance of any 'instrument' made by a Minister of the Crown (or the Scottish Executive or the National Assembly for Wales or the Welsh Ministers or the First Minister for Wales or the Counsel General to the Welsh Assembly Government) under any 'enactment';

- to comply with any condition or requirement imposed by a Minister of the Crown (and the devolved counterparts above) (whether before or after the passing of the Act) by virtue of any 'enactment'.

An 'enactment' for this purpose will include an Act of Parliament (including legislation of the Welsh Assembly and the Scottish Parliament), subordinate legislation (such as a statutory instrument) and any Order in Council,[44] whether passed or made before or after the date the DDA 1995 received the Royal Assent.[45] An 'instrument' clearly refers to subordinate legislation made by a Minister under statutory delegated authority, whether made before or after the passing of the DDA 1995.

---

delegated budget was held not to be the agent of an LEA when committing an alleged act of disability discrimination in recruitment and selection arrangements because the LEA had no statutory power to carry out the governors' functions: *Lancashire County Council v Mason* [1998] ICR 907, EAT. But see now *Murphy v Slough Borough Council* [2004] ICR 1163, EAT; [2005] EWCA Civ 122, CA; and Education (Modification of Enactments Relating to Employment) (England) Order 2003, SI 2003/1964 and Education (Modification of Enactments Relating to Employment) (Wales) Order 2006, SI 2006/1073.

[41] By virtue of DDA 1995, s 57(2). In *London Borough of Hammersmith & Fulham v Farnsworth* [2000] IRLR 691, EAT, the vicarious liability of the local authority for the actions of an occupational health physician (as an agent of the authority) informing an employment decision by the authority (and the relevance of the provisions of DDA 1995, ss 57–58) would have been in issue but for a concession made during the appeal.

[42] Under DDA 1995, s 58(5).

[43] Ibid, s 59(1), as amended. See the discussion and illustrations in the codes of practice.

[44] DDA 1995, s 68(1) (which cross-refers to Interpretation Act 1978, s 21), as amended by the Scotland Act 1998 (Consequential Modifications) Order 2000, SI 2000/2040. Also included (by virtue of Sch 8, para 47(1)) is any statutory provision within the meaning of Interpretation Act (Northern Ireland) 1954, s 1(f).

[45] DDA 1995, s 59(2) (namely, 8 November 1995).

10.2.9 The use of the phrase 'in pursuance of' any enactment or instrument is deliberate. In the comparable provisions of race discrimination law,[46] the draftsman also used this term rather than the phrasing 'under' any enactment or instrument. This has led to a narrow interpretation of the exception by the courts. The exemption applies only to actions reasonably necessary to comply with a statutory obligation and not to acts done in exercise of a power of discretion conferred by the enactment or instrument.[47] The use of the word 'under' (contained originally in the 1995 Bill) may well have had the effect of inviting a wider interpretation of the statutory authority exemption. The result may have been that the exception would have applied to anything done under statutory authority, whether of a discretionary nature or not, and that would have gone some way towards undermining the objectives of the 1995 legislation. That possibility has apparently been excluded.

10.2.10 An example of how this exception might operate was given by a Minister when the DDA 1995 was being enacted:

> 'Under s 12 of the Health and Safety at Work etc Act 1974, the Secretary of State is given the power to give the Health and Safety Commission directions about ways in which it carries out its functions. If one of those functions, in the Secretary of State's opinion, required the Commission to do something which adversely affected disabled people, it would not be unlawful and could not be challenged under the provisions of the [Act].'[48]

It was also made clear that it was important that the exception should apply to both existing and future enactments. This point was illustrated by reference to the hypothetical possibility that a future safety legislative provision might require employers to modify equipment for the protection of employee operators. As a result of that modification, a disabled person might find it no longer physically possible to operate the equipment. The exception ensures that, by refusing to remove or alter the modification, the employer would not be in breach of the duty to accommodate disabled persons under the DDA 1995. The new safety law would override the disability discrimination legislation to that extent alone, although other forms of reasonable adjustment might remain appropriate for the employee.[49]

---

[46] RRA 1976, s 41.

[47] *Hampson v Department of Education and Science* [1990] IRLR 302, HL. See also, under the DDA 1995, *Post Office v Jones* [2000] ICR 388, EAT; [2001] IRLR 324, CA.

[48] HC Deb Standing Committee E, col 428. See also the examples in respect of alterations to the highway or to listed buildings given at HL Deb, vol 565, col 673. An example under the DDA 1995 arose in *Lane Group plc v Farmiloe* EAT 0352/03 and 0357/03 (IDS Brief 772) where an employee was dismissed in circumstances where a skin condition prevented him from wearing protective footwear. The employer had attempted to make alternative arrangements and to make reasonable adjustments, but could not overcome the absolute duty under health and safety legislation in relation to protective footwear: DDA 1995, s 59 applied.

[49] There would be nothing to prevent a future enactment being made expressly subject to the DDA 1995. For example, the Local Government and Housing Act 1989, s 7 requires

10.2.11 In any proceedings in respect of discrimination in the employment field,[50] a certificate signed by or on behalf of a Minister of the Crown (or a Northern Ireland Department) which certifies that any conditions or requirements specified in the certificate were imposed by a Minister (or that Department), and were in operation at or throughout a specified time, shall be conclusive evidence of the matters certified.[51] A document purporting to be such a certificate shall be received in evidence and, unless the contrary is proved, is deemed to be such a certificate.[52] Similar provision is made in respect of proceedings under Part 3 of the DDA 1995 in respect of goods, facilities, services and premises[53] or the new Part 4 in respect of education.[54]

National security

10.2.12 Nothing in Part 2 of the DDA 1995 makes unlawful any act done for the purpose of safeguarding national security if the doing of the act was justified by that purpose. Nothing in Part 3 of the Act (to the extent that it relates to the provision of employment services) makes unlawful any act done for the purpose of safeguarding national security if the doing of the act was justified by that purpose. Otherwise, nothing in the DDA 1995 makes unlawful any act done for the purpose of safeguarding national security.[55] The implications of national security in proceedings before an employment tribunal under Part 2 of the DDA 1995 are now dealt with in the Employment Tribunals Act 1996 (ETA 1996), as amended.[56] As far as proceedings in services and premises cases before a court under Part 3 of the DDA 1995 are concerned, a certificate signed by or on behalf of a Minister of the Crown which certifies that an act specified in the certificate was done for the purpose of safeguarding national security is to be conclusive evidence of the matter certified.[57] A document purporting to be such a certificate shall be received in evidence

---

all local government staff to be appointed on merit. However, that has effect expressly subject to DDA 1995, ss 4, 4A, 4D and 4E (discrimination and duties to make reasonable adjustments in relation to employees and office-holders). Thus, while local government appointments must be made on merit, that is always subject to the duty to make reasonable adjustments for disabled persons. That may include transferring a disabled employee to a higher grade post (for which the employee is otherwise qualified) without a competitive interview: *Archibald v Fife Council* [2004] UKHL 32, [2004] IRLR 651, HL.

[50] DDA 1995, s 17A.

[51] Ibid, Sch 3, para 4(1)(a), as amended. Sch 3, para 4(1A) and (1B) makes similar provision in respect of the Welsh and Scottish devolved governments.

[52] Ibid, Sch 3, paras 4(2).

[53] Ibid, Sch 3, paras 8(1)(a) and (2) in respect of proceedings under s 25. The modification of this provision in the context of Northern Ireland is set out in Sch 8, para 50(4).

[54] Ibid, Sch 3, paras 11 and 15, in respect of proceedings under ss 28I, 28K, 28L and 28V.

[55] Ibid, s 59(2A) and (3).

[56] ETA 1996, ss 10–10B, and see the Employment Tribunals (National Security) Rules of Procedure 2004.

[57] DDA 1995, Sch 3, para 8(1)(b). In Northern Ireland, the relevant certificate must be signed by the Secretary of State (Sch 8, para 50(2)).

and, unless the contrary is proved, is deemed to be such a certificate.[58] There are no comparable provisions affecting education cases under the new Part 4 of the DDA 1995.

10.3 STATUTORY QUESTIONNAIRE

10.3.1 Section 56 of the DDA 1995 (as substituted by DDA 2005) makes provision for statutory questionnaires to be used in proceedings under Part 2 (employment) and Part 3 (services, public authorities, private clubs and premises cases).[59] This is designed to assist 'the person aggrieved'. This is a person who considers that he or she may have been discriminated against in contravention of Part 2 or 3, or subjected to harassment in contravention of Part 2 or s 21A(2).[60] A person against whom the person aggrieved may decide to institute (or has instituted) proceedings in respect of such discrimination or harassment is referred to as 'the respondent'.[61] This provision is designed with a view to helping the person aggrieved decide whether to institute proceedings and to formulate and present the case in the most effective manner.

10.3.2 The Secretary of State shall by order prescribe (a) forms by which the person aggrieved may question the respondent on the reasons for doing any relevant act (or on any other matter which is or may be relevant) and (b) forms by which the respondent may reply to any questions.[62] The Secretary of State may by order (a) prescribe the period within which questions must be duly served in order to be admissible in evidence and (b) prescribe the manner in which a question, and any reply by the respondent, may be duly served.[63] See the Disability Discrimination (Questions and Replies) Orders 2004 and 2005.[64]

---

[58] DDA 1995, Sch 3, para 8(2).

[59] Previously, the statutory questionnaire procedure applied in Part 2 cases only. These provisions are modelled after similar provisions for assisting aggrieved persons to obtain information in cases of potential sex or race discrimination: SDA 1975, s 74; RRA 1976, s 65. See generally: *Oxford v DHSS* [1977] IRLR 225, EAT; *Greater Glasgow Health Board v Carey* [1987] IRLR 484, EAT; *City of Bradford Metropolitan Council v Arora* [1989] IRLR 442, EAT; *Carrington v Helix Lighting Ltd* [1990] IRLR 6, EAT; *King v The Great Britain-China Centre* [1991] IRLR 513, CA; *Dattani v Chief Constable of Mercia Police* [2005] IRLR 327, EAT.

[60] DDA 1995, s 56(1)(a) as substituted by DDA 2005, s 17 and in force from 4 December 2006. In Northern Ireland, see SI 2006/312, art 17.

[61] DDA 1995, s 56(1)(b).

[62] Ibid, s 56(2).

[63] Ibid, s 56(4).

[64] SI 2004/1168 (as amended), Sch 1 and 2 (for employment tribunal proceedings) and SI 2005/2703, Sch 1 and 2 (for county court or sheriff court proceedings), revoking and replacing the Disability Discrimination (Questions and Replies) Order 1996, which prescribed a statutory questionnaire procedure in Part 2 cases only. See generally: Casserley and Gor, *Disability Discrimination Claims: An Adviser's Handbook* (2001, Bristol: Jordans), chapters 4 and 7–8.

10.3.3 Where the person aggrieved questions the respondent in accordance with the prescribed forms, the question (and any reply by the respondent) shall be admissible as evidence in any proceedings under Part 2 or 3.[65] It might appear to the court or tribunal in any such proceedings that the respondent deliberately, and without reasonable excuse, omitted to reply within the period of eight weeks beginning with the day on which the question was served on him or that the respondent's reply is evasive or equivocal. If so, the court or tribunal may draw any inference which it considers it just and equitable to draw, including an inference that the respondent committed an unlawful act.[66]

Employment tribunal proceedings

10.3.4 In employment tribunal proceedings under the DDA 1995, a question shall only be admissible as evidence in pursuance of s 56(3) as follows.[67] Where the question was served before a complaint had been presented to a tribunal, it is admissible if it was served within the period of three months beginning when the act complained of was done.[68] Where it was served after a complaint has been presented to a tribunal, it is admissible if it was served within the period of 28 days beginning with the day on which the complaint was presented, or if it was served with the leave of a tribunal, within the period specified by that tribunal.

Civil court proceedings

10.3.5 In Part 3 cases, rules of court may enable a court entertaining a claim under s 25 (enforcement, remedies and procedure in Part 3 cases) to determine, before the date fixed for the hearing of the claim, whether a question or reply is admissible under s 56 or not.[69] In proceedings in respect of a s 21B claim (discrimination by public authorities), s 56(3)(b) (discussed in **10.3.3**) does not apply in relation to a failure to reply (or a particular reply) if the following conditions are met.[70] First, at the time of doing any relevant act, the respondent was carrying out public investigator functions or was a public prosecutor.[71] Secondly, the respondent reasonably believes that a reply or (as the case may be) a different reply would be likely to prejudice any criminal investigation, any decision to institute criminal proceedings or any criminal proceedings or would reveal the reasons behind a decision not to institute, or a decision not to continue, criminal proceedings.[72] Regulations may provide for s 56

---

[65] DDA 1995, s 56(3)(a).
[66] Ibid, s 56(3)(b).
[67] SI 2004/1168 (as amended), reg 4. Rules of service are set out in reg 5.
[68] Or within the extended period within which proceedings may be brought as a result of reg 15 of Employment Act 2002 (Dispute Resolution) Regulations 2004.
[69] DDA 1995, s 56(5).
[70] Ibid, s 56(6).
[71] Ibid, s 56(6)(a).
[72] Ibid, s 56(6)(b).

not to have effect, or to have effect with prescribed modifications, in relation to s 21B claims of a prescribed description.[73]

10.3.6 In civil court proceedings (under the relevant provisions of Part 3), for the purposes of s 56(3), a question shall only be admissible as evidence in the proceedings as follows.[74] Where proceedings have not commenced, the question is admissible if it was served within the period of six months beginning on the date of the act complained of. Where the dispute has been referred by the Commission for Equality and Human Rights for conciliation,[75] it is admissible if it was served within the period of eight months beginning on the date of the act complained of. Where proceedings have commenced, the question is admissible only if it is served with leave of the court and within the period specified by it.

Generally

10.3.7 Section 56 is without prejudice to any other enactment or rule of law regulating interlocutory and preliminary matters in proceedings before a county court, the sheriff or an employment tribunal, and has effect subject to any enactment or rule of law regulating the admissibility of evidence in such proceedings.[76]

10.4 PART 2 CASES

10.4.1 A complaint by any person that another person has unlawfully discriminated against him or her (or subjected him or her to harassment) contrary to Part 2 (or, in respect of group insurance arrangements or employment services, Part 3) of the DDA 1995 may be presented to an employment tribunal.[77] A complaint survives the death of the claimant.[78] A Part 2 claim can only be brought via employment tribunal proceedings (except in those cases where the DRC or now the CEHR has statutory enforcement powers).[79] It does not give rise to any other civil or criminal proceedings, except by way of judicial review or through the Pensions Ombudsman.[80] The employment tribunal will also have jurisdiction to hear complaints where the claimant alleges that another person is to be

---

[73]   DDA 1995, s 56(7) and (9).
[74]   SI 2005/2703, reg 3. Rules of service are set out in reg 4.
[75]   In pursuance of arrangements under s 27(1) of Equality Act 2006.
[76]   DDA 1995, s 56(8).
[77]   Ibid, ss 17A and 25, as amended. The term 'person' includes an individual, a body corporate and an unincorporated association: Interpretation Act 1978, Sch 1.
[78]   Law Reform (Miscellaneous Provisions) Act 1934, s 1(1); *Harris (representative of Andrews) v Lewisham and Guy's Mental Health NHS Trust* [2000] IRLR 320, CA; *Executors of Soutar v James Murray and Co (Cupar) Ltd and Scottish Provident Institution* [2002] IRLR 22, EAT.
[79]   See Chapter 1.
[80]   DDA 1995, Sch 3, para 2.

treated as having acted unlawfully.[81] However, employment tribunal proceedings cannot be brought in respect of acts of qualifications bodies made unlawful under Part 2 of the DDA 1995 where an appeal (or proceedings in the nature of an appeal) may be brought under any enactment.[82]

10.4.2 It is not intended to rehearse the constitution and procedures of the employment tribunal here.[83] Proceedings are commenced by presenting a claim within the statutory time limits and the respondent may then present a defence in the form of a response.[84] Judgments of an employment tribunal are made unanimously or by a majority. An appeal from a judgment of an employment tribunal may be made to the Employment Appeal Tribunal (EAT) on a point of law, and from there to the Court of Appeal and, with leave, to the House of Lords. Employment tribunals are themselves subject to the DDA 1995 and will be covered by the rights of access to goods, facilities and services contained in Part 3 of the Act.[85]

Time-limits

10.4.3 An employment tribunal shall not consider a complaint under the DDA 1995 unless it is presented before the end of the period of three months, beginning when the act (or deliberate omission) complained of was done.[86] The time limit goes to the jurisdiction of the employment tribunal to hear the claim. In the case of an isolated act, the presumption will be that time starts to run from the date of the act (or omission). For example, time does not start to run in respect of a dismissal until the notice of dismissal expires and the employment ceases.[87] In a constructive dismissal, time runs from the date of termination rather than from the date of the breach.[88] In employment selection cases, time will start to run from when the applicant for employment is rejected.[89] A deliberate

---

[81]   DDA 1995, ss 57 (aiding unlawful acts) and 58 (liability of employers and principals). See generally **10.2**.

[82]   Ibid, s 17A(1A) by reference to s 14A(1) or (2).

[83]   Employment Tribunals (Constitution and Rules of Procedure) Regulations 2004, SI 2004/1861, as amended by SI 2004/2351; Industrial Tribunals (Constitution and Rules of Procedure) Regulations (Northern Ireland) 2004, SR 2004/165.

[84]   See generally: Casserley and Gor, *Disability Discrimination Claims: An Adviser's Handbook* (2001, Bristol: Jordans), chapters 5–6.

[85]   HC Deb Standing Committee E, col 279. See Chapter 5. Legal aid is not generally available in employment tribunal proceedings.

[86]   DDA 1995, s 68(1) and Sch 3, para 3(1). See *Ali v Office of National Statistics* [2005] IRLR 201, CA.

[87]   *British Gas Services Ltd v McCaull* [2001] IRLR 60, EAT (time did not start to run until an employer's failure to supply an employee with information about a proposed alternative job resulted in his refusing the alternative employment and his refusal resulted in his dismissal).

[88]   *Nottinghamshire County Council v Meikle* [2004] EWCA Civ 859, [2004] IRLR 703, CA.

[89]   *Tyagi v BBC World Service* [2001] EWCA Civ 549, [2001] IRLR 465, CA. See also *Virdi v Commissioner of Police of the Metropolis* [2007] IRLR 24, EAT.

omission is to be treated as done when the person in question decided upon it.[90] Subject to rebutting evidence, a person is treated as having decided upon an omission when he or she does an act inconsistent with doing the omitted act or, in the absence of such inconsistent behaviour, when the period expires within which he or she might reasonably have been expected to do the omitted act if it was to be done.[91] In the case of an act or omission which extends over a period of time, the three months' limitation provision will not start to run until the end of the period in question.[92] Where the alleged unlawful act is attributable to a term in a contract, time does not start to expire until the end of the contract. The unlawful act is said to extend throughout the duration of the contract.[93]

10.4.4 Even where a complaint has been presented out of time, an employment tribunal may nevertheless entertain it if, in all the circumstances of the case, it considers that it is just and equitable to do so.[94] This allows an employment tribunal considerable discretion to admit late claims.[95] Tribunal decisions to extend the time-limit in such cases are rarely challengeable on appeal.[96] For example, tribunals might allow a late claim to proceed where the claimant was unaware of a cause of action or the time-limits governing it.[97] However, the discretion to extend time is not without limitations. For example, the fact that the claimant has delayed presenting a claim to the tribunal because he or she was seeking to redress a grievance through an employer's internal grievance procedure before embarking on legal proceedings has not, as a general principle, made it just and equitable to extend time and to admit a late claim.[98] This was merely one factor to be taken into account. However, this is now subject to the new dispute resolution procedures.

---

[90] DDA 1995, Sch 3, para 3(3)(c).

[91] Ibid, Sch 3, para 3(4). Eg *Swithland Motors plc v Clarke* [1994] ICR 231, EAT.

[92] Ibid, Sch 3, para 3(3)(b). See *Amies v Inner London Education Authority* [1977] ICR 308, EAT; *Sougrin v Haringey Health Authority* [1991] ICR 791, EAT; *Calder v James Finlay Corporation Ltd* [1989] IRLR 55, EAT; *Littlewoods Organisation plc v Traynor* [1993] IRLR 154, EAT; *Hendricks v Commissioner of Police for the Metropolis* [2003] IRLR 96, CA. On continuing acts of discrimination generally, see *Barclays Bank plc v Kapur* [1991] ICR 208, HL; *Robertson v Bexley Community Centre* [2003] IRLR 434, CA.

[93] DDA 1995, Sch 3, para 3(3)(a).

[94] Ibid, Sch 3, para 3(2).

[95] *Hawkins v Ball* [1996] IRLR 258, EAT; *DPP v Marshall* [1998] ICR 518, EAT; *London Borough of Southwark v Afolabi* [2003] IRLR 220, CA.

[96] *Hutchinson v Westward Television Ltd* [1977] ICR 279, EAT.

[97] *Foster v South Glamorgan Health Authority* [1988] ICR 526, EAT.

[98] *Apelogun-Gabriels v London Borough of Lambeth* [2001] EWCA Civ 1853, [2002] IRLR 116, CA; *Robinson v Post Office* [2000] IRLR 804, EAT; *Aniagwu v London Borough of Hackney* [1999] IRLR 303, EAT (cf *Virdi v Commissioner of Police of the Metropolis* [2007] IRLR 24, EAT).

Dispute resolution procedures

10.4.5   From 1 October 2004, disability discrimination claims are subject to the new statutory dispute resolution procedures.[99] These are complex provisions and any detailed analysis of them is beyond the scope of this book. In any event, they seem very likely to be repealed by the Employment Bill 2008, presently before Parliament, probably with effect from April 2009. Their effect on disability discrimination claims may be summarised as follows.

10.4.6   When presenting a claim to the employment tribunal, the claimant must provide certain required information. That includes the details of the claim; whether or not the claimant is or was an employee of the respondent; whether or not the claim includes a complaint that the respondent has dismissed the claimant or has contemplated doing so; whether or not the claimant has raised the subject-matter of the claim with the respondent in writing at least 28 days prior to presenting the claim; and, if not, why not.[100] If that information is not provided, the claim will be rejected.[101] Put simply, unless the claim is about a dismissal (other than a constructive dismissal), the claimant must first raise a statutory grievance with the respondent.[102] He or she must do so no later than one month after the statutory time-limit of three months. The claimant must then wait 28 days before presenting a claim to the tribunal. He or she may then do so within a further three months of the end of the initial three-month time-limit.[103] These provisions are subject to various exceptions and qualifications.[104]

ACAS conciliation and arbitration

10.4.7   The DDA 1995 anticipates that there will be an attempt to reach a conciliated settlement between the parties before a complaint proceeds to a hearing by an employment tribunal.[105] Provision is made for a copy of a complaint of disability discrimination to be sent to a conciliation officer of the Advisory, Conciliation and Arbitration Service (ACAS).[106] In such a case, the conciliation officer must try to promote a settlement of the complaint, without a tribunal hearing, if requested to do so by both parties or if the conciliation officer considers that there is a reasonable

---

[99]   Employment Act 2002, ss 29–40 and Schs 2–5; Employment Act 2002 (Dispute Resolution) Regulations 2004, SI 2004/752; Employment Tribunals Rules of Procedure 2004, as amended, rules 1–9.

[100]   Employment Tribunals Rules of Procedure 2004, rule 1.

[101]   Ibid, rules 2–3.

[102]   Employment Act 2002, Sch 2.

[103]   Ibid, s 32 and Sch 4.

[104]   Employment Act 2002 (Dispute Resolution) Regulations 2004, SI 2004/752.

[105]   Employment Tribunals Act 1996, s 18, as amended (replacing DDA 1995, Sch 3, para 1).

[106]   Ibid, ss 18(1)(c), (2) and 42(1). In Northern Ireland, the Labour Relations Agency so acts: DDA 1995, Sch 8, para 50(1).

prospect of a successful attempt to promote a settlement being made.[107] This latter provision allows the conciliation officer to be proactive, even if only one of the parties has requested a conciliatory intervention. Moreover, where a complaint has yet to be presented to an employment tribunal, but a person is contemplating presenting such a complaint, the conciliation officer shall try to promote a settlement if asked to do so by the potential claimant or potential respondent.[108] Disability discrimination proceedings are not subject to the new provisions on fixed periods of conciliation during which the case cannot be listed for a hearing.[109]

10.4.8　If a conciliated settlement has been agreed with the assistance of an ACAS conciliation officer, the agreement will usually be recorded in writing using form COT3. An oral agreement would be equally valid, although less certain.[110] A conciliated settlement will be a valid agreement and will not be void if it merely records an agreement not to institute proceedings or an agreement to discontinue proceedings before an employment tribunal.[111] Unless the conciliated settlement is otherwise challengeable or invalid, the employment tribunal will then have no jurisdiction to hear the complaint which is the subject of the conciliation. Even if a respondent reneges on an ACAS-brokered settlement, the claimant will usually be required to sue on the agreement rather than seek to reopen the complaint. An agreement to submit the dispute to ACAS arbitration is also covered.[112]

Compromise contracts

10.4.9　A compromise contract is also valid if certain conditions are satisfied.[113] The contract must be in writing. It must relate to the particular complaint. The claimant must have received advice from a relevant independent adviser as to the terms and effect of the proposed contract and, in particular, its effect on his or her ability to pursue a complaint before an employment tribunal. There must be in force, when the adviser gives the advice, a contract of insurance (or an indemnity provided for members of a profession or professional body) covering the risk of a claim by the claimant in respect of loss arising in consequence of the advice. The contract must identify the adviser. It must state that the conditions regulating compromise contracts have been satisfied.

10.4.10　A person is a relevant independent adviser for these purposes if he or she is a qualified lawyer, as defined.[114] Also covered is an officer,

---

[107]　ETA 1996, s 18(2)

[108]　Ibid, s 18(3).

[109]　Employment Tribunals Rules of Procedure 2004, rules 22–24. In any event, the fixed conciliation periods are unlikely to survive the Employment Bill 2008.

[110]　*Gilbert v Kembridge Fibres Ltd* [1984] ICR 188, EAT.

[111]　DDA 1995, s 17C and Sch 3A, paras 1 and 2(1)(a).

[112]　Ibid, Sch 3A, para 2(8).

[113]　Ibid, s 17C and Sch 3A, paras 1, 2(1)(b) and 2(2).

[114]　Ibid, Sch 3A, para 2(5), as amended.

official, employee or member of an independent trade union who has been certified in writing by the trade union as competent to give advice and as authorised to do so on behalf of the trade union. A person is also a relevant independent adviser if he or she works at an advice centre (whether as an employee or a volunteer) and has been certified in writing by the centre as competent to give advice and as authorised to do so on behalf of the centre.[115] However, a person is not a relevant independent adviser for these purposes if he or she is, is employed by or is acting in the matter for the other party or a person who is connected with the other party.[116] In respect of a trade union or advice centre, it is not a relevant independent adviser if it is the other party or a person who is connected with the other party. In respect of an advice centre, it is not a relevant independent adviser if the claimant makes a payment for the advice received from the adviser.[117]

Restriction on publicity

10.4.11 Where evidence of a personal nature is likely to be heard by the employment tribunal hearing a complaint of disability discrimination, special provision is made for the restriction of publicity.[118] Evidence of a personal nature means any evidence of a medical or other intimate nature which might reasonably be assumed to be likely to cause significant embarrassment to the complainant if reported.[119] The Secretary of State is empowered to make regulations with respect to the procedure of employment tribunals so as to achieve this objective.[120] This is achieved in the employment tribunal procedural rules on restricted reporting orders.[121]

10.4.12 A restricted reporting order has the effect of prohibiting the publication in Great Britain (or Northern Ireland) of 'identifying matter' in a 'written publication' available to the public.[122] A written publication would obviously include a newspaper or magazine, but it also includes a film, a soundtrack and any other record in a permanent form.[123] A restricted reporting order will also have the effect of prohibiting the inclusion of any 'identifying matter' in a relevant radio or television programme for reception in Great Britain, or Northern Ireland, as the

---

[115] DDA 1995, Sch 3A, para 2(3), as amended.
[116] Ibid, Sch 3A, para 2(7): any two persons are to be treated as connected (a) if one is a company of which the other (directly or indirectly) has control; or (b) if both are companies of which a third person (directly or indirectly) has control.
[117] Ibid, Sch 3A, para 2(4).
[118] ETA 1996, s 12(1) (formerly DDA 1995, s 62(1)). See also *X v Stevens* [2003] IRLR 411, EAT.
[119] Ibid, s 12(7).
[120] Ibid, s 12(2).
[121] Employment Tribunals Rules of Procedure 2004, rules 18(7)(g) and 50.
[122] ETA 1996, s 12(7), Sch 8, para 42(2).
[123] Ibid, s 12(7).

case may be.[124] This will effectively prevent the press and broadcast media from reporting any 'identifying matter' about the case. In this context, 'identifying matter' means any matter which is likely to lead members of the public to identify the claimant or any other persons named in the restricted reporting order.[125]

10.4.13 A restricted reporting order has effect until the promulgation of the tribunal's decision in the case, unless the order is revoked earlier.[126] If the restricted reporting order is broken by a newspaper or periodical, the proprietor, editor or publisher of the newspaper or periodical is guilty of a summary offence, punishable by a fine not exceeding level 5 on the standard scale.[127] Where the order is breached in a publication in any other form, the publisher of the matter shall be so liable.[128] Where the identifying matter is published in breach of a restricted reporting order by a radio or television broadcast, the broadcast company and the programme editor face criminal liability.[129] In any case, it is a defence to prove that, at the time of the alleged offence, the person charged was not aware (and neither suspected nor had reason to suspect) that the publication or programme in question was of (or included) the matter in question.[130]

10.4.14 Provision is also made for the restriction of publicity on certain appeals from an employment tribunal to the EAT under the DDA 1995.[131] This applies to proceedings on an appeal against an employment tribunal's decision to make (or not make) a restricted reporting order in disability discrimination cases. It also applies in such cases on an appeal against any interim decision of an employment tribunal in proceedings in which the employment tribunal has made a restricted reporting order which it has not revoked.

Burden of proof

10.4.15 Where the claimant proves facts from which the employment tribunal could conclude, in the absence of an adequate explanation, that the respondent has acted in a way which is unlawful under Part 2 of the DDA 1995, the tribunal shall uphold the complaint unless the respondent

---

[124] ETA 1996, s 12(7), Sch 8, para 42(2).

[125] Ibid, s 12(7).

[126] Ibid, s 12(2)(a).

[127] Ibid, s 12(3)(a).

[128] Ibid, s 12(3)(b).

[129] Ibid, s 12(3)(c).

[130] Ibid, s 12(4). Note also s 12(5)–(6), which makes provision for offences of joint liability where the breach of a restricted reporting order is committed by a body corporate, with the consent or connivance of (or attributable neglect of) a director, manager, secretary or other similar officer.

[131] ETA 1996, s 32 (previously DDA 1995, s 63); Employment Appeal Tribunal Rules 1993, rule 23A, as amended.

proves that it did not so act.[132] This is the reversal of the burden of proof required by the EC Employment Framework Directive.[133] The Court of Appeal has recently given authoritative guidance on the reversal of the burden of proof and has updated the guidance given in earlier cases, which may be paraphrased and applied to disability discrimination as follows.[134]

10.4.16   It is for the claimant to prove on the balance of probabilities facts from which the tribunal could conclude, in the absence of an adequate explanation, that the respondent has committed an act of unlawful discrimination. If the claimant does not prove such facts, he or she will fail. It is unusual to find direct evidence of disability discrimination. Few employers would be prepared to admit such discrimination. In some cases, the discrimination will merely be based on an assumption that the claimant would not have fitted in. In deciding whether the claimant has proved such facts, the outcome will usually depend on what inferences it is proper to draw from the primary facts. It is important to note the word 'could' in s 17A(1C). At this stage, the tribunal does not have to reach a definitive determination that such facts would lead it to the conclusion that there was an act of unlawful discrimination. A tribunal is looking at the primary facts to see what inferences of secondary fact could be drawn from them. In considering what inferences or conclusions can be drawn from the primary facts, the tribunal must assume that there is no adequate explanation for those facts. These inferences can include any inferences that it is just and equitable to

---

[132] DDA 1995, s 17A(1C), as amended. On the general power of tribunals to draw inferences of discrimination before the statutory introduction of the reversal of the burden of proof, see *King v The Great Britain-China Centre* [1991] IRLR 513, CA; *Zafar v Glasgow City Council* [1998] ICR 125, HL; *Nagaragan v London Regional Transport* [1999] IRLR 572, HL; *Anya v University of Oxford* [2001] IRLR 364, CA; *Rowden v Dutton Gregory (a firm)* [2002] ICR 971, EAT; *Barton v Investec Henderson Crosthwaite Securities Ltd* [2003] IRLR 332, EAT; *University of Huddersfield v Wolff* [2004] IRLR 534, EAT; *Chamberlain Solicitors v Emokpae* [2004] IRLR 592, EAT; *Bahl v The Law Society* [2004] IRLR 799, CA; *Madden v Preferred Technical Group Cha Ltd* [2005] IRLR 46, CA.

[133] 2000/78/EC, Art 10. On the general power of tribunals to draw inferences of discrimination after the statutory introduction of the reversal of the burden of proof, see *Barton v Investec Henderson Crosthwaite Securities Ltd* [2003] IRLR 332, EAT; *University of Huddersfield v Wolff* [2004] IRLR 534, EAT; *Chamberlain Solicitors v Emokpae* [2004] IRLR 592, EAT; *Sinclair Roche and Temperly v Heard* [2004] IRLR 763, EAT; *Webster v Brunel University* EAT 0730/04.

[134] *Igen Ltd v Wong; Chamberlin Solicitors v Emokpae; Brunel University v Webster (EOC, CRE and DRC intervening)* [2005] EWCA Civ 142, [2005] IRLR 258, CA, overturning the decisions of the EAT in *Emokpae* (above) and in *Webster* (above), and revising the guidance given in *Barton* (above). See further: *Desdner Kleinwort Wasserstein Ltd v Adebayo* [2005] IRLR 514, EAT; *EB v BA* [2006] IRLR 471, CA; *Laing v Manchester City Council* [2006] IRLR 748, EAT; *Network Rail Infrastructure Ltd v Griffiths-Henry* [2006] IRLR 865, EAT; *Madarassy v Nomura International plc* [2007] IRLR 246, CA; *Brown v London Borough of Croydon* [2007] IRLR 259, CA; *Appiah v Governing Body of Bishop Douglass RC High School* [2007] IRLR 264, CA.

draw from an evasive or equivocal reply to a statutory questionnaire. Inferences may also be drawn from any failure to comply with any relevant code of practice.

10.4.17 Where the claimant has proved facts from which conclusions could be drawn that the respondent has treated the claimant less favourably on the ground of disability or for a disability-related reason, then the burden of proof moves to the respondent. It is then for the respondent to prove that it did not commit (or is not to be treated as having committed) that act. It is necessary for the respondent to prove, on the balance of probabilities, that the treatment was in no sense whatsoever on the ground of disability or for a disability-related reason. That requires a tribunal to assess not merely whether the respondent has proved an explanation for the facts from which such inferences can be drawn, but further that it is adequate to discharge the burden of proof on the balance of probabilities that disability was not a ground for the treatment in question. Since the facts necessary to prove an explanation would normally be in the possession of the respondent, a tribunal would normally expect cogent evidence to discharge that burden of proof. In particular, the tribunal will need to examine carefully explanations for failure to deal with the questionnaire procedure or a code of practice.

Remedies

10.4.18 Where an employment tribunal finds that a complaint of unlawful disability discrimination or harassment in the employment field contrary to Part 2 of the DDA 1995 is well founded, it shall take one or more of the following steps as it considers just and equitable.[135] First, it may make a declaration as to the rights of the claimant and the respondent in relation to the matters to which the complaint relates. Secondly, it may order the respondent to pay compensation to the claimant. Thirdly, it may recommend that the respondent take, within a specified period, action appearing to the tribunal to be reasonable, in all the circumstances of the case, for the purpose of obviating or reducing the adverse effect on the claimant of any matter to which the complaint relates.

Declaration of rights

10.4.19 Where a claimant has successfully brought a disability discrimination claim, the very least that the disabled person will be entitled to is a declaration that he or she has suffered unlawful discrimination or harassment in certain particulars or that his or her rights have been unlawfully transgressed.[136] A declaration of the claimant's rights alone is likely to be appropriate in those cases where he

---

[135] DDA 1995, s 17A(2).
[136] Ibid, s 17A(2)(a).

or she has suffered no measurable loss or where there is only a point of principle involved. A tribunal might occasionally use its declaratory powers to encourage the respondent to take some positive step towards the successful claimant (such as offer employment to or reinstate him or her), although the legal effect of such a declaration is of doubtful value.

Compensation and interest

10.4.20   The EAT has guided tribunals on the procedural approach to the assessment of compensation under the DDA 1995.[137] A separate remedies hearing will be appropriate. The parties' preparation for that hearing should be conducted under careful judicial case management, often involving the making of further case management orders and the exchange of statements of case and witness statements prior to the hearing. Where medical expert evidence is required (typically to assist the tribunal's findings as to the future employment prospects of the claimant for the purpose of assessing future loss of earnings), the listing of the case may need to take account of the availability of the expert witness.[138]

10.4.21   Where a tribunal orders compensation to be paid in an employment discrimination case,[139] the amount of the compensation is calculated according to the principles applicable to the calculation of damages in claims in tort (or, in Scotland, in reparation for breach of a statutory duty).[140] In other words, disability discrimination compensation will be assessed like any claim for damages in tort and according to common-law principles. Case-law under the other discrimination statutes will be instructive. There is no limit on the maximum amount of compensation that can be awarded for a breach of Part 2 of the DDA 1995.

10.4.22   A successful claimant will be entitled to be compensated for any actual financial or pecuniary loss up to the date of the tribunal decision, provided that it is caused by or attributable to the unlawful act or omission. The tribunal may also be invited to calculate future or continuing losses within the award.[141] The main head of damages is likely to be present or future loss of earnings which has resulted as a consequence of the unlawful act. This will include loss of basic wages or salary, together with any fringe benefits (such as a bonus, commission,

---

[137]   *Buxton v Equinox Design Ltd* [1999] IRLR 158, EAT.

[138]   See also generally the advice given in relation to expert witnesses and expert evidence in *De Keyser v Wilson* [2001] IRLR 324, EAT.

[139]   DDA 1995, s 17A(2)(b).

[140]   Ibid, s 17A(3). Where there is more than one respondent found liable, the award of compensation may be made against them on a joint and several basis: *Way v Crouch* [2005] IRLR 603, EAT.

[141]   Where the period of future loss is likely to exceed two years, the tribunal is likely to take the 'substantial loss' approach to its calculation as set out in the guidance to employment judges in *Compensation for Loss of Pension Rights: Orthet Ltd v Vince-Cain* [2004] IRLR 857, EAT.

company car, private health insurance, pension entitlements, and so on) to which the individual would have been entitled but for the discriminatory action. The claimant will be subject to a duty to mitigate any loss.[142]

10.4.23   The amount of compensation may also include compensation for injury to feelings, whether or not the award includes compensation under any other head.[143] It is suggested that such an element of damages will be appropriate (and easily implied without pleading) in most cases unless exceptional.[144] It will also include compensation for physical or psychiatric injury *caused by* an act of disability discrimination.[145] Such awards may be particularly in point in DDA cases where the claimant's disability is a mental illness which has been exacerbated by the act of discrimination. The tribunal will be careful to avoid an overlap with injury to feelings damages so as not to encourage double recovery. Aggravated damages may be awarded in exceptional cases where a respondent has acted in a high-handed, malicious, insulting or oppressive manner.[146] Exemplary damages were thought to be inappropriate in disability discrimination claims because of developments in the common law,[147] but now may be available in exceptional cases.[148]

---

[142] *Wilding v British Telecommunications plc* [2002] EWCA Civ 349, [2002] IRLR 524, CA (depending upon all the circumstances, a refusal to accept an offer of re-employment may amount to a failure to mitigate loss). This may require the compensation to take account of state benefits received: *Chief Constable of West Yorkshire Police v Vento (No. 2)* [2002] IRLR 177, EAT, and [2003] IRLR 102, CA. See also: *Atos Origin IT UK Ltd v Haddock* [2005] IRLR 20, EAT (allowance should also be made for payments which might be made under the employer's permanent health insurance scheme where the premiums have been paid by the employer without contribution from the employee).

[143] DDA 1995, s 17A(4). See generally: *Armitage v Johnson* [1997] IRLR 162, EAT; *Heil v Rankin* [2000] IRLR 334, CA; *Chief Constable of West Yorkshire v Khan* [2000] IRLR 324, CA; [2001] UKHL 48, [2001] IRLR 830, HL; *ICTS (UK) Ltd v Tchoula* [2000] IRLR 643, EAT; *O'Donoghue v Redcar and Cleveland Borough Council* [2001] IRLR 615, EAT; *Chief Constable of West Yorkshire Police v Vento (No. 2)* [2002] IRLR 177, EAT and [2003] IRLR 102, CA; *Doshoki v Draeger Ltd* [2002] IRLR 340, EAT; *British Telecommunications plc v Reid* [2004] IRLR 327, CA; *Scott v Commissioners of Inland Revenue* [2004] IRLR 713, CA; *Moyhing v Barts and London NHS Trust* [2006] IRLR 860, EAT; *R (on application of Elias) v Secretary of State for Defence* [2006] IRLR 934, CA.

[144] *Murray v Powertech (Scotland) Ltd* [1992] IRLR 257, EAT. The award is not, in principle, to be grossed-up for tax: *Orthet Ltd v Vince-Cain* [2004] IRLR 857, EAT.

[145] *Sheriff v Klyne Tugs (Lowestoft) Ltd* [1999] IRLR 481, CA. As to the judicial approach to the assessment of compensation for psychiatric injury, see *HM Prison Service v Salmon* [2001] IRLR 425, EAT; *Essa Ltd v Laing* [2003] IRLR 346, EAT.

[146] *Armitage v Johnson* [1997] IRLR 162, EAT; *HM Prison Service v Salmon* [2001] IRLR 425, EAT; *Chief Constable of West Yorkshire Police v Vento (No. 2)* [2002] IRLR 177, EAT; [2003] IRLR 102, CA; *Zaiwalla & Co v Walia* [2002] IRLR 697, EAT; *British Telecommunications plc v Reid* [2004] IRLR 327, CA; *Scott v Commissioners of Inland Revenue* [2004] IRLR 713, CA.

[147] *Alexander v Home Office* [1988] IRLR 190, CA; *City of Bradford Metropolitan Borough Council v Arora* [1991] IRLR 165, CA; *AB v South Western Water Services Ltd* [1993] 1 All ER 609, CA; *Deane v Ealing London Borough Council* [1993] IRLR 209, EAT.

[148] *Kuddus v Chief Constable of Leicestershire Constabulary* [2001] UKHL 29, [2001] 3 All ER 193, HL, overruling *AB v South Western Water Services Ltd* [1993] 1 All ER 609, CA.

10.4.24 The DDA 1995 also provided for regulations to be made to give tribunals the power to award interest on an award of compensation and to specify how that interest is to be determined.[149] The Employment Tribunals (Interest on Awards in Discrimination Cases) Regulations 1996 provide for the award of interest in proceedings for payment of compensation under the DDA 1995.[150]

10.4.25 In the case of an act which is *both* unfair dismissal *and* unlawful disability discrimination or harassment, recovery of the same loss under more than one provision is prohibited.[151] The employment tribunal shall not award compensation, for example, under the heading of disability discrimination in respect of any loss or matter which has already been accounted for in the award of compensation for unfair dismissal. The effect is to prevent double recovery of a loss already compensated for in the tribunal's award, whether the issue arises in the same proceedings before the tribunal in question or whether it arises in separate proceedings. For example, if the claimant has been dismissed and brought a successful unfair dismissal claim, it is likely that he or she will have been awarded compensation for loss of earnings to the date of the tribunal hearing and/or for future loss of earnings. A later tribunal considering a separate complaint of disability discrimination in respect of that dismissal must take account of the award for lost earnings when calculating any award under the DDA 1995.

10.4.26 However, problems are still likely to arise in respect of awards of loss of earnings. These will often be capped by the statutory maximum (from time to time) for an unfair dismissal compensatory award. As there is no statutory limit to awards under the DDA 1995, it is in the claimant's interest to ensure that the award of lost earnings is dealt with explicitly under the DDA 1995 rather than the 1996 Act. What is not clear is what should happen where such an award has already been made under the unfair dismissal compensation provisions of the 1996 Act and has then been capped by the statutory maximum. Is an employment tribunal considering making an award of loss of earnings under the DDA 1995 bound to decide that this is a loss which has already been taken into account in the earlier award (even though the amount of the loss has been artificially capped)? Alternatively, should the tribunal apportion the compensation awarded in the unfair dismissal claim and award the balance under the DDA 1995? The latter approach seems preferable, although it is not easily reconcilable with the statutory language.

---

[149] DDA 1995, s 17A(6).

[150] SI 1996/2803. For examples of the judicial approach to the award of interest, see *Derby Specialist Fabrication Ltd v Burton* [2001] IRLR 69, EAT, and *Bentwood Bros (Manchester) Ltd v Shepherd* [2003] IRLR 364, CA.

[151] ERA 1996, s 126, as amended. Where a claimant has been dismissed unfairly, that does not terminate liability for an earlier wrong of disability discrimination, and all further losses do not fall to be assessed as compensation for unfair dismissal subject to the statutory cap on such compensation: *HM Prison Service v Beart (No 2)* [2005] IRLR 171, EAT; [2005] IRLR 568, CA.

10.4.27 Where an employment tribunal in an unfair dismissal case makes a reinstatement or re-engagement order,[152] but the employer disobeys the order by refusing to re-employ the unfairly dismissed employee, the tribunal shall make an award of compensation for unfair dismissal,[153] plus an additional award of compensation to be paid by the employer to the employee.[154] An additional award will not be made if the employer satisfies the tribunal that it was not practicable to comply with the reinstatement or re-engagement order.[155] The appropriate amount of the additional award is usually between 13 and 26 weeks' pay.[156] However, the tribunal will award a higher additional award where the unfair dismissal was also found to be an unlawful act under the DDA 1995.[157] The higher additional award in such cases is between 26 and 52 weeks' pay.[158]

10.4.28 An award of compensation in a DDA case may also have to be adjusted up or down to reflect the extent to which either the claimant or the respondent previously failed to complete the new statutory dispute resolution procedures.[159]

Recommendations

10.4.29 Where the employment tribunal has upheld a complaint of disability discrimination or harassment, it may recommend that the respondent take, within a specified period, action appearing to the tribunal to be 'reasonable', in all the circumstances of the case, for the purpose of obviating or reducing the adverse effect on the claimant of any 'matter' to which the complaint relates.[160] It is clear that the power to make recommendations may only be used by the tribunal to attempt to obviate or reduce the adverse effects of the discrimination on the claimant. This does not give the tribunal broader powers to effect changes for the benefit of a wider class of persons who are not party to the proceedings. The recommendation must be directed towards an individualised remedy rather than a class-based remedy. So the respondent cannot be ordered to review the wider effect of the discriminatory act nor to cease committing such an act in the future.[161]

---

[152] ERA 1996, s 113.

[153] Ibid, ss 118–127, and see s 117(8).

[154] Ibid, s 117(3); *Morganite Electrical Carbon Ltd v Donne* [1988] ICR 8, EAT; *Motherwell Railway Club v McQueen* [1989] ICR 418, EAT.

[155] Ibid, s 117(4)(a), and see s 117(7).

[156] Ibid, s 117(5)(b). A 'week's pay' is subject to the statutory maximum.

[157] Ibid, s 117(6)(c), as amended.

[158] Ibid, s 117(5)(a).

[159] Employment Act 2002, s 31 and Sch 3.

[160] DDA 1995, s 17A(2)(c). See generally: *Chief Constable of West Yorkshire Police v Vento (No 2)* [2002] IRLR 177, EAT; [2003] IRLR 102, CA.

[161] But see the powers of the DRC discussed in Chapter 9.

The tribunal's attention must be entirely focused upon making a recommendation which will counteract or reduce the discriminatory effect upon the claimant.

10.4.30   This might include, for example, a recommendation that the respondent should consider the claimant for the next available suitable vacancy or reconsider the training opportunities or career development of a disabled claimant already in the respondent's employment. It might also include a recommendation that the employer take steps that would amount to the making of reasonable adjustments to arrangements or the physical features of premises if this would be within that employer's statutory duty and directed towards preventing a substantial disadvantage to the disabled claimant created by those unadjusted arrangements or physical features. Nevertheless, in one case, the EAT suggested that the tribunal should simply recommend that the respondent should take action to make reasonable adjustments within a specified time, rather than make a particular adjustment contended for.[162]

10.4.31   It is a moot point whether the employment tribunal's statutory powers allow it to recommend that the disabled claimant should actually be engaged for or promoted to the next available suitable vacancy. Such a power was clearly not within the letter or spirit of sex or race discrimination legislation because the respondent, in obeying such a recommendation, might then commit an act of unlawful positive or reverse discrimination.[163] That does not appear to be a problem under the DDA 1995 because the legislation is asymmetrical. The Act does not prohibit (but neither does it require) positive discrimination in favour of disabled persons, and a non-disabled person treated less favourably than a disabled person has no cause of action under the DDA 1995. In the other employment discrimination jurisdictions, compensation is frequently regarded as the primary remedy. Given the emphasis in the DDA 1995 upon the respondent's duties to make reasonable adjustments to accommodate disabled persons, it is perhaps surprising that there has not been a shift away in DDA cases from first reliance upon compensatory remedies and towards recommendations of positive action.

10.4.32   If the respondent fails 'without reasonable justification' to comply with a recommendation made by an employment tribunal, the tribunal may, if it thinks it just and equitable, order the payment of compensation or increase the amount of a compensation order already made.[164] What will amount to 'reasonable justification' is clearly a question of fact and will vary from case to case.[165] For example, if a recommendation has been made to the effect that the claimant should be

---

[162]   *Post Office v Jones* [2000] ICR 388, EAT.

[163]   *Noon v North West Thames Regional Health Authority (No 2)* [1988] IRLR 530, CA; *British Gas plc v Sharma* [1991] IRLR 101, EAT.

[164]   DDA 1995, s 17A(5).

[165]   *Nelson v Tyne and Wear Passenger Transport Executive* [1978] ICR 1183, EAT.

considered for promotion, but, in the meanwhile, he or she has lost his or her employment due to a genuine redundancy exercise, that would probably amount to a reasonable justification for the failure to comply with the recommendation. It is unlikely that justification could be advanced by reference to factors which are themselves made unlawful under the DDA 1995. So, for example, if the claimant was only selected as a redundancy candidate because he or she was a disabled person, that would not be a justifying reason.

10.4.33   In its final report, the DRTF made a number of recommendations for the future reform of employment tribunal powers and procedures in relation to the DDA 1995.[166] It suggested that employment tribunals should be able to order re-instatement or re-engagement in disability-related dismissal cases and be empowered to make enforceable recommendations regarding the future conduct of an employer found liable for discrimination. The DRTF recommended that the time-limits for completing the pre-proceedings statutory questionnaire should be fine-tuned and that, wherever possible, a tribunal hearing a DDA case should include at least one person with disability expertise. Those recommendations were taken up by the former DRC.[167] The Government indicated its intention to act when the legislative timetable permitted.[168] However, when that opportunity came with the DDA 2005, many of the DRTF recommendations in this area were largely ignored.

10.5   PART 3 CASES

Proceedings in the county court or sheriff court

10.5.1   Claims of disability discrimination arising under Part 3 of the DDA 1995 in respect of provision of services, functions of local authorities, private clubs and premises are the subject of civil proceedings in the same way as any other claim in tort (or, in Scotland, in reparation for breach of a statutory duty).[169] Proceedings in England and Wales, and in Northern Ireland, may be brought only in the county court.[170] In Scotland, proceedings may be brought only in a sheriff court.[171] No civil

---

[166] Disability Rights Task Force, *From Exclusion to Inclusion: A Report of the Disability Rights Task Force for Disabled People* (1999, London: DfEE), Chapter 3.

[167] *Legislative Review: First Review of the Disability Discrimination Act 1995: Consultation* (Disability Rights Commission, May 2002).

[168] *Towards Inclusion – Civil Rights for Disabled People: Government Response to the Disability Rights Task Force* (DfEE, March 2001), para 3.51. See also: Department for Work and Pensions, *Draft Disability Discrimination Bill*, Cm 6058 (December 2003); Joint Committee on the Draft Disability Discrimination Bill, *First Report* (April 2004); Department for Work and Pensions, *The Government's Response to the Report of the Joint Committee on the Draft Disability Discrimination Bill*, Cm 6276 (July 2004).

[169] DDA 1995, s 25(1). However, Part 3 employment services and group insurance arrangement cases are dealt with in the employment tribunal: s 25(7)–(9), as substituted.

[170] DDA 1995, s 25(3) and Sch 8, para 12.

[171] Ibid, s 25(4).

or criminal proceedings may be brought in respect of an act merely because the act is made unlawful under the provisions of Part 3 of the DDA 1995.[172] This does not prevent proceedings for judicial review arising in respect of any decision taken in relation to Part 3.[173] It is likely that, in many instances, Part 3 cases will brought under the small claims arbitration procedure.

Time-limits

10.5.2   The limitation period for Part 3 claims is six months. A county court or sheriff court shall not consider a Part 3 claim unless proceedings in respect of it have been instituted before the end of the period of six months beginning when the act complained of was done.[174] The court may consider a claim which is otherwise time-barred if, in all the circumstances of the case, the court considers that it is just and equitable to do so.[175]

10.5.3   Questions about the operation of this limitation period are likely to arise in a similar way to those which arise in respect of the comparable provisions affecting employment cases. In particular, in the case of an isolated act of disability discrimination, the presumption will be that time starts to run from the date of the act or the omission itself. A deliberate omission is to be treated as done when the person in question decided upon it.[176] Subject to rebutting evidence, a person is treated as having decided upon an omission when he or she does an act inconsistent with doing the omitted act or, in the absence of such inconsistent behaviour, when the period expires within which he or she might reasonably have been expected to do the omitted act if it was to be done.[177] However, in other cases, there is more flexibility in measuring the date upon which time starts to run. In the case of any act or omission which extends over a period of time, the six-months limitation provision will not start to run until the end of the period in question.[178] Moreover, where the alleged unlawful act of discrimination is attributable to a term in a contract, time does not start to expire until the end of the contract. The unlawful act is said to extend throughout the duration of the contract.[179]

Conciliation

10.5.4   The former arrangements made by the DRC for the provision of 'conciliation services' in relation to disputes arising under Part 3 of the

---

[172] DDA 1995, Sch 3, para 5(1).
[173] Ibid, Sch 3, para 5(2).
[174] Ibid, Sch 3, para 6(1) (but see **10.5.4**). An 'act' includes a deliberate omission (s 68(1)).
[175] Ibid, Sch 3, para 6(3).
[176] Ibid, Sch 3, para 6(4)(c).
[177] Ibid, Sch 3, para 6(5).
[178] Ibid, Sch 3, para 6(4)(b).
[179] Ibid, Sch 3, para 6(4)(a).

DDA 1995 have been repealed.[180] Instead, the Commission for Equality and Human Rights may now make arrangements for the provision of comparable conciliation services.[181] Normally, civil proceedings for an alleged breach of the provisions of Part 3 of the DDA 1995 must be commenced within six months of the act of discrimination.[182] However, if the dispute concerned is referred for conciliation in pursuance of statutory arrangements made by the CEHR before the end of the six-months limitation period, then the limitation period within which civil proceedings must be commenced is extended by a further three months.[183]

Settlements

10.5.5 Any term in a contract for the provision of goods, facilities or services is void so far as it purports to require any person to do anything which would contravene any provision of (or made under) Part 3 of the DDA 1995.[184] This invalidating principle also applies to any term in any other agreement (which would presumably include a tenancy agreement or lease) which purports to have that effect. In like manner, a term in a contract or agreement which purports to exclude or limit the operation of any provision of Part 3, or which seeks to prevent any person from making a claim under this part of the statute, is void.

10.5.6 The effect of such terms being voided is to make them unenforceable, but this does not apparently render the contract or agreement itself null and void. Instead, a person interested in an agreement containing such a void term may apply to a county court (or a sheriff court in Scotland) for an order modifying the agreement to take account of the effect of the term being void.[185] The court may make such an order as it thinks just and this may include provision as respects any period before the order was made.[186] The court may not make any such order unless the affected parties have been given notice of the application (subject to any rules of court to the contrary) and have been afforded an opportunity to make representations to the court.[187]

10.5.7 This provision concerning the validity of contract terms does not prevent parties to a dispute under Part 3 of the DDA 1995 settling legal proceedings by an agreement on terms. A Part 3 claim by a person in civil

---

[180] DDA 1995, s 28, as substituted by the Disability Rights Commission Act 1999, and now repealed by the Equality Act 2006.

[181] Equality Act 2006, s 27 as amended by SI 2006/1031, SI 2007/1895, SI 2007/2405 and SI 2007/2914 (and in force from 1 October 2007).

[182] DDA 1995, Sch 3, para 6(1).

[183] Ibid, Sch 3, para 6(2), as amended.

[184] Ibid, s 26(1). However, that is not the case in relation to any term in a contract (or other agreement) for the provision of employment services or group insurance arrangements: s 26(1A), as amended.

[185] Ibid, s 26(3).

[186] Ibid, s 26(6).

[187] Ibid, s 26(4)–(5).

proceedings may be settled by an agreement that has the effect of excluding or limiting the operation of any provision of Part 3 or prevents a person from pursuing or continuing a claim under the DDA 1995.[188] It cannot, of course, require any person to do anything that would contravene the statute.

Remedies

10.5.8 In any proceedings in respect of discrimination in non-employment cases under Part 3 of the DDA 1995, any damages awarded by the court in respect of discrimination found to be unlawful may include compensation for injury to feelings.[189] Such a head of damages may be awarded alone or in tandem with compensation for other heads of loss. However, the DDA 1995 provides for the possibility that the amount of any damages awarded for injury to feelings shall not exceed a figure to be prescribed by regulations.[190] No such figure has been prescribed to date. If such a figure were to be prescribed in the future (which does not appear likely), it would not be a general ceiling on compensation that may be awarded in non-employment cases. It would be a limit only upon that element of any award that reflects injury to feelings.[191] The effect might be that any such limitation would ensure that the majority of litigation brought under Part 3 of the DDA 1995 would be pursued through the county court small claims procedure for claims under £5,000 (as seems likely, in any event).[192] At the other end of the scale, it is likely that the civil courts will follow the authorities on awards for injury to feelings in employment discrimination cases. An award of less than £750 would be unusual.[193]

10.5.9 Otherwise, the remedies available in civil proceedings under DDA 1995, Part 3 are those which are available in the High Court or, in Scotland, the Court of Session.[194] In appropriate cases, therefore, a

---

[188] DDA 1995, s 26(2).

[189] Ibid, s 25(2). In one of the few reported Part 3 cases, a county court awarded £1,000 for injury to feelings and £2,000 aggravated damages to a school pupil discriminated against in relation to a school holiday: *White v Clitheroe Royal Grammar School*, a 2002 decision of District Judge Ashton in Preston County Court reported in *Equal Opportunities Review* No 106 (June 2002), 26–28. The damages awarded contained a reduction for contributory conduct, but reflected the fact that the school had persisted in its discriminatory actions despite the protests of the pupil's parents and others. Other examples of Part 3 awards are noted briefly on the former DRC website: www.drg-gb.org.

[190] Ibid, Sch 3, para 7.

[191] HL Deb, vol 566, col 1065.

[192] Ibid, vol 565, cols 734–735.

[193] *Purves v Joydisk Ltd* [2003] Scot SC 16, [2003] IRLR 420 (Sheriff Principal Iain McPhail QC). The court increased an award for injury to feelings from £350 to £1,000 in a case where a disabled person with a guide dog was refused service at a restaurant. In so doing, the court expressly referred to the authorities from Part 2 cases.

[194] DDA 1995, s 25(5).

successful claimant (or pursuer) may be enabled to seek a declaration of his or her rights or an injunction to prevent further or continuing acts of discrimination.

10.6 EDUCATION CASES: SCHOOLS

Special Educational Needs and Disability Tribunal

10.6.1 In England and Wales, the anti-discrimination provisions[195] applying to schools and disabled pupils (with the exception of claims relating to admissions or exclusion decisions) are enforceable in the Special Educational Needs and Disability Tribunal (SENDIST).[196] Regulations may make provision about the proceedings of SENDIST on a claim of unlawful discrimination under Part 4, Chapter 1 of the DDA 1995 and the making of a claim.[197] Regulations have been made in the form of the Special Educational Needs and Disability Tribunal (General Provisions and Disability Claims Procedure) Regulations 2002.[198] Schedule 3, Part 3 of the DDA 1995, makes further provision about enforcement of Part 4, Chapter 1 of the DDA 1995 and about procedure.[199]

10.6.2 Proceedings before the SENDIST are to be held in private, except in prescribed circumstances.[200] The Secretary of State may pay such allowances for the purpose of or in connection with the attendance of persons at the SENDIST as he or she may, with the consent of the Treasury, determine.[201] Part 1 of the Arbitration Act 1996 does not apply to proceedings before the SENDIST, but regulations may make provision (in relation to such proceedings) corresponding to any provision of that Part.[202] The regulations may make provision for a claim under Part 4, Chapter 1 of the DDA 1995, to be heard, in prescribed circumstances, with an appeal under Part 4 of the Education Act 1996.[203]

---

[195] See **7.4**.

[196] DDA 1995, s 28H, inserted by SENDA 2001, s 17(1), as amended by Education Act 2002, s 195 and Sch 18. In Wales, SENDIST is known as the Special Educational Needs and Disability Tribunal for Wales. See generally, Schools Code of Practice, Chapter 9. According to SENDIST, *Annual Report 2005–2006* (January 2006) there had been an increase of 45 per cent in Part 4 disability discrimination claims over the previous year, but that the number of claims registered (122) was still relatively small.

[197] DDA 1995, s 28J, as amended. See s 28J(1).

[198] SI 2002/1985, made under DDA 1995, s 28J(1)–(3), (8). An account of the practice and procedure of the tribunal is beyond the scope of this book.

[199] DDA 1995, s 28J(11).

[200] Ibid, s 28J(3).

[201] Ibid, s 28J(5). In relation to Wales, the power conferred by s 28J(5) may be exercised only with the agreement of the Welsh Ministers: s 28J(6), as amended.

[202] Ibid, s 28J(7).

[203] That is, an appeal under the SEN framework: ibid, s 28J(8). See Schools Code of Practice, paras 9.9–9.10.

Claim and remedies

10.6.3   A claim that a responsible body has discriminated against a person (A) in a way which is made unlawful under Part 4, Chapter 1 of the DDA 1995, may be made to the SENDIST by A's parent under s 28I.[204] This will include a claim where the responsible body is to be treated as having discriminated against a person (A) in such a way by virtue of being an employer or principal.[205] If the SENDIST considers that the claim is well founded it may declare that A has been unlawfully discriminated against and, if it does so, it may make such order as it considers reasonable in all the circumstances of the case.[206] The power to make such an order in particular may be exercised with a view to obviating or reducing the adverse effect on the person concerned of any matter to which the claim relates, but does not include power to order the payment of any sum by way of compensation.[207]

10.6.4   Special provision is made by s 28K of the DDA 1995 as to claims relating to admissions.[208] The provisions of s 28I do not apply to such claims.[209] Section 28K will apply if statutory arrangements (appeal arrangements) have been made[210] or a statutory agreement has been entered into between the responsible body for an academy and the Secretary of State[211] enabling an appeal to be made against the decision by A's parent.[212] If that condition is satisfied, then s 28K applies to a claim in relation to an 'admissions decision'[213] that a responsible body has discriminated against a person (A) in a way which is made unlawful under Part 4, Chapter 1 of the DDA 1995.[214] In such a case, the claim must be made under the appeal arrangements.[215] The body hearing the claim has the same powers as it has in relation to an appeal under the appeal arrangements.[216]

---

[204]   DDA 1995, s 28I(1), as amended. It does not apply to claims to which s 28K or s 28L apply (admissions or exclusions): DDA 1995, s 28I(2).

[205]   Ibid, s 58.

[206]   Ibid, s 28I(3). See Schools Code of Practice, para 9.11 for examples of the kinds of order the SENDIST might make.

[207]   Ibid, s 28I(4).

[208]   Ibid, s 28K, as amended.

[209]   Ibid, s 28I(2).

[210]   Under School Standards and Framework Act 1998, s 94.

[211]   Under Education Act 1996, s 482.

[212]   DDA 1995, s 28K(2).

[213]   An 'admissions decision' means a decision of a kind mentioned in the School Standards and Framework Act 1998, s 94(1) or (2), or a decision as to the admission of a person to a city academy taken by the responsible body or on its behalf: DDA 1995, s 28K(5).

[214]   DDA 1995, s 28K(1). This will include a claim where the responsible body is to be treated under s 58 as having discriminated against a person (A) in such a way by virtue of being an employer or principal.

[215]   Ibid, s 28K(3). See Schools Code of Practice, paras 9.14–9.20.

[216]   Ibid, s 28K(4).

10.6.5   Special provision is made by s 28L of the DDA 1995 as to claims relating to exclusions.[217] The provisions of s 28I do not apply to such claims.[218] Section 28L will apply if statutory arrangements (appeal arrangements) have been made[219] or a statutory agreement has been entered into between the responsible body for a city academy and the Secretary of State[220] enabling an appeal to be made against the decision by A or A's parent.[221] If that condition is satisfied, then s 28L applies to a claim in relation to an 'exclusion decision'[222] that a responsible body has discriminated against a person (A) in a way which is made unlawful under Part 4, Chapter 1 of the DDA 1995.[223] In such a case, the claim must be made under the appeal arrangements.[224] The body hearing the claim has the powers it has in relation to an appeal under the appeal arrangements.[225]

10.6.6   Except as provided for by ss 28I, 28K, 28L and 28N of the DDA 1995 as described above, no civil or criminal proceedings may be brought against any person in respect of an act merely because the act is unlawful under Part 4, Chapter 1 of the DDA 1995.[226] This does not prevent the making of an application for judicial review.

Time-limits

10.6.7   SENDIST shall not consider a claim under s 28I of the DDA 1995 unless proceedings in respect of the claim are instituted before the end of the period of six months beginning when the act complained of was done.[227] However, if in relation to proceedings (or prospective proceedings) under s 28I the dispute concerned is referred for

---

[217]   DDA 1995, s 28L, as amended. The meaning of an exclusion for the purpose of s 28L has been considered in *McAuley Catholic High School v (1) CC; (2) PC; and (3) Special Educational Needs and Disability Tribunal* [2003] EWHC 3045 (Admin), (2003) 6 CCLR 194. A temporary exclusion for a short fixed period did not exclude the subsequent jurisdiction of SENDIST under s 28I.

[218]   Ibid, s 28I(2).

[219]   Under Education Act 2002, s 52(3)(c).

[220]   Under Education Act 1996, s 482.

[221]   DDA 1995, s 28L(2).

[222]   An 'exclusion decision' means a decision of a kind mentioned the Education Act 2002, s 52(3)(c), or a decision not to reinstate a pupil who has been permanently excluded from an academy by its head teacher, taken by the responsible body or on its behalf: DDA 1995, s 28L(5). A responsible body in relation to a maintained school (as defined in s 28Q(5)) includes the discipline committee of the governing body if that committee is required to be established as a result of regulations made under Education Act 2002, s 19: DDA 1995, s 28L(6)–(7).

[223]   DDA 1995, s 28L(1). This will include a claim where the responsible body is to be treated under s 58 as having discriminated against a person (A) in such a way by virtue of being an employer or principal.

[224]   Ibid, s 28L(3). See Schools Code of Practice, paras 9.21–9.27.

[225]   Ibid, s 28L(4).

[226]   Ibid, Sch 3, Part 3, para 9, as amended.

[227]   Ibid, Sch 3, Part 3, para 10(1).

conciliation[228] before the end of that period of six months, the period is extended by three months.[229] Nevertheless, the SENDIST may consider a claim which is out of time if, in all the circumstances of the case, it considers that it is just and equitable to do so.[230] If an unlawful act of discrimination is attributable to a term in a contract, that act is to be treated as extending throughout the duration of the contract.[231] Any act extending over a period shall be treated as done at the end of that period.[232] A deliberate omission shall be treated as done when the person in question decided upon it.[233] In the absence of evidence establishing the contrary, a person shall be taken to decide upon an omission when he or she does an act inconsistent with doing the omitted act or (if he or she has done no such inconsistent act) when the period expires within which he or she might reasonably have been expected to do the omitted act if it was to be done.[234]

Roles of the Secretary of State and the Welsh Ministers

10.6.8 If the Secretary of State in England or the Welsh Ministers in Wales (in both cases referred to as the 'appropriate authority') is satisfied (whether on a complaint or otherwise) that a responsible body has acted (or is proposing to act) unreasonably in the discharge of a duty imposed by or under s 28D or s 28E of the DDA 1995 (or has failed to discharge a duty imposed by or under either of those sections) the appropriate authority may give that body such directions as to the discharge of the duty as appear to it to be expedient.[235] Particular provision is made in relation to special schools which are not maintained special schools (but which are approved by the Secretary of State or by the National Assembly[236]) and also for city academies.[237] In relation to such special schools and city academies, if the appropriate authority is satisfied (whether on a complaint or otherwise) that a responsible body has acted (or is proposing to act) unreasonably in the discharge of a duty which that

---

[228] In pursuance of arrangements under Equality Act 2006, s 27.

[229] DDA 1995, Sch 3, Part 3, para 10(2), as amended.

[230] Ibid, Sch 3, Part 3, para 10(3)–(4). But this does not permit the SENDIST to decide to consider a claim if a decision not to consider that claim has previously been taken under para 10(3).

[231] Ibid, Sch 3, Part 3, para 10(5)(a).

[232] Ibid, Sch 3, Part 3, para 10(5)(b).

[233] Ibid, Sch 3, Part 3, para 10(5)(c).

[234] Ibid, Sch 3, Part 3, para 10(6).

[235] Ibid, s 28M, as amended. Directions may be given even if the performance of the duty is contingent upon the opinion of the responsible body: DDA 1995, s 28M(4). Directions may be varied or revoked by the directing authority and may be enforced (on the application of the directing authority) by a mandatory order obtained in accordance with Supreme Court Act 1981, s 31 (prospectively, Senior Courts Act 1981, s 31): DDA 1995, s 28M(7). The term 'directing authority' means the Secretary of State in relation to a direction given by him or her, and the Welsh Ministers in relation to a direction given by them: ibid, s 28M(9).

[236] Under Education Act 1996, s 342.

[237] DDA 1995, s 28M(2).

body has in relation to the provision to the appropriate authority of copies of that body's accessibility plan or the inspection of that plan, or has failed to discharge that duty, the appropriate authority may give that body such directions as to the discharge of the duty as appear to it to be expedient.[238]

10.6.9 Where the SENDIST has made an order under s 28I(3) of the DDA 1995,[239] if the Secretary of State is satisfied (whether on a complaint or otherwise) that the responsible body concerned has acted (or is proposing to act) unreasonably in complying with the order or has failed to comply with the order, he or she may give that body such directions as to compliance with the order as appear to him or her to be expedient.[240]

Enforcement in Scotland

10.6.10 The position in Scotland regarding the enforcement of rights under DDA 1995, Part 4, Chapter 1 is somewhat different and simpler than the position in England and Wales,[241] although not necessarily more accessible. Section 28N of the DDA 1995 applies exclusively to Scotland. A claim that a responsible body in Scotland has discriminated against a person in a way which is unlawful under Part 4 of the DDA 1995 may be made the subject of civil proceedings in the same way as any other claim for the enforcement of a statutory duty.[242] Proceedings in Scotland may be brought only in a sheriff court.[243] The remedies available in such proceedings are those which are available in the Court of Session other

---

[238] DDA 1995, s 28M(3). Directions may be given even if the performance of the duty is contingent upon the opinion of the responsible body: ibid, s 28M(4). Directions may be varied or revoked by the directing authority and may be enforced (on the application of the directing authority) by a mandatory order obtained in accordance with Supreme Court Act 1981, s 31 (prospectively, Senior Courts Act 1981, s 31): DDA 1995, s 28M(7). The term 'directing authority' means the Secretary of State in relation to a direction given by him or her, and the Welsh Ministers in relation to a direction given by them: ibid, s 28M(9).

[239] If SENDIST considers that a claim is well founded, it may declare that A has been unlawfully discriminated against and, if it does so, it may make such order as it considers reasonable in all the circumstances of the case.

[240] DDA 1995, s 28M(5)–(6). Directions may be varied or revoked by the directing authority and may be enforced (on the application of the directing authority) by a mandatory order obtained in accordance with Supreme Court Act 1981, s 31 (prospectively, Senior Courts Act 1981, s 31): DDA 1995, s 28M(7). The term 'directing authority' means the Secretary of State in relation to a direction given by him or her, and the Welsh Ministers in relation to a direction given by them: ibid, s 28M(9).

[241] See generally, Schools Code of Practice, Chapter 8.

[242] DDA 1995, s 28N(1). This will include a claim where the responsible body is to be treated under s 58 as having discriminated against a person in such a way by virtue of being an employer or principal.

[243] Ibid, s 28N(2).

than an award of damages.[244] Financial compensation is not available, but a declaration of rights, an interdict or an order requiring positive action will be.[245]

Validity and revision of agreements of responsible bodies

10.6.11 Section 28P of the DDA 1995 makes provision for the validity and revision of agreements of responsible bodies.[246] By virtue of s 28P(1), any term in a contract or other agreement made by or on behalf of a responsible body is void so far as it purports to:

- require a person to do anything which would contravene any provision of (or made under);

- exclude or limit the operation of any provision of (or made under); or

- prevent any person from making a claim under,

Part 4, Chapter 1 of the DDA 1995.[247]

This does not prevent an agreement settling a claim under s 28I or s 28N or to which s 28K or s 28L apply.[248] On the application of any person interested in an agreement to which s 28P(1) applies, a county court (or a sheriff court in Scotland) may make such order as it thinks just for modifying the agreement to take account of the effect of s 28P(1).[249] No such order may be made unless all persons affected have been given notice of the application and afforded an opportunity to make representations to the court.[250] Such an order may include provision as respects any period before the making of the order.[251]

---

[244] DDA 1995, s 28N(3). Ibid, Sch 3, Part 3 makes further provision about enforcement in Scotland and about procedure: s 28N(4). In relation to civil proceedings in Scotland, in Sch 3, Part 3, references to s 28I are to be construed as a reference to s 28N, and references to the SENDIST are to be construed as references to the sheriff court: s 28N(5), as amended.

[245] Schools Code of Practice, paras 8.7–8.9. In an exclusion case, the sheriff court has the power to reduce (ie to annul or overturn) the decision to exclude.

[246] See Schools Code of Practice, paras 10.20–10.21.

[247] DDA 1995, s 28P(1).

[248] Ibid, s 28P(2).

[249] Ibid, s 28P(3).

[250] Ibid, s 28P(4), subject to any rules of court providing for notice to be dispensed with: s 28P(5).

[251] Ibid, s 28P(6).

Conciliation

10.6.12 Section 27 of the Equality Act 2006 makes provision for conciliation for disputes arising in education cases. This is not considered further here.

10.7 EDUCATION CASES: FURTHER AND HIGHER EDUCATION

10.7.1 Section 28V of the DDA 1995 makes provision for the enforcement of the anti-discrimination rights in further and higher education.[252] A claim by a person that a responsible body has discriminated against him or her (or subjected him or her to harassment) in a way which is unlawful under Part 4, Chapter 2 of the DDA 1995 may be made the subject of civil proceedings in the same way as any other claim in tort or (in Scotland) in reparation for breach of statutory duty.[253] Proceedings in England and Wales may be brought only in a county court, whereas proceedings in Scotland may be brought only in a sheriff court.[254] The fact that a person who brings proceedings under Part 4, Chapter 2 of the DDA 1995 (the education provisions) against a responsible body may also be entitled to bring proceedings against that body under Part 2 (the employment provisions) does not affect the proceedings under Part 4.[255] No civil or criminal proceedings may be brought against any person in respect of an act merely because the act is unlawful under Part 4, Chapter 2 of the DDA 1995, but this does not prevent the making of an application for judicial review.[256]

10.7.2 As in other areas of discrimination law, there is a statutory reversal of the burden of proof. Where a claim is brought under s 28V(1), and the claimant (or pursuer) proves facts from which the court could conclude in the absence of an adequate explanation that the defendant (or defender) has acted in a way which is unlawful, the court shall uphold the claim unless the defendant (or defender) proves that he, she or it did not so act.[257]

---

[252] DDA 1995, Sch 3, Part 4 makes further provision about the enforcement and about procedure: s 28V(7). See generally revised Post-16 Code of Practice 2006, Chapter 13.

[253] DDA 1995, s 28V(1). This includes a claim that a responsible body is by virtue of ibid, s 57 (aiding unlawful acts) or s 58 (liability of employers and principals) to be treated as having discriminated against him or her in such a way, or that a person is by virtue of s 57 (aiding unlawful acts) to be treated as having discriminated against him in such a way.

[254] Ibid, s 28V(3)–(4).

[255] Ibid, s 28V(6).

[256] Ibid, Sch 3, Part 4, para 12.

[257] Ibid, s 28V(1A) (from 1 September 2006). See SI 2006/1721, reg 4.

Time-limits

10.7.3 A county court (or a sheriff court in Scotland) shall not consider a claim under s 28V of the DDA 1995 unless proceedings in respect of the claim are instituted before the end of the period of six months beginning when the act complained of was done.[258] If, in relation to proceedings (or prospective proceedings) under s 28V, the dispute concerned is referred for conciliation[259] before the end of that period of six months, the period allowed shall be extended by three months.[260] Time is also extended where, in England and Wales, the dispute has not been referred to conciliation, but is a dispute relating to the act or omission of a qualifying institution, and is referred as a complaint under the student complaints scheme before the end of the period of six months.[261]

10.7.4 A court may consider any claim under s 28V which is out of time if, in all the circumstances of the case, it considers that it is just and equitable to do so.[262] If an unlawful act is attributable to a term in a contract, that act is to be treated as extending throughout the duration of the contract.[263] Any act extending over a period shall be treated as done at the end of that period.[264] A deliberate omission shall be treated as done when the person in question decided upon it.[265] In the absence of evidence establishing the contrary, a person shall be taken to decide upon an omission when he or she does an act inconsistent with doing the omitted act or, if he or she has done no such inconsistent act, when the period expires within which he or she might reasonably have been expected to do the omitted act if it was to be done.[266]

Remedies

10.7.5 The remedies available in proceedings brought under Part 4, Chapter 2 of the DDA 1995 are those which are available in the High Court or (in Scotland) the Court of Session.[267] These will include a declaration of rights, an injunction (an interdict in Scotland) and damages. Damages may include compensation for injury to feelings (whether or not they include compensation under any other head).[268]

---

[258] DDA 1995, Sch 3, Part 4, para 13(1).
[259] In pursuance of arrangements under Equality Act 2006, s 27.
[260] DDA 1995, Sch 3, Part 4, para 13(2)(a), as amended.
[261] Ibid, Sch 3, Part 4, para 13(2)(b) and (2A), as amended. See Higher Education Act 2004, ss 11–12.
[262] DDA 1995, Sch 3, Part 4, para 13(3).
[263] Ibid, Sch 3, Part 4, para 13(3)(a).
[264] Ibid, Sch 3, Part 4, para 13(3)(c).
[265] Ibid, Sch 3, Part 4, para 13(3)(a).
[266] Ibid, Sch 3, Part 4, para 13(4).
[267] Ibid, s 28V(5).
[268] Ibid, s 28V(2). The amount of any damages awarded as compensation for injury to feelings shall not exceed a prescribed amount: ibid, Sch 3, Part 4, para 14. No maximum amount has been prescribed.

Validity and revision of agreements of responsible bodies

10.7.6 Section 28P of the DDA 1995 makes provision for the validity and revision of agreements of responsible bodies.[269] This applies equally to claims brought against responsible bodies in further and higher education as it does in relation to schools.[270]

Conciliation

10.7.7 Section 27 of the Equality Act 2006 makes provision for conciliation for disputes arising in further and higher education cases. This is not considered further here.

10.8 EDUCATION CASES: GENERAL QUALIFICATIONS BODIES

10.8.1 Similar provisions to those that apply in the other areas of education now also apply to proceedings in relation to general qualifications bodies.[271] A claim by a person that a general qualifications body has unlawfully discriminated against him or her (or subjected him or her to unlawful harassment) may be made the subject of civil proceedings in the same way as any other claim in tort or (in Scotland) in reparation for breach of statutory duty.[272] Proceedings are brought in the county court or the sheriff court.[273] Otherwise, no other civil or criminal proceedings may be brought (except judicial review).[274]

10.8.2 A court shall not consider a claim against a general qualifications body unless proceedings are instituted before the end of the period of six months beginning when the act complained of was done.[275] However, if the dispute concerned is referred to conciliation[276] before the end of the period of six months, that period shall be extended by three months.[277] A court may consider any claim which is out of time if, in all the circumstances of the case, it considers that it is just and equitable to do so.[278]

---

[269] Inserted by SENDA 2001, s 24. See **10.5.11**.
[270] DDA 1995, s 28X. See Post-16 Code of Practice, paras 8.11–8.12.
[271] DDA 1995, s 31ADA and Sch 3, Part 5.
[272] Ibid, s 31ADA(1). This also applies where the body is to be treated as having done so under ss 57 or 58 or where a person is to be treated as having done so under s 57.
[273] Ibid, s 31ADA(4) and (5).
[274] Ibid, Sch 3, para 16.
[275] Ibid, Sch 3, para 17(1) and (4).
[276] Under arrangements made under Equality Act 2007, s 27.
[277] DDA 1995, Sch 3, para 17(2).
[278] Ibid, Sch 3, para 17(3).

10.8.3   There is a statutory reversal of the burden of proof.[279] The remedies available are those which are available in the High Court or the Court of Session.[280] Compensation in damages may include injury to feelings.[281]

---

[279] DDA 1995, s 31ADA(2).
[280] Ibid, s 31ADA(6).
[281] Ibid, s 31ADA(3).

APPENDIX I

DISABILITY DISCRIMINATION ACT 1995 (1995 C. 50)

(AS AMENDED)

ARRANGEMENT OF SECTIONS

PART I
DISABILITY

PART II
THE EMPLOYMENT FIELD AND MEMBERS OF LOCALLY-ELECTABLE AUTHORITIES

Meaning of 'discrimination' and 'harassment'

Employment

Contract Workers

Office-holders

Occupational pension schemes

Partnerships

PART III
DISCRIMINATION IN OTHER AREAS

Public authorities

Private Clubs etc

Premises

Enforcement, etc

PART IV
EDUCATION

Chapter 1
Schools

Duties of responsible bodies

PART V
PUBLIC TRANSPORT

PART I
DISABILITY

1 Meaning of 'disability' and 'disabled person'

(1) Subject to the provisions of Schedule 1, a person has a disability for the purposes of this Act if he has a physical or mental impairment which has a substantial and long-term adverse effect on his ability to carry out normal day-to-day activities.

(2) In this Act 'disabled person' means a person who has a disability.

2 Past disabilities

(1) The provisions of this Part and Parts II to 4 and 5A apply in relation to a person who has had a disability as they apply in relation to a person who has that disability.

(2) Those provisions are subject to the modifications made by Schedule 2.

(3) Any regulations or order made under this Act by the Secretary of State, the Scottish Ministers or the Welsh Ministers may include provision with respect to persons who have had a disability.

(4) In any proceedings under Part 2, 3 , 4 or 5A of this Act, the question whether a person had a disability at a particular time ('the relevant time') shall be determined, for the purposes of this section, as if the provisions of, or made under, this Act in force when the act complained of was done had been in force at the relevant time.

(5) The relevant time may be a time before the passing of this Act.

Amendment – Amended by Special Educational Needs and Disability Act 2001, s 38(1), (2); Disability Discrimination Act 2005, s 19(1), Sch 1, Pt 1, paras 1, 2(1), (2); SI 2007/1388, art 3, Sch 1, paras 47, 48.

3 Guidance

(A1) The Secretary of State may issue guidance about matters to be taken into account in determining whether a person is a disabled person.

(1) Without prejudice to the generality of subsection (A1) the Secretary of State may in particular, issue guidance about the matters to be taken into account in determining—

    (a)   whether an impairment has a substantial adverse effect on a person's ability to carry out normal day-to-day activities; or

    (b)   whether such an impairment has a long-term effect.

(2) Without prejudice to the generality of subsection (A1), guidance about the matters mentioned in subsection 1 may, among other things, give examples of—

(a) effects which it would be reasonable, in relation to particular activities, to regard for purposes of this Act as substantial adverse effects;

(b) effects which it would not be reasonable, in relation to particular activities, to regard for such purposes as substantial adverse effects;

(c) substantial adverse effects which it would be reasonable to regard, for such purposes, as long-term;

(d) substantial adverse effects which it would not be reasonable to regard, for such purposes, as long-term.

(3) An adjudicating body determining, for any purpose of this Act, whether a person is a disabled person, shall take into account any guidance which appears to it to be relevant.

(3A) 'Adjudicating body' means—

(a) a court;

(b) a tribunal; and

(c) any may decide a claim under Part 4.

(4) In preparing a draft of any guidance other person who, or body which,, the Secretary of State shall consult such persons as he considers appropriate.

(5) Where the Secretary of State proposes to issue any guidance, he shall publish a draft of it, consider any representations that are made to him about the draft and, if he thinks it appropriate, modify his proposals in the light of any of those representations.

(6) If the Secretary of State decides to proceed with any proposed guidance, he shall lay a draft of it before each House of Parliament.

(7) If, within the 40-day period, either House resolves not to approve the draft, the Secretary of State shall take no further steps in relation to the proposed guidance.

(8) If no such resolution is made within the 40-day period, the Secretary of State shall issue the guidance in the form of his draft.

(9) The guidance shall come into force on such date as the Secretary of State may appoint by order.

(10) Subsection (7) does not prevent a new draft of the proposed guidance from being laid before Parliament.

(11) The Secretary of State may—

(a) from time to time revise the whole or part of any guidance and re-issue it;

(b) by order revoke any guidance.

(12) In this section—

'40-day period', in relation to the draft of any proposed guidance, means—

(a) if the draft is laid before one House on a day later than the day on which it is laid before the other House, the period of 40 days beginning with the later of the two days, and

(b) in any other case, the period of 40 days beginning with the day on which the draft is laid before each House,

no account being taken of any period during which Parliament is dissolved or prorogued or during which both Houses are adjourned for more than 4 days; and

'guidance' means guidance issued by the Secretary of State under this section and includes guidance which has been revised and re-issued.

Amendment – Amended by Special Educational Needs and Disability Act 2001, s 38(1), (3), (4); Disability Discrimination Act 2005, s 19(1), Sch 1, Pt 1, paras 1, s 3(1), (2), (3) (a), (b), (4), (5).

PART II
THE EMPLOYMENT FIELD AND MEMBERS OF LOCALLY-ELECTABLE AUTHORITIES
Meaning of 'discrimination' and 'harassment'

Amendment – Amended by Disability Discrimination Act 2005, s 19(1), Sch 1, Pt 1, paras 1, 4; Disability Discrimination Act 1995 (Amendment) Regulations 2003, SI 2003/1673, regs 3(1), 4(1), (2); SI 2003/1673, regs 3(1), 4(1).

3A Meaning of 'discrimination'

(1) For the purposes of this Part, a person discriminates against a disabled person if—

(a) for a reason which relates to the disabled person's disability, he treats him less favourably than he treats or would treat others to whom that reason does not or would not apply, and

(b) he cannot show that the treatment in question is justified.

(2) For the purposes of this Part, a person also discriminates against a disabled person if he fails to comply with a duty to make reasonable adjustments imposed on him in relation to the disabled person.

(3) Treatment is justified for the purposes of subsection (1)(b) if, but only if, the reason for it is both material to the circumstances of the particular case and substantial.

(4) But treatment of a disabled person cannot be justified under subsection (3) if it amounts to direct discrimination falling within subsection (5).

(5) A person directly discriminates against a disabled person if, on the ground of the disabled person's disability, he treats the disabled person less favourably than he treats or would treat a person not having that

particular disability whose relevant circumstances, including his abilities, are the same as, or not materially different from, those of the disabled person.

(6) If, in a case falling within subsection (1), a person is under a duty to make reasonable adjustments in relation to a disabled person but fails to comply with that duty, his treatment of that person cannot be justified under subsection (3) unless it would have been justified even if he had complied with that duty.

Amendment – Inserted by Disability Discrimination Act 1995 (Amendment) Regulations 2003, SI 2003/1673, regs 3(1), 4(2).

3B   Meaning of 'harassment'

(1) For the purposes of this Part, a person subjects a disabled person to harassment where, for a reason which relates to the disabled person's disability, he engages in unwanted conduct which has the purpose or effect of—

   (a)   violating the disabled person's dignity, or
   (b)   creating an intimidating, hostile, degrading, humiliating or offensive environment for him.

(2) Conduct shall be regarded as having the effect referred to in paragraph (a) or (b) of subsection (1) only if, having regard to all the circumstances, including in particular the perception of the disabled person, it should reasonably be considered as having that effect.

Amendment – Inserted by Disability Discrimination Act 1995 (Amendment) Regulations 2003, SI 2003/1673, regs 3(1), 4(2).

Employment

Amendment – Inserted by Disability Discrimination Act 1995 (Amendment) Regulations 2003, SI 2003/1673, regs 3(1), 5.

4   Employers: discrimination and harassment

(1) It is unlawful for an employer to discriminate against a disabled person—

   (a)   in the arrangements which he makes for the purpose of determining to whom he should offer employment;
   (b)   in the terms on which he offers that person employment; or
   (c)   by refusing to offer, or deliberately not offering, him employment.

(2) It is unlawful for an employer to discriminate against a disabled person whom he employs—

   (a)   in the terms of employment which he affords him;
   (b)   in the opportunities which he affords him for promotion, a transfer, training or receiving any other benefit;

(c) by refusing to afford him, or deliberately not affording him, any such opportunity; or

(d) by dismissing him, or subjecting him to any other detriment.

(3) It is also unlawful for an employer, in relation to employment by him, to subject to harassment—

(a) a disabled person whom he employs; or

(b) a disabled person who has applied to him for employment.

(4) Subsection (2) does not apply to benefits of any description if the employer is concerned with the provision (whether or not for payment) of benefits of that description to the public, or to a section of the public which includes the employee in question, unless—

(a) that provision differs in a material respect from the provision of the benefits by the employer to his employees;

(b) the provision of the benefits to the employee in question is regulated by his contract of employment; or

(c) the benefits relate to training.

(5) The reference in subsection (2)(d) to the dismissal of a person includes a reference—

(a) to the termination of that person's employment by the expiration of any period (including a period expiring by reference to an event or circumstance), not being a termination immediately after which the employment is renewed on the same terms; and

(b) to the termination of that person's employment by any act of his (including the giving of notice) in circumstances such that he is entitled to terminate it without notice by reason of the conduct of the employer.

(6) This section applies only in relation to employment at an establishment in Great Britain.

Amendment – Amended by Disability Discrimination Act 1995 (Amendment) Regulations 2003, SI 2003/1673, regs 3(1), 5.

4A   Employers: duty to make adjustments

(1) Where—

(a) a provision, criterion or practice applied by or on behalf of an employer, or

(b) any physical feature of premises occupied by the employer,

places the disabled person concerned at a substantial disadvantage in comparison with persons who are not disabled, it is the duty of the employer to take such steps as it is reasonable, in all the circumstances of the case, for him to have to take in order to prevent the provision, criterion or practice, or feature, having that effect.

(2) In subsection (1), 'the disabled person concerned' means—

    (a)   in the case of a provision, criterion or practice for determining to whom employment should be offered, any disabled person who is, or has notified the employer that he may be, an applicant for that employment;

    (b)   in any other case, a disabled person who is—

        (i)   an applicant for the employment concerned, or

        (ii)   an employee of the employer concerned.

(3) Nothing in this section imposes any duty on an employer in relation to a disabled person if the employer does not know, and could not reasonably be expected to know—

    (a)   in the case of an applicant or potential applicant, that the disabled person concerned is, or may be, an applicant for the employment; or

    (b)   in any case, that that person has a disability and is likely to be affected in the way mentioned in subsection (1).

Amendment – Inserted by Disability Discrimination Act 1995 (Amendment) Regulations 2003, SI 2003/1673, regs 3(1), 5.

Contract Workers

Amendment-Inserted by SI 2003/1673.

4B   Contract workers

(1) It is unlawful for a principal, in relation to contract work, to discriminate against a disabled person who is a contract worker (a 'disabled contract worker')—

    (a)   in the terms on which he allows him to do that work;

    (b)   by not allowing him to do it or continue to do it;

    (c)   in the way he affords him access to any benefits or by refusing or deliberately omitting to afford him access to them; or

    (d)   by subjecting him to any other detriment.

(2) It is also unlawful for a principal, in relation to contract work, to subject a disabled contract worker to harassment.

(3) Subsection (1) does not apply to benefits of any description if the principal is concerned with the provision (whether or not for payment) of benefits of that description to the public, or to a section of the public which includes the contract worker in question, unless that provision differs in a material respect from the provision of the benefits by the principal to contract workers.

(4) This subsection applies to a disabled contract worker where, by virtue of—

    (a)   a provision, criterion or practice applied by or on behalf of all or most of the principals to whom he is or might be supplied, or

(b)   a physical feature of premises occupied by such persons,

he is likely, on each occasion when he is supplied to a principal to do contract work, to be placed at a substantial disadvantage in comparison with persons who are not disabled which is the same or similar in each case.

(5) Where subsection (4) applies to a disabled contract worker, his employer must take such steps as he would have to take under section 4A if the provision, criterion or practice were applied by him or on his behalf or (as the case may be) if the premises were occupied by him.

(6) Section 4A applies to any principal, in relation to contract work, as if he were, or would be, the employer of the disabled contract worker and as if any contract worker supplied to do work for him were an employee of his.

(7) However, for the purposes of section 4A as applied by subsection (6), a principal is not required to take a step in relation to a disabled contract worker if under that section the disabled contract worker's employer is required to take the step in relation to him.

(8) This section applies only in relation to contract work done at an establishment in Great Britain (the provisions of section 68 about the meaning of 'employment at an establishment in Great Britain' applying for the purposes of this subsection with the appropriate modifications).

(9) In this section—

'principal' means a person ('A') who makes work available for doing by individuals who are employed by another person who supplies them under a contract made with A;

'contract work' means work so made available; and

'contract worker' means any individual who is supplied to the principal under such a contract.

Amendment – Inserted by Disability Discrimination Act 1995 (Amendment) Regulations 2003, SI 2003/1673, regs 3(1), 5.

Office-holders

Amendment – Amended by SI 2003/1673.

4C   Office-holders: introductory

(1) Subject to subsection (5), sections 4D and 4E apply to an office or post if—

(a)   no relevant provision of this Part applies in relation to an appointment to the office or post; and

(b)   one or more of the conditions specified in subsection (3) is satisfied.

(2) The following are relevant provisions of this Part for the purposes of subsection (1)(a): section 4, section 4B, section 6A, section 7A, section 7C, section 14C and section 15B(3) (b).

(3) The conditions specified in this subsection are that—

    (a)   the office or post is one to which persons are appointed to discharge functions personally under the direction of another person, and in respect of which they are entitled to remuneration;

    (b)   the office or post is one to which appointments are made by a Minister of the Crown, a government department, the Welsh Ministers, the First Minister for Wales, the Counsel General to the Welsh Assembly Government or any part of the Scottish Administration;

    (c)   the office or post is one to which appointments are made on the recommendation of, or subject to the approval of, a person referred to in paragraph (b).

(4) For the purposes of subsection (3)(a) the holder of an office or post—

    (a)   is to be regarded as discharging his functions under the direction of another person if that other person is entitled to direct him as to when and where he discharges those functions;

    (b)   is not to be regarded as entitled to remuneration merely because he is entitled to payments—

        (i)   in respect of expenses incurred by him in carrying out the functions of the office or post, or

        (ii)   by way of compensation for the loss of income or benefits he would or might have received from any person had he not been carrying out the functions of the office or post.

(5) Sections 4D and 4E do not apply to—

    (a)   any office of the House of Commons held by a member of it,

    (b)   a life peerage within the meaning of the Life Peerages Act 1958, or any office of the House of Lords held by a member of it,

    (c)   any office mentioned in Schedule 2 (Ministerial offices) to the House of Commons Disqualification Act 1975,

    (d)   the offices of Leader of the Opposition, Chief Opposition Whip or Assistant Opposition Whip within the meaning of the Ministerial and other Salaries Act 1975,

    (e)   any office of the Scottish Parliament held by a member of it,

    (f)   a member of the Scottish Executive within the meaning of section 44 of the Scotland Act 1998, or a junior Scottish Minister within the meaning of section 49 of that Act,

    (g)   any office of the National Assembly for Wales held by a member of it,

    (ga)   a member of the Welsh Assembly Government ,

    (h)   in England, any office of a county council, a London borough council, a district council or a parish council held by a member of it,

(i)   in Wales, any office of a county council, a county borough council or a community council held by a member of it,

(j)   in relation to a council constituted under section 2 of the Local Government etc (Scotland) Act 1994 or a community council established under section 51 of the Local Government (Scotland) Act 1973, any office of such a council held by a member of it,

(k)   any office of the Greater London Authority held by a member of it,

(l)   any office of the Common Council of the City of London held by a member of it,

(m)   any office of the Council of the Isles of Scilly held by a member of it, or

(n)   any office of a political party.

Amendment – Inserted by Disability Discrimination Act 2005, s 19(1), Sch 1, Pt 1, paras 1, 5; Disability Discrimination Act 1995 (Amendment) Regulations 2003, SI 2003/1673, regs 3(1), 5; SI 2007/1388, art 3, Sch 1, paras 47, 49(1), (2), (3).

4D   Office-holders: discrimination and harassment

(1) It is unlawful for a relevant person, in relation to an appointment to an office or post to which this section applies, to discriminate against a disabled person—

(a)   in the arrangements which he makes for the purpose of determining who should be offered the appointment;

(b)   in the terms on which he offers him the appointment; or

(c)   by refusing to offer him the appointment.

(2) It is unlawful for a relevant person, in relation to an appointment to an office or post to which this section applies and which satisfies the condition set out in section 4C(3)(c), to discriminate against a disabled person—

(a)   in the arrangements which he makes for the purpose of determining who should be recommended or approved in relation to the appointment; or

(b)   in making or refusing to make a recommendation, or giving or refusing to give an approval, in relation to the appointment.

(3) It is unlawful for a relevant person, in relation to a disabled person who has been appointed to an office or post to which this section applies, to discriminate against him—

(a)   in the terms of the appointment;

(b)   in the opportunities which he affords him for promotion, a transfer, training or receiving any other benefit, or by refusing to afford him any such opportunity;

(c)   by terminating the appointment; or

(d)   by subjecting him to any other detriment in relation to the appointment.

(4) It is also unlawful for a relevant person, in relation to an office or post to which this section applies, to subject to harassment a disabled person—

(a)   who has been appointed to the office or post;

(b)   who is seeking or being considered for appointment to the office or post; or

(c)   who is seeking or being considered for a recommendation or approval in relation to an appointment to an office or post satisfying the condition set out in section 4C(3)(c).

(5) Subsection (3) does not apply to benefits of any description if the relevant person is concerned with the provision (for payment or not) of benefits of that description to the public, or a section of the public to which the disabled person belongs, unless—

(a)   that provision differs in a material respect from the provision of the benefits to persons appointed to offices or posts which are the same as, or not materially different from, that to which the disabled person has been appointed;

(b)   the provision of the benefits to the person appointed is regulated by the terms and conditions of his appointment; or

(c)   the benefits relate to training.

(6) In subsection (3)(c) the reference to the termination of the appointment includes a reference—

(a)   to the termination of the appointment by the expiration of any period (including a period expiring by reference to an event or circumstance), not being a termination immediately after which the appointment is renewed on the same terms and conditions; and

(b)   to the termination of the appointment by any act of the person appointed (including the giving of notice) in circumstances such that he is entitled to terminate the appointment by reason of the conduct of the relevant person.

(7) In this section—

(a)   references to making a recommendation include references to making a negative recommendation; and

(b)   references to refusal include references to deliberate omission.

Amendment – Inserted by Disability Discrimination Act 1995 (Amendment) Regulations 2003, SI 2003/1673, regs 3(1), 5.

4E   Office-holders: duty to make adjustments

(1) Where—

(a)   a provision, criterion or practice applied by or on behalf of a relevant person, or

(b)   any physical feature of premises—

    (i)   under the control of a relevant person, and

(ii) at or from which the functions of an office or post to which this section applies are performed,

places the disabled person concerned at a substantial disadvantage in comparison with persons who are not disabled, it is the duty of the relevant person to take such steps as it is reasonable, in all the circumstances of the case, for him to have to take in order to prevent the provision, criterion or practice, or feature, having that effect.

(2) In this section, 'the disabled person concerned' means—

(a) in the case of a provision, criterion or practice for determining who should be appointed to, or recommended or approved in relation to, an office or post to which this section applies, any disabled person who—

  (i) is, or has notified the relevant person that he may be, seeking appointment to, or (as the case may be) seeking a recommendation or approval in relation to, that office or post, or

  (ii) is being considered for appointment to, or (as the case may be) for a recommendation or approval in relation to, that office or post;

(b) in any other case, a disabled person—

  (i) who is seeking or being considered for appointment to, or a recommendation or approval in relation to, the office or post concerned, or

  (ii) who has been appointed to the office or post concerned.

(3) Nothing in this section imposes any duty on the relevant person in relation to a disabled person if the relevant person does not know, and could not reasonably be expected to know—

(a) in the case of a person who is being considered for, or is or may be seeking, appointment to, or a recommendation or approval in relation to, an office or post, that the disabled person concerned—

  (i) is, or may be, seeking appointment to, or (as the case may be) seeking a recommendation or approval in relation to, that office or post, or

  (ii) is being considered for appointment to, or (as the case may be) for a recommendation or approval in relation to, that office or post; or

(b) in any case, that that person has a disability and is likely to be affected in the way mentioned in subsection (1).

Amendment – Inserted by Disability Discrimination Act 1995 (Amendment) Regulations 2003, SI 2003/1673, regs 3(1), 5.

4F   Office-holders: supplementary

(1) In sections 4C to 4E, appointment to an office or post does not include election to an office or post.

(2) In sections 4D and 4E, 'relevant person' means—

    (a)   in a case relating to an appointment to an office or post, the person with power to make that appointment;

    (b)   in a case relating to the making of a recommendation or the giving of an approval in relation to an appointment, a person or body referred to in section 4C(3)(b) with power to make that recommendation or (as the case may be) to give that approval;

    (c)   in a case relating to a term of an appointment, the person with power to determine that term;

    (d)   in a case relating to a working condition afforded in relation to an appointment—

        (i)   the person with power to determine that working condition; or

        (ii)   where there is no such person, the person with power to make the appointment;

    (e)   in a case relating to the termination of an appointment, the person with power to terminate the appointment;

    (f)   in a case relating to the subjection of a disabled person to any other detriment or to harassment, any person or body falling within one or more of paragraphs (a) to (e) in relation to such cases as are there mentioned.

(3) In subsection (2)(d), 'working condition' includes—

    (a)   any opportunity for promotion, a transfer, training or receiving any other benefit; and

    (b)   any physical feature of premises at or from which the functions of an office or post are performed.

Amendment – Inserted by Disability Discrimination Act 1995 (Amendment) Regulations 2003, SI 2003/1673, regs 3(1), 5.

Occupational pension schemes

Amendment – Inserted by Disability Discrimination Act 1995 (Pensions) Regulations 2003, SI 2003/2770, regs 2, 3.

4G   Occupational pension schemes: non-discrimination rule

(1) Every occupational pension scheme shall be taken to include a provision ('the non-discrimination rule') containing the following requirements—

    (a)   a requirement that the trustees or managers of the scheme refrain from discriminating against a relevant disabled person in carrying out any of their functions in relation to the scheme (including in particular their functions relating to the admission of members to the scheme and the treatment of members of the scheme);

(b)   a requirement that the trustees or managers of the scheme do not subject a relevant disabled person to harassment in relation to the scheme.

(2) The other provisions of the scheme are to have effect subject to the non-discrimination rule.

(3) It is unlawful for the trustees or managers of an occupational pension scheme—

(a)   to discriminate against a relevant disabled person contrary to requirement (a) of the non-discrimination rule; or

(b)   to subject a relevant disabled person to harassment contrary to requirement (b) of the non-discrimination rule.

(4) The non-discrimination rule does not apply in relation to rights accrued, or benefits payable, in respect of periods of service prior to the coming into force of this section (but it does apply to communications with members or prospective members of the scheme in relation to such rights or benefits).

(5) The trustees or managers of an occupational pension scheme may, if—

(a)   they do not (apart from this subsection) have power to make such alterations to the scheme as may be required to secure conformity with the non-discrimination rule, or

(b)   they have such power but the procedure for doing so—
    (i)   is liable to be unduly complex or protracted, or
    (ii) involves the obtaining of consents which cannot be obtained, or can only be obtained with undue delay or difficulty,

by resolution make such alterations to the scheme.

(6) The alterations referred to in subsection (5) may have effect in relation to a period before the alterations are made (but may not have effect in relation to a period before the coming into force of this section).

Amendment – Inserted by Disability Discrimination Act 1995 (Pensions) Regulations 2003, SI 2003/2770, regs 2, 3.

4H   Occupational pension schemes: duty to make adjustments

(1) Where—

(a)   a provision, criterion or practice (including a scheme rule) applied by or on behalf of the trustees or managers of an occupational pension scheme, or

(b)   any physical feature of premises occupied by the trustees or managers, places a relevant disabled person at a substantial disadvantage in comparison with persons who are not disabled, it is the duty of the trustees or managers to take such steps as it is reasonable, in all the circumstances of the case, for them to have to take in order to prevent the provision, criterion or practice, or feature, having that effect.

(2) The making of alterations to scheme rules is (in addition to the examples set out in section 18B(2)) an example of a step which trustees or managers may have to take in order to comply with the duty set out in subsection (1).

(3) Nothing in subsection (1) imposes any duty on trustees or managers in relation to a disabled person if they do not know, and could not reasonably be expected to know—

    (a)   that the disabled person is a relevant disabled person; or

    (b)   that that person has a disability and is likely to be affected in the way mentioned in subsection (1).

Amendment – Inserted by Disability Discrimination Act 1995 (Pensions) Regulations 2003, SI 2003/2770, regs 2, 3.

4I   Occupational pension schemes: procedure

(1) Where under section 17A a relevant disabled person presents a complaint to an employment tribunal that the trustees or managers of an occupational pension scheme have acted in relation to him in a way which is unlawful under this Part, the employer in relation to that scheme shall, for the purposes of the rules governing procedure, be treated as a party and be entitled to appear and be heard in accordance with those rules.

(2) In this section, 'employer', in relation to an occupational pension scheme, has the meaning given by section 124(1) of the Pensions Act 1995 as at the date of coming into force of this section.

Amendment – Inserted by Disability Discrimination Act 1995 (Pensions) Regulations 2003, SI 2003/2770, regs 2, 3.

4J   Occupational pension schemes: remedies

(1) This section applies where—

    (a)   under section 17A a relevant disabled person presents to an employment tribunal a complaint that—

        (i)   the trustees or managers of an occupational pension scheme have acted in relation to him in a way which is unlawful under this Part; or

        (ii)   an employer has so acted in relation to him;

    (b)   the complaint relates to—

        (i)   the terms on which persons become members of an occupational pension scheme, or

        (ii)   the terms on which members of the scheme are treated;

(c)   the disabled person is not a pensioner member of the scheme; and

(d)   the tribunal finds that the complaint is well-founded.

(2) The tribunal may, without prejudice to the generality of its power under section 17A(2)(a), make a declaration that the complainant has a right—

(a)   (where subsection (1)(b)(i) applies) to be admitted to the scheme in question; or

(b)   (where subsection (1)(b)(ii) applies) to membership of the scheme without discrimination.

(3) A declaration under subsection (2)—

(a)   may be made in respect of such period as the declaration may specify (but may not be made in respect of any period before the coming into force of this section);

(b)   may make such provision as the tribunal considers appropriate as to the terms upon which, or the capacity in which, the disabled person is to enjoy such admission or membership.

(4) The tribunal may not award the disabled person any compensation under section 17A(2)(b) (whether in relation to arrears of benefits or otherwise) other than—

(a)   compensation for injury to feelings;

(b)   compensation pursuant to section 17A(5).

Amendment – Inserted by Disability Discrimination Act 1995 (Pensions) Regulations 2003, SI 2003/2770, regs 2, 3.

4K   Occupational pension schemes: supplementary

(1) In their application to communications, sections 4G to 4J apply in relation to a disabled person who is—

(a)   entitled to the present payment of dependants' or survivors' benefits under an occupational pension scheme; or

(b)   a pension credit member of such a scheme,

as they apply in relation to a disabled person who is a pensioner member of the scheme.

(2) In sections 4G to 4J and in this section—

'active member', 'deferred member', 'managers', 'pension credit member', 'pensioner member' and 'trustees or managers' have the meanings given by section 124(1) of the Pensions Act 1995 as at the date of coming into force of this section;

'communications' includes—

(i)   the provision of information, and

(ii)   the operation of a dispute resolution procedure;

'member', in relation to an occupational pension scheme, means any active, deferred or pensioner member;

'non-discrimination rule' means the rule in section 4G(1);

'relevant disabled person', in relation to an occupational pension scheme, means a disabled person who is a member or prospective member of the scheme; and

'prospective member' means any person who, under the terms of his contract of employment or the scheme rules or both—

    (i)   is able, at his own option, to become a member of the scheme,

    (ii)   will become so able if he continues in the same employment for a sufficiently long period,

    (iii)   will be admitted to it automatically unless he makes an election not to become a member, or

    (iv)   may be admitted to it subject to the consent of his employer.

Amendment – Inserted by Disability Discrimination Act 1995 (Pensions) Regulations 2003, SI 2003/2770, regs 2, 3.

5 *(repealed)*

Amendment – Repealed by Disability Discrimination Act 1995 (Amendment) Regulations 2003, SI 2003/1673, regs 3(1), 5.

6 *(repealed)*

Amendment – Repealed by Disability Discrimination Act 1995 (Amendment) Regulations 2003, SI 2003/1673, regs 3(1), 5.

Partnerships

Amendment – Inserted by SI 2003/1673.

6A Partnerships: discrimination and harassment

(1) It is unlawful for a firm, in relation to a position as partner in the firm, to discriminate against a disabled person—

    (a)   in the arrangements which they make for the purpose of determining who should be offered that position;

    (b)   in the terms on which they offer him that position;

    (c)   by refusing or deliberately omitting to offer him that position; or

    (d)   in a case where the person already holds that position—

        (i)   in the way they afford him access to any benefits or by refusing or deliberately omitting to afford him access to them; or

        (ii)   by expelling him from that position, or subjecting him to any other detriment.

(2) It is also unlawful for a firm, in relation to a position as partner in the firm, to subject to harassment a disabled person who holds or has applied for that position.

(3) Subsection (1) does not apply to benefits of any description if the firm are concerned with the provision (whether or not for payment) of benefits of that description to the public, or to a section of the public which includes the partner in question, unless that provision differs in a material respect from the provision of the benefits to other partners.

(4) The reference in subsection (1)(d)(ii) to the expulsion of a person from a position as partner includes a reference—

(a)   to the termination of that person's partnership by the expiration of any period (including a period expiring by reference to an event or circumstance), not being a termination immediately after which the partnership is renewed on the same terms; and

(b)   to the termination of that person's partnership by any act of his (including the giving of notice) in circumstances such that he is entitled to terminate it without notice by reason of the conduct of the other partners.

Amendment – Inserted by Disability Discrimination Act 1995 (Amendment) Regulations 2003, SI 2003/1673, regs 3(1), 6.

6B Partnerships: duty to make adjustments

(1) Where—

(a)   a provision, criterion or practice applied by or on behalf of a firm, or

(b)   any physical feature of premises occupied by the firm,

places the disabled person concerned at a substantial disadvantage in comparison with persons who are not disabled, it is the duty of the firm to take such steps as it is reasonable, in all the circumstances of the case, for them to have to take in order to prevent the provision, criterion or practice, or feature, having that effect.

(2) In this section, 'the disabled person concerned' means—

(a)   in the case of a provision, criterion or practice for determining to whom the position of partner should be offered, any disabled person who is, or has notified the firm that he may be, a candidate for that position;

(b)   in any other case, a disabled person who is—

(i)   a partner, or

(ii)   a candidate for the position of partner.

(3) Nothing in this section imposes any duty on a firm in relation to a disabled person if the firm do not know, and could not reasonably be expected to know—

(a)   in the case of a candidate or potential candidate, that the disabled person concerned is, or may be, a candidate for the position of partner; or

(b) in any case, that that person has a disability and is likely to be affected in the way mentioned in subsection (1).

(4) Where a firm are required by this section to take any steps in relation to the disabled person concerned, the cost of taking those steps shall be treated as an expense of the firm; and the extent to which such cost should be borne by that person, where he is or becomes a partner in the firm, shall not exceed such amount as is reasonable, having regard in particular to the proportion in which he is entitled to share in the firm's profits.

Amendment – Inserted by Disability Discrimination Act 1995 (Amendment) Regulations 2003, SI 2003/1673, regs 3(1), 6.

6C Partnerships: supplementary

(1) Sections 6A(1)(a) to (c) and (2) and section 6B apply in relation to persons proposing to form themselves into a partnership as they apply in relation to a firm.

(2) Sections 6A and 6B apply to a limited liability partnership as they apply to a firm; and, in the application of those sections to a limited liability partnership, references to a partner in a firm are references to a member of the limited liability partnership.

(3) In the case of a limited partnership, references in sections 6A and 6B to a partner shall be construed as references to a general partner as defined in section 3 of the Limited Partnerships Act 1907.

(4) In sections 6A and 6B and in this section, 'firm' has the meaning given by section 4 of the Partnership Act 1890.

Amendment – Inserted by Disability Discrimination Act 1995 (Amendment) Regulations 2003, SI 2003/1673, regs 3(1), 6.

7 (*repealed*)

Amendment – Repealed by Disability Discrimination Act 1995 (Amendment) Regulations 2003, SI 2003/1673, regs 3(1), 7.

Barristers and advocates

Amendment – Inserted by Disability Discrimination Act 1995 (Amendment) Regulations 2003, SI 2003/1673, regs 3(1), 8.

7A Barristers: discrimination and harassment

(1) It is unlawful for a barrister or a barrister's clerk, in relation to any offer of a pupillage or tenancy, to discriminate against a disabled person—

(a) in the arrangements which are made for the purpose of determining to whom it should be offered;

(b) in respect of any terms on which it is offered; or

(c) by refusing, or deliberately omitting, to offer it to him.

(2) It is unlawful for a barrister or a barrister's clerk, in relation to a disabled pupil or tenant in the set of chambers in question, to discriminate against him—

(a) in respect of any terms applicable to him as a pupil or tenant;

(b) in the opportunities for training, or gaining experience, which are afforded or denied to him;

(c) in the benefits which are afforded or denied to him;

(d) by terminating his pupillage or by subjecting him to any pressure to leave the chambers; or

(e) by subjecting him to any other detriment.

(3) It is unlawful for a barrister or barrister's clerk, in relation to a pupillage or tenancy, to subject to harassment a disabled person who is, or has applied to be, a pupil or tenant in the set of chambers in question.

(4) It is also unlawful for any person, in relation to the giving, withholding or acceptance of instructions to a barrister, to discriminate against a disabled person or to subject him to harassment.

(5) In this section and in section 7B—

'barrister's clerk' includes any person carrying out any of the functions of a barrister's clerk;

'pupil', 'pupillage' and 'set of chambers' have the meanings commonly associated with their use in the context of barristers practising in independent practice; and

'tenancy' and 'tenant' have the meanings commonly associated with their use in the context of barristers practising in independent practice, but they also include reference to any barrister permitted to practise from a set of chambers.

Amendment – Inserted by Disability Discrimination Act 1995 (Amendment) Regulations 2003, SI 2003/1673, regs 3(1), 8.

7B   Barristers: duty to make adjustments

(1) Where—

(a) a provision, criterion or practice applied by or on behalf of a barrister or barrister's clerk, or

(b) any physical feature of premises occupied by a barrister or a barrister's clerk,

places the disabled person concerned at a substantial disadvantage in comparison with persons who are not disabled, it is the duty of the barrister or barrister's clerk to take such steps as it is reasonable, in all the circumstances of the case, for him to have to take in order to prevent the provision, criterion or practice, or feature, having that effect.

(2) In a case where subsection (1) applies in relation to two or more barristers in a set of chambers, the duty in that subsection is a duty on

each of them to take such steps as it is reasonable, in all of the circumstances of the case, for him to have to take.

(3) In this section, 'the disabled person concerned' means—

    (a)   in the case of a provision, criterion or practice for determining to whom a pupillage or tenancy should be offered, any disabled person who is, or has notified the barrister or the barrister's clerk concerned that he may be, an applicant for a pupillage or tenancy;

    (b)   in any other case, a disabled person who is—

        (i)   a tenant;

        (ii)   a pupil; or

        (iii)   an applicant for a pupillage or tenancy.

(4) Nothing in this section imposes any duty on a barrister or a barrister's clerk in relation to a disabled person if he does not know, and could not reasonably be expected to know—

    (a)   in the case of an applicant or potential applicant, that the disabled person concerned is, or may be, an applicant for a pupillage or tenancy; or

    (b)   in any case, that that person has a disability and is likely to be affected in the way mentioned in subsection (1).

Amendment – Inserted by Disability Discrimination Act 1995 (Amendment) Regulations 2003, SI 2003/1673, regs 3(1), 8.

7C Advocates: discrimination and harassment

(1) It is unlawful for an advocate, in relation to taking any person as his pupil, to discriminate against a disabled person—

    (a)   in the arrangements which he makes for the purpose of determining whom he will take as his pupil;

    (b)   in respect of any terms on which he offers to take the disabled person as his pupil; or

    (c)   by refusing, or deliberately omitting, to take the disabled person as his pupil.

(2) It is unlawful for an advocate, in relation to a disabled person who is a pupil, to discriminate against him—

    (a)   in respect of any terms applicable to him as a pupil;

    (b)   in the opportunities for training, or gaining experience, which are afforded or denied to him;

    (c)   in the benefits which are afforded or denied to him;

    (d)   by terminating the relationship or by subjecting him to any pressure to leave; or

    (e)   by subjecting him to any other detriment.

(3) It is unlawful for an advocate, in relation to taking any person as his pupil, to subject to harassment a disabled person who is, or has applied to be taken as, his pupil.

(4) It is also unlawful for any person, in relation to the giving, withholding or acceptance of instructions to an advocate, to discriminate against a disabled person or to subject him to harassment.

(5) In this section and section 7D—

'advocate' means a member of the Faculty of Advocates practising as such; and

'pupil' has the meaning commonly associated with its use in the context of a person training to be an advocate.

Amendment – Inserted by Disability Discrimination Act 1995 (Amendment) Regulations 2003, SI 2003/1673, regs 3(1), 8.

7D   Advocates: duty to make adjustments

(1) Where—

(a)   a provision, criterion or practice applied by or on behalf of an advocate, or

(b)   any physical feature of premises occupied by, and under the control of, an advocate,

places the disabled person concerned at a substantial disadvantage in comparison with persons who are not disabled, it is the duty of the advocate to take such steps as it is reasonable, in all the circumstances of the case, for him to have to take in order to prevent the provision, criterion or practice, or feature, having that effect.

(2) In this section, 'the disabled person concerned' means—

(a)   in the case of a provision, criterion or practice for determining whom he will take as his pupil, any disabled person who has applied, or has notified the advocate that he may apply, to be taken as a pupil;

(b)   in any other case, a disabled person who is—

(i)   an applicant to be taken as the advocate's pupil, or

(ii)   a pupil.

(3) Nothing in this section imposes any duty on an advocate in relation to a disabled person if he does not know, and could not reasonably be expected to know—

(a)   in the case of an applicant or potential applicant, that the disabled person concerned is, or may be, applying to be taken as his pupil; or

(b)   in any case, that that person has a disability and is likely to be affected in the way mentioned in subsection (1).

Amendment – Inserted by Disability Discrimination Act 1995 (Amendment) Regulations 2003, SI 2003/1673, regs 3(1), 8.

8–12 (*repealed*)

Amendment – Sections and preceding cross-headings repealed by Disability Discrimination Act 1995 (Amendment) Regulations 2003, SI 2003/1673, regs 3(1), 12.

Trade and professional bodies

Amendment – Inserted by Disability Discrimination Act 1995 (Amendment) Regulations 2003, SI 2003/1673, regs 3(1), 13.

13   Trade organisations: discrimination and harassment

(1) It is unlawful for a trade organisation to discriminate against a disabled person—

(a) in the arrangements which it makes for the purpose of determining who should be offered membership of the organisation;

(b) in the terms on which it is prepared to admit him to membership of the organisation; or

(c) by refusing to accept, or deliberately not accepting, his application for membership.

(2) It is unlawful for a trade organisation, in the case of a disabled person who is a member of the organisation, to discriminate against him—

(a) in the way it affords him access to any benefits or by refusing or deliberately omitting to afford him access to them;

(b) by depriving him of membership, or varying the terms on which he is a member; or

(c) by subjecting him to any other detriment.

(3) It is also unlawful for a trade organisation, in relation to membership of that organisation, to subject to harassment a disabled person who—

(a) is a member of the organisation; or

(b) has applied for membership of the organisation.

(4) In this section and section 14 'trade organisation' means—

(a) an organisation of workers;

(b) an organisation of employers; or

(c) any other organisation whose members carry on a particular profession or trade for the purposes of which the organisation exists.

Amendment – Amended by Disability Discrimination Act 1995 (Amendment) Regulations 2003, SI 2003/1673, regs 3(1), 13.

14 Trade organisations: duty to make adjustments

(1) Where—

(a) a provision, criterion or practice applied by or on behalf of a trade organisation, or

(b) any physical feature of premises occupied by the organisation,

places the disabled person concerned at a substantial disadvantage in comparison with persons who are not disabled, it is the duty of the organisation to take such steps as it is reasonable, in all the circumstances of the case, for it to have to take in order to prevent the provision, criterion or practice, or feature, having that effect.

(2) In this section 'the disabled person concerned' means—

(a) in the case of a provision, criterion or practice for determining to whom membership should be offered, any disabled person who is, or has notified the organisation that he may be, an applicant for membership;

(b) in any other case, a disabled person who is—
(i)   a member of the organisation, or
(ii) an applicant for membership of the organisation.

(3) Nothing in this section imposes any duty on an organisation in relation to a disabled person if the organisation does not know, and could not reasonably be expected to know—

(a) in the case of an applicant or potential applicant, that the disabled person concerned is, or may be, an applicant for membership of the organisation; or

(b) in any case, that that person has a disability and is likely to be affected in the way mentioned in subsection (1).

Amendment – Amended by Disability Discrimination Act 1995 (Amendment) Regulations 2003, SI 2003/1673, regs 3(1), 13.

14A Qualifications bodies: discrimination and harassment

(1) It is unlawful for a qualifications body to discriminate against a disabled person—

(a) in the arrangements which it makes for the purpose of determining upon whom to confer a professional or trade qualification;

(b) in the terms on which it is prepared to confer a professional or trade qualification on him;

(c) by refusing or deliberately omitting to grant any application by him for such a qualification; or

(d) by withdrawing such a qualification from him or varying the terms on which he holds it.

(2) It is also unlawful for a qualifications body, in relation to a professional or trade qualification conferred by it, to subject to harassment a disabled person who holds or applies for such a qualification.

(3) In determining for the purposes of subsection (1) whether the application by a qualifications body of a competence standard to a disabled person constitutes discrimination within the meaning of section 3A, the application of the standard is justified for the purposes of section 3A(1)(b) if, but only if, the qualifications body can show that—

  (a)　the standard is, or would be, applied equally to persons who do not have his particular disability; and
  (b)　its application is a proportionate means of achieving a legitimate aim.

(4) For the purposes of subsection (3)—

  (a)　section 3A(2) (and (6)) does not apply; and
  (b)　section 3A(4) has effect as if the reference to section 3A(3) were a reference to subsection (3) of this section.

(5) In this section and section 14B—

  'qualifications body' means any authority or body which can confer a professional or trade qualification, but it does not include—
  (a)　a responsible body (within the meaning of Chapter 1 or 2 of Part 4),
  (b)　a local education authority in England or Wales, or
  (c)　an education authority (within the meaning of section 135(1) of the Education (Scotland) Act 1980);

  'confer' includes renew or extend;
  'professional or trade qualification' means an authorisation, qualification, recognition, registration, enrolment, approval or certification which is needed for, or facilitates engagement in, a particular profession or trade;
  'competence standard' means an academic, medical or other standard applied by or on behalf of a qualifications body for the purpose of determining whether or not a person has a particular level of competence or ability.

Amendment – Inserted by Disability Discrimination Act 1995 (Amendment) Regulations 2003, SI 2003/1673, regs 3(1), 13.

14B　Qualifications bodies: duty to make adjustments

(1) Where—

  (a)　a provision, criterion or practice, other than a competence standard, applied by or on behalf of a qualifications body; or
  (b)　any physical feature of premises occupied by a qualifications body,

places the disabled person concerned at a substantial disadvantage in comparison with persons who are not disabled, it is the duty of the qualifications body to take such steps as it is reasonable, in all the circumstances of the case, for it to have to take in order to prevent the provision, criterion or practice, or feature, having that effect.

(2) In this section 'the disabled person concerned' means—

    (a) in the case of a provision, criterion or practice for determining on whom a professional or trade qualification is to be conferred, any disabled person who is, or has notified the qualifications body that he may be, an applicant for the conferment of that qualification;

    (b) in any other case, a disabled person who—

        (i) holds a professional or trade qualification conferred by the qualifications body, or

        (ii) applies for a professional or trade qualification which it confers.

(3) Nothing in this section imposes a duty on a qualifications body in relation to a disabled person if the body does not know, and could not reasonably be expected to know—

    (a) in the case of an applicant or potential applicant, that the disabled person concerned is, or may be, an applicant for the conferment of a professional or trade qualification; or

    (b) in any case, that that person has a disability and is likely to be affected in the way mentioned in subsection (1).

Amendment – Inserted by Disability Discrimination Act 1995 (Amendment) Regulations 2003, SI 2003/1673, regs 3(1), 13.

Practical work experience

Amendment – Inserted by Disability Discrimination Act 1995 (Amendment) Regulations 2003, SI 2003/1673, regs 3(1), 13.

14C Practical work experience: discrimination and harassment

(1) It is unlawful, in the case of a disabled person seeking or undertaking a work placement, for a placement provider to discriminate against him—

    (a) in the arrangements which he makes for the purpose of determining who should be offered a work placement;

    (b) in the terms on which he affords him access to any work placement or any facilities concerned with such a placement;

    (c) by refusing or deliberately omitting to afford him such access;

    (d) by terminating the placement; or

    (e) by subjecting him to any other detriment in relation to the placement.

(2) It is also unlawful for a placement provider, in relation to a work placement, to subject to harassment—

   (a)   a disabled person to whom he is providing a placement; or

   (b)   a disabled person who has applied to him for a placement.

(3) This section and section 14D do not apply to—

   (a)   anything which is unlawful under any provision of section 4, sections 19 to 21A, sections 21F to 21J or Part 4; or

   (b)   to anything which would be unlawful under any such provision but for the operation of any provision in or made under this Act.

(4) In this section and section 14D—

   'work placement' means practical work experience undertaken for a limited period for the purposes of a person's vocational training;
   'placement provider' means any person who provides a work placement to a person whom he does not employ.

(5) This section and section 14D do not apply to a work placement undertaken in any of the naval, military and air forces of the Crown.

Amendment – Inserted by Disability Discrimination Act 1995 (Amendment) Regulations 2003, SI 2003/1673, regs 3(1), 13. Amended by Disability Discrimination Act 2005, s 19(1), Sch 1, Pt 1, paras 1, 6.

14D   Practical work experience: duty to make adjustments

(1) Where—

   (a)   a provision, criterion or practice applied by or on behalf of a placement provider, or

   (b)   any physical feature of premises occupied by the placement provider,

places the disabled person concerned at a substantial disadvantage in comparison with persons who are not disabled, it is the duty of the placement provider to take such steps as it is reasonable, in all the circumstances of the case, for him to have to take in order to prevent the provision, criterion or practice, or feature, having that effect.

(2) In this section, 'the disabled person concerned' means—

   (a)   in the case of a provision, criterion or practice for determining to whom a work placement should be offered, any disabled person who is, or has notified the placement provider that he may be, an applicant for that work placement;

   (b)   in any other case, a disabled person who is—

      (i)   an applicant for the work placement concerned, or

      (ii) undertaking a work placement with the placement provider.

(3) Nothing in this section imposes any duty on a placement provider in relation to the disabled person concerned if he does not know, and could not reasonably be expected to know—

(a)   in the case of an applicant or potential applicant, that the disabled person concerned is, or may be, an applicant for the work placement; or

(b)   in any case, that that person has a disability and is likely to be affected in the way mentioned in subsection (1).

Amendment – Inserted by Disability Discrimination Act 1995 (Amendment) Regulations 2003, SI 2003/1673, regs 3(1), 13.

15 (*repealed*)

Amendment – Repealed by Disability Discrimination Act 1995 (Amendment) Regulations 2003, SI 2003/1673, regs 3(1), 13.

Relationships between locally-electable authorities and their members

Amendment – Inserted by Disability Discrimination Act 2005, s 1.

15A   Interpretation of sections 15B and 15C

(1) Sections 15B and 15C apply to the following authorities—

(a)   the Greater London Authority;

(b)   a county council (in England and Wales);

(c)   a county borough council (in Wales);

(d)   a district council (in England);

(e)   a London borough council;

(f)   the Common Council of the City of London;

(g)   the Council of the Isles of Scilly;

(h)   a council constituted under section 2 of the Local Government etc (Scotland) Act 1994;

(i)   a parish council (in England); and

(j)   a community council (in Wales or Scotland).

(2) In relation to a member of an authority to which sections 15B and 15C apply, a reference in those sections to his carrying-out of official business is to his doing of anything—

(a)   as member of the authority;

(b)   as member of any body to which he is appointed by, or is appointed following nomination by, the authority or a group of bodies that includes the authority; or

(c)   as member of any other body if it is a public body.

(3) In this section and sections 15B and 15C 'member', in relation to the Greater London Authority, means Mayor of London or member of the London Assembly.

Amendment – Inserted by Disability Discrimination Act 2005, s 1.

15B Authorities and their members: discrimination and harassment

(1) It is unlawful for an authority to which this section applies to discriminate against a disabled person who is a member of the authority—

(a) in the opportunities which it affords the disabled person to receive training, or any other facility, for his carrying-out of official business;

(b) by refusing to afford, or deliberately not affording, the disabled person any such opportunities; or

(c) by subjecting the disabled person to any other detriment in connection with his carrying-out of official business.

(2) It is unlawful for an authority to which this section applies to subject a disabled person who is a member of the authority to harassment in connection with his carrying-out of official business.

(3) A member of an authority to which this section applies is not subjected to a detriment for the purposes of subsection (1)(c) by reason of—

(a) his not being appointed or elected to an office of the authority;

(b) his not being appointed or elected to, or to an office of, a committee or sub-committee of the authority; or

(c) his not being appointed or nominated in exercise of any power of the authority, or of a group of bodies that includes the authority, to appoint, or nominate for appointment, to any body.

(4) Regulations may make provision as to the circumstances in which treatment is to be taken to be justified, or is to be taken not to be justified, for the purposes of section 3A(1)(b) as it has effect for the interpretation of 'discriminate' in subsection (1).

(5) Regulations under subsection (4) may (in particular) provide for section 3A(3) to apply with prescribed modifications, or not to apply, for those purposes; but treatment of a disabled person cannot be justified under subsection (4) if it amounts to direct discrimination falling within section 3A(5).

(6) If, in a case falling within section 3A(1) as it has effect for the interpretation of 'discriminate' in subsection (1), an authority to which this section applies is under a duty imposed by section 15C in relation to a disabled person but fails to comply with that duty, its treatment of that person cannot be justified under subsection (4) unless it would have been justified even if it had complied with that duty.

Amendment – Inserted by Disability Discrimination Act 2005, s 1.

15C   Authorities and their members: duty to make adjustments

(1) Subsection (2) applies where—

(a) a provision, criterion or practice applied by or on behalf of an authority to which this section applies, or

(b) any physical feature of premises occupied by, or under the control of, such an authority,

places a disabled person who is a member of the authority at a substantial disadvantage, in comparison with members of the authority who are not disabled persons, in connection with his carrying-out of official business.

(2) It is the duty of the authority to take such steps as it is reasonable, in all the circumstances of the case, for it to have to take in order to prevent the provision, criterion or practice, or feature, having that effect.

(3) Subsection (2) does not impose any duty on an authority to which this section applies in relation to a member of the authority who is a disabled person if the authority does not know, and could not reasonably be expected to know, that the member

(a) has a disability; and

(b) is likely to be affected in the way mentioned in subsection (1).

(4) Regulations may make provision, for purposes of this section—

(a) as to circumstances in which a provision, criterion or practice, or physical feature, is to be taken to have the effect mentioned in subsection (1);

(b) as to circumstances in which a provision, criterion or practice, or physical feature, is to be taken not to have the effect mentioned in subsection (1);

(c) as to circumstances in which it is, or as to circumstances in which it is not, reasonable for an authority to have to take steps of a prescribed description;

(d) as to steps which it is always, or as to steps which it is never, reasonable for an authority to have to take;

(e) as to things which are, or as to things which are not, to be treated as physical features.]

Amendment – Inserted by Disability Discrimination Act 2005, s 1.

16   (*repealed*)

Amendment – Amendment section and preceding cross heading repealed by Disability Discrimination Act 1995 (Amendment) Regulations 2003, SI 2003/1673, regs 3(1), 14(2).

Other unlawful acts

Amendment – Inserted by Disability Discrimination Act 1995 (Amendment) Regulations 2003, SI 2003/1673, regs 3(1), 15(1).

16A   Relationships which have come to an end

(1) This section applies where—

   (a)   there has been a relevant relationship between a disabled person and another person ('the relevant person'), and
   (b)   the relationship has come to an end.

(2) In this section a 'relevant relationship' is—

   (a)   a relationship during the course of which an act of discrimination against, or harassment of, one party to the relationship by the other party to it is unlawful under any preceding provision of this Part; other than sections 15B and 15C; or
   (b)   a relationship between a person providing employment services and a person receiving such services.

(3) It is unlawful for the relevant person—

   (a)   to discriminate against the disabled person by subjecting him to a detriment, or
   (b)   to subject the disabled person to harassment,

where the discrimination or harassment arises out of and is closely connected to the relevant relationship.

(4) This subsection applies where—

   (a)   a provision, criterion or practice applied by the relevant person to the disabled person in relation to any matter arising out of the relevant relationship, or
   (b)   a physical feature of premises which are occupied by the relevant person,

places the disabled person at a substantial disadvantage in comparison with persons who are not disabled, but are in the same position as the disabled person in relation to the relevant person.

(5) Where subsection (4) applies, it is the duty of the relevant person to take such steps as it is reasonable, in all the circumstances of the case, for him to have to take in order to prevent the provision, practice or criterion, or feature, having that effect.

(6) Nothing in subsection (5) imposes any duty on the relevant person if he does not know, and could not reasonably be expected to know, that the disabled person has a disability and is likely to be affected in the way mentioned in that subsection.

(7) In subsection (2), reference to an act of discrimination or harassment which is unlawful includes, in the case of a relationship which has come to an end before the commencement of this section, reference to such an act which would, after the commencement of this section, be unlawful.

Amendment – Inserted by Disability Discrimination Act 1995 (Amendment) Regulations 2003, SI 2003/1673, regs 3(1), 15(1). Amended by Disability Discrimination Act 2005,
s 19(1), Sch 1, Pt 1, paras 1, 7(a),(b).

16B   Discriminatory advertisements

(1) It is unlawful for a person, to publish or cause to be published an
advertisement which—

   (a)   invites applications for that appointment or benefit; and

   (b)   indicates, or might reasonably be understood to indicate, that an
application will or may be determined to any extent by reference
to—

      (i)   the applicant not having any disability, or any particular
disability, or

      (ii)   any reluctance of the person determining the application to
comply with a duty to make reasonable adjustments or (in
relation to employment services) with the duty imposed by
section 21(1) as modified by section 21A(6).

(2) Subsection (1) does not apply where it would not in fact be unlawful
under this Part or, to the extent that it relates to the provision of
employment services, Part 3 for an application to be determined in the
manner indicated (or understood to be indicated) in the advertisement.

(2A) A person who publishes an advertisement of the kind described in
subsection (1) shall not be subject to any liability under subsection (1) in
respect of the publication of the advertisement if he proves—

   (a)   that the advertisement was published in reliance on a statement
made to him by the person who caused it to be published to the
effect that, by reason of the operation of subsection (2), the
publication would not be unlawful; and

   (b)   that it was reasonable for him to rely on the statement

(2B) A person who knowingly or recklessly makes a statement such as is
mentioned in subsection (2A)(a) which in a material respect is false or
misleading commits an offence, and shall be liable on summary conviction
to a fine not exceeding level 5 on the standard scale.

(2C) Subsection (1) does not apply in relation to an advertisement so far
as it invites persons to apply, in their capacity as members of an authority
to which sections 15B and 15C apply, for a relevant appointment or
benefit which the authority is intending to make or confer.

(3) In this section, 'relevant appointment or benefit' means—

   (a)   any employment, promotion or transfer of employment;

   (b)   membership of, or a benefit under, an occupational pension
scheme;

   (c)   an appointment to any office or post to which section 4D applies;

   (d)   any partnership in a firm (within the meaning of section 6A);

- (e) any tenancy or pupillage (within the meaning of section 7A or 7C);
- (f) any membership of a trade organisation (within the meaning of section 13);
- (g) any professional or trade qualification (within the meaning of section 14A);
- (h) any work placement (within the meaning of section 14C);
- (i) any employment services.

(4) In this section, 'advertisement' includes every form of advertisement or notice, whether to the public or not.

(5) Proceedings in respect of a contravention of subsection (1) may be brought only—

- (a) by the Commission for Equality and Human Rights, and
- (b) in accordance with section 25 of the Equality Act 2006.

Amendment – Inserted by Disability Discrimination Act 1995 (Amendment) Regulations 2003, SI 2003/1673, regs 3(1), 15(1). Amended by Disability Discrimination Act 2005, s 8(1), (2), (3); s 10 (1), (2), (3), (4); Equality Act 2006, s 40, Sch 3, paras 41, 42.

16C   Instructions and pressure to discriminate

(1) It is unlawful for a person—

- (a) who has authority over another person, or
- (b) in accordance with whose wishes that other person is accustomed to act,

to instruct him to do any act which is unlawful under this Part or, to the extent that it relates to the provision of employment services, Part 3, or to procure or attempt to procure the doing by him of any such act.

(2) It is also unlawful to induce, or attempt to induce, a person to do any act which contravenes this Part or, to the extent that it relates to the provision of employment services, Part 3 by—

- (a) providing or offering to provide him with any benefit, or
- (b) subjecting or threatening to subject him to any detriment.

(3) An attempted inducement is not prevented from falling within subsection (2) because it is not made directly to the person in question, if it is made in such a way that he is likely to hear of it.

(4) Proceedings in respect of a contravention of this section may be brought only—

- (a) by the Commission for Equality and Human Rights , and
- (b) in accordance with section 25 of the Equality Act 2006.

Amendment – Inserted by Disability Discrimination Act 1995 (Amendment) Regulations 2003, SI 2003/1673, regs 3(1), 15(1). Amended by Equality Act 2006, s 40, Sch 3, paras 41, 43.

17 (*repealed*)

Amendment – Section and preceding cross-heading repealed by Disability Discrimination Act 1995 (Pensions) Regulations 2003, SI 2003/2770, regs 2, 4(1).

Enforcement etc

Amendment – Inserted by Disability Discrimination Act 1995 (Amendment) Regulations 2003, SI 2003/1673, regs 3(1), 9(1).

17A   Enforcement, remedies and procedureg

(1) A complaint by any person that another person—

   (a)   has discriminated against him, or subjected him to harassment, in a way which is unlawful under this Part, or

   (b)   is, by virtue of section 57 or 58, to be treated as having done so,

may be presented to an employment tribunal.

(1A) Subsection (1) does not apply to a complaint under section 14A(1) or (2) of an act in respect of which an appeal, or proceedings in the nature of an appeal, may be brought under any enactment.

(1B) (*repealed*)

(1C) Where, on the hearing of a complaint under subsection (1), the complainant proves facts from which the tribunal could, apart from this subsection, conclude in the absence of an adequate explanation that the respondent has acted in a way which is unlawful under this Part, the tribunal shall uphold the complaint unless the respondent proves that he did not so act.

(2) Where an employment tribunal finds that a complaint presented to it under this section is well-founded, it shall take such of the following steps as it considers just and equitable—

   (a)   making a declaration as to the rights of the complainant and the respondent in relation to the matters to which the complaint relates;

   (b)   ordering the respondent to pay compensation to the complainant;

   (c)   recommending that the respondent take, within a specified period, action appearing to the tribunal to be reasonable, in all the circumstances of the case, for the purpose of obviating or reducing the adverse effect on the complainant of any matter to which the complaint relates.

(3) Where a tribunal orders compensation under subsection (2)(b), the amount of the compensation shall be calculated by applying the principles applicable to the calculation of damages in claims in tort or (in Scotland) in reparation for breach of statutory duty.

(4) For the avoidance of doubt it is hereby declared that compensation in respect of discrimination in a way which is unlawful under this Part may

include compensation for injury to feelings whether or not it includes compensation under any other head.

(5) If the respondent to a complaint fails, without reasonable justification, to comply with a recommendation made by an employment tribunal under subsection (2)(c) the tribunal may, if it thinks it just and equitable to do so—

    (a)   increase the amount of compensation required to be paid to the complainant in respect of the complaint, where an order was made under subsection (2)(b); or

    (b)   make an order under subsection (2)(b).

(6) Regulations may make provision—

    (a)   for enabling a tribunal, where an amount of compensation falls to be awarded under subsection (2)(b), to include in the award interest on that amount; and

    (b)   specifying, for cases where a tribunal decides that an award is to include an amount in respect of interest, the manner in which and the periods and rate by reference to which the interest is to be determined.

(7) Regulations may modify the operation of any order made under section 14 of the Employment Tribunals Act 1996 (power to make provision as to interest on sums payable in pursuance of employment tribunal decisions) to the extent that it relates to an award of compensation under subsection (2)(b).

(8) Part I of Schedule 3 makes further provision about the enforcement of this Part and about procedure.

Amendment – Amended by Employment Rights (Dispute Resolution) Act 1998, s 1(2)(a), (c); Disability Discrimination Act 2005, s 19, Sch 1, Pt 1, paras 1, 9; Disability Discrimination Act 1995 (Amendment) Regulations 2003, SI 2003/1673, regs 3(1), 9(1), (2)(a)–(c).

17B *(repealed)*

17C   Validity of contracts, collective agreements and rules of undertakings

Schedule 3A shall have effect.

Amendment – Inserted by Disability Discrimination Act 1995 (Amendment) Regulations 2003, SI 2003/1673, regs 3(1), 16(1).

Supplementary and general

Amendment—Inserted by SI 2003/1673, regs 3(1), 17(1).

18 (*repealed*)

18A   Alterations to premises occupied under leases

(1) This section applies where—

  (a)   a person to whom a duty to make reasonable adjustments applies ('the occupier') occupies premises under a lease;

  (b)   but for this section, the occupier would not be entitled to make a particular alteration to the premises; and

  (c)   the alteration is one which the occupier proposes to make in order to comply with that duty.

(2) Except to the extent to which it expressly so provides, the lease shall have effect by virtue of this subsection as if it provided—

  (a)   for the occupier to be entitled to make the alteration with the written consent of the lessor;

  (b)   for the occupier to have to make a written application to the lessor for consent if he wishes to make the alteration;

  (c)   if such an application is made, for the lessor not to withhold his consent unreasonably; and

  (d)   for the lessor to be entitled to make his consent subject to reasonable conditions.

(3) In this section—

  'lease' includes a tenancy, sub-lease or sub-tenancy and an agreement for a lease, tenancy, sub-lease or sub-tenancy; and

  'sub-lease' and 'sub-tenancy' have such meaning as may be prescribed.

(4) If the terms and conditions of a lease—

  (a)   impose conditions which are to apply if the occupier alters the premises, or

  (b)   entitle the lessor to impose conditions when consenting to the occupier's altering the premises,

the occupier is to be treated for the purposes of subsection (1) as not being entitled to make the alteration.

(5) Part I of Schedule 4 supplements the provisions of this section.

Amendment – Inserted by Disability Discrimination Act 1995 (Amendment) Regulations 2003, SI 2003/1673, regs 3(1), 14(2), (3)(a), (b).

18B   Reasonable adjustments: supplementary

(1) In determining whether it is reasonable for a person to have to take a particular step in order to comply with a duty to make reasonable adjustments, regard shall be had, in particular, to—

  (a)   the extent to which taking the step would prevent the effect in relation to which the duty is imposed;

  (b)   the extent to which it is practicable for him to take the step;

(c) the financial and other costs which would be incurred by him in taking the step and the extent to which taking it would disrupt any of his activities;

(d) the extent of his financial and other resources;

(e) the availability to him of financial or other assistance with respect to taking the step;

(f) the nature of his activities and the size of his undertaking;

(g) where the step would be taken in relation to a private household, the extent to which taking it would—

    (i) disrupt that household, or

    (ii) disturb any person residing there.

(2) The following are examples of steps which a person may need to take in relation to a disabled person in order to comply with a duty to make reasonable adjustments—

(a) making adjustments to premises;

(b) allocating some of the disabled person's duties to another person;

(c) transferring him to fill an existing vacancy;

(d) altering his hours of working or training;

(e) assigning him to a different place of work or training;

(f) allowing him to be absent during working or training hours for rehabilitation, assessment or treatment;

(g) giving, or arranging for, training or mentoring (whether for the disabled person or any other person);

(h) acquiring or modifying equipment;

(i) modifying instructions or reference manuals;

(j) modifying procedures for testing or assessment;

(k) providing a reader or interpreter;

(l) providing supervision or other support.

(3) For the purposes of a duty to make reasonable adjustments, where under any binding obligation a person is required to obtain the consent of another person to any alteration of the premises occupied by him—

(a) it is always reasonable for him to have to take steps to obtain that consent; and

(b) it is never reasonable for him to have to make that alteration before that consent is obtained.

(4) The steps referred to in subsection (3)(a) shall not be taken to include an application to a court or tribunal.

(5) In subsection (3), 'binding obligation' means a legally binding obligation (not contained in a lease (within the meaning of section 18A(3)) in relation to the premises, whether arising from an agreement or otherwise.

(6) A provision of this Part imposing a duty to make reasonable adjustments applies only for the purpose of determining whether a person has discriminated against a disabled person; and accordingly a breach of any such duty is not actionable as such.

Amendment – Inserted by Disability Discrimination Act 1995 (Amendment) Regulations 2003, SI 2003/1673, regs 3(1), 17(2).

18C   Charities and support for particular groups of persons

(1) Nothing in this Part—

    (a)   affects any charitable instrument which provides for conferring benefits on one or more categories of person determined by reference to any physical or mental capacity; or

    (b)   makes unlawful any act done by a charity or recognised body in pursuance of any of its charitable purposes, so far as those purposes are connected with persons so determined.

(2) Nothing in this Part prevents—

    (a)   a person who provides supported employment from treating members of a particular group of disabled persons more favourably than other persons in providing such employment; or

    (b)   the Secretary of State from agreeing to arrangements for the provision of supported employment which will, or may, have that effect.

(3) In this section—

    'charitable instrument' means an enactment or other instrument (whenever taking effect) so far as it relates to charitable purposes;

    'charity' has the same meaning as in the Charities Act 1993;

    'recognised body' means a body which is a recognised body for the purposes of Part I of the Law Reform (Miscellaneous Provisions) (Scotland) Act 1990; and

    'supported employment' means facilities provided, or in respect of which payments are made, under section 15 of the Disabled Persons (Employment) Act 1944.

(4) In the application of this section to England and Wales, 'charitable purposes' means purposes which are exclusively charitable according to the law of England and Wales.

(5) In the application of this section to Scotland, 'charitable purposes' shall be construed in the same way as if it were contained in the Income Tax Acts.

Amendment – Inserted by Disability Discrimination Act 1995 (Amendment) Regulations 2003, SI 2003/1673, regs 3(1), 11.

18D   Interpretation of Part 2

(1) Subject to any duty to make reasonable adjustments, nothing in this Part is to be taken to require a person to treat a disabled person more favourably than he treats or would treat others.

(2) In this Part—

'benefits', except in sections 4G to 4K, includes facilities and services;

'detriment', except in section 16C(2)(b), does not include conduct of the nature referred to in section 3B (harassment);

'discriminate', 'discrimination' and other related expressions are to be construed in accordance with section 3A;

'duty to make reasonable adjustments' means a duty imposed by or under section 4A, 4B(5) or (6), 4E, 4H, 6B, 7B, 7D, 14, 14B, 14D, 15C, 16A(5);

'employer' includes a person who has no employees but is seeking to employ another person;

'harassment' is to be construed in accordance with section 3B;

'physical feature', in relation to any premises, includes subject to any provision under section 15C (4) (e) any of the following (whether permanent or temporary)—

    (a)   any feature arising from the design or construction of a building on the premises,

    (b)   any feature on the premises of any approach to, exit from or access to such a building,

    (c)   any fixtures, fittings, furnishings, furniture, equipment or material in or on the premises,

    (d)   any other physical element or quality of any land comprised in the premises;

'provision, criterion or practice' includes any arrangements.

Amendment – Inserted by Disability Discrimination Act 1995 (Amendment) Regulations 2003, SI 2003/1673, regs 3(1), 18. Amended by Disability Discrimination Act 2005 s 19(1), Sch 1, Pt 1, paras 1, 11 (a), (b); Disability Discrimination Act 1995 (Pensions) Regulations 2003, SI 2003/2770, regs 2, 4(2)(a), (b);.

18E   Premises provided otherwise than in course of a Part 2 relationship

(1) This Part does not apply in relation to the provision, otherwise than in the course of a Part 2 relationship, of premises by the regulated party to the other party.

(2) For the purposes of subsection (1)—

    (a)   'Part 2 relationship' means a relationship during the course of which an act of discrimination against, or harassment of, one party to the relationship by the other party to it is unlawful under sections 4 to 15C; and

    (b)   in relation to a Part 2 relationship, 'regulated party' means the party whose acts of discrimination, or harassment, are made unlawful by sections 4 to 15C.

Amendment – Inserted by Disability Discrimination Act 2005, s 19(1), Sch 1, Pt 1, paras 1, 12.

PART III
DISCRIMINATION IN OTHER AREAS

Goods, facilities and services

19 Discrimination in relation to goods, facilities and services

(1) It is unlawful for a provider of services to discriminate against a disabled person—

- (a) in refusing to provide, or deliberately not providing, to the disabled person any service which he provides, or is prepared to provide, to members of the public;
- (b) in failing to comply with any duty imposed on him by section 21 in circumstances in which the effect of that failure is to make it impossible or unreasonably difficult for the disabled person to make use of any such service;
- (c) in the standard of service which he provides to the disabled person or the manner in which he provides it to him; or
- (d) in the terms on which he provides a service to the disabled person.

(2) For the purposes of this section and sections 20 to 21ZA

- (a) the provision of services includes the provision of any goods or facilities;
- (b) a person is 'a provider of services' if he is concerned with the provision, in the United Kingdom, of services to the public or to a section of the public; and
- (c) it is irrelevant whether a service is provided on payment or without payment.

(3) The following are examples of services to which this section and sections 20 and 21 apply—

- (a) access to and use of any place which members of the public are permitted to enter;
- (b) access to and use of means of communication;
- (c) access to and use of information services;
- (d) accommodation in a hotel, boarding house or other similar establishment;
- (e) facilities by way of banking or insurance or for grants, loans, credit or finance;
- (f) facilities for entertainment, recreation or refreshment;
- (g) facilities provided by employment agencies or under section 2 of the Employment and Training Act 1973;
- (h) the services of any profession or trade, or any local or other public authority.

(4) In the case of an act which constitutes discrimination by virtue of section 55, this section also applies to discrimination against a person who is not disabled.

(4A) Subsection (1) does not apply to anything that is governed by Regulation (EC) No 1107/2006 of the European Parliament and of the Council of 5 July 2006 concerning the rights of disabled persons and persons with reduced mobility when travelling by air.

(5) Regulations may provide for subsection (1) and section 21(1), (2) and (4) not to apply, or to apply only to a prescribed extent, in relation to a service of a prescribed description.

(5A) Nothing in this section or sections 20 to 21A applies to the provision of a service in relation to which discrimination is unlawful under Part 4.

(6) *(repealed)*

Amendments – Amended by Education Act 1996, s 582(1), Sch 37, Pt I, para 129; School Standards and Framework Act 1998, s 140(3), Sch 31; Teaching and Higher Education Act 1998, s 38; Learning and Skills Act 2000, ss 149, 153, Sch 9, paras 1, 49, Sch 11; Special Educational Needs and Disability Act 2001, ss 38(1), (5), (6), 42(6), Sch 9; Disability Discrimination Act 2005, s 19(1), Sch 1, Pt 1, paras 1, 13(1), (2); Civil Aviation (Access to Air Travel for Disabled Persons and Persons with Reduced Mobility) Regulations 2007, SI 2007/1895, reg 8.

20 Meaning of 'discrimination'

(1) For the purposes of section 19, a provider of services discriminates against a disabled person if—

- (a) for a reason which relates to the disabled person's disability, he treats him less favourably than he treats or would treat others to whom that reason does not or would not apply; and
- (b) he cannot show that the treatment in question is justified.

(2) For the purposes of section 19, a provider of services also discriminates against a disabled person if—

- (a) he fails to comply with a section 21 duty imposed on him in relation to the disabled person; and
- (b) he cannot show that his failure to comply with that duty is justified.

(3) For the purposes of this section, treatment is justified only if—

- (a) in the opinion of the provider of services, one or more of the conditions mentioned in subsection (4) are satisfied; and
- (b) it is reasonable, in all the circumstances of the case, for him to hold that opinion.

(4) The conditions are that—

- (a) in any case, the treatment is necessary in order not to endanger the health or safety of any person (which may include that of the disabled person);
- (b) in any case, the disabled person is incapable of entering into an enforceable agreement, or of giving an informed consent, and for that reason the treatment is reasonable in that case;

(c) in a case falling with section 19(1)(a), the treatment is necessary because the provider of services would otherwise be unable to provide the service to members of the public;

(d) in a case falling within section 19(1)(c) or (d), the treatment is necessary in order for the provider of services to be able to provide the service to the disabled person or to other members of the public;

(e) in a case falling within section 19(1)(d), the difference in the terms on which the service is provided to the disabled person and those on which it is provided to other members of the public reflects the greater cost to the provider of services in providing the service to the disabled person.

(5) Any increase in the cost of providing a service to a disabled person which results from compliance by a provider of services with a section 21 duty shall be disregarded for the purposes of subsection (4)(e).

(6) Regulations may make provision, for purposes of this section, as to circumstances in which—

(a) it is reasonable for a provider of services to hold the opinion mentioned in subsection (3)(a);

(b) it is not reasonable for a provider of services to hold that opinion.

(7) Regulations may make provision for subsection (4)(b) not to apply in prescribed circumstances where—

(a) a person is acting for a disabled person under a power of attorney;

(b) functions conferred by or under the Mental Capacity Act 2005 are exercisable in relation to a disabled person's property or affairs; or

(c) powers are exercisable in relation to a disabled person's property or affairs in consequence of the appointment, under the law of Scotland, of a guardian, tutor or judicial factor.

(8) Regulations may make provision, for purposes of this section, as to circumstances (other than those mentioned in subsection (4)) in which treatment is to be taken to be justified.

(9) In subsections (3), (4) and (8) 'treatment' includes failure to comply with a section 21 duty.

Amendments – Mental Capacity Act 2005, s 67(1), Sch 6, para 41; Disability Discrimination Act 2005, s 19(1), Sch 1, Pt 1, paras 1, 14.

21 Duty of providers of services to make adjustments

(1) Where a provider of services has a practice, policy or procedure which makes it impossible or unreasonably difficult for disabled persons to make use of a service which he provides, or is prepared to provide, to other members of the public, it is his duty to take such steps as it is reasonable,

in all the circumstances of the case, for him to have to take in order to change that practice, policy or procedure so that it no longer has that effect.

(2) Where a physical feature (for example, one arising from the design or construction of a building or the approach or access to premises) makes it impossible or unreasonably difficult for disabled persons to make use of such a service, it is the duty of the provider of that service to take such steps as it is reasonable, in all the circumstances of the case, for him to have to take in order to—

    (a)   remove the feature;
    (b)   alter it so that it no longer has that effect;
    (c)   provide a reasonable means of avoiding the feature; or
    (d)   provide a reasonable alternative method of making the service in question available to disabled persons.

(3) Regulations may prescribe—

    (a)   matters which are to be taken into account in determining whether any provision of a kind mentioned in subsection (2)(c) or (d) is reasonable; and
    (b)   categories of providers of services to whom subsection (2) does not apply.

(4) Where an auxiliary aid or service (for example, the provision of information on audio tape or of a sign language interpreter) would—

    (a)   enable disabled persons to make use of a service which a provider of services provides, or is prepared to provide, to members of the public, or
    (b)   facilitate the use by disabled persons of such a service,

it is the duty of the provider of that service to take such steps as it is reasonable, in all the circumstances of the case, for him to have to take in order to provide that auxiliary aid or service.

(5) Regulations may make provision, for the purposes of this section—

    (a)   as to circumstances in which it is reasonable for a provider of services to have to take steps of a prescribed description;
    (b)   as to circumstances in which it is not reasonable for a provider of services to have to take steps of a prescribed description;
    (c)   as to what is to be included within the meaning of 'practice, policy or procedure';
    (d)   as to what is not to be included within the meaning of that expression;
    (e)   as to things which are to be treated as physical features;
    (f)   as to things which are not to be treated as such features;
    (g)   as to things which are to be treated as auxiliary aids or services;
    (h)   as to things which are not to be treated as auxiliary aids or services.

(6) Nothing in this section requires a provider of services to take any steps which would fundamentally alter the nature of the service in question or the nature of his trade, profession or business.

(7) Nothing in this section requires a provider of services to take any steps which would cause him to incur expenditure exceeding the prescribed maximum.

(8) Regulations under subsection (7) may provide for the prescribed maximum to be calculated by reference to—

(a)   aggregate amounts of expenditure incurred in relation to different cases;

(b)   prescribed periods;

(c)   services of a prescribed description;

(d)   premises of a prescribed description; or

(e)   such other criteria as may be prescribed.

(9) Regulations may provide, for the purposes of subsection (7), for expenditure incurred by one provider of services to be treated as incurred by another.

(10) This section imposes duties only for the purpose of determining whether a provider of services has discriminated against a disabled person; and accordingly a breach of any such duty is not actionable as such.

21ZA   Application of services 19 to 21 to transport vehicles

(1) Section 19(1) (a), (c) and (d) do not apply in relation to a case where the service is a transport service and, as provider of that service, the provider of services discriminates against a disabled person—

(a)   in not providing, or in providing, him with a vehicle; or

(b)   in not providing, or in providing, him with services when he is travelling in a vehicle provided in the course of the transport service.

(2) For the purposes of section 21(1), (2) and (4), its is never reasonable for a provider of services, as a provider of a transport service—

(a)   to have to take steps which would involve the alteration or removal of a physical feature of a vehicle used in providing the service;

(b)   to have to take steps which would—

(i)   affect whether vehicles are provided in the course of service or what vehicles are so provided, or

(ii)   where a vehicle is provided in the course of the service, affect what happens in the vehicle while someone is traveling in it.

(3) Regulations may provide for subsection (1) or (2) not to apply, or to apply only to a prescribed extent, in relation to vehicles of a prescribed description.

(4) In this section—

'transport service' means a service which (to any extent) involves transport of people by vehicle;

'vehicle' means a vehicle for transporting people by land, air or water, and includes (in particular)—

(a)   a vehicle not having wheels, and

(b)   a vehicle constructed or adapted to carry passengers on a system using a mode of guided transport;

'guided transport' has the same meaning as in the Transport and Works Act 1992.

Amendment – Inserted by Disability and Discrimination Act 2005, s 5.

21A   Employment services

(1) In this Act, 'employment services' means—

(a)   vocational guidance;

(b)   vocational training; or

(c)   services to assist a person to obtain or retain employment, or to establish himself as self-employed.

(2) It is unlawful for a provider of employment services, in relation to such services, to subject to harassment a disabled person—

(a)   to whom he is providing such services, or

(b)   who has requested him to provide such services;

and section 3B (meaning of 'harassment') applies for the purposes of this subsection as it applies for the purposes of Part 2.

(3) In their application to employment services, the preceding provisions of this Part have effect as follows.

(4) Section 19 has effect as if—

(a)   after subsection (1)(a), there were inserted the following paragraph—

'(aa) in failing to comply with a duty imposed on him by subsection (1) of section 21 in circumstances in which the effect of that failure is to place the disabled person at a substantial disadvantage in comparison with persons who are not disabled in relation to the provision of the service;';

(b)   in subsection (1)(b), for 'section 21' there were substituted 'subsection (2) or (4) of section 21';

(c)   in subsection (2), for 'sections 20 and 21ZA' there is substituted 'sections 20 to 21A.

(5) Section 20 has effect as if—

    (a)   after subsection (1), there were inserted the following subsection—

'(1A) For the purposes of section 19, a provider of services also discriminates against a disabled person if he fails to comply with a duty imposed on him by subsection (1) of section 21 in relation to the disabled person.';

    (b)   in subsection (2)(a), for 'a section 21 duty imposed' there were substituted 'a duty imposed by subsection (2) or (4) of section 21';

    (c)   after subsection (3), there were inserted the following subsection—

'(3A) But treatment of a disabled person cannot be justified under subsection (3) if it amounts to direct discrimination falling within section 3A(5).'.

(6) Section 21 has effect as if—

    (a)   in subsection (1), for 'makes it impossible or unreasonably difficult for disabled persons to make use of' there were substituted 'places disabled persons at a substantial disadvantage in comparison with persons who are not disabled in relation to the provision of';

    (b)   after subsection (1), there were inserted the following subsection—

'(1A) In subsection (1), 'practice, policy or procedure' includes a provision or criterion.'.

Amendment – Inserted by Disability Discrimination Act 1995 (Amendment) Regulations 2003, SI 2003/1673, regs 3(1), 19(1). Amended by Disability Discrimination Act 2005, s 19(1).

Public authorities

Amendment – Inserted by Disability Discrimination Act 2005, s 2.

21B Discrimination by public authorities

(1) t is unlawful for a public authority to discriminate against a disabled person in carrying out its functions.

(2) In this section, and sections 21D and 21E, 'public authority'—

    (a)   includes any person certain of whose functions are functions of a public nature; but

    (b)   does not include any person mentioned in subsection (3).

(3) The persons are—

    (a)   either House of Parliament;

- (b) a person exercising functions in connection with proceedings in Parliament;
- (c) the Security Service;
- (d) the Secret Intelligence Service;
- (e) the Government Communications Headquarters; and
- (f) a unit, or part of a unit, of any of the naval, military or air forces of the Crown which is for the time being required by the Secretary of State to assist the Government Communications Headquarters in carrying out its functions.

(4) In relation to a particular act, a person is not a public authority by virtue only of subsection (2)(a) if the nature of the act is private.

(5) Regulations may provide for a person of a prescribed description to be treated as not being a public authority for purposes of this section and sections 21D and 21E.

(6) In the case of an act which constitutes discrimination by virtue of section 55, subsection (1) of this section also applies to discrimination against a person who is not disabled

(7) Subsection (1)—

- (a) does not apply to anything which is unlawful under any provision of this Act other than subsection (1); and
- (b) does not, subject to subsections (8) and (9), apply to anything which would be unlawful under any such provision but for the operation of any provision in or made under this Act.

(8) Subsection (1) does apply in relation to a public authority's function of appointing a person to, and in relation to a public authority's functions with respect to a person as holder of, an office or post if—

- (a) none of the conditions specified in section 4C(3) is satisfied in relation to the office or post; and
- (b) sections 4D and 4E would apply in relation to an appointment to the office or post if any of those conditions was satisfied.

(9) Subsection (1) does apply in relation to a public authority's functions with respect to a person as candidate or prospective candidate for election to, and in relation to a public authority's functions with respect to a person as elected holder of, an office or post if—

- (a) the office or post is not membership of a House of Parliament, the Scottish Parliament, the National Assembly for Wales or an authority mentioned in section 15A(1);
- (b) none of the conditions specified in section 4C(3) is satisfied in relation to the office or post; and
- (c) sections 4D and 4E would apply in relation to an appointment to the office or post if—
  - (i) any of those conditions was satisfied, and
  - (ii) section 4F(1) (but not section 4C(5)) was omitted.

(10) Subsections (8) and (9)—

    (a)   shall not be taken to prejudice the generality of subsection (1); but

    (b)   are subject to section 21C(5).]

Amendment – Inserted by Disability Discrimination Act 2005, s 2.

21C   Exceptions from section 21B(1)

(1) Section 21B(1) does not apply to—

    (a)   a judicial act (whether done by a court, tribunal or other person); or

    (b)   an act done on the instructions, or on behalf, of a person acting in a judicial capacity.

(2) Section 21B(1) does not apply to any act of, or relating to, making, confirming or approving—

    (a)   an Act, an Act of the Scottish Parliament, a Measure or Act of the National Assembly for Wales or an Order in Council; or

    (b)   an instrument made under an Act, or under an Act of the Scottish Parliament, or under a Measure or Act of the National Assembly for Wales, by—

        (i)   a Minister of the Crown;

        (ii)   a member of the Scottish Executive; or

        (iii)   the Welsh Ministers, the First Minister for Wales or the Counsel General to the Welsh Assembly Government.

(3) Section 21B(1) does not apply to any act of, or relating to, imposing conditions or requirements of a kind falling within section 59(1)(c).

(4) Section 21B(1) does not apply to—

    (a)   a decision not to institute criminal proceedings;

    (b)   where such a decision is made, an act done for the purpose of enabling the decision to be made;

    (c)   a decision not to continue criminal proceedings; or

    (d)   where such a decision is made—

        (i)   an act done for the purpose of enabling the decision to be made; or

        (ii)   an act done for the purpose of securing that the proceedings are not continued.

(5) Section 21B(1) does not apply to an act of a prescribed description.

Amendment – Inserted by Disability Discrimination Act 2005, s 2; SI 2007/1388.

21D   Meaning of 'discrimination' in section 21B

(1) For the purposes of section 21B(1), a public authority discriminates against a disabled person if—

(a)   for a reason which relates to the disabled person's disability, it treats him less favourably than it treats or would treat others to whom that reason does not or would not apply; and

(b)   it cannot show that the treatment in question is justified under subsection (3), (5) or (7)(c).

(2) For the purposes of section 21B(1), a public authority also discriminates against a disabled person if—

(a)   it fails to comply with a duty imposed on it by section 21E in circumstances in which the effect of that failure is to make it—

(i)   impossible or unreasonably difficult for the disabled person to receive any benefit that is or may be conferred, or

(ii)   unreasonably adverse for the disabled person to experience being subjected to any detriment to which a person is or may be subjected,

by the carrying-out of a function by the authority; and

(b)   it cannot show that its failure to comply with that duty is justified under subsection (3), (5) or (7)(c).

(3) Treatment, or a failure to comply with a duty, is justified under this subsection if—

(a)   in the opinion of the public authority, one or more of the conditions specified in subsection (4) are satisfied; and

(b)   it is reasonable, in all the circumstances of the case, for it to hold that opinion.

(4) The conditions are—

(a)   that the treatment, or non-compliance with the duty, is necessary in order not to endanger the health or safety of any person (which may include that of the disabled person);

(b)   that the disabled person is incapable of entering into an enforceable agreement, or of giving an informed consent, and for that reason the treatment, or non-compliance with the duty, is reasonable in the particular case;

(c)   that, in the case of treatment mentioned in subsection (1), treating the disabled person equally favourably would in the particular case involve substantial extra costs and, having regard to resources, the extra costs in that particular case would be too great;

(d)   that the treatment, or non-compliance with the duty, is necessary for the protection of rights and freedoms of other persons.

(5) Treatment, or a failure to comply with a duty, is justified under this subsection if the acts of the public authority which give rise to the treatment or failure are a proportionate means of achieving a legitimate aim.

(6) Regulations may make provision, for purposes of this section, as to circumstances in which it is, or as to circumstances in which it is not, reasonable for a public authority to hold the opinion mentioned in subsection (3)(a).

(7) Regulations may—

- (a) amend or omit a condition specified in subsection (4) or make provision for it not to apply in prescribed circumstances;
- (b) amend or omit subsection (5) or make provision for it not to apply in prescribed circumstances;
- (c) make provision for purposes of this section (in addition to any provision for the time being made by subsections (3) to (5)) as to circumstances in which treatment, or a failure to comply with a duty, is to be taken to be justified.

Amendment – Inserted by Disability Discrimination Act 2005, s 2.

21E Duties for purposes of section 21D(2) to make adjustments

(1) Subsection (2) applies where a public authority has a practice, policy or procedure which makes it—

- (a) impossible or unreasonably difficult for disabled persons to receive any benefit that is or may be conferred, or
- (b) unreasonably adverse for disabled persons to experience being subjected to any detriment to which a person is or may be subjected,

by the carrying-out of a function by the authority.

(2) It is the duty of the authority to take such steps as it is reasonable, in all the circumstances of the case, for the authority to have to take in order to change that practice, policy or procedure so that it no longer has that effect.

(3) Subsection (4) applies where a physical feature makes it—

- (a) impossible or unreasonably difficult for disabled persons to receive any benefit that is or may be conferred, or
- (b) unreasonably adverse for disabled persons to experience being subjected to any detriment to which a person is or may be subjected,

by the carrying-out of a function by a public authority.

(4) It is the duty of the authority to take such steps as it is reasonable, in all the circumstances of the case, for the authority to have to take in order to—

- (a) remove the feature;
- (b) alter it so that it no longer has that effect;
- (c) provide a reasonable means of avoiding the feature; or

    (d)   adopt a reasonable alternative method of carrying out the function.

(5) Regulations may prescribe—

    (a)   matters which are to be taken into account in determining whether any provision of a kind mentioned in subsection (4)(c) or (d) is reasonable;

    (b)   categories of public authorities to whom subsection (4) does not apply.

(6) Subsection (7) applies where an auxiliary aid or service would—

    (a)   enable disabled persons to receive, or facilitate the receiving by disabled persons of, any benefit that is or may be conferred, or

    (b)   reduce the extent to which it is adverse for disabled persons to experience being subjected to any detriment to which a person is or may be subjected,

by the carrying-out of a function by a public authority.

(7) It is the duty of the authority to take such steps as it is reasonable, in all the circumstances of the case, for the authority to have to take in order to provide that auxiliary aid or service.

(8) Regulations may make provision, for purposes of this section—

    (a)   as to circumstances in which it is, or as to circumstances in which it is not, reasonable for a public authority to have to take steps of a prescribed description;

    (b)   as to steps which it is always, or as to steps which it is never, reasonable for a public authority to have to take;

    (c)   as to what is, or as to what is not, to be included within the meaning of 'practice, policy or procedure';

    (d)   as to things which are, or as to things which are not, to be treated as physical features;

    (e)   as to things which are, or as to things which are not, to be treated as auxiliary aids or services.

(9) Nothing in this section requires a public authority to take any steps which, apart from this section, it has no power to take.

(10) This section imposes duties only for the purposes of determining whether a public authority has, for the purposes of section 21B(1), discriminated against a disabled person; and accordingly a breach of any such duty is not actionable as such.

Amendment – Inserted by Disability Discrimination Act 2005, s 2.

Private Clubs etc

Amendment – Inserted by Disability Discrimination Act 2005, s 5

21F Discrimination by private clubs etc

(1) This section applies to any association of persons (however described, whether corporate or unincorporate, and whether or not its activities are carried on for profit) if—

    (a)   it has twenty-five or more members;

    (b)   admission to membership is regulated by its constitution and is so conducted that the members do not constitute a section of the public within the meaning of section 19(2); and

    (c)   it is not an organisation to which section 13 applies.

(2) It is unlawful for an association to which this section applies, in the case of a disabled person who is not a member of the association, to discriminate against him—

    (a)   in the terms on which it is prepared to admit him to membership; or

    (b)   by refusing or deliberately omitting to accept his application for membership.

(3) It is unlawful for an association to which this section applies, in the case of a disabled person who is a member, or associate, of the association, to discriminate against him—

    (a)   in the way it affords him access to a benefit, facility or service;

    (b)   by refusing or deliberately omitting to afford him access to a benefit, facility or service;

    (c)   in the case of a member—

        (i)   by depriving him of membership, or

        (ii)   by varying the terms on which he is a member;

    (d)   in the case of an associate—

        (i)   by depriving him of his rights as an associate, or

        (ii)   by varying those rights; or

    (e)   in either case, by subjecting him to any other detriment.

(4) It is unlawful for an association to which this section applies to discriminate against a disabled person—

    (a)   in the way it affords him access to a benefit, facility or service,

    (b)   by refusing or deliberately omitting to afford him access to a benefit, facility or service, or

    (c)   by subjecting him to any other detriment,

in his capacity as a guest of the association.

(5) It is unlawful for an association to which this section applies to discriminate against a disabled person—

    (a)   in the terms on which it is prepared to invite him, or permit a member or associate to invite him, to be a guest of the association;

(b) by refusing or deliberately omitting to invite him to be a guest of the association; or

(c) by not permitting a member or associate to invite him to be a guest of the association.

(6) It is unlawful for an association to which this section applies to discriminate against a disabled person in failing in prescribed circumstances to comply with a duty imposed on it under section 21H.

(7) In the case of an act which constitutes discrimination by virtue of section 55, this section also applies to discrimination against a person who is not disabled.

Amendment – Inserted by Disability Discrimination Act 2005, s 5.

21G Meaning of 'discrimination'

(1) For the purposes of section 21F, an association discriminates against a disabled person if—

(a) for a reason which relates to the disabled person's disability, the association treats him less favourably than it treats or would treat others to whom that reason does not or would not apply; and

(b) it cannot show that the treatment in question is justified.

(2) For the purposes of subsection (1), treatment is justified only if—

(a) in the opinion of the association, one or more of the conditions mentioned in subsection (3) are satisfied; and

(b) it is reasonable, in all the circumstances, for it to hold that opinion.

(3) The conditions are that—

(a) the treatment is necessary in order not to endanger the health or safety of any person (which may include that of the disabled person);

(b) the disabled person is incapable of entering into an enforceable agreement, or giving an informed consent, and for that reason the treatment is reasonable in that case;

(c) in a case falling within section 21F(2)(a), (3)(a), (c)(ii), (d)(ii) or (e), (4)(a) or (c) or (5)(a), the treatment is necessary in order for the association to be able to afford members, associates or guests of the association, or the disabled person, access to a benefit, facility or service;

(d) in a case falling within section 21F(2)(b), (3)(b), (c)(i) or (d)(i), (4)(b) or (5)(b) or (c), the treatment is necessary because the association would otherwise be unable to afford members, associates or guests of the association access to a benefit, facility or service;

(e) in a case falling within section 21F(2)(a), the difference between—

(i)   the terms on which membership is offered to the disabled person, and

(ii)   those on which it is offered to other persons,

reflects the greater cost to the association of affording the disabled person access to a benefit, facility or service;

(f)   in a case falling within section 21F(3)(a), (c)(ii) or (d)(ii) or (4)(a), the difference between—

    (i)   the association's treatment of the disabled person, and

    (ii)   its treatment of other members or (as the case may be) other associates or other guests of the association,

reflects the greater cost to the association of affording the disabled person access to a benefit, facility or service;

(g)   in a case falling within section 21F(5)(a), the difference between—

    (i)   the terms on which the disabled person is invited, or permitted to be invited, to be a guest of the association, and

    (ii)   those on which other persons are invited, or permitted to be invited, to be guests of the association,

reflects the greater cost to the association of affording the disabled person access to a benefit, facility or service.

(4) Any increase in the cost of affording a disabled person access to a benefit, facility or service which results from compliance with a duty under section 21H shall be disregarded for the purposes of subsection (3)(e), (f) and (g).

(5) Regulations may—

(a)   make provision, for purposes of this section, as to circumstances in which it is, or as to circumstances in which it is not, reasonable for an association to hold the opinion mentioned in subsection (2)(a);

(b)   amend or omit a condition specified in subsection (3) or make provision for it not to apply in prescribed circumstances;

(c)   make provision as to circumstances (other than any for the time being mentioned in subsection (3)) in which treatment is to be taken to be justified for the purposes of subsection (1).

(6) For the purposes of section 21F, an association also discriminates against a disabled person if—

(a)   it fails to comply with a duty under section 21H imposed on it in relation to the disabled person; and

(b)   it cannot show that its failure to comply with that duty is justified.

(7) Regulations may make provision as to circumstances in which failure to comply with a duty under section 21H is to be taken to be justified for the purposes of subsection (6).

Amendment – Inserted by Disability Discrimination Act 2005, s 12.

21H　Duty to make adjustments

(1) Regulations may make provision imposing on an association to which section 21F applies—

    (a)　a duty to take steps for a purpose relating to a policy, practice or procedure of the association, or a physical feature, which adversely affects disabled persons who—

        (i)　are, or might wish to become, members or associates of the association, or

        (ii)　are, or are likely to become, guests of the association;

    (b)　a duty to take steps for the purpose of making an auxiliary aid or service available to any such disabled persons.

(2) Regulations under subsection (1) may (in particular)—

    (a)　make provision as to the cases in which a duty is imposed;

    (b)　make provision as to the steps which a duty requires to be taken;

    (c)　make provision as to the purpose for which a duty requires steps to be taken.

(3) Any duty imposed under this section is imposed only for the purpose of determining whether an association has, for the purposes of section 21F, discriminated against a disabled person; and accordingly a breach of any such duty is not actionable as such.

Amendment – Inserted by Disability Discrimination Act 2005, s 12.

21J　'Member', 'associate' and 'guest'

(1) For the purposes of sections 21F to 21H and this section—

    (a)　a person is a member of an association to which section 21F applies if he belongs to it by virtue of his admission to any sort of membership provided for by its constitution (and is not merely a person with certain rights under its constitution by virtue of his membership of some other association), and references to membership of an association shall be construed accordingly;

    (b)　a person is an associate of an association to which section 21F applies if, not being a member of it, he has under its constitution some or all of the rights enjoyed by members (or would have apart from any provision in its constitution authorising the refusal of those rights in particular cases).

(2) References in sections 21F to 21H to a guest of an association include a person who is a guest of the association by virtue of an invitation issued by a member or associate of the association and permitted by the association.

(3) Regulations may make provision, for purposes of sections 21F to 21H, as to circumstances in which a person is to be treated as being, or as to circumstances in which a person is to be treated as not being, a guest of an association.

Amendment – Inserted by Disability Discrimination Act 2005, s 12.

Premises

22   Discrimination in relation to premises

(1) It is unlawful for a person with power to dispose of any premises to discriminate against a disabled person—

    (a)   in the terms on which he offers to dispose of those premises to the disabled person;

    (b)   by refusing to dispose of those premises to the disabled person; or

    (c)   in his treatment of the disabled person in relation to any list of persons in need of premises of that description.

(2) Subsection (1) does not apply to a person who owns an estate or interest in the premises and wholly occupies them unless, for the purpose of disposing of the premises, he—

    (a)   uses the services of an estate agent, or

    (b)   publishes an advertisement or causes an advertisement to be published.

(3) It is unlawful for a person managing any premises to discriminate against a disabled person occupying those premises—

    (a)   in the way he permits the disabled person to make use of any benefits or facilities;

    (b)   by refusing or deliberately omitting to permit the disabled person to make use of any benefits or facilities; or

    (c)   by evicting the disabled person, or subjecting him to any other detriment.

(3A) Regulations may make provision, for purposes of subsection (3)—

    (a)   as to who is to be treated as being, or as to who is to be treated as not being, a person who manages premises;

    (b)   as to who is to be treated as being, or as to who is to be treated as not being, a person occupying premises.

(4) It is unlawful for any person whose licence or consent is required for the disposal of any premises comprised in, or (in Scotland) the subject of, a tenancy to discriminate against a disabled person by withholding his licence or consent for the disposal of the premises to the disabled person.

(5) Subsection (4) applies to tenancies created before as well as after the passing of this Act.

(6) In this section—

'advertisement' includes every form of advertisement or notice, whether to the public or not;

'dispose', in relation to premises, includes granting a right to occupy the premises, and, in relation to premises comprised in, or (in Scotland) the subject of, a tenancy, includes—

  (a) assigning the tenancy, and
  (b) sub-letting or parting with possession of the premises or any part of the premises;

and 'disposal' shall be construed accordingly;

'estate agent' means a person who, by way of profession or trade, provides services for the purpose of finding premises for persons seeking to acquire them or assisting in the disposal of premises; and

'tenancy' means a tenancy created—

  (a) by a lease or sub-lease,
  (b) by an agreement for a lease or sub-lease,
  (c) by a tenancy agreement, or
  (d) in pursuance of any enactment.

(7) In the case of an act which constitutes discrimination by virtue of section 55, this section also applies to discrimination against a person who is not disabled.

(8) This section applies only in relation to premises in the United Kingdom.

_____

Amendment – Amended by Disability Discrimination Act 2005 s 19(1), Pt 1, paras 1, 16.

22A Commonholds

(1) It is unlawful for any person whose licence or consent is required for the disposal of an interest in a commonhold unit by the unit-holder to discriminate against a disabled person by withholding his licence or consent for the disposal of the interest in favour of, or to, the disabled person.

(2) Where it is not possible for an interest in a commonhold unit to be disposed of by the unit-holder unless some other person is a party to the disposal of the interest, it is unlawful for that other person to discriminate against a disabled person by deliberately not being a party to the disposal of the interest in favour of, or to, the disabled person.

(3) Regulations may provide for subsection (1) or (2) not to apply, or to apply only, in cases of a prescribed description.

(4) Regulations may make provision, for purposes of this section—

  (a) as to what is, or as to what is not, to be included within the meaning of 'dispose' (and 'disposal');
  (b) as to what is, or as to what is not, to be included within the meaning of 'interest in a commonhold unit'.

(5) In this section 'commonhold unit', and 'unit-holder' in relation to such a unit, have the same meaning as in Part 1 of the Commonhold and Leasehold Reform Act 2002.

(6) In the case of an act which constitutes discrimination by virtue of section 55, this section also applies to discrimination against a person who is not disabled.

(7) This section applies only in relation to premises in England and Wales.

Amendment – Inserted by Disability Discrimination Act 2005, s 19(1).

23 Exemption for small dwellings

(1) Where the conditions mentioned in subsection (2) are satisfied, subsection (1), (3) or (as the case may be) (4) of section 22 does not apply.

(2) The conditions are that—

    (a)   the relevant occupier resides, and intends to continue to reside, on the premises;

    (b)   the relevant occupier shares accommodation on the premises with persons who reside on the premises and are not members of his household;

    (c)   the shared accommodation is not storage accommodation or a means of access; and

    (d)   the premises are small premises.

(3) For the purposes of this section, premises are 'small premises' if they fall within subsection (4) or (5).

(4) Premises fall within this subsection if—

    (a)   only the relevant occupier and members of his household reside in the accommodation occupied by him;

    (b)   the premises comprise, in addition to the accommodation occupied by the relevant occupier, residential accommodation for at least one other household;

    (c)   the residential accommodation for each other household is let, or available for letting, on a separate tenancy or similar agreement; and

    (d)   there are not normally more than two such other households.

(5) Premises fall within this subsection if there is not normally residential accommodation on the premises for more than six persons in addition to the relevant occupier and any members of his household.

(6) For the purposes of this section 'the relevant occupier' means—

    (a)   in a case falling within section 22(1), the person with power to dispose of the premises, or a near relative of his;

    (aa)   in a case falling within section 22(3), the person managing the premises, or a near relative of his;

(b)   in a case falling within section 22(4), the person whose licence or consent is required for the disposal of the premises, or a near relative of his.

(7) For the purposes of this section—

'near relative' means a person's spouse or civil partner, partner, parent, child, grandparent, grandchild, or brother or sister (whether of full or half blood or by marriage or civil partnership; and
'partner' means the other member of a couple consisting of—

    (a)   a man and a woman who are not married to each other but are living together as husband and wife, or

    (b)   two people of the same sex who are not civil partners of each other but are living together as if they were civil partners.

Amendment – Amended by Civil Partnership Act 2004, s 261(1), Sch 27, para 150(1), (2)(a), (b), (3); Disability Discrimination Act 2005, s 19(1).

24   Meaning of 'discrimination'

(1) For the purposes of section 22 and 22A, a person ('A') discriminates against a disabled person if—

(a)   for a reason which relates to the disabled person's disability, he treats him less favourably than he treats or would treat others to whom that reason does not or would not apply; and

(b)   he cannot show that the treatment in question is justified.

(2) For the purposes of this section, treatment is justified only if—

(a)   in A's opinion, one or more of the conditions mentioned in subsection (3) are satisfied; and

(b)   it is reasonable, in all the circumstances of the case, for him to hold that opinion.

(3) The conditions are that—

(a)   in any case, the treatment is necessary in order not to endanger the health or safety of any person (which may include that of the disabled person);

(b)   in any case, the disabled person is incapable of entering into an enforceable agreement, or of giving an informed consent, and for that reason the treatment is reasonable in that case;

(c)   in a case falling within section 22(3)(a), the treatment is necessary in order for the disabled person or the occupiers of other premises forming part of the building to make use of the benefit or facility;

(d)   in a case falling within section 22(3)(b), the treatment is necessary in order for the occupiers of other premises forming part of the building to make use of the benefit or facility.

(e)   in a case to which subsection (3A) applies, the terms are less favourable in order to recover costs which—

    (i)   as a result of the disabled person having a disability, are incurred in connection with the disposal of the premises, and

    (ii)   are not costs incurred in connection with taking steps to avoid liability under section 24G(1);

  (f)   in a case to which subsection (3B) applies, the disabled person is subjected to the detriment in order to recover costs which—

    (i)   as a result of the disabled person having a disability, are incurred in connection with the management of the premises, and

    (ii)   are not costs incurred in connection with taking steps to avoid liability under section 24A(1) or 24G(1)].

(3A) This subsection applies to a case if—

  (a)   the case falls within section 22(1)(a);

  (b)   the premises are to let;

  (c)   the person with power to dispose of the premises is a controller of them; and

  (d)   the proposed disposal of the premises would involve the disabled person becoming a person to whom they are let.

(3B) This subsection applies to a case if—

  (a)   the case falls within section 22(3)(c);

  (b)   the detriment is not eviction;

  (c)   the premises are let premises;

  (d)   the person managing the premises is a controller of them; and

  (e)   the disabled person is a person to whom the premises are let or, although not a person to whom they are let, is lawfully under the letting an occupier of them.

(3C) Section 24G(3) and (4) apply for the purposes of subsection (3A) as for those of section 24G; and section 24A(3) and (4) apply for the purposes of subsection (3B) as for those of section 24A.

(4) Regulations may make provision, for purposes of this section, as to circumstances in which—

  (a)   it is reasonable for a person to hold the opinion mentioned in subsection 2(a);

  (b)   it is not reasonable for a person to hold that opinion.

(4A) Regulations may make provision for the condition specified in subsection (3)(b) not to apply in prescribed circumstances.

(5) Regulations may make provision, for purposes of this section, as to circumstances (other than those mentioned in subsection (3)) in which treatment is to be taken to be justified.

Amendment – Amended by Disability Discrimination Act 2005, s 19(1), Sch 1.

24A   Let premises: discrimination in failing to comply with duty

(1) It is unlawful for a controller of let premises to discriminate against a disabled person—

- (a)   who is a person to whom the premises are let; or
- (b)   who, although not a person to whom the premises are let, is lawfully under the letting an occupier of the premises.

(2) For the purposes of subsection (1), a controller of let premises discriminates against a disabled person if—

- (a)   he fails to comply with a duty under section 24C or 24D imposed on him by reference to the disabled person; and
- (b)   he cannot show that failure to comply with the duty is justified (see section 24K).

(3) For the purposes of this section and sections 24B to 24F, a person is a controller of let premises if he is—

- (a)   a person by whom the premises are let; or
- (b)   a person who manages the premises.

(4) For the purposes of this section and sections 24B to 24F—

- (a)   'let' includes sub-let; and
- (b)   premises shall be treated as let by a person to another where a person has granted another a contractual licence to occupy them.

(5) This section applies only in relation to premises in the United Kingdom.

Amendment – Inserted by the Disability Discrimination Act 2005, s 13.

24B   Exceptions to section 24A(1)

(1) Section 24A(1) does not apply if—

- (a)   the premises are, or have at any time been, the only or principal home of an individual who is a person by whom they are let; and
- (b)   since entering into the letting—
  - (i)   the individual has not, and
  - (ii)   where he is not the sole person by whom the premises are let, no other person by whom they are let has,

used for the purpose of managing the premises the services of a person who, by profession or trade, manages let premises.

(2) Section 24A(1) does not apply if the premises are of a prescribed description.

(3) Where the conditions mentioned in section 23(2) are satisfied, section 24A(1) does not apply.

(4) For the purposes of section 23 'the relevant occupier' means, in a case falling within section 24A(1), a controller of the let premises, or a near relative of his; and 'near relative' has here the same meaning as in section 23.

Amendment – Inserted by Disability Discrimination Act 2005, s 13.

24C Duty for purposes of section 24A(2) to provide auxiliary aid or service

(1) Subsection (2) applies where—

(a)   a controller of let premises receives a request made by or on behalf of a person to whom the premises are let;

(b)   it is reasonable to regard the request as a request that the controller take steps in order to provide an auxiliary aid or service; and

(c)   either the first condition, or the second condition, is satisfied.

(2) It is the duty of the controller to take such steps as it is reasonable, in all the circumstances of the case, for him to have to take in order to provide the auxiliary aid or service (but see section 24E(1)).

(3) The first condition is that—

(a)   the auxiliary aid or service—

(i)   would enable a relevant disabled person to enjoy, or facilitate such a person's enjoyment of, the premises, but

(ii)   would be of little or no practical use to the relevant disabled person concerned if he were neither a person to whom the premises are let nor an occupier of them; and

(b)   it would, were the auxiliary aid or service not to be provided, be impossible or unreasonably difficult for the relevant disabled person concerned to enjoy the premises.

(4) The second condition is that—

(a)   the auxiliary aid or service—

(i)   would enable a relevant disabled person to make use, or facilitate such a person's making use, of any benefit, or facility, which by reason of the letting is one of which he is entitled to make use, but

(ii)   would be of little or no practical use to the relevant disabled person concerned if he were neither a person to whom the premises are let nor an occupier of them; and

(b)   it would, were the auxiliary aid or service not to be provided, be impossible or unreasonably difficult for the relevant disabled person concerned to make use of any benefit, or facility, which by reason of the letting is one of which he is entitled to make use.

Amendment – Inserted by Disability Discrimination Act 2005, s 13.

24D   Duty for purposes of section 24A(2) to change practices, terms etc

(1) Subsection (3) applies where—

- (a)   a controller of let premises has a practice, policy or procedure which has the effect of making it impossible, or unreasonably difficult, for a relevant disabled person—
  - (i)   to enjoy the premises, or
  - (ii)   to make use of any benefit, or facility, which by reason of the letting is one of which he is entitled to make use, or
- (b)   a term of the letting has that effect,

and (in either case) the conditions specified in subsection (2) are satisfied.

(2) Those conditions are—

- (a)   that the practice, policy, procedure or term would not have that effect if the relevant disabled person concerned did not have a disability;
- (b)   that the controller receives a request made by or on behalf of a person to whom the premises are let; and
- (c)   that it is reasonable to regard the request as a request that the controller take steps in order to change the practice, policy, procedure or term so as to stop it having that effect.

(3) It is the duty of the controller to take such steps as it is reasonable, in all the circumstances of the case, for him to have to take in order to change the practice, policy, procedure or term so as to stop it having that effect (but see section 24E(1)).

Amendment – Inserted by Disability Discrimination Act 2005, s 13.

24E   Sections 24C and 24D: supplementary and interpretation

(1) For the purposes of sections 24C and 24D, it is never reasonable for a controller of let premises to have to take steps consisting of, or including, the removal or alteration of a physical feature.

(2) Sections 24C and 24D impose duties only for the purpose of determining whether a person has, for the purposes of section 24A, discriminated against another; and accordingly a breach of any such duty is not actionable as such.

(3) In sections 24C and 24D 'relevant disabled person', in relation to let premises, means a particular disabled person—

- (a)   who is a person to whom the premises are let; or
- (b)   who, although not a person to whom the premises are let, is lawfully under the letting an occupier of the premises.

(4) For the purposes of sections 24C and 24D, the terms of a letting of premises include the terms of any agreement which relates to the letting of the premises.

Amendment – Inserted by Disability Discrimination Act 2005, s 13.

24F   Let premises: victimisation of persons to whom premises are let

(1) Where a duty under section 24C or 24D is imposed on a controller of let premises by reference to a person who, although not a person to whom the premises are let, is lawfully under the letting an occupier of the premises, it is unlawful for a controller of the let premises to discriminate against a person to whom the premises are let.

(2) For the purposes of subsection (1), a controller of the let premises discriminates against a person to whom the premises are let if—

   (a)   the controller treats that person ('T') less favourably than he treats or would treat other persons whose circumstances are the same as T's; and

   (b)   he does so because of costs incurred in connection with taking steps to avoid liability under section 24A(1) for failure to comply with the duty.

(3) In comparing T's circumstances with those of any other person for the purposes of subsection (2)(a), the following (as well as the costs' having been incurred) shall be disregarded—

   (a)   the making of the request that gave rise to the imposition of the duty; and

   (b)   the disability of each person who—

      (i)   is a disabled person or a person who has had a disability, and

      (ii)   is a person to whom the premises are let or, although not a person to whom the premises are let, is lawfully under the letting an occupier of the premises.

Amendment – Inserted by Disability Discrimination Act 2005, s 13.

24G   Premises that are to let: discrimination in failing to comply with duty

(1) Where—

   (a)   a person has premises to let, and

   (b)   a disabled person is considering taking a letting of the premises,

it is unlawful for a controller of the premises to discriminate against the disabled person.

(2) For the purposes of subsection (1), a controller of premises that are to let discriminates against a disabled person if—

   (a)   he fails to comply with a duty under section 24J imposed on him by reference to the disabled person; and

   (b)   he cannot show that failure to comply with the duty is justified (see section 24K).

(3) For the purposes of this section and sections 24H and 24J, a person is a controller of premises that are to let if he is—

(a)   a person who has the premises to let; or
(b)   a person who manages the premises.

(4) For the purposes of this section and sections 24H and 24J—

(a)   'let' includes sub-let;
(b)   premises shall be treated as to let by a person to another where a person proposes to grant another a contractual licence to occupy them;

and references to a person considering taking a letting of premises shall be construed accordingly.

(5) This section applies only in relation to premises in the United Kingdom.

Amendment – Inserted by Disability Discrimination Act 2005, s 13.

24H   Exceptions to section 24G(1)

(1) Section 24G(1) does not apply in relation to premises that are to let if the premises are, or have at any time been, the only or principal home of an individual who is a person who has them to let and—

(a)   the individual does not use, and
(b)   where he is not the sole person who has the premises to let, no other person who has the premises to let uses,

the services of an estate agent (within the meaning given by section 22(6)) for the purposes of letting the premises.

(2) Section 24G(1) does not apply if the premises are of a prescribed description.

(3) Where the conditions mentioned in section 23(2) are satisfied, section 24G(1) does not apply.

(4) For the purposes of section 23 'the relevant occupier' means, in a case falling within section 24G(1), a controller of the premises that are to let, or a near relative of his; and 'near relative' has here the same meaning as in section 23.

Amendment – Inserted by Disability Discrimination Act 2005, s 13.

24J   Duties for purposes of section 24G(2)

(1) Subsection (2) applies where—

(a)   a controller of premises that are to let receives a request made by or on behalf of a relevant disabled person;

(b) it is reasonable to regard the request as a request that the controller take steps in order to provide an auxiliary aid or service;

(c) the auxiliary aid or service—

(i) would enable the relevant disabled person to become, or facilitate his becoming, a person to whom the premises are let, but

(ii) would be of little or no practical use to him if he were not considering taking a letting of the premises; and

(d) it would, were the auxiliary aid or service not to be provided, be impossible or unreasonably difficult for the relevant disabled person to become a person to whom the premises are let.

(2) It is the duty of the controller to take such steps as it is reasonable, in all the circumstances of the case, for the controller to have to take in order to provide the auxiliary aid or service (but see subsection (5)).

(3) Subsection (4) applies where—

(a) a controller of premises that are to let has a practice, policy or procedure which has the effect of making it impossible, or unreasonably difficult, for a relevant disabled person to become a person to whom the premises are let;

(b) the practice, policy or procedure would not have that effect if the relevant disabled person did not have a disability;

(c) the controller receives a request made by or on behalf of the relevant disabled person; and

(d) it is reasonable to regard the request as a request that the controller take steps in order to change the practice, policy or procedure so as to stop it having that effect.

(4) It is the duty of the controller to take such steps as it is reasonable, in all the circumstances of the case, for him to have to take in order to change the practice, policy or procedure so as to stop it having that effect (but see subsection (5)).

(5) For the purposes of this section, it is never reasonable for a controller of premises that are to let to have to take steps consisting of, or including, the removal or alteration of a physical feature.

(6) In this section 'relevant disabled person', in relation to premises that are to let, means a particular disabled person who is considering taking a letting of the premises.

(7) This section imposes duties only for the purpose of determining whether a person has, for the purposes of section 24G, discriminated against another; and accordingly a breach of any such duty is not actionable as such.

Amendment – Inserted by Disability Discrimination Act 2005, s 13.

24K   Let premises and premises that are to let: justification

(1) For the purposes of sections 24A(2) and 24G(2), a person's failure to comply with a duty is justified only if—

> (a)   in his opinion, a condition mentioned in subsection (2) is satisfied; and
>
> (b)   it is reasonable, in all the circumstances of the case, for him to hold that opinion.

(2) The conditions are—

> (a)   that it is necessary to refrain from complying with the duty in order not to endanger the health or safety of any person (which may include that of the disabled person concerned);
>
> (b)   that the disabled person concerned is incapable of entering into an enforceable agreement, or of giving informed consent, and for that reason the failure is reasonable.

(3) Regulations may—

> (a)   make provision, for purposes of this section, as to circumstances in which it is, or as to circumstances in which it is not, reasonable for a person to hold the opinion mentioned in subsection (1)(a);
>
> (b)   amend or omit a condition specified in subsection (2) or make provision for it not to apply in prescribed circumstances;
>
> (c)   make provision, for purposes of this section, as to circumstances (other than any for the time being mentioned in subsection (2)) in which a failure is to be taken to be justified.

Amendment – Inserted by Disability Discrimination Act 2005, s 13.

24L   Sections 24 to 24K: power to make supplementary provision

(1) Regulations may make provision, for purposes of sections 24(3A) and (3B) and 24A to 24K—

> (a)   as to circumstances in which premises are to be treated as let to a person;
>
> (b)   as to circumstances in which premises are to be treated as not let to a person;
>
> (c)   as to circumstances in which premises are to be treated as being, or as not being, to let;
>
> (d)   as to who is to be treated as being, or as to who is to be treated as not being, a person who, although not a person to whom let premises are let, is lawfully under the letting an occupier of the premises;
>
> (e)   as to who is to be treated as being, or as to who is to be treated as not being, a person by whom premises are let;
>
> (f)   as to who is to be treated as having, or as to who is to be treated as not having, premises to let;
>
> (g)   as to who is to be treated as being, or as to who is to be treated as not being, a person who manages premises;

(h)   as to things which are, or as to things which are not, to be treated as auxiliary aids or services;

(i)   as to what is, or as to what is not, to be included within the meaning of 'practice, policy or procedure';

(j)   as to circumstances in which it is, or as to circumstances in which it is not, reasonable for a person to have to take steps of a prescribed description;

(k)   as to steps which it is always, or as to steps which it is never, reasonable for a person to have to take;

(l)   as to circumstances in which it is, or as to circumstances in which it is not, reasonable to regard a request as being of a particular kind;

(m)   as to things which are, or as to things which are not, to be treated as physical features;

(n)   as to things which are, or as to things which are not, to be treated as alterations of physical features.

(2) Regulations under subsection (1)(a) may (in particular) provide for premises to be treated as let to a person where they are a commonhold unit of which he is a unit-holder; and 'commonhold unit', and 'unit-holder' in relation to such a unit, have here the same meaning as in Part 1 of the Commonhold and Leasehold Reform Act 2002.

(3) The powers under subsections (1)(j) and (k) are subject to sections 24E(1) and 24J(5).

Amendment – Inserted by Disability Discrimination Act 2005, s 13.

24M   Premises provisions do not apply where other provisions operate

(1) Sections 22 to 24L do not apply—

(a)   in relation to the provision of premises by a provider of services where he provides the premises in providing services to members of the public;

(b)   in relation to the provision, in the course of a Part 2 relationship, of premises by the regulated party to the other party;

(c)   in relation to the provision of premises to a student or prospective student—

    (i)   by a responsible body within the meaning of Chapter 1 or 2 of Part 4, or

    (ii)   by an authority in discharging any functions mentioned in section 28F(1); or

(d)   to anything which is unlawful under section 21F or which would be unlawful under that section but for the operation of any provision in or made under this Act.

(2) Subsection (1)(a) has effect subject to any prescribed exceptions.

(3) In subsection (1)(a) 'provider of services', and providing services, have the same meaning as in section 19.

(4) For the purposes of subsection (1)(b)—

    (a) 'Part 2 relationship' means a relationship during the course of which an act of discrimination against, or harassment of, one party to the relationship by the other party to it is unlawful under sections 4 to 15C; and

    (b) in relation to a Part 2 relationship, 'regulated party' means the party whose acts of discrimination, or harassment, are made unlawful by sections 4 to 15C

(5) In subsection (1)(c) 'student' includes pupil

Amendment – Inserted by Disability Discrimination Act 2005, s 19(1), Sch 1, Pt 1, 20.

Enforcement, etc

25 Enforcement, remedies and procedure

(1) A claim by any person that another person—

    (a) has discriminated against him in a way which is unlawful under this Part; or

    (b) is by virtue of section 57 or 58 to be treated as having discriminated against him in such a way,

may be made the subject of civil proceedings in the same way as any other claim in tort or (in Scotland) in reparation for breach of statutory duty.

(2) For the avoidance of doubt it is hereby declared that damages in respect of discrimination in a way which is unlawful under this Part may include compensation for injury to feelings whether or not they include compensation under any other head.

(3) Proceedings in England and Wales shall be brought only in a county court.

(4) Proceedings in Scotland shall be brought only in a sheriff court.

(5) The remedies available in such proceedings are those which are available in the High Court or (as the case may be) the Court of Session.

(6) Part II of Schedule 3 makes further provision about the enforcement of this Part and about procedure.

(6A) Subsection (1) does not apply in relation to a claim by a person that another person—

    (a) has discriminated against him in relation to the provision under a group insurance arrangement of facilities by way of insurance; or

    (b) is by virtue of section 57 or 58 to be treated as having discriminated against him in relation to the provision under such an arrangement of such facilities.

(7) Subsection (1) does not apply in relation to a claim by a person that another person—

(a) has discriminated against him in relation to the provision of employment services; or

(b) is by virtue of section 57 or 58 to be treated as having discriminated against him in relation to the provision of employment services

(8) A claim—

(a) of the kind referred to in subsection (6A) or (7), or

(b) by a person that another—

(i) has subjected him to harassment in a way which is unlawful under section 21A(2), or

(ii) is by virtue of section 57 or 58 to be treated as having subjected him to harassment in such a way,

may be presented as a complaint to an employment tribunal.

(9) Section 17A(1A) to (7) and paragraphs 3 and 4 of Schedule 3 apply in relation to a complaint under subsection (8) as if it were a complaint under section 17A(1) (and paragraphs 6 to 8 of Schedule 3 do not apply in relation to such a complaint).

Amendment – Inserted by Disability Discrimination Act 1995 (Amendment) Regulations 2003, SI 2003/1673, regs 3(1), 19(2). Amended by Disability Discrimination Act 2005, s 11(2).

26   Validity and revision of certain agreements

(1) Any term in a contract for the provision of goods, facilities or services or in any other agreement is void so far as it purports to—

(a) require a person to do anything which would contravene any provision of, or made under, this Part,

(b) exclude or limit the operation of any provision of this Part, or

(c) prevent any person from making a claim under this Part.

(1A) Subsection (1) does not apply to—

(a) any term in a contract for the provision of employment services;

(b) any term in a contract which is a group insurance arrangement; or

(c) a term which—

(i) is in an agreement which is not a contract of either of those kinds, and

(ii) relates to the provision of employment services or the provision under a group insurance arrangement of facilities by way of insurance.

(2) Paragraphs (b) and (c) of subsection (1) do not apply to an agreement settling a claim to which section 25 applies.

(3) On the application of any person interested in an agreement to which subsection (1) applies, a county court or a sheriff court may make such order as it thinks just for modifying the agreement to take account of the effect of subsection (1).

(4) No such order shall be made unless all persons affected have been—

(a) given notice of the application; and
(b) afforded an opportunity to make representations to the court.

(5) Subsection (4) applies subject to any rules of court providing for that notice to be dispensed with.

(6) An order under subsection (3) may include provision as respects any period before the making of the order.

Amendment – Inserted by Disability Discrimination Act 1995 (Amendment) Regulations 2003, SI 2003/1673, regs 3(1), 19(3). Amended by Disability Discrimination Act 2005, s 19(1).

27   Alterations to premises occupied under leases

(1) This section applies where—

(a) a provider of services, a public authority (within the meaning given by section 21B) or an association to which section 21F applies ('the occupier') occupies premises under a lease;
(b) but for this section, the occupier would not be entitled to make a particular alteration to the premises; and
(c) the alteration is one which the occupier proposes to make in order to comply with a section 21 duty or a duty imposed under section 21E or 21H.

(2) Except to the extent to which it expressly so provides, the lease shall have effect by virtue of this subsection as if it provided—

(a) for the occupier to be entitled to make the alteration with the written consent of the lessor;
(b) for the occupier to have to make a written application to the lessor for consent if he wishes to make the alteration;
(c) if such an application is made, for the lessor not to withhold his consent unreasonably; and
(d) for the lessor to be entitled to make his consent subject to reasonable conditions.

(3) In this section—

'lease' includes a tenancy, sub-lease or sub-tenancy and an agreement for a lease, tenancy, sub-lease or sub-tenancy; and
'sub-lease' and 'sub-tenancy' have such meaning as may be prescribed.

(4) If the terms and conditions of a lease—

(a) impose conditions which are to apply if the occupier alters the premises, or

(b) entitle the lessor to impose conditions when consenting to the occupier's altering the premises,

the occupier is to be treated for the purposes of subsection (1) as not being entitled to make the alteration.

(5) Part II of Schedule 4 supplements the provisions of this section.

Amendment – Amended by Disability Discrimination Act 2005, s 19(1).

28 Conciliation of disputes

(*repealed*)

Amendment – Repealed by Equality Act 2006.

PART IV
EDUCATION

Chapter 1
Schools
Duties of responsible bodies

28A Discrimination against disabled pupils and prospective pupils

(1) It is unlawful for the body responsible for a school to discriminate against a disabled person—

(a) in the arrangements it makes for determining admission to the school as a pupil;

(b) in the terms on which it offers to admit him to the school as a pupil; or

(c) by refusing or deliberately omitting to accept an application for his admission to the school as a pupil.

(2) It is unlawful for the body responsible for a school to discriminate against a disabled pupil in the education or associated services provided for, or offered to, pupils at the school by that body.

(3) The Secretary of State may by regulations prescribe services which are, or services which are not, to be regarded for the purposes of subsection (2) as being—

(a) education; or

(b) an associated service.

(4) It is unlawful for the body responsible for a school to discriminate against a disabled pupil by excluding him from the school, whether permanently or temporarily.

(5) The body responsible for a school is to be determined in accordance with Schedule 4A, and in the remaining provisions of this Chapter is referred to as the 'responsible body'.

(6) In the case of an act which constitutes discrimination by virtue of section 55, this section also applies to discrimination against a person who is not disabled.

Amendment – Section and preceding Chapter heading and cross-heading inserted by Special Educational Needs and Disability Act 2001, s 11(1).

28B Meaning of 'discrimination'

(1) For the purposes of section 28A, a responsible body discriminates against a disabled person if—

  (a) for a reason which relates to his disability, it treats him less favourably than it treats or would treat others to whom that reason does not or would not apply; and

  (b) it cannot show that the treatment in question is justified.

(2) For the purposes of section 28A, a responsible body also discriminates against a disabled person if—

  (a) it fails, to his detriment, to comply with section 28C; and

  (b) it cannot show that its failure to comply is justified.

(3) In relation to a failure to take a particular step, a responsible body does not discriminate against a person if it shows—

  (a) that, at the time in question, it did not know and could not reasonably have been expected to know, that he was disabled; and

  (b) that its failure to take the step was attributable to that lack of knowledge.

(4) The taking of a particular step by a responsible body in relation to a person does not amount to less favourable treatment if it shows that at the time in question it did not know, and could not reasonably have been expected to know, that he was disabled.

(5) Subsections (6) to (8) apply in determining whether, for the purposes of this section—

  (a) less favourable treatment of a person, or

  (b) failure to comply with section 28C,

is justified.

(6) Less favourable treatment of a person is justified if it is the result of a permitted form of selection.

(7) Otherwise, less favourable treatment, or a failure to comply with section 28C, is justified only if the reason for it is both material to the circumstances of the particular case and substantial.

(8) If, in a case falling within subsection (1)—

  (a) the responsible body is under a duty imposed by section 28C in relation to the disabled person, but

  (b) it fails without justification to comply with that duty, its treatment of that person cannot be justified under subsection (7) unless that treatment would have been justified even if it had complied with that duty.

Amendment – Inserted by Special Educational Needs and Disability Act 2001, s 12.

28C   Disabled pupils not to be substantially disadvantaged

(1) The responsible body for a school must take such steps as it is reasonable for it to have to take to ensure that—

    (a)   in relation to the arrangements it makes for determining the admission of pupils to the school, disabled persons are not placed at a substantial disadvantage in comparison with persons who are not disabled; and

    (b)   in relation to education and associated services provided for, or offered to, pupils at the school by it, disabled pupils are not placed at a substantial disadvantage in comparison with pupils who are not disabled.

(2) That does not require the responsible body to—

    (a)   remove or alter a physical feature (for example, one arising from the design or construction of the school premises or the location of resources); or

    (b)   provide auxiliary aids or services.

(3) Regulations may make provision, for the purposes of this section—

    (a)   as to circumstances in which it is reasonable for a responsible body to have to take steps of a prescribed description;

    (b)   as to steps which it is always reasonable for a responsible body to have to take;

    (c)   as to circumstances in which it is not reasonable for a responsible body to have to take steps of a prescribed description;

    (d)   as to steps which it is never reasonable for a responsible body to have to take.

(4) In considering whether it is reasonable for it to have to take a particular step in order to comply with its duty under subsection (1), a responsible body must have regard to any relevant provisions of a code of practice issued under section 14 of the Equality Act 2006.

(5) Subsection (6) applies if, in relation to a person, a confidentiality request has been made of which a responsible body is aware.

(6) In determining whether it is reasonable for the responsible body to have to take a particular step in relation to that person in order to comply with its duty under subsection (1), regard shall be had to the extent to which taking the step in question is consistent with compliance with that request.

(7) 'Confidentiality request' means a request which asks for the nature, or asks for the existence, of a disabled person's disability to be treated as confidential and which satisfies either of the following conditions—

    (a)   it is made by that person's parent; or

    (b)   it is made by that person himself and the responsible body reasonably believes that he has sufficient understanding of the nature of the request and of its effect.

(8) This section imposes duties only for the purpose of determining whether a responsible body has discriminated against a disabled person; and accordingly a breach of any such duty is not actionable as such.

Amendment – Inserted by Special Educational Needs and Disability Act 2001, s 13. Amended by Equality Act 2006, s 40, Sch 3, paras. 41, 46.

28D Accessibility strategies and plans

(1) Each local education authority must prepare, in relation to schools for which they are the responsible body—

    (a)   an accessibility strategy;

    (b)   further such strategies at such times as may be prescribed.

(2) An accessibility strategy is a strategy for, over a prescribed period—

    (a)   increasing the extent to which disabled pupils can participate in the schools' curriculums;

    (b)   improving the physical environment of the schools for the purpose of increasing the extent to which disabled pupils are able to take advantage of education and associated services provided or offered by the schools; and

    (c)   improving the delivery to disabled pupils—

        (i)   within a reasonable time, and

        (ii) in ways which are determined after taking account of their disabilities and any preferences expressed by them or their parents,

of information which is provided in writing for pupils who are not disabled.

(3) An accessibility strategy must be in writing.

(4) Each local education authority must keep their accessibility strategy under review during the period to which it relates and, if necessary, revise it.

(5) It is the duty of each local education authority to implement their accessibility strategy.

(6) *(repealed)*

(7) Subsections (8) to (13) apply to—

    (a)   maintained schools and maintained nursery schools;

    (b)   independent schools; and

    (c)   special schools which are not maintained special schools but which are approved by the Secretary of State, or by the Welsh Ministers, under section 342 of the Education Act 1996.

(8) The responsible body must prepare—

    (a)   an accessibility plan;

    (b)   further such plans at such times as may be prescribed.

(9) An accessibility plan is a plan for, over a prescribed period—

    (a)   increasing the extent to which disabled pupils can participate in the school's curriculum;

    (b)   improving the physical environment of the school for the purpose of increasing the extent to which disabled pupils are able to take advantage of education and associated services provided or offered by the school; and

    (c)   improving the delivery to disabled pupils—

        (i)   within a reasonable time, and

        (ii)   in ways which are determined after taking account of their disabilities and any preferences expressed by them or their parents,

of information which is provided in writing for pupils who are not disabled.

(10) An accessibility plan must be in writing.

(11) During the period to which the plan relates, the responsible body must keep its accessibility plan under review and, if necessary, revise it.

(12) It is the duty of the responsible body to implement its accessibility plan.

(13) An inspection under Part 1 of the Education Act 2005 may extend to the performance by the responsible body of its functions in relation to the preparation, publication, review, revision and implementation of its accessibility plan.

(14) For a maintained school or maintained nursery school, the duties imposed by subsections (8) to (12) are duties of the governing body.

(15) Regulations may prescribe services which are, or services which are not, to be regarded for the purposes of this section as being—

    (a)   education; or

    (b)   an associated service.

(16) In this section and in section 28E, 'local education authority' has the meaning given in section 12 of the Education Act 1996.

(17) In this section—

'prescribed' means prescribed in regulations; and

'regulations' means —

(a) in relation to England, regulations made by the Secretary of State, and

(b) in relation to Wales, regulations made by the Welsh Ministers

(18) 'Disabled pupil' includes a disabled person who may be admitted to the school as a pupil.

(19) 'Maintained school' and 'independent school' have the meaning given in section 28Q(5).

Amendments – Inserted by Special Educational Needs and Disability Act 2001, s 14(1). Amended by Education Act 2002, s 215(1), Sch 21, para 26; Children Act 2004, s 64, Sch 5, Pt 3; Disability Discrimination Act 2005, s 19(1), Sch 1, Pt 1, paras 1, 24(1), (2); SI 2005/2913; SI 2007/1388.

28E Accessibility strategies and plans: procedure

(1) In preparing their accessibility strategy, a local education authority must have regard to—

(a) the need to allocate adequate resources for implementing the strategy; and

(b) any guidance issued as to—

   (i) the content of an accessibility strategy;

   (ii) the form in which it is to be produced; and

   (iii) the persons to be consulted in its preparation.

(2) A local education authority must have regard to any guidance issued as to compliance with the requirements of section 28D(4).

(3) Guidance under subsection (1)(b) or (2) may be issued—

(a) for England, by the Secretary of State; and

(b) for Wales, by the Welsh Ministers

(4) In preparing an accessibility plan, the responsible body must have regard to the need to allocate adequate resources for implementing the plan.

(5) If the Secretary of State asks for a copy of—

(a) the accessibility strategy prepared by a local education authority in England, or

(b) the accessibility plan prepared by the proprietor of an independent school (other than an Academy) in England,

the strategy or plan must be given to him.

(6) If the Welsh Ministers asks for a copy of—

(a) the accessibility strategy prepared by a local education authority in Wales, or

(b) the accessibility plan prepared by the proprietor of an independent school (other than an Academy) in Wales, the strategy or plan must be given to them.

(7) If asked to do so, a local education authority must make a copy of their accessibility strategy available for inspection at such reasonable times as they may determine.

(8) If asked to do so, the proprietor of an independent school which is not an Academy must make a copy of his accessibility plan available for inspection at such reasonable times as he may determine.

Amendments – Inserted by Special Educational Needs and Disability Act 2001, s 15. Amended by Education Act 2002, s 65(3), Sch 7, Pt 2, para 5(1), (2); SI 2007/1388.

Residual duty of education authorities

28F   Duty of education authorities not to discriminate

(1) This section applies to—

    (a)   the functions of a local education authority under the Education Acts; and

    (b)   the functions of an education authority under—

        (i)   the Education (Scotland) Act 1980;

        (ii)   the Education (Scotland) Act 1996;

        (iii)   the Standards in Scotland's Schools etc Act 2000; and

        (iv)   the Education (Additional Support for Learning (Scotland) Act 2004.

(2) But it does not apply to any prescribed function.

(3) In discharging a function to which this section applies, it is unlawful for the authority to discriminate against—

    (a)   a disabled pupil; or

    (b)   a disabled person who may be admitted to a school as a pupil.

(4) But an act done in the discharge of a function to which this section applies is unlawful as a result of subsection (3) only if no other provision of this Chapter makes that act unlawful.

(5) In the case of an act which constitutes discrimination by virtue of section 55, this section also applies to discrimination against a person who is not disabled.

(6) In this section and section 28G, 'local education authority' has the meaning given in section 12 of the Education Act 1996.

(7) 'The Education Acts' has the meaning given in section 578 of the Education Act 1996.

(8) In this section and section 28G, 'education authority' has the meaning given in section 135(1) of the Education (Scotland) Act 1980.

Amendment – Section and preceding cross-heading inserted by Special Educational Needs and Disability Act 2001, s 16. Amended by SI 2005/1791, art 1(1).

28G   Residual duty: supplementary provisions

(1) Section 28B applies for the purposes of section 28F as it applies for the purposes of section 28A with the following modifications—

  (a)   references to a responsible body are to be read as references to an authority; and
  (b)   references to section 28C are to be read as references to subsections (2) to (4).

(2) Each authority must take such steps as it is reasonable for it to have to take to ensure that, in discharging any function to which section 28F applies—

  (a)   disabled persons who may be admitted to a school as pupils are not placed at a substantial disadvantage in comparison with persons who are not disabled; and
  (b)   disabled pupils are not placed at a substantial disadvantage in comparison with pupils who are not disabled.

(3) That does not require the authority to—

  (a)   remove or alter a physical feature; or
  (b)   provide auxiliary aids or services.

(4) This section imposes duties only for the purpose of determining whether an authority has discriminated against a disabled person; and accordingly a breach of any such duty is not actionable as such.

(5) A reference in sections 28I, 28K(1), 28M(6) and 28P to a responsible body is to be read as including a reference to a local education authority in relation to a function to which section 28F applies.

(6) A reference in section 28N and 28P to a responsible body is to be read as including a reference to an education authority in relation to a function to which section 28F applies.

(7) 'Authority' means—

  (a)   in relation to England and Wales, a local education authority; and
  (b)   in relation to Scotland, an education authority.

Amendment – Inserted by Special Educational Needs and Disability Act 2001, s 16.

Enforcement: England and Wales

28H   Tribunals

(1) The Special Educational Needs Tribunal—

  (a)   is to continue to exist; but
  (b)   after the commencement date is to be known as the Special Educational Needs and Disability Tribunal.

(2) In this Chapter—

'the Tribunal' means the Special Educational Needs and Disability
Tribunal, and
'the Welsh Tribunal' means the Special Educational Needs Tribunal for
Wales.

(3) In addition to the jurisdiction of those tribunals under Part 4 of the
Education Act 1996, each of them is to exercise the jurisdiction conferred
on it by this Chapter.

(4) 'Commencement date' means the day on which section 17 of the
Special Educational Needs and Disability Act 2001 comes into force.

Amendments – Section and preceding cross-heading inserted by Special Educational Needs
and Disability Act 2001, s 17(1). Amended by Education Act 2002, s 195, Sch 18, paras 7,
8(1), (2).

28I Jurisdiction and powers of the Tribunal

(1) A claim that a responsible body—

(a) has discriminated against a person ('A') in a way which is made
unlawful under this Chapter, or
(b) is by virtue of section 58 to be treated as having discriminated
against a person ('A') in such a way,

may be made to the appropriate tribunal by A's parent.

(2) But this section does not apply to a claim to which section 28K or 28L
applies.

(3) If the appropriate tribunal considers that a claim under subsection (1)
is well founded—

(a) it may declare that A has been unlawfully discriminated against;
and
(b) if it does so, it may make such order as it considers reasonable in
all the circumstances of the case.

(4) The power conferred by subsection (3)(b)—

(a) may, in particular, be exercised with a view to obviating or
reducing the adverse effect on the person concerned of any
matter to which the claim relates; but
(b) does not include power to order the payment of any sum by way
of compensation.

(5) Subject to regulations under section 28J(8), the appropriate
tribunal—

(a) for a claim against the responsible body for a school in England,
is the Tribunal,
(b) for a claim against the responsible body for a school in Wales, is
the Welsh Tribunal.

Amendments – Inserted by Special Educational Needs and Disability Act 2001, s 18.
Amended by Education Act 2002, s 195, Sch 18, paras 7, 9(1)–(3).

28J   Procedure

(1) Regulations may make provision about—

   (a)   the proceedings of the Tribunal on a claim of unlawful discrimination under this Chapter; and

   (b)   the making of a claim.

(2) The regulations may, in particular, include provision—

   (a)   as to the manner in which a claim must be made;

   (b)   if the jurisdiction of the Tribunal is being exercised by more than one tribunal—

      (i)   for determining by which tribunal any claim is to be heard, and

      (ii)   for the transfer of proceedings from one tribunal to another;

   (c)   for enabling functions which relate to matters preliminary or incidental to a claim (including, in particular, decisions under paragraph 10(3) of Schedule 3) to be performed by the President, or by the chairman;

   (d)   enabling hearings to be conducted in the absence of any member other than the chairman;

   (e)   as to the persons who may appear on behalf of the parties;

   (f)   for granting any person such disclosure or inspection of documents or right to further particulars as might be granted by a county court;

   (g)   requiring persons to attend to give evidence and produce documents;

   (h)   for authorising the administration of oaths to witnesses;

   (i)   for the determination of claims without a hearing in prescribed circumstances;

   (j)   as to the withdrawal of claims;

   (k)   for enabling the Tribunal to stay proceedings on a claim;

   (l)   for the award of costs or expenses;

   (m)   for taxing or otherwise settling costs or expenses (and, in particular, for enabling costs to be taxed in the county court);

   (n)   for the registration and proof of decisions and orders; and

   (o)   for enabling prescribed decisions to be reviewed, or prescribed orders to be varied or revoked, in such circumstances as may be determined in accordance with the regulations.

(2A) If made with the agreement of the Welsh Ministers, the regulations apply to the Welsh Tribunal as they apply to the Tribunal, subject to such modifications as may be specified in the regulations.

(3) Proceedings before the Tribunal or the Welsh Tribunal are to be held in private, except in prescribed circumstances.

(4) *(repealed)*

(5) The Secretary of State may pay such allowances for the purpose of or in connection with the attendance of persons at the Tribunal or the Welsh Tribunal as he may, with the consent of the Treasury, determine.

(6) In relation to the Welsh Tribunal, the power conferred by subsection (5) may be exercised only with the agreement of the Welsh Ministers.

(7) Part 1 of the Arbitration Act 1996 does not apply to proceedings before the Tribunal or the Welsh Tribunal but regulations may make provision, in relation to such proceedings, corresponding to any provision of that Part.

(8) The regulations may make provision for a claim under this Chapter to be heard, in prescribed circumstances, with an appeal under Part 4 of the Education Act 1996, including provision—

(a)   for determining the appropriate tribunal for the purposes of section 28I for such a claim, and

(b)   for the transfer of proceedings between the Tribunal and the Welsh Tribunal.

(9) A person who without reasonable excuse fails to comply with—

(a)   a requirement in respect of the disclosure or inspection of documents imposed by the regulations by virtue of subsection (2)(f), or

(b)   a requirement imposed by the regulations by virtue of subsection (2)(g),

is guilty of an offence.

(10) A person guilty of an offence under subsection (9) is liable on summary conviction to a fine not exceeding level 3 on the standard scale.

(11) Part 3 of Schedule 3 makes further provision about enforcement of this Chapter and about procedure.

Amendments – Inserted by Special Educational Needs and Disability Act 2001, s 19(1). Amended by Education Act 2002, s 195, Sch 18, paras 7, 10(1)–(8); Government of Wales Act 2006, ss 46, 161(5); SI 2007/1388.

28K   Admissions

(1) If the condition mentioned in subsection (2) is satisfied, this section applies to a claim in relation to an admissions decision that a responsible body—

(a)   has discriminated against a person ('A') in a way which is made unlawful under this Chapter; or

(b)   is by virtue of section 58 to be treated as having discriminated against a person ('A') in such a way.

(2) The condition is that arrangements ('appeal arrangements') have been made—

(a) under section 94 of the School Standards and Framework Act 1998, or

(b) under an agreement entered into between the responsible body for an Academy and the Secretary of State under section 482 of the Education Act 1996,

enabling an appeal to be made against the decision by A's parent.

(3) The claim must be made under the appeal arrangements.

(4) The body hearing the claim has the powers which it has in relation to an appeal under the appeal arrangements.

(5) 'Admissions decision' means—

(a) a decision of a kind mentioned in section 94(1) or (2) of the School Standards and Framework Act 1998;

(b) a decision as to the admission of a person to an Academy taken by the responsible body or on its behalf.

Amendments – Inserted by Special Educational Needs and Disability Act 2001, s 20. Amended by Education Act 2002, s 65(3), Sch 7, Pt 2, para 5(1), (3).

28L Exclusions

(1) If the condition mentioned in subsection (2) is satisfied, this section applies to a claim in relation to an exclusion decision that a responsible body—

(a) has discriminated against a person ('A') in a way which is made unlawful under this Chapter; or

(b) is by virtue of section 58 to be treated as having discriminated against a person ('A') in such a way.

(2) The condition is that arrangements ('appeal arrangements') have been made—

(a) under section 52(3)(c) of the Education Act 2002, or

(b) under an agreement entered into between the responsible body for an Academy and the Secretary of State under section 482 of the Education Act 1996,

enabling an appeal to be made against the decision by A or by his parent.

(3) The claim must be made under the appeal arrangements.

(4) The body hearing the claim has the powers which it has in relation to an appeal under the appeal arrangements.

(5) 'Exclusion decision' means—

(a) a decision of a kind mentioned in section 52(3)(c) of the Education Act 2002;

(b) a decision not to reinstate a pupil who has been permanently excluded from an Academy by its head teacher, taken by the responsible body or on its behalf.

(6) 'Responsible body', in relation to a maintained school, includes the discipline committee of the governing body if that committee is required to be established as a result of regulations made under section 19 of the Education Act 2002·

(7) 'Maintained school' has the meaning given in section 28Q(5).

Amendments – Inserted by Special Educational Needs and Disability Act 2001, s 21. Amended by Education Act 2002, s 65(3), Sch 7, Pt 2, para 5(1), (4), s 215(1), Sch 21, para 27(1), (2).

28M   Roles of the Secretary of State and the Welsh Ministers

(1) If the appropriate authority is satisfied (whether on a complaint or otherwise) that a responsible body—

(a)   has acted, or is proposing to act, unreasonably in the discharge of a duty imposed by or under section 28D or 28E, or

(b)   has failed to discharge a duty imposed by or under either of those sections,

it may give that body such directions as to the discharge of the duty as appear to it to be expedient.

(2) Subsection (3) applies in relation to—

(a)   special schools which are not maintained special schools but which are approved by the Secretary of State, or by the Welsh Ministers, under section 342 of the Education Act 1996; and

(b)   city academies.

(3) If the appropriate authority is satisfied (whether on a complaint or otherwise) that a responsible body—

(a)   has acted, or is proposing to act, unreasonably in the discharge of a duty which that body has in relation to—

(i)   the provision to the appropriate authority of copies of that body's accessibility plan, or

(ii)   the inspection of that plan, or

(b)   has failed to discharge that duty,

it may give that body such directions as to the discharge of the duty as appear to it to be expedient.

(4) Directions may be given under subsection (1) or (3) even if the performance of the duty is contingent upon the opinion of the responsible body.

(5) Subsection (6) applies if the Tribunal or the Welsh Tribunal has made an order under section 28I(3).

(6) If the Secretary of State is satisfied (whether on a complaint or otherwise) that the responsible body concerned—

(a) has acted, or is proposing to act, unreasonably in complying with the order, or

(b) has failed to comply with the order,

he may give that body such directions as to compliance with the order as appear to him to be expedient.

(7) Directions given under subsection (1), (3) or (6)—

(a) may be varied or revoked by the directing authority; and

(b) may be enforced, on the application of the directing authority, by a mandatory order obtained in accordance with section 31of the Senior Courts Act 1981.

(8) 'Appropriate authority' means—

(a) in relation to England, the Secretary of State; and

(b) in relation to Wales, the Welsh Ministers.

(9) 'Directing authority' means—

(a) the Secretary of State in relation to a direction given by him; and

(b) the Welsh Ministers in relation to a direction given by them.

Amendments – Inserted (save in so far as it gives the National Assembly for Wales power to give directions under subss (1), (3) or makes provision in relation to such a direction) by Special Educational Needs and Disability Act 2001, s 22. Amended by Education Act 2002, s 195, Sch 18, paras 7, 11; Constitutional Reform Act 2005, s 148(1); SI 2007/1388, art 3, Sch 1, paras 47, 54(1), (4).

Enforcement: Scotland

Amendment – Inserted by Special Educational Needs and Disability Act 2001, s 23.

28N Civil proceedings

(1) A claim that a responsible body in Scotland—

(a) has discriminated against a person in a way which is unlawful under this Chapter, or

(b) is by virtue of section 58 to be treated as having discriminated against a person in such a way,

may be made the subject of civil proceedings in the same way as any other claim for the enforcement of a statutory duty.

(2) Proceedings in Scotland may be brought only in a sheriff court.

(3) The remedies available in such proceedings are those which are available in the Court of Session other than an award of damages.

(4) Part 3 of Schedule 3 makes further provision about the enforcement of this Chapter and about procedure.

(5) In relation to civil proceedings in Scotland, in paragraph 10 of that Schedule—

(a) references to sections 28I , are to be construed as a reference to this section;

(b) references to the Tribunal or Welsh Tribunal are to be construed as references to the sheriff court.

Amendment – Inserted by Special Educational Needs and Disability Act 2001, s 23; Disability Discrimination Act 2005, s 19(1), Sch 1, Pt 1, paras 1, 24(1), 3(a).

Agreements relating to enforcement

28P Validity and revision of agreements of responsible bodies

(1) Any term in a contract or other agreement made by or on behalf of a responsible body is void so far as it purports to—

(a) require a person to do anything which would contravene any provision of, or made under, this Chapter;

(b) exclude or limit the operation of any provision of, or made under, this Chapter; or

(c) prevent any person from making a claim under this Chapter.

(2) Paragraphs (b) and (c) of subsection (1) do not apply to an agreement settling a claim—

(a) under section 28I or 28N; or

(b) to which section 28K or 28L applies.

(3) On the application of any person interested in an agreement to which subsection (1) applies, a county court or a sheriff court may make such order as it thinks just for modifying the agreement to take account of the effect of subsection (1).

(4) No such order may be made unless all persons affected have been—

(a) given notice of the application; and

(b) afforded an opportunity to make representations to the court.

(5) Subsection (4) applies subject to any rules of court providing for notice to be dispensed with.

(6) An order under subsection (3) may include provision as respects any period before the making of the order.

Amendments – Section and preceding cross-heading inserted by Special Educational Needs and Disability Act 2001, s 24.

Interpretation of Chapter 1

28Q Interpretation

(1) This section applies for the purpose of interpreting this Chapter.

(2) 'Disabled pupil' means a pupil who is a disabled person.

(3) 'Pupil'—

    (a)   in relation to England and Wales, has the meaning given in section 3(1) of the Education Act 1996; and

    (b)   in relation to Scotland, has the meaning given in section 135(1) of the Education (Scotland) Act 1980.

(4) Except in relation to Scotland (when it has the meaning given in section 135(1) of the Education (Scotland) Act 1980) 'school' means—

    (a)   a maintained school;

    (b)   a maintained nursery school;

    (c)   an independent school;

    (d)   a special school which is not a maintained special school but which is approved by the Secretary of State, or by the National Assembly, under section 342 of the Education Act 1996;

    (e)   a pupil referral unit.

(5) In subsection (4)—

'maintained school' has the meaning given in section 20(7) of the School Standards and Framework Act 1998;

'maintained nursery school' has the meaning given in section 22(9) of the School Standards and Framework Act 1998;

'independent school' has the meaning given in section 463 of the Education Act 1996; and

'pupil referral unit' has the meaning given in section 19(2) of the Education Act 1996.

(6) 'Responsible body' has the meaning given in section 28A(5).

(7) 'Governing body', in relation to a maintained school, means the body corporate (constituted in accordance with regulations under section 19 of the Education Act 2002 which the school has as a result of that section.

(8) 'Parent'—

    (a)   in relation to England and Wales, has the meaning given in section 576 of the Education Act 1996; and

    (b)   in relation to Scotland, has the meaning given in section 135(1) of the Education (Scotland) Act 1980.

(9) In relation to England and Wales 'permitted form of selection' means—

    (a)   if the school is a maintained school which is not designated as a grammar school under section 104 of the School Standards and Framework Act 1998, any form of selection mentioned in section 99(2) or (4) of that Act;

    (b)   if the school is a maintained school which is so designated, any of its selective admission arrangements;

    (c)   if the school is an independent school, any arrangements which make provision for any or all of its pupils to be selected by reference to general or special ability or aptitude, with a view to admitting only pupils of high ability or aptitude.

(10) In relation to Scotland, 'permitted form of selection' means—

    (a)   if the school is managed by an education authority, such arrangements as have been approved by the Scottish Ministers for the selection of pupils for admission;

    (b)   if the school is an independent school or a self-governing school, any arrangements which make provision for any or all of its pupils to be selected by reference to general or special ability or aptitude, with a view to admitting only pupils of high ability or aptitude.

(11) In subsection (10), 'education authority', 'independent school' and 'self-governing school' have the meaning given in section 135(1) of the Education (Scotland) Act 1980.

(12) (*repealed*)

(13) 'Accessibility strategy' and 'accessibility plan' have the meaning given in section 28D.

(14) (*repealed*)

Amendments – Section and preceding cross-heading inserted by Special Educational Needs and Disability Act 2001, s 25. Amended by Education Act 2002, s 215 (1), Sch 21, para 28(a), (b), ss 65(3), 215 (2), Sch 7, Pt 2, para 5(1), (5), Sch 22 , Pt 3; Government of Wales Act 2006, ss 46, 161(5); SI 2004/1388.

Chapter 2
Further and Higher Education
Duties of responsible bodies

28R Discrimination against disabled students and prospective students

(1) It is unlawful for the body responsible for an educational institution to discriminate against a disabled person—

    (a)   in the arrangements it makes for determining admissions to the institution;

    (b)   in the terms on which it offers to admit him to the institution; or

    (c)   by refusing or deliberately omitting to accept an application for his admission to the institution.

(2) It is unlawful for the body responsible for an educational institution to discriminate against a disabled student in the student services it provides, or offers to provide.

(3) It is unlawful for the body responsible for an educational institution to discriminate against a disabled student by excluding him from the institution, whether permanently or temporarily.

(3A) It is unlawful for the body responsible for an educational institution to discriminate against a disabled person—

(a)   in the arrangements which it makes for the purpose of determining upon whom to confer a qualification;

(b)   in the terms on which it is prepared to confer a qualification on him;

(c)   by refusing or deliberately omitting to grant any application by him for a qualification; or

(d)   by withdrawing a qualification from him or varying the terms on which he holds it.

(3B) It is unlawful for the body responsible for an educational institution to subject to harassment a disabled person who—

(a)   holds or applies for a qualification conferred by the institution;

(b)   is a student at the institution; or

(c)   seeks admission as a student to the institution.

(4) In the case of an act which constitutes discrimination by virtue of section 55, this section also applies to discrimination against a person who is not disabled.

(5) The body responsible for an educational institution is to be determined in accordance with Schedule 4B, and in the remaining provisions of this Chapter is referred to as the 'responsible body'.

(6) 'Educational institution', in relation to England and Wales, means an institution—

(a)   within the higher education sector;

(b)   within the further education sector; or

(c)   designated in an order made by the Secretary of State.

(7) 'Educational institution', in relation to Scotland, means—

(a)   an institution within the higher education sector (within the meaning of section 56(2) of the Further and Higher Education (Scotland) Act 1992);

(b)   a college of further education with a board of management within the meaning of section 36 of that Act;

(c)   a central institution within the meaning of section 135 of the Education (Scotland) Act 1980;

(d)   a college of further education maintained by an education authority in the exercise of their further education functions in providing courses of further education within the meaning of section 1(5)(b)(ii) of that Act;

(e)   an institution designated in an order made by the Secretary of State.

(8) Subsection (6) is to be read with section 91 of the Further and Higher Education Act 1992.

(9) The Secretary of State may not make an order under subsection (6)(c) or (7)(e) unless he is satisfied that the institution concerned is wholly or partly funded from public funds.

(10) Before making an order under subsection (7)(e), the Secretary of State must consult the Scottish Ministers.

(11) 'Student services' means services of any description which are provided wholly or mainly for students.

(12) Regulations may make provision as to services which are, or are not, to be regarded for the purposes of subsection (2) as student services.

Amendment – Section and preceding Chapter heading and cross-heading inserted by Special Educational Needs and Disability Act 2001, s 26(1); SI 2006/1721, reg 4 (1), (5).

28S   Meaning of 'discrimination'

(1) For the purposes of this chapter, a responsible body discriminates against a disabled person if—

    (a)   for a reason which relates to his disability, it treats him less favourably than it treats or would treat others to whom that reason does not or would not apply; and

    (b)   it cannot show that the treatment in question is justified.

(2) For the purposes of this Chapter, a responsible body also discriminates against a disabled person if it fails to comply with a duty imposed on it by section 28T or 28UA(5) in relation to the disabled person.

(3) In relation to a failure to take a particular step, a responsible body does not discriminate against a person if it shows—

    (a)   that, at the time in question, it did not know and could not reasonably have been expected to know, that he was disabled; and

    (b)   that its failure to take the step was attributable to that lack of knowledge.

(4) *(repealed)*.

(5) Treatment, other than the application of a competence standard, is (subject to subsections (7) to (9)), justified for the purposes of subsection (1)(b) if, but only if, the reason for it is both material to the circumstances of the particular case and substantial.

(6) The application by a responsible body of a competence standard to a disabled person is (subject to subsections (8) and (9)) justified for the purposes of subsection (1)(b) if, but only if, the body can show that—

    (a)   the standard is, or would be, applied equally to persons who do not have his particular disability, and

    (b)   its application is a proportionate means of achieving a legitimate aim.

(7) If in a case falling within subsection (1), other than a case where the treatment is the application of a competence standard, a responsible body is under a duty under section 28T or 28UA(5) in relation to the disabled person, but fails to comply with that duty, its treatment of that person

cannot be justified under subsection (5) unless that treatment would have been justified even if it had complied with that duty.

(8) Subject to subsection (9), regulations may make provision, for purposes of this section, as to circumstances in which treatment is, or as to circumstances in which treatment is not, to be taken to be justified.

(9) Treatment of a disabled person by a responsible body cannot be justified under subsection (5), (6) or (8) if it amounts to direct discrimination falling within subsection (10).

(10) A responsible body directly discriminates against a disabled person if, on the ground of the disabled person's disability, it treats the disabled person less favourably than it treats or would treat a person not having that particular disability whose relevant circumstances, including his abilities, are the same as, or not materially different from, those of the disabled person.

(11) In this section and section 28T, 'competence standard' means an academic, medical or other standard applied by or on behalf of a responsible body for the purpose of determining whether or not a person has a particular level of competence or ability.

Amendment – Inserted by Special Educational Needs and Disability Act 2001, s 27. Amended by SI 2006/1721.

28SA   Meaning of 'harassment

(1) For the purposes of this Chapter, a responsible body subjects a disabled person to harassment where, for a reason which relates to the disabled person's disability, that body engages in unwanted conduct which has the purpose or effect of—

- (a)   violating the disabled person's dignity, or
- (b)   creating an intimidating, hostile, degrading, humiliating or offensive environment for him.

(2) Conduct shall be regarded as having the effect referred to in subsection (1)(a) or (b) only if, having regard to all the circumstances, including in particular the perception of the disabled person, it should reasonably be considered as having that effect.

Amendment – Inserted by SI 2006/1721.

28T   Responsible bodies' duties to make adjustments

(1) Where—

- (a)   a provision, criterion or practice, other than a competence standard, is applied by or on behalf of a responsible body,
- (b)   it is a provision, criterion or practice relating to—
  - (i)   the arrangements it makes for determining admissions to the institution, or

(ii)   student services provided for, or offered to, students by the responsible body, and

(c)   that provision, criterion or practice places disabled persons at a substantial disadvantage in comparison with persons who are not disabled,

it is the duty of the responsible body to take such steps as it is reasonable, in all the circumstances of the case, for it to have to take in order to prevent the provision, criterion or practice having that effect.

(1A) Where—

(a)   a provision, criterion or practice, other than a competence standard, is applied by or on behalf of a responsible body,

(b)   it is a provision, criterion or practice for determining on whom a qualification is to be conferred,

(c)   a disabled person is, or has notified the body that he may be, an applicant for the conferment of that qualification, and

(d)   the provision, criterion or practice places the disabled person at a substantial disadvantage in comparison with persons who are not disabled,

it is the duty of the responsible body to take such steps as it is reasonable, in all the circumstances of the case, for it to have to take in order to prevent the provision, criterion or practice having that effect.

(1B) Where—

(a)   a provision, criterion or practice, other than a competence standard, is applied by or on behalf of a responsible body,

(b)   it is a provision, criterion or practice other than one mentioned in subsection (1)(b) or (1A)(b), and

(c)   it places a disabled person who—
(i)   holds a qualification conferred by the responsible body, or
(ii)   applies for a qualification which the responsible body confers,

at a substantial disadvantage in comparison with persons who are not disabled,

it is the duty of the responsible body to take such steps as it is reasonable, in all the circumstances of the case, for it to have to take in order to prevent the provision, criterion or practice having that effect.

(1C) Where any physical feature of premises occupied by a responsible body places disabled persons at a substantial disadvantage in comparison with persons who are not disabled in relation to—

(a)   the arrangements which that body makes for determining admissions to the institution, or

(b)   student services provided for, or offered to, students by that body, it is the duty of the body to take such steps as it is reasonable, in all the circumstances of the case, for it to have to take in order to prevent the feature having that effect.

(1D) Where any physical feature of premises occupied by a responsible body places a disabled person who—

(a)   applies for a qualification which that body confers, or
(b)   holds a qualification which was conferred by that body,

at a substantial disadvantage in comparison with persons who are not disabled, it is the duty of the body to take such steps as it is reasonable, in all the circumstances of the case, for it to have to take in order to prevent the feature having that effect.

(2) In considering whether it is reasonable for it to have to take a particular step in order to comply with its duty under any of subsections (1) to (1D), a responsible body must have regard to any relevant provisions of a code of practice issued under section 14 of the Equality Act 2006.

(3) Subsection (4) applies if a person has made a confidentiality request of which a responsible body is aware.

(4) In determining whether it is reasonable for the responsible body to have to take a particular step in relation to that person in order to comply with its duty under any of subsections (1) to (1D), regard shall be had to the extent to which taking the step in question is consistent with compliance with that request.

(5) 'Confidentiality request' means a request made by a disabled person, which asks for the nature, or asks for the existence, of his disability to be treated as confidential.

(6) This section imposes duties only for the purpose of determining whether a responsible body has discriminated against a disabled person; and accordingly a breach of any such duty is not actionable as such.

Amendment – Inserted by Special Educational Needs and Disability Act 2001, s 28. Amended by Equality Act 2006, s 40, Sch 3, paras 41, 46; SI 2006/1721.

Other providers of further education or training facilities

28U   Further education etc provided by local education authorities and schools

(1) Part 1 of Schedule 4C modifies this Chapter for the purpose of its application in relation to higher and further education secured by a local education authority.

(2) Part 1A of that Schedule modifies this Chapter for the purpose of its application in relation to recreational or training facilities secured by a local education authority and further education provided by the governing body of a maintained school.

(3) Part 2 of that Schedule modifies this Chapter for the purpose of its application in relation to further education, within the meaning of section 1(5)(b)(iii) of the Education (Scotland) Act 1980.

(4) Part 2A of that Schedule modifies this Chapter for the purpose of its application in relation to facilities whose provision is secured by an education authority under section 1(3) of the Education (Scotland) Act 1980.

Amendment – Section and preceding cross-heading inserted by Special Educational Needs and Disability Act 2001, s 29(1). Substituted by SI 2006/1721, regs 4(1), 10.

Other unlawful acts

28UA   Relationships which have come to an end

(1) This section applies where—

    (a)   there has been a relevant relationship between a disabled person and a responsible body, and

    (b)   that relationship has come to an end.

(2) In this section a 'relevant relationship' is a relationship during the course of which an act of discrimination against, or harassment of, one party to the relationship by the other party to it is unlawful under any preceding provision of this Chapter.

(3) It is unlawful for the responsible body—

    (a)   to discriminate against the disabled person by subjecting him to a detriment, or

    (b)   to subject the disabled person to harassment,

where the discrimination or harassment arises out of and is closely connected to the relevant relationship.

(4) This subsection applies where—

    (a)   a provision, criterion or practice applied by the responsible body to the disabled person in relation to any matter arising out of the relevant relationship, or

    (b)   a physical feature of premises which are occupied by the responsible body,

places the disabled person at a substantial disadvantage in comparison with persons who are not disabled but are in the same position as the disabled person in relation to the responsible body.

(5) Where subsection (4) applies, it is the duty of the responsible body to take such steps as it is reasonable, in all the circumstances of the case, for him to have to take in order to prevent the provision, criterion or practice, or feature, having that effect.

(6) Subsection (5) imposes duties only for the purpose of determining whether a responsible body has discriminated against a disabled person; and accordingly a breach of any such duty is not actionable as such.

(7) Nothing in subsection (5) imposes any duty on the responsible body if it does not know and could not reasonably be expected to know, that the person has a disability and is likely to be affected in the way mentioned in that subsection.

(8) In subsection (2), reference to an act of discrimination or harassment which is unlawful includes, in the case of a relationship which has come to an end before the commencement of this section, reference to such an act which would, after the commencement of this section, be unlawful.

Amendment – Section and preceding cross-heading inserted by SI 2006/1721.

28UB Instructions and pressure to discriminate

(1) It is unlawful for a responsible body to instruct another person to do any act which is unlawful under this Chapter or to procure or attempt to procure the doing of any such unlawful act by that other person.

(2) It is also unlawful for a responsible body to induce, or attempt to induce, another person to do any act which is unlawful under this Chapter by—

    (a)   providing or offering to provide that person with any benefit, or
    (b)   subjecting or threatening to subject that person to any detriment.

(3) An attempted inducement is not prevented from falling within subsection (2) because it is not made directly to the person in question, if it is made in such a way that he is likely to hear of it.

(4) Proceedings in respect of a contravention of subsection (1) may be brought only—

    (a)   by the Commission for Equality and Human Rights, and
    (b)   in accordance with section 25 of the Equality Act 2006.

Amendment – Inserted by SI 2006/1721.

28UC Discriminatory advertisements

(1) It is unlawful for a responsible body to publish or cause to be published an advertisement which—

    (a)   invites applications in relation to any course or student service provided or offered by it, or any qualification conferred by it, and
    (b)   indicates, or might reasonably be understood to indicate, that such an application will or may be determined to any extent by reference to—
        (i)   the applicant not having any disability, or any particular disability, or

(ii) any reluctance on the part of the person determining the application to comply with a duty imposed on it by section 28T.

(2) Subsection (1) does not apply where it would not in fact be unlawful under this Chapter for an application to be determined in the manner indicated (or understood to be indicated) in the advertisement.

(3) In this section, 'advertisement' includes every form of advertisement or notice, whether to the public or not.

(4) Proceedings in respect of a contravention of subsection (1) may be brought only—

(a) by the Commission for Equality and Human Rights, and

(b) in accordance with section 25 of the Equality Act 2006.

Amendment – Inserted by SI 2006/1721.

Enforcement, etc

28V Enforcement, remedies and procedure

(1) A claim by a person—

(a) that a responsible body has discriminated against him, or subjected him to harassment, in a way which is unlawful under this Chapter,

(b) that a responsible body is by virtue of section 57 or 58 to be treated as having done so,

(c) that a person is by virtue of section 57 to be treated as having done so,,

may be made the subject of civil proceedings in the same way as any other claim in tort or (in Scotland) in reparation for breach of statutory duty.

(1A) Where—

(a) a claim is brought under subsection (1), and

(b) the claimant (or pursuer, in Scotland) proves facts from which the court could, apart from this subsection, conclude in the absence of an adequate explanation that the defendant (or defender, in Scotland) has acted in a way which is unlawful under this Chapter,

the court shall uphold the claim unless the defendant (or defender, in Scotland) proves that he did not so act.

(2) For the avoidance of doubt it is hereby declared that damages in respect of discrimination in a way which is unlawful under this Chapter may include compensation for injury to feelings whether or not they include compensation under any other head.

(3) Proceedings in England and Wales may be brought only in a county court.

(4) Proceedings in Scotland may be brought only in a sheriff court.

(5) The remedies available in such proceedings are those which are available in the High Court or (as the case may be) the Court of Session.

(6) The fact that a person who brings proceedings under this Part against a responsible body may also be entitled to bring proceedings against that body under Part 2 is not to affect the proceedings under this Part.

(7) Part 4 of Schedule 3 makes further provision about the enforcement of this Part and about procedure.

Amendment – Section and preceding cross-heading inserted by Special Educational Needs and Disability Act 2001, s 30(1). Amended by SI 2006/1721, regs 1(3), 4(1), 15(1), (2)(a).

28W   Occupation of premises by educational institutions

(1) This section applies if—

(a)   premises are occupied by an educational institution under a lease;

(b)   but for this section, the responsible body would not be entitled to make a particular alteration to the premises; and

(c)   the alteration is one which the responsible body proposes to make in order to comply with section 28T or section 28UA (5).

(2) Except to the extent to which it expressly so provides, the lease has effect, as a result of this subsection, as if it provided—

(a)   for the responsible body to be entitled to make the alteration with the written consent of the lessor;

(b)   for the responsible body to have to make a written application to the lessor for consent if it wishes to make the alteration;

(c)   if such an application is made, for the lessor not to withhold his consent unreasonably; and

(d)   for the lessor to be entitled to make his consent subject to reasonable conditions.

(3) In this section—

'lease' includes a tenancy, sub-lease or sub-tenancy and an agreement for a lease, tenancy, sub-lease or sub-tenancy; and

'sub-lease' and 'sub-tenancy' have such meaning as may be prescribed.

(4) If the terms and conditions of a lease—

(a)   impose conditions which are to apply if the responsible body alters the premises, or

(b)   entitle the lessor to impose conditions when consenting to the responsible body's altering the premises,

the responsible body is to be treated for the purposes of subsection (1) as not being entitled to make the alteration.

(5) Part 3 of Schedule 4 supplements the provisions of this section.

Amendment – Inserted by Special Educational Needs and Disability Act 2001, s 31(1). Amended by SI 2006/1721.

28X Validity and revision of agreements

Section 28P applies for the purposes of this Chapter as it applies for the purposes of Chapter 1, but with the substitution, for paragraphs (a) and (b) of subsection (2), of 'under section 28V'.

Amendment – Inserted by Special Educational Needs and Disability Act 2001, s 32.

29 (repealed)

Amendment – Repealed by Special Educational Needs and Disability Act 2001, ss 40(1), 42(6), Sch 9.

Duties of funding councils

Amendment – Cross-heading inserted by Special Educational Needs and Disability Act 2001, s 34(4).

30 Further and higher education of disabled persons

(1) The Further and Higher Education Act 1992 is amended as set out in subsections (2) to (6).

(2)–(4) (*repealed*)

(5) In section 62 (establishment of higher education funding councils), after subsection (7) insert—

'(7A) In exercising their functions, each council shall have regard to the requirements of disabled persons.

(7B) In subsection (7A) 'disabled persons' means persons who are disabled persons for the purposes of the Disability Discrimination Act 1995.'

(6)–(9) (*repealed*)

Amendments – Subsections (1) and (5) inserted by Further and Higher Education Act 1992, s 62(7A), (7B). Amended by Education Act 1996, s 582(2), Sch 38, Pt I; Learning and Skills Act 2000, s 153, Sch 11; Special Educational Needs and Disability Act 2001, ss 34(5), 42(6), Sch 9.

31 Further and higher education of disabled persons: Scotland

(1) The Further and Higher Education (Scotland) Act 1992 is amended as follows.

(2) In section 37 (establishment of Scottish Higher Education Funding Council) after subsection (4) insert—

'(4A) In exercising their functions, the Council shall have regard to the requirements of disabled persons.

(4B) In subsection (4A) above, 'disabled persons' means persons who are disabled persons for the purpose of the Disability Discrimination Act 1995.'

(3) (*repealed*)

Amendment – Subsections (1) and (2) inserted by Further and Higher Education (Scotland) Act 1992, s 37(4A), (4B). Amended by Special Educational Needs and Disability Act 2001, ss 34(6), 42(6), Sch 9.

Interpretation of Chapter 2

31A　Interpretation

(1) Subsections (2) to (10) apply for the purpose of interpreting this Chapter.

(2) 'Disabled student' means a student who is a disabled person.

(3) 'Student' means a person who is attending, or undertaking a course of study at, an educational institution.

(4) 'Educational institution', 'responsible body' and 'student services' have the meaning given in section 28R.

(5) 'Provision, criterion or practice' includes any arrangements.

(6) 'Qualification' means any authorisation, qualification, approval or certification conferred by a responsible body.

(7) 'Discriminate, 'discrimination' and other related expressions are to be construed in accordance with section 28S.

(8) 'Harassment' is to be construed in accordance with section 28SA.

(9) References (however expressed) to the conferment of a qualification on a person by a responsible body include—
    (i)　the renewal or extension of a qualification, and
    (ii)　the authentication of a qualification awarded to him by another person.

(10) 'Physical feature', in relation to any premises, includes any of the following (whether permanent or temporary)—

  (a)　any feature arising from the design or construction of a building on the premises,
  (b)　any feature on the premises of any approach to, exit from or access to such a building,
  (c)　any fixtures, fittings, furnishings, furniture, equipment or material in or on the premises, and
  (d)　any other physical element or quality of any land comprised in the premises.]

Amendment – Section and preceding cross-heading inserted by Special Educational Needs and Disability Act 2001, s 33. Amended by SI 2006/1721.

Chapter 2A
General Qualifications Bodies

31AA   General qualifications bodies: discrimination and harassment

(1) It is unlawful for a general qualifications body to discriminate against a disabled person—

   (a)   in the arrangements which it makes for the purpose of determining upon whom to confer a relevant qualification;

   (b)   in the terms on which it is prepared to confer a relevant qualification on him;

   (c)   by refusing or deliberately omitting to grant any application by him for such a qualification; or

   (d)   by withdrawing such a qualification from him or varying the terms on which he holds it.

(2) It is also unlawful for a general qualifications body, in relation to a relevant qualification conferred by it, to subject to harassment a disabled person who holds or applies for such a qualification.

(3) In the case of an act which constitutes discrimination by virtue of section 55, this section also applies to discrimination against a person who is not disabled.

(4) In this section and section 31AD, 'relevant qualification' means an authorisation, qualification, approval or certification of a prescribed description.

(5) But an authorisation, qualification, approval or certification may not be prescribed under subsection (4) if it is a professional or trade qualification (within the meaning given by section 14A(5)).

(6) In this Chapter—

   (a)   'general qualifications body' means any authority or body which can confer a relevant qualification, but it does not include—

      (i)   a responsible body (within the meaning of Chapter 1 or 2 of this Part),

      (ii)   a local education authority in England or Wales,

      (iii) an education authority (within the meaning of section 135(1) of the Education (Scotland) Act 1980), or

      (iv)   an authority or body of a prescribed description or in prescribed circumstances;

   (b)   references (however expressed) to the conferment of a qualification on a person include—

      (i)   the renewal or extension of a qualification, and

      (ii)   the authentication of a qualification awarded to him by another person.

Amendment – Section and preceding cross-heading Inserted by Disability Discrimination Act 2005, s 15.

31AB Meaning of 'discrimination

(1) For the purposes of section 31AA, a body discriminates against a disabled person if—

    (a)   for a reason which relates to the disabled person's disability, it treats him less favourably than it treats or would treat others to whom that reason does not or would not apply; and

    (b)   it cannot show that the treatment in question is justified.

(2) For the purposes of section 31AA, a body also discriminates against a disabled person if it fails to comply with a duty imposed on it by section 31AD in relation to the disabled person.

(3) Treatment, other than the application of a competence standard, is (subject to subsections (5) to (7)) justified for the purposes of subsection (1)(b) if, but only if, the reason for it is both material to the circumstances of the particular case and substantial.

(4) The application by a body of a competence standard to a disabled person is (subject to subsections (6) and (7)) justified for the purposes of subsection (1)(b) if, but only if, the body can show that—

    (a)   the standard is, or would be, applied equally to persons who do not have his particular disability; and

    (b)   its application is a proportionate means of achieving a legitimate aim.

(5) If, in a case falling within subsection (1) other than a case where the treatment is the application of a competence standard, a body is under a duty under section 31AD in relation to the disabled person but fails to comply with that duty, its treatment of that person cannot be justified under subsection (3) unless it would have been justified even if the body had complied with that duty.

(6) Regulations may make provision, for purposes of this section, as to circumstances in which treatment is, or as to circumstances in which treatment is not, to be taken to be justified (but see subsection (7)).

(7) Treatment of a disabled person cannot be justified under subsection (3), (4) or (6) if it amounts to direct discrimination falling within subsection (8).

(8) A body directly discriminates against a disabled person if, on the ground of the disabled person's disability, it treats the disabled person less favourably than it treats or would treat a person not having that particular disability whose relevant circumstances, including his abilities, are the same as, or not materially different from, those of the disabled person.

(9) In this section, 'competence standard' means an academic, medical or other standard applied by or on behalf of a general qualifications body for the purpose of determining whether or not a person has a particular level of competence or ability.

Amendment – Inserted by Disability Discrimination Act 2005, s 15.

31AC Meaning of 'harassment'

(1) For the purposes of section 31AA, a body subjects a disabled person to harassment where, for a reason which relates to the disabled person's disability, the body engages in unwanted conduct which has the purpose or effect of—

(a) violating the disabled person's dignity; or

(b) creating an intimidating, hostile, degrading, humiliating or offensive environment for him.

(2) Conduct shall be regarded as having the effect referred to in paragraph (a) or (b) of subsection (1) only if, having regard to all the circumstances, including in particular the perception of the disabled person, it should reasonably be considered as having that effect.

Amendment – Inserted by Disability Discrimination Act 2005, s 15.

31AD General qualifications bodies: duty to make adjustments

(1) Where—

(a) a provision, criterion or practice, other than a competence standard, is applied by or on behalf of a general qualifications body,

(b) it is a provision, criterion or practice for determining on whom a relevant qualification is to be conferred,

(c) a disabled person is, or has notified the body that he may be, an applicant for the conferment of that qualification, and

(d) the provision, criterion or practice places the disabled person at a substantial disadvantage in comparison with persons who are not disabled,

it is the duty of the body to take such steps as it is reasonable, in all the circumstances of the case, for it to have to take in order to prevent the provision, criterion or practice having that effect.

(2) Where—

(a) a provision, criterion or practice, other than a competence standard, is applied by or on behalf of a general qualifications body,

(b) it is a provision, criterion or practice other than one for determining on whom a relevant qualification is to be conferred, and

(c) it places a disabled person who—

(i) holds a relevant qualification conferred by the body, or

(ii) applies for a relevant qualification which the body confers, at a substantial disadvantage in comparison with persons who are not disabled,

it is the duty of the body to take such steps as it is reasonable, in all the circumstances of the case, for it to have to take in order to prevent the provision, criterion or practice having that effect.

(3) Where any physical feature of premises occupied by a general qualifications body places a disabled person who—

    (a)   holds a relevant qualification conferred by the body, or

    (b)   applies for a relevant qualification which the body confers,

at a substantial disadvantage in comparison with persons who are not disabled, it is the duty of the body to take such steps as it is reasonable, in all the circumstances of the case, for it to have to take in order to prevent the feature having that effect.

(4) Nothing in subsection (1), (2) or (3) imposes a duty on a general qualifications body in relation to a disabled person if the body does not know, and could not reasonably be expected to know—

    (a)   in the case of an applicant or potential applicant for the conferment of a relevant qualification, that the disabled person concerned is, or may be, such an applicant; or

    (b)   in any case, that that person has a disability and is likely to be affected in the way mentioned in that subsection.

(5) In this section—

    (a)   'provision, criterion or practice' includes (subject to any provision under subsection (6)(e)) any arrangements;

    (b)   'competence standard' has the meaning given by section 31AB(9).

(6) Regulations may make provision, for purposes of this section—

    (a)   as to circumstances in which a provision, criterion or practice is to be taken to have, or as to circumstances in which a provision, criterion or practice is to be taken not to have, the effect mentioned in subsection (1)(d) or (2)(c);

    (b)   as to circumstances in which a physical feature is to be taken to have, or as to circumstances in which a physical feature is to be taken not to have, the effect mentioned in subsection (3);

    (c)   as to circumstances in which it is, or as to circumstances in which it is not, reasonable for a body to have to take steps of a prescribed description;

    (d)   as to steps which it is always, or as to steps which it is never, reasonable for a body to have to take;

    (e)   as to what is, or as to what is not, to be included within the meaning of 'provision, criterion or practice';

    (f)   as to things which are, or as to things which are not, to be treated as physical features.

(7) This section imposes duties only for the purpose of determining whether a body has, for the purposes of section 31AA, discriminated against a disabled person; and accordingly a breach of any such duty is not actionable as such.

Amendment – Inserted by Disability Discrimination Act 2005, s 15.

31ADA   Enforcement, remedies and procedures

(1) A claim by a person—

(a)   that a general qualifications body has discriminated against him, or subjected him to harassment, in a way which is unlawful under this Chapter,

(b)   that a general qualifications body is by virtue of section 57 or 58 to be treated as having done so, or

(c)   that a person is by virtue of section 57 to be treated as having done so,

may be made the subject of civil proceedings in the same way as any other claim in tort or (in Scotland) in reparation for breach of statutory duty.

(2) Where—

(a)   a claim is brought under subsection (1), and

(b)   the claimant (or pursuer, in Scotland) proves facts from which the court could, apart from this subsection, conclude in the absence of an adequate explanation that the defendant (or defender, in Scotland) has acted in a way which is unlawful under this Chapter,

the court shall uphold the claim unless the defendant (or defender, in Scotland) proves that he did not so act.

(3) Damages in respect of discrimination in a way which is unlawful under this Chapter may include compensation for injury to feelings whether or not they include compensation under any other head.

(4) Proceedings in England and Wales may be brought only in a county court.

(5) Proceedings in Scotland may be brought only in a sheriff court.

(6) The remedies available in such proceedings are those which are available in the High Court or (as the case may be) the Court of Session.

(7) Part 5 of Schedule 3 makes further provision about the enforcement of this Part and about procedure and evidence.

Amendment – Inserted by SI 2007/2405.

31ADB   Alterations to premises occupied under leases

(1) This section applies where—

- (a)   a general qualifications body occupies premises under a lease;
- (b)   but for this section, the general qualifications body would not be entitled to make a particular alteration to the premises; and
- (c)   the alteration is one which the general qualifications body proposes to make in order to comply with the duty imposed by section 31AD(3).

(2) Except to the extent to which it expressly so provides, the lease shall have effect by virtue of this subsection as if it provided—

- (a)   for the general qualifications body to be entitled to make the alteration with the written consent of the lessor;
- (b)   for the general qualifications body to have to make a written application to the lessor for consent if it wishes to make the alteration;
- (c)   f such an application is made, for the lessor not to withhold his consent unreasonably; and
- (d)   for the lessor to be entitled to make his consent subject to reasonable conditions.

(3) In this section and in Part 4 of Schedule 4—

'lease' includes a tenancy, sub-lease or sub-tenancy and an agreement for a lease, tenancy, sub-lease or sub-tenancy;

'sub-lease' means any sub-term created out of, or deriving from, a leasehold interest; and

'sub-tenancy' means any tenancy created out of, or deriving from, a superior tenancy.

(4) For the purposes of subsection (1), the general qualifications body is to be treated as not being entitled to make the alteration, if the terms and conditions of the lease—

- (a)   impose conditions which are to apply if the general qualifications body alters the premises, or
- (b)   entitle the lessor to impose conditions when consenting to the general qualifications body's altering the premises.

(5) Part 4 of Schedule 4 supplements the provisions of this section.

Amendment – Inserted by SI 2007/2405.

31AE   Chapter 2A: claims, leased premises and certain agreements

(1) Regulations may make provision for, or in connection with, the making of a claim by a person—

(a) that a general qualifications body has discriminated against him, or subjected him to harassment, in a way which is unlawful under this Chapter;

(b) that a general qualifications body is by virtue of section 57 or 58 to be treated as having done so; or

(c) that a person is by virtue of section 57 to be treated as having done so.

(2) Regulations may, in relation to a case where premises are occupied by a general qualifications body under a lease—

(a) make provision modifying the lease, or make provision for its modification, in connection with the making of alterations to the premises in pursuance of a duty imposed on the body by section 31AD;

(b) make provision in connection with the determination of questions that are about the body's compliance with any such duty and are related to the making of alterations to the premises.

(3) Any term in a contract or other agreement made by or on behalf of a general qualifications body is void so far as it purports to—

(a) require a person to do anything which would contravene any provision of, or made under, this Chapter;

(b) exclude or limit the operation of any provision of, or made under, this Chapter; or

(c) prevent any person making a claim of a kind mentioned in subsection (1).

(4) Regulations may—

(a) make provision for subsection (3)(b) or (c) not to apply to an agreement settling a claim of a kind mentioned in subsection (1);

(b) make provision modifying an agreement to which subsection (3) applies, or make provision for the modification of such an agreement, in order to take account of the effect of that subsection.

(5) The provision that may be made under subsection (1), (2) or (4) includes (in particular)—

(a) provision as to the court or tribunal to which a claim, or an application in connection with a modification, may be made;

(b) provision for the determination of claims or matters otherwise than by the bringing of proceedings before a court or tribunal;

(c) provision for a person who is a lessor in relation to a lease under which a general qualifications body occupies premises to be made a party to proceedings;

(d) provision as to remedies;

(e) provision as to procedure;

(f) provision as to appeals;

(g) provision as to time limits;

(h)   provision as to evidence;

(i)   provision as to costs or expenses.

(6) Provision under subsection (1), (2) or (4) may take the form of amendments of this Act.

(7) Regulations may make provision as to the meaning of 'lease' or 'lessor' in this section.

(8) Except as provided in regulations under subsection (1), no civil or criminal proceedings may be brought against any person in respect of an act merely because the act is unlawful under this Chapter.

(9) Subsection (8) does not prevent the making of an application for judicial review

Amendment – Inserted by Disability Discrimination Act 2005, s 15.

31AF   Chapter 2A: duty to consult before making regulations

(1) Before making regulations under this Chapter, the Secretary of State shall consult such persons as it appears to him to be appropriate to consult, having regard to the substance and effect of the regulations in question.

(2) Without prejudice to the generality of subsection (1), the Secretary of State shall consult the Welsh Ministers and the Scottish Ministers before making regulations under this Chapter.

Amendment – Inserted by Disability Discrimination Act 2005, s 15. Amended by Government of Wales Act 2006, ss 46, 161(5); SI 2007/1388.

Chapter 3

Supplementary

31B   *(repealed)*

Amendment – Section and preceding Chapter heading inserted by Special Educational Needs and Disability Act 2001, s 37. Amended by Equality Act 2006, ss 40, 91, Sch 3, paras 41, 47, Sch 4.

31C   Application to Isles of Scilly

This Part applies to the Isles of Scilly—

(a)   as if the Isles were a separate non-metropolitan county (and the Council of the Isles of Scilly were a county council), and

(b)   with such other modifications as may be specified in an order made by the Secretary of State.

Amendment – Inserted by Special Educational Needs and Disability Act 2001.

PART V
PUBLIC TRANSPORT

Taxis

32 Taxi accessibility regulations

(1) The Secretary of State may make regulations ('taxi accessibility regulations') for the purpose of securing that it is possible—

(a) for disabled persons—
   (i)   to get into and out of taxis in safety;
   (ii) to be carried in taxis in safety and in reasonable comfort; and

(b) for disabled persons in wheelchairs—
   (i)   to be conveyed in safety into and out of taxis while remaining in their wheelchairs; and
   (ii) to be carried in taxis in safety and in reasonable comfort while remaining in their wheelchairs.

(2) Taxi accessibility regulations may, in particular—

(a) require any regulated taxi to conform with provisions of the regulations as to—
   (i)   the size of any door opening which is for the use of passengers;
   (ii)   the floor area of the passenger compartment;
   (iii) the amount of headroom in the passenger compartment;
   (iv)   the fitting of restraining devices designed to ensure the stability of a wheelchair while the taxi is moving;

(b) require the driver of any regulated taxi which is plying for hire, or which has been hired, to comply with provisions of the regulations as to the carrying of ramps or other devices designed to facilitate the loading and unloading of wheelchairs;

(c) require the driver of any regulated taxi in which a disabled person who is in a wheelchair is being carried (while remaining in his wheelchair) to comply with provisions of the regulations as to the position in which the wheelchair is to be secured.

(3) The driver of a regulated taxi which is plying for hire, or which has been hired, is guilty of an offence if—

(a) he fails to comply with any requirement imposed on him by the regulations; or

(b) the taxi fails to conform with any provision of the regulations with which it is required to conform.

(4) A person who is guilty of such an offence is liable, on summary conviction, to a fine not exceeding level 3 on the standard scale.

(5) In this section—

'passenger compartment' has such meaning as may be prescribed;
'regulated taxi' means any taxi to which the regulations are expressed
to apply;
'taxi' means a vehicle licensed under—
    (a)   section 37 of the Town Police Clauses Act 1847, or
    (b)   section 6 of the Metropolitan Public Carriage Act 1869,
    but does not include a taxi which is drawn by a horse or other
    animal.

33   Designated transport facilities

(1) In this section 'a franchise agreement' means a contract entered into
by the operator of a designated transport facility for the provision by the
other party to the contract of hire car services—

    (a)   for members of the public using any part of the transport facility;
        and
    (b)   which involve vehicles entering any part of that facility.

(2) The appropriate national authority may by regulations provide for the
application of any taxi provision in relation to—

    (a)   vehicles used for the provision of services under a franchise
        agreement; or
    (b)   the drivers of such vehicles.

(3) Any regulations under subsection (2) may apply any taxi provision
with such modifications as the authority making the regulations considers
appropriate.

(4) In this section—

'appropriate national authority' means—

    (a)   in relation to transport facilities in England and Wales, the
        Secretary of State, and
    (b)   in relation to transport facilities in Scotland, the Scottish
        Ministers (but see subsection (5));

'designated' means designated for the purposes of this section by an
    order made by the appropriate national authority;
'hire car' has such meaning as may be specified by regulations made by
    the appropriate national authority;
'operator', in relation to a transport facility, means any person who is
    concerned with the management or operation of the facility;
'taxi provision' means any provision of—
    (a)   this Act, or
    (b)   regulations made in pursuance of section 20(2A) of the
        Civic Government (Scotland) Act 1982,

which applies in relation to taxis or the drivers of taxis; and
'transport facility' means any premises which form part of any port,
    airport, railway station or bus station.

(5) The Secretary of State may, for the purposes mentioned in section 2(2) of the European Communities Act 1972 (implementation of Community obligations etc of the United Kingdom), exercise the powers conferred by this section on the Scottish Ministers.

Amendment – Amended by Disability Discrimination Act 2005, s 19(1), Sch 1, Pt 1.

34   New licences conditional on compliance with taxi accessibility regulations

(1) No licensing authority shall grant a licence for a taxi to ply for hire unless the vehicle conforms with those provisions of the taxi accessibility regulations with which it will be required to conform if licensed.

(2) Subsection (1) does not apply if such a licence was in force with respect to the vehicle at any time during the period of 28 days immediately before the day on which the licence is granted.

(3) The Secretary of State may by order provide for subsection (2) to cease to have effect on such date as may be specified in the order.

(4) Separate orders may be made under subsection (3) with respect to different areas or localities.

35   Exemption from taxi accessibility regulations

(1) The Secretary of State may make regulations ('exemption regulations') for the purpose of enabling any relevant licensing authority to apply to him for an order (an 'exemption order') exempting the authority from the requirements of section 34.

(2) Exemption regulations may, in particular, make provision requiring a licensing authority proposing to apply for an exemption order—

    (a)   to carry out such consultations as may be prescribed;
    (b)   to publish the proposal in the prescribed manner;
    (c)   to consider any representations made to it about the proposal, before applying for the order;
    (d)   to make its application in the prescribed form.

(3) A licensing authority may apply for an exemption order only if it is satisfied—

    (a)   that, having regard to the circumstances prevailing in its area, it would be inappropriate for the requirements of section 34 to apply; and
    (b)   that the application of section 34 would result in an unacceptable reduction in the number of taxis in its area.

(4) After considering any application for an exemption order and consulting the Disabled Persons Transport Advisory Committee and such other persons as he considers appropriate, the Secretary of State may—

    (a)   make an exemption order in the terms of the application;

(b) make an exemption order in such other terms as he considers appropriate; or
(c) refuse to make an exemption order.

(5) The Secretary of State may by regulations ('swivel seat regulations') make provision requiring any exempt taxi plying for hire in an area in respect of which an exemption order is in force to conform with provisions of the regulations as to the fitting and use of swivel seats.

(6) The Secretary of State may by regulations make provision with respect to swivel seat regulations similar to that made by section 34 with respect to taxi accessibility regulations.

(7) In this section—

'exempt taxi' means a taxi in relation to which section 34(1) would apply if the exemption order were not in force;
'relevant licensing authority' means a licensing authority responsible for licensing taxis in any area of England and Wales other than the area to which the Metropolitan Public Carriage Act 1869 applies; and
'swivel seats' has such meaning as may be prescribed.

36 Carrying of passengers in wheelchairs

(1) This section imposes duties on the driver of a regulated taxi which has been hired—

(a) by or for a disabled person who is in a wheelchair; or
(b) by a person who wishes such a disabled person to accompany him in the taxi.

(2) In this section—

'carry' means carry in the taxi concerned; and
'the passenger' means the disabled person concerned.

(3) The duties are—

(a) to carry the passenger while he remains in his wheelchair;
(b) not to make any additional charge for doing so;
(c) if the passenger chooses to sit in a passenger seat, to carry the wheelchair;
(d) to take such steps as are necessary to ensure that the passenger is carried in safety and in reasonable comfort;
(e) to give such assistance as may be reasonably required—
    (i) to enable the passenger to get into or out of the taxi;
    (ii) if the passenger wishes to remain in his wheelchair, to enable him to be conveyed into and out of the taxi while in his wheelchair;
    (iii) to load the passenger's luggage into or out of the taxi;
    (iv) if the passenger does not wish to remain in his wheelchair, to load the wheelchair into or out of the taxi.

(4) Nothing in this section is to be taken to require the driver of any taxi—

    (a)   except in the case of a taxi of a prescribed description, to carry more than one person in a wheelchair, or more than one wheelchair, on any one journey; or

    (b)   to carry any person in circumstances in which it would otherwise be lawful for him to refuse to carry that person.

(5) A driver of a regulated taxi who fails to comply with any duty imposed on him by this section is guilty of an offence and liable, on summary conviction, to a fine not exceeding level 3 on the standard scale.

(6) In any proceedings for an offence under this section, it is a defence for the accused to show that, even though at the time of the alleged offence the taxi conformed with those provisions of the taxi accessibility regulations with which it was required to conform, it would not have been possible for the wheelchair in question to be carried in safety in the taxi.

(7) If the licensing authority is satisfied that it is appropriate to exempt a person from the duties imposed by this section—

    (a)   on medical grounds, or

    (b)   on the ground that his physical condition makes it impossible or unreasonably difficult for him to comply with the duties imposed on drivers by this section,

it shall issue him with a certificate of exemption.

(8) A certificate of exemption shall be issued for such period as may be specified in the certificate.

(9) The driver of a regulated taxi is exempt from the duties imposed by this section if—

    (a)   a certificate of exemption issued to him under this section is in force; and

    (b)   the prescribed notice of his exemption is exhibited on the taxi in the prescribed manner.

37   Carrying of guide dogs and hearing dogs

(1) This section imposes duties on the driver of a taxi which has been hired—

    (a)   by or for a disabled person who is accompanied by his guide dog or hearing dog, or

    (b)   by a person who wishes such a disabled person to accompany him in the taxi.

(2) The disabled person is referred to in this section as 'the passenger'.

(3) The duties are—

    (a)   to carry the passenger's dog and allow it to remain with the passenger; and

    (b)   not to make any additional charge for doing so.

(4) A driver of a taxi who fails to comply with any duty imposed on him by this section is guilty of an offence and liable, on summary conviction, to a fine not exceeding level 3 on the standard scale.

(5) If the licensing authority is satisfied that it is appropriate on medical grounds to exempt a person from the duties imposed by this section, it shall issue him with a certificate of exemption.

(6) In determining whether to issue a certificate of exemption, the licensing authority shall, in particular, have regard to the physical characteristics of the taxi which the applicant drives or those of any kind of taxi in relation to which he requires the certificate.

(7) A certificate of exemption shall be issued—

    (a)   with respect to a specified taxi or a specified kind of taxi; and

    (b)   for such period as may be specified in the certificate.

(8) The driver of a taxi is exempt from the duties imposed by this section if—

    (a)   a certificate of exemption issued to him under this section is in force with respect to the taxi; and

    (b)   the prescribed notice of his exemption is exhibited on the taxi in the prescribed manner.

(9) The Secretary of State may, for the purposes of this section, prescribe any other category of dog trained to assist a disabled person who has a disability of a prescribed kind.

(10) This section applies in relation to any such prescribed category of dog as it applies in relation to guide dogs.

(11) In this section—

    'guide dog' means a dog which has been trained to guide a blind person; and

    'hearing dog' means a dog which has been trained to assist a deaf person.

37A   Carrying of assistance dogs in private hire vehicles

(1) It is an offence for the operator of a private hire vehicle to fail or refuse to accept a booking for a private hire vehicle—

    (a)   if the booking is requested by or on behalf of a disabled person, or a person who wishes a disabled person to accompany him; and

    (b)   the reason for the failure or refusal is that the disabled person will be accompanied by his assistance dog.

(2) It is an offence for the operator of a private hire vehicle to make an additional charge for carrying an assistance dog which is accompanying a disabled person.

(3) It is an offence for the driver of a private hire vehicle to fail or refuse to carry out a booking accepted by the operator of the vehicle—

    (a)   if the booking was made by or on behalf of a disabled person, or a person who wishes a disabled person to accompany him; and

    (b)   the reason for the failure or refusal is that the disabled person is accompanied by his assistance dog.

(4) A person who is guilty of an offence under this section is liable on summary conviction to a fine not exceeding level 3 on the standard scale.

(5) If the licensing authority is satisfied that it is appropriate on medical grounds to issue a certificate of exemption to a driver in respect of subsection (3) it must do so.

(6) In determining whether to issue a certificate of exemption, the licensing authority shall, in particular, have regard to the physical characteristics of the private hire vehicle which the applicant drives or those of any kind of private hire vehicle in relation to which he requires the certificate.

(7) A certificate of exemption shall be issued—

    (a)   with respect to a specified private hire vehicle or a specified kind of private hire vehicle; and

    (b)   for such period as may be specified in the certificate.

(8) No offence is committed by a driver under subsection (3) if—

    (a)   a certificate of exemption issued to him under this section is in force with respect to the private hire vehicle; and

    (b)   the prescribed notice is exhibited on the private hire vehicle in the prescribed manner.

(9) In this section—

'assistance dog' means a dog which—

    (a)   has been trained to guide a blind person;

    (b)   has been trained to assist a deaf person;

    (c)   has been trained by a prescribed charity to assist a disabled person who has a disability which—

        (i)   consists of epilepsy; or

        (ii)   otherwise affects his mobility, manual dexterity, physical co-ordination or ability to lift, carry or otherwise move everyday objects;

'driver' means a person who holds a licence granted under—

    (a)   section 13 of the Private Hire Vehicles (London) Act 1998 (c 34) ('the 1998 Act');

(b) section 51 of the Local Government (Miscellaneous Provisions) Act 1976 (c 57) ('the 1976 Act'); or

(c) an equivalent provision of a local enactment;

'licensing authority', in relation to any area of England and Wales, means the authority responsible for licensing private hire vehicles in that area;

'operator' means a person who holds a licence granted under—

(a) section 3 of the 1998 Act;

(b) section 55 of the 1976 Act; or

(c) an equivalent provision of a local enactment;

'private hire vehicle' means a vehicle licensed under—

(a) section 6 of the 1998 Act;

(b) section 48 of the 1976 Act; or

(c) an equivalent provision of a local enactment.

Amendment – Inserted by Private Hire Vehicles (Carriage of Guide Dogs etc) Act 2002, s 1(1).

38 Appeal against refusal of exemption certificate

(1) Any person who is aggrieved by the refusal of a licensing authority to issue an exemption certificate under section 36, 37 or 38A may appeal to a magistrates' court before the end of the period of 28 days beginning with the date of the refusal.

(2) On an appeal to it under this section, the court may direct the licensing authority concerned to issue the appropriate certificate of exemption to have effect for such period as may be specified in the direction.

(3) (*repealed*)

Amendment – Amended by Private Hire Vehicles (Carriage of Guide Dogs etc) Act 2002, s 3; Courts Act 2003, s 109(1), Sch 8, para 368(1), (2), (3), Sch 10.

39 Requirements as to disabled passengers in Scotland

(1) Part II of the Civic Government (Scotland) Act 1982 (licensing and regulation) is amended as follows.

(2) In subsection (4) of section 10 (suitability of vehicle for use as taxi)—

(a) after 'authority' insert '—(a)'; and

(b) at the end add '; and

(b) as not being so suitable if it does not so comply.'

(3) In section 20 (regulations relating to taxis etc) after subsection (2) insert—

'(2A) Without prejudice to the generality of subsections (1) and (2) above, regulations under those subsections may make such provision as appears to the Secretary of State to be necessary or expedient in relation to the carrying in taxis of disabled persons (within the meaning of section 1(2) of the Disability Discrimination Act 1995) and such provision may in particular prescribe—

(a) requirements as to the carriage of wheelchairs, guide dogs, hearing dogs and other categories of dog;

(b) a date from which any such provision is to apply and the extent to which it is to apply; and

(c) the circumstances in which an exemption from such provision may be granted in respect of any taxi or taxi driver,

and in this subsection—

'guide dog' means a dog which has been trained to guide a blind person;

'hearing dog' means a dog which has been trained to assist a deaf person; and

'other categories of dog' means such other categories of dog as the Secretary of State may prescribe, trained to assist disabled persons who have disabilities of such kinds as he may prescribe.'

Public service vehicles

40 PSV accessibility regulations

(1) The Secretary of State may make regulations ('PSV accessibility regulations') for the purpose of securing that it is possible for disabled persons—

(a) to get on to and off regulated public service vehicles in safety and without unreasonable difficulty (and, in the case of disabled persons in wheelchairs, to do so while remaining in their wheelchairs); and

(b) to be carried in such vehicles in safety and in reasonable comfort.

(2) PSV accessibility regulations may, in particular, make provision as to the construction, use and maintenance of regulated public service vehicles including provision as to—

(a) the fitting of equipment to vehicles;

(b) equipment to be carried by vehicles;

(c) the design of equipment to be fitted to, or carried by, vehicles;

(d) the fitting and use of restraining devices designed to ensure the stability of wheelchairs while vehicles are moving;

(e) the position in which wheelchairs are to be secured while vehicles are moving.

(3) Any person who—

(a) contravenes or fails to comply with any provision of the PSV accessibility regulations,

(b)   uses on a road a regulated public service vehicle which does not conform with any provision of the regulations with which it is required to conform, or

(c)   causes or permits to be used on a road such a regulated public service vehicle,

is guilty of an offence.

(4) A person who is guilty of such an offence is liable, on summary conviction, to a fine not exceeding level 4 on the standard scale.

(5) In this section—

'public service vehicle' means a vehicle which is—
    (a)   adapted to carry more than eight passengers; and
    (b)   a public service vehicle for the purposes of the Public Passenger Vehicles Act 1981;

'regulated public service vehicle' means any public service vehicle to which the PSV accessibility regulations are expressed to apply.

(6) Different provision may be made in regulations under this section—

(a)   as respects different classes or descriptions of vehicle;
(b)   as respects the same class or description of vehicle in different circumstances.

(7) Before making any regulations under this section or section 41 or 42 the Secretary of State shall consult the Disabled Persons Transport Advisory Committee and such other representative organisations as he thinks fit.

41   Accessibility certificates

(1) A regulated public service vehicle shall not be used on a road unless—

(a)   a vehicle examiner has issued a certificate (an 'accessibility certificate') that such provisions of the PSV accessibility regulations as may be prescribed are satisfied in respect of the vehicle; or

(b)   an approval certificate has been issued under section 42 in respect of the vehicle.

(2) The Secretary of State may make regulations—

(a)   with respect to applications for, and the issue of, accessibility certificates;

(b)   providing for the examination of vehicles in respect of which applications have been made;

(c)   with respect to the issue of copies of accessibility certificates in place of certificates which have been lost or destroyed.

(3) If a regulated public service vehicle is used in contravention of this section, the operator of the vehicle is guilty of an offence and liable on summary conviction to a fine not exceeding level 4 on the standard scale.

(4) In this section 'operator' has the same meaning as in the Public Passenger Vehicles Act 1981.

42   Approval certificates

(1) Where the Secretary of State is satisfied that such provisions of the PSV accessibility regulations as may be prescribed for the purposes of section 41 are satisfied in respect of a particular vehicle he may approve the vehicle for the purposes of this section.

(2) A vehicle which has been so approved is referred to in this section as a 'type vehicle'.

(3) Subsection (4) applies where a declaration in the prescribed form has been made by an authorised person that a particular vehicle conforms in design, construction and equipment with a type vehicle.

(4) A vehicle examiner may, after examining (if he thinks fit) the vehicle to which the declaration applies, issue a certificate in the prescribed form ('an approval certificate') that it conforms to the type vehicle.

(5) The Secretary of State may make regulations—

   (a)   with respect to applications for, and grants of, approval under subsection (1);
   (b)   with respect to applications for, and the issue of, approval certificates;
   (c)   providing for the examination of vehicles in respect of which applications have been made;
   (d)   with respect to the issue of copies of approval certificates in place of certificates which have been lost or destroyed.

(6) The Secretary of State may at any time withdraw his approval of a type vehicle.

(7) Where an approval is withdrawn—

   (a)   no further approval certificates shall be issued by reference to the type vehicle; but
   (b)   any approval certificate issued by reference to the type vehicle before the withdrawal shall continue to have effect for the purposes of section 41.

(8) In subsection (3) 'authorised person' means a person authorised by the Secretary of State for the purposes of that subsection.

43   Special authorisations

(1) The Secretary of State may by order authorise the use on roads of—

   (a)   any regulated public service vehicle of a class or description specified by the order, or
   (b)   any regulated public service vehicle which is so specified,

and nothing in section 40, 41, or 42 prevents the use of any vehicle in accordance with the order.

(2) Any such authorisation may be given subject to such restrictions and conditions as may be specified by or under the order.

(3) The Secretary of State may by order make provision for the purpose of securing that, subject to such restrictions and conditions as may be specified by or under the order, provisions of the PSV accessibility regulations apply to regulated public service vehicles of a description specified by the order subject to such modifications or exceptions as may be specified by the order.

44 Reviews and appeals

(1) Subsection (2) applies where—

  (a) the Secretary of State refuses an application for the approval of a vehicle under section 42(1); and
  (b) before the end of the prescribed period, the applicant asks the Secretary of State to review the decision and pays any fee fixed under section 45.

(2) The Secretary of State shall—

  (a) review the decision; and
  (b) in doing so, consider any representations made to him in writing, before the end of the prescribed period, by the applicant.

(3) A person applying for an accessibility certificate or an approval certificate may appeal to the Secretary of State against the refusal of a vehicle examiner to issue such a certificate.

(4) An appeal must be made within the prescribed time and in the prescribed manner.

(5) Regulations may make provision as to the procedure to be followed in connection with appeals.

(6) On the determination of an appeal, the Secretary of State may—

  (a) confirm, vary or reverse the decision appealed against;
  (b) give such directions as he thinks fit to the vehicle examiner for giving effect to his decision.

45 Fees

(1) Such fees, payable at such times, as may be prescribed may be charged by the Secretary of State in respect of—

  (a) applications for, and grants of, approval under section 42(1);
  (b) applications for, and the issue of, accessibility certificates and approval certificates;
  (c) copies of such certificates;
  (d) reviews and appeals under section 44.

(2) Any such fees received by the Secretary of State shall be paid by him into the Consolidated Fund.

(3) Regulations under subsection (1) may make provision for the repayment of fees, in whole or in part, in such circumstances as may be prescribed.

(4) Before making any regulations under subsection (1) the Secretary of State shall consult such representative organisations as he thinks fit.

Rail vehicles

46   Rail vehicle accessibility regulations

(1) The Secretary of State may make regulations ('rail vehicle accessibility regulations') for the purpose of securing that it is possible—

    (a)   for disabled persons—
        (i)   to get on to and off regulated rail vehicles in safety and without unreasonable difficulty;
        (ii) to be carried in such vehicles in safety and in reasonable comfort; and

    (b)   for disabled persons in wheelchairs—
        (i)   to get on to and off such vehicles in safety and without unreasonable difficulty while remaining in their wheelchairs, and
        (ii) to be carried in such vehicles in safety and in reasonable comfort while remaining in their wheelchairs.

(2) Rail vehicle accessibility regulations may, in particular, make provision as to the construction, use and maintenance of regulated rail vehicles including provision as to—

    (a)   the fitting of equipment to vehicles;
    (b)   equipment to be carried by vehicles;
    (c)   the design of equipment to be fitted to, or carried by, vehicles;
    (d)   the use of equipment fitted to, or carried by, vehicles;
    (e)   the toilet facilities to be provided in vehicles;
    (f)   the location and floor area of the wheelchair accommodation to be provided in vehicles;
    (g)   assistance to be given to disabled persons.

(3) If a regulated rail vehicle which does not conform with any provision of the rail vehicle accessibility regulations with which it is required to conform is used for carriage, the operator of the vehicle is guilty of an offence.[1]

(4) A person who is guilty of such an offence is liable, on summary conviction, to a fine not exceeding level 4 on the standard scale.[2]

[(4A) The Secretary of State shall exercise the power to make rail vehicle accessibility regulations so as to secure that on and after 1st January 2020 every rail vehicle is a regulated rail vehicle, but this does not affect the powers conferred by subsection (5) or section 47(1) or 67(2).][3]

(5) Different provision may be made in rail vehicle accessibility regulations—

    (a)   as respects different classes or descriptions of rail vehicle;

    (b)   as respects the same class or description of rail vehicle in different circumstances;

    (c)   as respects different networks.

(6) In this section—

'network' means any permanent way or other means of guiding or supporting rail vehicles or any section of it;

'operator', in relation to any rail vehicle, means the person having the management of that vehicle;[4]

'rail vehicle' means a vehicle—

    (a)   constructed or adapted to carry passengers on any railway, tramway or prescribed system; and

    (b)   first brought into use, or belonging to a class of vehicle first brought into use, after 31st December 1998;[5]

['rail vehicle' means a vehicle constructed or adapted to carry passengers on any railway, tramway or prescribed system;][5]

'regulated rail vehicle' means any rail vehicle to which *the* [provisions of][6] rail vehicle accessibility regulations are expressed to apply; and

'wheelchair accommodation' has such meaning as may be prescribed.

(7) In subsection (6)—

'prescribed system' means a system using a prescribed mode of guided transport ('guided transport' having the same meaning as in the Transport and Works Act 1992); and

'railway' and 'tramway' have the same meaning as in that Act.

(8) The Secretary of State may by regulations make provision as to the time when a rail vehicle, or a class of rail vehicle, is to be treated, for the purposes of this section, as first brought into use.

(9) Regulations under subsection (8) may include provision for disregarding periods of testing and other prescribed periods of use.

(10) For the purposes of this section and section 47, a person uses a vehicle for carriage if he uses it for the carriage of members of the public for hire or reward at separate fares.

(11) Before making any regulations under subsection (1) or section 47 the Secretary of State shall consult the Disabled Persons Transport Advisory Committee and such other representative organisations as he thinks fit.[7]

Amendments—The following prospective amendments are made from dates to be appointed:

[1] Subsection prospectively repealed by Disability Discrimination Act 2005, s 19, Sch 1, Pt 1, paras 1, as from a day to be appointed.

[2]Subsection prospectively repealed by Disability Discrimination Act 2005, s 19, Sch 1, Pt 1, paras 1, as from a day to be appointed.

[3] Subsection prospectively inserted by Disability Discrimination Act 2005, s 6(1), as from a day to be appointed.

[4] Definition prospectively repealed by Disability Discrimination Act 2005, s 19(2), Sch 2, as from a day to be appointed.

[5] Definition prospectively substituted by Disability Discrimination Act 2005, s 6(2), as from a day to be appointed.

[6] Word prospectively repealed and subsequent words substituted by Disability Discrimination Act 2005, s 19(1), Sch 1, Pt 1, paras 1, as from a day to be appointed.

[7] Subsections (8)-(10) prospectively repealed by Disability Discrimination Act 2005, s 19(2), Sch 2, as from a day to be appointed.

47   Exemption from rail vehicle accessibility regulations

(1) The Secretary of State may by order (an 'exemption order')—

    (a)   authorise the use for carriage of a regulated rail vehicle even though the vehicle does not conform with the provisions of rail vehicle accessibility regulations with which it is required to conform;

    (b)   authorise a regulated rail vehicle to be used for carriage otherwise than in conformity with the provisions of rail vehicle accessibility regulations with which use of the vehicle is required to conform.

(1A) Authority under subsection (1)(a) or (b) may be for—

    (a)   any regulated rail vehicle that is specified or is of a specified description; or

    (b)   use in specified circumstances of—

        (i)   any regulated rail vehicle, or

        (ii)   any regulated rail vehicle that is specified or is of a specified description

(2) Regulations may make provision with respect to exemption orders including, in particular, provision as to—

    (a)   the persons by whom applications for exemption orders may be made;

    (b)   the form in which such applications are to be made;

    (c)   information to be supplied in connection with such applications;

    (d)   the period for which exemption orders are to continue in force;

    (e)   the revocation of exemption orders.

(3) After considering any application for an exemption order and consulting the Disabled Persons Transport Advisory Committee and such other persons as he considers appropriate, the Secretary of State may—

    (a)   make an exemption order in the terms of the application;

    (b)   make an exemption order in such other terms as he considers appropriate;

    (c)   refuse to make an exemption order.

(4) An exemption order may be made subject to such restrictions and conditions as may be specified.

(5) In this section 'specified' means specified in an exemption order.

Amendment—Amended by Disability Discrimination Act 2005, s 6(3).

47A   Rail vehicle accessibility compliance certificates

(1) A regulated rail vehicle to which this subsection applies shall not be used for carriage unless a rail vehicle accessibility compliance certificate is in force for the vehicle.

(2) Subsection (1) applies to a regulated rail vehicle if the vehicle—

> *(a)   is prescribed; or*
> *(b)   is of a prescribed class or description.*

(3) A rail vehicle accessibility compliance certificate is a certificate that the Secretary of State is satisfied that the regulated rail vehicle conforms with those provisions of rail vehicle accessibility regulations with which the vehicle is required to conform.

(4) A rail vehicle accessibility compliance certificate may provide that it is subject to conditions specified in the certificate.

(5) Subsection (6) applies where—

> *(a)   the Secretary of State refuses an application for the issue of a rail vehicle accessibility compliance certificate for a regulated rail vehicle; and*
> *(b)   before the end of the prescribed period, the applicant asks the Secretary of State to review the decision and pays any fee fixed under section 47C*

(6) The Secretary of State shall—

> *(a)   review the decision; and*
> *(b)   in doing so, consider any representations made to him in writing, before the end of the prescribed period, by the applicant.*

Amendment – Section prospectively inserted by Disability Discrimination Act 2005, s 7(1).

47B   Rail vehicle accessibility compliance certificates: supplementary

(1) Regulations may make provision with respect to rail vehicle accessibility compliance certificates.

(2) The provision that may be made under subsection (1) includes (in particular)—

> *(a)   provision for certificates to be issued on application;*
> *(b)   provision specifying conditions to which certificates are subject;*
> *(c)   provision as to the period for which certificates are to continue in force or as to circumstances in which certificates are to cease to be in force;*

(d) provision (other than provision of a kind mentioned in paragraph (c)) dealing with failure to comply with a condition to which a certificate is subject;

(e) provision for the withdrawal of certificates issued in error;

(f) provision for the correction of errors in certificates;

(g) provision with respect to the issue of copies of certificates in place of certificates which have been lost or destroyed;

(h) provision for the examination of a rail vehicle before a certificate is issued in respect of it.

(3) In making provision of the kind mentioned in subsection (2)(a), regulations under subsection (1) may (in particular)—

(a) make provision as to the persons by whom applications may be made;

(b) make provision as to the form in which applications are to be made;

(c) make provision as to information to be supplied in connection with an application, including (in particular) provision requiring the supply of a report of a compliance assessment.

(4) For the purposes of this section, a 'compliance assessment' is an assessment of a rail vehicle against provisions of rail vehicle accessibility regulations with which the vehicle is required to conform.

(5) In requiring a report of a compliance assessment to be supplied in connection with an application, regulations under subsection (1) may make provision as to the person who has to have carried out the assessment, and may (in particular) require that the assessment be one carried out by a person who has been appointed by the Secretary of State to carry out compliance assessments (an 'appointed assessor').

(6) For the purposes of any provisions in regulations under subsection (1) with respect to the supply of reports of compliance assessments carried out by appointed assessors, regulations under that subsection—

(a) may make provision about appointments of appointed assessors, including (in particular)—

(i) provision for an appointment to be on application or otherwise than on application;

(ii) provision as to who may be appointed;

(iii) provision as to the form of applications for appointment;

(iv) provision as to information to be supplied with applications for appointment;

(v) provision as to terms and conditions, or the period or termination, of an appointment; and

(vi) provision for terms and conditions of an appointment, including any as to its period or termination, to be as agreed by the Secretary of State when making the appointment;

(b) may make provision authorising an appointed assessor to charge fees in connection with, or incidental to, its carrying-out of a compliance assessment, including (in particular)—

(i)   *provision restricting the amount of a fee;*

(ii)   *provision authorising fees that contain a profit element; and*

(iii) *provision for advance payment of fees;*

(c) *may make provision requiring an appointed assessor to carry out a compliance assessment, and to do so in accordance with any procedures that may be prescribed, if prescribed conditions, which may include conditions as to the payment of fees to the assessor, are satisfied;*

(d) *shall make provision for the referral to the Secretary of State of disputes between—*

(i)   *an appointed assessor carrying out a compliance assessment, and*

(ii)   *the person who requested the assessment,*

relating to which provisions of rail vehicle accessibility regulations the vehicle is to be assessed against or to what amounts to conformity with any of those provisions.

(7) In subsection (6)(b) to (d) 'compliance assessment' includes pre-assessment activities (for example, a consideration of how the outcome of a compliance assessment would be affected by the carrying-out of particular proposed work).

Amendment – Section prospectively inserted by Disability Discrimination Act 2005, s 7(1).

47C   Rail vehicle accessibility compliance certificates: fees

(1) Such fees, payable at such times, as may be prescribed may be charged by the Secretary of State in respect of—

(a) *applications for, and the issue of, rail vehicle accessibility compliance certificates;*

(b) *copies of such certificates;*

(c) *reviews under section 47A;*

(d) *referrals of disputes under provision that, in accordance with section 47B(6)(d), is contained in regulations under section 47B(1).*

(2) Any such fees received by the Secretary of State shall be paid by him into the Consolidated Fund.

(3) Regulations under subsection (1) may make provision for the repayment of fees, in whole or in part, in such circumstances as may be prescribed.

(4) Before making any regulations under subsection (1) the Secretary of State shall consult such representative organisations as he thinks fit.]

Amendment – Section prospectively inserted by Disability Discrimination Act 2005, s 7(1).

47D   Penalty for using rail vehicle without accessibility compliance certificate

If a regulated rail vehicle to which section 47A(1) applies is used for carriage at a time when no rail vehicle accessibility compliance certificate is in force for the vehicle, the Secretary of State may require the operator of the vehicle to pay a penalty.

Amendment – Section prospectively inserted by Disability Discrimination Act 2005, s 7(1).

47E   Penalty for using rail vehicle that does not conform with accessibility regulations

(1) Where it appears to the Secretary of State that a regulated rail vehicle does not conform with a provision of rail vehicle accessibility regulations with which the vehicle is required to conform, the Secretary of State may give to the operator of the vehicle a notice—

(a) *identifying the vehicle, the provision and how the vehicle fails to conform with the provision; and*

(b) *specifying the improvement deadline.*

(2) The improvement deadline specified in a notice under subsection (1) may not be earlier than the end of the prescribed period beginning with the day when the notice is given to the operator.

(3) Subsection (4) applies where—

(a) *the Secretary of State has given a notice under subsection (1);*

(b) *the improvement deadline specified in the notice has passed; and*

(c) *it appears to the Secretary of State that the vehicle still does not conform with the provision identified in the notice.*

(4) The Secretary of State may give to the operator a further notice—

(a) *identifying the vehicle, the provision and how the vehicle fails to conform to the provision; and*

(b) *specifying the final deadline.*

(5) The final deadline specified in a notice under subsection (4) may not be earlier than the end of the prescribed period beginning with the day when the notice is given to the operator.

(6) If—

(a) *the Secretary of State has given a notice under subsection (4) to the operator of a regulated rail vehicle, and*

(b) *the vehicle is used for carriage at a time after the final deadline when the vehicle does not conform with the provision identified in the notice,*

the Secretary of State may require the operator to pay a penalty.

Amendment – Section prospectively inserted by Disability Discrimination Act 2005, s 8(1).

47F Penalty for using rail vehicle otherwise than in conformity with accessibility regulations

(1) Where it appears to the Secretary of State that a regulated rail vehicle has been used for carriage otherwise than in conformity with a provision of rail vehicle accessibility regulations with which use of the vehicle is required to conform, the Secretary of State may give to the operator of the vehicle a notice—

  (a) *identifying the provision and how it was breached;*
  (b) *identifying which of the regulated rail vehicles operated by the operator is or are covered by the notice; and*
  (c) *specifying the improvement deadline.*

(2) The improvement deadline specified in a notice under subsection (1) may not be earlier than the end of the prescribed period beginning with the day when the notice is given to the operator.

(3) Subsection (4) applies where—

  (a) *the Secretary of State has given a notice under subsection (1);*
  (b) *the improvement deadline specified in the notice has passed; and*
  (c) *it appears to the Secretary of State that a vehicle covered by the notice has after that deadline been used for carriage otherwise than in conformity with the provision identified in the notice.*

(4) The Secretary of State may give to the operator a further notice—

  (a) *identifying the provision and how it was breached;*
  (b) *identifying which of the regulated rail vehicles covered by the notice under subsection (1) is or are covered by the further notice; and*
  (c) *specifying the final deadline.*

(5) The final deadline specified in a notice under subsection (4) may not be earlier than the end of the prescribed period beginning with the day when the notice is given to the operator.

(6) If—

  (a) *the Secretary of State has given a notice under subsection (4), and*
  (b) *a vehicle covered by the notice is at a time after the final deadline used for carriage otherwise than in conformity with the provision identified in the notice,*

the Secretary of State may require the operator of the vehicle to pay a penalty.

(7) For the purposes of subsection (1), a vehicle is operated by a person if that person is the operator of the vehicle.

Amendment – Section prospectively inserted by Disability Discrimination Act 2005, s 7(1).

47G   Sections 47E and 47F: inspection of rail vehicles

(1) Where the Secretary of State has reasonable grounds for suspecting that a regulated rail vehicle may not conform with provisions of rail vehicle accessibility regulations with which it is required to conform, a person authorised by the Secretary of State—

(a)   *may inspect the vehicle for conformity with the provisions;*

(b)   *for the purpose of exercising his power under paragraph (a)—*

    (i)   *may enter premises if he has reasonable grounds for suspecting the vehicle to be at those premises, and*

    (ii)   *may enter the vehicle; and*

(c)   *for the purpose of exercising his power under paragraph (a) or (b), may require any person to afford such facilities and assistance with respect to matters under that person's control as are necessary to enable the power to be exercised.*

(2) Where the Secretary of State has given a notice under section 47E(1) or (4), a person authorised by the Secretary of State—

(a)   *may inspect the vehicle concerned for conformity with the provision specified in the notice;*

(b)   *for the purpose of exercising his power under paragraph (a)—*

    (i)   *may enter premises if he has reasonable grounds for suspecting the vehicle to be at those premises, and*

    (ii)   *may enter the vehicle; and*

(c)   *for the purpose of exercising his power under paragraph (a) or (b), may require any person to afford such facilities and assistance with respect to matters under that person's control as are necessary to enable the power to be exercised.*

(3) A person exercising power under subsection (1) or (2) shall, if required to do so, produce evidence of his authority to exercise the power.

(4) Where a person obstructs the exercise of power under subsection (1), the Secretary of State may, for purposes of section 47E(1) or 47F(1), draw such inferences from the obstruction as appear proper.

(5) Where—

(a)   *a person obstructs the exercise of power under subsection (2), and*

(b)   *the obstruction occurs before a notice under section 47E(4) is given in respect of the vehicle concerned,*

the Secretary of State may treat section 47E(3)(c) as satisfied in the case concerned.

(6) Where a person obstructs the exercise of power under subsection (2) and the obstruction occurs—

(a)   *after a notice under section 47E(4) has been given in respect of the vehicle concerned, and*

(b)   as a result of the operator, or a person who acts on his behalf, behaving in a particular way with the intention of obstructing the exercise of the power,

the Secretary of State may require the operator of the vehicle to pay a penalty.

(7) In this section 'inspect' includes test.

Amendment – Section prospectively inserted by Disability Discrimination Act 2005, s 7(1).

47H   Sections 47E and 47F: supplementary powers

(1) For the purposes of section 47E, the Secretary of State may give notice to a person requiring the person to supply the Secretary of State, by a time specified in the notice, with a vehicle number or other identifier for a rail vehicle—

(a)   of which that person is the operator; and

(b)   which is described in the notice.

(2) The time specified in a notice given to a person under subsection *(1)* may not be earlier than the end of 14 days beginning with the day when the notice is given to the person.

(3) If a person to whom a notice is given under subsection *(1)* does not comply with the notice by the time specified in the notice, the Secretary of State may require the person to pay a penalty.

(4) Where the Secretary of State has given a notice to a person under section 47E(1) or (4) or 47F(1) or (4), the Secretary of State may request that person to supply the Secretary of State, by a time specified in the request, with a statement detailing the steps taken in response to the notice.

(5) The time specified in a request under subsection *(4)* must—

(a)   if the request relates to a notice under section 47E(1) or 47F(1), be no earlier than the improvement deadline; and

(b)   if the request relates to a notice under section 47E(4) or 47F(4), be no earlier than the final deadline.

(6) Where a request under subsection *(4)*—

(a)   relates to a notice under section 47E(1) or 47F(1), and

(b)   is not complied with by the time specified in the request,

the Secretary of State may treat section 47E(3)(c) or (as the case may be) section 47F(3)(c) as being satisfied in the case concerned.

Amendment – Section prospectively inserted by Disability Discrimination Act 2005, s 8(1).

47J   Penalties under sections 47D to 47H: amount, due date and recovery

(1) In this section 'penalty' means a penalty under any of sections 47D to 47H.

(2) The amount of a penalty—

    (a) must not exceed the maximum prescribed for the purposes of this subsection; and

    (b) must not exceed 10 per cent of the turnover of the person on whom it is imposed.

(3) For the purposes of subsection (2)(b), a person's turnover shall be determined in accordance with regulations.

(4) A penalty must be paid to the Secretary of State before the end of the prescribed period.

(5) Any sum payable to the Secretary of State as a penalty may be recovered by the Secretary of State as a debt due to him.

(6) In proceedings under subsection (5) for enforcement of a penalty, no question may be raised as to—

    (a) liability to the imposition of the penalty; or

    (b) its amount.

(7) Any sum paid to the Secretary of State as a penalty shall be paid by him into the Consolidated Fund.

(8) The Secretary of State shall issue a code of practice specifying matters to be considered in determining the amount of a penalty.

(9) The Secretary of State may from time to time revise the whole or any part of the code and issue the code as revised.

(10) Before issuing the first or a revised version of the code, the Secretary of State shall lay a draft of that version before Parliament.

(11) After laying the draft of a version of the code before Parliament, the Secretary of State may bring that version of the code into operation by order.

(12) The Secretary of State shall have regard to the code (in addition to any other matters he thinks relevant)—

    (a) when imposing a penalty; and

    (b) when considering under section 47K(6) a notice of objection under section 47K(4).

Amendment – Section prospectively inserted by Disability Discrimination Act 2005, s 8(1).

47K   *Penalties under sections 47D to 47H: procedure*

(1) In this section 'penalty' means a penalty under any of sections 47D to 47H.

(2) If the Secretary of State decides that a person is liable to a penalty, the Secretary of State must notify the person of the decision.

(3) A notification under subsection (2) must—

- *(a)   state the Secretary of State's reasons for deciding that the person is liable to the penalty;*
- *(b)   state the amount of the penalty;*
- *(c)   specify the date before which, and the manner in which, the penalty must be paid; and*
- *(d)   include an explanation of the steps that the person may take if he objects to the penalty.*

(4) Where a person to whom a notification under subsection (2) is issued objects on the ground that—

- *(a)   he is not liable to the imposition of a penalty, or*
- *(b)   the amount of the penalty is too high,*

the person may give a notice of objection to the Secretary of State.

(5) A notice of objection must—

- *(a)   be in writing;*
- *(b)   give the objector's reasons; and*
- *(c)   be given before the end of the prescribed period.*

(6) Where the Secretary of State receives a notice of objection to a penalty in accordance with this section, he shall consider it and—

- *(a)   cancel the penalty;*
- *(b)   reduce the penalty; or*
- *(c)   determine to do neither of those things.*

(7) Where the Secretary of State considers under subsection (6) a notice of objection under subsection (4), he shall—

- *(a)   inform the objector of his decision before the end of the prescribed period or such longer period as he may agree with the objector; and*
- *(b)   if he reduces the penalty, notify the objector of the reduced amount.*

Amendment – Section prospectively inserted by Disability Discrimination Act 2005, s 7(1).

47L   *Penalties under sections 47D to 47H: appeals*

(1) A person may appeal to the court against a penalty imposed on him under any of sections 47D to 47H on the ground that—

- *(a)   he is not liable to the imposition of a penalty; or*
- *(b)   the amount of the penalty is too high.*

(2) On an appeal under this section, the court may—

- *(a)   allow the appeal and cancel the penalty;*
- *(b)   allow the appeal and reduce the penalty; or*
- *(c)   dismiss the appeal.*

(3) An appeal under this section shall be a re-hearing of the Secretary of State's decision to impose a penalty, and shall be determined having regard to—

  (a) any code of practice under section 47J which has effect at the time of the appeal; and

  (b) any other matters which the court thinks relevant (which may include matters of which the Secretary of State was unaware).

(4) An appeal may be brought by a person under this section against a penalty whether or not—

  (a) he has given notice of objection under section 47K(4); or

  (b) the penalty has been reduced under section 47K(6).

(5) A reference in this section to 'the court' is a reference—

  (a) in England and Wales, to a county court; and

  (b) in Scotland, to the sheriff.

(6) The sheriff may transfer proceedings under this section to the Court of Session.

(7) Where the sheriff has made a determination under subsection (2), any party to the proceedings may appeal on a point of law, either to the Sheriff Principal or to the Court of Session, against that determination.

Amendment – Section prospectively inserted by Disability Discrimination Act 2005, s 7(1).

47M   Sections 46 to 47H: interpretation

(1) In sections 46 to 47H 'operator', in relation to any rail vehicle, means the person having the management of that vehicle.

(2) For the purposes of those sections, a person uses a vehicle for carriage if he uses it for the carriage of passengers.

(3) Where an exemption order under section 47 authorises use of a rail vehicle even though the vehicle does not conform with a provision of rail vehicle accessibility regulations, references in sections 47A to 47G to provisions of rail vehicle accessibility regulations with which the vehicle is required to conform do not, in the vehicle's case, include that provision.

Amendment – Section prospectively inserted by Disability Discrimination Act 2005, s 8(1).

Supplemental

48   Offences by bodies corporate etc

(1) Where an offence under section 40 or 46[1] committed by a body corporate is committed with the consent or connivance of, or is attributable to any neglect on the part of, a director, manager, secretary or other similar officer of the body, or a person purporting to act in such a capacity, he as well as the body corporate is guilty of the offence.

(2) In subsection (1) 'director', in relation to a body corporate whose affairs are managed by its members, means a member of the body corporate.

(3) Where, in Scotland, an offence under section 40 or *46*[2] committed by a partnership or by an unincorporated association other than a partnership is committed with the consent or connivance of, or is attributable to any neglect on the part of, a partner in the partnership of (as the case may be) a person concerned in the management or control of the association, he, as well as the partnership or association, is guilty of the offence.

Amendment

[1] Words prospectively repealed Disability Discrimination Act 2005, s 19(2).

[2] Words prospectively repealed Disability Discrimination Act 2005, s 19(2).

49   Forgery and false statements [, and impersonation][1]

(1) In this section 'relevant document' means—

   (a)   a certificate of exemption issued under section 36, 37 or 37A;
   (b)   a notice of a kind mentioned in section 36(9)(b), 37(8)(b) or 37A(8)(b);
   (c)   an accessibility certificate; or[2]
   (d)   an approval certificate[; or
   (e)   a rail vehicle accessibility compliance certificate][3].

(2) A person is guilty of an offence if, with intent to deceive, he—

   (a)   forges, alters or uses a relevant document;
   (b)   lends a relevant document to any other person;
   (c)   allows a relevant document to be used by any other person; or
   (d)   makes or has in his possession any document which closely resembles a relevant document.

(3) A person who is guilty of an offence under subsection (2) is liable—

   (a)   on summary conviction, to a fine not exceeding the statutory maximum;
   (b)   on conviction on indictment, to imprisonment for a term not exceeding two years or to a fine or to both.

(4) A person who knowingly makes a false statement for the purpose of obtaining an accessibility certificate or *an approval certificate,* [an approval certificate or a rail vehicle accessibility compliance certificate][4]is guilty of an offence and liable on summary conviction to a fine not exceeding level 4 on the standard scale.

[(5) A person who falsely pretends to be a person authorised to exercise power under section 47G is guilty of an offence and liable on summary conviction to a fine not exceeding level 4 on the standard scale.][5]

Amendment – Amended by Private Hire Vehicles (Carriage of Guide Dogs etc) Act 2002, s 4(1)–(3).

[1] Section Heading prospectively inserted by Disability Discrimination Act 2005, s 8(2), as from a date to be appointed.

[2] Words prospectively repealed by Disability Discrimination Act 2005, s 19(2), as from a date to be appointed.

[3] Words prospectively inserted by Disability Discrimination Act 2005, s 7(2)(a), as from a date to be appointed.

[4] Words prospectively repealed and subsequent words prospectively inserted by Disability Discrimination Act 2005, s 7(2)(b), as from a date to be appointed.

[5] Subsection prospectively inserted by Disability Discrimination Act 2005, s 8(2), as from a date to be appointed.

PART 5A
PUBLIC AUTHORITIES

Amendment – Inserted by Disability Discrimination Act 2005, s 3.

49A   General duty

(1) Every public authority shall in carrying out its functions have due regard to—

- (a)   the need to eliminate discrimination that is unlawful under this Act;
- (b)   the need to eliminate harassment of disabled persons that is related to their disabilities;
- (c)   the need to promote equality of opportunity between disabled persons and other persons;
- (d)   the need to take steps to take account of disabled persons' disabilities, even where that involves treating disabled persons more favourably than other persons;
- (e)   the need to promote positive attitudes towards disabled persons; and
- (f)   the need to encourage participation by disabled persons in public life.

(2) Subsection (1) is without prejudice to any obligation of a public authority to comply with any other provision of this Act.

Amendment – Inserted by Disability Discrimination Act 2005, s 3.

49B   Meaning of 'public authority' in Part 5A

(1) In this Part 'public authority'—

- (a)   includes any person certain of whose functions are functions of a public nature; but
- (b)   does not include—
  - (i)   any person mentioned in section 21B(3);
  - (ii)   the Scottish Parliament;
  - (iii) a person, other than the Scottish Parliamentary Corporate Body, exercising functions in connection with proceedings in the Scottish Parliament;
  - (iv)   the National Assembly for Wales; or

(v) a person, other than the National Assembly for Wales Commission, exercising functions in connection with proceedings in the National Assembly for Wales.

(2) In relation to a particular act, a person is not a public authority by virtue only of subsection (1)(a) if the nature of the act is private.

(3) Regulations may provide for a person of a prescribed description to be treated as not being a public authority for the purposes of this Part.

Amendment – Inserted by Disability Discrimination Act 2005, s 3. Amended by Government of Wales Act 2006, ss 46, s 161(5); SI 2007/1388.

49C Exceptions from section 49A(1)

(1) Section 49A(1) does not apply to—

(a) a judicial act (whether done by a court, tribunal or other person); or
(b) an act done on the instructions, or on behalf, of a person acting in a judicial capacity.

(2) Section 49A(1) does not apply to any act of, or relating to, making or approving an Act of Parliament, an Act of the Scottish Parliament, a Measure or Act of the National Assembly for Wales or an Order in Council.

(3) Section 49A(1)(c) and (d) do not apply to—

(a) an act done in connection with recruitment to any of the naval, military or air forces of the Crown; or
(b) an act done in relation to a person in connection with service by him as a member of any of those forces.

(4) Regulations may provide for one or more specified paragraphs of section 49A(1) not to apply to an act of a prescribed description.

Amendment – Inserted by Disability Discrimination Act 2005, s 3. Amended by Government of Wales Act 2006, ss 46, s 161(5); Equality Act 2006, s 88; SI 2007/1388.

49D Power to impose specific duties

(1) The Secretary of State may by regulations impose on a public authority, other than a relevant Scottish authority or a cross-border authority, such duties as the Secretary of State considers appropriate for the purpose of ensuring the better performance by that authority of its duty under section 49A(1).

(2) The Secretary of State may by regulations impose on a cross-border authority such duties as the Secretary of State considers appropriate for the purpose of ensuring the better performance by that authority of its duty under section 49A(1) so far as relating to such of its functions as are not Scottish functions.

(3) The Scottish Ministers may by regulations impose on a relevant Scottish authority such duties as the Scottish Ministers consider appropriate for the purpose of ensuring the better performance by that authority of its duty under section 49A(1).

(4) The Scottish Ministers may by regulations impose on a cross-border authority such duties as the Scottish Ministers consider appropriate for the purpose of ensuring the better performance by that authority of its duty under section 49A(1) so far as relating to its Scottish functions.

(5) Before making regulations under any of subsections (1) to (4), the person making the regulations shall consult the Commission for Equality and Human Rights.

(6) Before making regulations under subsection (1) or (2) in relation to functions exercisable in relation to Wales by a public authority that is not a relevant Welsh authority, the Secretary of State shall consult the Welsh Ministers.

(7) The Secretary of State shall not make regulations under subsection (1) or (2) in relation to a relevant Welsh authority except with the consent of the Welsh Ministers.

(8) Before making regulations under subsection (2), the Secretary of State shall consult the Scottish Ministers.

(9) Before making regulations under subsection (4), the Scottish Ministers shall consult the Secretary of State.

(10) In this section—

'relevant Scottish authority' means—

(a)   a member of the Scottish executive or a junior Scottish Minister;
(b)   the Registrar General of Births, Deaths and Marriages for Scotland, the Keeper of the Registers of Scotland or the Keeper of the Records of Scotland;
(c)   any office of a description specified in an Order in Council under section 126(8)(b) of the Scotland Act 1998 (other non-ministerial office in the Scottish Administration); or
(d)   a public body, public office or holder of a public office—
    (i)   which (or who) is not a cross-border authority or the Scottish Parliamentary Corporate Body;
    (ii)   whose functions are exercisable only in or as regards Scotland; and
    (iii)   some at least of whose functions do not (within the meaning of the Scotland Act 1998) relate to reserved matters;

'cross-border authority' means a cross-border public authority within the meaning given by section 88(5) of the Scotland Act 1998;

'Scottish functions' means functions which are exercisable in or as regards Scotland and which do not (within the meaning of the Scotland Act 1998) relate to reserved matters;

'relevant Welsh authority' means—

(a)   the National Assembly for Wales Commission;

(aa)   the Welsh Ministers, the First Minister for Wales or the Counsel General to the Welsh Assembly Government; or

(b)   a public authority whose functions are exercisable only in relation to Wales.

Amendment – Inserted by Disability Discrimination Act 2005, s 3. Amended by Equality Act 2006, s 40, Sch 3, paras 41, 48; Government of Wales Act 2006, ss 46, 161(5); SI 2007/1388.

49E–49F (*repealed*)

PART 5 B

IMPROVEMENTS TO DWELLING HOUSES

Amendment – Inserted by Disability Discrimination Act 2005, s 16(1).

49G   Improvements to let dwelling houses

(1) This section applies in relation to a lease of a dwelling house if—

(a)   the tenancy is not a protected tenancy, a statutory tenancy or a secure tenancy,

(b)   the tenant or any other person who lawfully occupies or is intended lawfully to occupy the premises is a disabled person,

(c)   the person mentioned in paragraph (b) occupies or is intended to occupy the premises as his only or principal home,

(d)   the tenant is entitled under the lease to make improvements to the premises with the consent of the landlord, and

(e)   the tenant applies to the landlord for his consent to make a relevant improvement.

(2) If the consent of the landlord is unreasonably withheld it must be taken to have been given.

(3) Where the tenant applies in writing for the consent—

(a)   if the landlord refuses to give consent, he must give the tenant a written statement of the reason why the consent was withheld;

(b)   if the landlord neither gives nor refuses to give consent within a reasonable time, consent must be taken to have been withheld.

(4) If the landlord gives consent to the making of an improvement subject to a condition which is unreasonable, the consent must be taken to have been unreasonably withheld.

(5) In any question as to whether—

(a) the consent of the landlord was unreasonably withheld, or

(b) a condition imposed by the landlord is unreasonable,

it is for the landlord to show that it was not.

(6) If the tenant fails to comply with a reasonable condition imposed by the landlord on the making of a relevant improvement, the failure is to be treated as a breach by the tenant of an obligation of his tenancy.

(7) An improvement to premises is a relevant improvement if, having regard to the disability which the disabled person mentioned in subsection (1)(b) has, it is likely to facilitate his enjoyment of the premises.

(8) Subsections (2) to (6) apply to a lease only to the extent that provision of a like nature is not made by the lease.

(9) In this section—

'improvement' means any alteration in or addition to premises and includes—

(a) any addition to or alteration in landlord's fittings and fixtures,

(b) any addition or alteration connected with the provision of services to the premises,

(c) the erection of a wireless or television aerial, and

(d) the carrying out of external decoration;

'lease' includes a sub-lease or other tenancy, and 'landlord' and 'tenant' must be construed accordingly;

'protected tenancy' has the same meaning as in section 1 of the Rent Act 1977;

'statutory tenancy' must be construed in accordance with section 2 of that Act;

'secure tenancy' has the same meaning as in section 79 of the Housing Act 1985.

Amendment – Inserted by Disability Discrimination Act 2005, s 16(1).

49H–49I (*repealed*)

PART VI
THE NATIONAL DISABILITY COUNCIL

50–52 (*repealed*)

Amendment – Repealed by Disability Rights Commission Act 1999, s 14(2), Sch 5.

PART VII
SUPPLEMENTAL

53A–54 (*repealed*)

55 Victimisation

(1) For the purposes of Part 2, or Part 4 or Part 3 other than sections 24A to 24L, a person ('A') discriminates against another person ('B') if—

    (a) he treats B less favourably than he treats or would treat other persons whose circumstances are the same as B's; and

    (b) he does so for a reason mentioned in subsection (2).

(2) The reasons are that—

    (a) B has—

        (i) brought proceedings against A or any other person under this Act or;

        (ii) given evidence or information in connection with such proceedings brought by any person; or

        (iii) otherwise done anything under or by reference to, this Act in relation to A or any other person; or

        (iv) alleged that A or any other person has (whether or not the allegation so states) contravened this Act; or

    (b) A believes or suspects that B has done or intends to do any of those things.

(3) Where B is a disabled person, or a person who has had a disability, the disability in question shall be disregarded in comparing his circumstances with those of any other person for the purposes of subsection (1)(a).

(3A) For the purposes of Chapter 1 of Part 4—

    (a) references in subsection (2) to B include references to–

        (i) a person who is, for the purposes of that Chapter, B's parent; and

        (ii) a sibling of B; and

    (b) references in that subsection to this Act are, as respects a person mentioned in sub-paragraph (i) or (ii) of paragraph (a), restricted to that Chapter.

(4) Subsection (1) does not apply to treatment of a person because of an allegation made by him if the allegation was false and not made in good faith.

(5) In the case of an act which constitutes discrimination by virtue of this section, sections 4, 4B, 4D, 4G, 6A, 7A, 7C, 13, 14A, 14C, 15B and 16A also apply to discrimination against a person who is not disabled.

(6) (*repealed*)

Amendment – Amended by Special Educational Needs and Disability Act 2001, s 38(1), (7), (8); Disability Discrimination Act 2005, s 19(1), Sch 1, Pt 1, paras 1, 29(1), (5), Sch 2; Disability Discrimination Act 1995 (Amendment) Regulations 2003, SI 2003/1673, regs 3(1), 21;. Disability Discrimination Act 1995 (Pensions) Regulations 2003, SI 2003/2770, regs 2, 4(3).

56   Help for aggrieved persons in obtaining information etc

(1) For the purposes of this section—

- (a)   a person who considers that he may have been—
    - (i)   discriminated against in contravention of Part 2 or 3, or
    - (ii)   subjected to harassment in contravention of Part 2 or section 21A(2),
    is referred to as 'the person aggrieved'; and

- (b)   a person against whom the person aggrieved may decide to institute, or has instituted, proceedings in respect of such discrimination or harassment is referred to as 'the respondent'.

(2) With a view to helping the person aggrieved decide whether to institute proceedings and, if he does so, to formulate and present his case in the most effective manner, the Secretary of State shall by order prescribe—

- (a)   forms by which the person aggrieved may question the respondent on his reasons for doing any relevant act, or on any other matter which is or may be relevant; and

- (b)   forms by which the respondent may if he so wishes reply to any questions.

(3) Where the person aggrieved questions the respondent in accordance with forms prescribed by an order under subsection (2)—

- (a)   the question, and any reply by the respondent (whether in accordance with such an order or not), shall be admissible as evidence in any proceedings under Part 2 or 3;

- (b)   f it appears to the court or tribunal in any such proceedings—
    - (i)   that the respondent deliberately, and without reasonable excuse, omitted to reply within the period of eight weeks beginning with the day on which the question was served on him, or
    - (ii)   that the respondent's reply is evasive or equivocal,
    it may draw any inference which it considers it just and equitable to draw, including an inference that the respondent committed an unlawful act.

(4) The Secretary of State may by order—

- (a)   prescribe the period within which questions must be duly served in order to be admissible under subsection (3)(a); and

- (b)   prescribe the manner in which a question, and any reply by the respondent, may be duly served.

(5) Rules of court may enable a court entertaining a claim under section 25 to determine, before the date fixed for the hearing of the claim, whether a question or reply is admissible under this section or not.

(6) In proceedings in respect of a section 21B claim, subsection (3)(b) does not apply in relation to a failure to reply, or a particular reply, if the following conditions are met—

>   (a)   that, at the time of doing any relevant act, the respondent was carrying out public investigator functions or was a public prosecutor; and

>   (b)   that the respondent reasonably believes that a reply or (as the case may be) a different reply would be likely to prejudice any criminal investigation, any decision to institute criminal proceedings or any criminal proceedings or would reveal the reasons behind a decision not to institute, or a decision not to continue, criminal proceedings.

(7) Regulations may provide for this section not to have effect, or to have effect with prescribed modifications, in relation to section 21B claims of a prescribed description.

(8) This section is without prejudice to any other enactment or rule of law regulating interlocutory and preliminary matters in proceedings before a county court, the sheriff or an employment tribunal, and has effect subject to any enactment or rule of law regulating the admissibility of evidence in such proceedings.

(9) In this section 'section 21B claim' means a claim under section 25 by virtue of section 21B.

Amendment – Substituted by Disability Discrimination Act 2005, s 17.

57   Aiding unlawful acts

(1) A person who knowingly aids another person to do an unlawful act is to be treated for the purposes of this Act as himself doing the same kind of unlawful act.

(2) For the purposes of subsection (1), an employee or agent for whose act the employer or principal is liable under section 58 (or would be so liable but for section 58(5)) shall be taken to have aided the employer or principal to do the act.

(3) For the purposes of this section, a person does not knowingly aid another to do an unlawful act if—

>   (a)   he acts in reliance on a statement made to him by that other person that, because of any provision of this Act, the act would not be unlawful; and

>   (b)   it is reasonable for him to rely on the statement.

(4) A person who knowingly or recklessly makes such a statement which is false or misleading in a material respect is guilty of an offence.

(5) Any person guilty of an offence under subsection (4) shall be liable on summary conviction to a fine not exceeding level 5 on the standard scale.

(6) 'Unlawful act' means an act made unlawful by any provision of this Act other than a provision contained in Chapter 1 of Part 4.

Amendment – Amended by Special Educational Needs and Disability Act 2001, s 38(1), (9), (10).

58   Liability of employers and principals

(1) Anything done by a person in the course of his employment shall be treated for the purposes of this Act as also done by his employer, whether or not it was done with the employer's knowledge or approval.

(2) Anything done by a person as agent for another person with the authority of that other person shall be treated for the purposes of this Act as also done by that other person.

(3) Subsection (2) applies whether the authority was—

(a)   express or implied; or
(b)   given before or after the act in question was done.

(4) Subsections (1) and (2) do not apply in relation to an offence under section 57(4).

(5) In proceedings under this Act against any person in respect of an act alleged to have been done by an employee of his, it shall be a defence for that person to prove that he took such steps as were reasonably practicable to prevent the employee from—

(a)   doing that act; or
(b)   doing, in the course of his employment, acts of that description.

59   Statutory authority and national security etc

(1) Nothing in this Act makes unlawful any act done—

(a)   in pursuance of any enactment;or
(b)   in pursuance of any instrument made under any enactment by—
    (i)   a Minister of the Crown,
    (ii)   a member of the Scottish Executive,
    (iii) the National Assembly for Wales constituted by the Government of Wales Act 1998, or
    (iv)   the Welsh Ministers, the First Minister for Wales or the Counsel General to the Welsh Assembly Government; or

(c)   to comply with any condition or requirement—
    (i)   imposed by a Minister of the Crown (whether before or after the passing of this Act) by virtue of any enactment,
    (ii)   imposed by a member of the Scottish Executive (whether before or after the coming into force of this sub-paragraph) by virtue of any enactment,

(iii) imposed by the National Assembly for Wales constituted by the Government of Wales Act 1998 (whether before or after the coming into force of this sub-paragraph) by virtue of any enactment, or

(iv) imposed by the Welsh Ministers, the First Minister for Wales or the Counsel General to the Welsh Assembly Government

(2) In subsection (1) 'enactment' includes one passed or made after the date on which this Act is passed and 'instrument' includes one made after that date.

(2A) Nothing in—

(a) Part 2 of this Act, or

(b) Part 3 of this Act to the extent that it relates to the provision of employment services,

makes unlawful any act done for the purpose of safeguarding national security if the doing of the act was justified by that purpose

(3) Nothing in any other provision of this Act makes unlawful any act done for the purpose of safeguarding national security.

Amendment – Amended by Disability Discrimination Act 2005, s 19(1), Sch 1, Pt 1; Disability Discrimination Act 1995 (Amendment) Regulations 2003, SI 2003/1673, regs 3(1), 23(a); SI 2007/1388.

59A National Security

(1) Rules of court may make provision for enabling a county court or sheriff court in which a claim is brought in respect of alleged discrimination contrary to this Act (including anything treated by virtue of this Act as amounting to discrimination contrary to this Act), where the court considers it expedient in the interests of national security—

(a) to exclude from all or part of the proceedings—
   (i) the claimant;
   (ii) the claimant's representatives;
   (iii) any assessors;

(b) to permit a claimant or representative who has been excluded to make a statement to the court before the commencement of the proceedings, or the part of the proceedings, from which he is excluded;

(c) to take steps to keep secret all or part of the reasons for the court's decision in the proceedings.

(2) The Attorney General or, in Scotland, the Advocate General for Scotland, may appoint a person to represent the interests of a claimant in, or in any part of, proceedings from which the claimant or his representatives are excluded by virtue of subsection (1).

(3) A person may be appointed under subsection (2) only—

    (a)   in relation to proceedings in England and Wales, if he has a general qualification (within the meaning of section 71 of the Courts and Legal Services Act 1990 (c 41)), or

    (b)   in relation to proceedings in Scotland, if he is—

        (i)   an advocate, or

        (ii)   qualified to practice as a solicitor in Scotland.

(4) A person appointed under subsection (2) shall not be responsible to the person whose interests he is appointed to represent.

Amendment – Inserted by Equality Act 2006, s 89.

PART VIII
MISCELLANEOUS

60 Appointment by Secretary of State of advisers

(1) The Secretary of State may appoint such persons as he thinks fit to advise or assist him in connection with matters relating to the employment of disabled persons and persons who have had a disability.

(2) Persons may be appointed by the Secretary of State to act generally or in relation to a particular area or locality.

(3) The Secretary of State may pay to any person appointed under this section such allowances and compensation for loss of earnings as he considers appropriate.

(4) The approval of the Treasury is required for any payment under this section.

(5) In subsection (1) 'employment' includes self-employment.

(6) The Secretary of State may by order—

    (a)   provide for section 17 of, and Schedule 2 to, the Disabled Persons (Employment) Act 1944 (national advisory council and district advisory committees) to cease to have effect—

        (i)   so far as concerns the national advisory council; or

        (ii)   so far as concerns district advisory committees; or

    (b)   repeal that section and Schedule.

(7) At any time before the coming into force of an order under paragraph (b) of subsection (6), section 17 of the Act of 1944 shall have effect as if in subsection (1), after 'disabled persons' in each case there were inserted ', and persons who have had a disability,' and as if at the end of the section there were added—

    '(3) For the purposes of this section—

(a) a person is a disabled person if he is a disabled person for the purposes of the Disability Discrimination Act 1995; and

(b) 'disability' has the same meaning as in that Act.'

(8) At any time before the coming into force of an order under paragraph (a)(i) or (b) of subsection (6), section 16 of the Chronically Sick and Disabled Persons Act 1970 (which extends the functions of the national advisory council) shall have effect as if after 'disabled persons' in each case there were inserted ', and persons who have had a disability,' and as if at the end of the section there were added—

'(2) For the purposes of this section—

(a) a person is a disabled person if he is a disabled person for the purposes of the Disability Discrimination Act 1995; and

(b) 'disability' has the same meaning as in that Act.'

61 Amendment of Disabled Persons (Employment) Act 1944

(1)–(7) (*repealed*)

(8) Any provision of subordinate legislation in which 'disabled person' is defined by reference to the Act of 1944 shall be construed as if that expression had the same meaning as in this Act.

(9) Subsection (8) does not prevent the further amendment of any such provision by subordinate legislation.

62, 63 (*repealed*)

Amendment – Repealed by Employment Tribunals Act 1996, s 45, Sch 3, Pt I.

64 Application to Crown etc

(A1) The following provisions bind the Crown—

(a) sections 21B to 21E and Part 5A, and
(b) the other provisions of this Act so far as applying for the purposes of provisions mentioned in paragraph (a);

and sections 57 and 58 shall apply for purposes of provisions mentioned in paragraph (a) as if service as a Crown servant were employment by the Crown.

(1) This Act other than the provisions mentioned in paragraphs (a) and (b) of subsection (A1), applies—

(a) to an act done by or for purposes of a Minister of the Crown or government department, or
(b) to an act done on behalf of the Crown by a statutory body, or a person holding a statutory office,

as it applies to an act done by a private person.

(2) Part II applies to service—

    (a)   for purposes of a Minister of the Crown or government department, other than service of a person holding a statutory office, or

    (b)   on behalf of the Crown for purposes of a person holding a statutory office or purposes of a statutory body,

as it applies to employment by a private person.

(2A) Subsections (A1) to (2) have effect subject to section 64A.

(3) The provisions of Parts II to IV of the 1947 Act apply to proceedings against the Crown under this Act as they apply to Crown proceedings in England and Wales;

(4) The provisions of Part V of the 1947 Act apply to proceedings against the Crown under this Act as they apply to proceedings in Scotland which by virtue of that Part are treated as civil proceedings by or against the Crown; but the proviso to section 44 of that Act (removal of proceedings from the sheriff court to the Court of Session) does not apply.

(5) (*repealed*)

(6) (*repealed*)

(7) Part II does not apply to service in any of the naval, military or air forces of the Crown.

(8) In this section—

    'the 1947 Act' means the Crown Proceedings Act 1947;

    'Crown proceedings' means proceedings which, by virtue of section 23 of the 1947 Act, are treated for the purposes of Part II of that Act as civil proceedings by or against the Crown;

    'service for purposes of a Minister of the Crown or government department' does not include service in any office for the time being mentioned in Schedule 2 (Ministerial offices) to the House of Commons Disqualification Act 1975;

    'statutory body' means a body set up by or under an enactment;

    'statutory office' means an office so set up.

Amendment – Amended by Disability Discrimination Act 2005, s 19(1); Disability Discrimination Act 1995 (Amendment) Regulations 2003, SI 2003/1673, regs 3(1), 24(a)-(e); SI 2005/2712.

64A   Police

(1) For the purposes of Part 2, the holding of the office of constable shall be treated as employment—

    (a)   by the chief officer of police as respects any act done by him in relation to a constable or that office;

    (b)   by the police authority as respects any act done by them in relation to a constable or that office.

(2) For the purposes of section 58—

   (a)   the holding of the office of constable shall be treated as employment by the chief officer of police (and as not being employment by any other person); and

   (b)   anything done by a person holding such an office in the performance, or purported performance, of his functions shall be treated as done in the course of that employment.

(3) There shall be paid out of the police fund—

   (a)   any compensation, costs or expenses awarded against a chief officer of police in any proceedings brought against him under Part or 3, and any costs or expenses incurred by him in any such proceedings so far as not recovered by him in the proceedings; and

   (b)   any sum required by a chief officer of police for the settlement of any claim made against him under Part 2 if the settlement is approved by the police authority.

(4) Any proceedings under Part 2 or 3 which, by virtue of this section, would lie against a chief officer of police shall be brought against—

   (a)   the chief officer of police for the time being, or

   (b)   in the case of a vacancy in that office, against the person for the time being performing the functions of that office;

and references in subsection (3) to the chief officer of police shall be construed accordingly.

(5) A police authority may, in such cases and to such extent as appear to it to be appropriate, pay out of the police fund—

   (a)   any compensation, costs or expenses awarded in proceedings under Part 2 or 3 of this Act against a person under the direction and control of the chief officer of police;

   (b)   any costs or expenses incurred and not recovered by such a person in such proceedings; and

   (c)   any sum required in connection with the settlement of a claim that has or might have given rise to such proceedings.

(6) Subsections (1) and (2) apply to a police cadet and appointment as a police cadet as they apply to a constable and the office of constable.

(7) Subject to subsection (8), in this section—

'chief officer of police'—

   (a)   in relation to a person appointed, or an appointment falling to be made, under a specified Act, has the same meaning as in the Police Act 1996,

   (b)   (*repealed*),

   (c)   in relation to a person appointed, or an appointment falling to be made, under the Police (Scotland) Act 1967, means the chief constable of the relevant police force,

(d)   in relation to any other person or appointment means the officer or other person who has the direction and control of the body of constables or cadets in question;

'police authority'—

(a)   in relation to a person appointed, or an appointment falling to be made, under a specified Act, has the same meaning as in the Police Act 1996,

(b)   (*repealed*)

(c)   in relation to a person appointed, or an appointment falling to be made, under the Police (Scotland) Act 1967, has the meaning given in that Act,

(d)   in relation to any other person or appointment, means the authority by whom the person in question is or on appointment would be paid;

'police cadet' means any person appointed to undergo training with a view to becoming a constable;

'police fund'—

(a)   in relation to a chief officer of police within paragraph (a) of the above definition of that term, has the same meaning as in the Police Act 1996,

(b)   and

(c)   in any other case means money provided by the police authority;

'specified Act' means the Metropolitan Police Act 1829, the City of London Police Act 1839 or the Police Act 1996.

(8) In relation to a constable of a force who is not under the direction and control of the chief officer of police for that force, references in this section to the chief officer of police are references to the chief officer of the force under whose direction and control he is, and references in this section to the police authority are references to the relevant police authority for that force.

Amendment – Inserted by Disability Discrimination Act 1995 (Amendment) Regulations 2003, SI 2003/1673, regs 3(1), 25. Amended by Disability Discrimination Act 2005, s 4(1), Serious Organised Crime and Police Act 2005, ss 59, 174(2).

65 Application to Parliament

(1) This Act applies to an act done by or for purposes of the House of Lords or the House of Commons as it applies to an act done by a private person.

(2) For the purposes of the application of Part II in relation to the House of Commons, the Corporate Officer of that House shall be treated as the employer of a person who is (or would be) a relevant member of the House of Commons staff for the purposes of section 195 of the Employment Rights Act 1996.

(3) Except as provided in subsection (4), for the purposes of the application of sections 19 to 21, the provider of services is—

    (a)   as respects the House of Lords, the Corporate Officer of that House; and

    (b)   as respects the House of Commons, the Corporate Officer of that House.

(4) Where the service in question is access to and use of any place in the Palace of Westminster which members of the public are permitted to enter, the Corporate Officers of both Houses jointly are the provider of that service.

(5) Nothing in any rule of law or the law or practice of Parliament prevents proceedings being instituted before an employment tribunal under Part 2or 3 before any court under Part III.

Amendments – Amended by Employment Rights Act 1996, s 240, Sch 1, para 69(1), (3); Employment Rights (Dispute Resolution) Act 1998, s 1(2)(a); Disability Discrimination Act 2005, s 19(1).

66   (*repealed*)

Amendment – Repealed by Disability Discrimination Act 1995 (Amendment) Regulations 2003, SI 2003/1673, regs 3(1), 26.

67   Regulations and orders

(1) Any power under this Act of the Secretary of State, the Scottish Ministers or the Welsh Ministers to make regulations or orders shall be exercisable by statutory instrument.

(2) Any such power may be exercised to make different provision for different cases, including different provision for different areas or localities.

(3) Any such power includes power—

    (a)   to make such incidental, supplemental, consequential or transitional provision as appears to the person by whom the power is exercisable to be expedient; and

    (b)   to provide for a person to exercise a discretion in dealing with any matter.

(3A) Where regulations under section 21D(7)(b) provide for the omission of section 21D(5), the provision that may be made by the regulations in exercise of the power conferred by subsection (3)(a) includes provision amending section 21D for the purpose of omitting references to section 21D(5).

(3B) The provision that may be made by regulations under section 21G(5)(b) in exercise of the power conferred by subsection (3)(a) includes provision amending or repealing section 21G(4).

(3C) The provision that may be made by regulations under any of subsections (1) to (4) of section 49D in exercise of the power conferred by subsection (3)(a) includes provision amending or repealing an enactment.

(4) Subsection (4A) applies to—

    (a)   the first regulations to be made under section 21H(1);

    (b)   the first regulations to be made under each of subsections (1), (2) and (4) of section 31AE;

    (c)   regulations under section 31AE(1), (2) or (4) that amend this Act;

    (d)   regulations under section 31AE(1) that make provision as to remedies;

    (e)   regulations under section 47J(3);

    (f)   regulations under section 49D(1) or (2) that, in exercise of the power under subsection (3)(a), amend or repeal an enactment contained in an Act[, in an Act of the Scottish Parliament, or in a Measure or Act of the National Assembly for Wales;

    (g)   regulations under section 67A(3);

    (h)   regulations under paragraph 6A(2) of Schedule 1.

(4A) No regulations to which this subsection applies shall be made unless a draft of the statutory instrument containing the regulations (whether containing the regulations alone or with other provisions) has been laid before, and approved by a resolution of, each House of Parliament.

(4B) Subsection (4C) applies to regulations under section 49D(3) or (4) that, in exercise of the power under subsection (3)(a), amend or repeal any enactment contained in an Act or in an Act of the Scottish Parliament.

(4C) No regulations to which this subsection applies shall be made unless a draft of the statutory instrument containing the regulations (whether containing the regulations alone or with other provisions) has been laid before, and approved by a resolution of, the Scottish Parliament.

(4D) A statutory instrument—

    (a)   that—

        (i)   contains regulations under section 49D(3) or (4), and

        (ii)   is not subject to the requirement in subsection (4C) that a draft of the instrument be laid before, and approved by, the Scottish Parliament, or

    (b)   that contains regulations or an order made by the Scottish Ministers under section 33,

shall be subject to annulment in pursuance of a resolution of the Scottish Parliament.

(5) A statutory instrument—

    (a)   that—

        (i)   contains regulations made by the Secretary of State under this Act, and

(ii)   is not subject to the requirement in subsection (4A) that a draft of the instrument be laid before, and approved by a resolution of, each House of Parliament, or

(b)   that contains an order made by the Secretary of State under this Act that is not an order under section 3(9), 47(1), or 70(3),

shall be subject to annulment in pursuance of a resolution of either House of Parliament.

(5A) A statutory instrument that contains an order under section 47(1), if made without a draft having been laid before, and approved by a resolution of, each House of Parliament, shall be subject to annulment in pursuance of a resolution of either House, but the exercise of the discretion conferred by this subsection is subject to section 67A.

(6) Subsection (1) does not require an order under section 43 which applies only to a specified vehicle, or to vehicles of a specified person, to be made by statutory instrument but such an order shall be as capable of being amended or revoked as an order which is made by statutory instrument.

(7) Nothing in section 34(4), 40(6) or 46(5) affects the powers conferred by subsections (2) and (3).

Amendment – Amended by Disability Rights Commission Act 1999, s 14(1), Sch 4, para 3(1), (2); Disability Discrimination Act 2005, s 19(1), Sch 1; Government of Wales Act 2006, ss 46, 161(5); Equality Act 2006, ss 40, 91, Sch 3.

67A   Exercise of discretion under section 67(5A)

(1) Before the Secretary of State decides which of the parliamentary procedures available under section 67(5A) is to be adopted in connection with the making of any particular order under section 47(1), he must consult the Disabled Persons Transport Advisory Committee.

(2) An order under section 47(1) may be made without a draft of the instrument that contains it having been laid before, and approved by a resolution of, each House of Parliament only if—

(a)   regulations under subsection (3) are in force; and
(b)   the making of the order without such laying and approval is in accordance with the regulations.

(3) Regulations may set out the basis on which the Secretary of State, when he comes to make an order under section 47(1), will decide which of the parliamentary procedures available under section 67(5A) is to be adopted in connection with the making of the order.

(4) Before making regulations under subsection (3), the Secretary of State must consult—

(a)   the Disabled Persons Transport Advisory Committee; and
(b)   such other persons as he considers appropriate

Amendment – Inserted by Disability Discrimination Act 2005, s 6(4).

67B Annual report on rail vehicle exemption orders

(1) The Secretary of State must after each 31st December prepare, in respect of the year that ended with that day, a report on—

(a) the exercise in that year of the power to make orders under section 47(1); and

(b) the exercise in that year of the discretion under section 67(5A).

(2) A report under subsection (1) must (in particular) contain—

(a) details of each order made under section 47(1) in the year in respect of which the report is made; and

(b) details of consultation carried out under sections 47(3) and 67A(1) in connection with orders made in that year under section 47(1).

(3) The Secretary of State must lay before each House of Parliament each report that he prepares under this section.

Amendment – Inserted by Disability Discrimination Act 2005, s 6(5).

68 Interpretation

(1) In this Act—

'accessibility certificate' means a certificate issued under section 41(1)(a);

'act' includes a deliberate omission;

'approval certificate' means a certificate issued under section 42(4);

'conciliation officer' means a person designated under section 211 of the Trade Union and Labour Relations (Consolidation) Act 1992;

'criminal investigation' has the meaning given in subsection (1A);

'criminal proceedings' includes—

(a) proceedings on dealing summarily with a charge under the Army Act 1955 or the Air Force Act 1955 or on summary trial under the Naval Discipline Act 1957;

(b) proceedings before a summary appeal court constituted under any of those Acts;

(c) proceedings before a court-martial constituted under any of those Acts or a disciplinary court constituted under section 52G of the Naval Discipline Act 1957;

(d) proceedings before the Courts-Martial Appeal Court; and

(e) proceedings before a Standing Civilian Court;]

['criminal proceedings' includes service law proceedings (as defined by section 324(5) of the Armed Forces Act 2006);][1]

'employment' means, subject to any prescribed provision, employment under a contract of service or of apprenticeship or a contract personally to do any work, and related expressions are to be construed accordingly;

'employment at an establishment in Great Britain' is to be construed in accordance with subsections (2) to (4A);

'employment services' has the meaning given in section 21A (1);

'enactment' includes subordinate legislation and any Order in Council, and includes an enactment comprised in, or in an instrument made under, an Act of the Scottish Parliament;;

'Great Britain' includes such of the territorial waters of the United Kingdom as are adjacent to Great Britain;

'group insurance arrangement' means an arrangement between an employer and another for the provision by the other of facilities by way of insurance to the employer's employees or to any class of those employees

'licensing authority' except in section 37A means—

    (a)   in relation to the area to which the Metropolitan Public Carriage Act 1869 applies, the Secretary of State or the holder of any office for the time being designated by the Secretary of State; or

    (b)   in relation to any other area in England and Wales, the authority responsible for licensing taxis in that area;

'mental impairment' does not have the same meaning as in the Mental Health Act 1983 but the fact that an impairment would be a mental impairment for the purpose of that Act does not prevent it from being a mental impairment for the purposes of this Act;

'Minister of the Crown' includes the Treasury and the Defence Council;

'occupational pension scheme' has the same meaning as in the Pension Schemes Act 1993;

'premises' includes land of any description;

'prescribed' means prescribed by regulations; except in section 28D (where is has the meaning given by section 28D (17));

'profession' includes any vocation or occupation;

'provider of services' has the meaning given in section 19(2)(b);

'public investigator functions' has the meaning given in subsection (1B);

'public service vehicle' and 'regulated public service vehicle' have the meaning given in section 40;

'PSV accessibility regulations' means regulations made under section 40(1);

'rail vehicle' and 'regulated rail vehicle' have the meaning given in section 46;

['rail vehicle accessibility compliance certificate' has the meaning given in section 47A(3);][2]

'rail vehicle accessibility regulations' means regulations made under section 46(1);

'regulations' means regulations made by the Secretary of State, except in sections 2(3), 28D, 28L(6), 28Q(7), 33, 49D and 67 (provisions where the meaning of 'regulations' is apparent);

'section 21 duty' means any duty imposed by or under section 21;

'subordinate legislation' has the same meaning as in section 21 of the Interpretation Act 1978;

'taxi' and 'regulated taxi' have the meaning given in section 32;

'taxi accessibility regulations' means regulations made under section 32(1);

'trade' includes any business;

'trade organisation' has the meaning given in section 13;

'vehicle examiner' means an examiner appointed under section 66A of the Road Traffic Act 1988.

(1A) In this Act 'criminal investigation' means—

(a) any investigation which a person in carrying out functions to which section 21B(1) applies has a duty to conduct with a view to it being ascertained whether a person should be charged with, or in Scotland prosecuted for, an offence, or whether a person charged with or prosecuted for an offence is guilty of it;

(b) any investigation which is conducted by a person in carrying out functions to which section 21B(1) applies and which in the circumstances may lead to a decision by that person to institute criminal proceedings which the person has power to conduct; or

(c) any investigation which is conducted by a person in carrying out functions to which section 21B(1) applies and which in the circumstances may lead to a decision by that person to make a report to the procurator fiscal for the purpose of enabling him to determine whether criminal proceedings should be instituted.

(1B) In this Act 'public investigator functions' means functions of conducting criminal investigations or charging offenders.

(1C) In subsections (1A) and (1B)—

'offence' includes *any offence of a kind triable by court-martial under the Army Act 1955, the Air Force Act 1955 or the Naval Discipline Act 1957* [any service offence within the meaning of the Armed Forces Act 2006],[3] and

'offender' is to be construed accordingly

(2) Employment (including employment on board a ship to which subsection (2B) applies or on an aircraft or hovercraft to which subsection (2C) applies) is to be regarded as being employment at an establishment in Great Britain if the employee—

(a) does his work wholly or partly in Great Britain; or

(b) does his work wholly outside Great Britain and subsection (2A) applies.

(2A) This subsection applies if—

   (a)   the employer has a place of business at an establishment in Great Britain;

   (b)   the work is for the purposes of the business carried on at the establishment; and

   (c)   the employee is ordinarily resident in Great Britain—

       (i)   at the time when he applies for or is offered the employment, or

      (ii)   at any time during the course of the employment.

(2B) This subsection applies to a ship if—

   (a)   it is registered at a port of registry in Great Britain; or

   (b)   it belongs to or is possessed by Her Majesty in right of the Government of the United Kingdom.

(2C) This subsection applies to an aircraft or hovercraft if—

   (a)   it is—

       (i)   registered in the United Kingdom, and

      (ii)   operated by a person who has his principal place of business, or is ordinarily resident, in Great Britain; or

   (b)   it belongs to or is possessed by Her Majesty in right of the Government of the United Kingdom.

(2D) The following are not to be regarded as being employment at an establishment in Great Britain—

   (a)   employment on board a ship to which subsection (2B) does not apply;

   (b)   employment on an aircraft or hovercraft to which subsection (2C) does not apply.

(4) Employment of a prescribed kind, or in prescribed circumstances, is to be regarded as not being employment at an establishment in Great Britain.

(4A) For the purposes of determining if employment concerned with the exploration of the sea bed or sub-soil or the exploitation of their natural resources is outside Great Britain, subsections (2)(a) and (b), (2A) and (2C) of this section each have effect as if 'Great Britain' had the same meaning as that given to the last reference to Great Britain in section 10(1) of the Sex Discrimination Act 1975 by section 10(5) of that Act read with the Sex Discrimination and Equal Pay (Offshore Employment) Order 1987.

(5) *(repealed)*

Amendment – Amended by Disability Discrimination Act 1995 (Amendment) Regulations 2003 SI 2003/1673, regs 3(1), 27(a)(i)–(iv); Private Hire Vehicles (Carriage of Guide Dogs etc) Act 2002, s 5; Disability Discrimination Act 1995 (Amendment) Regulations 2003, SI 2003/1673, regs 3(1), 27(b)–(d).

[1] Definition 'criminal proceedings' prospectively substituted by Armed Forces Act 2006, s 378(1) as from a date to be appointed.

[2] Definition 'rail vehicle accessibility compliance certificate' prospectively inserted by Disability Discrimination Act 2005 , s 7(3), as from a date to be appointed.

[3] Words prospectively repealed and subsequent words substituted by Armed Forces Act 2006, s 378(2) as from a date to be appointed.

69 Financial provisions

(1) There shall be paid out of money provided by Parliament—

    (a)   any expenditure incurred by a Minister of the Crown under this Act;

    (b)   any increase attributable to this Act in the sums payable out of money so provided under or by virtue of any other enactment.

70 Short title, commencement, extent etc

(1) This Act may be cited as the Disability Discrimination Act 1995.

(2) This section (apart from subsections (4), (5) and (7)) comes into force on the passing of this Act.

(3) The other provisions of this Act come into force on such day as the Secretary of State may by order appoint and different days may be appointed for different purposes.

(4) Schedule 6 makes consequential amendments.

(5) The repeals set out in Schedule 7 shall have effect.

(5A) Sections 7A, 7B and 49G extend to England and Wales only.

(5B) Sections 7C and 7D extend to Scotland only.

(6) Subject to subsections (5A) and (5B), this Act extends to England and Wales, Scotland and Northern Ireland; but in their application to Northern Ireland the provisions of this Act mentioned in Schedule 8 shall have effect subject to the modifications set out in that Schedule.

(7) *(repealed)*

(8) Consultations which are required by any provision of this Act to be held by the Secretary of State may be held by him before the coming into force of that provision.

Amendment – Amended by; Disability Rights Commission Act 1999, s 14(2), Sch 5; Disability Discrimination Act 2005, s 19(1), Sch 1; Equality Act 2006, s 40, Sch 3, paras 41, 55; Disability Discrimination Act 1995 (Amendment) Regulations 2003 SI 2003/1673, regs 3(1), 28(a), (b).

Schedules

Schedule 1
Provisions Supplementing Section 1

Section 1(1)

Impairment

1

(1) (*repealed*)

(2) Regulations may make provision, for the purposes of this Act—

    (a)   for conditions of a prescribed description to be treated as amounting to impairments;

    (b)   for conditions of a prescribed description to be treated as not amounting to impairments.

(3) Regulations made under sub-paragraph (2) may make provision as to the meaning of 'condition' for the purposes of those regulations.

Long-term effects

2

(1) The effect of an impairment is a long-term effect if—

    (a)   it has lasted at least 12 months;

    (b)   the period for which it lasts is likely to be at least 12 months; or

    (c)   it is likely to last for the rest of the life of the person affected.

(2) Where an impairment ceases to have a substantial adverse effect on a person's ability to carry out normal day-to-day activities, it is to be treated as continuing to have that effect if that effect is likely to recur.

(3) For the purposes of sub-paragraph (2), the likelihood of an effect recurring shall be disregarded in prescribed circumstances.

(4) Regulations may prescribe circumstances in which, for the purposes of this Act—

    (a)   an effect which would not otherwise be a long-term effect is to be treated as such an effect; or

    (b)   an effect which would otherwise be a long-term effect is to be treated as not being such an effect.

Severe disfigurement

3

(1) An impairment which consists of a severe disfigurement is to be treated as having a substantial adverse effect on the ability of the person concerned to carry out normal day-to-day activities.

(2) Regulations may provide that in prescribed circumstances a severe disfigurement is not to be treated as having that effect.

(3) Regulations under sub-paragraph (2) may, in particular, make provision with respect to deliberately acquired disfigurements.

Normal day-to-day activities

4

(1) An impairment is to be taken to affect the ability of the person concerned to carry out normal day-to-day activities only if it affects one of the following—

(a)   mobility;
(b)   manual dexterity;
(c)   physical co-ordination;
(d)   continence;
(e)   ability to lift, carry or otherwise move everyday objects;
(f)   speech, hearing or eyesight;
(g)   memory or ability to concentrate, learn or understand; or
(h)   perception of the risk of physical danger.

(2) Regulations may prescribe—

(a)   circumstances in which an impairment which does not have an effect falling within sub-paragraph (1) is to be taken to affect the ability of the person concerned to carry out normal day-to-day activities;
(b)   circumstances in which an impairment which has an effect falling within sub-paragraph (1) is to be taken not to affect the ability of the person concerned to carry out normal day-to-day activities.

Substantial adverse effects

5

Regulations may make provision for the purposes of this Act—

(a)   for an effect of a prescribed kind on the ability of a person to carry out normal day-to-day activities to be treated as a substantial adverse effect;
(b)   for an effect of a prescribed kind on the ability of a person to carry out normal day-to-day activities to be treated as not being a substantial adverse effect.

Effect of medical treatment

6

(1) An impairment which would be likely to have a substantial adverse effect on the ability of the person concerned to carry out normal day-to-day activities, but for the fact that measures are being taken to treat or correct it, is to be treated as having that effect.

(2) In sub-paragraph (1) 'measures' includes, in particular, medical treatment and the use of a prosthesis or other aid.

(3) Sub-paragraph (1) does not apply—

    (a)   in relation to the impairment of a person's sight, to the extent that the impairment is, in his case, correctable by spectacles or contact lenses or in such other ways as may be prescribed; or

    (b)   in relation to such other impairments as may be prescribed, in such circumstances as may be prescribed.

6A

(1) Subject to sub-paragraph (2), a person who has cancer, HIV infection or multiple sclerosis is to be deemed to have a disability, and hence to be a disabled person.

(2) Regulations may provide for sub-paragraph (1) not to apply in the case of a person who has cancer if he has cancer of a prescribed description.

(3) A description of cancer prescribed under sub-paragraph (2) may (in particular) be framed by reference to consequences for a person of his having it.]

Persons deemed to be disabled

7

(1) Sub-paragraph (2) applies to any person whose name is, both on 12th January 1995 and on the date when this paragraph comes into force, in the register of disabled persons maintained under section 6 of the Disabled Persons (Employment) Act 1944.

(2) That person is to be deemed—

    (a)   during the initial period, to have a disability, and hence to be a disabled person; and

    (b)   afterwards, to have had a disability and hence to have been a disabled person during that period.

(3) A certificate of registration shall be conclusive evidence, in relation to the person with respect to whom it was issued, of the matters certified.

(4) Unless the contrary is shown, any document purporting to be a certificate of registration shall be taken to be such a certificate and to have been validly issued.

(5) Regulations may provide for prescribed descriptions of person to be deemed to have disabilities, and hence to be disabled persons, for the purposes of this Act.

(5A) The generality of sub-paragraph (5) shall not be taken to be prejudiced by the other provisions of this Schedule

(6) Regulations may prescribe circumstances in which a person who has been deemed to be a disabled person by the provisions of sub-paragraph (1) or regulations made under sub-paragraph (5) is to be treated as no longer being deemed to be such a person.

(7) In this paragraph—

'certificate of registration' means a certificate issued under regulations made under section 6 of the Act of 1944; and

'initial period' means the period of three years beginning with the date on which this paragraph comes into force.

Progressive conditions

8

(1) Where—

(a) a person has a progressive condition (such as cancer, multiple sclerosis or muscular dystrophy or infection by the human immunodeficiency virus),

(b) as a result of that condition, he has an impairment which has (or had) an effect on his ability to carry out normal day-to-day activities, but

(c) that effect is not (or was not) a substantial adverse effect,

he shall be taken to have an impairment which has such a substantial adverse effect if the condition is likely to result in his having such an impairment.

(2) Regulations may make provision, for the purposes of this paragraph—

(a) for conditions of a prescribed description to be treated as being progressive;

(b) for conditions of a prescribed description to be treated as not being progressive.

Interpretation

9

In this Schedule 'HIV infection' means infection by a virus capable of causing the Acquired Immune Deficiency Syndrome

Amendment— Amended by Disability Discrimination Act 2005, ss 18(1), (2), 19(2), Sch 2.

Schedule 2
Past Disabilities

Section 2(2)

1

The modifications referred to in section 2 are as follows.

2

References in Parts II to 4 and 5A to a disabled person are to be read as references to a person who has had a disability.

2A

References in Chapter 1 of Part 4 to a disabled pupil are to be read as references to a pupil who has had a disability.

2B

References in Chapter 2 of Part 4 to a disabled student are to be read as references to a student who has had a disability.

2C

In section 3A(5), and 31AB (8), after 'not having that particular disability' insert 'and who has not had that particular disability'.

3

In sections 4A(1), 4B(4), 4E(1), 4H(1), 6B(1), 7B(1), 7D(1), 14(1), 14B(1), 14D(1), 15C (1) and 16A(4), section 21A(4)(a) (in the words to be read as section 19(1)(aa)) and section 21A(6)(a) (in the words to be substituted in section 21(1)), and section 31AD(1) (d),(2) (c) and (3), after 'not disabled' (in each place it occurs) insert 'and who have not had a disability'.

4

In sections 4A(3)(b), 4E(3)(b), 4H(3)(b), 6B(3)(b), 7B(4)(b), 7D(3)(b), 14(3)(b), 14B(3)(b), 14D(3)(b), 15C (3) (a), 16A(6), and 31AD (4) (b), for 'has' (in each place it occurs) substitute 'has had'.

4ZA

In section 24(3)(e)(i) and (f)(i), after 'having' insert 'had'

4ZB

In sections 24D(2)(a) and 24J(3)(b), for 'did not have' substitute 'had not had'.

4A

In section 28B(3)(a) and (4), after 'disabled' insert 'or that he had had a disability'.

4B

In section 28C(1), in paragraphs (a) and (b), after 'not disabled' insert 'and who have not had a disability'.

4C

In section 28S

(a) in subsection (3)(a), after 'disabled' insert 'or that he had had a disability',
(b) in subsection (6)(a), after 'who do not have' insert 'and have not had', and
(c) in subsection (10), for 'that particular disability' substitute 'and who has not had that particular disability and'.

4D

In subsections (1), (1A), (1B), (1C) and (1D) of section 28T, after 'not disabled' insert 'and who have not had a disability.

4E

In subsection (1) of that section as substituted by paragraphs 2 9, 14 and 21 of Schedule 4C, after 'not disabled' insert 'and who have not had a disability'.

5

For paragraph 2(1) to (3) of Schedule 1, substitute—

'(1) The effect of an impairment is a long-term effect if it has lasted for at least 12 months.

(2) Where an impairment ceases to have a substantial adverse effect on a person's ability to carry out normal day-to-day activities, it is to be treated as continuing to have that effect if that effect recurs.

(3) For the purposes of sub-paragraph (2), the recurrence of an effect shall be disregarded in prescribed circumstances.'

Amendment – Amended by Special Educational Needs and Disability Act 2001, s 38(1), (11)–(13) ; Disability Discrimination Act 2005, s 19(1), Sch 1, Pt 1, para 1; Disability Discrimination Act 1995 (Amendment) Regulations 2003 SI 2003/1673, regs 3(1), 28(a), (b); Disability Discrimination Act 1995 (Amendment) Regulations 2003, SI 2003/1673, regs 3(1), 29(1)(a)–(c) and Disability Discrimination Act 1995 (Pensions) Regulations 2003, SI 2003/2770, regs 2, 4(4)(a), (b).

Schedule 3
Enforcement and Procedure

Sections 17A(8), 25(6), 31ADA

Amendment – Amended by Disability Discrimination Act 1995 (Amendment) Regulations 2003, SI 2003/1673, regs 3(1), 29(2)(a); SI 2007/2405, regs 3(1), 29(2)(a).

PART I
EMPLOYMENT

Conciliation

1

(*repealed*)

Restriction on proceedings for breach of Part II

2

(1) Except as provided by Part 2, no civil or criminal proceedings may be brought against any person in respect of an act merely because the act is unlawful under that Part.

(2) Sub-paragraph (1) does not prevent the making of an application for judicial review or the investigation or determination of any matter in accordance with Part 10 (investigations) of the Pension Schemes Act 1993 by the Pensions Ombudsman.

(3) Sub-paragraph (1) does not prevent the bringing of proceedings in respect of an offence under section 16B(2B).

Amendment – Amended by Disability Discrimination Act 1995 (Amendment) Regulations 2003, SI 2003/1673, regs 3(1), 29(2)(b) and Disability Discrimination Act 1995 (Pensions) Regulations 2003, SI 2003/2770, regs 2, 4(5).

Period within which proceedings must be brought

3

(1) An employment tribunal shall not consider a complaint under section 17A or 25(8) unless it is presented before the end of the period of three months beginning when the act complained of was done.

(2) A tribunal may consider any such complaint which is out of time if, in all the circumstances of the case, it considers that it is just and equitable to do so.

(3) For the purposes of sub-paragraph (1)—

    (a)   where an unlawful act is attributable to a term in a contract, that act is to be treated as extending throughout the duration of the contract;

    (b)   any act extending over a period shall be treated as done at the end of that period; and

    (c)   a deliberate omission shall be treated as done when the person in question decided upon it.

(4) In the absence of evidence establishing the contrary, a person shall be taken for the purposes of this paragraph to decide upon an omission—

    (a)   when he does an act inconsistent with doing the omitted act; or

    (b)   if he has done no such inconsistent act, when the period expires within which he might reasonably have been expected to do the omitted act if it was to be done.

Amendment – Amended by Employment Rights (Dispute Resolution) Act 1998, s 1(2)(a) and Disability Discrimination Act 1995 (Amendment) Regulations 2003, SI 2003/1673, regs 3(1), 29(2)(c).

Evidence

4

(1) In any proceedings under section 17A or 25(8), a certificate signed by or on behalf of a Minister of the Crown and certifying—

    (a)   that any conditions or requirements specified in the certificate were imposed by a Minister of the Crown and were in operation at a time or throughout a time so specified, or

    (b)   *(repealed)*

shall be conclusive evidence of the matters certified.

(1A) In any proceedings under section 17A or 25(8), a certificate signed by or on behalf of the Scottish Ministers and certifying that any conditions or requirements specified in the certificate—

    (a)   were imposed by a member of the Scottish Executive, and

    (b)   were in operation at a time or throughout a time so specified,

shall be conclusive evidence of the matters certified.

(1B) In any proceedings under section 17A or 25(8), a certificate signed by or on behalf of the Welsh Ministers and certifying that any conditions or requirements specified in the certificate—

    (a)   were imposed by the National Assembly for Wales constituted by the Government of Wales Act 1998, the Welsh Ministers, the First Minister for Wales or the Counsel General to the Welsh Assembly Government, and

    (b)   were in operation at a time or throughout a time so specified, shall be conclusive evidence of the matters certified.

(2) A document purporting to be such a certificate as is mentioned in sub-paragraph (1), (1A) or (1B) shall be received in evidence and, unless the contrary is proved, be deemed to be such a certificate.

Amendment – Amended by Employment Relations Act 1999, ss 41, 44, Sch 8, para 7 Disability Discrimination Act 2005, s 19(1), Sch 1; Government of Wales Act 2006, ss 46, 161(5); Disability Discrimination Act 1995 (Amendment) Regulations 2003, SI 2003/1673, regs 3(1), 29(2)(e); SI 2007/1388.

PART II
DISCRIMINATION IN OTHER AREAS

Restriction on proceedings for breach of Part III

5

(1) Except as provided by section 25 no civil or criminal proceedings may be brought against any person in respect of an act merely because the act is unlawful under Part III.

(2) Sub-paragraph (1) does not prevent the making of an application for judicial review.

Period within which proceedings must be brought

6

(1) A county court or a sheriff court shall not consider a claim under section 25 unless proceedings in respect of the claim are instituted before the end of the period of six months beginning when the act complained of was done.

(2) Where, in relation to proceedings or prospective proceedings under section 25, the dispute concerned is referred for conciliation in pursuance of arrangements under section 27 of the Equality Act 2006 before the end of the period of six months mentioned in sub-paragraph (1), the period allowed by that sub-paragraph shall be extended by three months.

(3) A court may consider any claim under section 25 which is out of time if, in all the circumstances of the case, it considers that it is just and equitable to do so.

(4) For the purposes of sub-paragraph (1)—

    (a)   where an unlawful act of discrimination is attributable to a term in a contract, that act is to be treated as extending throughout the duration of the contract;

    (b)   any act extending over a period shall be treated as done at the end of that period; and

    (c)   a deliberate omission shall be treated as done when the person in question decided upon it.

(5) In the absence of evidence establishing the contrary, a person shall be taken for the purposes of this paragraph to decide upon an omission—

(a) when he does an act inconsistent with doing the omitted act; or

(b) if he has done no such inconsistent act, when the period expires within which he might reasonably have been expected to do the omitted act if it was to be done.

Staying or sisting proceedings on section 21B claim affecting criminal matters

6A

(1) Sub-paragraph (2) applies where a party to proceedings under section 25 which have arisen by virtue of section 21B(1) has applied for a stay or sist of those proceedings on the grounds of prejudice to—

(a) particular criminal proceedings;

(b) a criminal investigation; or

(c) a decision to institute criminal proceedings.

(2) The court shall grant the stay or sist unless it is satisfied that the continuance of the proceedings under section 25 would not result in the prejudice alleged.

Restriction of remedies for section 21B claim relating to criminal matters

6B

(1) Sub-paragraph (2) applies to a remedy other than—

(a) damages; or

(b) a declaration or, in Scotland, a declarator.

(2) In proceedings under section 25, the remedy shall be obtainable in respect of a relevant discriminatory act only if the court is satisfied that—

(a) no criminal investigation,

(b) no decision to institute criminal proceedings, and

(c) no criminal proceedings,

would be prejudiced by the remedy.

(3) In sub-paragraph (2) 'relevant discriminatory act' means an act—

(a) which is done, or by virtue of section 57 or 58 is treated as done, by a person—
   (i) in carrying out public investigator functions, or
   (ii) in carrying out functions as a public prosecutor; and

(b) which is unlawful by virtue of section 21B(1)

Compensation for injury to feelings

7

In any proceedings under section 25, the amount of any damages awarded as compensation for injury to feelings shall not exceed the prescribed amount.

Evidence

8

(1) In any proceedings under section 25, a certificate signed by or on behalf of a Minister of the Crown and certifying—

  (a) that any conditions or requirements specified in the certificate were imposed by a Minister of the Crown and were in operation at a time or throughout a time so specified, or

  (b) that an act specified in the certificate was done for the purpose of safeguarding national security,

shall be conclusive evidence of the matters certified.

(2) A document purporting to be such a certificate shall be received in evidence and, unless the contrary is proved, be deemed to be such a certificate.

(3) In any proceedings under section 25, a certificate signed by or on behalf of the Scottish Ministers and certifying that any conditions or requirements specified in the certificate—

  (a) were imposed by a member of the Scottish Executive, and

  (b) were in operation at a time or throughout a time so specified,

shall be conclusive evidence of the matters certified.

(4) In any proceedings under section 25, a certificate signed by or on behalf of the Welsh Ministers and certifying that any conditions or requirements specified in the certificate—

  (a) were imposed by the National Assembly for Wales constituted by the Government of Wales Act 1998, the Welsh Ministers, the First Minister for Wales or the Counsel General to the Welsh Assembly Government, and

  (b) were in operation at a time or throughout a time so specified,

shall be conclusive evidence of the matters certified.

(5) A document purporting to be such a certificate as is mentioned in sub-paragraph (3) or (4) shall be received in evidence and, unless the contrary is proved, be deemed to be such a certificate.

Amendment – Amended by Employment Tribunals Act 1996, s 45, Sch 3, Pt I; Disability Discrimination Act 2005, s 19(1), Sch 1; Government of Wales Act 2006, ss 46, 161(5); Disability Rights Commission Act 1999, s 14(1), Sch 4, para 3(1), (3); Equality Act 2006, s 40, Sch 3; SI 2007/1388.

PART 3

DISCRIMINATION IN SCHOOLS

Amendment – Inserted by Special Educational Needs and Disability Act 2001, s 19(2), Sch 3, para 1.

Restriction on proceedings for breach of Part 4, Chapter 1

9

(1) Except as provided by sections 28I, 28K, 28L and 28N, no civil or criminal proceedings may be brought against any person in respect of an act merely because the act is unlawful under Chapter 1 of Part 4.

(2) Sub-paragraph (1) does not prevent the making of an application for judicial review.

(3) Sub-paragraph (1) does not prevent the bringing of proceedings in respect of an offence under section 28J(9)

Period within which proceedings must be brought

10

(1) The Tribunal or the Welsh Tribunal[1] shall not consider a claim under section 28I unless proceedings in respect of the claim are instituted before the end of the period of six months beginning when the act complained of was done.

(2) If, in relation to proceedings or prospective proceedings under section 28I, the dispute concerned is referred for conciliation in pursuance of arrangements under section 27 of the Equality Act 2006 before the end of the period of six months mentioned in sub-paragraph (1), the period allowed by that sub-paragraph shall be extended by three months.

(3) The Tribunal or the Welsh Tribunal may consider any claim under section 28I which is out of time if, in all the circumstances of the case, it considers that it is just and equitable to do so.

(4) But sub-paragraph (3) does not permit the Tribunal or the Welsh Tribunal to decide to consider a claim if a decision not to consider that claim has previously been taken under that sub-paragraph.

(5) For the purposes of sub-paragraph (1)—

    (a)   if an unlawful act of discrimination is attributable to a term in a contract, that act is to be treated as extending throughout the duration of the contract;

    (b)   any act extending over a period shall be treated as done at the end of that period; and

    (c)   a deliberate omission shall be treated as done when the person in question decided upon it.

(6) In the absence of evidence establishing the contrary, a person shall be taken for the purposes of this paragraph to decide upon an omission—

(a) when he does an act inconsistent with doing the omitted act; or

(b) if he has done no such inconsistent act, when the period expires within which he might reasonably have been expected to do the omitted act if it was to be done.

Evidence

11

(1) In any proceedings under section 28I, 28K, 28L or 28N, a certificate signed by or on behalf of a Minister of the Crown and certifying that any conditions or requirements specified in the certificate—

(a) were imposed by a Minister of the Crown, and

(b) were in operation at a time or throughout a time so specified,

shall be conclusive evidence of the matters certified.

(1A) In any proceedings under section 28N, a certificate signed by or on behalf of the Scottish Ministers and certifying that any conditions or requirements specified in the certificate—

(a) were imposed by a member of the Scottish Executive, and

(b) were in operation at a time or throughout a time so specified,

shall be conclusive evidence of the matters certified.

(1B) In any proceedings under section 28I, 28K or 28L, a certificate signed by or on behalf of the Welsh Ministers and certifying that any conditions or requirements specified in the certificate—

(a) were imposed by the National Assembly for Wales constituted by the Government of Wales Act 1998, the Welsh Ministers, the First Minister for Wales or the Counsel General to the Welsh Assembly Government, and

(b) were in operation at a time or throughout a time so specified,

shall be conclusive evidence of the matters certified.

(2) A document purporting to be such a certificate as is mentioned in sub-paragraph (1), (1A) or (1B) shall be received in evidence and, unless the contrary is proved, be deemed to be such a certificate.

Amendment – Inserted by Special Educational Needs and Disability Act 2001, s 19(2), Sch 3, para 1. Amended by Education Act 2002, s 195, Sch 18, paras 7, 12; Disability Discrimination Act 2005, s 19(1), Sch 1; Equality Act 2006, s 40, Sch 3; Government of Wales Act 2006, ss 46; SI 2007/1388.

PART 4
DISCRIMINATION IN FURTHER AND HIGHER EDUCATION INSTITUTIONS

Restriction on proceedings for breach of Part 4, Chapter 2

12

(1) Except as provided by Chapter 2 of Part 4, no civil or criminal proceedings may be brought against any person in respect of an act merely because the act is unlawful under that Chapter.

(2) Sub-paragraph (1) does not prevent the making of an application for judicial review.

Amendment – Inserted by Special Educational Needs and Disability Act 2001, s 30(2), Sch 3, para 2; SI 2006/1721.

Period within which proceedings must be brought

13

(1) A county court or a sheriff court shall not consider a claim under section 28V unless proceedings in respect of the claim are instituted before the end of the period of six months beginning when the act complained of was done.

(2) If, in relation to proceedings or prospective proceedings under section 28V—

(a) the dispute concerned is referred for conciliation in pursuance of arrangements under section 27 of the Equality Act 2006 before the end of the period of six months mentioned in sub-paragraph (1), or

(b) in England and Wales, in a case not falling within paragraph (a), the dispute concerned relates to the act or omission of a qualifying institution and is referred as a complaint under the student complaints scheme before the end of that period,

the period of six months allowed by sub-paragraph (1) shall be extended by three months.

(2A) In sub-paragraph (2)(b)—

'qualifying institution' has the meaning given by section 11 of the Higher Education Act 2004;

'the student complaints scheme' means a scheme for the review of qualifying complaints, as defined by section 12 of that Act, that is provided by the designated operator, as defined by section 13(5)(b) of that Act.

(3) A court may consider any claim under section 28V which is out of time if, in all the circumstances of the case, it considers that it is just and equitable to do so.

(4) For the purposes of sub-paragraph (1)—

(a)   if an unlawful act is attributable to a term in a contract, that act is to be treated as extending throughout the duration of the contract;

(b)   any act extending over a period shall be treated as done at the end of that period; and

(c)   a deliberate omission shall be treated as done when the person in question decided upon it.

(5) In the absence of evidence establishing the contrary, a person shall be taken for the purposes of this paragraph to decide upon an omission—

(a)   when he does an act inconsistent with doing the omitted act; or

(b)   if he has done no such inconsistent act, when the period expires within which he might reasonably have been expected to do the omitted act if it was to be done.

Compensation for injury to feelings

14

In any proceedings under section 28V, the amount of any damages awarded as compensation for injury to feelings shall not exceed the prescribed amount.

Evidence

15

(1) In any proceedings under section 28V, a certificate signed by or on behalf of a Minister of the Crown and certifying that any conditions or requirements specified in the certificate—

(a)   were imposed by a Minister of the Crown, and

(b)   were in operation at a time or throughout a time so specified,

is conclusive evidence of the matters certified.

(1A) In any proceedings under section 28V, a certificate signed by or on behalf of the Scottish Ministers and certifying that any conditions or requirements specified in the certificate—

(a)   were imposed by a member of the Scottish Executive, and

(b)   were in operation at a time or throughout a time so specified,

is conclusive evidence of the matters certified.

(1B) In any proceedings under section 28V, a certificate signed by or on behalf of the Welsh Ministers and certifying that any conditions or requirements specified in the certificate—

(a) were imposed by the National Assembly for Wales constituted by the Government of Wales Act 1998, the Welsh Ministers, the First Minister for Wales or the Counsel General to the Welsh Assembly Government, and

(b) were in operation at a time or throughout a time so specified,

is conclusive evidence of the matters certified.

(2) A document purporting to be such a certificate as is mentioned in sub-paragraph (1), (1A) or (1B) is to be—

(a) received in evidence; and

(b) deemed to be such a certificate unless the contrary is proved.

Amendment – Inserted by Special Educational Needs and Disability Act 2001, s 30(2), Sch 3, para 2. Amended by Higher Education Act 2004, s 19(3);Disability Discrimination Act 2005, s 19(1); Equality Act 2006, s 40, Sch 3; SI 2006/1721; Government of Wales Act 2006, ss 46; SI 2007/1388.

PART 5
DISCRIMINATION IN GENERAL QUALIFICATIONS BODIES
Amendment – Inserted by SI 2007/2405.

Restriction on proceedings for breach of Part 4, Chapter 2A

16

(1) Except as provided by section 31ADA, no civil or criminal proceedings may be brought against any person in respect of an act merely because the act is unlawful under Chapter 2A of Part 4.

(2) Sub-paragraph (1) does not prevent the making of an application for judicial review

Amendment—Inserted by SI 2007/2405.

Period within which proceedings must be brought

17

(1) A county court or a sheriff court shall not consider a claim under section 31ADA unless proceedings in respect of the claim are instituted before the end of the period of six months beginning when the act complained of was done.

(2) If, in relation to proceedings or prospective proceedings under section 31ADA, the dispute concerned is referred to conciliation in pursuance of arrangements under section 27 of the Equality Act 2006 before the end of the period of six months mentioned in sub-paragraph (1), the period of six months allowed by that sub-paragraph shall be extended by three months.

(3) A court may consider any claim under section 31ADA which is out of time if, in all the circumstances of the case, it considers that it is just and equitable to do so.

(4) For the purposes of sub-paragraph (1)—

    (a)   if an unlawful act is attributable to a term in a contract, that act is to be treated as extending throughout the duration of the contract;

    (b)   any act extending over a period shall be treated as done at the end of that period; and

    (c)   a deliberate omission shall be treated as done when the person in question decided upon it.

(5) In the absence of evidence establishing the contrary, a person shall be taken for the purposes of this paragraph to decide upon an omission—

    (a)   when he does an act inconsistent with doing the omitted act; or

    (b)   if he has done no such inconsistent act, when the period expires within which he might reasonably have been expected to do the omitted act if it was to be done

Evidence

18

(1) In any proceedings under section 31ADA, a certificate signed by or on behalf of a Minister of the Crown and certifying that any conditions or requirements specified in the certificate—

    (a)   were imposed by a Minister of the Crown, and

    (b)   were in operation at a time or throughout a time so specified,

is conclusive evidence of the matters certified.

(2) In any proceedings under section 31ADA, a certificate signed by or on behalf of the Scottish Ministers and certifying that any conditions or requirements specified in the certificate—

    (a)   were imposed by a member of the Scottish Executive, and

    (b)   were in operation at a time or throughout a time so specified,

is conclusive evidence of the matters certified.

(3) In any proceedings under section 31ADA, a certificate signed by or on behalf of the Welsh Ministers and certifying that any conditions or requirements specified in the certificate—

    (a)   were imposed by them, and

    (b)   were in operation at a time or throughout a time so specified,

is conclusive evidence of the matters certified.

(4) A document purporting to be such a certificate as is mentioned in sub-paragraph (1), (2) or (3) is to be—

(a) received in evidence; and

(b) deemed to be such a certificate unless the contrary is proved

---

Amendment – Inserted by SI 2007/2405.

Schedule 3A
Validity of Contracts, Collective Agreements and Rules of Undertakings

Section 17C

PART 1
VALIDITY AND REVISION OF CONTRACTS

1

(1) A term of a contract is void where—

(a) the making of the contract is, by reason of the inclusion of the term, unlawful by virtue of this Part of this Act;

(b) it is included in furtherance of an act which is unlawful by virtue of this Part of this Act; or

(c) it provides for the doing of an act which is unlawful by virtue of this Part of this Act.

(2) Sub-paragraph (1) does not apply to a term the inclusion of which constitutes, or is in furtherance of, or provides for, unlawful discrimination against, or harassment of, a party to the contract, but the term shall be unenforceable against that party.

(3) A term in a contract which purports to exclude or limit any provision of this Part of this Act is unenforceable by any person in whose favour the term would operate apart from this paragraph.

(4) Sub-paragraphs (1), (2) and (3) apply whether the contract was entered into before or after the date on which this Schedule comes into force; but in the case of a contract made before that date, those sub-paragraphs do not apply in relation to any period before that date.

2

(1) Paragraph 1(3) does not apply—

(a) to a contract settling a complaint to which section 17A(1) or 25(8) applies where the contract is made with the assistance of a conciliation officer (within the meaning of the Trade Union and Labour Relations (Consolidation) Act 1992); or

(b) to a contract settling a complaint to which section 17A(1) or 25(8) applies if the conditions regulating compromise contracts under this Schedule are satisfied in relation to the contract.

(2) The conditions regulating compromise contracts under this Schedule are that—

(a) the contract must be in writing;

(b)   the contract must relate to the particular complaint;

(c)   the complainant must have received advice from a relevant independent adviser as to the terms and effect of the proposed contract and in particular its effect on his ability to pursue a complaint before an employment tribunal;

(d)   there must be in force, when the adviser gives the advice, a contract of insurance, or an indemnity provided for members of a profession or professional body, covering the risk of a claim by the complainant in respect of loss arising in consequence of the advice;

(e)   the contract must identify the adviser; and

(f)   the contract must state that the conditions regulating compromise contracts under this Schedule are satisfied.

(3) A person is a relevant independent adviser for the purposes of sub-paragraph (2)(c)—

(a)   if he is a qualified lawyer;

(b)   if he is an officer, official, employee or member of an independent trade union who has been certified in writing by the trade union as competent to give advice and as authorised to do so on behalf of the trade union;

(c)   if he works at an advice centre (whether as an employee or a volunteer) and has been certified in writing by the centre as competent to give advice and as authorised to do so on behalf of the centre; or

(d)   if he is a person of a description specified in an order made by the Secretary of State.

(4) But a person is not a relevant independent adviser for the purposes of sub-paragraph (2)(c) in relation to the complainant—

(a)   if he is, is employed by or is acting in the matter for the other party or a person who is connected with the other party;

(b)   in the case of a person within sub-paragraph (3)(b) or (c), if the trade union or advice centre is the other party or a person who is connected with the other party; or

(c)   in the case of a person within sub-paragraph (3)(c), if the complainant makes a payment for the advice received from him.

(5) In sub-paragraph (3)(a) 'qualified lawyer' means—

(a)   as respects England and Wales, a barrister (whether in practice as such or employed to give legal advice), a solicitor who holds a practising certificate, or a person other than a barrister or solicitor who is an authorised advocate or authorised litigator (within the meaning of the Courts and Legal Services Act 1990); and

(b)   as respects Scotland, an advocate (whether in practice as such or employed to give legal advice), or a solicitor who holds a practising certificate.

(6) In sub-paragraph (3)(b) 'independent trade union' has the same meaning as in the Trade Union and Labour Relations (Consolidation) Act 1992.

(7) For the purposes of sub-paragraph (4)(a) any two persons are to be treated as connected—

(a) if one is a company of which the other (directly or indirectly) has control; or

(b) if both are companies of which a third person (directly or indirectly) has control.

(8) An agreement under which the parties agree to submit a dispute to arbitration—

(a) shall be regarded for the purposes of sub-paragraph (1)(a) and (b) as being a contract settling a complaint if—

   (i) the dispute is covered by a scheme having effect by virtue of an order under section 212A of the Trade Union and Labour Relations (Consolidation) Act 1992, and

   (ii) the agreement is to submit it to arbitration in accordance with the scheme; but

(b) shall be regarded as neither being nor including such a contract in any other case.

3

(1) On the application of a disabled person interested in a contract to which paragraph 1(1) or (2) applies, a county court or a sheriff court may make such order as it thinks fit for—

(a) removing or modifying any term rendered void by paragraph 1(1), or

(b) removing or modifying any term made unenforceable by paragraph 1(2);

but such an order shall not be made unless all persons affected have been given notice in writing of the application (except where under rules of court notice may be dispensed with) and have been afforded an opportunity to make representations to the court.

(2) An order under sub-paragraph (1) may include provision as respects any period before the making of the order (but after the coming into force of this Schedule).

Amendment—Inserted by SI 2003/1673, regs 3(1). Amended by Disability Discrimination Act 2005, s 19(1), Sch 1.

PART 2
COLLECTIVE AGREEMENTS AND RULES OF UNDERTAKINGS

4

(1) This Part of this Schedule applies to—

(a) any term of a collective agreement, including an agreement which was not intended, or is presumed not to have been intended, to be a legally enforceable contract;

(b) any rule made by an employer for application to all or any of the persons who are employed by him or who apply to be, or are, considered by him for employment;

(c) any rule made by a trade organisation (within the meaning of section 13) or a qualifications body (within the meaning of section 14A) for application to—

(i) all or any of its members or prospective members; or

(ii) all or any of the persons on whom it has conferred authorisations or qualifications or who are seeking the authorisations or qualifications which it has power to confer.

(2) Any term or rule to which this Part of this Schedule applies is void where—

(a) the making of the collective agreement is, by reason of the inclusion of the term, unlawful by virtue of this Part of this Act;

(b) the term or rule is included in furtherance of an act which is unlawful by virtue of this Part of this Act; or

(c) the term or rule provides for the doing of an act which is unlawful by virtue of this Part of this Act.

(3) Sub-paragraph (2) applies whether the agreement was entered into, or the rule made, before or after the date on which this Schedule comes into force; but in the case of an agreement entered into, or a rule made, before the date on which this Schedule comes into force, that sub-paragraph does not apply in relation to any period before that date.

5

A disabled person to whom this paragraph applies may present a complaint to an employment tribunal that a term or rule is void by virtue of paragraph 4 if he has reason to believe—

(a) that the term or rule may at some future time have effect in relation to him; and

(b) where he alleges that it is void by virtue of paragraph 4(2)(c), that—

(i) an act for the doing of which it provides, may at some such time be done in relation to him, and

(ii) the act would be unlawful by virtue of this Part of this Act if done in relation to him in present circumstances.

6

In the case of a complaint about—

(a) a term of a collective agreement made by or on behalf of—
  (i) an employer,
  (ii) an organisation of employers of which an employer is a member, or
  (iii) an association of such organisations of one of which an employer is a member, or

(b) a rule made by an employer within the meaning of paragraph 4(1)(b),

paragraph 5 applies to any disabled person who is, or is genuinely and actively seeking to become, one of his employees.

7

In the case of a complaint about a rule made by an organisation or body to which paragraph 4(1)(c) applies, paragraph 5 applies to any disabled person—

(a) who is, or is genuinely and actively seeking to become, a member of the organisation or body;

(b) on whom the organisation or body has conferred an authorisation or qualification; or

(c) who is genuinely and actively seeking an authorisation or qualification which the organisation or body has power to confer.

8

(1) When an employment tribunal finds that a complaint presented to it under paragraph 5 is well-founded the tribunal shall make an order declaring that the term or rule is void.

(2) An order under sub-paragraph (1) may include provision as respects any period before the making of the order (but after the coming into force of this Schedule).

9

The avoidance by virtue of paragraph 4(2) of any term or rule which provides for any person to be discriminated against shall be without prejudice to the following rights (except in so far as they enable any person to require another person to be treated less favourably than himself), namely—

(a) such of the rights of the person to be discriminated against, and

(b)   such of the rights of any person who will be treated more favourably in direct or indirect consequence of the discrimination,

as are conferred by or in respect of a contract made or modified wholly or partly in pursuance of, or by reference to, that term or rule.

Amendment—Section and preceding cross heading inserted by SI 2003/1673.

PART 3
INTERPRETATION

10

In this Schedule 'collective agreement' means any agreement relating to one or more of the matters mentioned in section 178(2) of the Trade Union and Labour Relations (Consolidation) Act 1992 (meaning of trade dispute), being an agreement made by or on behalf of one or more employers or one or more organisations of employers or associations of such organisations with one or more organisations of workers or associations of such organisations.

11

Any reference in this Schedule to this Part of this Act shall be taken to include a reference to Part 3 of this Act, to the extent that it relates to—

(a)   the provision of employment services; or
(b)   the provision under a group insurance arrangement of facilities by way of insurance.

12

Where a term to which section 26(1A)(c) applies is a term in an agreement which is not a contract, Part 1 of this Schedule shall have effect as if the agreement were a contract

Amendment – Inserted by Disability Discrimination Act 1995 (Amendment) Regulations 2003, SI 2003/1673, regs 3(1), 16(2). Amended by Disability Discrimination Act 2005, s 19(1), Sch 1.

Schedule 4
Premises Occupied Under Leases

Sections 18A(5), 27(5), 31ADB

Amendment – Amended by Disability Discrimination Act 1995 (Amendment) Regulations 2003, SI 2003/1673, regs 3(1), 29(3)(a); SI 2007/2405, reg 1(2).

PART I
OCCUPATION BY EMPLOYER ETC

Amendment – Amended by Disability Discrimination Act 1995 (Amendment) Regulations 2003, SI 2003/1673, regs 3(1), 29(3)(b).

Failure to obtain consent to alteration

1

If any question arises as to whether the occupier has failed to comply with any duty to make reasonable adjustments, by failing to make a particular alteration to the premises, any constraint attributable to the fact that he occupies the premises under a lease is to be ignored unless he has applied to the lessor in writing for consent to the making of the alteration.

Amendment – Amended by Disability Discrimination Act 1995 (Amendment) Regulations 2003, SI 2003/1673, regs 3(1), 29(3)(c).

Joining lessors in proceedings under section 17A

2

(1) In any proceedings on a complaint under section 17A, in a case to which section 18A applies, the complainant or the occupier may ask the tribunal hearing the complaint to direct that the lessor be joined or sisted as a party to the proceedings

(2) The request shall be granted if it is made before the hearing of the complaint begins.

(3) The tribunal may refuse the request if it is made after the hearing of the complaint begins.

(4) The request may not be granted if it is made after the tribunal has determined the complaint.

(5) Where a lessor has been so joined or sisted as a party to the proceedings, the tribunal may determine—

    (a)   whether the lessor has—
        (i)   refused consent to the alteration, or
        (ii)   consented subject to one or more conditions, and

    (b)   if so, whether the refusal or any of the conditions was unreasonable.

(6) If, under sub-paragraph (5), the tribunal determines that the refusal or any of the conditions was unreasonable it may take one or more of the following steps—

    (a)   make such declaration as it considers appropriate;
    (b)   make an order authorising the occupier to make the alteration specified in the order;
    (c)   order the lessor to pay compensation to the complainant.

(7) An order under sub-paragraph (6)(b) may require the occupier to comply with conditions specified in the order.

(8) Any step taken by the tribunal under sub-paragraph (6) may be in substitution for, or in addition to, any step taken by the tribunal under section 17A(2).

(9) If the tribunal orders the lessor to pay compensation it may not make an order under section 17A(2) ordering the occupier to do so.

Amendment – Amended by Disability Discrimination Act 2005, s 19(1), Sch 1; Disability Discrimination Act 1995 (Amendment) Regulations 2003, SI 2003/1673, regs 3(1), 29(3)(d)–(f).

Regulations

3

Regulations may make provision as to circumstances in which—

    (a)   a lessor is to be taken, for the purposes of section 18A of this Part of this Schedule to have—
        (i)   withheld his consent;
        (ii)   withheld his consent unreasonably;
        (iii) acted reasonably in withholding his consent;

    (b)   a condition subject to which a lessor has given his consent is to be taken to be reasonable;
    (c)   a condition subject to which a lessor has given his consent is to be taken to be unreasonable.

Amendment – Amended by Disability Discrimination Act 1995 (Amendment) Regulations 2003, SI 2003/1673, regs 3(1), 29(3)(g).

Sub-leases etc

4

The Secretary of State may by regulations make provision supplementing, or modifying, the provision made by section 18A or any provision made by or under this Part of this Schedule in relation to cases where the occupier occupies premises under a sub-lease or sub-tenancy.

Amendment – Amended by Disability Discrimination Act 1995 (Amendment) Regulations 2003, SI 2003/1673, regs 3(1), 29(3)(g).

PART II
OCCUPATION BY PERSONS SUBJECT TO A DUTY UNDER SECTION 21, 21E OR 21H.

Amendment – Amended by SI 2003/1673; Disability Discrimination Act 2005, s 19(1), Sch 1, Pt 1, para 1.

Failure to obtain consent to alteration

5

If any question arises as to whether the occupier has failed to comply with the section 21 duty or a duty imposed under section 21E or 21H, by failing to make a particular alteration to premises, any constraint attributable to the fact that he occupies the premises under a lease is to be ignored unless he has applied to the lessor in writing for consent to the making of the alteration.

Reference to court

6

(1) If the occupier has applied in writing to the lessor for consent to the alteration and—

(a) that consent has been refused, or

(b) the lessor has made his consent subject to one or more conditions,

the occupier or a disabled person who has an interest in the proposed alteration to the premises being made, may refer the matter to a county court or, in Scotland, to the sheriff.

(2) In the following provisions of this Schedule 'court' includes 'sheriff'.

(3) On such a reference the court shall determine whether the lessor's refusal was unreasonable or (as the case may be) whether the condition is, or any of the conditions are, unreasonable.

(4) If the court determines—

(a) that the lessor's refusal was unreasonable, or

(b) that the condition is, or any of the conditions are, unreasonable,

it may make such declaration as it considers appropriate or an order authorising the occupier to make the alteration specified in the order.

(5) An order under sub-paragraph (4) may require the occupier to comply with conditions specified in the order.

Joining lessors in proceedings under section 25

7

(1) In any proceedings on a claim under section 25 in a case to which section 27 applies, other than a claim presented as a complaint under section 25(8), the plaintiff, the pursuer or the occupier concerned may ask the court to direct that the lessor be joined or sisted as a party to the proceedings.

(2) The request shall be granted if it is made before the hearing of the claim begins.

(3) The court may refuse the request if it is made after the hearing of the claim begins.

(4) The request may not be granted if it is made after the court has determined the claim.

(5) Where a lessor has been so joined or sisted as a party to the proceedings, the court may determine—

 (a) whether the lessor has—
   (i) refused consent to the alteration, or
   (ii) consented subject to one or more conditions, and

 (b) if so, whether the refusal or any of the conditions was unreasonable.

(6) If, under sub-paragraph (5), the court determines that the refusal or any of the conditions was unreasonable it may take one or more of the following steps—

 (a) make such declaration as it considers appropriate;
 (b) make an order authorising the occupier to make the alteration specified in the order;
 (c) order the lessor to pay compensation to the complainant.

(7) An order under sub-paragraph (6)(b) may require the occupier to comply with conditions specified in the order.

(8) If the court orders the lessor to pay compensation it may not order the occupier to do so.

7A

(1) In any proceedings on a complaint under section 25(8) in a case to which section 27 applies, the complainant or the occupier may ask the tribunal hearing the complaint to direct that the lessor be joined or sisted as a party to the proceedings.

(2) The request shall be granted if it is made before the hearing of the complaint begins.

(3) The tribunal may refuse the request if it is made after the hearing of the complaint begins.

(4) The request may not be granted if it is made after the tribunal has determined the complaint.

(5) Where a lessor has been so joined or sisted as a party to the proceedings, the tribunal may determine—

 (a) whether the lessor has—
   (i) refused consent to the alteration, or
   (ii) consented subject to one or more conditions; and

 (b) if so, whether the refusal or any of the conditions was unreasonable.

(6) If, under sub-paragraph (5), the tribunal determines that the refusal or any of the conditions was unreasonable it may take one or more of the following steps—

 (a) make such declaration as it considers appropriate;

 (b) make an order authorising the occupier to make the alteration specified in the order;

 (c) order the lessor to pay compensation to the complainant.

(7) An order under sub-paragraph (6)(b) may require the occupier to comply with conditions specified in the order.

(8) Any step taken by the tribunal under sub-paragraph (6) may be in substitution for, or in addition to, any step taken by the tribunal under section 17A(2).

(9) If the tribunal orders the lessor to pay compensation it may not make an order under section 17A(2) ordering the occupier to do so.

Amendment – Inserted by Disability Discrimination Act 2005, s 19(1), Sch 1, Pt 1, para 1.

Regulations

8

Regulations may make provision as to circumstances in which—

 (a) a lessor is to be taken, for the purposes of section 27 and this Part of this Schedule to have—

  (i) withheld his consent;

  (ii) withheld his consent unreasonably;

  (iii) acted unreasonably in withholding his consent;

 (b) a condition subject to which a lessor has given his consent is to be taken to be reasonable;

 (c) a condition subject to which a lessor has given his consent is to be taken to be unreasonable.

Sub-leases etc

9

The Secretary of State may by regulations make provision supplementing, or modifying, the provision made by section 27 or any provision made by or under this Part of this Schedule in relation to cases where the occupier occupies premises under a sub-lease or sub-tenancy.

Amendment – Amended by Disability Discrimination Act 2005, s 19(1), Sch 1, Pt 1, para 1.

PART 3
OCCUPATION BY EDUCATIONAL INSTITUTIONS
Failure to obtain consent

10

If any question arises as to whether a responsible body has failed to comply with the duty imposed by section 28T or section 28UA (5), by failing to make a particular alteration to premises, any constraint attributable to the fact that the premises are occupied by the educational institution under a lease is to be ignored unless the responsible body has applied to the lessor in writing for consent to the making of the alteration.

Reference to court

11

(1) If the responsible body has applied in writing to the lessor for consent to the alteration and—

   (a)   that consent has been refused, or
   (b)   the lessor has made his consent subject to one or more conditions,

that body or a disabled person who has an interest in the proposed alteration to the premises being made, may refer the matter to a county court or, in Scotland, to the sheriff.

(2) On such a reference the court must determine whether the lessor's refusal was unreasonable or (as the case may be) whether the condition is, or any of the conditions are, unreasonable.

(3) If the court determines—

   (a)   that the lessor's refusal was unreasonable, or
   (b)   that the condition is, or any of the conditions are, unreasonable,

it may make such declaration as it considers appropriate or an order authorising the responsible body to make the alteration specified in the order.

(4) An order under sub-paragraph (3) may require the responsible body to comply with conditions specified in the order.

Joining lessors in proceedings under section 28V

12

(1) In proceedings on a claim under section 28V, in a case to which this Part of this Schedule applies, the claimant, the pursuer or the responsible body concerned may ask the court to direct that the lessor be joined or sisted as a party to the proceedings.

(2) The request must be granted if it is made before the hearing of the claim begins.

(3) The court may refuse the request if it is made after the hearing of the claim begins.

(4) The request may not be granted if it is made after the court has determined the claim.

(5) If a lessor has been so joined or sisted as a party to the proceedings, the court may determine—

    (a)   whether the lessor has—
        (i)   refused consent to the alteration, or
        (ii)   consented subject to one or more conditions, and

    (b)   if so, whether the refusal or any of the conditions was unreasonable.

(6) If, under sub-paragraph (5), the court determines that the refusal or any of the conditions was unreasonable it may take one or more of the following steps—

    (a)   make such a declaration as it considers appropriate;
    (b)   make an order authorising the responsible body to make the alteration specified in the order;
    (c)   order the lessor to pay compensation to the complainant.

(7) An order under sub-paragraph (6)(b) may require the responsible body to comply with conditions specified in the order.

(8) If the court orders the lessor to pay compensation it may not order the responsible body to do so.

Regulations

13

Regulations may make provision as to circumstances in which—

    (a)   a lessor is to be taken, for the purposes of section 28W and this Part of this Schedule to have—
        (i)   withheld his consent;
        (ii)   withheld his consent unreasonably;
        (iii) acted reasonably in withholding his consent;

    (b)   a condition subject to which a lessor has given his consent is to be taken to be reasonable;
    (c)   a condition subject to which a lessor has given his consent is to be taken to be unreasonable.

Sub-leases etc

14

Regulations may make provision supplementing, or modifying, section 28W or any provision made by or under this Part of this Schedule in relation to cases where the premises of the educational institution are occupied under a sub-lease or sub-tenancy.

Amendment – Part inserted by Special Educational Needs and Disability Act 2001, s 31(2), Sch ; SI 2006/1721.

PART 4
OCCUPATION BY GENERAL QUALIFICATIONS BODIES
Amendment – Inserted by SI 2007/2405, regs 2(1), 6(1), (3).

Failure to obtain consent to alteration

15

If any question arises as to whether a general qualifications body has failed to comply with the duty imposed by section 31AD by failing to make a particular alteration to the premises, any constraint attributable to the fact that the body occupies the premises under a lease is to be ignored unless the body has applied to the lessor in writing for consent to the making of the alteration

Reference to court

16

(1) If the general qualifications body has applied in writing to the lessor for consent to the alteration and—

    (a)   that consent has been refused, or

    (b)   the lessor has made his consent subject to one or more conditions,

that general qualifications body or a disabled person who has an interest in the proposed alteration to the premises being made may refer the matter to a county court or, in Scotland, to the sheriff.

(2) On such a reference the court must determine whether the refusal was unreasonable or (as the case may be) whether the condition is, or any of the conditions are, unreasonable.

(3) If the court determines—

    (a)   that the refusal was unreasonable, or

    (b)   that the condition is, or any of the conditions are, unreasonable, it may make such declaration as it considers appropriate or an order authorising the general qualifications body to make the alteration specified in the order.

(4) An order under sub-paragraph (3) may require the general qualifications body to comply with conditions specified in the order.

Joining lessors in proceedings under section 31ADA

17

(1) In any proceedings on a claim under section 31ADA in which a question arises as to whether a general qualifications body has failed to comply with the duty imposed by section 31AD by failing to make an alteration to premises occupied by the general qualifications body under a lease—

    (a)   the claimant (or pursuer in Scotland), or
    (b)   the general qualifications body concerned,

may ask the court to direct that the lessor be joined (or sisted) as a party to the proceedings.

(2) The request shall be granted if it is made before the hearing of the claim begins.

(3) The court may refuse the request if it is made after the hearing of the claim begins.

(4) The request may not be granted if it is made after the court has determined the claim.

(5) Where a lessor has been so joined (or sisted) as a party to the proceedings, the court may determine—

    (a)   whether the lessor has—
        (i)   refused consent to the alteration, or
        (ii) consented subject to one or more conditions, and

    (b)   if so, whether the refusal or any of the conditions was unreasonable.

(6) If, under sub-paragraph (5), the court determines that the refusal or any of the conditions was unreasonable, it may take one or more of the following steps—

    (a)   make such declaration as it considers appropriate;
    (b)   make an order authorising the general qualifications body to make the alteration specified in the order;
    (c)   order the lessor to pay compensation to the claimant or pursuer.

(7) An order under sub-paragraph (6)(b) may require the general qualifications body to comply with the conditions specified in the order.

(8) If the court orders the lessor to pay compensation it may not order the general qualifications body to do so.

Amendment – Inserted by SI 2007/2405.

Schedule 4A
Responsible Bodies for Schools

Section 28A

1

(1) The bodies responsible for schools in England and Wales are set out in the following table.

(2) In that Table—

'the local education authority' has the meaning given by section 22(8) of the School Standards and Framework Act 1998; and
'proprietor' has the meaning given by section 579 of the Education Act 1996.

Table

Type of school	Responsible body
1 Maintained school or maintained nursery school.	The local education authority or governing body, according to which has the function in question.
2 Pupil referral unit.	The local education authority.
3 Maintained nursery school.	The local education authority.[2]
4 Independent school.	The proprietor.
5 Special school not maintained by a local education authority.	The proprietor.

2

(1) The bodies responsible for schools in Scotland are set out in the following table.

(2) In that Table 'board of management', 'education authority', 'managers' and 'proprietor' each have the meaning given in section 135(1) of the Education (Scotland) Act 1980.

Table

Type of school	Responsible body
1 School managed by an education authority.	The education authority.
2 Independent school.	The proprietor.
3 Self-governing school.	The board of management.
4 School in respect of which the managers are for the time being receiving grants under section 73(c) or (d) of the Education (Scotland) Act 1980.	The managers of the school.

Amendments – Inserted by Special Educational Needs and Disability Act 2001, s 11(2), Sch 2.

Schedule 4B
Responsible Bodies for Educational Institutions

Section 28R

1

(1) The bodies responsible for educational institutions in England and Wales are set out in the following table.

(2) In that Table 'governing body' has the meaning given by section 90 of the Further and Higher Education Act 1992.

Table

Type of institution	Responsible body
1 Institution within the further education sector.	The governing body.
2 University.	The governing body.
3 Institution, other than a university, within the higher education sector.	The governing body.
4 Institution designated under section 28R(6)(c).	The body specified in the order as the responsible body.

2

(1) The bodies responsible for relevant institutions in Scotland are set out in the following table.

(2) In that Table—

'board of management' has the meaning given in section 36(1) of the Further and Higher Education (Scotland) Act 1992 ('the 1992 Act');

'central institution', 'education authority' and 'managers' have the meaning given in section 135(1) of the Education (Scotland) Act 1980; and

'governing body' has the meaning given in section 56(1) of the 1992 Act.

Table

Type of institution	Responsible body
1 Designated institution within the meaning of Part 2 of the 1992 Act.	The governing body.
2 University.	The governing body.
3 College of further education with a board of management.	The board of management.
4 Institution maintained by an education authority in the exercise of their further education functions.	The education authority.
5 Central institution.	The governing body.
6 School in respect of which the managers are for the time being receiving grants under section 73(c) or (d) of the Education (Scotland) Act 1980.	The managers of the school.
7 Institution designated under section 28R(7)(e).	The body specified in the order as the responsible body.

Amendment – Inserted by Special Educational Needs and Disability Act 2001, s 26(2), Sch 4.

Schedule 4C
Modifications of Chapter 2 of Part 4

Section 28U

PART 1
MODIFICATIONS FOR ENGLAND AND WALES—FURTHER EDUCATION, ETC PROVIDED BY LOCAL EDUCATION AUTHORITIES

1

The following is substituted for section 28R—

'28R Higher and further education secured by local education authorities

(1) Subsections (2) and (4) apply in relation to—

    (a)   any course of higher education secured by a local education authority under section 120 of the Education Reform Act 1988', and

    (b)   any course of further education secured by a local education authority.—

(2) It is unlawful for the local education authority to discriminate against a disabled person—

    (a)   in the arrangements they make for determining who should be enrolled on the course;

    (b)   in the terms on which they offer to enrol him on the course; or

    (c)   by refusing or deliberately omitting to accept an application for his enrolment on the course.

(3) It is unlawful for the local education authority to discriminate against a disabled person who has enrolled on the course in the services which they provide, or offer to provide.

(4) It is unlawful for the local education authority to subject to harassment a disabled person who—

    (a)   seeks enrolment on the course,

    (b)   is enrolled on the course, or

    (c)   is a user of any services provided by that authority in relation to the course.

(5) 'Services', in relation to a course, means services of any description which are provided wholly or mainly for persons enrolled on the course.

(6) In relation to further education secured by a local education authority—

    (a)   'course' includes each of the component parts of a course of further education if, in relation to the course, there is no requirement imposed on persons registered for any component part of the course to register for any other component part of that course; and

    (b)   'enrolment', in relation to such a course, includes registration for any one of those parts

(7) In this Chapter—

    'responsible body' means a local education authority in relation to a course of further or higher education secured by them;

    'further education' in relation to a course secured by the local education authority, has the meaning given in section 2(3) of the Education Act 1996;

    'higher education' has the meaning given in section 579(1) of the Education Act 1996; and

    'local education authority' has the meaning given in section 12 of the Education Act 1996.'.'

2

Subsections (1A) to (1D) of section 28T (responsible bodies' duties to make adjustments) are omitted and the following subsection is substituted for subsection (1) of that section—

    '(1)Each responsible body must take such steps as it is reasonable for it to have to take to ensure that —

        (a)   in relation to its arrangements for enrolling persons on a course of further or higher education provided by it, and

        (b)   in relation to services provided, or offered by it,

    disabled persons are not placed at a substantial disadvantage in comparison with persons who are not disabled.'

3

In subsections (2) and (4) of section 28T, for 'any of subsections (1) to (1D)' there is substituted 'subsection (1)'.

4

In section 28W(1)(a) for 'by an educational institution' there is substituted 'by a responsible body wholly or partly for the purpose of its functions

5

Section 31A is omitted

Amendment – Substituted by SI 2006/1721.

PART 1A
MODIFICATIONS FOR ENGLAND AND WALES—FURTHER EDUCATION PROVIDED BY SCHOOLS, ETC

6

The following is substituted for section 28R—

28R Further education provided by schools and recreational or training facilities provided by local education authorities

(1) Subsections (2) and (3) apply in relation to any course of further education provided by the governing body of a maintained school under section 80 of the School Standards and Framework Act 1998.

(2) It is unlawful for the governing body to discriminate against a disabled person—

    (a)   in the arrangements they make for determining who should be enrolled on the course;

    (b)   in the terms on which they offer to enrol him on the course; or

    (c)   by refusing or deliberately omitting to accept an application for his enrolment on the course.

(3) It is unlawful for the governing body to discriminate against a disabled person who has enrolled on the course in the services which they provide or offer to provide.

(4) 'Services', in relation to a course, means services of any description which are provided wholly or mainly for persons enrolled on the course.

(5) It is unlawful for a local education authority to discriminate against a disabled person in the terms on which they provide or offer to provide recreational or training facilities.

(6) In this Chapter—

'Responsible body' means—

    (a)   the governing body of a maintained school, in relation to a course of further education provided under section 80 of the School Standards and Framework Act 1998, and

    (b)   a local education authority in relation to recreational or training facilities;

'Further education', in relation to a course provided under section 80 of the School Standards and Framework Act 1998, means education of a kind mentioned in subsection (1) of that section;

'Local education authority' has the meaning given in section 12 of the Education Act 1996;

'Governing Body' and 'maintained school' have the same meaning as in Chapter 1;

'Recreational or training facilities' means—

(a) in the case of a local education authority in England, any facilities secured by the authority under section 507A or 507B of the Education Act 1996 (functions of local education authorities in England in respect of recreation etc), and

(b) in the case of a local education authority in Wales, any facilities secured by the authority under subsection (1), or provided by them under subsection (1A), of section 508 of that Act (functions of local education authorities in Wales in respect of recreation and social and physical training).'

7

In section 28S (meaning of 'discrimination'), the following subsection is substituted for subsection (2)—

'(2) For the purposes of section 28R, a responsible body also discriminates against a disabled person if—

(a) it fails, to his detriment, to comply with section 28T; and

(b) it cannot show that its failure to comply is justified.'

8

In section 28S, the following subsections are substituted for subsections (5) to (11)—

'(5) Subsections (6) to (9) apply in determining whether for the purposes of this section—

(a) less favourable treatment of a person, or

(b) failure to comply with section 28T,

is justified.

(6) Less favourable treatment of a person is justified if it is necessary in order to maintain—

(a) academic standards; or

(b) standards of any other prescribed kind.

(7) Less favourable treatment is also justified if—

(a) it is of a prescribed kind;

(b) it occurs in prescribed circumstances; or

(c) it is of a prescribed kind and occurs in prescribed circumstances.

(8) Otherwise less favourable treatment, or a failure to comply with section 28T, is justified only if the reason for it is both material to the circumstances of the particular case and substantial.

(9) If, in a case falling within subsection (1)—

(a) the responsible body is under a duty imposed by section 28T in relation to the disabled person, but

(b) fails without justification to comply with that duty,

its treatment of that person cannot be justified under subsection (8) unless that treatment would have been justified even if it had complied with that duty.'.

9

Subsections (1A) to (1D) of section 28T (responsible bodies' duties to make adjustments) are omitted and the following subsection is substituted for subsection (1) of that section—

'(1) Each responsible body must take such steps as it is reasonable for it to have to take to ensure that—

(a) in relation to its arrangements for enrolling persons on a course of further education provided by it, and

(b) in relation to services provided or offered by it,

disabled persons are not placed at a substantial disadvantage in comparison with persons who are not disabled.'.

10

In subsections (2) and (4) of section 28T, for 'any of subsections (1) to (1D)' there is substituted 'subsection (1)'.

11

In section 28W(1)(a) for 'by an educational institution' there is substituted 'by a responsible body wholly or partly for the purpose of its functions'.

12

Sections 28SA, 28UA, 28UB, 28UC, 28V(1A) and 31A are omitted.

Amendment – Substituted by SI 2006/1721.

PART 2
MODIFICATIONS FOR SCOTLAND—FURTHER EDUCATION

13

The following is substituted for section 28R—

'**28R Further education etc provided by education authorities in Scotland**

(1) Subsections (2) and (3) apply to any course of further education secured by an education authority.

(2) It is unlawful for the education authority to discriminate against a disabled person—

(a) in the arrangements they make for determining who should be enrolled on the course;

(b) in the terms on which they offer to enrol him on the course; or

(c) by refusing or deliberately omitting to accept an application for his enrolment on the course.

(3) It is unlawful for the education authority to discriminate against a disabled person who has enrolled on the course in the services which they provide, or offer to provide.

(4) It is unlawful for the education authority to subject to harassment a disabled person who—

(a) seeks enrolment on a course offered by that authority,

(b) is enrolled on a course offered by that authority, or

(c) is a user of services provided by that authority

(5) 'Services', in relation to a course, means services of any description which are provided wholly or mainly for persons enrolled on the course.

It is unlawful for an education authority to discriminate against a disabled person in the terms on which they provide, or offer to provide, recreational or training facilities.

(6) In this Chapter—

'responsible body' means an education authority.

'Further education' has the meaning given in section 1(5) of the Education (Scotland) Act 1980.

'Education authority' has the meaning given in section 135(1) of that Act.'

14

Subsections (1A) to (1D) of section 28T are omitted and the following subsection is substituted for subsection (1) of that section—

'(1) Each responsible body must take such steps as it is reasonable for it to have to take to ensure that—

(a) in relation to its arrangements for enrolling persons on a course of further education provided by it, and

(b) in relation to services provided or offered by it,

disabled persons are not placed at a substantial disadvantage in comparison with persons who are not disabled.'

15

In subsections (2) and (4) of section 28T, for 'any of subsections (1) to (1D)' there is substituted 'subsection (1)'.

16

In section 28W(1)(a) for 'by an educational institution' there is substituted 'by a responsible body wholly or partly for the purpose of its functions

17

Section 31A is omitted.

Amendment – Schedule inserted by Special Educational Needs and Disability Act 2001, s 29(2), Sch 5; substituted by SI 2006/1721.

PART 2A
MODIFICATIONS FOR SCOTLAND—RECREATIONAL OR TRAINING FACILITIES

18

The following is substituted for section 28R—

28R Recreational or training facilities provided by education authorities

(1) It is unlawful for an education authority to discriminate against a disabled person in the terms on which they provide, or offer to provide, recreational or training facilities.

(2) In this Chapter—

'Responsible body' means an education authority;
'Education authority' has the meaning given in section 135(1) of the Education (Scotland) Act 1980.'.

19

In section 28S (Meaning of 'discrimination'), the following subsection is substituted for subsection (2)—

'(2) For the purposes of section 28R, a responsible body also discriminates against a disabled person if—

    (a)   it fails, to his detriment, to comply with section 28T; and
    (b)   it cannot show that its failure to comply is justified.'.

20

In section 28S (Meaning of 'discrimination'), the following subsections are substituted for subsections (5) to (11)—

'(5) Subsections (6) to (9) apply in determining whether for the purposes of this section—

    (a)   less favourable treatment of a person, or
    (b)   failure to comply with section 28T,

is justified.

(6) Less favourable treatment of a person is justified if it is necessary in order to maintain—

    (a)   academic standards; or
    (b)   standards of any other prescribed kind.

(7) Less favourable treatment is also justified if—

    (a)   it is of a prescribed kind;
    (b)   it occurs in prescribed circumstances; or
    (c)   it is of a prescribed kind and occurs in prescribed circumstances.

(8) Otherwise less favourable treatment, or a failure to comply with section 28T, is justified only if the reason for it is both material to the circumstances of the particular case and substantial.

(9) If, in a case falling within subsection (1)—

    (a)   the responsible body is under a duty imposed by section 28T in relation to the disabled person, but
    (b)   fails without justification to comply with that duty,

its treatment of that person cannot be justified under subsection (8) unless that treatment would have been justified even if it had complied with that duty.'

21

Subsections (1A) to (1D) of section 28T are omitted and the following subsection is substituted for subsection (1) of that section—

'(1) Each responsible body must take such steps as it is reasonable for it to have to take to ensure that, in relation to services provided or offered by it for any recreational or training facilities, disabled persons are not placed at a substantial disadvantage in comparison with persons who are not disabled.'.

22

In subsections (2) and (4) of section 28T, for 'any of subsections (1) to (1D)' there is substituted 'subsection (1)'.

23

In section 28W(1)(a) for 'by an educational institution' there is substituted 'by a responsible body wholly or partly for the purpose of its functions'.

24

Sections 28SA, 28UA, 28UB, 28UC, 28V(1A) and 31A are omitted.

Amendment – Inserted by SI 2006/1721.

Schedule 5

(repealed)

Amendment – Repealed by Disability Rights Commission Act 1999, s 14(2), Sch 5.

Schedule 6
Consequential Amendments

Section 70(4)

1–3 *(repealed)*

Companies Act 1985 (c. 6)

4

In paragraph 9 of Schedule 7 to the Companies Act 1985 (disclosure in directors' report of company policy in relation to disabled persons), in the definition of 'disabled person' in sub-paragraph (4)(b), for 'Disabled Persons (Employment) Act 1944' substitute 'Disability Discrimination Act 1995'.

Local Government and Housing Act 1989 (c. 42)

5

In section 7 of the Local Government and Housing Act 1989 (all staff of a local authority etc to be appointed on merit), in subsection (2)—

(a)   paragraph (a) shall be omitted;
(b)   the word 'and' at the end of paragraph (d) shall be omitted; and
(c)   after paragraph (e) insert—

'; and
(f)   sections 5 and 6 of the Disability Discrimination Act 1995 (meaning of discrimination and duty to make adjustments).'

Enterprise and New Towns (Scotland) Act 1990 (c. 35)

6

In section 16 of the Enterprise and New Towns (Scotland) Act 1990 (duty of certain Scottish bodies to give preference to ex-service men and women in exercising powers to select disabled persons for training), in subsection (2), for 'said Act of 1944' substitute 'Disability Discrimination Act 1995'.

Amendments – Amended by Employment Rights Act 1996, s 242, Sch 3, Pt I; Employment Tribunals Act 1996, s 45, Sch 3, Pt I; Employment Rights (Northern Ireland) Order 1996, SI 1996/1919 (NI 16), art 257, Sch 3. Repealed in part by the Companies Act 2006, s 1300(2).

Schedule 7
Repeals

Section 70(5)

Chapter	Short title	Extent of repeal
7 & 8 Geo. 6 c. 10.	The Disabled Persons (Employment) Act 1944.	Section 1.
		Sections 6 to 14.
		Section 19.
		Section 21.
		Section 22(4).
6 & 7 Eliz. 2 c. 33.	The Disabled Persons (Employment) Act 1958.	Section 2.
1970 c. 44.	The Chronically Sick and Disabled Persons Act 1970.	Section 16.
1978 c. 44.	The Employment Protection (Consolidation) Act 1978.	In Schedule 13, in paragraph 20(3), the word 'or' in the definitions of 'relevant complaint of dismissal' and 'relevant conciliation powers'.
1989 c. 42.	The Local Government and Housing Act 1989.	In section 7(2), paragraph (a) and the word 'and' at the end of paragraph (d).
1993 c. 62.	The Education Act 1993.	In section 161(5), the words from 'and in this subsection' to the end.

Schedule 8
Modifications of this Act in its Application to Northern Ireland

Section 70(6)

1

In its application to Northern Ireland this Act shall have effect subject to the following modifications.

2

(1) *In section 3(1) for 'Secretary of State' substitute 'Department'.*[1]

(2) In section 3 for subsections (4) to (12) substitute—

'(4) In preparing a draft of any guidance, the Department shall consult such persons as it considers appropriate.

(5) Where the Department proposes to issue any guidance, the Department shall publish a draft of it, consider any representations that are made to the Department about the draft and, if the Department thinks it appropriate, modify its proposals in the light of any of those representations.

(6) If the Department decides to proceed with any proposed guidance, the Department shall lay a draft of it before the Assembly.

(7) If, within the statutory period, the Assembly resolves not to approve the draft, the Department shall take no further steps in relation to the proposed guidance.

(8) If no such resolution is made within the statutory period, the Department shall issue the guidance in the form of its draft.

(9) The guidance shall come into force on such date as the Department may by order appoint.

(10) Subsection (7) does not prevent a new draft of the proposed guidance being laid before the Assembly.

(11) The Department may—

    (a)   from time to time revise the whole or any part of any guidance and re-issue it;

    (b)   by order revoke any guidance.

(12) In this section—

'the Department' means the Office of the First Minister and Deputy First Minister;
'guidance' means guidance issued by the Department under this section and includes guidance which has been revised and re-issued;
'statutory period' has the meaning assigned to it by section 41(2) of the Interpretation Act (Northern Ireland) 1954.'

3

In section 4(6) for 'Great Britain' substitute 'Northern Ireland'.

4

(1) In section 7(2) for 'Secretary of State' substitute 'Office of the First Minister and Deputy First Minister'.

(2) In section 7(4) to (10) for 'Secretary of State' wherever it occurs substitute 'Office of the First Minister and Deputy First Minister', for 'he' and 'him' wherever they occur substitute 'it' and for 'his' wherever it occurs substitute 'its'.

(3) In section 7(9) for 'Parliament' substitute 'the Assembly'.

5

(1) In section 8(3) omit 'or (in Scotland) in reparation'.

(2) In section 8(7) for 'paragraph 6A of Schedule 9 to the Employment Protection (Consolidation) Act 1978' substitute 'Article 16 of the Industrial Tribunals (Northern Ireland) Order 1996'.

6

(1) In section 9(2)(a) for 'a conciliation officer' substitute 'the Agency'.

(2) In section 9(4) in the definition of 'qualified lawyer' for the words from 'means' to the end substitute 'means a barrister (whether in practice as such or employed to give legal advice) or a solicitor of the Supreme Court who holds a practising certificate.'.

7

(1) In section 10(1)(b) omit 'or recognised body'.

(2) In section 10(2)(b) for 'Secretary of State' substitute 'Department of Higher and Further Education, Training and Employment'.

(3) In section 10(3) in the definition of 'charity' for '1993' substitute '(Northern Ireland) 1964', omit the definition of 'recognised body' and in the definition of 'supported employment' for 'Act 1944' substitute 'Act (Northern Ireland) 1945'.

(4) In section 10(4) for 'England and Wales' where it twice occurs substitute 'Northern Ireland'.

(5) Omit section 10(5).

8

In section 12(5) for 'Great Britain' where it twice occurs substitute 'Northern Ireland'.

9

(1) In section 19(3)(g) for 'section 2 of the Employment and Training Act 1973' substitute 'sections 1 and 2 of the Employment and Training Act (Northern Ireland) 1950'.

(2) (*repealed*)

(3) (*repealed*)

10

In section 20(7) for paragraphs (b) and (c) substitute '; or

    (b)   functions conferred by or under Part VIII of the Mental Health (Northern Ireland) Order 1986 are exercisable in relation to a disabled person's property or affairs.'

11

In section 22(4) and (6) omit 'or (in Scotland) the subject of'.

12

(1) In section 25(1) omit 'or (in Scotland) in reparation'.

(2) In section 25(3) for 'England and Wales' substitute 'Northern Ireland'.

(3) Omit section 25(4).

(4) In section 25(5) omit the words from 'or' to the end.

13

In section 26(3) omit 'or a sheriff court'.

14

(1) In section 28 for 'Secretary of State' wherever it occurs substitute 'Office of the First Minister and Deputy First Minister'.

(2) In section 28(3) and (4) for 'he' substitute 'it'.

(3) In section 28(5) for 'Treasury' substitute 'Department of Finance and Personnel in Northern Ireland'.

15

Omit sections 29, 30 and 31.

16

(1) In section 32(1) for 'Secretary of State' substitute 'Department of the Environment'.

(2) In section 32(5) for the definition of 'taxi' substitute—

    "taxi' means a vehicle which—
        (a)   is licensed under Article 61 of the Road Traffic (Northern Ireland) Order 1981 to stand or ply for hire; and
        (b)   seats not more than 8 passengers in addition to the driver'.

17

In section 33, for 'Secretary of State', wherever it occurs, substitute 'Department of the Environment'.

18

For section 34 substitute—

> **'34 New licences conditional on compliance with accessibility taxi regulations**
>
> (1) The Department of the Environment shall not grant a public service vehicle licence under Article 61 of the Road Traffic (Northern Ireland) Order 1981 for a taxi unless the vehicle conforms with those provisions of the taxi accessibility regulations with which it will be required to confirm if licensed.
>
> (2) Subsection (1) does not apply if such a licence was in force with respect to the vehicle at any time during the period of 28 days immediately before the day on which the licence is granted.
>
> (3) The Department of the Environment may by order provide for subsection (2) to cease to have effect on such date as may be specified in the order.'

19

Omit section 35.

20

In section 36(7) for 'licensing authority' substitute 'Department of the Environment'.

21

(1) In section 37(5) and (6) for 'licensing authority' substitute 'Department of the Environment'.

(2) In section 37(9) for 'Secretary of State' substitute 'Department of the Environment'.

21A

(1) In section 37A(5) and (6) for 'licensing authority' substitute 'Department of the Environment'.

(2) In section 37A(9) for the definitions of 'driver', 'licensing authority', 'operator' and 'private hire vehicle' substitute—

> 'driver' means a person who holds a taxi driver's licence under Article 79A of the Road Traffic (Northern Ireland) Order 1981;

'operator' means a person who in the course of a business makes provision for the invitation or acceptance of bookings for a private hire vehicle;

'private hire vehicle' means a vehicle which—

    (a)   seats not more than 8 passengers in addition to the driver; and

    (b)   is licensed under Article 61 of the Road Traffic (Northern Ireland) Order 1981 to carry passengers for hire (but not to stand or ply for hire)'.

22

(1) In section 38(1) for 'a licensing authority' substitute 'the Department of the Environment'.

(2) In section 38(2) for 'licensing authority concerned' substitute 'Department of the Environment'.

(3) In section 38(3) for the words from 'the magistrates' court' to the end substitute 'a court of summary jurisdiction acting for the petty sessions district in which the aggrieved person resides'.

23

Omit section 39.

24

(1) In section 40 for 'Secretary of State' wherever it occurs substitute 'Department of the Environment'.

(2) In section 40(5) for the definition of 'public service vehicle' substitute—

    "public service vehicle' means a vehicle which—

    (a)   seats more than 8 passengers in addition to the driver; and

    (b)   is a public service vehicle for the purposes of the Road Traffic (Northern Ireland) Order 1981;'.

(3) In section 40(7) for the words for 'the Disabled' to the end substitute 'such representative organisations as it thinks fit'.

25

(1) In section 41(2) for 'Secretary of State' substitute 'Department of the Environment'.

(2) In section 41 for subsections (3) and (4) substitute—

'(3) Any person who uses a regulated public service vehicle in contravention of this section is guilty of an offence and liable on summary conviction to a fine not exceeding level 4 on the standard scale.'.

26

(1) In section 42 for 'Secretary of State' wherever it occurs substitute 'Department of the Environment'.

(2) In section 42(1) for 'he' substitute 'it'.

(3) In section 42(6) for 'his' substitute 'its'.

27

In section 43 for 'Secretary of State' wherever it occurs substitute 'Department of the Environment'.

28

(1) In section 44 for 'Secretary of State' wherever it occurs substitute 'Department of the Environment'.

(2) In section 44(2) for 'him' substitute 'it'.

(3) In section 44(6) for 'he' substitute 'it' and for 'his' substitute 'its'.

29

(1) In section 45 for 'Secretary of State' wherever it occurs substitute 'Department of the Environment'.

(2) In section 45(2) for 'him' substitute 'it' and at the end add 'of Northern Ireland'.

(3)nIn section 45(4) for 'he' substitute 'it'.

30

(1) In section 46 for 'Secretary of State' wherever it occurs substitute 'Department for Regional Development'.

(2) In section 46(6) in the definition of 'rail vehicle' for the words 'on any railway, tramway or prescribed system' substitute 'by rail'.

(3) Omit section 46(7).

(4) In section 46(11) for the words from 'the Disabled' to the end substitute 'such representative organisations as it thinks fit'.

31

(1) In section 47 for 'Secretary of State' wherever it occurs substitute 'Department for Regional Development'.

(2) In section 47(3) for the words 'the Disabled Persons Transport Advisory Committee and such other persons as he' substitute 'such persons as it' and for 'he' substitute 'it'.

32

Omit section 48(3).

33

(1) In sections 50 to 52 for 'the Council' substitute, in each place, the 'Equality Commission for Northern Ireland'.

(1A) Section 50(1) shall have no effect.

(2) In section 50(2) for 'Secretary of State' in the first place where it occurs substitute 'a Northern Ireland department' and in the other place where it occurs substitute 'that department'.

(3) In section 50(3) for 'Secretary of State' substitute 'Office of the First Minister and Deputy First Minister'.

(4) In section 50(7) for 'Secretary of State' substitute 'a Northern Ireland department' and after 'Crown' insert 'or a Northern Ireland department'.

(5) In section 50(9)(a) for sub-paragraphs (i) to (iv) substitute—

'(i)		the Disabled Persons (Employment) Act (Northern Ireland) 1945;
(ii)		the Contracts of Employment and Redundancy Payments Act (Northern Ireland) 1965;
(iii)		the Employment and Training Act (Northern Ireland) 1950;
(iv)		the Employment Rights (Northern Ireland) Order 1996; or'.

(6) In section 50(10) for the words from 'time when' to the end substitute 'time when—

(a) there are no committees in existence under section 17 of the Disabled Persons (Employment) Act (Northern Ireland) 1945; and

(b) there is no person appointed to act generally under section 60(1) of this Act.'.

34

(1) In section 51(1) for 'the Secretary of State' substitute 'any Northern Ireland department' and for 'the Secretary of State's' substitute 'that department's'.

(2) In section 51(2) for 'The Secretary of State' substitute 'A Northern Ireland department'.

(3) In section 51(4) for 'a county court or a sheriff court' substitute 'or a county court'.

(4) In section 51(6) for 'the Secretary of State' substitute 'a Northern Ireland department'.

35

For section 52 substitute—

'52 Further provisions about codes issued under section 51

(1) In this section—

'proposal' means a proposal made by the Equality Commission for Northern Ireland to a Northern Ireland department under section 51;

'responsible department'—

    (a)   in relation to a proposal, means the Northern Ireland department to which the proposal is made,

    (b)   in relation to a code, means the Northern Ireland department by which the code is issued; and

'statutory period' has the meaning assigned to it by section 41(2) of the Interpretation Act (Northern Ireland) 1954.

(2) In preparing any proposal, the Equality Commission for Northern Ireland shall consult—

    (a)   such persons (if any) as the responsible department has specified in making its request to the Equality Commission for Northern Ireland; and

    (b)   such other persons (if any) as the Equality Commission for Northern Ireland considers appropriate.

(3) Before making any proposal the Equality Commission for Northern Ireland shall publish a draft, consider any representations made to it about the draft and, if it thinks it appropriate, modify its proposal in the light of any of those representations.

(4) Where the Equality Commission for Northern Ireland makes any proposal, the responsible department may—

    (a)   approve it;

    (b)   approve it subject to such modifications as that department thinks appropriate; or

    (c)   refuse to approve it.

(5) Where the responsible department approves any proposal (with or without modifications) that department shall prepare a draft of the proposed code and lay it before the Assembly.

(6) If, within the statutory period, the Assembly resolves not to approve the draft, the responsible department shall take no further steps in relation to the proposed code.

(7) If no such resolution is made within the statutory period, the responsible department shall issue the code in the form of its draft.

(8) The code shall come into force on such date as the responsible department may appoint by order.

(9) Subsection (6) does not prevent a new draft of the proposed code from being laid before the Assembly.

(10) If the responsible department refuses to approve a proposal, that department shall give the Council a written statement of the department's reasons for not approving it.

(11) The responsible department may by order revoke a code.'

36

(1) In section 53 for 'Secretary of State' wherever it occurs substitute 'Office of the First Minister and Deputy First Minister'.

(2) In section 53(1) for 'he' substitute 'it'.

(3) In section 53(3) for 'a county court or a sheriff court' substitute 'or a county court'.

37

For section 54 substitute—

'54 Further provisions about codes issued under section 53

(1) In preparing a draft of any code under section 53, the Department shall consult such organisations representing the interests of employers or of disabled persons in, or seeking, employment as the Department considers appropriate.

(2) Where the Department proposes to issue a code, the Department shall publish a draft of the code, consider any representations that are made to the Department about the draft and, if the Department thinks it appropriate, modify its proposals in the light of any of those representations.

(3) If the Department decides to proceed with the code, the Department shall lay a draft of it before the Assembly.

(4) If, within the statutory period, the Assembly resolves not to approve the draft, the Department shall take no further steps in relation to the proposed code.

(5) If no such resolution is made within the statutory period, the Department shall issue the code in the form of its draft.

(6) The code shall come into force on such date as the Department may appoint by order.

(7) Subsection (4) does not prevent a new draft of the proposed code from being laid before the Assembly.

(8) The Department may by order revoke a code.

(9) In this section—

'the Department' means the Office of the First Minister and Deputy
First Minister; and

'statutory period' has the meaning assigned to it by section 41(2) of the
Interpretation Act (Northern Ireland) 1954.'

38

In section 56(2) and (4) for 'Secretary of State' substitute 'Office of the
First Minister and Deputy First Minister'.

39

In section 59(1) after 'Crown' where it twice occurs insert 'or a Northern
Ireland department'.

40

(1) In section 60(1) to (3) for 'Secretary of State' wherever it occurs
substitute 'Office of the First Minister and Deputy First Minister' and for
'he' and 'him' wherever they occur substitute 'it'.

(2) In section 60(4) for 'Treasury' substitute 'Department of Finance and
Personnel in Northern Ireland'.

(3) For section 60(6) substitute—

'(6) The Office of the First Minister and Deputy First Minister may
by order repeal section 17 of, and Schedule 2 to, the Disabled
Persons (Employment) Act (Northern Ireland) 1945 (district
advisory committees).'

(4) In section 60(7) omit 'paragraph (b) of', for '1944' substitute '1945'
and omit 'in each case'.

(5) In section 60, omit subsection (8).

41

For section 61 substitute—

**'61 Amendments of Disabled Persons (Employment) Act (Northern
Ireland) 1945**

(1) Section 15 of the Disabled Persons (Employment) Act
(Northern Ireland) 1945 (which gives the Office of the First Minister
and Deputy First Minister power to make arrangements for the
provision of supported employment) is amended as set out in
subsection (2) to (5).

(2) In subsection (1)—

   (a)   for 'persons registered as handicapped by disablement'
           substitute 'disabled persons';
   (b)   for 'their disablement' substitute 'their disability'; and

(c)   for 'are not subject to disablement' substitute 'do not have a disability'.

(3) In subsection (2) for the words from 'any of one or more companies' to 'so required and prohibited' substitute 'any company, association or body'.

(4) After subsection (2) insert—

'(2A) The only kind of company which the Department itself may form in exercising its powers under this section is a company which is—

(a)   required by its constitution to apply its profits, if any, or other income in promoting its objects; and

(b)   prohibited by its constitution from paying any dividend to its members.'

(5) After subsection (5) insert—

'(5A) For the purposes of this section—

(a)   a person is a disabled person if he is a disabled person for the purposes of the Disability Discrimination Act 1995; and

(b)   'disability' has the same meaning as in that Act.'

(6) The provisions of section 16 of the Act of 1945 (preference to be given under section 15 of that Act to ex-service men and women) shall become subsection (1) of that section and at the end insert—

'and whose disability is due to that service.

(2) For the purposes of subsection (1) of this section, a disabled person's disability shall be treated as due to service of a particular kind only in such circumstances as may be prescribed.'

(7) The following provisions of the Act of 1945 shall cease to have effect—

(a)   section 1 (definition of 'disabled person');

(b)   sections 2 to 4 (training for disabled persons);

(c)   sections 6 to 8 (the register of disabled persons);

(d)   sections 9 to 11 (obligations on employers with substantial staffs to employ quota of registered persons);

(e)   section 12 (the designated employment scheme for persons registered as handicapped by disablement);

(f)   section 13 (interpretation of provisions repealed by this Act);

(g)   section 14 (records to be kept by employer);

(h)   section 19 (proceedings in relation to offences);

(j)   sections 21 and 22 (supplementary).

(8) Any statutory provision in which 'disabled person' is defined by reference to the Act of 1945 shall be construed as if that expression had the same meaning as in this Act.'

42

(*repealed*)

43

Omit section 63.

44

(1) In section 64(3) for 'England and Wales' substitute 'Northern Ireland'.

(2) Omit section 64(4).

(3) In section 64(5)(a) omit the words from ', the British' to the end.

(4) In section 64(8)—

    (a)   omit the definitions of 'British Transport Police', 'Royal Parks Constabulary' and 'United Kingdom Atomic Energy Authority Constabulary';

    (b)   in the definition of 'the 1947 Act' at the end add 'as it applies both in relation to the Crown in right of Her Majesty's Government in Northern Ireland and in relation to the Crown in right of Her Majesty's Government in the United Kingdom';

    (c)   in the definition of 'fire brigade' for the words from 'means' to the end substitute 'has the same meaning as in the Fire Services (Northern Ireland) Order 1984';

    (d)   in the definition of 'prison officer' for the words from 'means' to the end substitute 'means any individual who holds any post, otherwise than as a medical officer, to which he has been appointed under section 2(2) of the Prison Act (Northern Ireland) 1953 or who is a prison custody officer within the meaning of Chapter III of Part VIII of the Criminal Justice and Public Order Act 1994';

    (e)   in the definition of 'service for purposes of a Minister of the Crown or government department' at the end add 'or service as the head of a Northern Ireland department'.

45

Omit section 65.

46

For section 67 substitute—

'67 Regulations and orders etc

(1) Any power under this Act to make regulations or orders shall be exercisable by statutory rule for the purposes of the Statutory Rules (Northern Ireland) Order 1979.

(2) Any such power may be exercised to make different provision for different cases, including different provision for different areas or localities.

(3) Any such power, includes power—

(a)   to make such incidental, supplementary, consequential or transitional provision as appears to the Northern Ireland department exercising the power to be expedient; and

(b)   to provide for a person to exercise a discretion in dealing with any matter.

(4) No order shall be made under section 50(3) unless a draft of the order has been laid before and approved by a resolution of the Assembly.

(5) Any other order made under this Act, other than an order under section 3(9), 52(8), 54(6) or 70(3), and any regulations made under this Act shall be subject to negative resolution within the meaning of section 41(6) of the Interpretation Act (Northern Ireland) 1954 as if they were statutory instruments within the meaning of that Act.

(6) Section 41(3) of the Interpretation Act (Northern Ireland) 1954 shall apply in relation to any instrument or document which by virtue of this Act is required to be laid before the Assembly as if it were a statutory instrument or statutory document within the meaning of that Act.

(7) Subsection (1) does not require an order under section 43 which applies only to a specified vehicle, or to vehicles of a specified person, to be made by statutory rule.

(8) Nothing in section 40(6) or 46(5) affects the powers conferred by subsections (2) and (3).'

47

(1) For section 68(1) substitute—

'(1) In this Act—

'accessibility certificate' means a certificate issued under section 41(1)(a);
'act' includes a deliberate omission;
'the Agency' means the Labour Relations Agency;
'approval certificate' means a certificate issued under section 42(4);
'the Assembly' means the Northern Ireland Assembly;

'benefits', in Part II, has the meaning given in section 4(4);

'the Department of Economic Development' means the Office of the First Minister and Deputy First Minister in Northern Ireland;

'the Department of the Environment' means the Department of the Environment for Northern Ireland;

'the Department of Health and Social Services' means the Office of the First Minister and Deputy First Minister for Northern Ireland;

'employment' means, subject to any prescribed provision, employment under a contract of service or of apprenticeship or a contract personally to do work and related expressions are to be construed accordingly;

'employment at an establishment in Northern Ireland' is to be construed in accordance with subsections (2) to (5);

'enactment' means any statutory provision within the meaning of section 1(f) of the Interpretation Act (Northern Ireland) 1954;

'government department' means a Northern Ireland department or a department of the Government of the United Kingdom;

'Minister of the Crown' includes the Treasury;

'Northern Ireland department' includes (except in sections 51 and 52) the head of a Northern Ireland department;

'occupational pension scheme' has the same meaning as in the Pension Schemes (Northern Ireland) Act 1993;

'premises', includes land of any description;

'prescribed' means prescribed by regulations;

'profession' includes any vocation or occupation;

'provider of services' has the meaning given in section 19(2)(b);

'public service vehicle' and 'regulated public service vehicle' have the meaning given in section 40;

'PSV accessibility regulations' means regulations made under section 40(1);

'rail vehicle' and 'regulated rail vehicle' have the meaning given in section 46;

'rail vehicle accessibility regulations' means regulations made under section 46(1);

'regulations' means—

(a)   in Parts I and II of this Act, section 66, the definition of 'employment' above and subsections (3) and (4) below, regulations made by the Department of Economic Development;

(b)   in Part V of this Act, regulations made by the Department of the Environment;

(c)   in any other provision of this Act, regulations made by the Department of Health and Social Services;

'section 6 duty' means any duty imposed by or under section 6;

'section 15 duty' means any duty imposed by or under section 15;

'section 21 duty' means any duty imposed by or under section 21;

'taxi' and 'regulated taxi' have the meaning given in section 32;

'taxi accessibility regulations' means regulations made under section 32(1);

'trade' includes any business;

'trade organisation' has the meaning given in section 13;

'vehicle examiner' means an officer of the Department of the Environment authorised by that Department for the purposes of sections 41 and 42.'.

(2) In section 68—

   (a)   for subsection (2) substitute—

   '(2) Where an employee does his work wholly outside Northern Ireland, his employment is not to be treated as being work at an establishment in Northern Ireland.'; and

   (b)   in subsections (3) and (4) for 'Great Britain' wherever it occurs substitute

   'Northern Ireland'.

48

(1) In section 70(3) for 'Secretary of State' substitute 'Office of the First Minister and Deputy First Minister'.

(2) In section 70(8) for 'the Secretary of State' substitute 'a Northern Ireland department' and for 'him' substitute 'it'.

49

(1) In Schedule 1 in paragraph 7(1) for 'Act 1944' substitute 'Act (Northern Ireland) 1945'.

(2) In Schedule 1 in paragraph 7(7) for '1944' substitute '1945'.

50

(1) (*repealed*)

(2) In Schedule 3 for paragraph 4(1) substitute—

   '(1) In any proceedings under section 8—

   (a)   a certificate signed by or on behalf of a Minister of the Crown or a Northern Ireland department and certifying that any conditions or requirements specified in the certificate were imposed by that Minister or that department (as the case may be) and were in operation at a time or throughout a time so specified; or
   (b)   a certificate signed by or on behalf of the Secretary of State and certifying that an act specified in the certificate was done for the purpose of safeguarding national security,

   shall be conclusive evidence of the matters certified.'.

(3) In Schedule 3 in paragraph 6(1) omit 'or a sheriff court'.

(4) In Schedule 3 for paragraph 8(1) substitute—

'(1) In any proceedings under section 25—

    (a) a certificate signed by or on behalf of a Minister of the Crown or a Northern Ireland department and certifying that any conditions or requirements specified in the certificate were imposed by that Minister or that department (as the case may be) and were in operation at a time or throughout a time so specified; or

    (b) a certificate signed by or on behalf of the Secretary of State and certifying that an act specified in the certificate was done for the purpose of safeguarding national security,

shall be conclusive evidence of the matters certified.'

51

(1) In Schedule 4 in paragraphs 2(1) and (5) and 7(1) and (5) omit 'or sisted'.

(2) In Schedule 4 in paragraph 4 for 'Secretary of State' substitute 'Office of the First Minister and Deputy First Minister'.

(3) In Schedule 4 in paragraph 6(1) omit 'or, in Scotland, to the sheriff'.

(4) In Schedule 4 omit paragraph 6(2).

(5) In Schedule 4 in paragraph 9 for 'Secretary of State' substitute 'Office of the First Minister and Deputy First Minister'.

52

(1) Schedule 5, except paragraph 7(a) to (c), shall have no effect.

(2) In paragraph 7(a) to (c), for 'Secretary of State' wherever it occurs substitute 'Department of Health and Social Services'.

53

For Schedules 6 and 7 substitute—

Schedule 6
Consequential Amendments

The Industrial Relations (Northern Ireland) Order 1976 (NI 16)

1

In Article 68(6) of the Industrial Relations (Northern Ireland) Order 1976 (reinstatement or re-engagement of dismissed employees)—

(a) in the definition of 'relevant complaint of dismissal', omit 'or' and at the end insert 'or a complaint under section 8 of the Disability Discrimination Act 1995 arising out of a dismissal';

(b) in the definition of 'relevant conciliation powers' omit 'or' and at the end insert 'or paragraph 1 of Schedule 3 to the Disability Discrimination Act 1995';

(c) in the definition of 'relevant compromise contract' for 'or Article' substitute 'Article' and at the end insert 'or section 9(2) of the Disability Discrimination Act 1995'.

The Companies (Northern Ireland) Order 1986 (NI 6)

3

In paragraph 9 of Schedule 7 to the Companies (Northern Ireland) Order 1986 (disclosure in directors' report of company policy in relation to disabled persons) in the definition of 'disabled person' in sub-paragraph (4)(b) for 'Disabled Persons (Employment) Act (Northern Ireland) 1945' substitute 'Disability Discrimination Act 1995'.

Schedule 7
Repeals

Chapter	Short Title	Extent of repeal
1945 c. 6 (N.I.)	The Disabled Persons (Employment) Act (Northern Ireland) 1945.	Sections 1 to 4.
		Sections 6 to 14.
		In section 16 the words 'vocational training and industrial rehabilitation courses and', the words 'courses and' and the words from 'and in selecting' to 'engagement'.
		Section 19.
		Section 21.
		Section 22.
1960 c. 4 (N.I.)	The Disabled Persons (Employment) Act (Northern Ireland) 1960.	The whole Act.

Chapter	Short Title	Extent of repeal
1976 NI16	The Industrial Relations (Northern Ireland) Order 1976.	In Article 68(6) the word 'or' in the definitions of 'relevant complaint of dismissal' and 'relevant conciliation powers'.

Amendments—Amended by Employment Rights(Northern Ireland) Order 1996, SI 1996/1919 (NI 16), art 255, Sch 1; Industrial Tribunals (Northern Ireland) Order 1996, SI 1996/1921 (NI 18), arts 26, 28 (1), Sch 1, para 12, Sch 3; Northern Ireland Act 1988, s 99, Sch 13, para 16; Departments Transfer and Assignment of Functions) Order (Northern Ireland) 1999, SR 1999/481, arts 4, 6(d), 8(a), Schs 2, 4, 6:Equal Opportunities (Employment Legislation) (Territorial Limits) Regulations (Northern Ireland)2000, SR 200/8, reg 3.Prospectively amended in relation to Northern Ireland by Employment Rughts (Dispute Resolution) (Northern Ireland) Order 1998, SI 1998/1265 (N18), art 16, Sch 2.

[1] Sub—paragraph prospectively repealed by Disability Discrimination (Northern Ireland) Order 2006, SI 2006/312, art 19, Sch 1, as from a day to be appointed.

[2] Paragraph prospectively inserted by Private Hire Vehicles (Carriage of Guide Dogs etc) Act 2002, s 6 (2).

[3] Sub—paragraph prospectively repealed by Disability Discrimination (Northern Ireland) Order 2006, SI 2006/312, art 19, Sch 1, as from a day to be appointed.

INDEX

References are to paragraph numbers.